OSTSEE
Königsberg
Danzig
Stettin
Oder
Berlin
Frankfurt a. d. Oder
Posen
Warschau
POLEN
Cottbus
Oder
Neisse
Breslau
Prag
TSCHECHOSLOWAKEI
Donau
Linz
Wien
Graz
DEUTSCHLAND
SCHWEIZ und ÖSTERREICH
KILOMETER
0 50 100 200
MEILEN
0 50 100 200
Staatsgrenze
Administrativgrenze
Landeshauptstadt
© C. S. HAMMOND & Co., Maplewood., N. J.
S0-BZC-577

GERMAN ONE

For Laboratory and Classroom

FREDERICK C. ELLERT
PETER HELLER
University of Massachusetts

GERMAN ONE

For Laboratory
and Classroom

D. C. HEATH AND COMPANY Boston

Cover: City Lights
Prinzregentenstraße, Munich
Photo by Peter Keetman

Printed in the United States of America (6 E 3)

Library of Congress Catalog Card Number: 62–9967

PREFACE

The authors of this book have long felt the need for an elementary German text that would mediate between the strictly traditional and the purely audio-lingual method. Prepared over a period of several years and revised after extensive testing in classroom and laboratory, GERMAN ONE attempts to fill this need.

Within each unit of this book the material is arranged according to a progressive sequence, leading from the training of ear and tongue toward the attainment, on the beginner's level, of the four language skills. The reading and writing of German is approached, then, by way of the spoken language.

Moreover, our experiments convinced us that students can begin to achieve maturity in a foreign language even in the early stages of their training. Students derive pleasure, of course, in communicating in a foreign tongue within the context of everyday situations and events. This is, no doubt, an important consideration in language learning and teaching. What is perhaps even more important, however, is that students be persuaded to move beyond this type of communication to a more significant level. In substance, therefore, the present text introduces at an early stage material of intrinsic cultural and literary interest.

GERMAN ONE consists of ten units. Each unit is divided into three lessons. The first lesson in each unit contains:

1. BASIC DIALOGUE
2. DRILL PATTERNS
   a. German Drill
   b. English-German Drill
   c. Pronunciation Drill *
3. GRAMMAR

The second lesson in each unit contains:

1. QUESTIONNAIRE (*Wer bin ich?*)
2. DRILL PATTERNS
   a. German Drill
   b. English-German Drill
   c. Pronunciation Drill
3. GRAMMAR

* The Pronunciation Drills are restricted to Units I–V.

The third lesson in each unit contains:

1. VOCABULARY BUILDING
2. PRONUNCIATION DRILL
3. READINGS

While individual teachers will vary methods and procedure according to their needs and preferences, the following observations and suggestions may prove helpful.

1. The *Basic Dialogues* introducing each unit should be drilled intensively in class or laboratory by way of individual or choral response and repetition *before* being assigned as homework. Each of these dialogues should then be thoroughly memorized by the students.

2. *a*) The majority of the German *Drill Patterns* provide for variations on the materials of the Basic Dialogues. They are designed to break the rigidity of the memorized phrases so as to give the student greater range and flexibility. Such patterns, while not intended for memorization, should be drilled and assigned for active mastery.

   Suggested procedures:
   (1) Introduce (selected) Drill Patterns by way of choral and individual repetition.
   (2) Drill for active mastery by spot-checking within a given pattern series, for example, by asking individual students in quick succession to give German equivalents for the instructor's English versions. This should be an open-book test to start with.

   Illustration (Drill Patterns, Lesson 8, p. 56):

   1. Nein, ich kann es mir nicht vorstellen.
   2. Nein, wir können es uns nicht vorstellen.
   3. Nein, du kannst es dir nicht vorstellen.
   4. Nein, Sie können es sich nicht vorstellen.
   5. Nein, ihr könnt es euch nicht vorstellen.
   6. Nein, sie kann es sich nicht vorstellen.
   7. Nein, er kann es sich nicht vorstellen.
   8. Nein, sie können es sich nicht vorstellen.

   Instructor (addressing English version of 7 to student A): "No, he cannot imagine it."
   Student A (after locating the correct statement): "Nein, er kann es sich nicht vorstellen."
   Instructor (to student B): "No, we cannot imagine it."
   Student B: "Nein, wir können es uns nicht vorstellen."

   And so on through this series to the next.

(3) Intensify active drill by way of question and answer. Note: Many questions designed for this purpose are already part of the Drill Pattern sections; others can easily be drawn from the same material. The student's answers, in turn, should adhere closely to the patterns provided in each section.

(4) The question-and-answer method leads naturally to a conversation practice, involving at first teacher and student, and, finally, student and student, with the teacher acting as director, prompter, and participator.

b) Above and beyond the exercises based directly on the Basic Dialogues or on other preceding areas of active command, such as the Questionnaire, the Drill Patterns also include material which anticipates subsequent topics (grammatical topics, for example). Hence, not all sections will lend themselves equally well to question-and-answer or to conversation practice. In the initial units some patterns are intended purely for rapid individual and choral repetition; in the latter part of the book some patterns will serve as comprehension exercises as well as material for active command. Still others clarify grammatical principles or illustrate word order. Yet all material included in the Drills can and should be treated within the framework of oral communication.

3. The *English to German* sections are closely related to the preceding German Drills and should be assigned as *written* homework. The *directional symbols* concerning the position of German verbs (see pp. 37–38) are intended to help students to form good habits in the crucial area of word order.

4. The *Pronunciation Drills*, like many of the other Drill Patterns, are designed for rhythmic (individual or choral) response.

5. The presentation of the *Grammar* is selective. The grammar sections include (*1*) *subject matter to be assigned for intensive study and active command, and* (*2*) *areas of reference*. These sections deal with material anticipated in the preceding Basic Dialogues, Questionnaires, and Drills, and they point ahead to the Readings of a given unit as well as to the subject matter of subsequent units. The grammar sections that are intended as areas of reference deal rather comprehensively with each topic as it comes up. Their purpose, however, is not to burden the student with detail for detail's sake, but to serve as explanatory guides through immediate difficulties and as orientation areas. A summary of major grammatical topics (verbs, nouns, pronouns, adjectives) is presented in the Appendix.

6. Heading the second lesson of each unit, the *Questionnaire* entitled "*Wer bin ich?*" provides added opportunity for oral response and active vocabulary building, and a further range in practice conversations pertaining to first person situations and events within the student's own immediate

sphere of experience. The Questionnaire also introduces the grammatical topics of the lesson and serves as a basis for the Drill Patterns. Both questions and sample answers should be assigned for active command.

7. The *Vocabulary Building* sections review some of the material covered, but primarily prepare for the Readings which they precede. They include listings, explanations, and exercises on such topics as German-English cognates, idiomatic expressions, the so-called "little words," synonyms and antonyms, words with multiple meanings, words based on strong verb stems, word formations involving prefixes and suffixes, and the like. The Vocabulary Building sections should be carefully discussed in class so as to aid and quicken the student's memory and reading ability. Distinction in assignment should be made between areas of active command and material intended for so-called "passive" or reading comprehension.

8. The *Readings*, selected for their topical, cultural, or literary interest, include a variety of subjects and styles. Unadulterated excerpts from the works of well-known German authors proved surprisingly adaptable to our purpose, particularly since we felt that students should be introduced to some complexities of verbal structure at an early stage. The visible vocabularies, as well as the Readings generally, are intended primarily for passive comprehension. In answering the questions (*Fragen*) on the Readings, students should consult the text rather than the end vocabularies.

   The brief *bilingual passages*, normally to be assigned as homework, serve to extend the available range and to anticipate, without much added labor, some further linguistic intricacies. Such passages should not be subjected to grammatical analysis, but spot-checked for comprehension, for example, by questions eliciting the appropriate phrase from the German original or by way of a rapid *viva-voce* reading practice interspersed with brief (English or German) summaries.

   The *poems*, freely translated into English,* should be read for comprehension and enjoyment. Some of the shorter poems may be assigned for memorization. *Additional reading material* in German type is provided in the Appendix.

9. The *end vocabularies* aim at extensive coverage. The German-English vocabulary covers virtually all German words used in the book, except the footnoted vocabulary of some added readings in the Appendix. The English-German vocabulary refers not only to the English-German Drills or to the Basic Dialogues, but to all areas of active command, including the German Drill Patterns, the Questionnaires (*Wer bin ich?*), and the active Vocabulary Building areas. The English-German vocabulary is

* By F. C. Ellert

designed to help students formulate a variety of German phrases and sentences appropriate to free conversation practice, based particularly on the Questionnaires.

10. GERMAN ONE may be used with or without access to a language laboratory. A set of tapes is available which includes all of the Basic Dialogues, German Drill Patterns, Pronunciation Drills, *Wer bin ich?* sections, and passages for comprehension, together with testing tapes.

ACKNOWLEDGMENTS

GERMAN ONE was written during a series of language experiments sponsored by a Carnegie Foundation grant shared by the language departments of the University of Massachusetts. We are pleased to acknowledge the help given us by many people. To cite all of them by name would make too lengthy a list. We should like, however, to express special thanks to Mrs. Christiane Heller, to Dr. Cioffari and Mrs. Dermer of D. C. Heath and Company, to Professor Meessen of Indiana University, to Mrs. Ingrid Mushroe, as well as to the members of the German Department at the University of Massachusetts, above all to Miss Eva Schiffer, for their many valuable suggestions.

We should also like to express our thanks to Mrs. Alma Mahler Werfel for permission to use lines from Franz Werfel's *Fünf Sinngedichte*.

F. C. E.
P. H.

CONTENTS

PRONUNCIATION

Consonant and Vowel Sounds

For the most part, German consonant sounds and vowel sounds are not equivalent to those of English. This is especially true of vowel sounds and consonant sounds like **ch, j, l, r, z,** and others. The comparative sound values listed below, however, can be helpful as a reference guide. They give the English-speaking student a more or less close approximation of German sounds. Needless to say, the classroom teacher and the language laboratory are the best guides on the way toward correct pronunciation of German.

Most of the examples given below appear in the first pages of this book. It will, therefore, be of immediate benefit to the student to exercise his pronunciation skill by way of these examples.

CONSONANTS

The following German consonants closely approximate the corresponding English consonants:

b when at the beginning of a word or syllable, or medially between vowels: Bleistift, Buch, Arbeit, Fußboden, Aufgabe

c infrequent in German except in combinations like **ch, chs, sch,** etc. When it occurs uncombined, it is normally like English *k*: Café, Courage

ck Stück, Decke, rücken

d when initial or medial: deutlich, wiederholen, Kreide

f, ff Frau, hoffentlich

h when initial: haben, heißen

k Kapitel, Korb, klar

l, ll more liquid than in English: legen, Zeile, alle

m, mm man, zusammen

n, nn neun, Donnerstag

p, pp Pult, Hauptsatz, Lippe

q only in **qu** combination, pronounced like English *kv:* Qualität, Quatsch

ss wissen, müssen; alternate spelling **ß** is used after a long vowel or a diphthong, at the end of a word, or before a consonant: Grüße, beißen, Fluß, ihr wißt

t, tt more explosive than in English: Tag, Wort, bitte

y as a consonant occurs only in words of foreign origin. It is pronounced like the English *y* in *city*.

The following consonants differ radically from the corresponding English consonants:

b at the end of a word or syllable is like English *p*: Korb, ab, abwarten, Absatz

ch This has no actual equivalent in English. It has two sound formations in German, the so-called front **ch** and back **ch.** The best way to learn them is to hear them demonstrated by your classroom teacher and in the laboratory,and then to imitate the sounds carefully. The front **ch** is preceded by **ä, äu, e, ei, eu, i, ie, ö:** sprechen, recht, ich, Licht; the back **ch** is preceded by **a, au, o,** or **u:** Sprachen, auch, noch, Buch. Both **ch** sounds are aspirated, i.e., breathed out (*h*) sounds, the front **ch** being a fricative produced by raised tongue and hard palate, the back **ch** a fricative produced by the back of the tongue raised toward the soft palate.

chs when part of a stem is like English *x*, as in *ox:* Ochs, wechseln

d when at the end of a word or syllable is pronounced *t*: und, niemand, Wand, Landkarte, endlich

g when at the beginning of a word or syllable, or medial, is like English *g* in *go:* gehen, eigentlich, folgen, morgen

when final after vowels, it is like English *k*: Tag, Krieg. (Many German-speaking people, however, pronounce this **g** like **ch** in **ich,** particularly **-ig:** langweilig, richtig)

when followed by **t** or **st,** it is also like *k*: sagst, sagt

when combined with **n,** it is like *-ng* in *sing, singer*, but never as in "finger": streng, Englisch, lang, langweilig

h after a vowel or diphthong within the same syllable is silent; it serves as a vowel-lengthening sign: Lehrer, Ihnen, erzählen, Weihnachten

j is like the English *y* in *year:* ja, jeder, jetzt, Jahr

r unlike English, is tongue-trilled or uvular. The first is simpler to master, but either one is acceptable.

s at the beginning of a word or syllable and followed by a vowel or diphthong, or medial between vowels, is like the *s* in *prism* or *rose:* Sie, sein, sagen, Absatz, Esel, Wesen

when it falls between **m, n, l, r** and a vowel, it is also voiced as above: Verse, also, Felsen

otherwise **s** is pronounced like *s* in *sing:* es, das, erst, Fenster

sch is like English *sh* in *shop:* schreiben, schlagen, Schularbeit, Geschichte

sp, st at the beginning of a word or syllable are pronounced as though the **s** were **sch:** sprechen, spät, stehen, verstehen, studieren

tz is like *ts* in *cats:* Satz, übersetzen

v is pronounced like **f:** von, Vater, vier

w is pronounced like English *v*: was, wie, wer, wo, Wand, wiederholen, antworten

x (occurring infrequently) is pronounced like German **chs** (see page xvi)

z is pronounced like **tz** (see above): zwei, zu, erzählen, Zeile

VOWELS

In German there are normally two different sounds for each vowel, termed long and short. A vowel is long when it is directly followed by an **h** within the same syllable, e.g., **Ohr;** when it is doubled, e.g., **Boot;** and usually when it is followed by a single consonant, e.g., **los.** (Commonly occurring exceptions are verbal prefixes, e.g., **verantworten, erinnern, umarmen.**) The vowel is short in most other cases.

Long **a** is like the *a* in *ah:* kahl, Vater, Tafel, Paar

Short **a** is like the *a* in *garden:* Garten, Wand, Blatt, Absatz

Long **e** is like the *a* in *gave:* geben, sehen, Feder, sehr

Short **e** is like the *e* in *met:* sprechen, setzen, Decke

Unaccented **e** is like the *e* in *the boat:* Zeile, schlagen, bitte

Long **i** is like the *i* in *marine:* ihn, Berlin
The combination **ie** has the same sound; the **e** is used to make the **i** long. The combination **ie** is therefore not a real diphthong. Examples: schließen, dies, Sie, die

Short **i** is like the *i* in *sit:* sitzen, ich, bin, Tisch

Long **o** is like the *o* in *tone:* Sohn, los, Boden

Short **o** is like the *o* in *won:* Sonne, sollen, hoffen

Long **u** is like the *u* in *Lulu:* Buch, Fuß, Stuhl, gut

Short **u** is like the *u* in *put:* Pult, Mutter, dumm, wußte

y occurs mostly in words of Greek origin and is pronounced like German **ü** (see page xviii): Lyrik, Physik, Symbol

UMLAUTED VOWELS

Long **ä** is much like the German long **e:** spät, Universität, erzählen

Short **ä** is like the German short **e:** kälter, Männer

Long **ö**, though it does not exist as a sound in English, can be approximated by saying the German long **e** (as in **sehr**) with lips rounded and pushed outward: schön, mögen, hören

Short **ö**, long and short **ü** are also lacking in English. Short **ö** can be formed by saying the German short **e** (as in **sprechen**) with lips rounded and pushed outward: öffnen, möchten

Long **ü** can be formed by saying the German long **i** (as in **ihn**) with lips rounded and pushed outward: über, Tür, Bücher

Short **ü** can be formed by saying the German short **i** (as in **bitte**) with lips rounded and pushed outward: müssen, rücken, Stück

DIPHTHONGS

au is like the *ou* in *out:* aus, Frau, Haupt

ei is like the *ei* in *Einstein:* ein, Stein, heißen, klein

äu and **eu** are like the *oy* in *coy:* Fräulein, neun, Deutsch

Word Accent

In words of German origin the stem normally takes the accent:
ge'ben, gege'ben; ge'hen, entge'hen; ste'hen, verste'hen; kom'men, bekom'men; Verbin'dung, Entschul'digung; gewöhn'lich

However, note the stress in many words of foreign origin:
Student', Kapi'tel, Person', Gramma'tik, Genie', Soldat', Papier'

Words with separable prefixes take the accent on the prefix:
auf'geben, durch'gehen, an'kommen, An'fang, Durch'bruch, Ab'satz, zu'künftig

Glottal Stop

The so-called glottal stop, a special characteristic of spoken German, refers to a kind of sound (normally unprinted or unwritten) that is caused by the closing and abrupt reopening of the glottis. It occurs just before the pronunciation of a stressed initial vowel, as in: Ihre ʔalten ʔEltern.

INSTRUCTIONAL PHRASES AND SENTENCES FOR CLASSROOM USE

(The instructor is urged to make use of these gradually and as the occasion arises.)

Guten Morgen (Guten Tag), meine Damen und Herren!	*Good morning (How do you do), Ladies and Gentlemen.*
Rücken Sie (ganz) nach vorne!	*Move (all the way) to the front.*
Setzen Sie sich, bitte! Bitte, nehmen Sie Platz!	*Sit down, please.* *Please take a seat.*
Öffnen Sie Ihr Buch! Machen Sie Ihr Buch auf! Schlagen Sie Ihr Buch auf!	*Open your book.*
Schlagen Sie Ihr Buch (Ihre Bücher) auf Seite zwei auf!	*Open your book (your books) to page two.*
Schlagen Sie nun Seite sechzehn auf!	*Now turn to page sixteen.*
Oben — (ganz) unten — in der Mitte.	*The top of the page — at the (very) bottom — in the middle.*
Erster (zweiter, dritter, usw.) Absatz (Paragraph), Abschnitt.	*First (second, third, etc.) paragraph, section.*
Zeile eins (zwei, drei, vier, fünf, sechs, sieben, acht, neun, zehn, usw.).	*Line one (two, three, four, five, six, seven, eight, nine, ten, etc.).*
Sprechen Sie mir nach!	*Repeat after me.*
Auf deutsch, bitte!	*In German, please.*
Alle zusammen, bitte!	*All together, please.*
Wiederholen Sie, bitte! Noch einmal, bitte!	*Repeat, please. Once again, please.*
Wie sagt man das auf deutsch, bitte?	*How do you say that in German, please?*
Wie heißt das auf englisch?	*What does that mean in English?*
Bitte, lesen Sie auf deutsch, Fräulein —— (Frau ——, Herr ——)!	*Please read in German, Miss —— (Mrs. ——, Mr. ——).*
Übersetzen Sie, bitte! Ins Deutsche! Ins Englische!	*Translate, please. Into German. Into English.*
Sagen Sie das auf englisch, bitte!	*Say that in English, please.*
Gut! Sehr gut! Das ist richtig. Das ist nicht richtig!	*Good! Very good! That's right!* *That's not right.*
Versuchen Sie es noch einmal, bitte!	*Try it once again, please.*
Jetzt geht es (schon) besser, nicht (nicht wahr)?	*It's (already) improving, isn't it?*
Was bedeutet das (das Wort, der Satz)?	*What does that mean (the word, the sentence)?*
Verstehen Sie das? Verstehen Sie das nicht?	*Do you understand (that)?* *Don't you understand (that)?*
Haben Sie eine Frage? Hat jemand eine Frage?	*Do you have a question? Does anybody have a question?*

Hat noch jemand eine Frage? Hat niemand eine Frage?	*Does anybody else have a question?* *Nobody has a question?*
Bitte, beantworten Sie (die) folgende Frage! Bitte, antworten Sie auf (die) folgende Frage!	*Please, answer the following question.*
Sprechen Sie etwas lauter, bitte!	*Speak a little louder, please.*
Verzeihen Sie, bitte! Verzeihung, bitte! Ich habe das (Sie) nicht verstanden.	*I beg your pardon.* *I didn't understand that (you).*
Ich verstehe das nicht. Ja, ich verstehe das.	*I don't understand that.* *Yes, I understand that.*
Danke schön! Ich danke Ihnen.	*Thank you very much. (I) thank you.*
Bitte schön!	*You're welcome.*
Was haben Sie gesagt? Wie meinen Sie, bitte? Wie, bitte?	*What did you say?*
Antworten Sie, bitte!	*Answer, please.*
Klar und deutlich, bitte!	*Clearly and distinctly, please.*
Sprechen Sie etwas langsamer, bitte!	*Speak a little more slowly, please.*
Schließen Sie Ihr Buch!	*Close your book.*
Legen Sie Ihr Buch (Ihre Bücher) beiseite!	*Put your book (your books) aside.*
Rücken Sie auseinander, bitte!	*Move apart (Spread out), please.*
Nehmen Sie ein Stück Papier!	*Take a sheet of paper.*
Bitte, schreiben Sie mit Tinte (mit Bleistift)!	*Please, write in ink (with a pencil).*
Schreiben Sie Ihren Namen oben auf das Papier!	*Write your name at the top of the paper.*
Schreiben Sie folgendes!	*Write the following.*
Die Zeit ist um.	*(The) time is up.*
Geben Sie Ihre Arbeit (Schularbeit, Hausarbeit) ab, bitte!	*Please hand in your work (homework).*
Machen Sie, bitte, das Fenster (die Fenster) auf (zu)!	*Please open (close) the window (the windows).*
Bitte, machen Sie die Tür (die Türen) auf (zu)!	*Please open (close) the door (the doors).*
Öffnen Sie das Fenster (die Tür)!	*Open the window (the door).*
Schließen Sie das Fenster (die Tür)!	*Close the window (the door).*
Schalten Sie das Licht an! Machen Sie das Licht an!	*Turn (put) the light on.*
Schalten Sie das Licht aus! Machen Sie das Licht aus!	*Turn (put) the light out.*
Gehen Sie, bitte, an die Tafel!	*Please go to the (black)board.*

Schreiben Sie folgendes (an die Tafel)!	*Write the following (on the board).*
Die Aufgabe für das (fürs) nächste Mal ist . . .	*The assignment for next time is . . .*
Die Aufgabe für Montag (Dienstag, Mittwoch, Donnerstag, Freitag, Samstag) ist (die) folgende . . .	*The assignment for Monday (Tuesday, Wednesday, Thursday, Friday, Saturday) is as follows . . .*
Die Stunde ist um.	*(The) class is over (dismissed).*
Auf Wiedersehen!	*Good-bye!*
Das ist ein (der) Bleistift. Dies ist eine (die) Feder. Dies ist ein (das) Notizbuch. } Dies ist ein (das) Heft. } Das ist ein (das) Buch. Das (dies) sind Bücher.	*That is a (the) pencil.* *This is a (the) pen.* *This is a (the) notebook.* *That is a (the) book.* *Those (These) are books.*
Was ist das? Das ist eine (die) Füllfeder. Das ist ein (der) Kugelschreiber. Was ist dies? Dies ist ein (der) Stuhl, ein (der) Tisch ein (das) Pult, ein (das) Lesepult ein (der) Papierkorb	*What is that?* *That is a (the) fountain pen.* *That is a (the) ballpoint pen.* *What is this?* *This is a (the) chair, a (the) table* *a (the) desk, a (the) lectern* *a (the) wastebasket*
Womit schreiben Sie? Ich schreibe mit einem Bleistift (einer Feder, einer Füllfeder, der Kreide).	*With what are you writing?* *I am writing with a pencil (a pen, a fountain pen, the chalk).*
Das ist die Wand (die Tafel, das Fenster, die Decke, der Fußboden, das Licht, die Landkarte, die Kreide, der Schwamm). Das ist ein (das) Wort ein (der) Satz (Hauptsatz, Nebensatz) eine (die) Zeile ein (der) Absatz eine (die) Seite ein (das) Kapitel	*That is the wall (the blackboard, the window, the ceiling, the floor, the light, the map, the chalk, the [sponge] eraser).* *That is a (the) word* *a (the) sentence (main clause, dependent clause)* *a (the) line* *a (the) paragraph* *a (the) page* *a (the) chapter*

GERMAN ONE

For Laboratory and Classroom

ERSTER TEIL

Frankfurt am Main: Eschenheimer Turm

Eine Vorlesung im Anatomischen Institut in Wien. Viele Studenten stehen auf der Galerie oder sitzen auf den Stufen, da sie in den Bänken keinen Platz mehr finden.

1. Aufgabe

ZWEI STUDENTEN *

Read and memorize the following dialogue:

SCHMIDT: Guten Morgen! Mein Name ist Schmidt, Karl Schmidt. Ich bin Student. — Und Sie? Wie heißen Sie?

MÜLLER: Mein Name ist Müller. Ich bin Student wie Sie.

SCHMIDT: Was studieren Sie, Herr Müller?

MÜLLER: Ich studiere Mathematik, Philosophie, Naturwissenschaften und Sprachen. Ich will auch Geschichte studieren.

SCHMIDT: Das möchte ich auch.

* *Note:* The English version of this Basic Dialogue is on the reverse side. Each Unit of this book begins with a Basic Dialogue, the German and English versions of which are placed back to back, as they are here.

TWO STUDENTS

SCHMIDT: Good morning. My name is Schmidt, Karl Schmidt. I am a student. — And you? What is your name?

MÜLLER: My name is Müller. I am a student too (*lit.* "like you").

SCHMIDT: What courses are you taking, Mr. Müller? (*lit.* "What are you studying . . . ?")

MÜLLER: I am studying mathematics, philosophy, science, and languages. I want to take history too.

SCHMIDT: So would I. (*lit.* "I should like [to take] that too.")

DRILL PATTERNS

Repeat the following drills after your instructor or after the speaker on the tape. Imitate the pronunciation very carefully.

1. Guten Morgen, Herr [1] Müller.
Guten Tag,[2] Herr Müller.
Guten Abend,[3] Herr Müller.

2. Guten Morgen, Frau [4] Müller.
Guten Tag, Frau Müller.
Guten Abend, Frau Müller.

3. Guten Morgen, Fräulein [5] Müller.
Guten Tag, Fräulein Müller.
Guten Abend, Fräulein Müller.

4. Sind Sie Student, Herr Müller?
Sind Sie Amerikaner, Herr Müller?
Sind Sie Lehrer,[6] Herr Müller?

5. Sind Sie Studentin, Fräulein Müller?
Sind Sie Amerikanerin, Fräulein Müller?
Sind Sie Lehrerin,[7] Fräulein Müller?

6. Ja, ich bin Student.
Ja, ich bin Amerikaner.

7. Ja, ich bin Studentin.
Ja, ich bin Amerikanerin.

8. Nein, ich bin kein [8] Student.
Nein, ich bin kein Amerikaner.
Nein, ich bin kein Lehrer.

9. Nein, ich bin keine Studentin.
Nein, ich bin keine Amerikanerin.
Nein, ich bin keine Lehrerin.

10. Ja, er ist Student.
Ja, er ist Amerikaner.
Ja, er ist Lehrer.

11. Ja, sie ist Studentin.
Ja, sie ist Amerikanerin.
Ja, sie ist Lehrerin.

12. Was ist Herr Müller?
Ist Herr Müller Lehrer?
Was ist Fräulein Müller?
Ist Fräulein Müller Lehrerin?

13. Nein, er ist kein Student.
Nein, er ist kein Amerikaner.
Nein, er ist kein Lehrer.

14. Nein, sie ist keine Studentin.
Nein, sie ist keine Amerikanerin.
Nein, sie ist keine Lehrerin.

15. Was studieren Sie, Fräulein Schmidt?
Was studieren Sie, Herr Müller?

16. Ich studiere Mathematik.
Ich studiere Philosophie.
Ich studiere Geschichte.

17. Er studiert Mathematik.
Er studiert Philosophie.
Er studiert Geschichte.

18. Sie studiert Mathematik.
Sie studiert Philosophie.
Sie studiert Geschichte.

19. Studieren Sie Mathematik?
Studieren Sie Philosophie?
Studieren Sie Geschichte?

20. Ich will Mathematik studieren.
Ich will Philosophie studieren.
Ich will Geschichte studieren.

21. Er will Mathematik studieren.
Er will Philosophie studieren.
Er will Geschichte studieren.

22. Sie will Mathematik studieren.
Sie will Philosophie studieren.
Sie will Geschichte studieren.

[1] **der Herr** gentleman; Mr. [2] **der Tag** day; **Guten Tag** *equivalent to:* How do you do? *or* Hello! [3] **der Abend** evening [4] **die Frau** woman; Mrs. [5] **das Fräulein** young lady; Miss [6] **der Lehrer** teacher (*masc.*) [7] **die Lehrerin** teacher (*fem.*) [8] **kein** (*adj.*) no, not a, not any

23. Das möchte ich auch.
Das möchte er auch.
Das möchte sie auch.

24. Ich möchte das auch.
Er möchte das auch.
Möchten Sie das auch?

25. Das möchte ich nicht.[1]
Das möchte er nicht.
Das möchte sie nicht.

26. Ich möchte das nicht.
Er möchte das nicht.
Möchten Sie das nicht?

Now use the patterns to make up your own questions and answers.

English to German

Prepare this exercise beforehand in writing so that you can give the German fluently and without hesitation.

1) Good morning, Miss Müller.
2) Are you an American,[2] Miss Müller?
3) Yes, I am an American. — I am a student.
4) What courses are you taking (*lit.* "What are you studying"[3]), Mr. Fischer?
5) I am taking mathematics, philosophy, and history.
6) I should like to take languages too.
7) Are you studying languages?
8) Yes, I want to study languages and science.

PRONUNCIATION DRILL

(vowels; **ch**)

Repeat after the instructor, imitating carefully the variation in vowel sounds and the **ch**-*sounds, and practice the following:*

Stădt[4] — Stāāt[5]	du weißt — ihr wĭßt	sie wĭssen — sie mü̆ssen
wēr — wīr	du mü̆ßt — ihr müßt	Sie mü̆ssen das wĭssen.
ēr — īhr	er sīeht — ihr sēht	sie wö̆llen — sie sö̆llen
dēr — dīr	er līest — ihr lēst	Sie sö̆llen das wö̆llen.

Das Buch möchte ich auch.
Ich möchte auch Geschichte studieren.
In der Nacht leuchtet das Licht.
Lichter leuchten in allen Nächten.

[1] **nicht** not [2] *In stating occupation, profession, or nationality, the indefinite article is usually omitted:* e.g., **Er ist Lehrer (Amerikaner)**. [3] *Note that there are no so-called progressive (or emphatic) forms in German. For example:* He is coming today. = He comes today. = **Er kommt heute.** Is he coming today? = "Comes he today?" = **Kommt er heute?** *Similarly:* Does he know you? = "Knows he you?" = **Kennt er Sie?** [4] ˘ = *short vowel* [5] ¯ = *long vowel*

GRAMMAR

1. Verbs

The following verbs appear in Lessons 1–3. They serve to illustrate practically all you need to know formally about the present tense of German verbs.

a. Most Common Verbs:

sein *to be*

	SINGULAR		FORMAL SING. OR PL.		PLURAL	
1st Person:	ich bin	*I am*			wir sind	*we are*
2nd Person:	du bist	*you are*	Sie sind	*you are*	ihr seid	*you are*
3rd Person:	sie ist	*she is*			sie sind	*they are*
	es ist	*it is*				
	er ist	*he is*				

Note that there are three ways of saying "you" in German: **du, Sie,** and **ihr.** The distinctions among them will be made clear in Unit II.

haben *to have*

	SINGULAR		FORMAL SING. OR PL.		PLURAL	
1st Person:	ich hab**e**	*I have*			wir hab**en**	*we have*
2nd Person:	du ha**st**	*you have*	Sie hab**en**	*you have*	ihr hab**t**	*you have*
3rd Person:	sie ha**t**	*she has*			sie hab**en**	*they have*
	es ha**t**	*it has*				
	er ha**t**	*he has*				

werden *to become*

	SINGULAR		FORMAL SING. OR PL.		PLURAL	
1st Person:	ich werde	*I become*			wir werd**en**	*we become*
2nd Person:	du wir**st**	*you become*	Sie werd**en**	*you become*	ihr werd**et**	*you become*
3rd Person:	sie wird	*she becomes*			sie werd**en**	*they become*
	es wird	*it becomes*				
	er wird	*he becomes*				

Sein, like its English equivalent, follows no regular pattern in the present tense.

Haben has personal endings that are common to the great majority of German verbs in the present tense:

	* SINGULAR	FORMAL SING. OR PL.	PLURAL
* *1st Person:*	**–e**		**–en**
2nd Person:	**–st**	**–en**	**–t**
3rd Person:	**–t**		**–en**

Note that the forms **hast** and **hat** lack the stem ending **b.**

* The same arrangement of person and number will be observed in subsequent examples.

Werden shows a vowel change (**e** to **i**) that will be seen in a number of so-called strong verbs. Such a vowel change, when it does occur, invariably appears in the **du, sie** (*she*), **es, er** forms. The absence of the stem ending **d** in **wirst** and of the personal ending **t** in **wird** should be carefully noted; also the –**et** ending in **ihr werdet.**

Sein, haben, and **werden** are multifunctional verbs and therefore appear frequently. **Werden,** for example, besides having independent function and meaning (*to become*) is also used:

(1) as the auxiliary for the future tense:

Ich werde Mathematik studieren.	*I am going to study mathematics.*

(2) as the auxiliary in the passive voice:

Philosophie wird auf der Universität studiert.	*Philosophy is studied at the university.*

It is also used in imaginative situations and will be illustrated in this connection later.

Memorize the forms of **sein, haben,** *and* **werden!**

b. Verbs Used Frequently:

sagen *to say*

ich sage		wir sagen
du sagst	Sie sagen	ihr sagt
sie sagt		sie sagen
es sagt		
er sagt		

sehen *to see*

ich sehe		wir sehen
du siehst	Sie sehen	ihr seht
sie sieht		sie sehen
es sieht		
er sieht		

antworten *to answer*

ich antworte		wir antworten
du antwortest	Sie antworten	ihr antwortet
sie antwortet		sie antworten
es antwortet		
er antwortet		

heißen *to be called*

ich heiße		wir heißen
du heißt	Sie heißen	ihr heißt
sie heißt		sie heißen
es heißt		
er heißt		

Sagen has the most regularly recurring endings you will encounter in the present tense of verbs. The following verbs in Lessons 1–3 conform exactly to the ending pattern of **sagen:**

studieren, erzählen, kommen, stehen, verstehen

Sehen shows the vowel change **e** to **ie.** Like the **e** to **i** change, this also will be encountered in a number of strong verbs in the **du, sie** (*she*), **es, er** forms.

Antworten requires an **e** throughout its ending pattern. The **e** obviously is necessary for the sake of pronunciation in the **du, sie** (*she*), **es, er, ihr** forms.

A verb like **finden** (*to find*) or **öffnen** (*to open*) follows the same ending pattern as **antworten,** and for the same reason; e.g., "Er findet nichts." [1] "Du öffnest alles." [2]

Heißen, whose stem ends in an **s**-sound, needs only a **t**-ending in the **du**-form. This makes it identical with the **er**-form: **du heißt, er heißt.**

Most verbs whose stem ends in a sibilant sound will follow the same pattern: **du sitzt,**[3] **er sitzt; du liest,**[4] **er liest. Wissen** and the modal auxiliary **müssen** (see section c. below) are exceptions to this.

c. Common Auxiliaries:

müssen *to have to, must*

ich muß	Sie müssen	wir müssen
du mußt		ihr müßt
sie muß		sie müssen
es muß		
er muß		

wollen *to want to*

ich will	Sie wollen	wir wollen
du willst		ihr wollt
sie will		sie wollen
es will		
er will		

Müssen and **wollen,** like the four other modal auxiliaries (which you will learn in Lesson 14), lack endings in the **ich, sie** (*she*), **es, er** forms. The only other verb displaying the same pattern in the present tense is **wissen.** (Compare with forms of **müssen** above.)

wissen *to know*

ich weiß	Sie wissen	wir wissen
du weißt		ihr wißt
sie weiß		sie wissen
es weiß		
er weiß		

Note the vowel change in **müssen** and **wollen;** also in **wissen.**

[1] **nichts** nothing [2] **alles** everything [3] **sitzen** sit [4] **lesen** read

NOTE:

A. All verbs in the present tense except **sein** go back to the infinitive spelling in the **wir, Sie, sie** (*they*) forms.

B. In the same tense the great majority of verbs reveal an identity in the **sie** (*she*), **es, er, ihr** forms. The only two "unique" forms in these verbs are those associated with **ich** and **du.** (See **sagen** on page 8.)

2. Questions

In German questions are asked in the following ways:

(a) By putting the verb in first position:

Sind Sie Student? **Studiert** er Sprachen? **Heißen** Sie Müller?

(b) By using a question word at the beginning:

Wie heißen Sie? **Was** studieren Sie?

(c) By intonation. Any declarative statement can be changed into a question:

Er studiert Mathematik? So ein kleines Buch? (*Such a small book?*)
Sie ist Amerikanerin?

3. Word Order I *(Position of Verb)*

LEARN

The position of the verb is the key to the understanding of German word order, and therefore to the understanding of the German clause or sentence. The verb may be either the first, the second, or the last *unit* in a German clause.

VERB-FIRST POSITION

(a) In questions that require a "yes" or "no" answer (except for those in 2 c. above):

Studieren Sie Sprachen?

(b) In commands:

Verstehen Sie mich recht, Herr Professor! *Understand me correctly, professor!*

VERB-SECOND POSITION

(a) In questions introduced by a question word:

Warum kommen Sie immer zu spät? *Why do you always come late?*

(b) In independent declarative statements:

Ich studiere Mathematik.
Mathematik studiere ich.

Der Student kommt eines Morgens zu spät in die Klasse.
Eines Morgens kommt der Student zu spät in die Klasse. } *One morning the student comes late to class.*

Er setzt sich schnell.
Schnell setzt er sich. } *He sits down quickly.*

VERB-LAST POSITION

(a) In dependent clauses and phrases:

Er weiß alles, was in dem Buch **steht.**	*He knows everything that's in the book.*
Ich finde es nicht schwer, den Professor zu **verstehen.**	*I don't find it difficult to understand the professor.*

(b) In independent clauses, whether statements or questions, dependent infinitives go to the end.

Ich möchte Ihnen nun eine kleine Anekdote **erzählen.**	*I should now like to tell you a little anecdote.*
Ich will auch Geschichte **studieren.**	
Wollen Sie Lehrer **werden?**	

Ulm an der Donau mit Blick auf das Münster. Die Geschichte dieser alten württembergischen Stadt reicht über tausend Jahre bis in das frühe Mittelalter zurück.

2. Aufgabe

WER[1] BIN ICH?

SAMPLE ANSWERS AND SUGGESTIONS

a. Wie heißen Sie? — *Ich heiße . . . (Mein Name ist . . .)*

b. Wo[2] sind Sie geboren?[3] — *Ich bin in . . . geboren.*[4]

c. Wo leben[5] Sie?
in welchem Land? — *Ich lebe in Amerika (in den Vereinigten Staaten[6]).*

d. Wo wohnen[7] Sie? — *Ich wohne in . . .*
in welcher Stadt?[8]
in welcher Straße?[9] — *Ich wohne in der . . .-straße.*
in welchem Staat?[10]

e. Was machen Sie[11] auf der Universität?

f. Studieren Sie auch Literatur?

DRILL PATTERNS

Repeat the following drills after your instructor or after the speaker on the tape. Imitate the pronunciation very carefully. Then, using the patterns, make up your own questions and answers.

1. Wie heißen Sie?
Wie heißt er?
Wie heißt sie?

2. Heißen Sie Müller?
Heißt er Müller?
Heißt sie Müller?

3. Ich heiße Müller.
Er heißt Müller.
Sie heißt Müller.

4. Was studieren Sie?
Was studiert er?
Was studiert sie?

5. Studieren Sie Sprachen?
Studiert er Sprachen?
Studiert sie Sprachen?

6. Ich studiere Sprachen.
Er studiert Sprachen.
Sie studiert Sprachen.

7. Ich bin Student wie Sie.
Ich bin Student wie er.
Ich bin Studentin wie Sie.
Ich bin Studentin wie sie.

8. Hier[12] ist der Student.
Hier ist die Studentin.
Hier ist der Lehrer.
Hier ist die Lehrerin.

9. Hier ist ein[13] Student.
Hier ist eine[13] Studentin.

10. Hier ist ein Lehrer.
Hier ist eine Lehrerin.

[1] **wer** who [2] **wo** where [3] **sind . . . geboren** were . . . born [4] **bin . . . geboren** was . . . born [5] **leben** live [6] **die Vereinigten Staaten** the United States [7] **wohnen** live (dwell) [8] **die Stadt** city [9] **die Straße** street [10] **der Staat** state [11] **Was machen Sie . . .?** What are you doing . . .? [12] **hier** here [13] **ein, eine** a

11. Haben Sie ein Buch?
Nein, ich habe kein Buch.
Hat Fräulein Müller ein Buch?
Nein, sie hat kein Buch.

12. Wer hat das Buch?
Ich habe es nicht.
Hat der Lehrer das Buch?
Ja, er hat es.

13. Das Kind [1] wird groß.[2]
Der Mann [3] wird alt.[4]
Es wird spät.
Die Nacht [5] wird kalt.

14. Ich will Lehrer werden.
Werden Sie Lehrerin?
Ja, ich werde Lehrerin.
Ja, sie will Lehrerin werden.

15. Es wird Morgen.
Es wird Tag.
Es wird Abend.
Es wird Nacht.

English to German

Prepare this exercise in writing.

1) What is your name? (*use* **heißen**)
What is his name?
What is her name?

2) Is your name Müller?
No, my name is Martin.

3) I am a student too (like you).
She is not a student. She is a teacher.
He is not a teacher. He is a student.

4) He would like to study philosophy.
I should like to take that too.

5) I have a book.
Don't you have a book?
The teacher has the book.
He has it.

6) It is getting late.

7) He is growing old.

PRONUNCIATION DRILL

(vowels; **ie, ei; h** lengthens preceding vowel; double consonants [**tt, mm, nn**] shorten preceding vowel; **w, v, f**)

Repeat after the instructor, imitating carefully the variation in length of vowels, and practice the following:

sieht — seid
zieht — Zeit
Lieder — leider
schrieben — schreiben

ihnen — einen
werde — wurde
würde — wird
wäre — war

vier — für
viele — fühle
viele — Fülle
Tier — Tür

wohne — Wonne
von — wann
wir — vier
Mutter — guter

zusammen — Namen
zusammen — nahmen
nimmt — nehmt
Sonne — Sohn

Sohn — Söhne
kennt — könnt
können — kennen
euch — auch

[1] **das Kind** child [2] **groß** tall, big [3] **der Mann** man [4] **alt** old [5] **die Nacht** night

GRAMMAR

4. Nouns

CLASSES OF NOUNS

For the sake of convenience we shall assume in this book that there are five classes of nouns. These classes can best be identified by the nominative plural endings.

	PLURAL ENDING	SINGULAR	PLURAL	
Class 1	—	der Morgen	die Morgen	*morning*(*s*)
Class 2	**–e**	der Tag	die Tage	*day*(*s*)
Class 3	**–er**	das Buch	die Bücher	*book*(*s*)
Class 4	**–n** or **–en**	der Student	die Studenten	*student*(*s*)
Class 5	**–s**	das Auto	die Autos	*car*(*s*)

However, no matter what the nominative plural endings may be, *all dative plurals*, except in nouns of Class 5, will end in **–n** or **–en.**

DATIVE PLURALS

1.	2.	3.	4.	5.
den Morgen	den Tagen	den Büchern	den Studenten	den Autos

Note that there are *three genders* in German. *Learn nouns together with definite articles.*

FEMININE	NEUTER	MASCULINE
die Frau (*woman*)	**das** Kind (*child*)	**der** Mann (*man*)

Grammatical gender does *not* necessarily agree with natural gender, for example:

die Nacht (*night*) **das** Fräulein (*young lady*) **der** Hund (*dog*)

Further explanation of nouns will be taken up later.

5. Cases, Pronouns, Definite Articles

a. The *nominative* is the case of the subject.

Der Student studiert Philosophie.
Er studiert Philosophie.

Die Studentin studiert Philosophie.
Sie studiert Philosophie.

b. The *accusative* is the case of the direct object.

Der Student sieht **den Professor** nicht.
Der Student sieht **ihn** (*him*) nicht.

Der Student sieht **die Studentin** nicht.
Der Student sieht **sie** (*her*) nicht.

c. The *dative* is the case of the indirect object.

> Der Student erzählt[1] **dem Lehrer** ([*to*] *the teacher*) eine Anekdote.[2]
> Der Student erzählt **ihm** ([*to*] *him*) eine Anekdote.

The dative is also frequently governed by adjectives.

> Das Buch ist **der Studentin** (*for the student*) zu[3] schwer.[4]
> Das Buch ist **ihr** (*for her*) zu schwer.

The dative and the accusative are also used after prepositions, for example:

> Er kommt **mit**[5] **der Lehrerin in die Klasse.**

Prepositions will be discussed in greater detail later.

German normally requires strict formal agreement between a pronoun and the word to which it refers.

Das Buch ist **dem Lehrer** nicht zu schwer.	**Die Studentin** erzählt **eine Anekdote.**
Es ist **ihm** nicht zu schwer.	**Sie** erzählt **sie.**
Er versteht **die Sprache** nicht.	Er kennt **den Namen** nicht.
Er versteht **sie** nicht.	Er kennt **ihn** nicht.

The following table shows the correspondence of pronouns and definite articles:

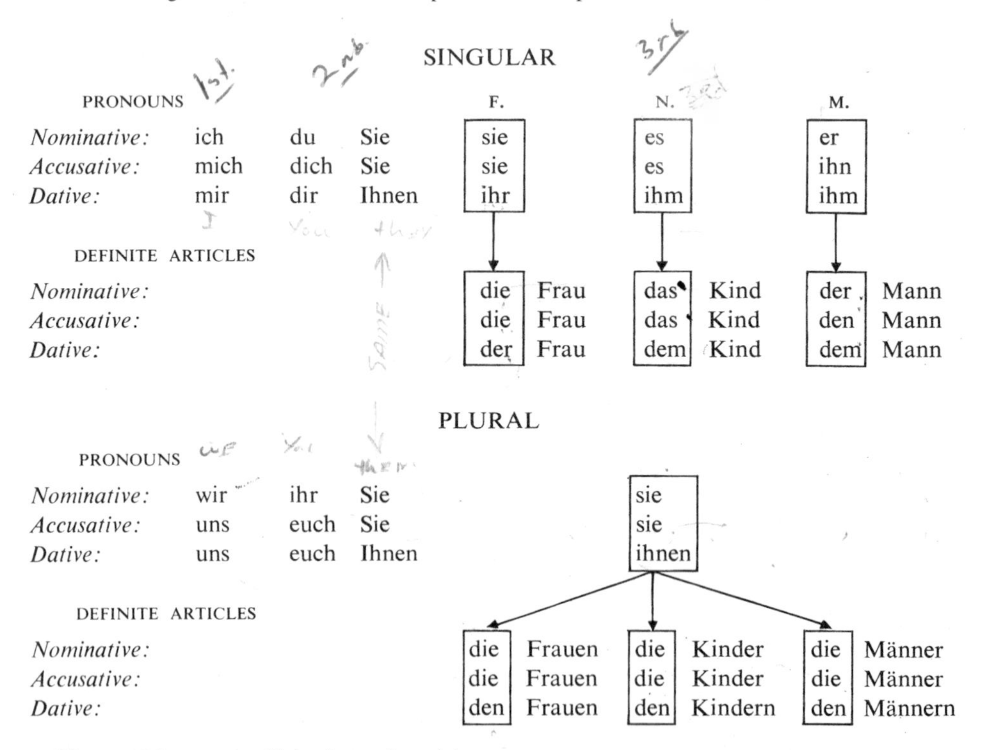

SINGULAR

PRONOUNS				F.	N.	M.
Nominative:	ich	du	Sie	sie	es	er
Accusative:	mich	dich	Sie	sie	es	ihn
Dative:	mir	dir	Ihnen	ihr	ihm	ihm

DEFINITE ARTICLES	F.		N.		M.	
Nominative:	die	Frau	das	Kind	der	Mann
Accusative:	die	Frau	das	Kind	den	Mann
Dative:	der	Frau	dem	Kind	dem	Mann

PLURAL

PRONOUNS				
Nominative:	wir	ihr	Sie	sie
Accusative:	uns	euch	Sie	sie
Dative:	uns	euch	Ihnen	ihnen

DEFINITE ARTICLES						
Nominative:	die	Frauen	die	Kinder	die	Männer
Accusative:	die	Frauen	die	Kinder	die	Männer
Dative:	den	Frauen	den	Kindern	den	Männern

The genitive case will be introduced later.

[1] **erzählen** tell [2] **die Anekdote** anecdote [3] **zu** too [4] **schwer** difficult; heavy [5] **mit** with

3. Aufgabe

VOCABULARY BUILDING

LINGUISTIC KINSHIP BETWEEN GERMAN AND ENGLISH

According to linguistic scholars, there existed about 5,000 years ago a more or less uniform language which is now generally taken to be the prototype of the majority of languages spoken or written today by vast numbers of people in Europe, the Americas, Asia, Australia, New Zealand, and South Africa. As this loosely unified, ancient language began to break up, sharper and sharper divisions and differences gradually became evident until finally in the long, slow course of time clearly defined separate units became established. Taken together these became identified as the Indo-European family of languages, consisting essentially of eight to twelve major divisions.

The one factor that is constant about languages is their changeability. "Nothing is perfectly static [in language]. Every word, every grammatical element, every locution, every sound and accent is a slowly changing configuration, molded by the invisible and impersonal drift that is the life of language." * If this is characteristic of languages today, it was even more so in a radical sense of languages in earlier times. In the case of Indo-European a series of transformations began to occur, for example, some 4,000 years ago, so basic as to effect a sharp cleavage within this language community. The result was that there gradually emerged within the Indo-European family a language segment that ultimately became clearly differentiated from the rest of the Indo-European. This large language segment is now designated as the Germanic subfamily of languages.

It is estimated that the changes which produced this Germanic subfamily were practically fulfilled by 500 B.C. and ran their final course from about 500 B.C. to ca. 250 A.D. These changes, operating by way of some cause still baffling to the best observers among language scientists, involved particularly, though not exclusively, the voiced and unvoiced stops, **b d g** and **p t k.**

One of the first to see unmistakable evidence of a systematic series of consonant changes (once actively operative within the Indo-European language community) was the philologist Jakob Grimm,† more popularly known as a collector of folk tales. So prevalent throughout the Indo-European were the changes that Grimm observed and so regularly recurring that he (like his Danish contemporary Rasmus Rask) was forced to conclude they followed some kind of linguistic law. It was one of Grimm's great contributions to linguistic science to formulate such a law and thus to become one of the founders of comparative philology.

Grimm's Law (later corrected, modified, and elaborated) is conceived as having basically two parts, both concerned with consonant changes or sound shifts. Whereas the first sound shift was instrumental in producing the difference between Indo-European and Germanic, the second sound shift (ca. 350–750 A.D.), operating within the West Germanic group of the Germanic subfamily, was subsequently instrumental in producing the difference between Low German (e.g. English) and High German.

Low and High are purely geographical terms referring to lowlands and highlands. English, for example, since the 5th century Germanic invasions is closely related most particularly to the language spoken on the low-lying Frisian Islands off the Netherlands (the Low Countries). English is thus essentially a Low German tongue, with substantial "borrowings" from Latin roots following the Norman Conquest in the 12th century. The estimate is that Modern English comprises about 50% Latin roots, 30% Germanic roots, 10% Greek roots; the remaining 10% are scattered.

* Sapir, Edward. *Language: An Introduction to the Study of Speech.* New York: Harcourt, Brace and Company, 1921, p. 183.
† (1785–1863)

THE GERMANIC LANGUAGES

East Germanic: Gothic

North Germanic: Scandinavian

Swedish	Danish
Norwegian	Icelandic
Old Norse	

West Germanic: Low German

Old Saxon or Low German	Dutch
English: Old English (*Beowulf*)	Flemish
Middle English (*Chaucer*)	Frisian
Modern English	

High German

Old High German	Yiddish
Middle High German	Pennsylvania Dutch
New High German	

In their historical development English and High German fall into three periods that show an approximate chronological correspondence.

Old English Old High German	800–1100
Middle English Middle High German	1100–1500
Modern English New High German	1500–

As indicated above, English and German are much more intimately related to each other organically than are English and Latin or any linguistic descendant of Latin — French, for example. Many cognates in German and English plainly testify to this close linguistic kinship between them. The following are some familiar examples:

Finger	*finger*	Schuh	*shoe*
Hand	*hand*	Freund	*friend*
Arm	*arm*	Schere	*shears*
Haar	*hair*	Feld	*field*
Lippe	*lip*	finden	*find*
Knie	*knee*	singen	*sing*
Land	*land*	geboren	*born*
Hund	*hound*	mußt	*must*
Name	*name*	hängen	*hang*

The majority of cognate pairs in German and English are, however, not so clearly identifiable as those in this list simply because of the consonant shift (mentioned above in terms of Grimm's Law) that helped to differentiate German, that is to say High German, from English (Low German). Many German words which you will come to know will really be English words in disguise. You will learn them more readily and even more permanently if you have some systematic way of penetrating their disguises.

Knowledge of the following table of consonant correspondencies and careful attention to recognition exercises (see below) can be helpful here. It should be noted now and for future reference that a list like the following does not try to account for vowel differences between German and English. Vowel relationships come under a different "system."

COGNATES

Study the following pairs:

GERMAN	ENGLISH	GERMAN	ENGLISH
b (*medial or final*)	**v** (*sometimes* **f**)	**cht**	**ght**
haben	have	recht	right
halb	half	die Macht	might
ch	**k**	**d**	**th**
brechen	break	die	the
das Buch	book	denken	think

Can you recognize the English for the following German words from the examples given above?

das Silber, das Weib; machen, die Milch; das Licht, die Nacht; dick, dünn

GERMAN	ENGLISH	GERMAN	ENGLISH
f, ff (*medial or final*)	**p**	**g**	**i** *or* **y**
helfen	help	gestern	yesterday
öffnen	open	legen	lay
pf (*initial or medial*)	**p, pp**	**k**	**ch**
der Apfel	apple	die Kammer	chamber
das Pfund	pound	der Käse	cheese

Can you recognize the English for the following German words from the examples given above?

hoffen, scharf; die Pfanne, der Pfennig; sagen, der Tag; die Kirche, das Kinn

GERMAN	ENGLISH	GERMAN	ENGLISH
s, ss, ß (*medial or final*)	**t**	**z**	**t**
das	that	das Herz	heart
die Straße	street	zwei	two
tz	**t**	**t**	**d**
setzen	set	gut	good
sitzen	sit	die Seite	side (page)

Can you recognize the English for the following German words from the above examples?

der Fuß, das Wasser; der Sitz, die Hitze; zehn, zwanzig; laut, das Wort

WORD STUDY

The following "little" words in German recur frequently. It is easy to minimize their value. On the other hand, ready knowledge of them becomes increasingly indispensable at each stage in the learning of the language. Fix these words in your mind as firmly as possible and refer to them constantly until they become part of your active vocabulary. (Almost all these words will have been used by the end of Lesson 3.)

WORDS COMMONLY USED

also therefore, accordingly, well then, well now (*never English* "also")
als ob as if
auch too, also
auch wenn even when (if)
eigentlich really, actually
ein a, an, one
hinein′ in, into (*with verbs of motion*)
immer always
kein not any, not a, no
  Er hat kein Buch.
nein no (*negative answer to questions*)
nicht not
nur only
viel much; **viele** many
warum′ why
was what
  Was ist das? Ich weiß nicht, was das ist.

COORDINATING CONJUNCTIONS

aber but (however)
  Es ist interessant aber schwer.
denn for (because)
oder or
sondern but (on the contrary)
  Es ist nicht kalt sondern warm.
und and

WORDS WITH MULTIPLE MEANINGS

an *to:* Er geht an die Tafel. *He goes to the blackboard.*
on: Er schreibt an die Tafel. *He is writing on the blackboard.*
at: Er steht (*stands, is standing*) an der Tafel.

das *the;* as pronoun, demonstrative or relative: *that*
Das ist das Buch, das ich suche (*am looking for*).

ja *yes;* but in medial position: *of course; you see; why!*
Ich habe ja ein Buch.

nun *now;* but in initial position when followed by a comma: *well, well now*
Nun, das ist sehr gut.

schwer *heavy:* Eisen (*iron*) ist schwer.
difficult: Deutsch ist nicht schwer.

sich (reflexive pronoun) *herself, himself, itself, oneself, yourself* (formal), *yourselves* (formal), *themselves*

so *such:* So ein Buch?
so: So spät?
this (*that*) *way:* Ich will es auch so.

von *of:* Er ist ein Freund von Karl.
from: Es ist nicht weit (*far*) von hier.
by: Die Oper ist von Wagner.

wie *as:* Er kommt spät wie immer (*always*).
like: Du bist wie eine Blume (*flower*).
how: Wie schwer ist das? Ich weiß nicht, wie schwer das ist.

zu *at:* Sie ist zu Hause (*home*).
to (with inf.): Das Buch ist nicht schwer zu verstehen (*understand*).
to (prep.): Kommen Sie zu uns!
too (degree): Ist es zu schwer?

IDIOMATIC EXPRESSIONS

Er ist ein guter Freund von **mir** (*of mine*). (Note the use of the personal pronoun.)
Er setzt sich. *He sits down.* (*lit.* "He sets (seats) himself.")

los = *free, disengaged, loose* — in both a neutral and unrestrained sense, as indicated:
Es geht nun los. *It's starting now.*
Also los! *Go ahead (then)! (Let's) get going!*
Was ist hier los? *What's the matter here? What's going on here?*

ansehen is a prefixed verb: **an** + **sehen** *look at*
Sie sieht ihn scharf **an.** *She looks at him sharply.* (Note the position of the prefix **an.**)

Recall here: Machen Sie, bitte, das Fenster **auf** (**zu**)!

PRONUNCIATION DRILL

(**a — ä; o — ö; u — ü; au — äu;** intonation: question-statement)

Repeat after the instructor, imitating carefully the variation in vowel sounds and the intonation patterns, and practice the following:

Hand — Hände	mochte — möchte	Kommt er? Kommt sie? Kommt ihr?
Land — Länder	Gott — Götter	Ja, er kommt.
Mann — Männer	Ton — Töne	Ja, sie kommt.
Nacht — Nächte	schon — schön	Ja, wir kommen.
schlagen — schlägt	Buch — Bücher	Du kommst.
halten — hält	Bruder — Brüder	Du kommst?
spät — schnell	Haupt — Häupter	Sie kommen.
geht — hell	Fräulein — Frau	Sie kommen?

Reading

SCHWER IST SCHWER

„Ich möchte Ihnen nun eine kleine Anekdote erzählen," sagt Fischer zu Müller.
„Hoffentlich wird das nicht zu langweilig," meint Müller.
„Nun, das muß man abwarten," antwortet Fischer.
„Also los!" sagt Müller.

LINE
2 hoffentlich — *I hope*
langweilig — *boring*
meint (*inf.:* meinen) — *says*

LINE
3 das . . . abwarten — *you'll have to* (lit. "*one must*") *wait and see about that*

MEMORIZE

„Eines Morgens kommt ein Student, ein guter Freund von mir, spät wie immer in die Klasse. Er setzt sich schnell, aber er öffnet sein Buch nicht. Der Professor sieht ihn scharf an und sagt streng: ‚Was ist mit Ihnen los, Herr Martin? Warum kommen Sie immer zu spät? Warum haben Sie kein Buch?'

5 ‚Kein Buch? Ich habe ja ein Buch. Es ist mir nur viel zu schwer.'

‚Zu schwer? Unsinn! So ein kleines, dünnes Buch?'

‚Verstehen Sie mich recht, Herr Professor. Das Buch, wissen Sie, das ist mir eigentlich nicht zu schwer, sondern nur was in dem Buch steht! — Das ist es.'"

FRAGEN

1. Was möchte Fischer erzählen? 2. Wem (*to whom*) möchte er die Anekdote erzählen? 3. Kommt der Student oft zu spät? 4. Wohin ("*whereto*," *to what place*) kommt der Student oft zu spät? 5. Ist der Student ein Freund von Ihnen? 6. Setzt er sich schnell? 7. Öffnet er sein Buch? 8. Was sagt der Professor zu ihm? 9. Was antwortet der Student? 10. Was ist ihm zu schwer: Das Buch selbst (*itself*)? Oder nur, was in dem Buch steht?

EXERCISES

1. Replace **Ihnen** in the following sentence with the appropriate forms of **du, sie, es, er,** and **sie** (*plural*). Rewrite the sentence each time. Check your answers against the personal pronoun declension chart on page 16.

   Ich möchte Ihnen nun eine kleine Anekdote erzählen.

2. Replace **ihn** in the following sentence with the appropriate forms of **ich, du, sie, es, wir, ihr, sie** (*plural*), and **Sie.** Rewrite the sentence each time. Check your answers.

   Der Professor sieht ihn scharf an.

3. Give the German equivalent for the following sentences, using the dative forms of the personal pronouns.

   Example: Er ist ein guter Freund von mir.

   He's a good friend of hers.
   He's a good friend of his.
   He's a good friend of ours.
   He's a good friend of yours. (*3 ways*)
   He's a good friend of theirs.

4. WORD-ORDER DRILL

   The following are all simple, complete declarative sentences. Bear in mind as you rewrite them that in each case the verb must be the second *unit* (but not necessarily the second *word*) and that the subject is the first or third unit.

LINE
3 streng — *sternly*
6 der Unsinn — *nonsense*

LINE
8 sondern nur — *but only*
was . . . steht — *what it says in the book*

a. Rewrite beginning with **nun:** Er kommt nun.
b. Rewrite beginning with **in die Klasse:** Er kommt in die Klasse.
c. Rewrite beginning with **nun:** Er kommt nun in die Klasse.
d. Rewrite beginning with **in die Klasse:** Er kommt nun in die Klasse.
e. Rewrite the following sentence twice, beginning with (1) **mir** and (2) **zu schwer:** Das Buch ist mir nicht zu schwer.
f. Rewrite the following sentence three times beginning with (1) **Ihnen,** (2) **nun,** and (3) **eine kleine Anekdote:** Ich möchte Ihnen nun eine kleine Anekdote erzählen.

DU BIST WIE EINE BLUME

Du bist wie eine Blume
So hold und schön und rein;
Ich schau' dich an und Wehmut
Schleicht mir ins Herz hinein.

Mir ist, als ob ich die Hände
Aufs Haupt dir legen sollt',
Betend, daß Gott dich erhalte
So rein und schön und hold.

Heinrich Heine
(1797–1856)

YOUR BEAUTY IS LIKE A FLOWER

Your beauty is like a flower,
Immaculate and fair,
I look on you and sadness
Steals through me unaware.

It seems that softly I should lay
My hands upon your head,
Imploring God to keep you
Fair and immaculate.

Memorize this poem!

ZWEITER TEIL

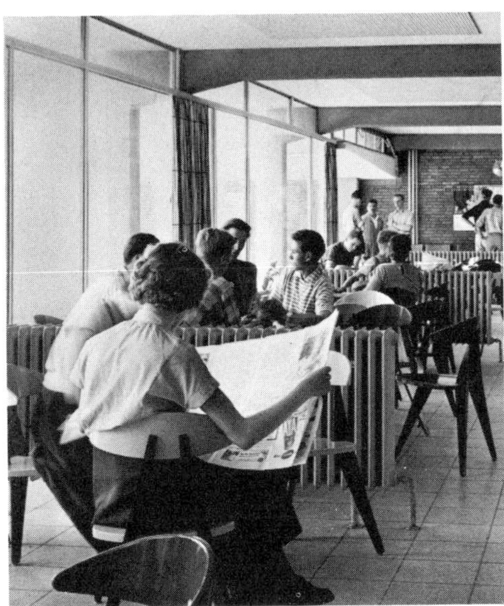

Freistunde in einem Gymnasium

Volkstrachten am Bodensee

Zwei Freunde im Gespräch in einer stillen Ecke eines deutschen Restaurants.

4. Aufgabe

FREUNDE SAGEN „DU" ZUEINANDER

Read and memorize the following dialogue:

MÜLLER: Guten Tag, Herr Fischer! Wie geht es Ihnen?

FISCHER: Danke, gut. Und Ihnen, Herr Müller?

MÜLLER: Es geht mir ausgezeichnet. Hören Sie, Herr Fischer, ich möchte Ihnen einen Vorschlag machen. Sollten wir nicht „du" zueinander sagen? Was halten Sie davon? Unter Freunden soll man nicht zu formell sein. Freunde sagen „du" zueinander.

FISCHER: Sie haben recht. Das heißt, du hast recht. Wir kennen uns zwar erst seit acht Tagen, aber ich weiß schon, daß du mein Freund bist. Ich sage gerne „du" zu dir.

MÜLLER: Wenn wir „du" zueinander sagen, müssen wir uns natürlich beim Vornamen nennen. Aber dein Vorname ist mir leider nicht bekannt.

FISCHER: Also gut. Von dieser Stunde an nennst du mich Karl.

MÜLLER: Und du sag Peter zu mir, bitte.

FISCHER: Also, auf Wiedersehen, Peter.

MÜLLER: Wiedersehen, Karl.

FRIENDS SAY "DU" TO EACH OTHER

MÜLLER: How do you do (*lit.* "Good day"), Mr. Fischer. How are you?

FISCHER: Fine, thanks! And you, Mr. Müller?

MÜLLER: I am very well. Listen, Mr. Fischer, I'd like to make a suggestion to you. Shouldn't we say "du" to each other? What do you think (of that)? Among friends one shouldn't be too formal. Friends say "du" to each other.

FISCHER: You're right. That is, "*du* hast recht." It's true we've known each other only a week (*lit.* "for eight days"), but I already know that you are my friend. I'll be pleased to say (*lit.* "I gladly say") "du" to you.

MÜLLER: If we say "du" to each other, of course we'll have to call each other by our first names. But unfortunately I don't know your first name (*lit.* "your first name is not known to me").

FISCHER: All right then. From now on (*lit.* "from this hour on") you call me Karl.

MÜLLER: And you call me Peter, please.

FISCHER: Well, I'll be seeing you, Peter. (wiedersehen *to see again*)

MÜLLER: So long, Karl.

DRILL PATTERNS

Repeat the following drills after your instructor or after the speaker on the tape. Imitate the pronunciation very carefully.

1. Sie sind mein Lehrer.
Sie sind mein Professor.
Sie sind mein Student.

2. Du bist mein Freund.
Du bist mein Vater.[1]
Du bist mein Bruder.[2]
Du bist mein Kind.[3]
Du bist mein Onkel.[4]
Du bist mein Großvater.[5]

3. Sie sind meine Lehrerin.
Sie sind meine Professorin.
Sie sind meine Studentin.

4. Du bist meine Freundin.
Du bist meine Mutter.
Du bist meine Tante.[6]
Du bist meine Schwester.[7]

5. Ist Karl dein Freund?
Ja, Karl ist mein Freund.
Ist Gretchen deine Freundin?
Ja, Gretchen ist meine Freundin.

6. Ihr seid meine Freunde.
Ihr seid meine Brüder.
Ihr seid meine Kinder.
Ihr seid meine Schwestern.

7. Seid ihr meine Freunde?
Ja, wir sind deine Freunde.
Seid ihr meine Brüder?
Ja, wir sind deine Brüder.

8. Möchten Sie ein Buch?
Wollen Sie ein Buch?
Haben Sie kein Buch?
Kennen Sie das Buch?

9. Du möchtest ein Buch.
Du willst das Buch.
Du hast kein Buch.
Du kennst das Buch.

10. Dieses Buch möchten Sie?
Dieses Buch wollen Sie?
Dieses Buch haben Sie?
Dieses Buch kennen Sie?

11. Dieses Buch möchtest du?
Dieses Buch willst du?
Dieses Buch hast du?
Dieses Buch kennst du?

12. Möchtet ihr das?
Wollt ihr das?
Habt ihr das?
Kennt ihr das?
Studiert ihr das?

13. Was sagen Sie?
Was wissen Sie?
Was müssen Sie (tun)? [8]
Was sollen Sie (tun)?

14. Was sagst du?
Was weißt du?
Was mußt du (tun)?
Was sollst du (tun)?

15. Sie haben recht.
Du hast recht.
Ich habe recht.
Wir haben recht.

16. Er sagt es Ihnen.
Er sagt es dir.
Er sagt es mir.
Er sagt es uns.

[1] **der Vater** father [2] **der Bruder** brother [3] **das Kind** child [4] **der Onkel** uncle [5] **der Großvater** grandfather [6] **die Tante** aunt [7] **die Schwester** sister [8] **tun** do

17. Man sagt es Ihnen.
Man sagt es dir.
Man sagt es mir.
Man sagt es uns.

18. Er sagt „du“ zu mir.
Sie sagt „du“ zu dir.
Sagt sie zu Ihnen „du“?

19. Sie kennt mich.
Er kennt mich.
Man kennt mich.

20. Kennen wir Sie?
Kennen wir *sie?* (*2 meanings*)
Kennen wir uns?

21. Kennt er Sie?
Kennt man Sie?
Kennt er *sie?* (*2 meanings*)
Kennt sie Sie?
Kennen sie Sie?
Kennen sie *sie?* (*2 meanings*)

22. Wir sind Freunde.
Wir sind Amerikaner.
Wir sind Studenten.
Wir sind Freundinnen.
Wir sind Amerikanerinnen.
Wir sind Studentinnen.

23. Sind sie Freunde?
Sind sie Amerikaner?
Sind sie Studenten?
Sind sie Freundinnen?
Sind sie Amerikanerinnen?
Sind sie Studentinnen?

English to German

Prepare this exercise in writing.

1) I am a student.
You are my professor.
You are my child.
She is my girl friend.
You are my friends.
Are you my friends?
Is she a student?

2) Do you know the book, mother?
Do you want the book, father?
Do you have the book, Mr. Smith?

3) What are you saying, Mr. Müller?
What are you saying, father?

4) Does he know this book?
No, he doesn't know this book.

5) He is right.
You are right, my child.
She says we are right.

6) She knows me.
They (*use* **man**) know me.
They (*use* **sie**) know me.
We know him.

7) She says "du" to you. (*2 ways*)

PRONUNCIATION DRILL

(vowels; **z[w]**; intonation: question — statement)

Repeat after the instructor, imitating carefully the vowel sounds and intonation patterns, and practice the following:

ein — mein	an — am	von — vor
nein — kein	außer — aus	zwischen — zu
die — wie	in — im	zum — zur
ihr — mir	bei — beim	neben — nach

hinter — unter	sieht — seid	Er kennt Sie nicht?
unter — über	wieder — leider	Kennt er Sie nicht?
kennen — können	fahren — fährt	Sie kennen ihn nicht?
kommt — kann	Häuser — Haus	Kennen Sie ihn nicht?
		Er kennt Sie nicht.
		Sie kennen ihn nicht.

GRAMMAR

6. Speech Patterns

It is evident even to the casual observer of language that each language has its own peculiar speech patterns. We take for granted the meaning of such an expression as "If only he were king." Upon closer examination we would find that there are departures from the customary in this statement: "only" does not really mean what it usually does, and "were" in this case does not convey a past tense meaning. Actually the expression "If only he were king" is a complicated linguistic phenomenon. In the first place "were" points to an *imaginary* situation, not an actual state of affairs, in *present* time. Moreover, the word "only" suggests a strongly projected wish. Finally, logically speaking, the statement is incomplete. The independent clause remains unspoken. What the words really are trying to say in an elliptical way is: He is not king, but I wish he might be, for then we could hope for better things. Note how close German is to English here: "Wenn er nur König **wäre!**" "If only he *were* king." The only real idiomatic difference between the two has to do with the position of the verb.

You have already discovered that it is frequently possible to understand completely the meaning of German statements by taking them word by word. It is often simply a matter of knowing the basic meaning of each word:

Ich kenne ihn.	*I know him.*
Dies ist mein guter Freund.	*This is my good friend.*

There is often, however, no such close idiomatic correspondence between the two languages. The expression "Was halten Sie davon?" for example, taken word for word, would read: "What hold you thereof?" Not only is this not English idiom, it makes no sense.

German idioms then will often need to be understood in terms of their equivalents in English. The acquisition of such knowledge is a matter of time and repeated experience. And the "feel" of a foreign language can follow only upon such knowledge. It is frequently possible to *get at* the meaning of a German statement by a verbatim procedure:

Kennen wir Sie?	("Know we you?")	*Do we know you?*
Ja, wir kennen uns.	("Yes, we know us.")	*Yes, we know each other.*
Es tut mir weh.	("It does me woe [pain].")	*It hurts me.*

Note the following idioms that have already occurred up to this point:

Wie heißen Sie?
Sie haben recht.
Ich sage gerne „du" zu dir.
Was halten Sie davon?
Er ist ein guter Freund von mir.
Er setzt sich schnell.
Was ist mit Ihnen los?
Das möchte ich auch.

7. Dative Prepositions

The parts of speech that are perhaps the most elusive and puzzling from language to language are the prepositions. As you are already aware from your knowledge of English, prepositions have not only basic meanings. Actually they have also a wide range of idiomatic meanings. Note, for example, some of the subtleties and complexities which we usually take for granted in the preposition "by":

by the roadside
by the way
by then
by chance
step by step
a light to read by
too late by an hour
by and by

Corresponding subtleties will be found in German as well. They can be mastered not by listing all meanings for each preposition at once, but by using the prepositions as they come along.

The following is a list of prepositions that take the *dative only*. Some of their meanings are included.

aus out of, from
außer outside of, besides, except
bei near, at, at the home of, by (*proximity*)
mit with (*means or accompaniment*)
nach after, to, according to
seit since, for
von from, by (*agency*), of
zu to, at

Memorize these prepositions!

Illustrations

Er kommt **aus** der Klasse.
Außer uns ist niemand (*nobody*) hier.
Wohnt er **bei** Ihnen?
(*Does he live with you?*)
Sie kommt **mit** dem Professor in die Klasse.
Wir sehen uns **nach** dem Sommer (*summer*) wieder.
Du bist **seit** einer Woche hier.
Du bist ein guter Freund **von** mir.
Er sagt „du" **zu** der Frau.
Sag „du" **zu** mir!

Three of these prepositions are also used in *contractions* with definite articles:

beim = bei dem
vom = von dem
zum = zu dem
zur = zu der

Illustrations

Er nennt ihn **beim** Vornamen.
Das Kind fällt **vom** Stuhl.
(*The child falls from the chair.*)
Man sagt „Du" **zum** lieben Gott.
Man sagt „du" **zur** Tante.

8. Dative or Accusative Prepositions

The following prepositions take the *dative* or *accusative*, depending upon the presence or absence of motion *and* goal.

Dative: Er ist in **der** Klasse. (*no motion, no goal*)

Accusative: Er kommt in **die** Klasse.
(*motion*) (*goal*)

an at, on, to
auf on, upon, at, to
hinter behind
in in, into
neben near, beside
über over, above, about
unter under, among
vor in front of (*spatial*), before (*temporal*), ago
zwischen between, among

Memorize these prepositions!

Illustrations

Er weiß alles, was in **dem** Buch steht.
Auf **der** Universität studiert er Philosophie.
Sie steht an **der** Tafel (*at the blackboard*).

Er schreibt in **das** Buch.
Er geht auf **die** Universität.
Sie geht an **die** Tafel (*to the blackboard*).

Contractions you may encounter:

ans = **an das**
am = **an dem**
aufs = **auf das**
hinterm = **hinter dem**
ins = **in das**
im = **in dem**
vors = **vor das**
vorm = **vor dem**

Illustrations

Vater unser, der Du bist **im** Himmel (*in heaven*).
Er weiß alles, was **im** Buch steht.
Er steht **am** Fenster.
Sie geht **ans** Fenster.

Im Sommer gehen wir immer **aufs** Land (*to the country*).
Ich schreibe etwas **ins** Heft (*into the notebook*).
Sie stehen **vorm** Haus.
Sie gehen **vors** Haus.

9. Word Order II *(Position of Verb)*

Whenever a verb-last clause or phrase introduces a complex sentence, the verb of the main clause will immediately follow such an introductory clause or phrase.

Wenn sie „du" zueinander **sagen, sind** sie wohl [1] Freunde.
Wenn man zu seinem Vater **spricht,**[2] **sagt** man „du," nicht „Sie."
Zu Kindern „Sie" zu **sagen, ist** wirklich [3] sehr albern.[4]

NOTE:

These may be considered verb-second situations, if the dependent clause (or phrase) is taken as a single unit modifying the verb of the main clause in each case.

(Wenn sie „du" zueinander sagen,) **sind** sie wohl Freunde.

[1] **wohl** probably [2] **spricht** (*inf.* **sprechen**) speaks [3] **wirklich** really [4] **albern** silly

Johann Wolfgang Goethe Universität, Frankfurt am Main: neue und alte Universitätsgebäude. Wie überall steigt auch hier die Zahl der Studenten ständig.

5. Aufgabe

WER BIN ICH?

SAMPLE ANSWERS AND SUGGESTIONS

a. Wo wohnen Sie hier auf der Universität? — *... in einem Studentenheim* [1]
Wo essen [2] Sie? — *... in der Mensa* [3]
Wo verbringen [4] Sie Ihre [5] Freizeit? [6] — *... auf dem Tennisplatz,* [7] *zu Hause,* [8] *im Kino* [9]
Wo studieren Sie lieber? [10] Auf Ihrem Zimmer [11] oder in der Bibliothek? [12] — *Ich studiere lieber ...*

b. Wie verbringen Sie Ihr Wochenende? [13]
Fahren [14] Sie nach Hause? [15]
Bleiben [16] Sie hier?
Besuchen [17] Sie Freunde?
Gehen Sie tanzen? [18]
Gehen Sie ins Kino? ins Theater? in ein Konzert?

c. Wie heißen Ihre Freunde?
Wie heißt Ihr bester Freund? — *Mein bester Freund ...*
Wie heißt Ihre beste Freundin? — *Meine beste Freundin ...*

DRILL PATTERNS

Repeat the following drills after your instructor or after the speaker on the tape. Imitate the pronunciation very carefully.

1. Sie weiß es.
Er weiß es.
Man weiß es.

2. Wissen Sie das nicht?
Weißt du es nicht?
Weiß sie das nicht?
Weiß er es nicht?
Weiß man es nicht?

3. Heißen Sie Müller, mein Herr?
Brauchen [19] Sie ein Buch, mein Fräulein?
Sprechen Sie Deutsch, meine Herren?

4. Sie sind meine Lehrerin.
Sie sind meine Studentin.
Ich bin Ihre Lehrerin.
Ich bin Ihre Studentin.

[1] **das Studentenheim** students' dormitory [2] **essen** eat [3] **die Mensa** students' dining hall *or* cafeteria [4] **verbringen** spend [5] **Ihr, Ihre** your [6] **die Freizeit** free time, leisure [7] **der Tennisplatz** tennis court [8] **zu Hause** at home [9] **das Kino** movie theater [10] **Wo studieren Sie lieber?** Where do you prefer to study? [11] **das Zimmer** room [12] **die Bibliothek** library [13] **das Wochenende** week end [14] **fahren** drive, go, travel [15] **nach Hause** home [16] **bleiben** stay [17] **besuchen** visit [18] **tanzen** dance [19] **brauchen** need

5. Sind Sie mein Lehrer, Herr Müller?
Ja, ich bin Ihr Lehrer, Herr Schmidt.
Sind Sie mein Student, Herr Fischer?
Ja, ich bin Ihr Student, Herr Professor.

6. Wie heißt Ihre Lehrerin, Fräulein Fischer?
Spricht Ihre Lehrerin Deutsch?
Wie heißt Ihr Lehrer, Herr Müller?
Spricht Ihr Lehrer Deutsch?

7. Seid ihr meine Kinder?
Seid ihr meine Studenten?
Seid ihr meine Studentinnen?
Seid ihr meine Freunde?

8. Wie verbringst du dein Wochenende?
Wie verbringst du deine Freizeit?
Wie verbringt er sein Wochenende?
Wie verbringt er seine Freizeit?
Wie verbringt sie ihr Wochenende?
Wie verbringt sie ihre Freizeit?
Wie verbringen Sie Ihr Wochenende?
Wie verbringen Sie Ihre Freizeit?
Wie verbringt ihr euer[1] Wochenende?
Wie verbringt ihr eure Freizeit?

9. Heißt du Karl, mein Kind?
Sprichst du Deutsch, mein Kind?
Kommst du nach Hause, mein Kind?
Bekommst[2] du keinen Pfennig,[3] mein Kind?
Brauchst du einen Pfennig, mein Kind?

10. Ich möchte mit Ihnen sprechen.
Ich möchte mit dir sprechen.
Mit Ihnen möchte er sprechen.
Mit dir möchte er sprechen.
Mit Ihnen möchte sie sprechen.
Wir möchten mit Ihnen sprechen.
Mit ihnen möchten wir sprechen.

11. Möchtest du mit ihnen sprechen?
Möchtest du mit mir sprechen?
Möchtest du mit uns sprechen?
Möchten Sie mit mir sprechen?
Möchten Sie mit uns sprechen?
Möchte sie mit dir sprechen?

12. Wenn er möchte, kommt er.
Wenn er will, kommt er.
Wenn er muß, kommt er.
Wenn er das weiß, kommt er.

13. Wenn er das weiß, sagt er es Ihnen.
Wenn er es muß, kann er es auch.
Wenn er es will, kann er es auch.

14. Wenn er es muß, kann er es tun.
Wenn er es will, kann er es tun.

15. Wenn sie „du" zueinander sagen, sind sie wohl Freunde.
Wenn wir Freunde sind, müssen wir „du" zueinander sagen.
Wenn wir „du" zueinander sagen, müssen wir uns beim Vornamen nennen.

16. Sie kennen sich erst seit acht Tagen.
Erst seit acht Tagen kennen sie sich.
Kennen sie sich erst seit acht Tagen?
Kennen Sie sich erst seit acht Tagen?
Wir kennen uns erst seit acht Tagen.

[1] **euer** your (*pl.*) [2] **bekommen** get [3] **der Pfennig** penny

English to German

The symbols at the end of sentences and clauses on page 38 (and in subsequent English to German sections) are intended as helpful reminders about the position of verb forms. Obey their directions carefully, and quite likely you will begin to follow more and more naturally basic, indispensable word-order rules that are often, unfortunately, violated by careless beginners.

Remember that it is as *wrong* in German to say: "Wenn er weiß das, er kommt" as it is in English to say: "If he that knows, comes he."

Conversely, it is just as correct (and really as easy) to say in German: **Wenn er das weiß, kommt er** as it is in English to say: *If he knows that, he'll come.*

KEY TO SYMBOLS

vf = verb first

Agreement here between German and English is unmistakable:

Sind Sie Studentin, Fräulein Müller?
Verstehen Sie mich recht, Herr Professor!

vs = verb second

Es	**ist**	mir eigentlich nicht zu schwer.
Mir	**ist**	es eigentlich nicht zu schwer.
Eigentlich	**ist**	es mir nicht zu schwer.
Zu schwer	**ist** [1]	es mir eigentlich nicht.

vl = verb last

Ich weiß nicht, was in dem Buch **steht.**
Wir bleiben hier, wenn er heute **kommt.**

vl/v = verb last/verb

occurring in situations where a dependent clause precedes an independent clause:

Was in dem Buch **steht, weiß** ich nicht.
Wenn er heute **kommt, bleiben** wir hier.

vs/vl = verb second/verb last

occurring in situations requiring modal-and-infinitive combinations or in compound tense situations:

Er **möchte** Ihnen eine kleine Anekdote **erzählen.**
Sie **würde** das nicht **sagen.** (*She would not say that.*)
Er **hat** das **studiert.** (*He has studied that.*)

[1] *Keep bearing in mind that in independent statements and clauses the verb is the second* unit, *though not necessarily the second* word.

vf/vl = verb first/verb last

Möchte er Ihnen eine kleine Anekdote **erzählen?**
Würde sie das nicht **sagen?**
Hat er das **studiert?**

Prepare the following exercise in writing.

1) Is your name Karl, my child? **vf**
Do you need a book, Miss Fischer? **vf**

2) We should like to talk to them. **vs/vl**
Would you (**du**) like to talk to him? **vf/vl**
Would you (**Sie**) like to talk to him? **vf/vl**

3) If he wants to, he'll come. (*use pres.*) **vl/v**
If he has to, he'll come. **vl/v**
If he knows that, he'll come. **vl/v**

4) If they say "du" to each other, they are friends. **vl/v**
They are friends **vs** if they say "du" to each other. **vl**
If we are friends, we must say "du" to each other. **vl/v/vl**
We must say "du" to each other **vs/vl** if we are friends. **vl**

5) They have known (*use pres.*) each other for a week. **vs**
We have known them for a week. **vs**
Only for a week have we known them. **vs**

Write the following sentences without the help of the key:

6) He is my friend.
She is my girl friend.
He is your (*2 ways*) friend.
She is your (*2 ways*) girl friend.
Is he your (*2 ways*) teacher?

PRONUNCIATION DRILL

(**w, v, f [ph]**; intonation in longer phrases [questions])

Repeat after the instructor, imitating carefully the above consonants and intonation patterns, and practice the following:

wer — war
wie — wir
wenn — wann
was — wo

vier — vor
von — vom
wir — vier
Wand — fand

Wo wohnt Vaters Freund?
Wo wohnt Werners Freundin?
Wer weiß, wo wir wohnen?
Wer weiß etwas davon?

Will Werners Freundin studieren?
Was will Werners Freundin studieren?
Will Werners Freundin auf der Universität Physik studieren?
Warum will Werners Freundin auf der Universität Physik und Philosophie studieren?

GRAMMAR

10. mein-Words

DECLENSIONAL ENDINGS OF **mein**

Note the identical or similar endings as you compare the forms of the definite article and the forms of **mein** (*my*).

	FEM.	NEUT.	MASC.	PLURAL
Nom.	d ie (Frau)	d as (Kind)	d er (Mann)	d ie (Frauen, Kinder, Männer)
Acc.	ie	as	en	ie
Dat.	er	em	em	en
Gen.	er	es	es	er
Nom.	mein e	* mein —	* mein —	mein e
Acc.	e	* mein —	en	e
Dat.	er	em	em	en
Gen.	er	es	es	er

NOTE:

A. (1) There are only three radical differences between the definite article and the **mein**-words: The latter lack endings in the areas indicated by the asterisk (*).

(2) Less radical is the –**ie** to –**e** change as indicated in the nominative and accusative of the feminine singular and the plural.

B. The following words take the same endings as **mein: ein, kein, dein** (*your*), **ihr** (*her*), **sein** (*its, his*), **unser** (*our*), **euer** (*your*), **ihr** (*their*), **Ihr** (*your*). (**Ein** has, of course, no plural forms.)

Illustrations and Exercises

Nom. Sie ist meine Freundin.
Acc. Sie kennt meine Freundin.
Dat. Sie sagt „du" zu meiner Freundin.

In the above sentences substitute **Lehrerin** for **Freundin** and use the proper forms of **ein** instead of **mein.**

Nom. Er ist mein Freund.
Acc. Er kennt meinen Freund.
Dat. Er sagt „du" zu meinem Freund.

In the above sentences substitute **Lehrer** for **Freund** and use the proper forms of **ein** instead of **mein.**

Nom. Das ist mein Kind.
Acc. Er kennt mein Kind.
Dat. Er sagt „du" zu meinem Kind.

In the above sentences substitute **Fräulein** for **Kind** and use the proper forms of **ein** instead of **mein.**

Nom. Das sind meine Freunde (Freundinnen, Kinder).
Acc. Er kennt meine Freunde (Freundinnen, Kinder).
Dat. Er sagt „du“ zu meine**n** Freunden (Freundinnen, Kindern).

Nom. Seine Freundin heißt Anna.
Acc. Anna kennt seine Mutter.
Dat. Sie spricht mit seine**r** Mutter.

Nom. Sein Freund heißt Karl.
Acc. Karl kennt seine**n** Vater.
Dat. Er spricht mit seine**m** Vater.

Nom. Sein Kind heißt Anna.
Acc. Karl kennt sein Kind.
Dat. Er spricht mit seine**m** Kind.

Nom. Seine Freunde sagen „du“ zu ihm.
Acc. Karl kennt seine Freunde.
Dat. Er spricht mit seine**n** Freunden.

In the above sentences, starting with **Das sind meine Freunde,** substitute the proper forms of **ihr** for **mein** and **sein.**

Now substitute the correct definite article form for each of the **mein-**words in all the sentences of this exercise (beginning on page 39).

11. Genitive Case

	FEMININE	NEUTER	MASCULINE
Singular:	der (meiner) Frau	des (meines) Kindes	des (meines) Mannes
Plural:	der (keiner) Frauen	der (keiner) Kinder	der (keiner) Männer

NOTE:

A. The genitive forms of the *neuter* and *masculine* definite article are identical; so are the genitive forms of the *neuter* and *masculine* **mein-**words.

B. The genitive singular of *neuter* and *masculine* nouns normally ends in **–s** or **–es.**

The genitive case indicates ownership or belonging together.

das Buch des (meines) Kindes
des (meines) Kindes Buch

der Freund des (meines) Vaters
des (meines) Vaters Freund

das Kind der Frau
die Bücher der Kinder, der Frauen, der Männer

Substitute the proper form of **sein** for **mein** in the following sentences:

Das ist das Buch meine**r** Freundin.
Das ist das Buch meine**s** Kindes.
Das ist das Buch meine**s** Freundes.

Das sind die Bücher meine**r** Freundinnen, Kinder und Freunde.

The genitive also appears with some prepositions. These will be discussed later.

The genitive is used to express indefinite time:

Eines Morgens kommt der Student spät wie immer in die Klasse.

6. Aufgabe

VOCABULARY BUILDING

Study the following pairs:

COGNATES

GERMAN	ENGLISH	GERMAN	ENGLISH
b (*medial or final*)	**v** (*sometimes* **f**)	**cht**	**ght**
über	over	acht	eight
leben	live	wichtig	"weighty," important
ch	**k**	**d**	**th**
sprechen (*note* **r**)	speak	beide	both
die Woche	week	danken	thank

Can you recognize the English for the following German words from the examples given above?

sieben, das Kalb; das Wochenende, rechnen; leicht, achtzehn; der Bruder, das Leder

GERMAN	ENGLISH	GERMAN	ENGLISH
f, ff (*medial or final*)	**p, pp**	**k**	**ch**
auf	up (on)	die Kapelle	chapel
tief	deep	das Kind	child
g	**i** *or* **y**	**s, ss, ß** (*medial or final*)	**t**
mag	may	daß	that
das Auge	eye	essen	eat

Can you recognize the English for the following German words?

das Schiff, der Affe; der Weg, der Nagel; der Kanal, die Karte; aus

GERMAN	ENGLISH	GERMAN	ENGLISH
tz	**t**	**t**	**d**
die Katze	cat	der Gott	God
der Witz	wit	unter	under
z	**t**	*Note the double consonant correspondence between*	
zu	to, too	Zeit	"tide," time
zwischen	betwixt and between		

Can you recognize the English for the following German words?

das Netz, witzig; der Zoll, zwölf; kalt, tanzen

WORD STUDY

Most of the following words and idiomatic expressions appear in Unit II. Fix them in your mind as firmly as possible and refer to them constantly until they become part of your active vocabulary.

WORDS COMMONLY USED

da there, then, here
dahin to that place (*with motion verbs*)
  dahin, dorthin this way, that way
dann then
daß (*subordinating conj.*) that
  Ich weiß, daß ich muß.
dennoch nevertheless
dort there
dorthin to that place (*with motion verbs*)
eben just; you see
einmal once (**ein** + **Mal** = one time)
erst first; (*with expr. of time*) only, not until
  Er kommt erst heute.
fort away, gone
  Er geht fort. Er ist fort.
gar even, quite
  gar nicht not at all
jawohl′ yes indeed
jetzt now
man (*indef. pron.*) one, they, we, you
nichts nothing
nie never
niemals never
schon already
sogar′ even, as a matter of fact
sonst otherwise, or else; formerly
weg away, gone (*see* **fort**)
wohl well; probably
zwar to be sure; it's true

IDIOMATIC EXPRESSIONS

Wie geht's? *How are you?* (lit. "*How goes it?*")
Es geht mir (uns) gut (ausgezeichnet). *I* (*we*) *feel fine* (*very well*).

halten + **von** *have an opinion of* or *about*
  Was halten Sie **davon?** *What's your opinion of it* (***thereof***)*? What do you think about it?*

recht haben *be right*
  Ich **habe** recht. *I* ***am*** *right.* (Note the verb difference between these two.)

Sie **kennen** sich seit einer Woche. *They* ***have known*** *each other for a week.*
Er **ist** seit einer Woche hier. *He* ***has been*** *here for a week.*
  Note the difference in tense between German and English in the last two sentences. The tense of the German verbs points to a continuation in the present of a state or action begun in the past.

Nicht wahr? *Isn't it* (*so*)*? Don't you? Haven't you? Doesn't he? Hasn't he? etc.*
  Es ist kalt, nicht wahr? Du siehst es, nicht wahr? Sie haben ein Buch, nicht wahr?

PRONUNCIATION DRILL

(s [ss, ß], sch, sp, st, z [ts, tz])

Repeat after the instructor and practice the following:

sie — sich
seit — sein
sagt — sagen
so — sogar

Sind Sie sein Sohn?

diese — dieses
dieser — diesen
unser — Unsinn
also — Esel

Soll sie diesen Unsinn lesen?

zu — zum
zur — zwar
Zeit — Freizeit
zählen — erzählen

Übersetzen Sie das also!

was — das
dies — daß
los — groß
fassen — lassen

Was erzählt uns der Professor?

ist — bist
wissen — müssen

meistens — niemals
alles — nichts

Ist das alles, was du weißt?

Sprachen — sprechen
Sprache — spricht
Bleistift — Beispiel
stehen — versteht

Mensch — Menschen
scheinen — schön
deutsch — englisch
komisch — schwer

Dieses Beispiel zu verstehen, scheint für uns zu schwer zu sein.

Reading

DU UND SIE

Wenn man zu einem Freund spricht, zu einem Hund, einem Kind, einer Katze — ja sogar wenn man zu einem Esel spricht, sagt man immer „du," niemals „Sie."

Wenn man zu der Mutter spricht, zu dem Vater, der Tante, dem Onkel, dem Großvater, oder zu anderen Verwandten, sagt man auch „du" und nicht „Sie." 5 Unsere Verwandten sind ja meistens keineswegs Kinder, Hunde, oder Esel, und dennoch sagt man „du," niemals „Sie" zu ihnen.

Ja, auch wenn man zum lieben Gott spricht, sagt man „Du," niemals „Sie." Zum Beispiel: „Vater unser, der Du bist im Himmel . . ."

Müller aber sagt immer „Sie" zu Tobler. Und umgekehrt. Sie kennen einander 10 zwar, aber sie sind nicht intime Freunde, sonst würden sie wohl „du" zueinander sagen.

Komisch, nicht wahr? Aber so ist das eben im Deutschen. Es ist also wichtig, daß man sich das merkt und danach handelt. Wenn man es nicht tut, kann man leicht in Verlegenheit kommen: 15

Zur reichen Tante Augusta, zum Beispiel, immer „Sie" zu sagen, ist nicht nur

LINE
2 der Esel — *donkey, jackass*
6 die Verwandten — *relatives*
meistens — *for the most part*
keineswegs — *by no means*
8 zum lieben Gott — *to God*
9 zum Beispiel — *for example*
„Vater unser . . ." — (the beginning of the Lord's prayer)
10 umgekehrt — *vice versa*
11 sonst würden sie — *otherwise they would*
13 im Deutschen — *in (the) German (language)*
14 wichtig — *important*
sich (etwas) merken — *remember (something)*
danach handelt — *acts accordingly*
15 in Verlegenheit kommen — *get into embarrassing situations*

albern, es kann auch kalt und fremd wirken. Womöglich bekommt man am Ende keinen Pfennig von ihr.

Anderseits braucht ein junger Bursche, der gar nicht heiraten will, nur einmal unversehens „du" zu einer reichen, heiratslustigen, alten Dame zu sagen, und im 5 Nu ist er in der Falle.

So ist das Leben und so sind die Menschen, und so steht es in der deutschen Sprache mit einem so einfachen Wort wie „du."

FRAGEN

1. Zu wem sagt man „du"? 2. Sagt man zu Kindern „Sie"? 3. Sagt man zu Gott „Du" oder „Sie"? 4. Warum sagen Müller und Tobler nicht „du" zueinander? 5. Was soll man sich im Deutschen merken? 6. Warum soll man zu Tante Augusta nicht „Sie" sagen? 7. Wer soll „Sie" zu einer heiratslustigen, alten Dame sagen?

SCHAUDER

Jetzt bist du da, dann bist du dort.
Jetzt bist du nah, dann bist du fort.
Kannst du's fassen? Und über eine Zeit
gehen wir beide die Ewigkeit
dahin — dorthin. Und was blieb? . . .
Komm, schließ die Augen, und hab mich lieb!

Christian Morgenstern (1871–1914)

SHUDDER

Now you are here, then you are there.
Now you are near, then you are — where?
Can you fathom it? And after time diurnal
We two will go a way eternal —
Separately. And what remains? . . .
Come, close your eyes and love before love wanes.

AUS GOETHES *Maximen und Reflexionen*

„Wenn ich irre, kann es jeder bemerken, wenn ich lüge, nicht."
„Der Schmutz ist glänzend, wenn die Sonne scheinen mag."
„Wer fremde Sprachen nicht kennt, weiß nichts von seiner eigenen."

FROM GOETHE'S *Maxims and Reflections*

"*If I err, everybody can notice it, but not if I lie.*"
"*Dirt sparkles when the sun deigns to shine upon it.*"
"*He who does not know foreign languages knows nothing about his own.*"

LINE

1 albern — *silly*
fremd — *strange, alien(ating)*
wirken — *have* or *produce an effect*
womöglich — *possibly, perhaps*
3 anderseits — *on the other hand*
der Bursche — *fellow*
der — *who*
heiraten — *marry*

LINE

4 unversehens — *inadvertently*
heiratslustig — *bent on marrying*
4–5 im Nu — *in a twinkling, instantly*
5 in der Falle sein — *be trapped*
6 so steht es — *that's the way it is*
7 ein- so — *such a*
einfach — *simple*

DRITTER TEIL

Johann Wolfgang von Goethe

Ludwig van Beethoven

Albert Einstein

Straßenszene in Köln am Rhein. Der Kölner Dom gehört zu den berühmtesten gotischen Kathedralen Deutschlands.

7. Aufgabe

ALLER ANFANG IST SCHWER

Read and memorize the following dialogue:

MÜLLER: Hallo, Karl! Wie geht es dir?

FISCHER: Danke, Peter. Es geht.

MÜLLER: Wir haben uns lange nicht gesehen.

FISCHER: Ich habe immer schrecklich viel zu tun. Ich glaube, ich arbeite vierundzwanzig Stunden am Tag.

MÜLLER: So? Warum arbeitest du denn so viel?

FISCHER: Ich muß so viel arbeiten, denn Mathematik und Geschichte machen mir viel Mühe. Besonders Geschichte. Dieser Geschichtskurs, den Professor Braun gibt! — Kennst du ihn?

MÜLLER: Nein, aber ich habe von ihm gehört. Verlangt er denn so viel von euch?

FISCHER: Ja, wir müssen bei ihm alles auswendig lernen. Wir müssen, zum Beispiel, von allen großen Männern wissen, wann sie geboren und wann sie gestorben sind.

MÜLLER: Ich kann mir nicht vorstellen, daß ihr das wirklich wissen müßt.

FISCHER: Oh, doch! Denn Braun gibt jede Woche ein oder zwei Prüfungen. Und wenn man nicht alles weiß, bekommt man schlechte Noten.

THE FIRST STEP IS THE HARDEST

MÜLLER: Hello, Karl! How are you?

FISCHER: Pretty well, Peter, thanks. (*lit.* "It goes.")

MÜLLER: We haven't seen each other for a long time.

FISCHER: I am always terribly busy. (*lit.* "I always have terribly much to do.") I guess I am working twenty-four hours a day.

MÜLLER: Really? Why in the world are you working so hard? (*lit.* "Why, then, do you work so much?")

FISCHER: I have to work that hard, because math and history give (*lit.* "make") me a great deal of trouble. Especially history. That history course of Professor Braun's (*lit.* "which Professor Braun gives")! — Do you know him?

MÜLLER: No, but I've heard about him. Does he really ask so much of you?

FISCHER: Yes, we have to learn everything by heart in his course (*lit.* "with him"). For example, we have to know about all the famous men (we are studying), when they were born and when they died.

MÜLLER: I can't imagine that you really have to know (all) that.

FISCHER: Oh yes, we do, because Braun gives one or two exams every week. And if you don't know everything, you get low grades.

DRILL PATTERNS

Repeat the following drills after your instructor or after the speaker on the tape. Imitate the pronunciation very carefully.

1. Wie geht es dir?
Wie geht es Ihnen?
Wie geht es euch?
Wie geht es ihm?
Wie geht es ihr?
Wie geht es ihnen?

2. Es geht mir gut.
Es geht uns gut.
Es geht ihm gut.
Es geht ihr gut.
Es geht ihnen gut.

3. Mir geht es nicht gut.
Uns geht es nicht gut.
Ihm geht es nicht gut.
Ihr geht es nicht gut.
Ihnen geht es nicht gut. (*2 meanings*)

4. Ich kenne dich.
Ich kenne Sie.
Ich kenne sie (*her*).
Ich kenne es schon.
Ich kenne ihn schon.
Ich kenne euch schon.
Ich kenne sie (*them*).

5. Ich habe von ihm gehört.
Ich habe von dir gehört.
Ich habe von Ihnen gehört.
Ich habe von euch gehört.
Ich habe von ihr gehört.
Ich habe von ihnen gehört.

6. Hast du von Professor Braun gehört?
Hat er von Professor Braun gehört?
Habt ihr von Professor Braun gehört?
Haben Sie von Professor Braun gehört?
Ach ja, wir haben von ihm gehört.

7. Sie muß bei ihm alles auswendig lernen.
Bei mir muß sie alles auswendig lernen.
Bei dir muß sie alles auswendig lernen.

8. Bei euch muß man alles auswendig lernen.
Muß man bei ihr alles auswendig lernen?
Man muß bei ihnen alles auswendig lernen.
Muß man bei uns alles auswendig lernen?

9. Ja, ich kenne ihn schon lange.
Ja, wir kennen ihn schon lange.
Ja, du kennst ihn schon lange.
Ja, Sie kennen ihn schon lange.
Ja, ihr kennt ihn schon lange.
Ja, sie kennt ihn schon lange.
Ja, sie kennen ihn schon lange.
Ja, er kennt ihn schon lange.

10. Bist du sein Freund?
Ist er dein Freund?
Ist sie Ihre Freundin?
Sind Sie ihr Freund?

11. Kennen Sie das Haus meines Vaters?
Ja, wir kennen es.
Kennen Sie die Kinder Ihres Lehrers?
Nein, wir kennen sie nicht.
Kennst du die Freundin deines Freundes?
Ja, ich kenne sie.
Kennt ihr die Freunde meiner Freundin?
Nein, wir kennen sie nicht.

12. Ich arbeite jeden Tag eine Stunde.
Er arbeitet jeden Tag zwei Stunden.
Du arbeitest jeden Montag[1] drei Stunden.
Sie arbeitet jeden Mittwoch[2] vier Stunden.
Sie arbeiten jeden Sonnabend[3] fünf Stunden. (*2 meanings*)
Wir arbeiten jeden Dienstag[4] sechs Stunden.
Ihr arbeitet jeden Freitag[5] sieben Stunden.

13. Vater arbeitet jeden Tag acht Stunden.
Sein Vater arbeitet jeden Tag neun Stunden.
Mein Vater arbeitet jeden Tag zehn Stunden.
Meine Mutter arbeitet jeden Tag elf Stunden.
Jeden Tag arbeitet ihre Mutter zwölf Stunden.

14. Du mußt jede Woche dreizehn Stunden arbeiten.
Du mußt jede Woche vierzehn Stunden arbeiten.
Mußt du jede Woche siebzehn Stunden arbeiten?
Jede Woche mußt du zwanzig Stunden arbeiten.

15. Er muß jede Woche sechsundzwanzig Stunden arbeiten.
Sie muß jede Woche dreißig Stunden arbeiten.
Ihr müßt jede Woche dreiunddreißig Stunden arbeiten.
Muß ich jede Woche vierzig Stunden arbeiten?

16. Wir wissen, wann er geboren ist.
Wir wissen, wann sie geboren ist.
Wir wissen, wann Sie geboren sind.
Wir wissen, wann sie geboren sind.
Wir wissen, wann ihr geboren seid.

English to German

KEY TO SYMBOLS

vf — verb first	**vl** — verb last	**vs/vl** — verb second/verb last
vs — verb second	**vl/v** — verb last/verb	**vf/vl** — verb first/verb last

Prepare this exercise in writing.

1) How are you, Mrs. Müller? **vs**
How are you, my child? **vs**
How is she? **vs**
How are they? **vs**

2) He is well. **vs**
They are well. **vs**
I am well. **vs**
We are well. **vs**

3) I have known her (*use pres. tense*) for a long time. **vs**
I have known him for a long time. **vs**
I have known them for a long time. **vs**
I have known it for a long time. **vs**
I have known you (*3 ways*) for a long time. **vs**

[1] **der Montag** Monday [2] **der Mittwoch** Wednesday [3] **der Sonnabend** Saturday [4] **der Dienstag** Tuesday [5] **der Freitag** Friday

4) I have heard about you. (*3 ways*) **vs/vl**
He has heard about them. **vs/vl**
We have heard about her. **vs/vl**
They have heard about us. **vs/vl**

Translate the following sentences without the aid of the key:

5) He is your teacher. (*3 ways*)
Are you his student? (*3 ways*)
She is your mother. (*3 ways*)
Are you his father? (*2 ways*)

6) Do they know the friend (the girl friend, the friends, the girl friends) of her brother?
No, they don't know him (her, them).

7) Is he the teacher of her child (her brother, her girl friend, her children)?

PRONUNCIATION DRILL

(sibilants; accent and intonation in long words [compounds])

Repeat after the instructor and practice the following:

Zeit — seit
Zahl — Saal
reisen — reißen
lesen — lassen

unversehens — heiratslustig
anderseits — keineswegs

sterben — gestorben
stundenlang — Geschichtskurs

Sonnabend, Sonntag, Montag, Dienstag
Mittwoch, Donnerstag, Freitag
Samstag

Frühling, Sommer, Herbst und Winter

Januar, Februar, März, April
Mai, Juni, Juli, August
September, Oktober
November, Dezember

eins, zwei, drei — vier, fünf, sechs, sieben
neunundsechzig — siebenundachtzig
zweiundzwanzig — sechsunddreißig
siebzehnhundertsiebenundzwanzig — achtzehnhundertsechsundsechzig

GRAMMAR

12. Present Perfect Tense

The present perfect tense is formed by using as auxiliary the present tense forms of **haben** or **sein,** combined with the past participle of the main verb.

Illustrations

1. Ich **habe** von ihm **gehört.** — *I have heard of him.*
2. Wir wissen, wann sie **gestorben ist.** — *We know when she died.*

NOTE:

A. The past participle normally has a **ge–** prefix and a **–t** or **–en** suffix (see **gehört** and **gestorben** above). The reason for the difference in suffix will be discussed later.

B. (1) Intransitive verbs denoting change of place or change of state use **sein** as auxiliary in the present perfect, past perfect, and future perfect tenses. (An intransitive verb in German is one that does not take the accusative, e.g., **kommen, werden.)**

sterben (*die*): Sokrates **ist** vor vielen, vielen Jahren **gestorben.**
gehen (*go*): Mein Bruder **ist** nach Europa **gegangen.**
werden (*become*): Wir **sind** leider alt **geworden.**

(2) **Sein** and **bleiben** (*stay*) use **sein** as auxiliary in the same tenses as indicated in B (1) above, even though neither one expresses change of state or change of condition.

C. In independent clauses the auxiliary takes verb-second position, the past participle takes verb-last position (see No. 1 of Illustrations on page 51).

D. In dependent clauses the auxiliary comes last, preceded by the past participle (see No. 2 of Illustrations on page 51).

13. Cardinal Numerals

1	eins	11	elf	21	einundzwanzig
2	zwei	12	zwölf	22	zweiundzwanzig, *etc.*
3	drei	13	dreizehn	30	**dreißig**
4	vier	14	vierzehn	40	vierzig
5	fünf	15	fünfzehn	50	fünfzig
6	sechs	16	**sechzehn**	60	**sechzig**
7	sieben	17	**siebzehn**	70	**siebzig**
8	acht	18	achtzehn	80	achtzig
9	neun	19	neunzehn	90	neunzig
10	zehn	20	zwanzig	100	hundert

101	hundert(und)eins	10 000	zehntausend
122	hundert(und)zweiundzwanzig	100 000	hunderttausend
540	fünfhundertvierzig	1 000 000	eine Million′
785	siebenhundertfünfundachtzig	1 000 000 000	eine Milliar′de (*1 billion*)
1000	tausend		

1794 (ein)tausendsiebenhundertvierundneunzig
or (*as a date*) siebzehnhundertvierundneunzig
1827 (ein)tausendachthundertsiebenundzwanzig
or (*as a date*) achtzehnhundertsiebenundzwanzig
1962 (ein)tausendneunhundertzweiundsechzig
or (*as a date*) neunzehnhundertzweiundsechzig

14. Days of the Week, Months of the Year, and the Seasons

The days of the week, the months of the year, and the seasons are all masculine.

Montag	*Monday*	am Montag (*on Monday, etc.*)
Dienstag	*Tuesday*	am Dienstag
Mittwoch	*Wednesday*	am Mittwoch
Donnerstag	*Thursday*	am Donnerstag
Freitag	*Friday*	am Freitag
Sonnabend (*or* Samstag)	*Saturday*	am Sonnabend (*or* am Samstag)
Sonntag	*Sunday*	am Sonntag

Januar	im Januar (*in January, etc.*)	Juli	im Juli
Februar	im Februar	August	im August
März	im März	September	im September
April	im April	Oktober	im Oktober
Mai	im Mai	November	im November
Juni	im Juni	Dezember	im Dezember

der Frühling	im Frühling (*in the spring, etc.*)
der Sommer	im Sommer
der Herbst	im Herbst
der Winter	im Winter

der Tag (*day*), die Woche (*week*), der Monat (*month*), das Jahr (*year*)

Feierabend. Ein deutscher Arbeiter mit seinen Kindern.

8. Aufgabe

WER BIN ICH?

SAMPLE ANSWERS AND SUGGESTIONS

a. Wann sind Sie geboren? — *Ich bin im Jahr(e) . . . geboren.*
In welchem Monat sind Sie geboren? — *Ich bin im . . . geboren.*
b. Wie alt sind Sie? — *Ich bin . . . Jahre alt.*
c. Welche Nummer [1] hat das Haus, in dem [2] Sie wohnen? — *Das Haus, in dem ich wohne, hat Nummer . . .*
d. Wo wohnen Ihre Eltern? [3] — *Meine Eltern wohnen in . . .*
e. Wo sind Ihre Eltern geboren?
Wie alt ist Ihr Vater?
Wie alt ist Ihre Mutter?
Was ist der Mädchenname [4] Ihrer Mutter? — *Meine Mutter ist eine geborene [5] . . .*
f. Wo arbeitet Ihr Vater?
g. Haben Sie Geschwister? [6]
Wie viele [7] Geschwister haben Sie?
Wie heißen sie?
Wie alt ist Ihr Bruder?
Wie alt sind Ihre Brüder?
Wie alt ist Ihre Schwester?
Wie alt sind Ihre Schwestern?

DRILL PATTERNS

Repeat the following drills after your instructor or after the speaker on the tape. Imitate the pronunciation very carefully.

1. Herr Schmidt hat jeden [8] Morgen eine Klasse.
Fräulein Müller hat jeden Morgen zwei Klassen.
Dienstag und Donnerstag haben wir drei Klassen.
Montag, Mittwoch und Freitag haben wir vier Klassen.
Haben Sie jede Woche drei (vier, fünf, sechs) Stunden Deutsch?

2. In dieser Klasse sind sieben (acht, neun, zehn) Studenten.
In manchen [9] Klassen sind achtzehn (neunzehn, zwanzig, dreißig) Studenten.
Wie viele Studentinnen sind in Ihrer Klasse?
Wie viele Studenten lernen hier Deutsch?

[1] **die Nummer** number [2] **dem** (*relative pronoun*) which [3] **die Eltern** (*plural noun*) parents [4] **der Mädchenname** maiden name [5] **Meine Mutter ist eine geborene (Schmidt)** (*lit.* "My mother is a born [Schmidt]") My mother's maiden name is (Schmidt) [6] **die Geschwister** (*plural noun*) brothers and sisters [7] **wieviel, wie viele** how much, how many [8] **jed**– (**–e, –es, –er**) each, every [9] **manch**– (**–e, –es, –er**) many a; (*plural*) some

3. Sokrates ist im Jahre vierhundertneunundsechzig v. Chr.[1] geboren.
Der heilige Augustinus [2] ist im Jahre dreihundertvierundfünfzig n. Chr.[3] geboren.
Columbus ist im Jahre fünfzehnhundert(und)sechs gestorben.
Shakespeare ist im Jahre sechzehnhundertsechzehn gestorben.
Johannes Kepler ist im Jahre sechzehnhundertdreißig gestorben.
Johann Wolfgang von Goethe ist im Jahre siebzehnhundertneunundvierzig geboren.
Albert Einstein ist im Jahre achtzehnhundertneunundsiebzig geboren.
Hemingway ist im Jahre achtzehnhundertachtundneunzig geboren.
Churchill ist im Jahre achtzehnhundertvierundsiebzig geboren.
Roosevelt ist im Jahre neunzehnhundertfünfundvierzig gestorben.
Stalin ist im Jahre neunzehnhundertdreiundfünfzig gestorben.

4. Verlangt er viel von dir?
Verlangt er viel von Ihnen?
Verlangt er viel von euch?
Verlangt er viel von ihr?
Verlangt er viel von ihm?
Verlangt er viel von ihnen?

5. Verlange ich zuviel von euch?
Verlangen wir zuviel von euch?
Hat sie von euch zuviel verlangt?
Hat er von euch zuviel verlangt?
Verlangt man zuviel von euch?

6. Wir haben uns lange nicht gesehen!
Ich habe Sie doch gestern [4] gesehen!
Gestern haben Sie mich gesehen?
Ja, ihr habt euch gestern gesehen.

7. Nein, ich kann es mir nicht vorstellen.
Nein, wir können es uns nicht vorstellen.
Nein, du kannst es dir nicht vorstellen.
Nein, Sie können es sich nicht vorstellen.
Nein, ihr könnt es euch nicht vorstellen.
Nein, sie kann es sich nicht vorstellen.
Nein, er kann es sich nicht vorstellen.
Nein, sie können es sich nicht vorstellen.

8. Ich kann mir nicht vorstellen, daß ich das tun muß.
Ich kann mir nicht vorstellen, daß wir das tun müssen.
Er kann sich nicht vorstellen, daß du das tun mußt.
Sie kann sich nicht vorstellen, daß Sie das müssen.

9. Wenn man das weiß, bekommt man gute Noten.
Wenn du das weißt, bekommst du gute Noten.
Wenn wir das wissen, bekommen wir gute Noten.

10. Wenn ich das nicht weiß, bekomme ich schlechte Noten.
Wenn Sie das nicht wissen, bekommen Sie schlechte Noten.
Wenn ihr das nicht wißt, bekommt ihr schlechte Noten.

11. In welchem [5] Jahr ist er geboren?
In welchem Monat ist er geboren?
In diesem Monat? In diesem Jahr?

12. Wie viele Tage hat der Monat?
Welcher Monat? — Dieser Monat.
Wie viele Tage hat das Jahr?
Welches Jahr? Jedes Jahr?

[1] **v. Chr. = vor Christi (Geburt)** B.C. [2] **der heilige Augustinus** St. Augustine [3] **n. Chr. = nach Christi (Geburt)** A.D. [4] **gestern** yesterday [5] **welch– (–e, –es, –er)** which

13. Arbeiten Sie jeden Tag?
Arbeiten Sie jeden Montag?
Ich studiere dieses Jahr.
Dieses Jahr muß ich studieren.

14. Ist dir diese Woche zu lang?
Jede Woche ist mir zu lang.
Jede Woche muß ich studieren.
Diese Woche studiere ich nicht.

15. Ist das das Haus, in dem [1] Sie wohnen?
Das ist das Haus, in dem ich wohne.
Sind das die Häuser, in denen [1] ihr wohnt?
Das sind die Häuser, in denen wir wohnen.

16. Ist der Geschichtskurs, den Braun gibt, schwer?
Alle Kurse, die Braun gibt, sind schwer.
Wie sind die Noten, die Professor Braun gibt?
Alle Noten, die Braun gibt, sind schlecht.

English to German

KEY TO SYMBOLS

vf — verb first	**vl** — verb last	**vs/vl** — verb second/verb last
vs — verb second	**vl/v** — verb last/verb	**vf/vl** — verb first/verb last

Prepare this exercise in writing.

1) She has to learn everything by heart. **vs/vl**

2) I have to work five hours every day. **vs/vl**
We have to work twelve hours every day. **vs/vl**
You (*3 ways*) have to work forty hours every week. **vs/vl**

3) In which year (month) was she born? **vs/vl**
We know **vs** when they were born. **vl**
He knows **vs** when I was born. **vl**

4) Does he ask a great deal of you (*3 ways*)? **vf**
He asks too much of me. **vs**

5) I cannot imagine **vs/vl** that you (*3 ways*) have to do that. **vl**
If you (*formal*) do not know that, you will get (*use pres. tense*) low grades. **vl/v**

Translate the following sentences without the help of the key:

6) I have seen him.
He has seen me.
They have seen us.
We have seen them.
We have seen each other.

7) Does every year have 365 days? (*write out numerals*)
Does every month have 30 days? (*write out numerals*)

8) Is that the house in which he lives?
Is that the house in which they live?
Are these (**Sind das**) the houses in which the students live?

[1] **in dem, in denen** in which

PRONUNCIATION DRILL

(ch)

Repeat after the instructor, imitating carefully the variation in the **ch**-*sounds, and practice the following:*

acht — achtzig	ich — mich	schlecht — recht
Nacht — ach	sich — dich	sprechen — sprecht
machen — lachen	wichtig — richtig	sechzehn — sechzig
nach — danach	Geschichte — Gedicht	sechzehn — sechs
brauchen — braucht	leicht — licht	Sprache — spricht
auch — Bauch	reich — nicht	Nacht — Nächte
Buch — Tuch	weich — dicht	Buch — Bücher
Woche — doch	schleicht — Gesicht	mochte — möchte

GRAMMAR

15. dies-Words

We have already seen the system of endings of the **mein**-words emerging from the definite article pattern (see Grammar Section 10). An even closer formal relationship exists between the definite article and words like **dies**– (*this*) and **jen**– (*that*, archaic "yon").

	FEM.	NEUT.	MASC.	PLURAL
Nom.	d ie (Frau)	d as (Kind)	d er (Mann)	d ie (Frauen, Kinder, Männer)
Acc.	ie	as	en	ie
Dat.	er	em	em	en
Gen.	er	es	es	er
Nom.	dies e	dies es *	dies er *	dies e
Acc.	e	es *	en	e
Dat.	er	em	em	en
Gen.	er	es	es	er

Note that the starred forms (*) have endings where the **mein**-word does not. This constitutes the only difference between the **mein**-words and the **dies**-words.

The following words have the same pattern as **dies**– (**–e, –es, –er**) and **jen**– (**–e, –es, –er**):

jed– each, every
manch– many a (*sing.*), some (*pl.*)
solch– such a, such
welch– which, what

16. The Relative Pronoun

The relative pronoun declension is the same as that of the definite article (see above), except for the starred forms in the following columns:

	FEM.	NEUT.	MASC.	PLURAL
Nom.	die	das	der	die
Acc.	die	das	den	die
Dat.	der	dem	dem	denen *
Gen.	deren *	dessen *	dessen *	deren *

The demonstrative pronoun forms are exactly like those of the relative pronoun. The function and meanings of the demonstrative pronoun will be discussed later.

The relative pronoun **die, das, der** (*who, which, that*)

a. introduces verb-last word order;
b. must always be expressed in German;
c. agrees with its antecedent in number and gender; its case depends upon its use within its own clause.

Illustrations

Ein Mann, der (*masc. sing.; nom.*) Musik macht, ist ein Musikant.	lit. *A man who makes music is a musician.*
Der Geschichtskurs, von dem ich dir erzählen will, ist schwer.	
Der Dichter, dessen Gedicht ich auswendig gelernt habe, heißt Morgenstern.	lit. *The poet, whose poem I learned by heart, is called Morgenstern.*
Die Prüfung, die Professor Braun gibt, ist schwer.	
Die Prüfungen, die unsere Professoren geben, sind schwer.	
Der Geschichtskurs, den (*masc. sing.; acc.*) Professor Braun gibt, ist schwer.	*Professor Braun's history course is hard.* (lit. "*The history course, which Professor Braun gives, is difficult.*")

17. Accusative Prepositions

The following prepositions are used only with the accusative:

durch through, by, by means of	**ohne** without
für for, on behalf of	**um** around, at
gegen against, toward	**wider** against

Memorize the above prepositions!

Illustrations

Geht die Reise **um** die ganze Welt?	*Does the journey go around the whole world?*
Wir fahren mit unserem Wagen **durch** die Schweiz.	*We drive with our car through Switzerland.*

Wer nicht **für** mich ist, ist **gegen (wider)** mich.	*Who(ever) is not for me is against me.*
An der Grenze hielt der Paßbeamte meinen Paß **gegen** das Licht.	*At the border the passport officer held my passport against the light.*
Ohne dich kann ich nicht leben.	*I cannot live without you.*

Contractions:

durchs = **durch das** **fürs** = **für das** **ums** = **um das**

Geht die Reise durchs ganze Land?	*Does the trip go through the whole country?*
Fürs Kind ist das gut genug.	*That's good enough for the child.*
Sie läuft immer ums Haus.	*She keeps running around the house.*

9. Aufgabe

VOCABULARY BUILDING

COGNATES

Study the following pairs:

GERMAN	ENGLISH	GERMAN	ENGLISH
b (*medial or final*)	**v** (*sometimes* **f**)	**g**	**i** *or* **y**
der Dieb	thief	die Magd	maid
geben (gibt)	give (gives)	der Tag	day
d	**th**	**s, ss,** *or* **ß** (*medial or final*)	**t**
dies	this	lassen (läßt)	let (lets)
drei	three	beißen	bite

Can you recognize the English for the following German words?

eben, streben; das Bad, die Erde; lag, der Honig; grüßen, die Nuß

What season of the year is **der Herbst?**
How much is **ein bißchen?**
What color is **weiß?**
What color is **gelb?**
What is the meaning of the two opposites: **dick und dünn?**

GERMAN	ENGLISH	GERMAN	ENGLISH
t	**d**	**z**	**t**
tun	do	das Zeichen	token
der Tod	death	die Zeitung	tidings (newspaper)

Can you recognize the English for the following German words?

hart, alt, kalt, halten, falten; trinken, trank, getrunken; gut

Give the meaning for:

Zehnmal zwei ist zwanzig.
Zehnmal zwanzig ist zweihundert.
Zehnmal zwölf ist hundertzwanzig.

Complete the following sentences in English:

What part of the body is **die Zunge?**
Domestic animals are usually **zahm.**
One usually sleeps **in einem Bett.**
Some cans **sind aus Zinn gemacht.**

Give the meaning for:

Der Wind treibt den Regen.
An so einem traurigen Tag tanzen die Trunkenen tief in dem Tal.

WORD STUDY

The following words and idiomatic expressions appear frequently. They should become fixed in your memory as soon as possible.

WORDS COMMONLY USED

alles everything
ander– other
anders otherwise, different(ly)
beinahe almost
ein bißchen a little (bit)
drüben over there
eigentlich really
etwas some, something, somewhat
  etwas Brot some bread
  etwas Neues something new
  etwas spät somewhat late
fast almost (*see* **beinahe**)
genau' exact(ly)
genug' enough
gern(e) gladly
gewiß' certain(ly)
her here, this way (*denoting direction toward speaker*)
hin there, that way (*denoting direction away from speaker*)
  hin und her to and fro, back and forth
jemand someone, somebody
kaum hardly
lange for a long time
mal (*adds emphasis to imperative*) please, do, just
mehr more
meistens mostly, generally
nie never
niemand nobody, no one
nimmer = **nie mehr** nevermore
noch still (*temporal*)
  noch einmal once more
recht right
  Er hat recht. He is right.
richtig right, correct
  Es ist richtig. It is right.
sehr very
weder . . . noch neither . . . nor
wirklich really
zweierlei two kinds of

IDIOMATIC EXPRESSIONS

denn in medial or final position in questions expresses surprise, bewilderment, anger, impatience:
Wer ist er denn? *Who in the world is he?*
Warum siehst du mich denn so an? *Tell me, why are you looking at me that way?*
Was ist denn hier los? *What the deuce is going on here?*

geben: es gibt *there is, there are* (Note that the case governed by the verb is accusative.)
Es gibt wirklich eine seelische Armut. *There is really a spiritual (kind of) poverty.*
Es gibt auch zweierlei Reichtum. *There are also two kinds of wealth.*

gern haben *like* (**gern(e)** with other verbs: *like to*)
Wir haben den Kurs gern. *We like the course.*
Ich studiere nicht gern. *I don't like to study.*
Ich sage gerne „du" zu dir.

heißen *be called*
Sie heißt nicht Anna, sondern Augusta. *Her name is not Anna but Augusta.*
das heißt *that is (to say)*
Professor Braun verlangt viel von seinen Studenten, das heißt, sie müssen bei ihm fast alles auswendig lernen.

schon plus time expressions used with *present* tense of verbs denotes situations or actions begun in the past and continuing in the present:
Kennen Sie dieses Gedicht schon lange? *Have you known this poem for a long time?*

PRONUNCIATION DRILL

(ch, sch; r)

Repeat after the instructor and practice the following:

acht — beachten
Furcht — furchtbar
nah — nächste
dicht — Dichtung

manche — Mädchen
welche — solche
dennoch — möglich
einfach — üblich

wirklich — hoffentlich
persönlich — empfindlich
eigentlich — natürlich
wöchentlich — gewöhnlich

tragisch — wesentlich — melancholisch
deutsch — deutlich — bißchen traurig

Herr — Herren
starr — starren
knurrt — knurren
irren — irrt

sprechen — brechen
groß — Gras
tragisch — traurig
drehen — dreht

Reading

DER LEIERMANN

Drüben hinter'm Dorfe
Steht ein Leiermann,
Und mit starren Fingern
Dreht er, was er kann.

Barfuß auf dem Eise
Wankt er hin und her,
Und sein kleiner Teller
Bleibt ihm immer leer.

Keiner mag ihn hören,
Keiner sieht ihn an,
Und die Hunde knurren
Um den alten Mann.

Und er läßt es gehen
Alles, wie es will,
Dreht, und seine Leier
Steht ihm nimmer still.

Wunderlicher Alter,
Soll ich mit dir geh'n?
Willst zu meinen Liedern
Deine Leier dreh'n?

THE ORGAN GRINDER

Over near the village
Stands an organ man,
He winds with frozen fingers
As briskly as he can.

Barefoot on the ice now
Back and forth he sways,
And his little platter
Always empty stays.

No one cares to hear him,
People look away,
And the dogs are growling
In the old man's way.

And he lets things happen
As they may and will,
Grinds his little organ,
And it's never still.

Strange old organ grinder,
Shall I go with thee?
Will you play your music
To my poetry?

STUMPF LERNT VON MÜLLER

STUMPF: Von wem ist das Gedicht?

MÜLLER: Müller heißt der Dichter, Wilhelm Müller.

LINE
1 das Gedicht — *poem*

LINE
2 der Dichter — *poet*

STUMPF: Ach so, ein Verwandter von Ihnen, nicht wahr?

MÜLLER: (*lachend*) Oh ja, gewiß! Alle Müllers sind miteinander verwandt.

STUMPF: Er ist wohl Ihr Großvater?

MÜLLER: Das kann kaum sein. Ich habe ihn persönlich nicht gekannt, er ist im
5 Jahre siebzehnhundertvierundneunzig geboren.

STUMPF: Furchtbar lange ist das her.

MÜLLER: Furchtbar lange.

STUMPF: Und wo ist er denn geboren? In Deutschland oder in Österreich, oder gar in der Schweiz?

10 MÜLLER: Er ist in Dessau geboren, einer Stadt, die jetzt in der russischen Zone liegt, nicht sehr weit von Berlin.

STUMPF: Sie wissen aber furchtbar viel.

MÜLLER: Ja, furchtbar viel. Ich weiß auch, daß er im Jahre achtzehnhundertsiebenundzwanzig gestorben ist, denn ich habe es eben in meinem Litera-
15 turgeschichtsbuch gelesen.

STUMPF: Kennen Sie dieses Gedicht schon lange?

MÜLLER: Seit gestern. Ich habe es sehr gern. Sie auch?

STUMPF: Doch! Es gefällt mir, weil es so einfach ist.

MÜLLER: Und musikalisch?

20 STUMPF: Ja, und melancholisch.

MÜLLER: Melancholisch? Das finde ich nicht. Traurig ist es, beinahe tragisch, wenn auch ein bißchen sentimental, aber melancholisch ist es nicht.

STUMPF: Nun, sagen Sie mal, was will der Dichter mit seinem Gedicht denn eigentlich sagen?

25 MÜLLER: Na, was glauben S i e?

LINE

1 ach so — *oh, I see*
2 lachend — *laughing*
4 gekannt (kennen — *know*)
6 furchtbar — *terribly*
lange . . . her — *long ago*
8 Deutschland — *Germany*
Österreich — *Austria*
9 gar — *perhaps, even*
die Schweiz — *Switzerland*
10 die Stadt — *town, city*
russisch — *Russian*

LINE

11 liegen — *lie*
weit — *far*
14 eben — *just (now)*
15 gelesen (lesen — *read*)
17 gestern — *yesterday*
18 gefallen — *please*
weil — *because*
21 traurig — *sad*
23 mal — here: *just*
25 na — *well*

STUMPF: Was ich glaube? Nichts, als daß der arme Leiermann einen schlechten Eindruck mit seiner Musik macht.

MÜLLER: Arm, elend und zerlumpt ist er wohl, und niemand beachtet ihn und seine Musik. Das heißt: sie macht keinen Eindruck, weder einen guten noch einen schlechten. 5

STUMPF: Sie haben recht. Da steht es ja: „Keiner mag ihn hören,/Keiner sieht ihn an."

MÜLLER: Keiner? Wirklich? Gar keiner?

STUMPF: Hm! Na ja, der Dichter sieht ihn an. Der Dichter „mag ihn hören." Er allein. 10

MÜLLER: Gewiß! Die Welt wendet sich von dem Leiermann ab. Nur der Dichter erkennt seinen Wert. Er allein weiß, daß es zweierlei Armut gibt.

STUMPF: Wieso denn? Das verstehe ich nicht.

MÜLLER: Die eine, sehen Sie, ist die Geldarmut. „Und sein kleiner Teller/Bleibt 15 ihm immer leer." Diese Armut, meint der Dichter, ist schlimm genug, aber bei weitem nicht die schlimmere.

STUMPF: So, und die andere?

MÜLLER: Ist eine Armut, die wirklich arm macht — eine seelische Armut.

STUMPF: Und wir alle leiden daran? 20

MÜLLER: Alle, die nicht hören mögen. Das scheint mir klar zu sein.

STUMPF: Und es gibt also auch zweierlei Reichtum?

MÜLLER: Natürlich. Es gibt einen materiellen und einen seelischen Reichtum. Und dies, so scheint es mir, ist das Wesentliche an dem Gedicht: Der Singende ist auch meistens der Leidende, weil er auch der Sehende und 25 Duldende ist.

LINE
1 glauben — *believe, think*
als — *but, except*
arm — *poor*
1–2 schlechten Eindruck — *bad impression*
3 elend — *miserable*
zerlumpt — *ragged, shabby*
wohl — *indeed*
beachten — *notice*
8 Gar keiner? — *Nobody at all?*
11 sich abwenden — *turn away*
12 erkennen — *recognize*
der Wert — *worth, value*
zweierlei — *two kinds of*
die Armut — *poverty*
14 wieso — *how so*

LINE
15 das Geld — *money*
16 schlimm genug — *bad enough*
17 schlimmere — *worse*
19 die seelische Armut — *poverty of soul*
20 leiden daran — *suffer from this*
21 scheinen — *seem*
22 der Reichtum — *wealth*
24 das Wesentliche — *the essential thing, point*
25 der Singende — *the singer* (lit. "*the singing one*")
der Leidende — *the sufferer* (lit. "*the suffering one*")
der Sehende — *the one who sees*
26 der Duldende — *the patient one*

„Und er läßt es gehen
Alles, wie es will,
Dreht, und seine Leier
Steht ihm nimmer still.“

5 STUMPF: Wie können Sie das eigentlich sagen? Das meint der Dichter doch nicht.

MÜLLER: Warum denn nicht?

STUMPF: Nun, genau genommen singt der Leiermann ja nicht, sondern er dreht nur seinen Leierkasten.

10 MÜLLER: Genauer genommen — das heißt, symbolisch genommen — ist der Leiermann kein gewöhnlicher Leiermann.

STUMPF: Wieso denn? Das verstehe ich wieder nicht.

MÜLLER: Nun, er scheint mir ein Musiker zu sein — ein Künstler, einer, der Musik macht, fast in dem Sinne wie, zum Beispiel, der Tondichter Musik
15 macht.

STUMPF: Wie der Tondichter Schubert etwa?

MÜLLER: Gewiß, Herr Stumpf! Da haben Sie's genau getroffen, denn eben dieses Gedicht ist eins von Franz Schuberts Liedern. Es ist aus der „Winterreise,“ einem berühmten Zyklus von Liedern.

FRAGEN

1. Von wem (*by whom*) ist das Gedicht „Der Leiermann“? 2. Wann ist Wilhelm Müller geboren? 3. Wo ist Wilhelm Müller geboren? — In welchem Land? In welcher Stadt? 4. Wann ist der Dichter gestorben? 5. Beschreiben Sie (*describe*) das Gedicht! Ist es melancholisch? 6. Gefällt es Ihnen? Warum? (Warum nicht?) 7. Was für einen (*what sort of*) Eindruck macht der Leiermann mit seiner Musik? 8. Was für einen Eindruck macht er auf Sie? 9. Wer hört den Leiermann an? 10. Wer erkennt seinen Wert? 11. Wer wendet sich von ihm ab? 12. Gibt es zweierlei Armut? Gibt es zweierlei Reichtum? 13. An welcher Armut leidet der Leiermann? 14. An welcher Armut leidet die Welt? 15. Was hält Müller für (*what does Müller consider to be*) das Wesentliche in dem Gedicht? 16. Finden Sie, daß Müller recht hat? 17. Was hält Müller für die symbolische Bedeutung (*significance*) des Leiermanns? 18. Zu welchem Liederzyklus gehört das Gedicht? 19. Wer hat aus dem Gedicht ein Lied gemacht?

LINE
5 doch — *surely*
8 genau genommen — *taken precisely*
9 der Leierkasten — *hand organ, hurdy-gurdy*
10 genauer — *more precisely*
11 gewöhnlich — *ordinary*
12 wieder — *again*

LINE
13 der Künstler — (*creative*) *artist*
14 in dem Sinne wie — *in the sense that*
der Tondichter — *composer*
16 etwa — *maybe*
17 genau getroffen — *hit center, guessed right*
denn — *for* (*because*)

EXERCISE (Numbers)

Read the German text and compare it with the English version. Then fill in the missing numbers.

ELEFANTEN WERDEN TEURER

Die Regierung von Kenya in Ostafrika macht sich Sorgen um den Großwildbestand. Im Jahr neunzehnhundertsiebenundfünfzig betrug die Strecke dort: zweihundertdreizehn Elefanten, zweihundertvier Rhinos, sechsundachtzig Löwen und hundertvierundzwanzig Leoparden. Die zuständigen Stellen haben jetzt die Jagdgebühren so empfindlich erhöht, daß fortan wohl nur noch Maharadschas und Wall-Street-Prinzen auf Safari gehen können. Der Jagdschein allein kostet jetzt fast sechshundert DM, zu dem jeder Bezirk noch einmal einen Zuschlag von hundertzwanzig DM erhebt. Die Abschußerlaubnis für einen Elefanten beträgt neunhundert DM für den ersten und zwölfhundert DM für jeden weiteren Elefanten. Ein Löwe ist preiswerter, er kommt auf dreihundert DM. Mit allem Zubehör kostet eine richtige Safari je Tag etwa vierhundert DM, die übliche vierwöchentliche Jagdexpedition also rund zwölftausend DM.

Aus: *Die Zeit*, Freitag, den ersten August, neunzehnhundertachtundfünfzig

ELEPHANTS ARE GETTING MORE EXPENSIVE

The government of Kenya in East Africa is concerned about its big-game stock. In ——, the number of big game killed there came to —— elephants, —— rhinos, —— lions, and —— leopards. The authorities have now raised the hunting fees so sharply that henceforth perhaps only maharajas and Wall Street magnates will still be able to afford to go on safari. The hunting license alone now costs almost —— marks, in addition to which every district imposes a fee of —— marks. The permit to kill an elephant amounts to —— marks for the first, and —— marks for every additional elephant. A lion is less expensive, the charge being —— marks. Including all incidentals, a real safari costs about —— marks per day, the usual four-week hunting expedition costs therefore about —— marks.

From: *Die Zeit*, Friday, August ——, ——

VIERTER TEIL

Frankfurt nach dem Krieg

Das neue Frankfurt

Hamburg: Mönkebergstraße. Die alte Hansestadt, die heute etwa 1,7 Millionen Einwohner zählt, ist der bedeutendste Hafen Westdeutschlands.

10. Aufgabe

KRIEG UND FRIEDEN

Of the following dialogue memorize the section on this page only. The rest (see page 73) is to be treated as reading assignment.

ADLER: Guten Abend, Herr Berger. Was gibt es Neues?

BERGER: Immer dasselbe. In der heutigen Zeitung ist schon wieder von Krieg die Rede.

ADLER: So geht es. Kriege wird es immer geben.

BERGER: Warum eigentlich?

ADLER: Es wird immer Kriege geben, weil es immer Kriege gegeben hat.

BERGER: Nein, das verstehe ich nicht. Das sehe ich nicht ein. Das ist ja Unsinn!

ADLER: Unsinn? — So war es immer. So sieht die Wirklichkeit aus. So ist der Mensch.

BERGER: Überlegen Sie mal: Verändern sich die Menschen nicht? Waren die Menschen einst nicht roher und primitiver als heute?

ADLER: Mag sein. Aber Streit gab es immer, denn Streit und Konflikt gehören zum Wesen der Welt. Der Krieg — so sagte schon ein weiser, alter Grieche — ist der Vater aller Dinge.

BERGER: Müssen Streitigkeiten denn mit Bomben und mit Gewehren entschieden werden?

ADLER: Nicht alle Streitigkeiten, aber wohl manche. Oder glauben Sie wirklich an einen ewigen Frieden?

BERGER: Ja, ich glaube an einen zukünftigen, dauernden Frieden auf dieser Welt.

WAR AND PEACE

ADLER: Good evening, Mr. Berger. What's new?

BERGER: It's always the same. There is talk of war in today's newspaper once again.

ADLER: That's the way it goes. There'll always be wars.

BERGER: Why do you say that? (*lit.* "Why, actually?")

ADLER: There'll always be wars because there always have been wars.

BERGER: No, I don't understand that. I don't see that. That's nonsense.

ADLER: Nonsense? — That's how it always was. These are the realities. (That is what reality looks like.) That's the way man is.

BERGER: Just consider for a moment: Don't human beings change? Weren't people at one time more brutal and more primitive than (they are) today?

ADLER: Maybe. But there was always strife, for strife and conflict belong to the essential character of the world. War — said a wise old Greek — is the father of all things.

BERGER: But do quarrels really have to be settled by bombs and guns?

ADLER: Not all quarrels, but probably some. Or do you really believe in an eternal peace?

BERGER: Yes, I believe in a future lasting peace in this world.

ADLER: Daran kann ich nicht glauben.

BERGER: Sie halten sich für sehr weise. In Wirklichkeit sind Sie bloß ein Pessimist. Sie sehen die Menschen schwärzer als sie sind.

ADLER: Sie hingegen halten sich für etwas Besseres und sind in Wirklichkeit nur ein ganz gewöhnlicher Optimist. 5

BERGER: Sie wollen damit sagen, daß ich ein Mensch bin, der in Illusionen lebt?

ADLER: Ja, Sie sehen alles rosiger als es ist.

BERGER: Die Hoffnung auf eine bessere Welt gebe ich nie und nimmer auf.

ADLER: Das Beste, was es für uns gibt, ist die Wahrheit. 10

BERGER: Und ist nicht das Schlimmste der Krieg?

ADLER: Nein, mein Lieber. Das Schlimmste sind die falschen Hoffnungen, von denen man betrogen wird.

BERGER: Ist es nicht besser, in einer Welt von Illusionen zu leben als in einer Welt ohne Hoffnung — in einer Welt, die gar keine Welt ist? 15

ADLER: Hm. Das ist allerdings die Frage.

DRILL PATTERNS

Repeat the following drills after your instructor or after the speaker on the tape. Imitate the pronunciation very carefully.

1. Das glaube ich nicht. Das verstehe ich nicht. Das kann ich nicht verstehen.
Das glaubst du nicht? Das verstehst du nicht? Das kannst du nicht verstehen?
Das glaubt er nicht. Das versteht er nicht. Das kann er nicht verstehen.
Glaubt *sie* das nicht? Versteht *sie* das nicht? Kann *sie* das nicht verstehen?
Man glaubt das nicht. Man versteht das nicht. Man kann das nicht verstehen.
Glauben Sie das nicht? Verstehen Sie das nicht? Können Sie das nicht verstehen?
Wir glauben das nicht. Wir verstehen das nicht. Wir können das nicht verstehen.
Glaubt ihr das nicht? Versteht ihr das nicht? Könnt ihr das nicht verstehen?
Sie glauben das nicht. Sie verstehen das nicht. Sie können das nicht verstehen.

LINE
1 daran — *in that*
2 bloß — *merely*
3 schwärzer — *blacker*
4 etwas Besseres — *something better*
9 die Hoffnung — *hope*

LINE
9 aufgeben — *give up*
11 das Schlimmste — *the worst*
13 betrogen — *deceived*
16 allerdings — *to be sure*

2. Die Menschen verändern sich nicht.
Die Menschen haben sich nicht verändert.
Die Menschen werden sich nicht verändern.
Der Mensch verändert sich nicht.

3. Gibt es heute etwas Neues?
Gibt es heute denn nichts Neues?
Es gibt wieder etwas Neues.
Es gibt immer etwas Neues.
Immer gibt es etwas Neues.

4. Gab es gestern etwas Neues?
Gestern gab es etwas Neues.
Gestern gab es in der Zeitung doch schon wieder etwas Neues.
Gab es gestern im Theater denn schon wieder etwas Neues?
In der Schule gab es gestern leider wieder gar nichts Neues.

5. Gestern hat es etwas Neues gegeben, nicht wahr?
Im Kino hat es etwas Neues gegeben, nicht wahr?
In der Stadt hat es etwas Neues gegeben, nicht wahr?

6. Morgen gibt es etwas Neues.
Morgen wird es etwas Neues geben.
In der Zeitung wird es morgen wieder etwas Neues geben.

7. Ja, wir werden ihn morgen sehen.
Ja, Sie werden ihn morgen sehen.
Ja, sie werden Sie sehen.
Ja, ich werde euch sehen.

8. Wird sie dich morgen sehen?
Wirst du sie morgen sehen?
Werdet ihr uns morgen sehen?

9. Der Krieg muß entschieden werden.
Der Kampf[1] muß entschieden werden.
Die Sache[2] muß entschieden werden.
Die Frage muß entschieden werden.
Der Streit muß entschieden werden.

10. Kriege müssen entschieden werden.
Fragen müssen entschieden werden.
Streitigkeiten müssen entschieden werden.

11. Von Krieg ist nicht die Rede.
Von Krieg war nicht die Rede.
Von Krieg wird nicht die Rede sein.
Von Krieg ist nicht die Rede gewesen.

12. Ist von Krieg die Rede?
Wird von Krieg die Rede sein?
Ist von Krieg die Rede gewesen?

13. Heute bin ich reich. Gestern war ich arm.
Gestern war er reich. Heute ist er arm.
Warst du gestern arm? Bist du heute reich?

14. Ist es immer so?
War es immer so?
Ist es immer so gewesen?
Wird es immer so sein?

15. Sieht die Wirklichkeit so aus?
Sah die Wirklichkeit so aus?
Wird die Wirklichkeit immer so aussehen?

16. Siehst du das nicht ein?
Sahst du das nicht ein?
Sieht er das nicht ein?
Kann er das nicht einsehen?

17. Er sieht sie. Er sah sie.
Sie sieht ihn. Sie sah ihn.
Er sieht es. Er sah es.
Sie sieht es. Sie sah es.

18. Ich sehe sie an. Ich sah sie an.
Sie sieht mich an. Sie sah mich an.
Er sieht mich an. Er sah mich an.

19. Du siehst ihn an. Du sahst ihn an.
Du siehst sie an. Du sahst sie an.
Ihr seht ihn an. Ihr saht ihn an.
Ihr seht mich an. Ihr saht mich an.

[1] **der Kampf** battle, struggle [2] **die Sache** matter

English to German

Prepare this exercise in writing.

1) You (*3 ways*) cannot understand that? **vs/vl**
He does not understand that. **vs**
She cannot understand it. **vs/vl**

2) Is there any news today? **vf**
Was there any news today? **vf**
Will there be any news tomorrow? **vf/vl**
Has there been anything new today? **vf/vl**
There has always been something new. **vs/vl**
There will always be something new. **vs/vl**

3) I shall see him tomorrow. **vs/vl**
He will see her tomorrow. **vs/vl**
We will see them tomorrow. **vs/vl**
They will see me tomorrow. **vs/vl**
Will you (*3 ways*) see us tomorrow? **vf/vl**

4) This quarrel must be decided now. **vs/vl**
These quarrels must be decided now. **vs/vl**

Translate the following sentences without the help of the key:

5) People change.
People will change.
He does not change.
He will not change.

6) I saw her.*
You (*3 ways*) saw him.
He saw us.
We saw them.

7) He looked at her.
She looked at him.
They looked at us.
We looked at them.

PRONUNCIATION DRILL

(**r**; accents in verbs with separable and inseparable prefixes)

Repeat after the instructor and practice the following:

Rat — Rede
Räder — rollen
reiten — Reiter
rote — Rotten

Ruf — Russen
reißen — rasen
Recht — Unrecht
Rache — Rauch

zerfal'len — zerstört'
zerbro'chen — zerris'sen
verlo'ren — verges'sen
verfal'len — vertan'

an'kommen
an'sehen
an'fangen
An'fang

ab'gehen
ab'reisen
ab'fahren
Ab'fahrt

aus'sehen
ein'sehen
hin'sehen
um'sehen

her'kommen
hin'gehen
da'bleiben
weg'gehen

fort'gehen
mit'gehen
nach'gehen
zurück'gehen

su'chen — versu'chen
ste'hen — verste'hen
le'gen — verle'gen
ge'hen — verge'hen

besu'chen — beste'hen
bege'hen — bele'gen
bese'hen — bekom'men
berich'ten — befrei'en

ü'bersetzen — überset'zen
ü'bergehen — überge'hen

* See page 76 for past tense of **sehen**.

GRAMMAR

18. Past Tense

a. The past tense of **sein, sehen,** and **geben:**

sein (ist), war, ist gewesen

ich war	*I was*			wir war**en**	*we were*
du war**st**	*you were*	Sie war**en**	*you were*	ihr war**t**	*you were*
sie war	*she was*			sie war**en**	*they were*
es war	*it was*				
er war	*he was*				

This ending pattern is not new to you. You have already encountered it in the *present tense* of **wissen** and the modals (see Grammar Section 1*c*.). This same pattern will be seen in the *past tense* of the great majority of verbs that show stem vowel changes; for example:

sehen (sieht), sah, gesehen

ich sah	*I saw*			wir sah**en**	*we saw*
du sah**st**	*you saw*	Sie sah**en**	*you saw*	ihr sah**t**	*you saw*
sie sah	*she saw*			sie sah**en**	*they saw*
es sah	*it saw*				
er sah	*he saw*				

Note that the only two unduplicated forms within this pattern are **sahst** and **saht.**

geben (gibt), gab, gegeben

ich gab	*I gave*		wir gab**en**
du gab**st**	*etc.*	Sie gab**en**	ihr gab**t**
sie gab			sie gab**en**
es gab			
er gab			

Note that the only two unduplicated forms are **gabst** and **gabt.**

b. The past tense of **haben, werden,** and **sagen:**

haben (hat), hatte, gehabt

ich hatte	*I had*		wir hatt**en**
du hatt**est**	*etc.*	Sie hatt**en**	ihr hatt**et**
sie hatte			sie hatt**en**
es hatte			
er hatte			

Werden follows the same ending pattern as **haben.**

werden (wird), wurde, ist geworden

ich wurde	*I became*		wir wurd**en**
du wurd**est**	*etc.*	Sie wurd**en**	ihr wurd**et**
sie wurde			sie wurd**en**
es wurde			
er wurde			

Note that the only unduplicated forms are **hattest, hattet** and **wurdest, wurdet.**

This same ending pattern will be seen in the past tense of all verbs that show no stem vowel change; for example:

sagen, sagte, gesagt

ich sag**te**	*I said*		wir sag**ten**
du sag**test**	*etc.*	Sie sag**ten**	ihr sag**tet**
sie sag**te**			sie sag**ten**
es sag**te**			
er sag**te**			

19. Future Tense

The future tense is formed by employing as auxiliary the *present tense* forms of **werden** combined with the main verb *infinitive*. (A fuller discussion of the future tense will come later.)

suchen, suchte, gesucht *seek, look for*

ich werde suchen	*I shall seek*		wir werden suchen
du wirst suchen	*etc.*	Sie werden suchen	ihr werdet suchen
sie wird suchen			sie werden suchen
es wird suchen			
er wird suchen			

20. Passive Voice

The passive voice tenses also use **werden** as an auxiliary, but combined with the main verb *past participle;* for example, the present passive runs as follows:

ich werde gesucht	*I am being sought*		wir werden gesucht
du wirst gesucht	*etc.*	Sie werden gesucht	ihr werdet gesucht
sie wird gesucht			sie werden gesucht
es wird gesucht			
er wird gesucht			

Illustrations

Die Lieder **werden** von ihr **gesungen.**	*The songs are sung by her.*
Du **wirst** von ihnen **gesehen.**	*You are seen by them.*
Das Geld muß gefunden werden.	*The money must be found.*
Das muß gesehen werden.	*That must be seen.*
Das Lied muß gesungen werden.	*The song must be sung.*
Es muß gesagt werden.	*It must be said.*

Note the difference in the word order between the German and English passive infinitive forms:

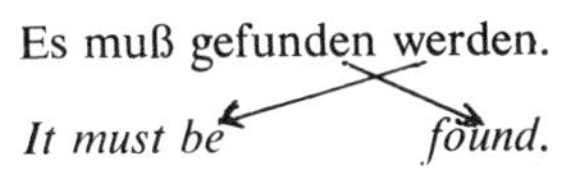

21. Verb Prefixes

German distinguishes between separable and inseparable verb prefixes.

a. SEPARABLE PREFIXES

Such prefixes are *not always* separated from their verbs, but *only* in the present tense and the past tense in independent declarative clauses and questions, and, normally, in commands. When separated, these prefixes stand alone and unattached at the end of their clauses.

Ich kann das nicht einsehen.

Er sieht / sah } das nicht ein.

Many prepositions are used as separable prefixes:

Der Professor sieht den Studenten scharf **an.** (**ansehen** *look at*)

Er ruft die Nummern von Regimentern und Kompanien **aus.** (**ausrufen** *call out*)

Kommen Sie **mit?** (**mitkommen** *come along*)

So sieht die Wirklichkeit **aus.** (**aussehen** *look like*)

There are a number of adverbs that are also used as separable prefixes, like **ab** (*away, down, off*), **hin** and **her** (alone or combined with prepositions, they are directional signs: **hin** — away from the speaker; **her** — toward the speaker), **weg** (*away*), **zusammen** (*together*).

Illustrations

Die Welt wendet sich von dem Leiermann **ab.** (*away*)

Er kommt nun **herein.** (*in*)
Sie geht dann **hinaus.** (*out*)

Wir liegen alle **herum.** (*around*) *We are all lying around.*

Wir treten zu ihm **hin.** (*over to, up to*) *We step up to him.*

Er geht heute **weg.** (*away*)

Wir kommen oft in dieser Stadt **zusammen.** (*together*)

Whenever the separable prefix is combined with its verb, it takes the accent: ab′wenden, herein′kommen, weg′gehen.

b. INSEPARABLE PREFIXES

Some inseparable prefixes you have already encountered, or will encounter within these pages, are:

be–	**er–**	**ver–**
emp–	**ge–**	**zer–**
ent–		

Inseparable prefixes are always unaccented. They often have distinct meanings or functions; for example:

zerfallen *fall to pieces*
entrinnen *run away (from), escape*

be– quite frequently changes intransitive verbs to transitive:

kommen *come* — bekommen *get*
stehen *stand* — bestehen *pass* (an examination)
gehen *go* — begehen *commit* (a crime)
treten *step* — betreten *enter* (a house)

Illustrations

Nur der Dichter erkennt seinen Wert.
Das verstehe ich nicht.

Wenn man nicht alles weiß, bekommt man schlechte Noten.

Er kann dem Tod nicht entrinnen.
(*He cannot escape death.*)

Die Zeit vergeht.

NOTE:

A. The difference between the past participles of separable and inseparable compound verbs:

Inseparable: Er hat schlechte Noten **bekommen.** (no **ge**– prefix)
Separable: Er ist spät dort **hingekommen.** (**ge**– prefix between separable prefix and stem)

B. The position of **zu** in relation to the following dependent infinitives:

Inseparable: Es ist schwer, den Lehrer **zu verstehen.**
Separable: Es ist schwer, früh morgens **auf*zu*stehen.** (**aufstehen** *get up*)

C. There is no difference in the position of the separable and the inseparable prefixes in dependent clauses:

Inseparable: Ich weiß, daß er sich alles genau **besieht.** *I know that he examines everything closely.*
Separable: Der Dichter sagt, daß keiner den alten Leiermann **ansieht.**

11. Aufgabe

WER BIN ICH?

	SAMPLE ANSWERS AND SUGGESTIONS
a. In welche Schule sind Sie gegangen?	*Ich bin in die Volksschule*[1] (*in die Oberschule*[2]) *gegangen.*
b. Auf welcher Universität studieren Sie?	
c. Welche Kurse nehmen Sie (haben Sie belegt)?[3]	*Ich nehme . . . Ich habe . . . belegt.*
Welche Naturwissenschaften studieren Sie?	*Ich studiere Zoologie und Geologie.*
Wie viele Sprachen haben Sie studiert? Haben Sie Französisch — Latein — Englisch — Deutsch — Italienisch — Russisch — Spanisch — Polnisch — Griechisch — Japanisch — Chinesisch — studiert?	
d. Was ist Ihr Hauptfach?[4]	
e. Wie viele Stunden arbeiten Sie am Tag?	

Before answering the following questions, study Grammar Section 22.

f. Wann stehen Sie auf?[5]	*Ich stehe um . . . Uhr auf.*
g. Wann fangen Ihre Klassen an?[6]	*Meine Klassen fangen um . . . Uhr an.*
h. Wann essen Sie zu Mittag?	*Ich esse um . . . Uhr zu Mittag.*
i. Studieren Sie am Nachmittag?	
j. Um wieviel Uhr[7] essen Sie zu Abend?	
k. Studieren Sie am Abend?	
Wann fangen Sie zu studieren an?	
Um wieviel Uhr hören Sie auf?[8]	*Ich höre um . . . Uhr zu studieren auf.*
l. Wann gehen Sie zu Bett?	*Ich gehe um . . . Uhr zu Bett.*

Now answer similar questions using the past tense:

m. Wann standen Sie gestern auf?	*Ich stand gestern um . . . Uhr auf.*
Wann fingen Ihre Klassen an?	*Meine Klassen fingen um . . . Uhr an.*
Wann aßen Sie zu Mittag?	*Ich aß . . .*
Studierten Sie am Nachmittag? am Abend?	
Wann fingen Sie zu studieren an?	*Ich fing um . . . Uhr zu studieren an.*
Wann hörten Sie zu studieren auf?	*Ich hörte um . . . Uhr zu studieren auf.*
Hatten Sie gestern viel zu tun?	
Wer hatte gestern viel zu tun?	

[1] **die Volksschule** grammar school [2] **die Oberschule** secondary school [3] **einen Kurs belegen** register for a (university) course, take a (university) course [4] **das Hauptfach** major (subject) [5] **aufstehen** get up [6] **anfangen** begin [7] **Um wieviel Uhr?** At what time? [8] **aufhören** stop, end

Now use the future tense:

n. Wann werden Sie morgen aufstehen? — *Ich werde morgen um . . . Uhr aufstehen.*
Wann werden Sie morgen zu Mittag essen? — *Ich werde morgen um . . . Uhr zu Mittag essen.*

Werden Sie am Nachmittag studieren?
Wann werden Sie zu Bett gehen?
Werden Sie morgen viel zu tun haben?

DRILL PATTERNS

Repeat the following drills after your instructor or after the speaker on the tape. Imitate the pronunciation carefully.

1. Er war schwach.[1] Er war müde.
Ihr wart schwach. Ihr wart müde.
Wir waren schwach. Wir waren todmüde.[2]

2. Das kleine Kind war müde.
Der arme Mann war müde.
Die gute Frau war müde.

3. Er war so müde wie du.
Wir waren so arm wie du.
Sie war so schwach wie du.
Ich war so hilflos [3] wie du.

4. War er denn hilflos?
Wart ihr denn hilflos?
War er denn so hilflos wie du?

5. Ich wurde müde.
Sie wurde müde.
Wurdest du müde?
Wurdet ihr müde?

6. Sie wurde alt.
Er wurde arm.
Es wurde spät.
Es war zu spät.

7. Hattest du gestern viel zu tun?
Gestern hattet ihr keine Kurse.
Ich hatte gestern keine Zeit.
Hatten Sie gestern Französisch und Deutsch?

8. Er hatte Geld.[4]
Ich hatte kein Geld.
Sie hatten Geld.
Wir hatten kein Geld.

9. Was sagte er?
Was sagten Sie?
Was sagtest du?
Was sagtet ihr?

10. Er glaubte das.
Ich glaubte das nicht.
Glaubtest du das?
Wir glaubten das nicht.

11. Glauben Sie an den ewigen Frieden?
Glaubt er an den ewigen Krieg?

12. In der heutigen Zeitung ist von Krieg die Rede.
In der heutigen Zeitung war von Krieg die Rede.
In der heutigen Zeitung wird von Krieg die Rede sein.
In der heutigen Zeitung ist von Krieg die Rede gewesen.

13. Sokrates war ein weiser Grieche.
Er war ein weiser, alter Grieche.
Dieser weise Grieche lebte in Athen.
Dieser weise, alte Grieche lebte etwa [5] vierhundert Jahre vor Christi Geburt.

[1] **schwach** weak [2] **todmüde** dead tired [3] **hilflos** helpless [4] **das Geld** money [5] **etwa** about

Goethehaus in Weimar: Goethes Arbeitszimmer. Hier schuf der größte deutsche Dichter seine Werke.

14. Der heilige Augustinus ist in Nordafrika geboren.
Dieser große Mann hat auch in Rom gelebt.
Der große deutsche Dichter Goethe ist in Frankfurt am Main geboren.
Er lebte lange in der schönen Stadt Weimar.

15. In diesen Städten bin ich nie gewesen.
In diesen schönen Städten bin ich nie gewesen.

16. Die Klasse beginnt in einer halben Stunde.
Unsere Klasse beginnt um drei Viertel elf.
Meine Klasse beginnt um halb neun.
Diese Klasse beginnt um Viertel zehn.

17. Unsere Schule beginnt in einem halben Jahr.
Diese Schule beginnt in einem Viertel Jahr.

18. Ich suchte das kleine Buch.
Wir suchten das kleine Buch.
Ich suchte mein kleines Buch
Wir suchten unsere kleinen Bücher.

19. Kennen Sie diesen Mann?
Kennen Sie diesen großen Mann?
Kennen Sie seine Frau?
Kennen Sie diese gute Frau?

20. Kennt ihr diese großen Männer?
Kennt ihr diese guten Frauen?

21. Der Zug [1] geht um sieben Uhr fünfundvierzig.
Der Zug geht um Viertel vor acht.
Der Zug geht um drei Viertel acht.
Der Zug geht um neunzehn Uhr fünfundvierzig.

22. Ich stehe um halb sieben auf.
Ich stehe um sechs Uhr dreißig auf.
Ich stehe um Viertel nach sieben auf.

English to German

Prepare this exercise in writing.

1) He was dead tired. **vs** They were tired. **vs**
She got tired. **vs** They got tired. **vs**
You (*3 ways*) were dead tired. **vs**
You (*3 ways*) got tired. **vs**

2) Was she as weak as you (*sing. fam.*)? **vf**
Were they as weak as she? **vf**
I was as helpless as you. **vs**

Begin each one in this group with the prepositional phrase:

3) There is talk of war *in today's newspaper.* **vs**
There was talk of war *in the newspaper.* **vs**
There has been talk of war *in the newspaper.* **vs /vl**
There will be talk of war *in the newspaper.* **vs /vl**

4) He was a wise old man. **vs**
Do you know this great man? **vf**
This great man lived in Rome. **vs**

5) Our class begins in half an hour. **vs**
I have never been in this beautiful city. **vs /vl**
I have never been in these beautiful cities. **vs /vl**

[1] **der Zug** train

6) We get up at six forty-five (*3 ways*). **VS**
We eat at eleven thirty (*2 ways*). **VS**
We go to bed at ten o'clock. **VS**

Translate the following sentences without the aid of the key:

7) Did you (*3 ways*) say that?
Did you (*3 ways*) see that?
Did you (*3 ways*) believe that?

8) Yesterday I had time.
Yesterday we had no money.
Did you (*3 ways*) have money?
Did they have time?

PRONUNCIATION DRILL

(vowels; **ch; f** [v], **w; r; s; z**[w]; accent, rhythm, and intonation in time-telling and in attributive phrases [adjective(s) + noun])

Repeat after the instructor and practice the following:

null Uhr fünfzehn
Viertel nach zwölf
zwölf Uhr fünfzehn
Viertel eins

zwanzig Uhr fünfzehn
Viertel nach acht
acht Uhr fünfzehn
Viertel neun

Viertel vier
drei Viertel drei
zwei Uhr zwanzig
zwanzig nach zwei

Ist es noch nicht acht?
Geht die Uhr nicht nach?

Ist es schon so spät?
Geht der Wecker vor?

Wann ist diese Klasse aus?
Steht die Uhr denn still?

Wo ist mein Freund, mein guter Freund, mein guter, alter Freund?
Wer ist dieser Mann, dieser gute Mann, dieser gute, alte Mann?

Wer kennt meinen Freund, meinen guten Freund, meinen guten, alten Freund?
Wer kennt diesen Mann, diesen guten Mann, diesen guten, alten Mann?

Wo ist mein Buch, mein kleines Buch, mein kleines, dünnes Buch?
Wo ist dieses Buch, dieses kleine Buch, dieses kleine, dünne Buch?

Wo ist meine Uhr, meine alte Uhr, meine gute, alte Uhr?
Wo ist diese Uhr, diese alte Uhr, diese gute, alte Uhr?

GRAMMAR

22. Telling Time

a. Wieviel Uhr ist es, bitte?
Wie spät ist es, bitte? } *What time is it, please?*

In German, as in English, there are different ways of telling time:

Es ist acht Uhr fünfzehn. — *It is eight fifteen.*
Es ist Viertel nach acht. — *It is quarter past eight.*

BUSINESS AND TRAVEL TIME

The twenty-four hour system is much more commonly used in Europe than in the United States.

Es ist zwanzig Uhr fünfzehn = 20.15 = 8:15 P.M.

According to this system:

null Uhr = midnight
1.00 = 1:00 = 1 A.M.
12.00 = 12:00 = 12 noon
13.00 = 13:00 = 1 P.M.
16.00 = 16:00 = 4 P.M.

German (unlike English) also commonly tells the quarter, the half, and the three-quarter hours by using a system in which the hour to come is anticipated:

Es ist Viertel neun. = "*It is a quarter on the way to nine.*" = *It is quarter past eight.*

halb neun = 8:30
drei Viertel neun = 8:45
halb eins = 12:30

Viertel sieben = 6:15
drei Viertel elf = 10:45

The following prepositions are used in time-telling:

nach (*after*): Es ist Viertel nach acht.
Es ist einundzwanzig Minuten nach acht.

vor (*of* or *to*): Es ist Viertel vor neun.
Es ist zwanzig Minuten vor neun.

um (*at*): Er kommt um acht Uhr in Paris an.
Er kommt um Mitternacht an.

bis (*until*): Er wartet bis acht Uhr auf uns.

b. The following prepositional prefixes are used in time-telling:

nach ("*slow*"): Meine alte Uhr geht immer nach. *My old watch is always slow.*

vor ("*fast*"): Seine alte Uhr geht immer vor. *His old watch is always fast.*

Die neue Uhr geht richtig. *The new watch is on time.*

NOTE:

die Uhr watch *or* clock
die Taschenuhr pocket watch
die Armbanduhr wrist watch

die Wanduhr (Küchenuhr) clock (kitchen clock)
die Weckuhr (der Wecker) alarm clock

23. Adjective Endings

The schematic pattern on page 86 can be used as an effective way to visualize and then to comprehend and control the inflected adjective system in German. *Do not start by memorizing these declensional endings.* You can more effectively make them part of your total memory experience in German by first using them (1) as a reference check on adjective-noun phrases as they occur in German sentences and (2) as a guide in going from English to German.

Before your instructor begins to explain how to use this reference pattern, you should be clearly aware of the following points:

a. The **dies**-word designation, for the purpose at hand, includes the definite article. As a matter of fact, you have already seen that the endings of the **dies**-word and the definite article are very closely related. The differences lie in only two areas:

die — **diese**
das — **dieses** (as neuter nominative and accusative forms)
(See Grammar Section 15)

b. The **dies**-word and the **mein**-word endings are the same except for the starred items, where the **mein**-word shows *no ending*.

c. The simplest way to check or follow the proper procedure is to associate by pairs the corresponding columns on both sides of the vertical line. The numbers at the top of each column will help you to do this. Your instructor will now help you to put the system into operation.

1. Know whether the noun is singular or plural.
2. Know the gender of the noun *if singular*.
3. Know the case of the noun.

	dies-word or **mein**-word preceding →				attributive adjectives				noun
	1. F.	2. N.	3. M.	4. PL.	1. F.	2. N.	3. M.	4. PL.	
Nom.	**e**	**es** (–) *	**er** (–) *	**e**	**e**	**e** (**es**)	**e** (**er**)	**en**	
Acc.	**e**	**es** (–) *	**en**	**e**	**e**	**e** (**es**)	**en**	**en**	
Dat.	**er**	**em**	**em**	**en**	**en**	**en**	**en**	**en**	
Gen.	**er**	**es**	**es**	**er**	**en**	**en**	**en**	**en**	
	no **dies**-word or **mein**-word preceding →								
Nom.					**e**	**es**	**er**	**e**	
Acc.					**e**	**es**	**en**	**e**	
Dat.					**er**	**em**	**em**	**en**	
Gen.					**er**	**en**	**en**	**er**	

As an example of how to use the chart, let us consider the phrase "this good child." The phrase would appear in the declensional pattern as follows:

	dies-word preceding	attributive adjective	noun (*not on chart*)
	2.	2.	
	N.	N.	(NEUT.)
Nom.	dieses	gut**e**	(Kind)
Acc.	dieses	gut**e**	(Kind)
Dat.	dies**em**	gut**en**	(Kind)
Gen.	dieses	gut**en**	(Kindes)

ADJECTIVE-ENDING DRILL

With the help of the chart on page 86 supply the endings that are lacking in the following sentences. Keep in mind that in three particular instances the **mein**-words have no ending.

a. 1. Er ist ein– gut– Freund von mir. 2. Er hat ein– reich– Tante. 3. Wenn man zu d– lieb– Gott spricht, sagt man immer „Du," niemals Sie. 4. Die Hunde knurren um d– alt– Mann. (*acc.*) 5. Es gibt ein– materiell– und ein– seelisch– Reichtum. 6. Ich möchte Ihnen ein– klein– Anekdote erzählen. 7. Er ist kein– gewöhnlich– Leiermann. 8. So ein– klein–, dünn– Buch will ich nicht kaufen. 9. Wir müssen vieles von dies– groß– Männern wissen. 10. Und sein– klein– Teller bleibt ihm immer leer. 11. Er sagt nie „du" zu d– alt– Dame. 12. Er ist kein– jung– Bursche. 13. In d– heutig– Zeitung ist schon wieder von Krieg die Rede. 14. Das Gedicht ist aus ein– berühmt– Zyklus von Liedern. 15. Er ist in ein– klein– Stadt geboren, die jetzt in d– russisch– Zone liegt. 16. So steht es in d– deutsch– Sprache mit ein– so einfach– Wort wie „du." 17. Dies– arm– Leiermann macht ein– schlecht– Eindruck. 18. Das ist ein– seelisch– Armut. (*fem.*) 19. Es gibt kein– klein– Kriege. 20. Für dies– alt– Mann sieht das anders aus.

b. 1. Wunderlich– Alter, soll ich mit dir gehen? 2. Er bekommt immer schlecht– Noten. 3. Sie sind nicht intim– Freunde. 4. Mit starr– Fingern dreht er, was er kann. 5. Er hat zwei intim– Freunde. 6. Gut– Wein ist teuer. (*masc.*) 7. Ich habe frisch– Brot gerne. (*neut.*) 8. Er trinkt immer schlecht– Wein. 9. Frisch– Milch trinkt er gern. (*fem.*) 10. Er ist in groß– Armut gestorben.

12. Aufgabe

VOCABULARY BUILDING

COGNATES

Study the following pairs:

GERMAN	ENGLISH
b (*medial or final*)	**v** (*sometimes* **f**)
leben	live
lieben	love
der Herbst	autumn (harvest)
halb	half

Can you recognize the English for the following German words from the examples given above?

die Salbe, das Grab, das Kalb

Replace the German with their English equivalents in the following sentences:

1. **Die Leber** is a vital human organ. 2. **Ein Sieb** is a kitchen utensil. 3. Her father is a tailor and his father **ein Weber.**

GERMAN	ENGLISH
ch *	**k**
machen	make
das Buch	book
riechen	smell ("reek")
suchen	seek

Can you recognize the English for the following German words from the examples given above?

erwachen, brechen, kochen

Give the English equivalent for each of the following:

1. Die Woche hat sieben Tage. 2. Der Koch bäckt Apfelkuchen in der Küche. 3. Das riecht gut. 4. Er trinkt Wein aus einem Becher. 5. Er ist Mathematiker; er kann gut rechnen.

GERMAN	ENGLISH
cht	**ght**
acht	eight
die Nacht	night
das Licht	light
brachte	brought

* There are some **ch** examples that correspond to *gh* rather than the usual *k*: **hoch** high; **lachen** laugh; **durch** through.

Give the English equivalent for the following:

1. Du hast recht. 2. Wer wacht um Mitternacht? 3. Sie brachten achtzig Lichter in die Kirche.

GERMAN	ENGLISH
d	**th**
durch	through
doch	though, but
dies	this
danken	thank

Can you recognize the English for the following German words from the examples given above?

das Ding, das Leder, die Nordsee, Südamerika

Give the English equivalent for the following:

1. Die Disteln auf der Heide haben scharfe Dornen. 2. Er hielt das Glas mit drei Fingern: mit dem Mittelfinger, mit dem Zeigefinger (*index finger*) und mit dem Daumen. 3. Diebe mögen (*may*) denken, aber sie danken nicht.

GERMAN	ENGLISH
f, ff (*medial or final*)	**p, pp**
greifen (griff)	grip (gripped)
hilflos	helpless
offen	open
pf	**p**
pfeifen	pipe, whistle
der Pfeffer	pepper
das Pfund	pound

Give the English equivalent for each of the following:

die Harfe, schlaflos; stampfen, der Pfennig; Der Affe ißt den Apfel.

GERMAN	ENGLISH
s, ss, *or* **ß**	**t**
groß	great
schießen (schoß)	shoot (shot)
tz	**t**
schmutzig	dirty ("smutty")
sitzen	sit
setzen	set
z	**t**
kurz	short ("curt")
zittern	tremble ("teeter," "totter")

Give the English equivalents for each of the following:

die Zunge, der Witz, der Fuß, das Netz, das Salz, beißen, ein bißchen

1. Der Wasserkessel ist heiß. 2. Affen essen Nüsse gerne. 3. Die Katze sitzt auf dem Sessel.

GERMAN	ENGLISH
t	**d**
alt	old
der Tag	day
hart	hard
der Tanz	dance

Give the English equivalent for each of the following:

das Blut, das Tal, kalt, halt!   Der Reiter reitet talaus talein.

Each of the following shows two consonant correspondencies. Give the English equivalents:

tief, der Tropfen, die Taube (*a bird*), der Silberschmied, der Dieb, treiben, durch

Give the English equivalent for each of the following (using the consonant pairs in the columns above as guides):

Weiß sind die Tauben und schwarz sind die Raben,
Und traurig die Herzen, die keine Waffen haben.

Lieben ist nicht Hassen,
Halten nicht Lassen;
Trinken ist nicht Essen,
Wissen kein Vergessen.
Schlafen ist nicht Wachen
Und Denken kein Lachen;
Hoffen ist nicht Haben
Und Dürsten nicht Laben; *
Sechs ist nicht sieben,
Aber Lieben ist Lieben.

* *See* **laben** (lave) refresh

WORD STUDY

Fix these words and idiomatic expressions in your mind as firmly as possible and refer to them frequently until they become part of your active vocabulary.

WORDS COMMONLY USED

alle all
allerdings′ of course, by all means
als than, as, when
an . . . vorü′ber past
bloß only, bare
dahin′ter behind (it, them)
damit′ with it *or* them; so that, in order that
doch but, though, nevertheless

draußen outside
ehe (*conj.*) before
einst once (upon a time), some time ago, some day
fest fixed, firm
ganz completely, quite
gera'de just, even, straight
grau gray
heim home
herum' around
heute today
hinauf' up
hinaus' out
hinge'gen on the other hand, on the contrary
immer + *comparative*
  immer höher higher and higher
  immer schöner more and more beautiful
lange her long ago
leise softly
manchmal sometimes
müde tired
nachdem' (*conj.*) after
noch still
  noch einmal once more
  noch immer (*or* **immer noch**) still
oben above, upstairs
paar: ein paar mal a couple of times
plötzlich suddenly
weil because
wenig little (*pl.* **wenige** few)
  Er hat wenig Zeit.
  Er hat wenige Freunde.
zusam'men together

IDIOMATIC EXPRESSIONS

halten + **für** *think* (in the sense of "consider, take to be")
  Du hältst dich für sehr weise. *You think you're very wise.*

Recall **halten** + **von** *think* (in the sense of holding an opinion about something)
  Was halten Sie davon?
  Ich halte nicht viel von ihm. *I do not think much of him.*

glauben + **an** + acc. *believe in*
  Müller glaubt an den ewigen Frieden.

hören with infinitive (*not* with participle)
  Noch einmal hören wir unsere Namen **rufen.** *Once again we hear our names* ***called.***

Das sind alle. *That's all there are* (of a series).
Das ist alles. *That's all there is* (of a substance).

Ich sehe nach. *I check* (*to see*).
Ich sehe ihm nach. *I watch him as he leaves* (*goes past, walks away, etc.*).

Ich sehe **mich** um. *I look around.*
Er sieht **sich** um. *He looks around.*
Wir sehen **uns** um. *We look around.*
} Note the need for the reflexive pronoun.

her *ago* (indicates a temporal instead of the customary spatial meaning)
  Wie lange ist das her? *How long ago is that* (*has that been*)?

an . . . vorüber with dat. = *past*
  An den Fenstern gleitet die Landschaft **vorüber.** *The landscape glides past the windows* (*of the train*).

Future tense with **wohl** (sometimes omitted) expresses present probability:
  Es **wird** (wohl) meine Schwester **sein.** *It* ***is*** *probably my sister.*

sprechen + **vor** + acc. reflexive pronoun + **hin** = *speak to oneself*
  Ich spreche den Namen vor mich hin. *I speak the name to myself.*

PRONUNCIATION DRILL

(**j**; **d** [final **d** pronounced **t**]; **b** [final **b** pronounced **p**])

Repeat after the instructor and practice the following:

der junge Mann — die junge Frau
ein junger Mann — eine junge Frau
der gute Junge — das junge Mädchen
ein guter Junge — ein junges Mädchen

jeder junge Mann — jede junge Frau
jener gute Junge — jenes junge Mädchen
jene jungen Männer — jene jungen Frauen
jene guten Jungen — jene jungen Mädchen

jedes Jahr
ja, Jahr um Jahr
jahrelang
jahraus, jahrein

niemand — jemand
diesseits — jenseits
niemals — jemals
immer — jetzt

Lied — Lieder
Land — Länder
Hand — Hände
Wand — Wände
Feld — Felder
Wald — Wälder

schwinden — schwand
finden — fand
binden — band
Linde — Wind

Bahn — Abend
ab — herab
oben — ob
Graben — Grab

Reading

E. M. REMARQUE

Nach der *Süddeutschen Zeitung*, Nr. 148, Samstag/Sonntag, 21./22. Juni 1958. (Seite 8)

ERICH MARIA REMARQUE, einer der meistgedruckten zeitgenössischen Schriftsteller, wurde am 22. Juni 1898 geboren. Weltberühmt machte den in Osnabrück Gebürtigen sein erstes Werk, mit dem er monatelang hausieren gehen mußte: der Anti-Kriegsroman *Im Westen nichts Neues*. Das Buch erreichte die Auflage von sechs Millionen. Als es 1930 verfilmt worden war, ließ Goebbels bei der Berliner Premiere Mäuse laufen, um das „pazifistische" Publikum auf die Stühle zu treiben, 1929 verließ Remarque seine Heimat, ging über die Schweiz nach Frankreich und wurde später amerikanischer Staatsbürger. In seinen Romanen *Drei Kameraden*, *Zeit zu leben und Zeit zu sterben*,

From the *Süddeutsche Zeitung*, No. 148, Saturday/Sunday, June 21/22, 1958. (Page 8)

ERICH MARIA REMARQUE, one of the most widely published contemporary authors, was born on June 22, 1898. Born in Osnabrück, he rose to fame through his first work, the antiwar novel *All Quiet on the Western Front*, which had to go begging for months in search of a publisher. The book reached an edition of 6,000,000 copies. It was made into a movie in 1930, and at its Berlin première Goebbels had a swarm of mice let loose through the theater in order to get the "pacifists" up on their chairs. In 1929 Remarque left his native land and went to France via Switzerland. Later he became an American citizen. In his novels *Three Comrades*, *A Time to Live and a Time to Die*,

Der schwarze Obelisk, *Arc de Triomphe*, *Der Funke Leben* versuchte er, die dunkelsten Punkte der deutschen Geschichte — Inflation, früher Nazismus, Emigrantenschicksal, Krieg und Konzentrationslager — literarisch zu fassen, wobei ihm freilich niemals mehr die unmittelbare explosive Wirkung seines ersten Buches gelang.

The Black Obelisk, *Arch of Triumph*, *The Spark of Life* he endeavored to recapture through the medium of literature the darkest periods of German history — inflation, early Nazism, the fate of the refugees, war, and the concentration camp. But never again did he really succeed in equaling the direct and explosive effect of his first book.

Aus: IM WESTEN NICHTS NEUES

I. An der Front

Trommelfeuer, Sperrfeuer, Gardinenfeuer, Minen, Gas, Tanks, Maschinengewehre, Handgranaten — Worte, Worte, aber sie umfassen das Grauen der Welt.

Unsere Gesichter sind verkrustet, unser Denken ist verwüstet, wir sind todmüde; — wenn der Angriff kommt, müssen manche mit Fäusten geschlagen werden, damit sie erwachen und mitgehen; — die Augen sind entzündet, die Hände zerrissen, die Knie bluten, die Ellbogen sind zerschlagen. 5

Vergehen Wochen — Monate — Jahre? Es sind nur Tage. Wir sehen die Zeit neben uns schwinden in den farblosen Gesichtern der Sterbenden, wir löffeln Nahrung in uns hinein, wir laufen, wir werfen, wir schießen, wir töten, wir liegen herum, wir sind schwach und stumpf, und nur das hält uns, daß noch Schwächere, 10 noch Stumpfere, noch Hilflosere da sind, die mit aufgerissenen Augen uns ansehen als Götter, die manchmal dem Tode entrinnen können.

II. Die Gefallenen *

Wir werden abgelöst. Die Räder rollen unter uns weg, wir stehen dumpf... Die Wagen halten... An den Seiten, dunkel, stehen Leute und rufen die Nummern von Regimentern, von Kompanien aus... 15

Nun ruft jemand die Nummer unserer Kompanie. Es ist, man hört es, der

* die Gefallenen — *the fallen, the dead*

LINE

1 das Trommelfeuer — *drumfire*
das Sperrfeuer — *barrage*
das Gardinenfeuer — *curtain fire*
2 umfassen — *encompass*
das Grauen — *horror*
3 die Gesichter (das Gesicht) — *faces*
verkrustet — *crusted with mud and dirt*
verwüstet — *desolate*
4 der Angriff — *attack*
die Fäuste (die Faust) — *fists*
geschlagen — *beaten*
5 entzündet — *inflamed*
5–6 zerrissen — *torn*
6 zerschlagen — *badly bruised*
8 schwinden — *melt* or *fade away*

LINE

8 farblos — *colorless*
der Sterbenden — *of the dying men*
8–9 löffeln . . . hinein — *spoon, stuff, pour*
9 die Nahrung — *food, nourishment*
werfen — *throw*
10 stumpf — *dull, apathetic*
und nur das hält uns — *and the only thing that keeps us going* (*is*)
11 aufgerissen — *gaping*
13 abgelöst — *relieved*
dumpf — *dull, listless*
14 halten — *stop*
dunkel — *dark*
die Leute — *people*
16 jemand — *someone, somebody*

Kompanieführer. . . Wir treten zu ihm hin, und ich erkenne Kat und Albert, wir stellen uns zusammen, lehnen uns aneinander und sehen uns an.

Und noch einmal und noch einmal hören wir unsere Nummer rufen. Er kann lange rufen, man hört ihn nicht in den Lazaretten und den Trichtern.

5 Noch einmal: „Zweite Kompanie hierher!"

Und dann leiser: „Niemand mehr zweite Kompanie?"

Er schweigt und ist etwas heiser als er fragt: „Das sind alle?" und befiehlt: „Abzählen!"

Der Morgen ist grau, es war noch Sommer, als wir hinausgingen, und wir waren 10 hundertfünfzig Mann. Jetzt friert uns, es ist Herbst, die Blätter rascheln, die Stimmen flattern müde auf: „Eins — zwei — drei — vier," und bei zweiunddreißig schweigen sie. Und es schweigt lange, ehe die Stimme fragt: „Noch jemand?" — und wartet und dann leise sagt: „In Gruppen —" und abbricht und nur vollenden kann: „Zweite Kompanie —," mühselig: „Zweite Kompanie — 15 ohne Tritt marsch!"

Eine Reihe, eine kurze Reihe tappt in den Morgen hinaus.

Zweiunddreißig Mann.

III. Urlaub *

Der Kompanieführer wünscht mir gute Reise. Ich sehe nach, wieviel Urlaub ich habe. Siebzehn Tage — vierzehn sind Urlaub, drei Reisetage . . .

20 Am nächsten Morgen, nachdem ich entlaust bin, marschiere ich zur Feldbahn. Albert und Kat begleiten mich. Wir nehmen Abschied. Sie gehen und winken ein paarmal. Dann sind sie verschwunden.

An den Fenstern gleitet die Landschaft vorüber, mit Dörfern, Kornfeldern, Obstgärten, Scheunen und alten Linden.

25 Die Namen der Stationen werden zu Begriffen, bei denen mein Herz zittert.

* der Urlaub — *furlough*, (*military*) *leave*

LINE

1 der Führer — *leader*
Kat und Albert (*the narrator's "buddies"*)
2 stellen uns zusammen — *gather in a group*
lehnen — *lean*
4 das Lazarett — *field hospital*
der Trichter — *shell hole*
6 leiser — *more softly*
7 schweigen — *be silent*
etwas heiser — *somewhat hoarse*
befiehlt — *commands*
8 Abzählen! — *Count off!*
9 hinausgingen — *went out, set out*
10 Mann — here: *men*
Jetzt friert uns — *Now we are freezing*
der Herbst — *fall* (compare "*harvest*")
die Blätter (das Blatt) — *leaves*
11 Stimmen flattern müde auf — *voices flutter up wearily*
13 abbricht — *breaks off*
14 vollenden — *say finally*

LINE

14 mühselig — *with an effort*
15 ohne Tritt — *at ease*
16 die Reihe — *column*
kurz — *short*
tappt . . . hinaus — *grope their way out*
18 nachsehen — *verify, check*
20 entlaust — *deloused*
die Feldbahn — *military train* (*R.R.*)
21 begleiten — *accompany*
Abschied nehmen — *take leave of one another*
winken — *wave*
22 verschwinden — *disappear*
23 vorübergleiten — *glide past*
24 der Obstgarten — *orchard*
die Scheune — *barn*
25 werden zu Begriffen — *turn into ideas* or *images*
bei denen — *at which*
zittern — *tremble*

Der Zug stampft und stampft, ich stehe am Fenster und halte mich an den Rahmenhölzern fest. Diese Namen umgrenzen meine Jugend.

Flache Wiesen, Felder, Höfe, eine Schranke, vor der Bauern warten, Mädchen, die winken, Kinder, die am Bahndamm spielen, Wege, die ins Land führen, glatte Wege, ohne Artillerie. 5

Es ist Abend. Ich erkenne die charakteristische Linie des Dolbenberges. Dahinter muß die Stadt kommen.

Ein Bahnübergang. Ich stehe am Fenster, ich kann mich nicht trennen. Die andern bereiten ihre Sachen zum Aussteigen vor. Ich spreche den Namen der Straße, die wir überqueren, vor mich hin — Bremer Straße — Bremer Straße — 10

Radfahrer, Wagen, Menschen sind da unten, es ist eine graue Straße . . .

Dann hält der Zug, und der Bahnhof ist da mit Lärm, Rufen und Schildern. Auf dem Perron sehe ich mich um; ich kenne niemand von den Leuten, die da hasten . . .

Draußen vor dem Bahnhof aber rauscht der Fluß neben der Straße, er zischt weiß aus den Schleusen der Mühlenbrücke hervor. Der alte Wartturm steht 15 daran, und vor ihm die große Linde, und dahinter der Abend.

Hier haben wir gesessen, oft — wie lange ist das her; über diese Brücke sind wir gegangen; wir haben uns über die ruhige Flut diesseits der Schleuse gebeugt und wir haben uns jenseits der Schleuse an heißen Tagen über den spritzenden Schaum gefreut und von unseren Lehrern geschwätzt. 20

Ich gehe über die Brücke, ich schaue rechts und links; das Wasser ist immer noch voll Algen, und es schießt immer noch in hellem Bogen herab. Hunde trotten durch die schmale Straße, vor den Haustüren stehen Menschen und sehen mir nach, wie ich schmutzig und bepackt vorübergehe.

In dieser Konditorei haben wir Eis gegessen und uns im Zigarettenrauchen 25 geübt. In dieser Straße kenne ich jedes Haus, das Kolonialwarengeschäft, die Drogerie, die Bäckerei. Und dann stehe ich vor der braunen Tür mit der abgegriffenen Klinke, und die Hand wird mir schwer. Ich öffne sie. . .

LINE

1 stampfen — *stamp, pound*
1–2 die Rahmenhölzer — *window frames*
2 umgrenzen — *encompass*
3 die Höfe (der Hof) — *farms*
die Schranke — *barrier*
der Bauer — *peasant, farmer*
4 der Bahndamm — *railway embankment*
glatt — *smooth*
6 der Dolbenberg — *Dolben mountain*
8 der Bahnübergang — *railway crossing*
ich kann mich nicht trennen — *I can't tear myself away*
9 vorbereiten — *get ready*
aussteigen — *get off*
10 überqueren — *cross*
11 der Radfahrer — *cyclist*
12 der Lärm — *noise*
die Schilder (das Schild) — *signs*
13 der Perron — *platform*
14–15 hervorzischen — *gush forth*

LINE

15 die Schleuse — *sluice*
die Mühlenbrücke — *mill bridge*
der Wartturm — *watchtower*
18 sich beugen — *bend, lean*
19–20 sich freuen über — *enjoy*
19 spritzend — *spraying*
der Schaum — *foam*
20 schwätzen — *gossip*
22 herabschießen — *shoot down*
der Bogen — *arc*
23 schmal — *narrow*
23–4 nachsehen — *watch*
24 schmutzig — *dirty*
bepackt — *loaded down*
25 die Konditorei — *pastry shop, bakery*
25–6 sich üben — *practice*
26 das Kolonialwarengeschäft — *grocery*
27 die Drogerie — *pharmacy, drugstore*
27–8 abgegriffen — *worn*
28 die Klinke — *handle, latch*

Unter meinen Stiefeln knarrt die Treppe. Oben klappt eine Tür, jemand blickt über das Geländer. Es ist die Küchentür — sie backen dort gerade Kartoffelpuffer, das Haus riecht danach, heute ist ja auch Sonnabend, und es wird meine Schwester sein, die sich herunterbeugt. Ich schäme mich einen Augenblick und
5 senke den Kopf, dann nehme ich den Helm ab und sehe hinauf. Ja, es ist meine älteste Schwester.

„Paul," ruft sie, „Paul —!"

Ich nicke, mein Tornister stößt gegen das Geländer, mein Gewehr ist plötzlich so schwer.

10 Sie reißt eine Tür auf und ruft: „Mutter, Mutter, Paul ist da."

Ich kann nicht weitergehen . . .

Und so stehe ich auf der Treppe, unglücklich, hilflos, in einem furchtbaren Krampf, und will nicht, und die Tränen laufen mir immer nur so über das Gesicht.

FRAGEN

1. Was wissen Sie über Erich Maria Remarque? 2. Was ist der Titel seines ersten Romans? 3. Wovon handelt *Im Westen nichts Neues?* 4. Was ist die Tendenz dieses Romans? 5. Beschreiben Sie das Leben der Frontsoldaten, wie (*as*) Remarque es sieht! 6. Wieviel Mann hatte die zweite Kompanie, als sie im Sommer an die Front kam? 7. Wieviel Mann waren im Herbst noch am Leben? 8. Beschreiben Sie mit den Worten Remarques den Urlaub seines Helden!

ES SITZT EIN VOGEL AUF DEM LEIM

Es sitzt ein Vogel auf dem Leim,
er flattert sehr und kann nicht heim.
Ein schwarzer Kater schleicht herzu,
die Krallen scharf, die Augen gluh.
Am Baum hinauf und immer höher
kommt er dem armen Vogel näher.

Der Vogel denkt: Weil das so ist
und weil mich doch der Kater frißt,
so will ich keine Zeit verlieren,
will noch ein wenig quinquillieren
und lustig pfeifen wie zuvor —
Der Vogel, scheint mir, hat Humor.

Wilhelm Busch (1832–1908)

A BIRD SITS LIME-SNARED IN A TREE

A bird sits lime-snared in a tree,
It flutters wild and can't get free.
A tomcat creeps up black and lean,
Claws sharp, eyes fixed a glowing green.
Up in the branches high and higher
He nears his victim sly and slyer.

Since this is it, the bird thinks now,
And since he'll eat me anyhow,
I mustn't lose a moment's time
To sing my swan song on the lime
And gaily warble as I've done —
The bird, it seems, is full of fun.

LINE

1 der Stiefel — *boot*
knarren — *creak*
klappen — *click, slam*
2 das Geländer — *banister*
2–3 der Kartoffelpuffer — *potato pancake*
3 riecht danach — *smells of it*
der Sonnabend — *Saturday*
4 herunterbeugen — *lean down*
sich schämen — *be ashamed* or *embarrassed*

LINE

4 der Augenblick — *moment*
5 senken — *lower*
8 nicken — *nod*
der Tornister — *pack*
stoßen — *push*
10 auf — here: *open*
12–13 in einem furchtbaren Krampf — *in terrible tension*
13 die Tränen — *tears*

FÜNFTER TEIL

Süddeutsches Gasthaus

Das Hofbräuhaus in München

„Wir befinden uns in dem Speisesaal eines eleganten deutschen Restaurants.“ Bei Kempinski, Kurfürstendamm, Berlin.

13. Aufgabe

IM RESTAURANT

Read and memorize the dialogue in this selection:

Wir befinden uns in dem Speisesaal eines eleganten deutschen Restaurants. Jeder Tisch ist mit einem weißen Tischtuch bedeckt. Die Teller und Tassen, die Messer, Gabeln, Löffel und Gläser blitzen vor Sauberkeit.

Hans Werner, ein junger Mann, und seine Freundin, Anna Wagner, kommen von links herein. Sie setzen sich an einen freien Tisch in der Mitte des Raumes.

HANS: (*laut*) Ah, was für ein schönes Restaurant! Ich bin neugierig darauf, was es hier zu essen gibt.

ANNA: (*leise*) Ja, es ist hübsch hier. Aber ist es nicht etwas zu teuer, Hans?

HANS: Zu teuer? — Wem? — Darüber mach' ich mir heute keine Sorgen. Sehen wir uns nur die Speisekarte an, Anna. (*Er vertieft sich in das Menu.*) Womit fängst du an? Mit einer Vorspeise?

ANNA: (*welche ebenfalls die lange Liste von Speisen studiert*) Ich glaube, mit einer Suppe. Ja. Mit einer Gemüsesuppe.

HANS: Gut. Und was weiter? Fleisch? Geflügel? Fisch? Braten? Backhuhn mit Erbsen und Reis? Forelle blau?

ANNA: (*zögernd*) Man weiß gar nicht, wozu man sich entschließen soll. (*Eine Pause, in welcher Hans die Speisekarte weiter mit den Augen verschlingt*). O doch! Ich bestelle mir Wiener Schnitzel mit Kartoffeln und Gurkensalat.

HANS: (*überzeugt*) Ja, das ist das Beste. Und dazu eine Flasche Rheinwein!

ANNA: Und danach ein Stück Torte.

HANS: Und eine Tasse Kaffee! (*Er sieht sich ungeduldig um.*) Aber wo bleibt jetzt der Kellner? Wird man uns hier bedienen!?

ANNA: Er wird schon kommen, Hans. Wir können uns ja inzwischen —

HANS: (*laut*) Herr Ober!

ANNA: — von etwas anderem unterhalten.

HANS: (*welcher sie nicht beachtet*) Herr Ober! Wird man hier nicht bedient!?

ANNA: (*leise*) Oder bist du dazu zu hungrig?

IN A RESTAURANT

We are (*lit.* "We find ourselves") in the dining hall of an elegant German restaurant. Each table is covered with a white tablecloth. The plates and cups, the knives, forks, spoons, and glasses sparkle with cleanliness.

Hans Werner, a young man, and Anna Wagner, his girl friend, enter from the left. They sit down at a free table in the middle of the room.

HANS: (*loudly*) Ah, what a beautiful restaurant! I'm curious to find out what there is to eat here.

ANNA: (*softly*) Yes, it is nice here. But isn't it a little too expensive, Hans?

HANS: Too expensive? For whom? I'm not going to worry about that today. Just let's look at the menu, Anna. (*He becomes engrossed in the menu.*) What are you going to start with? An appetizer?

ANNA: (*who likewise is studying the long food list*) With soup, I guess. Yes. With a vegetable soup.

HANS: Fine. And what next? Meat? Foul? Fish? Roast? Fried chicken with peas and rice? Blue trout?

ANNA: (*hesitant*) It's really difficult to know what to choose. (*lit.* "One does not know at all what one should decide on.") (*A pause in which Hans continues to devour the menu with his eyes.*) Oh yes (I do)! I'm going to order veal cutlet (Viennese style) with potatoes and cucumber salad.

HANS: (*convinced*) Yes, that's the best. And a bottle of Rhine wine to go with it!

ANNA: And after that a piece of cake.

HANS: And a cup of coffee. (*He looks around impatiently.*) But where is the waiter now? Are we going to get service here?

ANNA: He'll come, don't worry, Hans. Meanwhile we could —

HANS: (*loudly*) Waiter (headwaiter)!

ANNA: — talk about something else.

HANS: (*who pays no attention to her*) Waiter! Don't they serve people here? (*lit.* "Isn't one being served here?")

ANNA: (*softly*) Or are you too hungry to do that (*lit.* "for that")?

DRILL PATTERNS

Repeat the following drills after your instructor or after the speaker on the tape. Imitate the pronunciation very carefully.

1. Was für ein Restaurant ist das?
   Wissen Sie, wem das Restaurant gehört?
   Wer sind die jungen Leute,[1] die dort sitzen?
   Wessen Freundin ist dieses Mädchen?
   Was bestellen die beiden?[2]
   Wen ruft der junge Mann so laut?

2. Sie kommt herein.
   Er kommt ihr nach.
   Sie setzt sich hin.
   Er setzt sich zu ihr.
   Sie wendet sich ab.
   Er sieht sie an.
   Sie geht hinaus.
   Er geht mit ihr mit.

3. Fängt er mit der Vorspeise an?
   Womit fangen wir an?
   Fängst du mit der Suppe an?
   Womit fängst du an?

4. Fängt man mit der Nachspeise[3] an?
   Nein, damit hört man auf.
   Hört man mit der Vorspeise auf?
   Nein, damit fängt man an.

5. Was gibt es hier? Was ißt man hier?
   Was gibt es hier zu essen?
   Ich weiß, was es hier zu essen gibt.
   Alles, was es hier gibt, ist gut.

6. Alles, was er sagt, ist die Wahrheit.
   Nichts, was er sagt, ist die Wahrheit.
   Das Beste, was es gibt, ist die Wahrheit.

7. Was sagt Annas Freund? Wovon spricht ihr Freund? Ich kann ihn nicht verstehen.
   Ihr Freund spricht nur vom Essen.
   Nur davon spricht ihr Freund.

8. Ist das alles, was er sagt?
   Das ist alles, was er sagt.
   Das ist alles, was er denkt.
   Ist denn der Mensch, was er ißt?

9. Ist Anna ein Kind, das in Illusionen lebt?
   Ist Anna eine Frau, die in Illusionen lebt?
   Ist Anna ein Mädchen, das in Illusionen lebt?
   Ist Hans ein Mensch, der in Illusionen lebt?
   Sind das Menschen, die in Illusionen leben?
   Kennen Sie Männer (Frauen, Kinder), die nicht in Illusionen leben?
   Kennen Sie einen Menschen, der nicht in Illusionen lebt?

10. Wo bleibt der Kellner, der sie bedient?
    Wo bleibt die Kellnerin, die sie bedient?
    Ist hier niemand, der sie bedient?

11. Hier kommt ein Kellner, den ich kenne.
    Hier kommt die Kellnerin, die ich kenne.
    Sind das die Leute, die ihr kennt?

12. Müller ist ein Mann, den ich gut kenne.
    Marie ist eine Frau, die ich gut kenne.
    Paul ist ein Kind, das ich gut kenne.
    Das sind Menschen, die ich gut kenne.

[1] **die jungen Leute** the young people [2] **beide** both; **die beiden** the two [3] **die Nachspeise** dessert

13. Das ist ein Mann, von dem ich nichts weiß.
Das ist eine Frau, von der ich nichts weiß.
Das ist ein Kind, von dem ich nichts weiß.
Das sind Männer, Frauen und Kinder, von denen ich wirklich nichts weiß.

14. Dort ist das Zimmer,[1] in welchem die Kinder schlafen.
Dort ist das Zimmer, in dem die Kinder schlafen.
Das ist der Raum,[2] in welchem ich studiere.
Das ist der Raum, in dem ich studiere.
Da ist die Küche,[3] in welcher wir kochen.
Da ist die Küche, in der wir kochen.
Das sind die Räume, in welchen wir tanzen.
Das sind die Räume, in denen wir tanzen.

15. Der Mann, der gestern kam, heißt Müller.
Die Frau, die gestern gestorben ist, hieß Fischer.
Das Fräulein, das jetzt hereinkommt, heißt Ida.
Der deutsche Junge, der bei uns wohnen wird, heißt Anton.

16. Der Student steht am Fenster.
Er steht daran.
Setzt der Lehrer sich an den Tisch?
Ja, er setzt sich daran.
Wer glaubt an einen dauernden Frieden?
Herr Berger glaubt daran.

17. Setzt Anna sich auf den Stuhl?
Ja, sie setzt sich darauf.
Setzen die beiden sich auf die Stühle?
Ja, sie setzen sich darauf.

18. Habt ihr von Müllers Gedicht gehört?
Ja, wir haben davon gehört.
Habt ihr von Schuberts Liedern gehört?
Ja, davon haben wir gehört.
Hat man je[4] von so einem Unsinn gehört?
Ja, davon hat man hier viel gehört.

19. Haben Sie von diesem jungen Mann gehört?
Ja, wir haben von ihm gehört.
Hat er von seiner Freundin gehört?
Ja, er hat von ihr gehört.
Hat sie von seinem Kind gehört?
Ja, sie hat von ihm gehört.

English to German

Prepare this exercise in writing.

1) Who is this young man? **vs**
Whose friend is he? **vs**
Whom does he know here? **vs**

2) Are they coming in? **vf**
Are they sitting down? **vf**
Are they leaving ("going outside")? **vf**

3) She is sitting down at the table. **vs**
Why are you (*3 ways*) standing at the window? **vs**
Why are you standing at it? **vs**

4) Are you (*3 ways*) starting your meal (**die Mahlzeit**) with a soup (with an appetizer)? **vf**

[1] **das Zimmer** room [2] **der Raum** room, space [3] **die Küche** kitchen [4] **je** ever

5) She is a girl **vs** who lives in illusions. **vl**
She is the young girl **vs** who lives in this house. **vl**
I know the young girl **vs** who lives in this house. **vl**
I know the young man **vs** who lives in this house. **vl**
I know a young man **vs** who lives in this house. **vl**
I know a child **vs** who lives in this house. **vl**
These are the people **vs** who live in this house. **vl**
I know the people **vs** who live in this house. **vl**

6) This is a book **vs** I know well. **vl**
These are books **vs** that he knows well. **vl**

Translate the following sentences without the help of the key:

7) He is a man I know nothing about.
She is a girl (a woman, a child) I know nothing about.

8) Is that all she says? Was that all they said?
Everything he says is the truth. All he said was the truth.

9) We believe in a lasting peace. We believe in it.

10) Has she ever heard about this poem? She has heard of it.
I have never heard of such nonsense. I have never heard of it.
They have heard about this man. They have heard about him.

COMPOUND NOUNS — EXERCISE

In compound nouns the last unit determines the gender:

die Speise — der Saal: der Speisesaal
die Speise — das Zimmer: das Speisezimmer
die Speise — die Karte: die Speisekarte

Bearing this in mind, combine the following nouns. Determine the meaning of each component part as well as the meaning of the compound.

der Tisch — das Tuch
der Abend — das Essen
der Mittag — das Essen
der Schinken [1] — das Brot [2]
der Wein — das Glas
das Bier — das Glas
der Rhein — der Wein
die Mosel [3] — der Wein

die Kartoffel [4] — der Salat
die Gurken — der Salat
das Obst [5] — der Salat
die Frucht — der Saft [6]
das Gemüse — die Suppe
die Nudel — die Suppe
das Fett — der Fleck [7]

Compound Nouns — Patterns

Das Zimmer, in dem die Kinder schlafen, wird wohl ihr Schlafzimmer sein.[8]
Die Zimmer, in denen die Kinder spielen, sind leider nicht nur Kinderspielzimmer.
Der Bach,[9] in dem die Forelle schwimmt, wird wohl ein Forellenbach sein.
Die Forelle, die in dem Bach schwimmt, mag wohl eine Bachforelle sein.
Teller, in denen Suppe serviert wird, heißen Suppenteller.

[1] **der Schinken** ham [2] **das Brot** bread [3] **die Mosel** (*river in Germany*) [4] **die Kartoffel** potato [5] **das Obst** fruit [6] **der Saft** juice [7] **der Fleck** spot [8] **wird wohl . . . sein** will probably be, is probably [9] **der Bach** brook

Der Teelöffel [1] eignet sich [2] dazu, den Zucker [3] im Tee zu rühren.[4]
Löffelt man aber mit einem Kaffeelöffel einen Teller Suppe aus?
Oder rührt man Kaffee mit einem Suppenlöffel?
Vor– und Nachspeise sollen zur Hauptspeise [5] passen.
Weißwein ist zwar [6] nie weiß, aber Rotwein muß rot sein.

PRONUNCIATION DRILL

(**pf**; accent and intonation in compound nouns)

Repeat after the instructor and practice the following:

Kampf — Krampf
stampfen — Gestampf′
Pferd — Pferde
Pfer′degestampf′

pfeifen — pfeift
pfiffen — gepfif′fen
stumpf — stumpfer
Stumpfsinn

Speisesaal — Speisezimmer — Speisekarte
Vorspeise — Nachspeise — Hauptspeise — Süßspeise

Obst′salat′ — Kartof′felsalat′
Frucht′salat′ — Gur′kensalat′

Butter — Brot
Butterbrot
Käsebrot
Milch′kaffee′

Ei — Eier
Spiegeleier
Eiertorte
Eierkuchen

Lehrer — Schullehrer
Hochschullehrer

Zimmer — Spielzimmer
Kinderspielzimmer

Tag — Geburt′ — Geburts′tag
Kind — Kinder — Kin′dergeburts′tag

GRAMMAR

24. Interrogative and Relative Pronouns

a. **Wer** (*who*) is declined like the masculine singular of the relative pronoun **der**.

Nom.	der	wer
Acc.	den	wen
Dat.	dem	wem
Gen.	dessen	wessen

Illustrations

Wer ist am zwölften Februar geboren?

Wen begleiten sie heute zur Bahn? — *Whom are they accompanying to the train today?*

Wem wünscht der Kompanieführer gute Reise? — *Whom does the commander of the company wish a good journey?*

[1] **der Teelöffel** teaspoon [2] **sich eignen** be fit *or* suited for [3] **der Zucker** sugar [4] **rühren** stir
[5] **die Hauptspeise** main dish [6] **zwar** to be sure

Wessen Namen ruft der Kompanieführer aus?	*Whose name is called out by the commander of the company?*

Wer has no plural forms, but may refer to the plural:

Wer sind diese Leute?	*Who are these people?*

Wer is also used as a compound relative (*he who, whoever*):

Wer fremde Sprachen nicht kennt, weiß nichts von seiner eigenen.	*He who does not know foreign languages knows nothing about his own language.*

b. Was is both nominative and accusative in form:

Was ist denn hier los? **Was** macht ihr denn hier?	*What is the matter here?* *What are you doing here?*

Was has no plural forms, but may refer to the plural:

Was sind diese Menschen?	*What are these people?*

Was is also used as a compound relative (*that which, whatever*):

Was er tut, ist mir ganz gleich.	*Whatever he does is all the same to me.*

Was is also used as a replacement for the relative pronoun **das** following indefinite pronouns and substantives like **alles, nichts, das Gute, das Beste,** and the like:

Das Beste, **was** es für uns gibt, ist die Wahrheit.	*The best there is for us is the truth.*
Alles, **was** er sagt, ist die Wahrheit.	*Everything he says is the truth.*
Nichts, **was** der Sohn macht, gefällt dem Vater.	(lit. "*Nothing which the son does pleases the father.*")

There is no genitive of **was**.

c. Wo-COMPOUNDS

Prepositional compounds with **wo** in place of **was** are very common in German.

Womit (lit. *wherewith*) schreibt er?	[womit = mit was]
Wovon (lit. *whereof*) spricht er?	[wovon = von was]
Worauf (lit. *whereon*) sitzt sie?	[worauf = auf was]

Note the introduction of **r** in compounds that use a preposition beginning with a vowel:

Woraus macht man Butter?	[woraus = aus was]	*What is butter made of?*
Woran denkt er?	[woran = an was]	*What is he thinking of?*
Worin sitzt er?	[worin = in was]	*What is he sitting in?*
Worüber denkst du nach?	[worüber = über was]	*What are you thinking about?*

Note also that the commonly used interrogative **warum** has undergone a vowel change: **o** to **a. Warum** means literally "wherefore" (*why*).

d. Welche, welches, welcher (meaning *which? what?*) is also used as a relative pronoun replacing **die, das, der** (*who, that, which*).

Welch– has no genitive forms and therefore borrows from the latter.

As a relative pronoun **welch**– has been gradually vanishing from both the spoken and written language, but inasmuch as the bulk of German literature includes the forms of **welch–**, it is necessary to know them.

In its inflectional system the relative pronoun **welch**– follows the pattern of **dies–**, except for the genitive (cf. Grammar Section 15).

	FEM.	NEUT.	MASC.	PLURAL
Nom.	welch e	welch es	welch er	welch e
Acc.	e	es	en	e
Dat.	er	em	em	en
Gen.	(deren)	(dessen)	(dessen)	(deren)

e. Da-COMPOUNDS

Da is frequently a replacement for any personal pronoun of the third person singular or plural when it

(1) occurs in a prepositional phrase *and*
(2) has an inanimate reference.

Illustrations

In the following sequence note the final phrase:

Do you know Professor Braun's history book?
What is your opinion *of it?*

Rendered literally, the final phrase would read: **von ihm.**

Under the given circumstances, however, such a phrase will appear regularly as: **davon.**

Kennen Sie Professor Brauns Geschichtsbuch?
Was halten Sie davon?

NOTE:

A. In the above case ambiguity is avoided by the use of the **da-**compound.

B. The arrow points out the shifted position of the preposition.

Da may also be used as a replacement for a demonstrative pronoun having a general or indefinite reference:

Ich möchte Ihnen einen Vorschlag machen, Herr Fischer. Sollten wir nicht „du" zueinander sagen? Was halten Sie **davon?** (*What do you think of that?*)

Additional Illustrations

He is writing with it (i.e. *pen, pencil, chalk, or the like*).
Er schreibt **damit.**

She is sitting on it (i.e. *chair, couch, bench, or the like*).
Sie sitzt **darauf.**

We are sitting on them (i.e. *chairs, couches, benches, or the like*).
Wir sitzen **darauf.**

He is walking beside it, behind it, in it.
Er geht **daneben, dahinter, darin.**

DER WERWOLF

Ein Werwolf eines Nachts entwich
von Weib und Kind und sich begab
an eines Dorfschullehrers Grab
und bat ihn: „Bitte, beuge mich!"

Der Dorfschulmeister stieg hinauf
auf seines Blechschilds Messingknauf
und sprach zum Wolf, der seine Pfoten
geduldig kreuzte vor dem Toten:

„Der Werwolf," sprach der gute Mann,
„des Weswolfs, Genitiv sodann,
dem Wemwolf, Dativ, wie mans nennt,
den Wenwolf, — damit hats ein End."

Dem Werwolf schmeichelten die Fälle,
er rollte seine Augenbälle.
„Indessen," bat er, „füge doch
zur Einzahl auch die Mehrzahl noch!"

Der Dorfschulmeister aber mußte
gestehn, daß er von ihr nichts wußte.
Zwar Wölfe gäbs in großer Schar,
doch „Wer" gäbs nur im Singular.

Der Wolf erhob sich tränenblind —
er hatte ja doch Weib und Kind!!
Doch da er kein Gelehrter eben,
so schied er dankend und ergeben.

Christian Morgenstern

THE WERWOLF

One night a werwolf, ill at ease,
Left wife and child in their dark cave,
Sought out a village teacher's grave
And asked point-blank: "Decline me, please."

The schoolmaster then upward lurched
And on his grave-sign top he perched,
Addressed the wolf who kept his paws
Crossed patiently, and with good cause.

"'Der Werwolf,' quoth he unperplexed,
'Des Weswolfs,' genitive comes next,
'Dem Wemwolf,' dative, as you see,
'Den Wenwolf,' there! 'voilà! fini!'"

The werwolf, flattered by the cases,
Now rolled his eyeballs in their places.
"While you're about it, Sir, please do it,
Just add a little plural to it."

The schoolmaster perforce admitted
He knew no plural forms that fitted.
Now wolves existed by the score,
But "Wer" came only singular.

The wolf rose shedding tear on tear —
He had a wife and child, 'twas clear,
But since he was no scholar, dumbly
He nodded thanks and withdrew humbly.

14. Aufgabe

WER BIN ICH?

Study the grammar of this lesson before you answer the following questions.

	SAMPLE ANSWERS AND SUGGESTIONS
a. Wissen Sie alles, was in Ihrem Textbuch steht?	*Ich weiß nicht alles, was . . .*
b. Werden Sie oft geprüft? Von wem werden Sie geprüft?	*Ja, ich werde oft geprüft. Nein, . . . nicht oft . . .*
c. Können Sie Deutsch (sprechen)? Wollen Sie Deutsch sprechen? Müssen Sie Deutsch sprechen?	*Ja, ich kann Deutsch (sprechen).*
d. Darf man in der Klasse rauchen?	*Nein, man darf in der Klasse nicht rauchen.*
e. Wann sind Sie gestern aufgestanden?	*Ich bin gestern um . . . Uhr aufgestanden.*
Haben Sie sich ordentlich [1] gewaschen? Haben Sie sich rasiert? [2] Haben Sie sich geschminkt? [3] Haben Sie sich schnell angezogen? [4]	*Ja, ich habe mich . . . gewaschen.*
f. Wann gingen Sie in die Schule? Kamen Sie zur rechten Zeit in die Klasse? Sind Sie etwa [5] zu spät gekommen?	
g. Um wieviel Uhr begann die erste Klasse?	
h. Welche Klassen besuchten Sie?	*Ich besuchte . . .*
i. Wie lange blieben Sie in der Schule?	*Ich blieb bis . . . Uhr . . .*
j. Was gab es gestern zu Mittag zu essen?	*Es gab . . .*
k. Studierten Sie nachmittags, oder hatten Sie etwas anderes zu tun?	
Haben Sie sich ein Buch gekauft?	*Ja, ich habe mir ein Buch gekauft. Nein, ich habe mir kein Buch gekauft.*
l. Trafen Sie einen von Ihren Freunden?	*Ja, ich traf einen von . . . Nein, ich traf keinen von . . .*
Wie heißt Ihr bester Freund?	
Trafen Sie eine von Ihren Freundinnen?	*Ja, ich traf eine von meinen Freundinnen. Nein, ich . . .*
Wie heißt Ihre beste Freundin?	
m. Sprachen Sie über das Wetter? War von den neuesten Nachrichten die Rede? Haben Sie über Ihre Klassen gesprochen? Worüber sprachen Sie?	*Wir sprachen über . . .*

[1] **ordentlich** thoroughly [2] **sich rasieren** shave [3] **sich schminken** put on make-up [4] **sich anziehen** dress [5] **etwa** perhaps

SAMPLE ANSWERS AND SUGGESTIONS

n. Wie war das Wetter in den letzten Tagen?
Regnete [1] es? — *Ja, es regnete. Nein, es regnete nicht.*
Schneite [2] es?
Schien die Sonne?

o. Hatten Sie in den letzten zwei Wochen viel zu tun?
Fanden Sie Ihre Klassen interessant?

DRILL PATTERNS

Repeat the following drills after your instructor or after the speaker on the tape. Imitate the pronunciation very carefully.

1. Sie sieht ihn scharf an. Sie sieht mich scharf an. Sie sieht uns scharf an. Sie sieht euch scharf an. Sie sieht sie (*her*) scharf an. Sie sieht Sie scharf an. Sie sieht sie (*them*) scharf an. Sie sieht es scharf an. Sie sieht dich scharf an.

2. Ich sehe mich um.
Du siehst dich um.
Er sieht sich um.
Sie sieht sich um.

3. Ich sehe mir das Menu an.
Siehst du dir das Menu an?
Er sieht sich das Menu an.
Sieht sie sich das Menu an?

4. Wir sehen uns um.
Ihr seht euch um.
Sie sehen sich um.
Man sieht sich um.

5. Wir sehen uns das Menu an.
Seht ihr euch das Menu an?
Sie sehen sich das Menu an.
Sieht man sich das Menu an?

6. Setzt du dich?
Setzen Sie sich?
Setzt ihr euch?
Setzen wir uns?

7. Worüber machst du dir Sorgen?
Worüber macht sie sich Sorgen?
Ich mache mir keine Sorgen.
Wir machen uns keine Sorgen.

8. Wo befindet sich Anna? — In einem Restaurant.
Wo befinden wir uns? — In einem Klassenzimmer.

9. Ich vertiefe mich in das Menu.
Was soll ich mir wohl bestellen?
Er sieht sich jetzt das Menu an.
Was wird er sich wohl bestellen?

10. Wozu soll man sich entschließen?
Wovon soll man sich unterhalten?
Wozu sollen wir uns entschließen?
Wovon sollen wir uns unterhalten?

11. Hans rasiert sich. Er hat sich rasiert.
Anna schminkt sich. Sie hat sich geschminkt.
Wäscht das Kind sich? Es hat sich gewaschen.

[1] **regnen** rain [2] **schneien** snow

12. Muß er immer das Beste haben? Er hat immer das Beste. Immer hatte er das Beste. Immer hat er das Beste gehabt.

Das wird zu teuer sein. Das ist zu teuer. Das war zu teuer. Das ist zu teuer gewesen.

Wo bleibt der Kellner? Wo mag er bleiben? Wo blieb er? Wo ist er geblieben?

Wie findet sie ihre Kurse? Wie fand sie ihren Kurs? Wie hat sie ihren Kurs gefunden? Wie wird sie ihre Kurse finden?

Wo befindet er sich heute? Wo hat er sich gestern befunden? Wo befand er sich? Wo wird er sich morgen befinden?

Ißt er? Aß er? Hat er gegessen? — Zu essen gibt es hier nichts.

Er spricht Englisch. Er sprach Englisch. Er hat Englisch gesprochen. — Englisch sprechen ist leicht.

Fängt man an? Fing man an? Hat man angefangen? — Anzufangen ist immer schwer.

Hat er das gesagt? Sagte er das? Wird er das sagen? Sagt er das?

Es regnet. Es regnete. Es hat geregnet. Es wird regnen.

Sie wird ihn schon kennen. Sie kennt ihn schon lange. Sie kannte ihn. Sie hat ihn gekannt.

13. Kann er Deutsch? Konnte er Deutsch? — Nein, Deutsch wird er nicht können. Nein, Deutsch hat er nie gekonnt.

Geht sie in die Schule? Ist sie in die Schule gegangen? Ging sie gestern in die Schule? Wird sie in die Schule gehen?

Ist er gekommen? Kam er? Kommt er? Wird er je wieder kommen?

Man tut zuviel. Man tat zuviel. Man hat zuviel zu tun. — Hast du so viel getan?

14. Du wirst heute geprüft.
Ihr werdet heute geprüft.
Er wird heute geprüft.
Sie wird heute geprüft.
Ja, heute wird geprüft.

15. Ja, ich werde heute geprüft.
Ja, wir werden heute geprüft.
Ja, sie werden heute geprüft.
Werden Sie heute geprüft?

16. Du wirst von ihnen gesehen.
Ihr werdet von ihnen gesehen.
Er wird von ihr gesehen.
Sie wird von ihm gesehen.

17. Das Lied wird überall gehört.
Überall werden die Lieder gehört.
Sein Lied wird überall gehört.
Man hört seine Lieder überall.

18. Von wem wird man hier bedient? Man wird von dem Kellner bedient.
Von wem wird der Braten serviert? Der Braten wird von dem Ober serviert.
Womit wird der Braten geschnitten? Der Braten wird mit dem Messer geschnitten.

19. Mein Lehrer hört mich nie. Ich werde von ihm nie gehört.
Meine Lehrerin beachtet mich nicht. Ich werde von ihr nicht beachtet.
Unsere Lehrer sehen uns nie. Wir werden von ihnen nie gesehen.
Prüfen euere Lehrer euch nicht? — Oh doch, wir werden von ihnen geprüft.

English to German

Prepare this exercise in writing.

1) The matter is being decided now. **vs / vl**
2) He is taking his examination today. (*use passive of* **prüfen**) **vs / vl**
3) They are taking their examination today. (*use passive of* **prüfen**) **vs / vl**
4) I am (being) seen by them. **vs / vl**
   He is (being) seen by us. **vs / vl**
5) His song is heard everywhere. **vs / vl**
   His songs are heard everywhere. **vs / vl**
6) They never see us. **vs**
   We are never seen by them. **vs / vl**

Translate the following sentences without the help of the key:

7) He looks at you (*3 ways*).
   He looked at her. (*past*)
8) She is looking around.
9) He is looking at the menu. (*use reflexive*)
10) What is he worrying about?
11) Is he ordering beer or wine for himself?
12) What are you (*2 ways*) ordering for yourself?
13) Can't you (*3 ways*) make up your mind?
14) He shaves every morning.
    He shaved every morning.

In the following sentences use (1) *present perfect,* (2) *past tense:*

15) How did she find his course?
    Did he come?
    Did they speak English?
    Did he know her?
    Did he know German?

PRONUNCIATION DRILL

(vowels, vowel change, and accent in verb forms; **x [nks, ngs]**)

Repeat after the instructor and practice the following:

bleiben — blieb — geblie'ben
schließen — schloß — geschlos'sen
singen — sang — gesun'gen
sehen — sah — gese'hen

fallen — fällt
halten — hält
fangen — fängt
schlagen — schlägt

nannte — nennt
kannte — kennt
rannte — rennt
brannte — brennt

dürfen — durfte
können — konnte
mögen — mochte
müssen — mußte

gegan'gen — gehabt'
gekom'men — gewe'sen
gestan'den — getan' — gewor'den

links — Tanks
explosiv'
längst — tags
engste — Ängste

denkst du? dankst du?
sangst du? sankst du?
winkst du? wankst du?
bangst du? schwankst du?

GRAMMAR

25. Strong Verbs

German strong verbs are those capable of making vowel changes. These changes, which occur in the verb stem, cannot easily be committed to memory unless the memory is aided by some kind of classification system. No system exists in German, however, that can arrange *all* variations according to a neat, all-inclusive pattern. The following classification system is no exception to this, but it can be far more helpful to your memory than any haphazard encounters with strong verbs. Used discriminately, it can help to bring shape and order out of potential difficulty and confusion in the whole verb area. For the sake of brevity and convenience this system has only five classes rather than a possible seven or eight.

CLASS	INFINITIVE	PRESENT	PAST	PAST PARTICIPLE
1.	**ei**	(—)	**ie, i**	**ie, i**
2.	**ie** (*often* **e**)	(—)	**o**	**o**
3.	**i**	(—)	**a**	**u, o**
4.	**e**	**(i, ie)**	**a**	**e, o**
5.	**a**	(¨)	**i, ie, u**	**a**

Do not attempt to memorize this vowel gradation scheme, but rather memorize the principal parts of the verbs in Grammar Sections 25 *and* 26.

The following verbs are reference models. Enter these and every new strong verb in your notebook, each according to its proper class.

Models taken from the first five units:

CLASS	INFINITIVE	3RD SING. PRESENT	3RD SING. PAST	PAST PARTICIPLE	
1.	bleiben	(bleibt)	blieb	geblieben	*remain*
	reißen	(reißt)	riß	gerissen	*tear*
2.	schließen	(schließt)	schloß	geschlossen	*close*
	heben	(hebt)	hob	gehoben	*lift*
3.	singen	(singt)	sang	gesungen	*sing*
	beginnen	(beginnt)	begann	begonnen	*begin*
4.	sehen	(sieht)	sah	gesehen	*see*
	sprechen	(spricht)	sprach	gesprochen	*speak*
5.	fangen	(fängt)	fing	gefangen	*catch*
	halten	(hält) *	hielt	gehalten	*hold*
	schlagen	(schlägt)	schlug	geschlagen	*strike*

* Note the shortened form **hält.**

a. The following verbs taken from Units I–V belong to Class 1. They are either like:

bleiben	or like	**reißen**
entscheiden (*decide*)		gleiten (*glide*)
scheinen (*shine*)		greifen (*seize, grasp*)
schreiben (*write*)		leiden (*suffer*)
schweigen (*be silent*)		pfeifen (*whistle, pipe*)
steigen (*climb*)		schleichen (*creep*)
verzeihen (*pardon*)		schneiden (*cut*)

Take note of the double consonants in the past tenses of:

gleiten: glitt, geglitten
greifen: griff, gegriffen
leiden: litt, gelitten
pfeifen: pfiff, gepfiffen
schneiden: schnitt, geschnitten

Since the **i** is short in the past and past participle forms, more than one consonant is required immediately after the vowel. (Note that in **leiden** and **schneiden** the change is from **d** to **tt.**)

b. The following verbs from Units I–V belong to Class 2. They are like:

schließen

anziehen [1] (*put on, dress*)
frieren (*freeze*)
riechen (*smell*)
schießen (*shoot*)
verlieren (*lose*)
ziehen [1] (*go, move, pull*)

NOTE:

Except for the present tense, **betrügen** (*deceive*) and **lügen** (*lie, tell a lie*) belong here too.

c. The following verbs from Units I–V belong to Class 3. They are either like:

singen	or like	**beginnen**
finden (*find*)		entrinnen (*run away from, escape*)
(ver)schwinden (*disappear, dwindle*)		

d. The following verbs from Units I–V belong to Class 4.[2] They are either like:

sehen	or like	**sprechen**
essen [3] (*eat*)		abbrechen (*break off*)
fressen (*eat* [of animals])		befehlen (*command*)
geben (*give*)		nehmen [3] (*take*)
lesen (*read*)		sterben (*die*)
treten [3] (*step*)		treffen [3] (*meet*)

[1] *Note consonantal irregularities in:* anziehen (zieht an), zog an, angezogen; ziehen (zieht), zog, gezogen. [2] *Note that* lesen *and* befehlen *change their stem vowel from* **e** to **ie** (liest, befiehlt); *the others change from* **e** to **i** (*e.g.*, geben [gibt]). [3] *Note consonantal irregularities in:* essen (ißt), aß, gegessen; treten (tritt), trat, getreten; nehmen (nimmt), nahm, genommen; treffen (trifft), traf, getroffen.

NOTE:

Except for the infinitive and the present tense, **bitten** [1] (*ask*), **liegen** (*lie*), and **sitzen** [1] (*sit*) belong with **sehen;** and **gebären** (*bear, give birth to*), with **sprechen.**

e. The following verbs from Units I–V belong to Class 5. They are either like:

halten	or like	**schlagen**
fallen [2] (*fall*)		fahren (*ride, travel, go*)
lassen (*let*)		backen [2] (*bake*)
		waschen (*wash*)
		wachsen (*grow*)

NOTE:

The following four verbs are like **halten** in the past: **heißen** (*be named*), **laufen** (*run*), **rufen** (*call*), **stoßen** (*push*). Regardless of the differences among them in infinitive vowel (or diphthong), they all show **ie** in the past tense: **hielt, hieß, lief, rief, stieß.**

Characteristic of Class 5 is the identity of the infinitive and past participle stem vowel within a given verb:

heißen — geheißen	laufen — gelaufen
stoßen — gestoßen	rufen — gerufen

This characteristic then bars **heißen** from Class 1.

Compare:	bleiben	(bleibt)	blieb	geblieben
	heißen	(heißt)	hieß	geheißen

All verbs in Class 5 except **heißen, rufen, schaffen** (*create, do*) and compounds of them take umlaut in the present indicative.

NOTE:

A. As indicated above, the past participle ending of *strong verbs* is normally **–en.**

B. The past participle ending of *weak verbs* is normally **–t** (**–et** after stem ending **t, d,** or stem combinations like **atm–, regn–**):

INFINITIVE	PAST	PAST PARTICIPLE	
sagen	sagte	gesagt	(*say*)
warten	wartete	gewartet	(*wait*)
reden	redete	geredet	(*speak*)
regnen	regnete	geregnet	(*rain*)

C. The *weak-strong verbs*, modal auxiliaries, **wissen** (*know*), and **haben** (*have*) all show a **–t** ending in the past participle.

[1] *Note consonantal irregularities in:* bitten (bittet), bat, gebeten; sitzen (sitzt), saß, gesessen.
[2] *Note consonantal irregularities in:* fallen (fällt), fiel, gefallen; backen (bäckt), buk, gebacken.

26. Weak-Strong Verbs, Modals, Irregular Verbs

a. The following verbs from Units I–V have strong-verb as well as weak-verb characteristics.

kennen	(kennt)	kannte	gekannt	(*know*)
nennen	(nennt)	nannte	genannt	(*name, call*)
rennen	(rennt)	rannte	gerannt	(*run*)

NOTE:

A. The past tense endings are like **sagte.**

B. The past participle endings are like **gesagt.**

There are five others similar to these:

brennen (*burn*) denken (*think*)
bringen (*bring*) senden (*send*)
wenden (*turn*)

Note the following consonant changes in **bringen** and **denken.** Compare with English:

bringen	brachte	gebracht
denken	dachte	gedacht

b. MODALS AND **wissen:**

The modal auxiliaries and **wissen** can also be considered weak-strong verbs for the same reasons as stated in a. above. Note, however, (1) the radical difference in vowel gradations and (2) the present tense ending pattern, which is similar to the *past tense of strong verbs:*

INFINITIVE	3RD SING. PRESENT	3RD SING. PAST	PAST PARTICIPLE	
dürfen	(darf)	durfte	gedurft	(*be permitted to*)
können	(kann)	konnte	gekonnt	(*can*)
mögen	(mag)	mochte	gemocht	(*like, like to*)
müssen	(muß)	mußte	gemußt	(*must*)
sollen	(soll)	sollte	gesollt	(*shall, should*)
wollen	(will)	wollte	gewollt	(*will, want to*)
wissen	(weiß)	wußte	gewußt	(*know*)

NOTE:

A. **Dürfen** = *may* (*be permitted to*).

B. Only **mögen** shows a consonant change: **mocht–.**

C. **Sollen** shows no vowel change and is, therefore, strictly speaking, not a weak-strong verb.

D. The only umlauts in the principal parts are within the block. (**Möchte** [*would like to*] is a past subjunctive form.)

E. **Darf, kann, mag** have a common vowel.

c. The following seven verbs may be classified simply as irregulars. Since they are used with great frequency, *they should be memorized thoroughly:*

INFINITIVE	3RD SING. PRESENT	3RD SING. PAST	PAST PARTICIPLE	
gehen	(geht)	ging	gegangen	(*go*)
haben	(hat)	hatte	gehabt	(*have*)
kommen	(kommt)	kam	gekommen	(*come*)
sein	(ist)	war	gewesen	(*be*)
stehen	(steht)	stand	gestanden	(*stand*)
tun	(tut)	tat	getan	(*do*)
werden	(wird)	wurde	geworden	(*become*)

Note that **hatte** and **wurde** follow the ending pattern of the past tense of *weak verbs.*

27. Prepositions and Passive Voice

Prepositional phrases expressing *personal* agency in passive voice situations (cf. Grammar Section 20) regularly use **von.** Instrument and means are expressed by **mit** and **durch:**

Das Gedicht wurde **von** Heinrich Heine geschrieben.	*The poem was written by Heinrich Heine.*
Brot, Fleisch und Butter werden **mit** einem Messer geschnitten.	*Bread, meat, and butter are cut with a knife.*
Remarques Ruhm wurde **durch** seinen Roman *Im Westen nichts Neues* begründet.	*Remarque's fame was established by his novel,* All Quiet on the Western Front.

28. Reflexive Pronouns

a. Of the regular personal pronouns the following may be used reflexively:

mich, mir, dich, dir, uns, euch

Illustrations

Ich wasche mich.
Du wäschst dich.

Ich kaufe mir ein Buch.
Du kaufst dir ein Buch.

b. The reflexive pronoun **sich** (which has already occurred a number of times in Units I–V) is an immutable form. It may serve as an accusative or a dative form:

Sie wäscht sich.
Sie kauft sich ein Buch.

Sich may mean: *herself, himself, itself, oneself, themselves*, and (when used with **Sie**) *yourself, yourselves:*

Er wäscht sich. Er kauft sich ein Buch.	Sie waschen sich. (*What are the possible English equivalents?*)
Die Katze wäscht sich. Die Katze kauft sich kein Buch.	Sie kaufen sich Bücher. (*What are the possible English equivalents?*)

c. With many verbs in German reflexives are used where English feels no need for them:

Der Soldat fürchtet sich nicht. Wir haben uns sehr gefreut.	*The soldier is not afraid.* *We were very happy.*
Die Verwandten wunderten sich sehr darüber.	*The relatives were greatly surprised at that.*

15. Aufgabe

VOCABULARY BUILDING

SUFFIXES

I. ADJECTIVE-ADVERB SUFFIXES: –**ig** and –**lich** (English *-y*, *-ily*, *-ful*, *-ous*, and the like)

These two suffixes, often combined with noun or verb stems, produce adjectives, most of which, in their uninflected form, may be used adverbially. (All the examples given below are from Units I–V.)

A. The following examples should be immediately recognizable:

hungrig	freundlich
richtig	natürlich
rosig	persönlich
traurig	täglich
witzig	monatlich

B. Consider the following examples:

auswendig	deutlich
ewig	hoffentlich
heutig	plötzlich
langweilig	schrecklich
neugierig	unglücklich
ruhig	verständlich
zukünftig	wirklich

A number of the above examples are used in the following sentences. Some of these will be immediately recognizable; others you will need to guess at. Check in the end vocabulary for the correct answers, after you have made your choices.

Sprechen Sie langsam und **deutlich.**
Was Sie sagen, ist mir nicht **verständlich.**

Hoffentlich wird die Anekdote nicht zu **langweilig.**

Er glaubt **wirklich** an einen **ewigen** Frieden.

In der **heutigen** Zeitung ist wieder von Krieg die Rede, von einem **zukünftigen, schrecklichen** Atomkrieg.

C. The following examples show adjectives formed by adding the suffix –**ig** to noun stems:

die Neugier *curiosity* : neugierig *curious*
die Ruhe *peace, quiet* : ruhig *peaceful, quiet*

Form adjectives ending in –**ig** from the following nouns and give their English meanings:

die Geduld *patience*
die Lust *pleasure, joy*
der Witz *wit*
der Schmutz *dirt*
die Ungeduld *impatience*
das Blut *blood*

D. The following examples show adjectives formed by adding **–lich** to the noun stem:

das Wunder *wonder* : wunderlich *strange*
die Gefahr *danger* : gefährlich *dangerous*

Form adjectives ending in **–lich** from the following nouns and give their English meanings. (Add umlaut wherever possible.)

die Angst *anxiety*
das Glück *luck, happiness*
der Verstand *understanding*
die Person *person*
der Tag *day*
das Jahr *year*

II. NOUN SUFFIXES: –heit, –keit, –ung

The English suffix *–hood* is the cognate of **–heit:** childhood, falsehood.
Besides *–hood* there are other English equivalents for **–heit:** *–dom, –(i)ty, –ment, –ness.* **–heit** forms feminine abstract nouns (Class 4, **–en**) when combined particularly with adjective stems.

A. Note how the following adjectives are changed to feminine abstract nouns by attaching **–heit:**

gelegen *opportune* : die Gelegenheit *opportunity*
gesund *sound, healthy* : die Gesundheit *soundness, health*

Form similar nouns in the same way by using the following adjectives. Give the meanings of the nouns thus formed:

blind
klar
krank
stumpf (*dull*)
rein
schön
wahr
weise (*drop the final* **e**)

Form similar feminine abstracts by suffixing **–heit** to each of the following:

der Gott
das Kind
der Tor (*fool*)
der Mensch

B. **–keit** replaces **–heit** after adjectival suffixes **–lich, –ig, –bar,** and others:

freundlich *friendly* : die Freundlichkeit *friendliness*
ewig *eternal* : die Ewigkeit *eternity*

Form feminine abstract nouns ending in –**keit** from the following adjectives and give their English meanings:

ängstlich	plötzlich
deutlich	traurig
natürlich	verständlich
persönlich	wirklich

C. –**ung** is frequently attached to verb stems to form feminine nouns:

achten *pay attention to* : die Achtung *attention*
vergeben *forgive* : die Vergebung *forgiveness*

Form similar nouns from the following verbs:

drehen	prüfen
erzählen	vernichten
meinen	wiederholen
melden (*announce*)	wohnen

WORD STUDY

IDIOMATIC EXPRESSIONS

was für ein *what kind of*
Was für einen Garten (*garden*) haben Sie?
Was für ein Restaurant ist das?
Was für Menschen sind das?

einholen *catch up* (*with*)
Erich holte mich zur rechten Zeit ein. *Erich caught up with me at the right time.*

sprechen + **über** + acc. *speak about, discuss*
Der Professor sprach über das Wesen der Sprache. *The professor discussed the nature of language.*

Richard warf **mit** Steinen **nach** ihnen. *Richard threw stones* ***at*** *them.*

Er stellte mir ein Bein. *He tripped me up.*

ein Tagebuch (*lit.* "daybook") **führen** *keep a diary*
Vom vierzehnten Juni neunzehnhundertzweiundvierzig bis zum ersten August neunzehnhundertvierundvierzig führte Anne Frank ihr Tagebuch.

sich verstecken vor *hide from*
Bei jeder Gelegenheit hat sie sich vor mir versteckt. *At every opportunity she hid from me.*

schuld sein an *be guilty of, be to blame for*
Sie sind alle schuld an ihrem Tod (daran). *They are all to blame for her death* (*for it*).

sich erinnern an + acc. *remember*
Sie erinnert sich wenig an ihre Jugend (daran). *She remembers little of her youth* (*of it*).

erinnern an + acc. of personal pronoun *remind*
Es erinnert mich an meine Jugend (daran). *It reminds me of my youth* (*of it*).

Aus wichtigen, persönlichen **Gründen** ist er nicht geblieben. *For important personal reasons he did not stay.*

PRONUNCIATION DRILL

(**qu**; vowel + **h**; **mm**, **nn**, **pp**, **tt**)

Repeat after the instructor and practice the following:

Qual — quält
Quelle — quillt
quinquillie'ren
kreuz und quer

querfeldein — überque'ren
quatschen — quaken — quäken — quieken

Quantum — Quanten — Quantitä'ten
Quart — Quartet'te — Quark
Quecksilber — inkonsequent'

Hans — Hahn
Hanna — Huhn
Ahn — Ahnung — ahnungslos
da — ah — ach — ja
du — Ruh — Tuch — zu

Emma — immer
Anna — Amme
tappen — Treppe
treppauf' — treppab'

Wetter — Gewit'ter
Donnerwetter!

Reading

ERICH KÄSTNER

ERICH KÄSTNER wurde am 23. Februar 1899 in Dresden geboren. In den zwanziger Jahren wurden Verse aus seinen Gedichtbänden *Herz auf Taille*, *Lärm im Spiegel* und *Ein Mann gibt Auskunft* weithin zitiert. Aber das Herz der kleinen und großen Leute gewann er sich erst durch Kinderbücher wie *Emil und die Detektive*, *Pünktchen und Anton* und *Das fliegende Klassenzimmer*. Die kurze Erzählung „Der Feind" stammt aus Kästners 5 Autobiographie *Als ich ein kleiner Junge war*. Kästners ironische und auf indirekte Weise erzieherische Art gibt auch seinen journalistischen Arbeiten den großen Reiz. Erich Kästner lebt heute in München.

Aus: ALS ICH EIN KLEINER JUNGE WAR

Der Feind

Er war einen Kopf größer als ich, ein ganz netter Kerl, und konnte mich nicht leiden. Daß es so war, hätte ich zur Not hingenommen. Aber ich wußte nicht 10 warum. Und das verwirrte mich.

Unsere Mütter hatten schon nebeneinander auf den grünen Bänken im Garten

LINE
1–2 zwanziger Jahre — *nineteen-twenties*
3 weithin zitiert — *widely quoted*
6–7 auf indirekte Weise — *indirectly*
7 erzieherisch — *didactic, pedagogical*
die Art — *manner*

LINE
7 der Reiz — *charm*
9 der Kerl — *fellow*
10 hätte . . . hingenommen — *would have accepted*
11 verwirren — *confuse*

Bodensee: Segelregatta vor der Insel Lindau. Der größte See im deutschen Sprachgebiet liegt an der Grenze zwischen Österreich, der Schweiz und Westdeutschland.

des Japanischen Palais an der Elbe gesessen, als wir noch im Kinderwagen lagen. Später hockten wir zusammen auf dem Spielplatz im Sandkasten und buken Sandkuchen. Wir gingen gemeinsam in den Turnverein Neu- und Antonstadt, in der Alaunstraße, und in die Vierte Bürgerschule. Und bei jeder Gelegenheit suchte er mir eins auszuwischen. 5

Er warf mit Steinen nach mir. Er stellte mir ein Bein. Er stieß mich hinterrücks, daß ich hinfiel. Er lauerte mir, der ahnungslos des Wegs kam, in Haustoren auf, schlug mich und lief kreischend davon. Ich rannte ihm nach, und wenn ich ihn einholen konnte, hatte er nichts zu lachen. Ich war nicht ängstlich. Aber ich verstand ihn nicht. Warum überfiel er mich? Warum ließ er mich nicht in 10 Frieden? Ich tat ihm doch nichts. Ich hatte ihn ganz gern. Warum griff er mich an?

Eines Tages sagte meine Mutter, der ich davon erzählt hatte: „Er kratzte dich schon, als ihr noch im Kinderwagen saßt." „Aber warum denn?" fragte ich ratlos. Sie dachte eine Weile nach. Dann antwortete sie: „Vielleicht weil dich alle so 15 hübsch fanden! Die alten Frauen, die Gärtner und die Kinderfräuleins, die an unserer Bank vorüberkamen, schauten in eure Kinderwagen hinein und fanden dich viel reizender als ihn. Sie lobten dich über den grünen Klee!" „Und du meinst, das hat er verstanden? Als Baby?" „Nicht die Worte. Aber den Sinn. Und den Ton, womit sie es sagten." „Und daran erinnert er sich noch? Obwohl 20 er es gar nicht verstand?" „Vielleicht," meinte die Mutter. „Und nun mach deine Schularbeiten." „Ich habe sie längst gemacht," antwortete ich. „Ich gehe spielen."

Und als ich aus dem Haus trat, stolperte ich über Naumann Richards Bein. Ich sauste hinter ihm her, holte ihn ein und gab ihm eins hinter die Ohren. Es 25 konnte schon sein, daß er mich seit unsrer Kinderwagenzeit haßte. Daß er sich daran erinnerte. Daß er mich gar nicht angriff, wie ich geglaubt hatte. Sondern daß er sich nur verteidigte. Doch ein Bein stellen ließ ich mir deshalb noch lange nicht.

FRAGEN

1. Wer ist Erich Kästner? Was wissen Sie über ihn und sein Werk? 2. In welchem Alter (*age*) wurde Richard Erichs Feind? 3. Wie lange kannten sich die beiden? 4. Was tat

LINE
1 die Elbe — *the Elbe river*
der Kinderwagen — *baby carriage*
2 hocken — *squat*
3 der Turnverein — *athletic club*
4 die Bürgerschule — *high school*
die Gelegenheit — *opportunity*
5 mir eins auszuwischen — *"poke," hit me*
6–7 hinterrücks — *from the back*
7–8 auflauern — *lay in wait*
7 ahnungslos — *unsuspecting*
das Haustor — *doorway*
8 kreischend — *screaming*
10 überfallen — *pounce upon*

LINE
11 doch — *after all*
11–12 angreifen — *attack*
13 kratzen — *scratch*
14 ratlos — *perplexed*
15 nachdenken — *think, ponder*
16 das Kinderfräulein — *governess*
18 reizender — *more charming*
Sie lobten . . . Klee — *They praised you to the skies*
24 stolpern — *stumble*
25 sausen — *rush*
28 verteidigen — *defend*
28–9 noch lange nicht — *not by a long shot*

Richard, um Erich zu ärgern? (**um . . . zu** *in order to;* **ärgern** *annoy*) 5. Warum griff Richard Erich immer an? 6. Was hielt Erichs Mutter für die Ursache (*cause*) von Richards Feindschaft (*hostility*)? 7. Was halten Sie von ihrer Erklärung (*explanation*)? 8. Ist ein Minderwertigkeitskomplex (*inferiority complex*) eine Entschuldigung (*excuse*) für schlechtes Benehmen (*behavior*)?

AUS DEM TAGEBUCH DER ANNE FRANK

Anne Frank war fünfzehn Jahre alt, als die Nazis sie und ihre Familie verhafteten. Sie starb sieben Monate später in dem Konzentrationslager Bergen-Belsen, drei Wochen bevor die britischen Truppen die überlebenden Gefangenen befreiten. Vom 14. Juni 1942 bis zum 1. August 1944 führte Anne Frank ihr Tagebuch. Die Franks lebten 5 während dieser Zeit in Holland. Sie mußten sich aus „rassischen Gründen" vor den Deutschen, die das Land besetzt hielten, versteckt halten.

Mittwoch, 3. Mai 1944

Liebe Kitty! . . .

Warum ist überhaupt Krieg? Warum können die Menschen nicht in Frieden leben? Warum alle die Verwüstungen? Diese Fragen sind verständlich, aber eine erschöpfende Antwort hat bisher noch niemand gefunden. Warum werden 10 täglich Millionen für den Krieg verwendet, aber für die Heilkunde, die Künstler und auch für die Armen ist kein Pfennig verfügbar? Warum müssen Menschen hungern, wenn in anderen Weltteilen Nahrungsmittel umkommen? Warum sind die Menschen so töricht?

Ich glaube nicht, daß allein die führenden Männer, die Regierenden und Kapi- 15 talisten am Kriege schuld sind. Nein, der kleine Mann anscheinend auch, sonst würden die Völker als solche nicht mitmachen! Der Drang zur Vernichtung ist nun einmal in den Menschen, der Drang zum Töten, Morden und Wüten, und solange nicht die gesamte Menschheit eine völlige Metamorphose durchgemacht hat, wird es Kriege geben. Was gebaut, gepflegt und gewachsen ist, wird niedergetreten 20 und vernichtet, und die Menschheit muß von neuem beginnen.

LINE
1 verhaften — *arrest*
3 überleben — *survive*
der Gefangene — *prisoner*
5 aus „rassischen Gründen" — *for racial reasons*
6 besetzt — *occupied*
versteckt — *hidden*
7 überhaupt — *anyway*
8 die Verwüstung — *devastation*
verständlich — *understandable*
9 erschöpfend — *exhaustive*
10 verwenden — *spend*
die Heilkunde — *medicine, medical science*
11 verfügbar — *available*
12 der Weltteil — *part of the world, continent*
die Nahrungsmittel (*pl.*) — *food*

LINE
12 umkommen — *go to waste*
13 töricht — *foolish*
14 die Regierenden — *rulers*
15 anscheinend — *apparently*
sonst — *otherwise*
16 mitmachen — *participate*
der Drang — *urge*
die Vernichtung — *destruction*
17 nun einmal — *simply*
wüten — *rage, go berserk*
18 gesamt — *entire*
durchmachen — *undergo*
19 pflegen — *cultivate*
niedertreten — *trample underfoot*
20 von neuem — *anew*

Ich war oft niedergeschlagen, aber nie verzweifelt. Dieses Untertauchen betrachte ich als gefährliches Abenteuer, das romantisch und interessant ist. Ich habe mir nun einmal vorgenommen, daß ich ein anderes Leben führen werde als Mädels im allgemeinen und später auch nicht das Alltagsleben einer Hausfrau. . .

Anne

FRAGEN

1. Wer war Anne Frank? 2. Wie alt war sie, als sie starb? 3. Wo starb Anne Frank? 4. In welcher Zeit führte sie ihr Tagebuch?

EXERCISES

a. Change the verbs in the passage indicated from present to past tense:

Page 95, lines 8–16: from "Ich stehe am Fenster" to ". . . und dahinter der Abend."

b. Change the verbs in the passage indicated from past to present tense:

Page 123, lines 6–12: from "Er warf mit Steinen . . ." to "Warum griff er mich an?"

c. ADJECTIVE ENDINGS

By using the adjective ending chart in Grammar Section 23, supply the missing endings in the following sentences.

Note: Since some of these sentences among the first twenty are familiar to you already, try first of all to get at the correct endings by ear. Then check immediately against the chart to see how reliable the aural impression has been.

1. D– Best–, was es für uns gibt, ist die Wahrheit. 2. Am nächst– Morgen begleiten mich Albert und Kat zur klein– Feldbahn. 3. D– ganz– Haus riecht danach. (*neut.*) 4. Er glaubt nicht an ein– ewig– Frieden. 5. An d– Fenstern gleitet d– wunderschön– Landschaft vorüber. (*fem.*) 6. Wir lernen die Namen d– alt– Straßen. (*pl.*) 7. Wir müssen jed– einzeln– Wort auswendig lernen. (*neut.*) 8. Am breit– Fenster (*neut.*) gleiten flach– Wiesen vorüber. 9. Er gibt die Hoffnung auf ein– besser– Welt nicht auf. 10. Haben Sie je von dies– gut– Frau gehört? 11. Schreiben Sie mit ein– neu– Feder? (*fem. dat.*) 12. Das ist ein– schwierig– Frage. 13. Schreibst du mit ein– rot– Bleistift? (*masc. dat.*) 14. Herr Berger, Sie sind doch nur ein– ganz gewöhnlich– Optimist. 15. Ich erkenne d– charakteristisch– Linie (*fem.*) d– schön– Dolbenberges. 16. Sind Sie je über dies– klein– Brücke gegangen? 17. D– ander– Leute bereiten ihre Sachen zum Aussteigen vor. 18. Adler sieht nur d– ewig– Krieg voraus. 19. Hunde trotten durch d– schmal–,

LINE
1 niedergeschlagen — *downcast*
verzweifelt — *in despair*
das Untertauchen — *going underground*
1–2 betrachten — *regard*
2 gefährlich — *dangerous*

LINE
2 das Abenteuer — *adventure*
3 sich (etwas) vornehmen — *resolve*
4 Mädels — *girls*
im allgemeinen — *in general*
das Alltagsleben — *everyday routine*

grau– Straße. (*fem. acc. sing.*) 20. Adler glaubt an kein– zukünftig–, dauernd– Frieden. 21. Das ist mein– ältest– Schwester. 22. Ich stehe da in ein– furchtbar– Krampf. (*masc.*) 23. D– britisch– Truppen befreiten d– überlebend– Gefangenen. (*pl.*) 24. Die Franks lebten während dies– ganz– Zeit in Holland. (*fem. gen. sing.*) 25. Bisher hat noch niemand ein– erschöpfend– Antwort gefunden. (*fem.*) 26. In ander– Weltteilen hungern viele Menschen. (*pl.*) 27. D– führend– Männer sind nicht allein am Kriege schuld. (*pl.*) Nein, d– klein– Mann anscheinend auch. 28. D– gesamt– Menschheit muß ein– völlig– Metamorphose durchmachen. (*both fem. sing.*) 29. Ich werde ein– ander– Leben führen als Mädels im allgemeinen. (*neut.*) 30. Er war ein– ganz nett– Kerl. 31. Unser– lieb– Mütter saßen immer auf jen– grün– Bänken. (*both pl.*) 32. Sie lobten dich über d– grün– Klee. (*masc. acc. sing.*) 33. D– alt– Frauen schauten in eur– klein– Kinderwagen hinein. (*pl.*)

SECHSTER TEIL

Bayrische Alpenstraße

Bahnhof in Hamburg-Altona

Das bayrische Städtchen Oberammergau ist durch seine Passionsspiele weltbekannt.

16. Aufgabe

EINE REISE

Of the following dialogue memorize only the section on this page. The rest (see page 131) is to be treated as reading assignment.

WERNER: Hast du ein paar Minuten Zeit, Karl? Ich habe dir etwas Wichtiges mitzuteilen.

KARL: (*zögernd*) Tu das lieber ein anderes Mal, wenn ich besserer Laune bin als heute morgen. Und wenn ich weniger zu tun habe.

WERNER: (*strahlend*) Nein, Karl. Höre! Wir werden diesen kommenden Sommer während der Ferien eine große Reise machen. Die größte Reise unseres Lebens.

KARL: Wir? Eine Reise?

WERNER: (*aufgeregt*) Anfang Juni, am ersten oder zweiten, geht es los. Wir fliegen abends gegen neun Uhr dreißig von Boston in unserem Privatflugzeug ab. Am nächsten Morgen frühstücken wir in London.

KARL: Was? Wo? In London?

WERNER: Leider haben wir für London nur bis Nachmittag Zeit. Zum Abendessen müssen wir schon in Paris sein.

KARL: (*ironisch*) Wo man uns aufs beste empfangen wird!

A TRIP

WERNER: Do you have a minute or two (*lit.* "a few minutes' time"), Karl? I have something important to tell you.

KARL: (*reluctant*) I'd rather have you tell me some other time (*lit.* "Do that rather another time") when I am in a better mood than this morning. And when I have less (work) to do.

WERNER: (*beaming*) No, Karl. Listen! This coming summer during vacation we are going to take a big trip, the biggest trip of our lives.

KARL: We? A trip?

WERNER: (*excited*) At the beginning of June, on the first or second, the trip starts. About nine-thirty P.M. we take off in our private plane from Boston. Next morning we have breakfast in London.

KARL: What?! Where? In London?

WERNER: Unfortunately we have time only until that afternoon to see London (*lit.* "for London"). We have to be in Paris by dinnertime.

KARL: (*with irony*) Where we'll be received most cordially.

WERNER: (*ohne ihn zu beachten*) Von da aus geht es mit unserem Wagen quer durch Frankreich nach Westdeutschland, an den schönen Rhein, nach Köln und nach Bonn, dem Sitz der Regierung, dann durch die norddeutsche Ebene zu der prächtigen Hafenstadt Hamburg, und jetzt fliegen wir wieder, aber diesmal über ostdeutsches Gebiet, in eine der interessantesten und lebendigsten Städte Europas: nach Berlin! 5

KARL: Geht die Reise etwa um die ganze Welt?

WERNER: Nicht ganz. Wir wenden uns nun dem Süden zu. Wir besuchen die malerischen Universitätsstädte, Marburg und Heidelberg, und 10 trinken Bier im Münchner Hofbräuhaus. Dann ruhen wir uns an einem See in den österreichischen Alpen ein wenig aus. Ob wir auch nach Wien kommen, weiß ich nicht, aber das märchenhafte Venedig, die herrliche Stadt Florenz und das ewige Rom stehen auf unserem Programm. 15

KARL: Entschuldige, aber ich glaube, du bist verrückt.

WERNER: Über Italien, die Schweiz und Frankreich begeben wir uns zu guter letzt wieder nach London, und am einunddreißigsten August landen wir im Flughafen von Boston.

KARL: Woher nehmen wir denn das Geld für diese Reise? Du bist wohl 20 plötzlich ein Wall-Street-Millionär geworden! Oder hast du eine Erbschaft gemacht?

WERNER: Wir reisen ohne Geld.

KARL: Es ist schade um dich, Werner. Du warst doch ein ganz vernünftiger Junge. 25

WERNER: Nein, Karl, das Beste kommt noch, wir reisen auf Kosten einer Reisegesellschaft, die zwei Studenten mitnehmen will.

KARL: Und warum gerade uns?

WERNER: Warum? Weil du Italienisch und Deutsch sprichst und weil ich Französisch und Deutsch spreche. Ich habe es dir immer gesagt: 30 Die Fremdsprachen sind doch zu etwas gut.

LINE
2 quer durch — *(diagonally) across, (right) through*
4 die Ebene — *plain*
prächtig — *magnificent, splendid*
die Hafenstadt — *port (city), harbor*
6 das Gebiet — *territory, region, area*
9 zuwenden — *turn toward*
12 der See — *lake*
13 märchenhaft — *enchanting*
16 verrückt — *crazy*
17 sich begeben — *go*
17–18 zu guter letzt — *at long last, finally*
19 der Flughafen — *airport*
22 die Erbschaft — *inheritance, legacy*
24 Es ist schade um dich — *I feel sorry for you (It's a shame about you)*
24–5 vernünftig — *sensible*
27 die Reisegesellschaft — *travel group*
31 die Fremdsprache — *foreign language*

DRILL PATTERNS

Repeat the following drills after your instructor or after the speaker on the tape. Imitate the pronunciation very carefully.

1. Haben Sie eine Viertelstunde Zeit?
Ich habe leider nur ein paar Minuten.
Du hast eine halbe Stunde Zeit.
In einer dreiviertel Stunde fahren wir ab.

2. Anfang Mai geht es los.
Anfang Mai sollte es losgehen.
Ging es Mitte Juni los?
Nein, Ende August ist es losgegangen.

3. Wann fliegt ihr ab?
Wann flogt ihr ab?
Wann seid ihr abgeflogen?

4. Gegen zehn Uhr dreißig.
Um halb elf.
Um zweiundzwanzig Uhr dreißig.

5. Wann kommen Sie denn in London an?
Wann kamt ihr in London an?
Wann bist du in London angekommen?

6. Um Viertel vor drei.
Um drei Viertel drei.
Um zwei Uhr fünfundvierzig.

7. Wie empfängt man sie?
Wie empfing man Sie?
Wie hat man euch empfangen?

8. Man gab uns zu essen.
Man gab uns zu trinken.
Man hat uns aufs beste empfangen.

9. Wart ihr in Wien?
Ja, wir waren in Wien.
Wie hat euch Wien gefallen?

10. Wien ist eine große Stadt.
Ist Wien auch eine schöne Stadt?
Berlin ist eine größere Stadt.
Ist Berlin auch die schönere Stadt?
London ist eine noch größere Stadt.
Ist New York die größte Stadt der Welt?
Ist New York die schönste Stadt der Welt?

11. Frankfurt ist eine große deutsche Stadt.
München ist eine größere Stadt als Frankfurt.
Berlin ist die größte deutsche Stadt.

12. Vorgestern war er guter Laune.
Gestern war er besserer Laune.
Heute ist er bester Laune.

13. Ich habe dir noch etwas Wichtiges mitzuteilen.
Sie hat dir noch etwas Wichtigeres mitzuteilen.
Er hat dir noch das Wichtigste mitzuteilen.

14. Heute hat sie wenig zu tun.
Morgen wird sie weniger zu tun haben als heute.
Übermorgen [1] hat sie am wenigsten zu tun.

15. Machen Sie eine große Reise?
Du machst eine größere Reise.
Wir machen die größte Reise unseres Lebens.

16. Ich weiß nicht soviel wie er.
Er weiß mehr als ich.
Von uns allen weiß er am meisten.

[1] **übermorgen** day after tomorrow

17. Das ist die größte Reise ihres Lebens.
War das die größte Reise Ihres Lebens?
Was war die größte Reise eueres Lebens?

18. Anfang August fahren wir mit unserem neuen Wagen in die Schweiz.
Ende August fahren wir mit dem Zug nach Österreich.
Mitte September sind wir in Italien.
Gegen Ende des Monats fliegen wir nach Spanien.
Zwei Wochen später fahren wir mit dem Auto quer durch Frankreich.

19. „Will er in ihrem Wagen fahren?" (*2 meanings*)
„Nein, in Ihrem Wagen."
„Warum nicht in euerem Wagen?"
„In unserem Wagen fährt er nicht."

20. Sein Vater kennt ihre Mutter; ihre Mutter kennt seinen Vater.
Kennt ihr Vater Ihre Mutter? Kennt seine Mutter Ihren Vater?

21. Die Arbeit ist gut. Er macht seine Arbeit gut.
Seine Arbeit ist besser als deine. Er macht seine Arbeit besser als du.

22. Sie ist fleißig. Sie ist fleißiger als du.
Sie arbeitet fleißig. Sie arbeitet fleißiger als alle andern.
Sie ist ein fleißiges Mädchen. Sie ist das fleißigste Mädchen in der Klasse.

23. In den Bergen wird es im Winter sehr kalt.
In den Alpen wird es im Winter äußerst[1] kalt.

24. Wenn die Nächte länger werden, werden die Tage kürzer.
Wann sind die Tage am längsten, im Juni oder im Juli?
Am heißesten wird es bei uns im August.
Wann ist die längste Nacht des Jahres?
Am kältesten wird es vor Sonnenaufgang.[2]

English to German

Prepare this exercise in writing:

1) Was this the biggest trip of your life? **vf**
2) Is Berlin larger than Paris? **vf**
3) What is the largest German city? **vs**
4) What is the name of the largest German city? **vs**
5) Tomorrow he will be in a better mood. **vs/vl**
6) We know as much as your teacher. **vs**
7) They knew less than we. **vs**
8) The plane will leave at 9:15 P.M. **vs** (*use pres.*)
9) The plane left at 9:45 A.M. **vs/vl** (*use pres. perf.*)
10) He does not want to ride in your car. **vs/vl** (*3 ways*)
11) I'll see them (him, her, you, it) next Friday. **vs/vl**

[1] **äußerst** very, extremely [2] **der Sonnenaufgang** sunrise

VERB EXERCISES

Rewrite the following sentences, changing the verbs (1) *to past tense*, (2) *to present perfect tense.*

NOTE: *In preparing this exercise, consult the end vocabulary to make sure of the principal parts and proper auxiliaries* (**sein** *or* **haben**) *of the boldface verbs used in these sentences.*

1. Anfang Juni **geht** es **los.** 2. Wir **fliegen** in unserem Privatflugzeug **ab.** 3. Am nächsten Morgen **frühstücken** wir in London. 4. Leider **haben** wir für London nur bis Nachmittag Zeit. 5. Zum Abendessen **müssen** wir in Paris sein, wo man uns aufs beste **empfängt.** (*Change to past tense only*). 6. Von da aus **fahren** wir mit unserem Wagen nach Westdeutschland. 7. **Geht** die Reise etwa um die ganze Welt? 8. Wir **wenden** uns nun dem Süden **zu.** 9. Dann **ruhen** wir uns ein wenig **aus.** 10. Über Italien und Frankreich **begeben** wir uns wieder nach London. 11. Am 31. August **landen** wir im Flughafen von Boston. 12. Wir **reisen** auf Kosten einer Reisegesellschaft, die zwei Studenten mitnehmen **will.** (*Change to past tense only.*) 13. Die Fremdsprachen **sind** doch zu etwas gut.

GRAMMAR

29. Adjectives

a. Predicate adjectives have no declensional endings.

Das Buch ist schwer. Die Bücher sind schwer.

b. POSSESSIVES

The possessive adjectives are:

mein	my			**unser**	our
dein	your	**Ihr**	your	**euer**	your
ihr	her, its			**ihr**	their
sein	his, its				

and the following complete the list of **mein**-words:

ein a, an
kein no, not a, not any

See Grammar Section 10 for the declensional pattern.

NOTE:

The form **ihr** has appeared previously with two separate meanings, which are in turn distinct from the meanings indicated above.

Ihr habt keine Bücher gehabt. — Er hat **ihr** die Bücher gegeben.

There is no mistaking the meaning of **ihr** in each of these two illustrations. In each case no additional context is necessary for identification purposes. This is not so in the following illustrations:

Dort liegen **ihre** Bücher. — **Ihre** Verwandten sind mir nicht bekannt.

How many possible meanings are there for the boldface words in each of these two illustrations?

c. COMPARISON OF ADJECTIVES

1. The comparative degree is formed by attaching **–er** to the basic stem.
2. The superlative degree is formed by attaching **–st** to the basic stem, or **–est** after **t, d,** and sibilants. A stem ending in a vowel sound normally takes **–est: froh — frohest; genau — genauest.**
3. Some adjectives add umlaut to the stem vowel.

Illustrations

heiß (*hot*)	heißer	heißest–
interessant	interessanter	interessantest–
klar	klarer	klarst–
klein	kleiner	kleinst–
blau	blauer	blauest–
roh	roher	rohest–
primitiv	primitiver	primitivst–
spät	später	spätest–
still	stiller	stillst–
traurig	trauriger	traurigst–
weise	weiser	weisest–
alt	älter	ältest–
arm	ärmer	ärmst–
hart	härter	härtest–
jung	jünger	jüngst–
kalt	kälter	kältest–
kurz	kürzer	kürzest–
lang	länger	längst–
scharf	schärfer	schärfst–
warm	wärmer	wärmst–

The following is a list of frequently occurring irregulars:

groß	größer	größt–
gut	besser	best–
hoch (*high*)	höher	höchst–
nahe	näher	nächst–
viel	mehr	meist–

Note that German does not use **mehr** and **meist** to form the comparative and superlative however many syllables the adjective may have:

Berlin ist eine der interessantesten und lebendigsten Städte in ganz Europa.

4. The declensional pattern of the comparative and superlative corresponds to the declensional pattern of the positive degree (see Grammar Section 23):

Positive: der junge Bursche (jung + e)
Comparative: der jüngere Bursche (jünger + e)
Superlative: der jüngste Bursche (jüngst– + e)

Positive: ein armer Mann (arm + er)
Comparative: ein ärmerer Mann (ärmer + er)

Positive: Er weiß nicht, was in diesem kleinen Buch steht. (klein + en)
Comparative: Er weiß nicht, was in jenem kleineren Buch steht. (kleiner + en)
Superlative: Er weiß nicht, was in dem kleinsten Buch steht. (kleinst– + en)

Superlative: Von allen Philosophen, die ich kenne, ist Sokrates der weiseste. (weisest– + e)

5. Special superlatives:

a) In the following sentence a comparison is made. Since it is, however, a comparison of the subject with itself and nothing else, the special **am-**construction is required, as indicated.

Die Zeitung ist sonntags am interessantesten.

Additional Illustrations

Sie sieht in dem roten Kleid immer am schönsten aus.
Im Winter sind die Tage am kürzesten, im Sommer am längsten.

b) This same **am-**construction is used adverbially:

Von allen Studenten kommt er am spätesten in die Klasse.

(Compare this with the last illustration in 4 above.)

Er trinkt Milch gern, Kaffee lieber, aber Wein am liebsten.

c) In the superlative when no comparison is involved, where English uses *most* or *very*, German uses **höchst, äußerst, sehr** (+ positive degree), and **aufs** (+ superlative degree):

Das ist höchst interessant. (sehr interessant)
Das Wetter ist äußerst kalt. (sehr kalt)
Das verletzt mein Gerechtigkeitsgefühl aufs tiefste.
(*That offends my sense of justice most deeply.*)

NOTE:

A. **aufs** with the superlative forms only adverbial phrases.

B. Compare the ending –**e** in the *superlative* and the lack of ending in the *positive* degree in the last group of illustrations.

17. Aufgabe

WER BIN ICH?

SAMPLE ANSWERS AND SUGGESTIONS

a. Reisen Sie gerne?
Wohin reisen Sie gewöhnlich? [1] — *Ich reise gewöhnlich (nach) . . .*
nach Boston? nach New York?
Wohin möchten Sie diesen kommenden Sommer reisen? — *Ich möchte diesen Sommer (nach . . . , in die . . . , an[s] . . .) reisen.*
in die Berge? [2] an einen See? ans Meer? [3] nach Florida? an die Westküste? nach Kalifornien?

Note: Before answering the following questions, study the section on ordinals in the grammar of this lesson.

b. Wann wollen Sie abreisen? in welchem Monat? — *Ich will im Juni abreisen.*
im Juni? am wievielten Juni?
am ersten? am zehnten? am einundzwanzigsten? — *Ich will am zehnten . . . abreisen.*
Wie lange dauern Ihre Ferien?
Wie viele Wochen? Wie viele Tage?

c. Reisen Sie lieber im Auto oder im Zug?
Reisen Sie gern im Flugzeug?
Oder reisen Sie am liebsten auf einem Dampfer? [4]

d. Sind Sie je in Europa gewesen?
Möchten Sie während der großen Ferien nach Europa reisen? — *Ich möchte . . . reisen.*
nach England? nach Irland?
nach Südeuropa? — nach Italien?
nach Mitteleuropa? — in die Schweiz? in die bayrischen Alpen?
nach Westeuropa? — nach Frankreich? nach Holland?
nach Osteuropa? — nach Ostdeutschland? nach Rußland?
Wollen Sie das nördliche Europa besuchen? — *Ich will . . . besuchen.*
die skandinavischen Länder? — Dänemark? Norwegen? Schweden?

e. Welche europäischen Städte möchten Sie sehen?
die großen Städte?

[1] **gewöhnlich** usually [2] **der Berg** mountain [3] **das Meer** sea, ocean [4] **der Dampfer** steamer

SAMPLE ANSWERS AND SUGGESTIONS

Möchten Sie nach London? Oder sind Sie schon in London gewesen?
Möchten Sie nach Paris, nach Rom, nach Moskau, nach Westberlin, nach Madrid, nach Zürich fahren?
Oder gefallen Ihnen die kleineren Städte besser? — *Die . . . Städte gefallen mir . . .*
Wollen Sie nicht Oxford und Cambridge besuchen? Oder an die Riviera fliegen — nach Cannes und Nizza?
Wollen Sie die Passionsspiele in Oberammergau besuchen?
Wollen Sie nicht zu den Festspielen nach Bayreuth, oder nach Salzburg reisen?
Möchten Sie in einem Düsenflugzeug [1] in die Vereinigten Staaten zurückfliegen?

f. Wohin möchten Sie lieber reisen?
nach Kanada oder nach Südamerika?
nach China oder nach Japan?

g. Wohin möchten Sie am liebsten reisen?

h. Was war die größte Reise Ihres Lebens? — *Die . . . Reise meines Lebens war eine Reise (nach) . . .*

Wohin fuhren Sie? — *Ich fuhr nach . . .*
Von wo fuhren Sie ab? — *Ich fuhr von . . . ab.*
Welche Länder, Staaten, Städte, Berge, Meere, Seen, Flüsse sahen Sie auf ihrer Reise?

DRILL PATTERNS

Repeat the following drills after your instructor or after the speaker on the tape. Imitate the pronunciation very carefully.

1. Während unserer Sommerferien möchten wir eine Reise machen.
Während unserer Osterferien haben wir dazu nicht genug Zeit.
Während des Frühlings haben wir weniger Zeit als im Sommer.
Während des Semesters haben wir überhaupt keine Zeit [2] zu reisen.

2. „Sie reisen quer durch ganz Europa? Und reisen ganz ohne Geld?"
„Ja, ohne einen Pfennig und um die ganze Welt."

3. Im kommenden Sommer werden wir eine große Reise machen.
Im vergangenen [3] Winter wollten wir eine lange Reise machen.
Vorigen [4] Herbst machten wir eine schöne, kleine Reise.
Nächsten Frühling wollen wir eine lange, schöne Reise machen.

[1] **das Düsenflugzeug** jet plane [2] **überhaupt keine Zeit** no time at all [3] **vergangen** past [4] **vorig** last, preceding

4. Wegen stürmischen[1] Wetters konnte das Schiff nicht landen.
Wegen schlechten Wetters wurde der Flug verschoben.[2]
Trotz des stürmischen Wetters flogen wir ab.
Trotz des schlechten Wetters kamen wir rechtzeitig an.

5. Er war aufgeregt.[3]
Er ist aufgeregt.
Er regt sich über alles auf.
Er ist ein aufgeregter Mensch.

6. Ist ihr Freund so aufgeregt wie Sie?
Sind Sie aufgeregter als ihr Freund?
Ich bin der aufgeregteste von allen.

7. Das Ganze ist größer als der Teil.
Die Hälfte ist besser als nichts.

8. Das Alte hat er nicht gern.
Das Neue hat er gern.
Das Neuere hat er lieber.
Das Neueste hat er am liebsten.

9. Alles Neue muß geprüft werden.
Alles Alte sollte man nicht verwerfen.[4]

10. Am ersten Juni sind wir in Boston.
Am zweiten Juli sind wir in London.
Am dritten August sind wir in Paris.
Am zwanzigsten September sind wir in Berlin.
Am einunddreißigsten Oktober sind wir wieder in Boston.

11. Im Mai gibt es strahlendes[5] Wetter.
Im Frühling ist das Wetter strahlend.
Das strahlendste Wetter gibt es bei uns im Herbst.

12. Die Alten bleiben zu Hause, die Jungen fahren in die weite Welt hinaus.

English to German

Prepare this exercise in writing.

1) He will arrive on the third of May. **vs /vl**
2) I shall be in Paris toward the middle of June. **vs /vl**
3) Your father and your uncle are more excited than you (*3 ways*). **vs**
4) Why are they so excited? **vs**
5) They had something more important to do. **vs /vl**
6) Her brother was often excited. **vs**
7) Our train leaves in half an hour (in a half hour). **vs**
8) On the twenty-fourth of March we go to Germany. **vs**
9) The new is not always better than the old. **vs**
10) During the winter we had little time for sport. **vs /vl** (*use pres. perf.*)
11) Because of bad weather the trip was postponed. **vs /vl** (*use past*)
12) The train will leave in half an hour. **vs** (*use pres.*)
13) Last summer I took a trip to Europe. **vs /vl** (*use pres. perf.*)

[1] **stürmisch** stormy [2] **verschieben** delay, postpone [3] **aufgeregt** excited [4] **verwerfen** reject
[5] **strahlend** radiant

GRAMMAR

30. Adjectives as Nouns

a. Most adjectives may be used as nouns.

Der alte Mann steht barfuß auf dem Eise.
Der **Alte** steht barfuß auf dem Eise.

Die arm**en** Menschen müssen im Winter frieren.
Die Arm**en** müssen im Winter frieren.

NOTE:

A. the identity in declensional endings within each pair above;
B. the capitalized form of the adjective-nouns.

b. Adjectives are often changed into neuter nouns having general or abstract meanings.

neu = *new;* nichts Neues = *nothing* (*that is*) *new*
Im Westen nichts Neues = *Nothing New in the West* (*All Quiet on the Western Front*)
In der Zeitung gibt es immer etwas Neues.

schön = *beautiful;* das Schöne = *the beautiful*
Plato glaubt an das Gute, das Wahre, das Schöne.

Note that nouns based on adjectives must follow the declensional pattern of adjectives. (See Grammar Section 23.)

31. mein-Words as Pronouns

When **mein-**words are used as pronouns they are declined exactly like the **dies-**words:

Ist das dein Buch?
Ja, es ist meines (meins).

Hast du seine Feder (sein Heft, seinen Bleistift)?
Ja, ich habe seine (seines, seinen).

„Keiner mag ihn hören.
Keiner sieht ihn an.“

32. Participles as Adjectives

Present and past participles of verbs are frequently used as adjectives.

a. Present participle: infinitive + **d** (**beten** + **d** = *praying*)

Mir ist, als ob ich die Hände
Aufs Haupt dir legen sollt',
Betend, daß Gott dich erhalte
So rein und schön und hold. (*See* p. 23)

Das Mädchen betet für ihren **sterbenden** Bruder.
Diese **kommende** Woche habe ich viel zu tun.

b. Past-participle adjectives:

In der **vergangenen** Woche hatte ich viel zu tun.

Das Volk betet für seine **gefallenen** Soldaten.

Er ist ein **aufgeregter** Mensch. (*He is an excitable person*).

c. Present and past-participle adjectives are often changed to nouns.

Sie betet für den **Sterbenden.**
Das Volk betet für die **Gefallenen.**

Während des Sommers gibt es in Europa viele **Reisende.**

33. Adjectives as Adverbs

a. The uninflected forms of most adjectives may be used as adverbs.

Er ist nicht gut.
Es geht ihm nicht gut.

Das Kind ist jetzt still.
Das Kind liegt jetzt still in seinem Bett.

b. An –**s** or –**ens** ending is required to change some adjectives to adverbs:

link–: links *to the left*
recht: rechts *to the right*
ander–: anders *differently*
bereit: bereits *already*
Er ist bereit zu gehen.
Er ist bereits da.

höchst: höchstens *at most, at best*
meist–: meistens *mostly (usually)*
zweit–: zweitens *secondly*

NOTE:

Some nouns are changed to adverbs through an –**s** suffix:

die Nacht: nachts *at night*
der Abend: abends *in the evening*
der Nachmittag: nachmittags *in the afternoon*
der Morgen: morgens *in the morning*
der Teil: teils *partly*

34. Ordinal Numerals as Adjectives

Formation: Ordinal numerals are based on cardinal numbers. (See Grammar Section 13.) To form the stems of ordinals add –**t** to cardinal numbers through nineteen (the three boldface forms on page 142 are exceptions), –**st** to all other cardinal numbers. Ordinal adjectives follow the declensional pattern of attributive adjectives (e.g., die erst**e** Frau, das zweit**e** Jahr, der dritt**e** Mann).

erst–	neunt–	siebzehnt–
zweit–	zehnt–	achtzehnt–
dritt–	elft–	neunzehnt–
viert–	zwölft–	zwanzigst–
fünft–	dreizehnt–	einundzwanzigst–
sechst–	vierzehnt–	dreißigst–
siebent–	fünfzehnt–	sechsundsechzigst–
acht– (*no* –t *added*)	sechzehnt–	hundertst–

Die Abschußerlaubnis für einen Elefanten beträgt neunhundert DM für den **ersten,** zwölfhundert DM für den **zweiten,** fünfzehnhundert DM für den **dritten,** zweitausend DM für den **vierten** und zweitausendsechshundert DM für jeden weiteren Elefanten. Der **hundertste,** ja sogar der **zehntausendste** würde also auch zweitausendsechshundert DM kosten. Aber was sollten wir denn mit so vielen Elefanten tun?

35. Fractions

To form fractions add –(t)**el** (= **Teil** = *part*) to cardinals from 4–19 and –**stel** from 20 on.

sechs (*six*) + –tel: ein Sechstel (*one sixth*)

ein halb, die Hälfte	ein Sieb(en)tel
ein Drittel	ein Achtel (*no* –t *added*)
ein Viertel	ein Zwanzigstel
ein Fünftel	

36. Genitive Prepositions

The following prepositions take the genitive:

längs along (*also takes dat.*)	**während** during
(an)statt instead of	**wegen** on account of, because of
trotz in spite of	

NOTE:

In modern German **trotz** is frequently used with the dative.

Memorize the above prepositions!

Illustrations

Wir sind immer längs des Flusses gegangen.
Wegen der Kriegsgefahr verließen alle Ausländer das Land.
Während der Ferien werden wir eine Reise machen.
Trotz seiner Krankheit war er immer munter.
Er sollte heute arbeiten. Statt dessen geht er ins Kino.

Some other genitive prepositions that occur less frequently:

diesseits on this side of	**oberhalb** above
jenseits on that side of	**unterhalb** below

Memorize these prepositions!

37. Conjunctions

COORDINATING CONJUNCTIONS

Coordinating conjunctions are simply connecting links between phrases or clauses (of equal rank) and as such play no active part in determining word order:

Wir fliegen abends gegen neun Uhr von Boston ab, und am nächsten Morgen frühstücken wir in London.

Ich sollte eigentlich nicht ins Kino gehen, denn ich habe heute noch viel zu tun.

The following have already been used:

aber but (however)
denn for
oder or
sondern but (on the contrary)
und and

SUBORDINATING CONJUNCTIONS

The subordinating conjunctions introduce verb-last word order:

Ich weiß nicht, ob wir diesen Sommer nach Wien kommen.
Tu das lieber ein anderes Mal, wenn ich besserer Laune bin.

Many of the following have already been used:

als as (*temporal*), when
als ob as if
als wenn as if
bevor′ before
bis until
da when, since (*causal*), as (*temporal* or *causal*)
damit′ in order that
daß that
ehe before
nachdem′ after
ob whether, if
obgleich′ although
ohne . . . zu (*with inf.*) without
seit(dem)′ since (*temporal*)
sobald′ as soon as
trotzdem′ in spite of the fact that
um . . . zu (*with inf.*) in order to
während while
weil because
wenn if, when, whenever
wenn . . . auch (*or* **auch wenn**) even if
wie when (*see* **als**)

1. **Daß** is often omitted in indirect statements. In such an event, normal word order prevails.

    Ich weiß, daß Sie sich für weise halten.
    Ich weiß, Sie halten sich für weise.

2. **Ob** in **als ob** is often omitted. In such an event, the finite verb moves into the position of the omitted conjunction.

    Es schien, als ob er das tun wollte.
    Es schien, als wollte er das tun.

3. Similarly, **wenn** can be omitted in the combination **als wenn.**

4. **Wenn,** meaning *if,* may be omitted when the **wenn**-clause comes first in a series. In such an event, the finite verb moves into the position of the omitted conjunction.

   Wenn er nicht kommt, (so) gehen wir ohne ihn.
   Kommt er nicht, so gehen wir ohne ihn.

   Wenn wir „du" zueinander sagen, (so) müssen wir uns beim Vornamen nennen.
   Sagen wir „du" zueinander, so müssen wir uns beim Vornamen nennen.

NOTE:

Particularly when **wenn** is omitted, the particle **so** is often introduced between the two clauses.

5. *Question words* in indirect-question clauses introduce verb-last word order.

   Ich weiß nicht, wann er geboren ist.
   Ich weiß nicht, wie er in Wirklichkeit heißt.
   Ich weiß nicht, was das eigentlich bedeutet.

18. Aufgabe

VOCABULARY BUILDING

The following strong (and irregular) verbs appeared for the first time in Units V and VI in this book. Included as new verbs are inseparable compounds, even though they may have appeared as simple verbs previous to Unit V, e.g., **befinden, erhalten, verbringen.** This list is to remind you of the principal parts of these verbs. Frequent reference to this list will help you in the formation of the past tenses.

CLASS 1

ei ie ie

* scheiden *depart, separate*
treiben *drive, push*

ei i i

* entweichen *escape*
schneiden *cut*
vergleichen *compare*
zerreißen *tear to pieces*

CLASS 2

ie o o

beschließen *decide*
beziehen *draw, receive* (salary, payment)
entschließen *decide*
* fliegen *fly*
verbieten *forbid*

e o o

erheben *raise* (refl. *rise, arise*)

CLASS 3

i a u

(sich) befinden *be, feel*
schwingen *swing*
trinken *drink*

i a o

* schwimmen *swim*

CLASS 4

e (i, ie) a e

(sich) begeben (i) *go, happen*
(sich) ergeben (i) *happen, come to pass*
* geschehen (ie) *happen*
vergessen (i) *forget*

e (i) a o

entnehmen (i) *take from* or *away*
versprechen (i) *promise*

CLASS 5

a (ä) i a

anfangen [1] *begin, do*
empfangen *receive, welcome*

a (ä) ie a

erhalten *receive, get*
schlafen *sleep*
unterhalten *entertain*
(sich über [etwas] unterhalten *converse about* [*something*])

a (ä) u a

einladen [1] *invite*
erschaffen [2] *create, produce*
tragen *carry, wear*

IRREGULARS

bedürfen (bedarf), bedurfte, bedurft *need*
* entstehen (entsteht), entstand, entstanden *arise, originate*
gestehen (gesteht), gestand, gestanden *admit, confess*
verbringen (verbringt), verbrachte, verbracht *spend* (*time*)

* These verbs take **sein** as auxiliary.

[1] These verbs have separable prefixes. [2] All but (**er**)**schaffen** in Class 5 take umlaut in the **du, sie, es, er** forms of the present tense.

WORD STUDY

Some of the following nouns have already been used and should be part of your active vocabulary. Others will be used in the Readings of the present unit and in subsequent units. A number of them you will be able to guess at, even though they have not yet appeared. Look up the ones you do not know in the end vocabulary.

Der menschliche Körper (*The human body*)

(das Skelett, das Glied, das Organ, die Figur)

das Haupt	das Gesicht	die Hand	der Fuß
der Kopf	das Auge	der Finger	die Sohle
das Haar	die Augenbrauen	der Daumen	die Zehe
die Stirn(e)	die Augenlider	der Fingernagel	
der Hals	die Nase	die Faust	
	der Mund	das Handgelenk	
	die Lippe	der Arm	
	der Zahn	die Schulter	
	die Zunge		
	die Kehle		
	das Kinn		
	die Wange		
	das Ohr		
das Gehirn	die Brust	die Hüfte	die Haut
das Herz	der Bauch	der Schenkel	das Fleisch
die Lunge	die Rippe	das Knie	das Blut
der Magen	der Rücken	das Bein	der Puls
die Leber	das Rückgrat		der Nerv
die Niere			der Muskel
			der Knochen

Was trägt man? (*What do you wear?*)

der Hut	die Jacke	der Schlafanzug	der Schuh
der Mantel	die Hose	das Hemd	der Handschuh
der Regenmantel	die Tasche	das Nachthemd	die Brille
der Schlips *or* die Krawatte	das Taschentuch	der Kragen	die Halskette
der Strumpf	das Kleid	der Ärmel	das Armband
der Anzug	der Rock	der Knopf	der Ring
	der Schlafrock	die Socke	die Uhr

Was sieht man in einem Zimmer? (*What do you see in a room?*)

(das Zimmer, die Stube, der Raum, der Saal; das Wohnzimmer, das Speisezimmer, das Schlafzimmmer, das Badezimmer, die Küche)

die Tür	das (elektrische) Licht	der Spiegel	das Sofa
der Fußboden	die Lampe	das Fenster	das Bett
der Teppich	das Bild	der Vorhang	der Schrank
die Wand	die Tapete	der Tisch	der Bücherschrank
die Decke	die Wanduhr	der Stuhl	der Schreibtisch

IDIOMATIC EXPRESSIONS

Each of the following sentences involves a prepositional phrase in which the meaning of the preposition departs radically from what may be considered its primary meaning (or meanings):

Es ist schade **um** dich. *It's a shame **about** you. I feel sorry **for** you.*
Der Schaffner bittet **um** die Fahrkarten. *The conductor asks **for** the tickets.*

Fremdsprachen sind doch **zu** etwas gut. *Foreign languages are good **for** something after all.*

Er interessiert sich nur **für** seine Sprachforschungen. *He is interested only **in** his linguistic research.*

Ich freue mich schon lange **auf** die Sommerferien. *I have long been looking forward with pleasure **to** the summer vacation.*

Vor sechs Jahren war sie **zum** ersten Mal in Salzburg. *Six years **ago** she was in Salzburg **for** the first time.*

Er rettet sich **vor** dem Regenguß. *He rescues himself (escapes) **from** the downpour.*

All of the following sentences involve idioms that will appear in the next reading selections.

Mir ist sehr wohl zumute. *I feel very well.*
Mir ist recht verschmitzt zumute. *I feel very clever (cunning).*

Er kommt oft in Verlegenheit. *He often gets into difficulties (embarrassing situations).*

Sie macht sich Sorgen um das nötige Geld. *She is concerned (worried) about the necessary money (funds).*

Sein Paß sollte in Ordnung sein, doch dem ist leider nicht so. *His passport should be in order, but unfortunately that's not the case.*

lassen — Two primary and recurrent meanings are *leave* and, perhaps more commonly, *let:*

Er läßt es da. *He leaves it there.*
Er läßt es da liegen (stehen). *He leaves it lying (standing) there. He lets it lie (stand) there.*

Sie läßt ihn zu Hause. *She leaves him at home.*
Sie läßt ihn ins Haus. *She lets him into the house.*

Er läßt es **gehen.** *He lets it **go.***
Er läßt mich **kommen.** *He lets me **come.***

Er läßt es **machen.** *He lets it **be done.***
Er läßt sich **sehen.** *He lets himself **be seen.***

Note the treatment of the infinitives in the last pair. English speech pattern demands a passive infinitive when *let* is associated with a transitive verb. In German no such distinction is made: **machen** and **sehen** are transitive, active infinitives.

But note the following:

Er läßt es mich **machen.** *He lets me **do** it.*

Like German, English uses the active infinitive (*do*) whenever both *let* and the infinitive take a direct object.

Give the meaning of the following:

Er läßt ihn das Buch sehen.
Er läßt es sehen.
Er ließ es nicht machen.
Er läßt es zum Fenster hinausfliegen.
Er läßt alles gehen, wie es will.

Er ließ das Kind ins Zimmer.
Er ließ das Kind im Zimmer.
Er ließ das Kind dort stehen.
Er ließ das Kind die Sachen sehen.
Er ließ das Kind rufen.

The last example may be interpreted two ways:

He let the child call. He let the child be called (*summoned*).

The context will normally indicate which meaning is required. In this last English example, *let* takes on the meaning of *had* in the sense of "caused":

He had the child summoned (i.e. *caused it to be summoned*).

This is a commonly used meaning for **lassen,** as indicated in the following sentences:

Das Kind wurde plötzlich krank. Da ließ die Mutter schnell den Doktor kommen. *The child suddenly became sick. So the mother had the doctor come right away.*

Er läßt sich jede Woche die Haare schneiden. *He has his hair cut every week.*

Der Reiter ließ sein Pferd einen Schritt vorwärts tun. *The rider* (*horseman*) *had his horse take one step forward.*

Used reflexively with an impersonal subject, **lassen** has the meaning *can:*

Es läßt sich nicht machen (sehen). *It cannot be done* (*seen*).
Dieses Problem läßt sich leicht lösen. *This problem can be solved easily.*

Reading

Aus: DER KLEINE GRENZVERKEHR [1] (Kästner)

Die folgenden Abschnitte sind Erich Kästners Erzählung *Der kleine Grenzverkehr* entnommen. Die Erzählung ist in Form eines Tagebuchs geschrieben. Der Autor des Tagebuchs, Georg Rentmeister aus Berlin, ist ein junger Gelehrter, der sich für nichts interessiert als für seine Sprachforschungen. Wie schon sein Name besagt, ist er ein bemittelter junger Mann, der eine Rente bezieht. Sein Freund Karl, ein Künstler, hat Georg eingeladen, den Sommer zusammen mit ihm in der österreichischen Stadt Salzburg zu verbringen, wo jährlich die berühmten Festspiele abgehalten werden. Die Ereignisse spielen in der Nazizeit, im Jahre 1937, als die Deutschen, die nach Österreich reisten, nicht mehr als zehn Mark mitnehmen durften. „Nun habe ich mathematisch einwandfrei festgestellt," schreibt Georg Rentmeister in sein Tagebuch, „daß ich in diesem Falle an jedem Tag — den Monat zu dreißig Tagen gerechnet — genau 33,33333 [2] Pfennige ausgeben kann, noch genauer 33,3333333 Pfennige."

The following selections are taken from Erich Kästner's novelette *Der kleine Grenzverkehr*. The story is written in the form of a diary. The author of the diary, George Rentmeister from Berlin, is a young scholar who is interested solely in linguistic research. As his very name suggests, he is a young man of means, living on his private income. His artist friend, Karl, has invited George to spend the summer together with him in the Austrian city of Salzburg, famous for its annual [music and theater] festivals. The events take place during the Nazi period, in the year 1937, at a time when Germans travelling to Austria were allowed to take out no more than ten marks (per month). "By a mathematical procedure, which is accurate beyond any doubt," George Rentmeister writes in his diary, "I arrived at the conclusion that in this case, figuring on the basis of thirty days per month, I shall be able to spend every day exactly 33.33333 [German] pennies, or, to be even more precise, 33.3333333 pennies."

[1] The title is actually a technical term used to designate the local and "small-time" traffic or trade across a frontier. [2] 33,33333 = 33.33333 (In German a comma is used instead of the decimal point.)

Solange Georg auf deutschem Boden bleibt, braucht er sich um das nötige Geld keine Sorgen zu machen. Er beschließt deshalb, in einem deutschen Kurort, Bad Reichenhall, zu wohnen, der nah an der Grenze liegt und von dem aus man Salzburg in einer halben Stunde erreichen kann. „Ich habe," teilt er dem Leser mit, „mit dem Hotel Axelmannstein in Bad Reichenhall telephoniert und ein Zimmer mit Bad bestellt. Ich kenne das Hotel von früher. Sehr komfortabel: Golfplatz, Schwimmbad, Tennisplätze, alles im Hause." Georg beabsichtigt, die Nächte in seinem Hotel in Deutschland zu verbringen, die Tage aber in Salzburg mit seinem Freund Karl. Von den folgenden Auszügen aus dem Tagebuch ist der erste von Georg in dem Nachtzug, der von Berlin nach Reichenhall fährt, geschrieben, der zweite in Reichenhall nach Georgs Rückkehr von seinem ersten Ausflug über die Grenze.

As long as George remains on German territory, he does not have to worry about the necessary funds. Therefore, he decides to stay in a German resort, Bad Reichenhall, which is close to the border and within half an hour's journey to Salzburg. "I phoned the Hotel Axelmannstein in Bad Reichenhall," he informs the reader, "and I reserved a room with bath. I know this hotel from previous visits. It's very comfortable: golf course, swimming pool, tennis courts, everything is included." George plans to spend the nights in his hotel in Germany, but the days in Salzburg together with his friend Karl. The first of the following diary excerpts is written by George on the night train from Berlin to Reichenhall, the second in Reichenhall, after his return from his first trip across the border.

Im Schlafwagen, 19. August

Mir ist recht verschmitzt zumute. Es ist Nacht. Der Zug donnert durch Franken. Ich liege im Bett, trinke eine halbe Flasche Roten, rauche und freue mich auf Karls dummes Gesicht.

Er wird kein klügeres ziehen als vor wenigen Stunden der alte Justizrat Scheinert am Anhalter Bahnhof. „Hallo, Doktor" rief er, als er mich sah, „wo fahren Sie denn hin?" 5

„Nach Salzburg!" antwortete ich.

„Nach Salzburg? Sie Glücklicher! Wo werden Sie denn wohnen?"

„In Reichenhall!"

Der gute Mann hat schon von Hause aus kein sehr durchgeistigtes Antlitz, doch 10 jetzt wirkte er tatsächlich wie ein Schaf mit Hornbrille.

In Österreich ins Theater gehen, in Deutschland essen und schlafen: die Ferien versprechen einigermaßen originell zu werden! Mein alter Schulatlas hat mich davon überzeugt, daß Reichenhall und Salzburg keine halbe Bahnstunde auseinanderliegen. Eisenbahnverbindungen sind vorhanden. Der Paß ist in Ordnung. 15 So werde ich denn für meine Person den sogenannten kleinen Grenzverkehr permanent gestalten.

LINE

1 mir ist recht verschmitzt zumute — *I feel very clever* (*cunning*)
2 Franken — *Franconia*
Roten — here: *red wine*
4 er wird kein klügeres ziehen — *he won't have a brighter expression on his face*
der Justizrat — *counsellor*
5 Anhalter Bahnhof (*railroad station in Berlin*)
10 von Hause aus — *by nature*

LINE

10 durchgeistigtes Antlitz — *intelligent face*
11 wirkte er — here: *he looked*
tatsächlich — *actually, indeed*
die Hornbrille — *horn-rimmed spectacles*
13 einigermaßen — *rather*
14 überzeugen — *convince*
15 die Verbindung — *connection*
vorhanden — *available*
17 gestalten — *establish, engage in*

Die Festspielstadt Salzburg mit Salzach (Österreich). Hier, am Geburtsort Mozarts, finden jeden Sommer die berühmten Musik- und Theateraufführungen statt.

In Reichenhall werde ich als Grandseigneur leben, in Salzburg als Habenichts; und jeden Tag werde ich der eine und der andere sein. Welch komödienhafte Situation! Und da haben die Herren Dichter Angst, die Erde könnte, infolge des sogenannten Fortschritts, unromantisch werden!

Man sollte sich diesbezüglich keine Sorgen machen. Die meisten Länder haben schon ihre Devisengesetze. — Die Flasche ist leer. Drum schließ ich meine Äuglein zu. 5

Im Speisewagen,* 20. August

Das Frühstück ist die schönste Tageszeit. Der Schnellzug eilt durch die bayrischen Berge. Die Bauern spießen das Heu, damit es trockne, auf in den Wiesengrund gerammte Pflöcke. Und die Sommerlandschaft dreht sich heiter um uns, „wie eine Platte auf Gottes großem Grammophon." 10

Ich sitze im Raucherabteil und habe soeben eine Feststellung gemacht. Die Eisenbahngesellschaften aller Länder haben zwei Sorten Coupés in Betrieb, die Raucher- und Nichtraucherabteile. Soweit scheint die Sache in Ordnung — doch sie scheint es nur. Im Nichtraucherabteil ist das Rauchen verboten; demzufolge müßte im Rauchercoupé das Nichtrauchen verboten sein! Doch dem ist nicht so und derartige Inkonsequenzen verletzen mein Gerechtigkeitsgefühl aufs tiefste. Wie schön wäre das, wenn der Schaffner jetzt ins Raucherabteil träte und diejenigen, die nicht rauchen, in Strafe nähme und streng ins Nichtrauchercoupé spedierte! 15 20

Nichts auf der Welt ist vollkommen. Doch ich muß aufhören. Wir haben Freilassing passiert. Die nächste Station heißt Reichenhall.

Reichenhall, 20. August

Eben bin ich aus Salzburg zurückgekommen; nun hock' ich, Mitternacht ist vorbei, in der Hotelbar und trinke das vielgeliebte „Charlottenburger Pilsner," wie die Freunde die herzhafte Mischung aus Sekt und Bier getauft haben. 25

* der Speisewagen — *dining car*

LINE

2 komödienhaft — *fraught with comic possibilities*
3 infolge — *as a result of*
4 der Fortschritt — *progress*
5 diesbezüglich — *in this respect*
6 die Devisengesetze — *laws regulating the exchange of foreign currency*
drum = darum
9–10 spießen das Heu . . . auf in den Wiesengrund gerammte Pflöcke — *load the hay (with forks) on to stakes rammed into the meadowland . . .*
10 heiter — *gaily*
11 die Platte — *record*
12 das Raucherabteil — *smoking compartment*
soeben — *just*
die Feststellung — *observation*
13 die Gesellschaft — *company*
das Coupé — *compartment*

LINE

13 in Betrieb haben — *maintain*
15–16 demzufolge — *accordingly*
16 müßte sein — *would have to be*
16–17 dem ist nicht so — *that is not the case*
17 derartige Inkonsequenzen verletzen mein Gerechtigkeitsgefühl — *such inconsistencies offend my sense of justice*
18 wie schön wäre das — *how nice it would be*
der Schaffner — *conductor*
träte — *stepped (into)*
19 diejenigen — *those*
in Strafe nähme — *would punish* or *penalize*
20 spedierte — *would send (them)*
21 vollkommen — *perfect*
22 Freilassing (*name of a town*)
23 hocken — *sit hunched*
25 herzhaft — *hearty*
der Sekt — *champagne*
taufen — *name, christen*

Vor sechs Jahren war ich zum letztenmal in Salzburg. Doch als Karl und ich heute mittag im Garten des Stieglbräus saßen und auf die Stadt der streitbaren und kunstsinnigen Erzbischöfe hinabschauten, war ich von neuem überwältigt. Auch Anmut kann erschüttern.

5 * Der Blick auf das halbe Dutzend durch Portale, Kolonnaden und Portikusse miteinander verbundener Paläste und auf die vielgestaltigen Türme und Dächer, die den Grundriß des komplexen Platzgefüges klar und doch lebendig wiederholen — dieser Anblick ist nördlich der Alpen einzig. Kein Wunder, denn jene geistlichen Fürsten, die Salzburg erschufen, wollten und bauten eine italienische Resi-
10 denz.

Der Zusammenklang der verschiedenen Farben und Farbtöne, die alle ins Heitere zielen, vollendet, was eigentlich keiner Vollendung bedarf. Die Dächer schimmern grün, schiefergrau und mennigrot. Über allem ragen die marmorweißen Türme des Doms, das dunkelgrau, weinrot und weiß gesprenkelte Dach
15 der Franziskanerkirche, die altrosa Türme der Kollegienkirche mit ihren weißen Heiligenfiguren, der graugrüne Turm des Glockenspiels und andre rostrote und oxydgrüne Kuppeln und Turmhelme. Man sieht eine Symphonie.

An unserem Tisch im Stieglbräu saßen Einheimische. Sie sprachen über das Theater, als seien sie, ob Bäcker, Schuster oder Schneider, Leute vom Bau. Sie
20 verglichen die verschiedenen im Lauf der Jahre aufgetretenen Titelhelden des „Jedermann," debattierten wie Kritiker vom Fach und einigten sich dahin, daß M. als Jedermann mit Abstand „am schönsten gestorben" sei.

* Der Blick auf das halbe Dutzend . . . einzig. — *The view looking down upon the half dozen palaces connected by portals, colonnades, and porticos, and upon the variously shaped towers and roofs reflecting in a clear and lively manner the complex ground plan of the whole area — this sight is unique north of the Alps.*

LINE
2 Stieglbräu (*a restaurant in Salzburg*)
streitbar — *aggressive, valiant*
3 kunstsinnig — *artistic*
der Erzbischof — *archbishop*
überwältigt — *overwhelmed*
4 die Anmut — *charm, gracefulness*
erschüttern — *move deeply*
8 kein Wunder — *small wonder* (*this is not surprising*)
8–9 die geistlichen Fürsten — *church dignitaries*
9 erschaffen — *create*
11 der Zusammenklang — *harmony*
die Farbtöne — *shades*
12 zielen — *aim at*
ins Heitere zielen — *tend to produce a cheerful* or *serene effect*
vollenden — *complete, perfect*
bedürfen — *require*
13 schiefergrau — *slate grey*
mennigrot — *minium red*
ragen — *rise up*

LINE
14 gesprenkelt — *dappled*
16 die Heiligen — *saints*
das Glockenspiel — *chimes, carillon*
rostrot — *rusty red*
17 oxydgrün — *verdigris*
der Turmhelm — *dome*
18 Einheimische — *natives*
19 als seien sie . . . Leute vom Bau — *as if they were experts*
der Schuster — *shoemaker*
der Schneider — *tailor*
20 der Lauf — *course*
die verschiedenen im Lauf der Jahre aufgetretenen Titelhelden — *the various actors who, in the course of the years, had appeared in the leading role*
21 „Jedermann" — *"Everyman"*
Kritiker vom Fach — *professional critics*
sich einigen — *agree*
22 mit Abstand — *by far*

Reichenhall, 20. August, spät nachts

Die Bar war schließlich so leer, daß ich es vorgezogen habe, mich mit zwei Flaschen Pilsner in mein Zimmer zurückzuziehen.

Ich liege im Bett und studiere eine Salzburger Zeitung. Die Redaktion teilt mit, daß in dieser Festspielzeit mehr als 60 000 Fremde in Salzburg abgestiegen sind und daß diese Fremden etwa 15 000 Automobile mitgebracht haben. Wenn man 5 unterstellt, daß in einem Wagen durchschnittlich drei bis vier Personen reisen, so ergibt sich zweifelsfrei, daß ich der einzige Zugereiste bin, der nicht im Auto angekommen ist.

Ich fahre im Autobus. Er hält in Reichenhall vor meinem Hotel und trifft, trotz zweier Paßkontrollen, kaum eine halbe Stunde später auf dem Residenzplatz 10 in Salzburg ein.

Die zehn Mark, die ich in einem Monat drüben verleben darf, habe ich bereits heute ausgegeben. Der Leichtsinn zwickte mich förmlich. Ich habe alles gekauft, was mir vors Portemonnaie kam: Mozartkugeln, Ansichtskarten, Brezeln. Sogar englische Gummibonbons! 15

Bald kommt Georg infolge seines Geldmangels in Salzburg in Verlegenheit. Er rettet sich vor einem Regenguß in ein Cafehaus, bestellt einen Kaffee — und stellt fest, daß er nicht bezahlen kann, weil er keinen Groschen bei sich hat. So muß er ein hübsches junges Mädchen, das ihm gegenübersitzt, bitten, für ihn zu bezahlen. — Damit sind wir allerdings erst am Anfang der Handlung. Das Weitere läßt sich nicht in ein paar Worten sagen. Wie zu erwarten, verliebt sich Georg in das österreichische Mädchen, und wie ebenfalls zu erwarten, geht es bei „dem kleinen Grenzverkehr" zwischen Georg und Konstanze (so heißt sie) nicht ohne Schwierigkeiten ab. Am Ende geht alles gut aus. Georg heiratet Konstanze und kehrt aus den Salzburger Ferien mit seiner jungen Frau nach Berlin zurück.

Soon George's lack of money causes him some embarrassment in Salzburg. He seeks shelter from a heavy rain storm in a café, orders coffee, and finds himself unable to pay since he hasn't any money with him. Therefore he is forced to ask a pretty young girl, who is sitting at a table facing his, to pay for him. This, to be sure, takes us merely into the beginning of the plot. What follows cannot be told in a few words. As expected, George falls in love with the Austrian girl, and, again as expected, "der kleine Grenzverkehr" between George and the girl (her name is Constance) is beset with difficulties. In the end all turns out well. George marries Constance and returns to Berlin from his Salzburg vacation, accompanied by his young wife.

LINE

1 schließlich — *finally*
2 sich zurückziehen — *withdraw*
3 die Redaktion teilt mit — here: *the newspaper discloses*
4 Fremde — *foreign visitors*
absteigen — *make a stop*
6 unterstellen — *assume*
durchschnittlich — *on the average*
7 ergibt sich zweifelsfrei — *it follows without doubt, it is obvious*
der Zugereiste — *stranger, visitor*

LINE

9–11 trifft ein (*inf.* eintreffen) — *arrives*
12 verleben — *spend* (*use up*)
13 ausgeben — *spend*
der Leichtsinn zwickte mich förmlich — *frivolity really spurred me on*
14 das Portemonnaie — *purse*
die Mozartkugeln — *marzipan balls* (candy)
die Ansichtskarte — *picture postcard*
15 die Gummibonbons — *gum drops*

FRAGEN

1. Wer ist Georg Rentmeister? 2. Wo und wie will Georg seine Ferien verbringen? 3. Wo ist Reichenhall? Wo ist Salzburg? 4. Wie lange fährt man von Reichenhall nach Salzburg? 5. Was gibt es in Salzburg zu sehen und zu hören? 6. Wen trifft Georg in Salzburg? 7. Wie geht die Geschichte aus?

EINE STATUE WIRD LEBENDIG

Vor dem Eingang zu Whitehall in London halten, still und hoch zu Pferde, zwei Reiter Wache. Tagaus, tagein. Ihre weißen Reithosen leuchten in der Sonne, ihr Waffenrock ist scharlachrot, die schwarzen Stiefel glänzen, ihre Brust ist mit schimmerndem Metall bedeckt, und die silbernen Helme blitzen. Jeder Tourist in 5 London sieht sich diese „horse guardsmen" an.

Eines Tages stand ein greiser, geschwätziger Fremdenführer vor einem von diesen Reitern. „Diese Wachen," erklärte er einer Gruppe von amerikanischen Touristen, „sind ausgesuchte Soldaten. Ihre Disziplin ist die härteste der Welt. Meine Damen und Herren, das sind keine Spielzeugsoldaten, sondern erfahrene 10 Krieger. Sie und ihre Pferde können stundenlang stillstehen, reglos und unbeweglich, wie Statuen aus Stein."

Die Touristen gafften den Reiter bewundernd an, der keine Miene verzog und kein Wort zu hören schien.

„Höchst interessant ist auch die Tatsache," fuhr der Fremdenführer fort, „daß 15 man dieses unbefleckbare Metall nie zu polieren braucht und daß man diese Lackstiefel nie putzen muß. Folglich haben diese Leute den ganzen Tag nichts anderes zu tun als Wache zu halten."

Da geschah das Unerhörte. Der Reiter ließ plötzlich sein Pferd einen Schritt vorwärts tun, senkte sein blankes Schwert und richtete es gegen die Kehle des 20 Fremdenführers.

„Das ist eine Lüge," sagte er ruhig. „Stundenlang muß man sie putzen — diese verfluchten Stiefel."

FRAGEN

1. Wer hält am Eingang zu Whitehall Wache? 2. Beschreiben Sie die Kleidung (*dress*) der Reiter! 3. Was behauptet (*maintains, asserts*) der Fremdenführer? 4. In welcher

LINE
1–2 Wache halten — *stand guard*
2 die Reithosen — *riding breeches*
leuchten — *shine*
3 der Waffenrock — *tunic*
glänzen — *glisten, shine*
6 ein greiser, geschwätziger Fremdenführer — *an old, garrulous guide*
8 ausgesucht — *selected, choice*
9 die Spielzeugsoldaten — *toy soldiers*
erfahren — *experienced*
10 reglos — *motionless*
10–11 unbeweglich — *fixed*
12 angaffen — *gape at, stare at*

LINE
12 bewundernd — *admiringly*
der keine Miene verzog — *who did not move a muscle*
14 die Tatsache — *fact*
15 unbefleckbar — *untarnishable*
15–16 die Lackstiefel — *patent leather boots*
16 folglich — *consequently*
19 vorwärts tun — *move forward*
blank — *shiny*
richten — *point*
die Kehle — *throat*
22 verflucht — *blasted*

Weise (*in what manner*) antwortet der Reiter auf die Behauptung (*assertion*) des Fremdenführers?

DER GEDANKENAUSTAUSCH *

Eines Tages besuchte Alexander Weill den deutschen Dichter Heinrich Heine, der lange schon in Paris in seiner Matratzengruft lag, körperlich gelähmt und schwach, aber dennoch geisteskräftig und munter. Herr Weill war ein guter Freund von Heine, er war aber weder interessant noch unterhaltend. Also langweilte es Heine immer, wenn ihn Weill besuchte. 5

Dieses Mal, nachdem Herr Weill gegangen war, begrüßte Heine seinen nächsten Besucher mit folgenden Worten:

„Ach, Sie finden mich heute ganz dumm!"

„Dumm? Nicht dumm, sondern krank, nicht wahr?" sagte der Freund und sah Heine fragend an. 10

„Nein, dumm, ganz dumm!" erwiderte Heine. „Denn eben war Herr Alexander Weill bei mir, und wir tauschten Gedanken aus."

FRAGEN

1. Wer war Heinrich Heine? 2. Wer war Alexander Weill? 3. Wie kommt es (*how come*), daß der Gedankenaustausch mit Weill den Dichter „dumm" macht?

MANFRED HAUSMANN

Manfred Hausmann wurde am 10. September 1898 in Kassel geboren. Er schrieb eine Reihe von Romanen und Erzählungen, darunter „Abel mit der Mundharmonika" und die leicht ironische Reisebeschreibung „Kleine Liebe zu Amerika." 15

IN DER VIERTEN KLASSE

In Isenbüttel-Gifhorn öffnet ein feiner Herr die Tür und steigt elastisch ein. Er trägt Kragen und Schlips, sein Haar ist gescheitelt, seine Nase spitz. Er schließt sofort alle Fenster auf der rechten Seite des Wagens und belehrt uns, daß sonst ein Durchzug entstehe, dessen Gefahr für Hals, Nase und Ohren eines jeden Menschen gar nicht abzuschätzen sei. 20

„Auch muß man," so belehrt er uns weiter, „auf die Lüftung an der Decke

* der Gedankenaustausch — *exchange of ideas*

LINE

2 die Matratzengruft — "*mattress grave*," *sick bed*
gelähmt — *paralysed*
3 geisteskräftig — *with an active mind*
munter — *alert*
4 unterhaltend — *entertaining*
12 austauschen — *exchange*
16 Isenbüttel-Gifhorn (*a little town near Braunschweig*)

LINE

17 Kragen und Schlips — *starched collar and tie*
gescheitelt — *parted*
18 belehren — *enlighten, instruct*
19 der Durchzug — *draft*
entstehe — here: *there would be*
der Hals — *throat*
20 gar nicht abzuschätzen sei — *would be incalculable*
21 die Lüftung — *ventilation*

achten. Diese hier ist zum Beispiel unbedingt zu schließen. Erlauben Sie bitte! So! Noch eins! Wo befindet sich in diesem Abteil die Notbremse? Dort und dort, aha! Ich bin befriedigt.“

Er breitet ein Taschentuch auf seinem Platz aus und setzt sich nieder. Dann 5 betrachtet er nacheinander die Decke, die Wände, den Fußboden.

„Sieh da,“ sagt er und hebt lächelnd etwas auf. „Wer von den Herrschaften vermißt seinen Fahrtausweis?“

Wir fassen in unsere Taschen, einer holt seinen Hut herunter, aber jedermann findet seine Karte.

10 „Auf dem Abort weilt niemand?“ fragt der Herr.

„Nein.“

„Sehr wohl, dann wollen wir das Dokument lieber vernichten, damit niemand in Versuchung kommt, es zu mißbräuchlichen Zwecken zu benutzen.“

Er zerreißt die graue Pappe kreuz und quer und läßt sie zum Fenster hinaus- 15 wehen.

Nicht lange danach schwingt sich der Schaffner von außen herein und bittet um die Fahrkarten, die er bereitwillig von allen erhält. Nur der elastische Herr kann seine nicht auftreiben. Er hat sie wohl gerade in die weite Welt gestreut.

FRAGEN

1. Beschreiben Sie den Herrn, der in Isenbüttel-Gifhorn einsteigt! 2. Was macht der feine Herr? 3. Wer von den Leuten im Coupé hat seinen Fahrtausweis verloren?

WINDGESPRÄCH

Hast nie die Welt gesehn?
Hammerfest — Wien — Athen?

„Nein, ich kenne nur dies Tal,
bin nur so ein Lokalwind —
kennst du Kuntzens Tanzsaal?“

Nein, Kind.
Servus! Muß davon!
Köln — Paris — Lissabon.

Christian Morgenstern

WIND TALK

You've never seen the world? Siena?
Athens — Hammerfest — Vienna?

"This valley's all the world I know,
I'm just a local wind, quite mild.
Perhaps you know Kurt's dancehall though?"

No, child!
So long! I'm on the run —
Paris — Cologne — Lisbon.

LINE

1 unbedingt — *absolutely*
2 sich befinden — *be situated*
die Notbremse — *emergency brake*
3 befriedigt — *satisfied*
4 ausbreiten — *spread*
das Taschentuch — *handkerchief*
5 betrachten — *look at, examine*
der Fußboden — *floor*
6 die Herrschaften — *ladies and gentlemen*
7 der Fahrtausweis — *ticket*
8 fassen — here: *reach*

LINE

10 der Abort — *washroom*
13 die Versuchung — *temptation*
mißbräuchlich — *improper, illegal*
der Zweck — *purpose*
benutzen — *use*
14 die Pappe — *pasteboard (ticket)*
kreuz und quer — here: *to pieces*
14–15 hinauswehen — *blow out*
17 bereitwillig — *readily*
18 auftreiben — *find, produce*
streuen — *scatter*

SIEBENTER TEIL

Bergschlucht bei Liechtenstein

Gedenktafel für einen abgestürzten Bergsteiger

Zell am See. Ein charakteristisches Bild aus dem österreichischen Alpenland.

19. Aufgabe

AM MÜHLSTURZHORN

Memorize the dialogue on this page only. The rest (see pages 161–162) is to be treated as reading assignment.

Zeit der Handlung: Frühling 1958.

Ort: Ein Krankenzimmer in dem Kreiskrankenhaus von Berchtesgaden. In dem Bett liegt der siebzehnjährige Otto H. Neben ihm sitzt ein Reporter mit Notizblock. Am Fußende des Bettes steht der Arzt.

DER ARZT: (*zu dem Reporter*) Bitte vergessen Sie nicht, daß der Patient geschont werden muß. Er ist erst gestern eingeliefert worden.

DER REPORTER: (*zu Otto*) Also, Otto, erzähl mir, wie das gewesen ist. Sonntag früh hat man euch losziehn sehen — dich und deinen Freund Preml.

OTTO: Ja, das stimmt.

DER REPORTER: Ihr habt auf das große Mühlsturzhorn klettern wollen. So war uns das berichtet worden.

OTTO: Wir hatten miteinander ja schon viel schwierigere Kletterpartien gemacht.

DER REPORTER: Ich weiß.

OTTO: Mein Freund hat zu mir noch gesagt: „Paß auf! In sechs Stunden werden wir das erledigt haben. Eh' es dämmert, sind wir zurück."

DER ARZT: Ihr habt nicht einmal Schlafsäcke mitgenommen?

OTTO: Die hielten wir für überflüssig.

DER ARZT: (*zu dem Reporter*) Das hat dem andern Jungen das Leben gekostet.

DER REPORTER: (*zu Otto*) Warum seid ihr nicht umgekehrt, als das Wetter wechselte? Die ganze Gegend wurde doch durch das Radio vor dem Wetterumsturz gewarnt.

ON THE MÜHLSTURZHORN

Time of Action: Spring 1958.

Place: A room in the district hospital of Berchtesgaden. In the bed lies Otto H., 17 years of age. Next to him a reporter is seated, notebook in hand. At the foot of the bed stands the doctor.

THE DOCTOR: (*to the reporter*) Please don't forget that the patient must be treated with care. He was brought in only yesterday.

THE REPORTER: (*to Otto*) All right, Otto, tell me how it was. Sunday morning you were seen starting out — you and your friend Preml.

OTTO: Yes, that's right.

THE REPORTER: You intended to climb the great Mühlsturzhorn. That's how it had been reported to us.

OTTO: The two of us, you see, had done much harder climbs together before this.

THE REPORTER: I know.

OTTO: My friend even said to me: "Wait and see. We'll do it (*lit.* "We'll have accomplished it") in six hours. We'll be back before it gets dark."

THE DOCTOR: You didn't even take sleeping bags with you?

OTTO: We considered them superfluous.

THE DOCTOR: (*to the reporter*) That cost the other boy his life.

THE REPORTER: (*to Otto*) Why didn't you turn back when the weather changed? After all, the whole region was given a warning over the radio about the abrupt change in weather.

OTTO: Verzeihen Sie, Herr Journalist, da waren wir längst in der Wand. Zuerst ging alles ja programmgemäß. Den Aufstieg hatten wir in ein paar Stunden geschafft. Zurück ging es zuerst auch ganz glatt. Und das Wetter schien uns prächtig. 5

DER REPORTER: Aber der Sturm!

OTTO: Den haben wir ja nicht kommen sehen. Wir wurden ganz einfach von dem Sturm überrascht. In dem zerklüfteten Fels hat man nichts gemerkt, bis es zu spät war, denn da war das Schneetreiben schon da, und da hatte sich auch 10 das Seil verhakt, so daß wir weder nach vorn noch nach rückwärts konnten. Wir haben grade noch eine Ecke im Südkamin finden können, wo man vor dem Ärgsten geschützt war.

DER REPORTER: Und dann? 15

OTTO: Und dann? Dann war nichts. Immer kälter ist es geworden, der Kamin war bald völlig vereist, und wir haben ununterbrochen um Hilfe geschrien, bis die Bergwacht uns hörte.

DER REPORTER: Wenn die Bergwacht euch gehört hat, warum hat man 20 euch dann nicht gleich heruntergeholt?

DER ARZT: (*zu dem Reporter*) Entschuldigen Sie, es war die Witterung, welche alle Rettungsversuche unmöglich machte, auch wenn die Rufverbindung noch weiterbestand. Man sah ja die Hand nicht vor den Augen. 25

OTTO: Sonntag abend ging uns die Verpflegung aus. Die letzte Rolle Traubenzucker, welche wir noch besaßen, habe ich dem Preml geschenkt. Am Montag setzten wir alle Hoffnung auf die Bergwacht, denn wir hatten sie den Tag über immer rufen hören; und sie uns auch. Nur ist dann mein 30

LINE
2 die Wand — here: *sheer rock wall*
gemäß — *according to*
2–3 der Aufstieg — *ascent*
3 schaffen — *make, complete*
4 glatt — *smoothly*
5 prächtig — *splendid*
8 überrascht — *taken by surprise*
8–9 der zerklüftete Fels — *jagged* or *cleft rock*
10 das Schneetreiben — *blizzard*
10–11 hatte sich . . . verhakt — *got caught*
11 das Seil — *rope*
13 der Südkamin — *south chimney, fissure*
das Ärgste — *the worst*

LINE
14 geschützt — *protected*
17 vereist — *covered with ice*
18 ununterbrochen — *continually*
die Bergwacht — *mountain watch*
22 die Witterung — *weather conditions*
23 der Rettungsversuch — *attempt at rescue*
24 noch weiterbestand — *was still maintained*
26 ging . . . aus — *was exhausted*
die Verpflegung — *food supply*
27 die Rolle Traubenzucker — *pack of grape sugar tablets*
noch besaßen — *had left*
29 den Tag über — *the whole day long*

Kamerad so müde geworden, daß ich mir Sorgen um ihn zu machen begann.

DER REPORTER: So verging der Montag — der Dienstag — ohne ein Stück Brot . . .

5 OTTO: Und am Mittwoch brach die Rufverbindung ab. Da waren wir wirklich verzweifelt. Am nächsten Morgen hat der Preml sich nicht mehr gerührt. Steif hat er an der Felswand gekauert. Nachdem ich begriffen hatte: Er ist tot! — bin ich ausgebrochen und habe versucht, die Wand zu queren.

10 DER ARZT: (*zu dem Reporter*) Das war sein Glück. Sie müssen wissen, daß die beiden aufgegeben waren, aber jetzt sah ihn die Bergwacht durch das Glas, und im Eiltempo ging es zur Einstiegstelle.

OTTO: „Wer ist hier?!" hat einer durch sein Sprachrohr gebrüllt, 15 und ich konnte noch grade zurückrufen, daß ich es nicht mehr aushalten konnte.

DER ARZT: (*zu dem Reporter*) Über zwei Stunden brauchten die Leute, um sich zu ihm abzuseilen. Nach vier Eisnächten, fünf Tagen bei Schneeorkan und Temperaturen bis zu minus zehn Grad, 20 ohne Verpflegung, ohne Schutz an der Südkante des großen Mühlsturzhorns, wird der Junge hier eingeliefert: Völlig erschöpft, mit leichten Erfrierungen — aber sonst fehlt ihm nichts, Sie sehen es ja! Und dabei ist es ein glattes Wunder, daß der Junge überhaupt noch lebt!

Nach einem Bericht der *Süddeutschen Zeitung* vom 3./4. Mai 1958, Seite 3.

DRILL PATTERNS

Repeat the following drills after your instructor or after the speaker on the tape. Imitate the pronunciation very carefully.

1. Zuerst ging alles programmgemäß.
Zuerst geht alles programmgemäß.

Zuerst ist alles programmgemäß gegangen.

LINE

1–2 sich Sorgen machen — *worry*
6 verzweifelt — *desperate*
7 sich rühren — *move*
8 begreifen — *understand*
ausbrechen — *break away, venture out*
9 queren — *cross*
12 das Eiltempo — *great speed*
12–13 die Einstiegstelle — *take-off point* (for the rescue)
14 das Sprachrohr — *megaphone*
brüllen — *shout, scream*

LINE

18 sich . . . abzuseilen — *lower themselves by ropes*
19 der Schneeorkan — *severe blizzard*
der Grad — *degree* (– 10 Grad = 14° F)
20 der Schutz — *protection*
die Südkante — *southern edge*
22 erschöpft — *exhausted*
leichte Erfrierungen — *minor frostbites*
22–3 fehlt ihm nichts — *nothing is wrong with him*
23 glatt — *sheer*

Zuerst war alles programmgemäß gegangen.
Zuerst wird alles programmgemäß gehen.

2. Nehmt ihr keine Schlafsäcke mit?
Nahmt ihr keine Schlafsäcke mit?
Habt ihr keine Schlafsäcke mitgenommen?
Hattet ihr keine Schlafsäcke mitgenommen?
Werdet ihr keine Schlafsäcke mitnehmen?

3. Die hält er für überflüssig.
Die hielt er für überflüssig.
Die hat er für überflüssig gehalten.
Die hatte er für überflüssig gehalten.
Die wird er für überflüssig halten.
Die wird er für überflüssig gehalten haben.

4. Kehren sie nicht um?
Sind sie nicht umgekehrt?
Werden sie nicht umgekehrt sein?
Werden sie nicht umkehren?
Waren sie nicht umgekehrt?
Kehrten sie nicht um?

5. Wie ist das?
Wie war das?
Wie ist das gewesen?
Wie wird das wohl gewesen sein?

6. Haben sie gewußt, was das kostet?
Wußte sie, was das gekostet hatte?
Wissen Sie, was das kosten wird?

7. Was sagt er dazu?
Was sagte er denn?
Was wird er wohl dazu zu sagen haben?

8. Darauf paßte ich nicht auf. [1]
Darauf hatte ich nicht aufgepaßt.
Schmidt, warum passen Sie nicht auf?
Schmidt! Warum haben Sie nicht aufgepaßt?

9. Das weiß ich nicht.
Ich wußte das nicht.
Ich hatte das nicht gewußt.

10. Das wußten Sie nicht? — Das mußten Sie wissen!
Das wissen Sie nicht? — Das müssen Sie wissen!
Sie haben das nicht wissen müssen? — Oh doch, Sie hatten das wissen müssen.
Das werden Sie niemals wissen? — Oh doch, Sie werden das wissen müssen.

11. Vergaß er das?
Hat er das wirklich vergessen?
Wie konnte er das vergessen!
Wie hat er das vergessen können!
Wir vergessen so etwas nie.
Wie könnten wir so etwas vergessen!
Ach, ihr werdet das auch bald vergessen.
Bis morgen werdet auch ihr das vergessen haben.

12. Eh' es dämmert, sind sie zurück.
Eh' es dämmert, werden sie zurück sein.
Eh' es dämmerte, waren sie zurück.
Eh' es gedämmert hatte, waren sie zurück.

13. Sonntag früh hat man euch losziehn sehen.
Sonntag früh hatte man euch losziehn sehen.
Sonntag früh sah man sie losziehn.
Sonntag früh sieht man sie losziehn.
Sonntag früh wird man sie losziehn sehen.

14. Er wollte auf das Mühlsturzhorn klettern.
Er will auf das Mühlsturzhorn klettern.

[1] **aufpassen** pay attention

Er hat auf das Mühlsturzhorn klettern wollen.
Er wird auf das Mühlsturzhorn klettern wollen.
Er hatte auf das Mühlsturzhorn klettern wollen.

15. Das wollen sie? Das wollen sie tun?
Ihr wolltet das? Das wolltet ihr tun?
Sie haben das gewollt? Das haben Sie tun wollen?
Ja, wir hatten es so gewollt. Ja, wir hatten das tun wollen.

16. Er hat den Sturm nicht kommen sehen.
Er wird den Sturm nicht kommen sehen.
Er sah den Sturm nicht kommen.
Er sieht den Sturm nicht kommen.
Er hatte den Sturm nicht kommen sehen.

17. Eh' es dämmert, sind wir zurück.
Wir sind zurück, eh' es dämmert.
Als das Wetter wechselte, kehrten sie um.
Sie kehrten um, als das Wetter wechselte.

18. Er schenkte ihm die letzte Rolle Traubenzucker, {welche / die} er noch besaß.

Das letzte Stück Brot, {welches / das} er noch besaß, hat er seinem Freund geschenkt.

Schenkte er ihm den einzigen Rock, {welchen / den} er besaß?

19. Es gab einen anderen Weg, {welcher / der} nicht in die Wand führte.

Es gab keinen anderen Weg, {auf welchem / auf dem} er umkehren konnte.

English to German

Prepare this exercise in writing.

1) You (*3 ways*) wanted to climb [1] the Matterhorn. **vs/vl**

2) Didn't you (*3 ways*) see the storm coming? **vf/vl** (*use pres. perf.*)

3) I knew **vs** you (*3 ways*) had wanted to come [2] yesterday. **vs/vl**

4) Did everything go according to plan? **vf** (*use past*)
Has everything gone according to plan? **vf/vl** (*use pres. perf.*)
Had everything gone according to plan? **vf/vl**
Will everything go according to plan? **vf/vl**
Everything will have gone [3] according to plan. **vs/vl**

5) We were back **vs** before it got dark. **vl**
We were back **vs** when it got dark. **vl**

6) We turned back **vs** because it got dark. **vl**
If it gets dark, we'll turn back. **vl/v** (*use pres.*)

[1] Use *present perfect* and *double infinitive* as explained in Grammar Section 39. [2] Translate without using **daß** and use *double infinitive.* [3] Use *future perfect* as illustrated in Grammar Section 38.

7) *Rewrite sentences in 5 and 6, interchanging the position of the two clauses in each case.*

Translate the following sentences without the help of the key:

8) He doesn't pay attention.
He hasn't paid attention.
He didn't pay attention.
He hadn't paid attention.
He won't pay attention.

9) You (*3 ways*) (they, we) have wanted to do that.

GRAMMAR

VERBS

Review the materials dealing with:

a. Present tense (Grammar Section 1)
b. Past tense (Grammar Section 18)
c. Present perfect tense (Grammar Section 12)
d. Future tense (Grammar Section 19)
e. Strong verbs (Grammar Section 25)
f. Weak verbs (Grammar Sections 1, p. 8, and 18, p. 77; also 25, Note B, p. 114)
g. Weak-strong verbs (Grammar Section 26)
h. Modals (Grammar Section 26)
i. Irregular verbs (Grammar Section 26)

38. The Six Tenses

A simple and efficient way to get at the tenses of verbs is to begin with the principal parts. For example:

INFINITIVE	3RD SING. PRESENT	3RD SING. PAST	3RD SING. PRESENT PERFECT
sagen	sagt	sagte	hat gesagt

Present: Sie **sagt** nichts Neues. *She says nothing new.*
Past: Sie **sagte** nichts Neues. *She said nothing new.*
Present perfect: Sie **hat** nichts Neues **gesagt.** *She has said nothing new.*

A simple change in the auxiliary from present to past tense produces the *past perfect:*

Sie **hatte** nichts Neues **gesagt.** *She had said nothing new.*

The *future* tense, as already noted, uses as auxiliary forms of **werden:**

Sie **wird** nichts Neues **sagen.** *She will say nothing new.*

To form the *future perfect* merely replace the present infinitive with the *perfect infinitive:*

Sie **wird** nichts Neues **gesagt haben.** *She will have said nothing new.*

Illustrations

INFINITIVE	PRESENT	PAST	PRESENT PERFECT
sprechen	spricht	sprach	hat gesprochen

Present: Der junge Mann **spricht** mit ihr darüber. *The young man speaks to her about it.*
Past: Der junge Mann **sprach** mit ihr darüber. *The young man spoke to her about it.*
Present perfect: Der junge Mann **hat** mit ihr darüber **gesprochen.** *The young man has spoken to her about it.*
Past perfect: Der junge Mann **hatte** mit ihr darüber **gesprochen.** *The young man had spoken to her about it.*
Future: Der junge Mann **wird** mit ihr darüber **sprechen.** *The young man will speak to her about it.*
Future perfect: Der junge Mann **wird** mit ihr darüber **gesprochen haben**. *The young man will have spoken to her about it.*

INFINITIVE	PRESENT	PAST	PRESENT PERFECT
versprechen	verspricht	versprach	hat versprochen

Present: Der Onkel **verspricht** es meiner Mutter.
Past: Der Onkel **versprach** es meiner Mutter.
Present perfect: Der Onkel **hat** es meiner Mutter **versprochen.**
Past perfect: Der Onkel **hatte** es meiner Mutter **versprochen.**
Future: Der Onkel **wird** es meiner Mutter **versprechen.**
Future perfect: Der Onkel **wird** es meiner Mutter **versprochen haben.**

INFINITIVE	PRESENT	PAST	PRESENT PERFECT
kommen	kommt	kam	ist gekommen

Present: Mein bester Freund **kommt** dadurch in Verlegenheit.
Past: Mein bester Freund **kam** dadurch in Verlegenheit.
Present perfect: Mein bester Freund **ist** dadurch in Verlegenheit **gekommen.**
Past perfect: Mein bester Freund **war** dadurch in Verlegenheit **gekommen.**
Future: Mein bester Freund **wird** dadurch in Verlegenheit **kommen.**
Future perfect: Mein bester Freund **wird** dadurch in Verlegenheit **gekommen sein.**

INFINITIVE	PRESENT	PAST	PRESENT PERFECT
zurückkommen	kommt zurück	kam zurück	ist zurückgekommen

Present: Am nächsten Donnerstag **kommt** sein jüngstes Kind **zurück.**
Past: Am nächsten Donnerstag **kam** sein jüngstes Kind **zurück.**
Present perfect: Am nächsten Donnerstag **ist** sein jüngstes Kind **zurückgekommen.**
Past perfect: Am nächsten Donnerstag **war** sein jüngstes Kind **zurückgekommen.**
Future: Am nächsten Donnerstag **wird** sein jüngstes Kind **zurückkommen.**
Future perfect: Am nächsten Donnerstag **wird** sein jüngstes Kind **zurückgekommen sein.**

INFINITIVE	PRESENT	PAST	PRESENT PERFECT
wollen	will	wollte	hat gewollt

Present:	Die ganze Klasse **will** es.
Past:	Die ganze Klasse **wollte** es.
Present perfect:	Die ganze Klasse **hat** es **gewollt.**
Past perfect:	Die ganze Klasse **hatte** es **gewollt.**
Future:	Die ganze Klasse **wird** es **wollen.**
Future perfect:	Die ganze Klasse **wird** es **gewollt haben.**

39. Double Infinitive

Die ganze Klasse hat (hatte) es **tun** / **lesen** } **wollen.**

*The whole class has (had) wanted **to do** / **read** } it.*

a. Note the conditions under which the *modal infinitive form* replaces the past participle:

(1) The tense must be present perfect or past perfect, and
(2) the dependent infinitive (**tun, lesen,** or the like) must be expressed.

b. Note that the modal infinitive in all such cases still has the force and meaning of the past participle.

Ich habe es nicht tun können, aber sie hat es gekonnt.

c. Note that such double infinitives always take the last two positions in the clause, whether the clause is dependent or independent.

Die ganze Klasse hatte das Buch **lesen wollen.**
Er wußte nicht, ob die ganze Klasse das Buch hatte **lesen wollen.**

d. Note that there are at least four other verbs that conform to the double infinitive pattern. The conditions are the same as those for the modals.

1. Ich habe ihn kommen **sehen.**	*I have seen* (or *I saw*) *him come.*
2. Er hat mich nicht kommen **hören.**	*He has not heard* (or *He did not hear*) *me come.*
3. Ihr habt es uns tun **lassen.**	*You have let* (or *You let*) *us do it.*
4. Sie hat ihnen das Geld suchen **helfen.**	*She has helped* (or *She helped*) *them look for the money.*

(Note that **helfen** governs the dative.)

VERB EXERCISES

I. Write the following sentences in all tenses (present, present perfect, past, past perfect, future, future perfect).

1. Die hielten wir für überflüssig. 2. Ihr kehrt um. 3. Du nimmst ihn mit. 4. Sie geht mit. 5. Wir wollen das nicht. 6. Ich weiß das. 7. Er muß das wissen. (*omit fut. perf.*) 8. Werden Sie das vergessen? 9. Ich kann das nicht vergessen. (*omit fut. perf.*)

II. Conjugate the following statements in the past perfect. Use all persons: **ich; du; sie, es, er; Sie; wir; ihr; sie.**

1. Er hatte den Schlafsack mitgenommen. 2. Er war umgekehrt.

III. Conjugate the sentences in II in the future perfect tense.

20. Aufgabe

WER BIN ICH?

SAMPLE ANSWERS AND SUGGESTIONS

a. Was wollen Sie werden? — *Ich will . . . werden.*

Note: Most German terms indicating professions can be used in the feminine gender by adding the ending **–in.**

Wissenschaftler
  Bakteriolog(e)
  Physiolog(e)
  Entomolog(e)
  Biolog(e)
  Geolog(e)
  Chemiker
  Physiker
Soziolog(e)
Psycholog(e)
  Psychiater
  Psychoanalytiker
Künstler [1]
  Maler [2]
Musiker
Schriftsteller [3]
Journalist

Arzt [4]
  Tierarzt [5]
  Zahnarzt [6]
  Ärztin
Ingenieur
Nationalökonom [7]
Kaufmann [8] *
Geschäftsmann [9] *
  Industrieller *
  Handlungsreisender [10] *
  Abteilungsleiter [11]
Lehrer
  Professor
  Pädagog(e)
  Kindergärtnerin
Staatsbeamter [12] *
Politiker

Historiker
Diplomat
Soldat *
  Offizier *
Matrose [13] *
  Schiffskapitän *
Flieger
Mathematiker
Krankenpflegerin [14]
Hausfrau
Pastor *
Priester *
Pfarrer [15] *
Advokat [16]
Polizist
Detektiv *

b. Sind Sie ein guter Student (eine gute Studentin)?
Was für Noten bekommen Sie gewöhnlich? [17] — *Ich bekomme gewöhnlich gute (schlechte) Noten.*

Werden Sie oft gelobt? [18] — *Ja, ich werde oft gelobt.* *Nein, ich werde nicht oft gelobt.*

  Von welchem Professor?
Wurden Sie oft getadelt? [19] — *Ja, ich wurde . . . getadelt.*
Sagte der Professor: „Seien Sie nicht so faul! Arbeiten Sie mehr!"?

[1] **der Künstler** artist [2] **der Maler** painter [3] **der Schriftsteller** writer [4] **der Arzt** (medical) doctor [5] **der Tierarzt** veterinarian [6] **der Zahnarzt** dentist [7] **der Nationalökonom** economist [8] **der Kaufmann** (*pl.* **–leute**) businessman, merchant [9] **der Geschäftsmann** (*pl.* **–leute**) businessman [10] **der Handlungsreisende** (**ein Handlungsreisender**) traveling salesman [11] **der Abteilungsleiter** department manager [12] **der Beamte** (**ein Beamter**) official [13] **der Matrose** sailor [14] **die Krankenpflegerin** nurse [15] **der Pfarrer** clergyman [16] **der Advokat** lawyer [17] **gewöhnlich** usually [18] **loben** praise, commend [19] **tadeln** criticize, find fault with

* The feminine form for **Geschäftsmann** is **Geschäftsfrau.** To form the feminine of **Handlungsreisender** and **Staatsbeamter** change the **–er** ending to **–e.** (**Staatsbeamtin** is possible.) There are no feminine forms for **Kaufmann, Industrieller, Soldat, Offizier, Matrose,** and **Schiffskapitän.** (**Detektivin** is possible.) **Frau Pastor** (**Pfarrer**) is the title given to a minister's wife. **Priesterin** is the term for *priestess* in pagan cults and religions.

Eine deutsche Studentin bei der Arbeit im Chemischen Institut, Bonn.

SAMPLE ANSWERS AND SUGGESTIONS

Oder sagte er: „Sie werden diesen Kurs nicht bestehen,[1] wenn Sie nicht fleißiger studieren!"?
Sagte er: „Gehen Sie nicht so oft tanzen! Bleiben Sie mal zu Hause!"?
Oder: „Hänschen, Hänschen, denke dran, was aus dir noch werden kann!"?
Lassen Sie sich gerne prüfen?

Ja, ich lasse mich gerne prüfen.
Nein, ich lasse mich nicht gerne prüfen.

Sind Sie in den letzten Tagen geprüft worden?

Ja, ich bin . . . geprüft worden.
Nein, ich bin . . . nicht geprüft worden.

Wollen Sie heute in Deutsch geprüft werden?

Ich will (nicht) . . . geprüft werden.

Warum nicht? Sind Sie nicht vorbereitet?[2]
Fürchten Sie sich davor, geprüft zu werden?

Ich fürchte mich (nicht) davor, geprüft zu werden.

Werden Sie morgen besser vorbereitet sein?
Wann werden die großen Prüfungen abgehalten?[3]

Die . . . Prüfungen werden im . . . abgehalten.

DRILL PATTERNS

Repeat the following drills after your instructor or after the speaker on the tape. Imitate the pronunciation very carefully.

1. Erzähl mir, wie das gewesen ist!
   Erzähl mir! Wie ist das gewesen?
   Erzählen Sie mir, wie das war!
   Erzählen Sie mir! Wie war das?
   Erzählt mir, wie das werden soll!
   Erzählt mir! Wie soll das werden?

2. Was war, das ist gewesen.
   Was sein muß, wird sein.
   Was immer ist, ist immer gewesen.
   Was immer gewesen ist, wird immer sein.

3. Paß auf!
   Passen Sie auf!
   Paßt auf!
   Aufpassen!
   Aufgepaßt!

4. Bitte, vergessen Sie nicht!
   Bitte, vergiß nicht!
   Bitte, vergeßt nicht!
   Nicht vergessen!

5. „Herein!" — „Hinaus!"
   „Steh auf!" — „Leg dich nieder!"
   „Geh fort!" — „Komm her!"
   „Sprich lauter!" — „Sei ruhig!"

6. „Treten Sie näher!" — „Bleiben Sie stehen!"
   „Fangen Sie an!" — „Hören Sie auf!"
   „Antworten Sie!" — „Schweigen Sie!"
   „Lernen Sie das!" — „Erklären Sie's mir!"

[1] **bestehen** pass [2] **vorbereiten** prepare [3] **abhalten** hold

7. „Denkt nicht daran!" — „Vergeßt das nicht!"
„Hört ihm nicht zu!" — „Seid nicht so ungezogen!" [1]

8. Was soll aus mir werden?
Was wird aus mir werden?
Was kann aus mir werden?
Was will ich werden?

9. Müller wollte Matrose werden.
Was ist aus Müller geworden?
Wurde Müller wirklich Matrose?
Nein, Müller wird nie Matrose werden.
Müller ist Zahnarzt geworden.

10. Meier hat als [2] Kind Detektiv werden wollen.
Will Meier das auch heute noch werden?
Meier *ist* Detektiv geworden.
Meier ist Detektiv.

11. „Ist Anna Psychologin geworden?"
„Psychologin? — Sie sollte doch Journalistin werden."
„Ich dachte, sie wollte Fliegerin werden."
„Ach nein, sie ist längst eine Hausfrau geworden."

12. Erst war sie Studentin.
Dann wurde sie Lehrerin.
Jetzt will sie Schriftstellerin werden.

13. Erst war sie Musikerin gewesen.
Dann wurde sie Mathematikerin.
Jetzt ist sie Staatsbeamtin.
Bald wird sie Abteilungsleiterin sein.

14. Er ist heute eingeliefert worden.
Er wird heute eingeliefert.
Er wurde heute eingeliefert.
Er wird heute eingeliefert werden.
Er wird heute eingeliefert worden sein.
Er war eben eingeliefert worden.

15. Ich wurde vor dem Sturm gewarnt.
Du wurdest vor dem Sturm gewarnt.
Sie wurde vor dem Sturm gewarnt.
Wir wurden vor dem Sturm gewarnt.
Ihr wurdet vor dem Sturm gewarnt.
Sie wurden vor dem Sturm gewarnt.

16. Er muß geschont werden.
Er mußte geschont werden.
Er wird geschont werden müssen.

17. So ist ihm das berichtet worden.
So wurde mir das berichtet.
So war ihnen das berichtet worden.
So wird uns das berichtet.
So wird Ihnen das berichtet werden.
So wird euch das berichtet worden sein.

18. Sie werden von dem Sturm überrascht.
Sie werden von dem Sturm überrascht werden.
Sie werden von dem Sturm überrascht worden sein.
Sie wurden von dem Sturm überrascht.
Sie sind von dem Sturm überrascht worden.
Sie waren von dem Sturm überrascht worden.

19. Ich weiß, daß er geschont werden muß.
Ich weiß, er muß geschont werden.
Daß er geschont werden muß, das weiß ich.

20. „Ist es wahr, daß Sie gestern geprüft worden sind?"
„Allerdings.[3] Ich wurde gestern geprüft."
„Von wem?" — „Von Professor Braun."
„Und heute werden Sie auch geprüft?"

[1] **ungezogen** ill-mannered [2] **als** as [3] **allerdings** to be sure, indeed, certainly

„Gewiß! Heute werden alle geprüft."
„Von wem?" — „Von Professor Braun."
„Ist es wahr, daß Sie morgen geprüft werden werden?"
„Gewiß doch! Wir werden täglich geprüft."
„Von wem?" — „Von Professor Braun."

21. Wer läßt sich gerne prüfen? Wer will sich heute prüfen lassen?
Heute lasse ich mich gerne prüfen. Heute bin ich gut vorbereitet.
Wenn man gut vorbereitet ist, läßt man sich gerne prüfen.

22. Als er das begriff, war er verzweifelt.
Nachdem er das begriffen hatte, war er verzweifelt.
Wenn er das begreift, wird er verzweifelt sein.
Begreift er das, so wird er verzweifelt sein.
Seitdem er das begriffen hat, ist er verzweifelt.
Weil er das nicht begriff, war er verzweifelt.
Er war verzweifelt, weil er das nicht begriff.
Bevor er das begriff, war er verzweifelt.
Wenn er das auch begriff, so war er doch verzweifelt.
Auch wenn er das begreift, wird er verzweifelt sein.

English to German

Prepare this exercise in writing. NOTE: *Study Grammar Section 41* (*Imperative*) *on page 175 before preparing sentences 1–6.*

1) Come here! **vf** (*3 ways*)
2) Sit down! **vf** (*3 ways*)
3) Tell them **vf** how it was, **vl** Peter.
4) Be careful, children. **vf**
Be careful, Marie. **vf**
Be careful, Mr. Müller. **vf**
5) Don't forget your sleeping bags, children. **vf**
Don't forget your money, Karl. **vf**
Don't forget your book, Miss Berger. **vf**
6) Speak more slowly. **vf** (*3 ways*)
7) He was warned only today. **vs/vl** (*use* [1] *past*, [2] *pres. perf.*)
8) He will never become a good student. **vs/vl**
9) They will be overtaken by the storm. **vs/vl**
They had been overtaken by the blizzard. **vs/vl**
10) She must be treated with care. **vs/vl**
11) She doesn't know **vs** that they have been warned about the storm. **vl**
12) That's the way it has been reported to us. **vs/vl**
13) She informs them **vs** that he was just brought in. **vl**
14) He can do it today. **vs/vl**
She couldn't do it today. **vs/vl**
They will not be able to do it today. **vs/vl**
I haven't been able to do it today. **vs/vl**

15) I saw (*use pres. perf.*) them start out Sunday morning. **vs/vl**
16) They didn't even take (*use pres. perf.*) sleeping bags with them. **vs/vl**
17) If you don't understand it, **vl** you will get a low mark. **vf/vl** (*Rewrite omitting* **wenn.**)
18) They must be warned about the storm. **vs/vl**
They must have been warned. **vs/vl**
19) I shall not forget **vs/vl** that the patient needs to be treated with care. **vl**

GRAMMAR

40. Passive Voice Tenses

As you know, **werden** may be used as an independent verb:

INFINITIVE	3RD SING. PRESENT	3RD SING. PAST	3RD SING. PRESENT PERFECT
werden	wird	wurde	ist geworden

Present:	Er wird älter. *He is getting older.*
Past:	Er wurde älter. *He got older.*
Present perfect:	Er ist älter geworden. *He has got older.*
Past perfect:	Er war älter geworden. *He had got older.*
Future:	Er wird älter werden. *He will get older.*
Future perfect:	Er wird älter geworden sein. *He will have got older.*

The passive voice, as you have already seen (Grammar Sections 20, 27), uses **werden** as auxiliary in combination with the *past participle* of the main verb.

You are familiar with the present passive and the present passive infinitive. For example:

Wir **werden abgelöst.**	*We are being relieved.*
Manche müssen mit den Fäusten **geschlagen werden . . .**	*Some must be beaten with fists . . .*

Note the abbreviated form of the auxiliary (**geworden — worden**) in the three perfect tenses in the following synopsis.

Present:	Jenes Lied wird von ihnen gesungen. *That song is sung by them.*
Past:	Jenes Lied wurde von ihnen gesungen. *That song was sung by them.*
Present perfect:	Jenes Lied ist von ihnen gesungen **worden.** *That song has been sung by them.*
Past perfect:	Jenes Lied war von ihnen gesungen **worden.** *That song had been sung by them.*

Future: Jenes Lied wird von ihnen gesungen werden.
That song will be sung by them.

Future perfect: Jenes Lied wird von ihnen gesungen **worden** sein.
That song will have been sung by them.

41. Imperative Mood

There are three imperative forms for each verb.

Singe uns das Lied vor, bitte! (*fam. sing.*)
Singt uns das Lied vor, bitte! (*fam. pl.*)
Singen Sie uns das Lied vor, bitte! (*formal sing. and pl.*)
} *Sing the song for us, please!*

a. The –**e** of the familiar singular is often dropped:

Erzähl uns eine kleine Anekdote! — *Tell us a little anecdote.*
Komm doch her! — *Come here!*

b. The **e** to **i** or **ie** change occurring in verbs like **sehen, sprechen, treten,** etc. is regularly transferred to the imperative, but only to the familiar singular:

Sieh dich im Spiegel an! — *Look at yourself in the mirror!*
Sprich langsamer! — *Speak more slowly!*
Tritt mal etwas näher, bitte! — *Just step a little closer, please!*

NOTE:

A. The –**e** ending is regularly dropped wherever the **e** to **i** or **ie** change appears.

B. **Werden** is the only verb that does not permit the **e** to **i** change to enter the imperative:

Werde nur nicht böse! — *Please don't get angry.*

c. The verb **sein** has irregular forms:

Sei brav, mein liebes Kind! — *Be good, my dear child!*
Seid nicht so ungezogen! — *Don't be so ill-mannered!*
Seien Sie bitte ruhig, gnädiges Fräulein! — *Please be calm* (*quiet*), *Miss!*

d. The formal **Sie** is always expressed; **du** and **ihr** sometimes, to lend stronger emphasis or to express impatience:

Gehen Sie nach Hause! — *Go home!*
Geh du doch fort! — *Just go away!*
Geht ihr mir aus dem Weg! — *You get out of my way!*

e. Infinitives and past participles are often used as imperatives, particularly the infinitives of separable-compound verbs:

Aufstehen!
Aufgestanden!
} *Stand up!* (*Get up!*)

Aufpassen!
Aufgepaßt!
} *Watch out! Attention!*

Infinitives of many verbs are frequently used as imperatives, especially when accompanied by verb modifiers:

Langsam fahren! *Drive slowly!*
Bremsen! *Step on the brake!*
Nicht vergessen! *Don't forget!*

42. Demonstrative Pronouns

There are two indeclinable demonstrative pronouns in German: **das** and **dies.**

Das (dies) ist mein Vater.	Das (dies) sind meine Eltern.
Das (dies) ist meine Frau.	Das (dies) sind meine Kinder.

The demonstrative pronoun **die, das, der** follows exactly the declensional pattern of the relative pronoun (Grammar Section 16). This demonstrative is used as an emphatic substitute for the personal pronoun, except in the genitive area where it is used as a substitute for the possessive adjectives.

Aufpassen! Da kommt die Mutter! Die weiß nichts davon.	*Watch out! Here comes Mother!* ***She*** *knows nothing about it.*
Mit denen will ich nichts zu tun haben.	*I don't want to have anything to do with these people.*
Deren Haus betrete ich nicht.	*I will not enter their house.*

„Das ist der Weisheit letzter Schluß:
Nur der verdient sich Freiheit wie das Leben,
Der täglich sie erobern muß."

Goethe

"This is the ultimate law of wisdom,
He only merits freedom and life,
Who must win them day after day."

21. Aufgabe

VOCABULARY BUILDING

The words listed below are based on strong and irregular verb stems. They comprise a selection from Units I–VII.

Examine them closely. You will be asked to identify some of them by way of exercises following this list.

backen *bake*
der Bäcker *baker*
die Bäckerei *bakery*
das Backhuhn *fried chicken*
das Gebäck *pastry*

beißen *bite*
ein bißchen *a little bit*

bitten *ask*
bitte! *please!*
bitten um *ask for*
die Bitte *request*

braten *roast, fry*
der Braten *roast*

denken *think*
der Denker *thinker*
der Gedanke *thought, idea*

essen *eat*
das Essen *food*
das Abendessen *supper, evening meal*
das Mittagessen *noon meal, dinner*

fahren *go, travel, fare*
erfahren *experience(d)*
die Fahrkarte *ticket*

fliegen *fly*
der Ausflug *excursion*
der Flieger *flyer, airman*
der Flughafen *airport*
das Flugzeug *airplane*

fließen *flow*
die Flut *flood, water*
der Fluß *river*
überflüssig *superfluous*

geben *give*
die Aufgabe *assignment, lesson*
aufgeben *assign*
die Gabe *gift* (*do not confuse with:* das Gift *poison*)

gehen *go*
der Gang *corridor, gangway*
der Eingang *entrance*
der Bahnübergang *railroad crossing*

haben *have*
der Habenichts *penniless person*

kennen *know*
bekannt *well-known*
unbekannt *unknown*

klingen *(re)sound, ring*
der Zusammenklang *harmony*

leiden *suffer*
der Leidende *sufferer*
das Leid *injury, sorrow*
Es tut mir leid. *I am sorry.*
leider *unfortunately*

mögen *may, like (to)*
möglich *possible, likely*
unmöglich *impossible*

schaffen *create, do*
das Geschäft *shop, business*
der Schaffner *conductor (R.R.)*

schlafen *sleep*
schläfrig *sleepy*
der Schlafsack *sleeping bag*
der Schlafwagen *sleeping car*
das Schlafzimmer *bedroom*

schneiden *cut*
der Schneider *tailor*

schrecken *frighten*
schrecklich *frightful, terrible*

schwimmen *swim*
der Schwamm *sponge, (blackboard) eraser*
das Schwimmbad *swimming pool*

sehen *see*
die Ansichtskarte *picture postcard*
das Gesicht *face*
der Sehende *one who sees*
der Seher *seer*

sein *be*
das Wesen *being, essence, creature*
das Wesentliche *the essential thing (point)*

singen *sing*
der Gesang *singing, song*
der Singende *one who sings*

sitzen *sit*
besessen *possessed, mad*
der Besitz *possession*
der Sitzplatz *seat*

sprechen *speak*
das Gespräch *conversation*
die Sprache *language, speech*
die Fremdsprache *foreign language*
das Sprachrohr *megaphone*

springen *spring, leap*
der Sprung *leap*

tun do
die Tat *act, deed*
die Tatsache *fact*
tatsächlich *actually*

wissen *know*
gewiß *certain(ly)*
die Wissenschaft *science*
der Wissenschaftler *scientist*

ziehen *go, move, draw, pull*
der Zug *train*
der D-Zug (Durchgangszug) *through-(way) train*
der Schnellzug *express train*

Übersetzen Sie, bitte, die folgenden Sätze:

Der Habenichts hat nichts, auch kein kleines bißchen.

Die Wissenschaftler führten ein langes Gespräch in einer uns unbekannten Fremdsprache.

Eine Fahrkarte ist keine Ansichtskarte. Die Fahrkarte muß man dem Schaffner im Zug zeigen [1]; die Ansichtskarte schickt man an einen Freund.

Die Gedanken eines wahren Denkers sind ebenso [2] klar wie [2] tief.

Beantworten Sie, bitte, die folgenden Fragen auf Deutsch!

Hat jeder Zug einen Schlafwagen?
Gibt es Sitzplätze in einem Schnellzug?
Hält [3] ein D-Zug an jeder Station?
Ist ein Gift eine Gabe?
Gibt Ihr Lehrer Ihnen Gaben? Oder gibt er Ihnen Aufgaben auf?
Was kauft man beim Bäcker (in der Bäckerei)?
Braten? Brot? ein Backhuhn? Gebäck?

WORD STUDY

These words and phrases are from the reading material immediately following. The starred items should become part of your active vocabulary.

WORDS COMMONLY USED

bloß only (*syn.:* **nur**)
* **dadurch** thereby
* **deswegen** therefore (*syn.:* **darum**)
* **fertig** ready (*syn.:* **bereit**)
* **gleich** immediately; equal to, like
lauter pure, nothing but, sheer

[1] **zeigen** show [2] **ebenso . . . wie** just as . . . as [3] **halten** stop

noch einmal once more
recht very (*often a substitute for* **sehr**)
schon wieder (once) again
so was = * **so etwas** a thing like this
So was kann bloß ein Esel machen. Only a jackass can do a thing like this.
überhaupt niemand no one at all
* **zornig** angry (*syn.:* **böse**)

IDIOMATIC EXPRESSIONS

In the following sentences note the difference between German and English in the use of prepositions. The German sentences are based on material taken from Unit VII:

Die ganze Gegend wurde **vor** dem Sturm gewarnt. *The whole region was warned* ***about*** *the storm.*

Wir waren glücklicherweise noch **vor** dem Ärgsten geschützt. *We were fortunately still protected* ***from*** *the worst* (*of the storm*).

Vom Fenster **aus** konnte man **auf** den Dorfplatz sehen. *From the window you could look* ***down upon*** *the village square.*

Es kostet achtzig Mark **im** Monat. *It costs eighty marks* ***per*** *month* (*a month*).

Der Onkel wartete schon **auf** mich. *Uncle was already waiting* ***for*** *me.*

Wir haben ununterbrochen **um** Hilfe gerufen. *We called incessantly* ***for*** *help.*

Paß **auf!** *Watch* ***out!***

Du bist **daran** schuld, weil du **beim** Abschreiben Fehler gemacht hast. *You are to blame* ***for it,*** *because you made mistakes* ***in*** *copying.*

Reading

The following story is one of a quasi-autobiographical series entitled, "Lausbuben-geschichten" by Ludwig Thoma (1867–1921). All the events in this series are related from the vantage point and in the language of an impudent and nimble-minded adolescent, who exposes the pretense and pompousness of his superiors.

ONKEL FRANZ

Da bekam meine Mutter einen Brief von Onkel Franz, welcher ein pensionierter Major war. Und sie sagte, daß sie recht froh ist, weil der Onkel schrieb, er will schon einen ordentlichen Menschen aus mir machen, und es kostet achtzig Mark im Monat. Dann mußte ich in die Stadt, wo Onkel wohnte. Das war sehr traurig. Es war über vier Stiegen, und es waren lauter hohe Häuser herum und kein Garten. 5
Ich durfte nie spielen, und es war überhaupt niemand da. Bloß der Onkel Franz und die Tante Anna, welche den ganzen Tag herumgingen und achtgaben, daß nichts passierte. Aber der Onkel war so streng zu mir und sagte immer, wenn er mich sah: „Warte nur, du Lausbub, ich krieg dich schon noch."

LINE
1 pensioniert — *retired*
3 ordentlich — *respectable*
4 mußte ich — here: *I had to go*
5 über vier Stiegen — *four flights up*

LINE
7 achtgeben — *see to it*
9 der Lausbub — *rascal*
kriegen — *get*

Vom Fenster aus konnte man auf die Straße hinunterspucken, und es klatschte furchtbar, wenn es daneben ging. Aber wenn man die Leute traf, schauten sie zornig herum und schimpften abscheulich. Da habe ich oft gelacht, aber sonst war es gar nicht lustig.

5 Der Professor konnte mich nicht leiden, weil er sagte, daß ich einen sehr schlechten Ruf mitgebracht hatte.

Der Onkel Franz hat ihn gut gekannt und ist oft hingegangen zu ihm.

Dann haben sie ausgemacht, wie sie mich alle zwei erwischen können.

Wenn ich von der Schule heimkam, mußte ich mich gleich wieder hinsetzen und 10 die Aufgaben machen.

Der Onkel schaute mir immer zu und sagte: „Machst du es wieder recht dumm? Wart nur, du Lausbub, ich komm' dir schon noch."

Einmal mußte ich eine Arithmetikaufgabe machen. Die brachte ich nicht zusammen, und da fragte ich den Onkel, weil er zu meiner Mutter gesagt hatte, 15 daß er mir nachhelfen will. Und die Tante hat auch gesagt, daß der Onkel so gescheit ist, und daß ich viel lernen kann bei ihm.

Deswegen habe ich ihn gebeten, daß er mir hilft, und er hat sie dann gelesen und gesagt: „Kannst du schon wieder nichts, du nichtsnutziger Lausbub? Das ist doch ganz leicht."

20 Und dann hat er sich hingesetzt und hat es probiert. Es ging aber gar nicht schnell. Er rechnete den ganzen Nachmittag, und wie ich ihn fragte, ob er es noch nicht fertig hat, schimpfte er mich fürchterlich und war sehr grob.

Erst vor dem Essen brachte er mir die Rechnung und sagte: „Jetzt kannst du es abschreiben; es war doch ganz leicht, aber ich habe noch etwas anderes tun 25 müssen, du Dummkopf."

Ich habe es abgeschrieben und dem Professor gegeben. Am Donnerstag kam die Aufgabe heraus, und ich meinte, daß ich einen Einser kriege. Es war aber wieder ein Vierer, und das ganze Blatt war rot, und der Professor sagte: „So eine dumme Rechnung kann bloß ein Esel machen."

30 „Das war mein Onkel," sagte ich, „der hat es gemacht, und ich habe es bloß abgeschrieben."

Die ganze Klasse hat gelacht, und der Professor wurde aber rot.

„Du bist ein gemeiner Lügner," sagte er, „und du wirst noch im Zuchthaus

LINE

1 spucken — *spit*
1–2 es klatschte furchtbar, wenn es daneben ging — *it landed with a slap whenever it missed its mark*
3 schimpfen — *scold, curse*
abscheulich — *horribly*
6 der Ruf — *reputation*
8 ausmachen — *agree, arrange*
erwischen — *catch, trap*
11 zuschauen — *watch*
12 ich komm' dir schon noch — *"I'll get you yet"*
13–14 zusammenbringen — *solve*
15 nachhelfen — *help along*

LINE

16 gescheit — *intelligent, bright*
18 nichtsnutzig — *good for nothing*
20 probieren — *try*
21 rechnen — *work on a mathematical problem*
22 grob — *gruff*
23 die Rechnung — here: *"the problem all solved"*
24 abschreiben — *copy*
27 heraus = zurück
27–8 ein Einser, ein Vierer (1 = *A*, 2 = *B*, 3 = *C*, 4 = *F*)
28 das Blatt — *page*
33 der Lügner — *liar*
das Zuchthaus — *jail*

enden.“ Dann sperrte er mich zwei Stunden ein. Der Onkel wartete schon auf mich, weil er mich immer durchhaute, wenn ich eingesperrt war. Ich schrie aber gleich, daß er schuld ist, weil er die Rechnung so falsch gemacht hat, und daß der Professor gesagt hat, so was kann bloß ein Esel machen.

Da haute er mich erst recht durch, und dann ging er fort. Der Greither Heinrich, mein Freund, hat ihn gesehen, wie er auf der Straße mit dem Professor gegangen ist, und wie sie immer stehen blieben und der Onkel recht eifrig geredet hat. 5

Am nächsten Tag hat mich der Professor aufgerufen und sagte: „Ich habe deine Rechnung noch einmal durchgelesen; sie ist ganz richtig, aber nach einer alten Methode, welche es nicht mehr gibt. Es schadet dir aber nichts, daß du eingesperrt warst, weil du es eigentlich immer verdienst, und weil du beim Abschreiben Fehler gemacht hast.“ 10

Das haben sie miteinander ausgemacht, denn der Onkel sagte gleich, wie ich heimkam: „Ich habe mit deinem Professor gesprochen. Die Rechnung war schon gut, aber du hast beim Abschreiben nicht aufgepaßt, du Lausbub.“ 15

Ich habe schon aufgepaßt, es war nur ganz falsch.

Aber meine Mutter schrieb mir, daß ihr der Onkel geschrieben hat, daß er mir nicht mehr nachhelfen kann, weil ich die einfachsten Rechnungen nicht abschreiben kann, und weil er dadurch in Verlegenheit kommt. 20

Das ist ein gemeiner Mensch.

FRAGEN

1. Bei wem wohnt der „Lausbub“? 2. Gefällt es ihm in der Stadt? 3. Ist Onkel Franz ein besserer Mathematiker als der Erzähler (*narrator*)? 4. Glauben Sie, daß Onkel Franz die Aufgabe, an der er den ganzen Nachmittag arbeitete, richtig löste? 5. Glauben Sie, daß der Lausbub beim Abschreiben wirklich Fehler gemacht hat? 6. Was schrieb Onkel Franz der Mutter des Erzählers? 7. Warum ist Onkel Franz ein gemeiner Mensch?

SICH SELBST WEGEN BIGAMIE ANGEZEIGT *

Ingolstadt (Eigener Bericht) — Vor dem Schöffengericht mußte sich der 43jährige Klempner Ruprecht D. wegen Bigamie verantworten. D. stammt aus Odessa, wo er mit 18 Jahren eine volksdeutsche Fabrikarbeiterin heiratete, die ihm eine Tochter gebar. 1943 wurde er zu einer deutschen Polizeieinheit eingezogen. Am Ende 25

* jemanden wegen . . . anzeigen — *denounce someone for, charge someone with*

LINE

1 einsperren — *lock up*
2 durchhauen — *give a thrashing*
5 erst recht — *all the more; really*
7 stehen bleiben — *stop*
eifrig — *excitedly, animatedly*
9 aufrufen — *call on*
11 schaden — *harm*
12 verdienen — *deserve*
21 gemein — *vulgar, mean*
22 der Bericht — *report*

LINE

22 das Schöffengericht — *court of judge and jury*
22–3 sich . . . wegen Bigamie verantworten — *answer the charge of bigamy*
23 der Klempner — *plumber*
stammt aus — *comes from, was born in*
24 volksdeutsch — *of German origin*
25 die Polizeieinheit — *police unit*
eingezogen — *drafted*

des Krieges geriet er in amerikanische Gefangenschaft, aus der er 1946 entlassen wurde. Seine Angehörigen waren inzwischen nach Westen geflohen. Von Berlin aus erhielt er im April 1945 die letzte Nachricht von seiner Familie. Von da an fehlte jede Spur. Es hieß, alle Rußlanddeutschen seien nach Osten verschleppt 5 worden. D. baute sich in Regensburg eine Existenz auf und heiratete 1952 in der Annahme, daß seine erste Frau tot sei, eine Landwirtstochter. Dabei verschwieg er, daß er bereits verheiratet war. Seine Eltern und Geschwister hatte er für tot erklären lassen. 1956 erhielt er vom Roten Kreuz die Mitteilung, daß seine erste Frau, seine Tochter und seine bereits totgesagten Eltern in Ostsibirien lebten, 10 wohin sie verschleppt worden waren. D. ging daraufhin zur Polizei und zeigte sich selbst wegen Bigamie an. Unter Zubilligung mildernder Umstände verurteilte ihn das Schöffengericht Ingolstadt zu sechs Monaten Gefängnisstrafe und einer Buße von 100 Mark. D. hat inzwischen — allerdings ohne Erfolg — alles versucht, um die Rückführung seiner Angehörigen aus Rußland zu erreichen.

Nach einem Bericht der *Süddeutschen Zeitung*,
Nr. 124/125, Pfingsten 1958, Seite 15.

FRAGEN

1. Wer zeigte Ruprecht D. an? 2. Weswegen (*On account of what*) mußte sich Ruprecht D. verantworten? 3. Woher stammte Ruprecht D.? 4. Wen heiratete er? Was war seine erste Frau? 5. Was war sein Schicksal (*fate*) während des Krieges? 6. Wann erhielt er die letzte Nachricht von seiner Familie? 7. Wo baute er sich eine neue Existenz auf? 8. In welcher Annahme heiratete er zum zweiten Mal? 9. Was war seine zweite Frau? 10. Was verschwieg Ruprecht D. seiner zweiten Frau? 11. Wen hatte er für tot erklären lassen? 12. Welche Mitteilung erhielt er 1956 vom Roten Kreuz? 13. Was tat er daraufhin? 14. Wie lautete (*What was*) das Urteil des Schöffengerichts Ingolstadt? 15. Gelang es Ruprecht D. (*Did Ruprecht D. succeed in*), die Rückführung seiner Angehörigen aus Rußland zu erreichen?

LINE

1 geraten — *get into*
geriet in amerikanische Gefangenschaft — *was captured by the Americans*
entlassen — *release*
2 die Angehörigen — *relatives*
inzwischen — *meanwhile*
3 die Nachricht — *report, news*
4 die Spur — *trace*
die Rußlanddeutschen — *Russo-Germans*
seien — *had*
verschleppen — *"drag away," transport forcibly*
6 die Annahme — *supposition, assumption*
die Landwirtstochter — *farmer's daughter*
verschweigen — *keep secret*

LINE

7 bereits — *already*
verheiratet — *married*
7–8 Seine Eltern und Geschwister . . . erklären lassen — *He had his parents, brothers, and sisters officially declared dead*
9 totgesagten — *declared dead*
10 daraufhin — *thereupon*
11 Unter Zubilligung mildernder Umstände — *Allowing for extenuating circumstances*
verurteilen — *sentence, condemn*
12 sechs Monate Gefängnisstrafe — *six months' imprisonment*
13 die Buße — *fine*
14 die Rückführung — *return*
erreichen — *bring about*

MILLIONENSTRAFE FÜR UHRENSCHMUGGEL

Warschau (up) — Die beiden österreichischen Staatsbürger Bernhardt Bass und Franz Keymar sind von einem Warschauer Gericht wegen Uhrenschmuggels zu je 1 825 000 Zlotys (nach amtlichem Kurs etwa 1,9 Millionen Mark) verurteilt worden. Sie sollen im vergangenen Jahr versucht haben, 4 806 Uhren nach Polen einzuschmuggeln. Das Gericht ordnete ferner die Beschlagnahme der Uhren und des Wagens an, in dem die Uhren gefunden worden waren.

Aus der *Süddeutschen Zeitung*,
Nr. 124/125, Pfingsten 1958, Seite, 16.

A MILLION MARK FINE FOR WATCH SMUGGLING

Warsaw (UP) — Two Austrians, Bernhardt Bass and Franz Keymar, were each fined by a Warsaw court 1,825,000 zlotys (about 1,900,000 marks according to the official rate of exchange) for smuggling watches. It is reported they tried to smuggle 4,806 watches into Poland during the past year. Furthermore, the court ordered the seizure of the watches and the car in which the watches had been found.

From the *Süddeutsche Zeitung*,
No. 124/125, Pentecost 1958, page 16.

VICE VERSA

Ein Hase sitzt auf einer Wiese,
des Glaubens, niemand sähe diese.

Doch, im Besitze eines Zeißes,
betrachtet voll gehaltnen Fleißes

vom vis-à-vis gelegnen Berg
Ein Mensch den kleinen Löffelzwerg.

Ihn aber blickt hinwiederum
ein Gott von fern an, mild und stumm.

Christian Morgenstern

VICE VERSA

A hare sits on a meadow green,
Believing it's by no one seen.

But through field lenses made by Zeiss
A man intently trains his eyes

Now, vis-à-vis, from hilltop height
Upon this tiny spoon-eared mite.

A God far off though, following suit,
Watches the watcher, gently, mute.

ACHTER TEIL

Frühling in Marburg

Bayrischer Volkstanz

Die enge Drosselgasse in Rüdesheim am Rhein. Dieses altertümliche kleine Städtchen liegt in der Heimat der besten deutschen Weine.

22. Aufgabe

GESPRÄCH IM FRÜHLING

Read and memorize the following dialogue:

HANS: Liebste Maria, wenn ich dir nur sagen könnte, wie sehr ich dich liebe!

MARIA: Mir scheint, als hättest du das schon vielen Mädchen gesagt, lieber Hans.

HANS: Wenn du wüßtest, wie aufrichtig ich bin, würdest du das nicht sagen, liebste Maria.

MARIA: Wenn du wirklich aufrichtig wärest, lieber Hans, so hättest du mir gewiß keine Liebeserklärung gemacht.

HANS: Du tust so, als gäbe es keine wahre Liebe. Glaubst du denn nicht an die Liebe, Liebste?

MARIA: Oh doch, lieber Hans. Und lieber wäre es mir, wenn ich auch dir glauben könnte.

HANS: Das kannst du. Wer soll dich daran hindern, Geliebte?

MARIA: Meine Freundin Grete, mein lieber Hans.

HANS: Liebe Maria — als ginge das deine Freundin etwas an!

MARIA: Wenn sie mir nur nicht erzählt hätte, was du ihr gestern gesagt hast, lieber Hans!

HANS: Und was wäre das, was ich — angeblich — zu ihr gesagt haben sollte?

MARIA: Liebste Grete, hast du gesagt, wenn ich dir doch nur sagen könnte, wie sehr ich dich liebe!

CONVERSATION IN SPRING

HANS: Dearest Maria, if I could just tell you how very much I love you.

MARIA: It seems to me as if you had already said this to many girls, dear Hans.

HANS: If you knew how sincere I am, you wouldn't say this, dearest Maria.

MARIA: If you were really sincere, my dear Hans, you certainly would not have made any declaration of love to me.

HANS: You act as if there were no such thing as true love. Don't you really believe in love, my love?

MARIA: I certainly do, my dear Hans. And I would prefer it if I could believe you too.

HANS: You can. Who is to prevent you, beloved?

MARIA: My friend Grete, my dear Hans.

HANS: Dear Maria — as if this concerned your friend at all!

MARIA: If only she hadn't told me what you told her yesterday, dear Hans.

HANS: And what might it be that I — allegedly — was supposed to have told her?

MARIA: Dearest Grete, you said, if only I could tell you how very much I love you.

DRILL PATTERNS

Repeat the following drill after your instructor or after the speaker on the tape. Imitate the pronunciation very carefully.

1. Wenn er aufrichtig wäre, { täte er das nicht. / würde er das nicht tun.

Wenn sie aufrichtig wären, { würden sie das nicht tun. / täten sie das nicht.

Wenn ihr aufrichtig wäret, { würdet ihr das nicht tun. / tätet ihr das nicht.

2. Wenn er aufrichtig gewesen wäre, { würde er das nicht gesagt haben. / hätte er das nicht gesagt.

Wenn sie aufrichtig gewesen wären, { hätten sie das nicht gesagt. / würden sie das nicht gesagt haben.

Wenn ihr aufrichtig gewesen wäret, { hättet ihr das nicht gesagt. / würdet ihr das nicht gesagt haben.

3. Wenn er sie liebte, könnte er das nicht tun.
Wenn sie ihn liebte, könnte sie das nicht tun.

4. Wenn er sie geliebt hätte, hätte er das nicht tun können.
Wenn sie ihn geliebt hätte, hätte sie das nicht tun können.

5. Hätte er sie geliebt, so hätte er das nicht getan.
Hätte sie ihn geliebt, so hätte sie das nicht tun können.

6. Wenn sie ihm nur nicht glaubte!
Hätte sie ihm nur nicht geglaubt!
An ihrer Stelle[1] hätte ich ihm kein Wort geglaubt.

7. Wer hätte gedacht, daß Hans so etwas tun könnte!
Ich hätte das einfach[2] nicht tun können.
Ich hätte das an seiner Stelle bestimmt nicht getan.

8. Hätten Sie an ihrer Stelle etwas anderes gesagt?
Hätten Sie an ihrer Stelle nicht dasselbe sagen müssen?
Hätten Sie an ihrer Stelle etwas anderes tun können?

9. Er tut so, { als ginge ihn das etwas an. / als ob ihn das etwas anginge.

Warum tut er so, { als ginge euch das etwas an? / als ob euch das etwas anginge?

10. Warum hat er so getan, als wäre ihn das etwas angegangen?
Wäre ihn das etwas angegangen, so hätte er uns nichts davon erzählt.

11. Wenn ich das wüßte, würde ich es dir sagen.
Wenn du das wüßtest, würdest du es mir sagen.

[1] **an ihrer Stelle** in her place [2] **einfach** simple, simply

Wüßten sie es, so würden sie es euch sagen.
Auch wenn wir das wüßten, würden wir es Ihnen nicht sagen.
Warum würdet ihr es uns nicht sagen, wenn ihr es wüßtet?

12. „Möchten Sie nicht ins Kino gehen?"
„Das möchte ich schon, aber ich sollte studieren."
„Könnten Sie nicht morgen studieren? Ich dächte, dazu wäre morgen noch Zeit."

13. „Wäre es Ihnen recht, wenn ich heute käme?"
„Ein ander Mal wäre mir lieber."
„Wäre es Ihnen recht, wenn wir morgen kämen?"
„Ich sähe Sie lieber nächste Woche."

14. Mir wäre es lieber, wenn sie nicht käme.
Ihr wäre es lieber, wenn Sie nicht kämen.
Uns wäre es lieber, wenn er nicht käme.
Ihm wäre es lieber, wenn ihr nicht kämet.

15. Wäre es Ihnen lieber, wenn sie nicht käme?
Sie sähe Sie gerne, bevor sie abreist.
Sie hätte Sie gerne noch gesehen.
Es wäre mir lieber, wenn Sie sie gesehen hätten.
Hätten Sie sie vor ihrer Abreise nicht noch sehen können?
Wenn ihr das recht gewesen wäre, hätte ich es gerne getan.

16. Wenn er reich [1] wäre, hätte er sich längst [2] ein Haus gekauft.
Wenn er das Haus gesehen hätte, so hätte er es sich gekauft.
Hätte er das Haus gesehen, so hätte er es auch gekauft.

17. Wenn er Geld hat, kauft er sich einen neuen Wagen.
Man kauft sich doch keinen neuen Wagen, wenn man kein Geld hat.
Wenn er Geld hätte, würde er sich einen neuen Wagen kaufen.
Wenn er kein Geld hätte, würde er sich doch keinen neuen Wagen kaufen.
Wenn er kein Geld gehabt hätte, hätte er sich doch keinen neuen Wagen gekauft.

18. Wenn ich nicht Schlittschuhlaufen [3] gegangen wäre, hätte ich mich nicht erkältet.
Wärt ihr nicht Skilaufen [4] gegangen, so hättet ihr euch nicht erkältet.

19. Wenn er nicht hier geblieben wäre, { so würde er ihr keine Liebeserklärung gemacht haben. / so hätte er ihr keine Liebeserklärung gemacht. }
Er hätte ihr keine Liebeserklärung gemacht, wenn er nicht hier geblieben wäre.

English to German

Study Grammar Section 43 before preparing the following exercise in writing.

1) If I could only tell you **vl** how much I love you! **vl**
If they could only tell us **vl** who she is! **vl**

[1] **reich** rich [2] **längst** a long time ago [3] **das Schlittschuhlaufen** skating [4] **das Skilaufen** skiing

2) Would you tell (it) me, **vf/vl** if you knew that? **vl** (*3 ways*)
Would you have told (it) me, **vf/vl** if you had known that? **vl** (*3 ways*)

3) It seems to me **vs** as if you had said that before.[1] **vl**

4) Would it be all right with you (*3 ways*), **vf** if we came today? **vl**
Would they prefer it, **vf/vl** if we came tomorrow? **vl**

5) If the weather should change, **vl** we would turn back. **vf/vl** (*Use* **würde** *for the conclusion.*)
If you were sincere, **vl** you would not say this. **vf/vl** (*Use* **würde** *for the conclusion.*)

6) You could do that? **vs/vl**
You should hear her. **vs/vl**

7) If you had been sincere, **vl** you would not have said this. **vf/vl** (*Express the conclusion in two different ways.*)

8) What would you do in her place? **vs**
What would you have done in her place? **vs/vl**

9) If I had enough money, **vl** I would buy a car. **vf/vl**
If he were rich, **vl** he would buy this house. **vf/vl**

10) If I had been rich, **vl** I would have bought that house. **vf/vl**
I would have taken a trip, **vs/vl** if I had had enough money. **vl**

11) If only she loved me! **vl**
If only she had loved him! **vl**

Translate the following sentences without the help of the key:

12) If only he would believe her!
If only he had believed us!

13) He acts as if he were in love.[2]

14) Who would have thought that!

15) It would be good, if she could do it. (*Express the first clause in two different ways.*)
It would be nice, if I could speak German. (*Express the first clause in two different ways.*)

GRAMMAR

43. Subjunctive

a. FORMATION

In contrast to the indicative, the subjunctive forms show few irregularities:

1. Personal Endings:

With the exception of the present tense of **sein** (see page 192 [3]) all tenses of all verbs follow a uniform personal-ending pattern.

ich **–e**		wir **–en**
du **–est**	Sie **–en**	ihr **–et**
sie (es, er) **–e**		sie **–en**

[1] before **schon** [2] in love **verliebt**

2. Present Subjunctive:

Neither vowel changes nor other irregularities sometimes found in the present indicative appear in the present subjunctive.

ich	seh**e**		wir	seh**en**
du	seh**est**	Sie seh**en**	ihr	seh**et**
sie (es, er)	seh**e**		sie	seh**en**
ich	hab**e**		wir	hab**en**
du	hab**est**	Sie hab**en**	ihr	hab**et**
sie (es, er)	hab**e**		sie	hab**en**
ich	werd**e**		wir	werd**en**
du	werd**est**	Sie werd**en**	ihr	werd**et**
sie (es, er)	werd**e**		sie	werd**en**

3. Present Subjunctive of **sein:**

ich	sei		wir	sei**en**
du	sei**(e)st**	Sie sei**en**	ihr	sei**et**
sie (es, er)	sei		sie	sei**en**

4. Past Subjunctive:

(i) *Weak verbs*

Since weak verbs show no vowel changes throughout and since their past tense endings are exactly like the subjunctive pattern, there is then no formal difference whatever between indicative past and subjunctive past in weak verbs:

ich	sag**te**		wir	sag**ten**
du	sag**test**	Sie sag**ten**	ihr	sag**tet**
sie (es, er)	sag**te**		sie	sag**ten**

(ii) *Strong verbs*

Strong-verb stem vowels capable of carrying umlaut regularly do so in the past subjunctive:

ich	säh**e**		wir	säh**en**
du	säh**est**	Sie säh**en**	ihr	säh**et**
sie (es, er)	säh**e**		sie	säh**en**

NOTE:

A. Six of the seven verbs classified as irregulars in this book have umlaut in the past subjunctive:

hätte, käme, täte, wäre, stände (*or* stünde), würde

B. The past subjunctive of the modals and **wissen:**

dürfte, könnte, müßte, möchte, sollte, wollte, wüßte

Sollte and **wollte** serve as both indicative and subjunctive forms.

C. The past subjunctive of weak-strong verbs:

brächte, brennte, dächte, kennte, nennte, rennte, sendete, wendete

The last two are sometimes used as indicative as well as subjunctive forms.

D. The past subjunctive of **helfen** and **sterben** show **ü** instead of **ä**:
hülfe, stürbe

5. Third person singular synopsis of the subjunctive of **sein, haben, kaufen, sehen:**

Present:	sei	habe	kaufe	sehe
Present perfect:	sei gewesen	habe gehabt	habe gekauft	habe gesehen
Past:	**wäre**	**hätte**	**kaufte**	**sähe**
Past perfect:	**wäre gewesen**	**hätte gehabt**	**hätte gekauft**	**hätte gesehen**
Future:	werde sein	werde haben	werde kaufen	werde sehen
Future perfect:	werde gewesen sein	werde gehabt haben	werde gekauft haben	werde gesehen haben

b. IMAGINATIVE FORMS

For the purpose of the immediate discussion we are concerned only with the past and the past perfect tenses (as indicated in boldface type above):

wäre	*were, would be*	wäre gewesen	*had been, would have been*
hätte	*had, would have*	hätte gehabt	*had had, would have had*
kaufte	*bought, would buy*	hätte gekauft	*had bought, would have bought*
sähe	*saw, would see*	hätte gesehen	*had seen, would have seen*

Consider the following sentence:

Wenn ich schwer krank wäre, wäre ich ja nicht hier.
(*If I were seriously ill, I wouldn't of course be here.*)

NOTE:

A. The above sentence expresses a contrary-to-fact or imagined situation.
B. The subjunctive forms are based on past tense stems (see **wäre** *were*), but:
C. The situation refers to *present time.*
D. It is therefore a present imaginative situation.
E. The verb forms may then also be termed *present imaginative.*
F. The conclusion of a present imaginative statement often can refer to the future, implied or clearly indicated:

Wenn ich Geld hätte, kaufte ich mir (sogleich, heute, morgen) einen neuen Wagen.
(*If I had the money, I would buy myself a new car* [*right away, today, tomorrow*].)

Examples of the *past perfect subjunctive* or, as it will be called hereafter, the *past imaginative:*

Wenn ich schwer krank gewesen wäre, dann wäre ich ja nicht hier gewesen.
Wenn ich Geld gehabt hätte, hätte ich mir einen neuen Wagen gekauft.
Hätte ich Geld gehabt, so hätte ich mir einen neuen Wagen gekauft.
Hätte er das gesehen, so wäre er gewiß zu Hause geblieben.

Imaginative forms with **als ob:**

Mir ist, als ob ich die Hände
Aufs Haupt dir legen sollt' . . . (*See page 23.*)

Es schien, { als ob sein Freund Werner verrückt wäre.
als wäre sein Freund Werner verrückt.

c. CONDITIONAL FORMS

There are two conditional tenses, present and past. Notice the similarity between the conditional forms and the future and future perfect subjunctive forms:

	werde : würde
Future subj.:	sie (es, er) werde sein (haben, kaufen, sehen, *etc.*)
Future perf. subj.:	sie (es, er) werde gewesen sein (gehabt haben, gekauft haben, gesehen haben, *etc.*)
Present conditional:	sie (es, er) würde sein (haben, kaufen, sehen, *etc.*)
Past conditional:	sie (es, er) würde gewesen sein (gehabt haben, gekauft haben, gesehen haben, *etc.*)

The present and past conditional forms are frequently used as replacements for the present and past imaginative, respectively, in the conclusion clauses of contrary-to-fact or imaginative statements:

Wenn ich schwer krank wäre, { wäre ich ja nicht hier.
würde ich ja nicht hier sein.

Wenn ich schwer krank gewesen wäre, { wäre ich ja nicht hier gewesen.
würde ich ja nicht hier gewesen sein.

Wenn ich Geld hätte, { kaufte ich mir einen neuen Wagen.
würde ich mir einen neuen Wagen kaufen.

Wenn ich Geld gehabt hätte, { hätte ich mir einen neuen Wagen gekauft.
würde ich mir einen neuen Wagen gekauft haben.

Wenn er gestern wirklich so krank gewesen wäre, { könnte er heute nicht ins Kino gehen.
würde er heute nicht ins Kino gehen können.

d. IMAGINATIVE FORMS EXPRESSING A HOPE OR WISH

These are simply the forms found in abbreviated contrary-to-fact or imaginative statements. **Nur** or **doch** (or the like) is used for emphasis:

Wenn ich nur Geld gehabt hätte! Hätte ich nur Geld gehabt!	*If I only had had money!*
Wenn ich doch Geld hätte!	*If I only had money!*
Wenn er doch ginge!	*If he would only go!*
Wenn ich nur mitgegangen wäre! Wäre ich nur mitgegangen!	*If I only had gone along!*

23. Aufgabe

WER BIN ICH?

	SAMPLE ANSWERS AND SUGGESTIONS
a. Was täten Sie, wenn Sie viel Geld hätten?	*Wenn ich viel Geld hätte, würde ich . . .*
Würden Sie eine Weltreise machen?	
Welche Länder möchten Sie besuchen?	
Würden Sie sich einen neuen Wagen kaufen?	*Ja, ich würde mir einen neuen Wagen kaufen. Nein, ich würde mir keinen neuen Wagen kaufen.*
Haben Sie einen Führerschein? [1]	
Welcher Wagen wäre Ihnen am liebsten?	*Am liebsten wäre mir . . .*
Hätten Sie lieber einen amerikanischen oder einen französischen (italienischen, deutschen, englischen) Wagen?	
Würden Sie sich ein Flugzeug kaufen?	
b. Was täten Sie, wenn Sie viel Zeit hätten?	
Wie oft würden Sie tanzen gehen?	
Welchen Sport würden Sie betreiben? [2]	
Würden Sie gerne Tennis oder Golf spielen?	
Würden Sie viele Bücher lesen?	
Was für Bücher würden Sie lesen?	
c. Was hätten Sie am letzten Wochenende am liebsten getan?	
Wären Sie gerne ins Theater oder ins Kino gegangen?	*Ich wäre gerne ins . . . gegangen.*
Welchen Film [3] hätten Sie sehen wollen?	*Ich hätte gerne . . . sehen wollen.*
Haben Sie je [4] einen deutschen Film gesehen?	
Hätten Sie gerne Baseball gespielt?	
Wären Sie gerne aufs Land [5] gefahren?	
Wären Sie gerne fischen oder jagen [6] gegangen?	
Hätten Sie gerne einen Berg bestiegen?	
Hätten Sie lieber Bridge oder Schach [7] gespielt?	
Hätten Sie nicht Ihren Eltern schreiben können?	
Oder hatten Sie dazu keine Zeit?	
Hätten Sie nicht studieren sollen?	*Ja, ich hätte studieren sollen.*
Oder haben Sie das nicht nötig? [8]	

[1] **der Führerschein** driver's license [2] **betreiben** engage *or* participate in [3] **der Film** moving picture [4] **je** ever [5] **aufs Land** to the country [6] **jagen** hunt [7] **das Schach** chess [8] **Haben Sie das nicht nötig?** Don't you need to?

Skiläufer in den Alpen nahe der Schweizer Grenze.

DRILL PATTERNS

Repeat the following drill after your instructor or after the speaker on the tape. Imitate the pronunciation very carefully.

1. Es sah so aus, als ob es regnen würde.
Es sah aus, als würde es schneien.
Es sah aus, als ob die Sonne wieder scheinen würde.

2. Er sollte so etwas nicht sagen.
Er würde das nicht sagen.
Er wird das wohl nicht gesagt haben.

3. Er hat es gewollt.
Er hatte es gewollt.
Er hatte es tun wollen.
Er hätte es tun wollen.

4. Er hätte es tun dürfen.
Er hätte es tun müssen.
Er hätte es tun können.
Er hätte es tun sollen.
Er hätte das nicht sagen sollen.

5. Das hätte er gewiß nicht tun müssen.
Das hätte sie vielleicht nicht tun wollen.
Das hätten auch Sie nicht tun sollen.
Das hätte sie eben [1] nicht glauben dürfen.

6. Wenn ich dir nur glauben könnte!
Hätte ich dir nur geglaubt!
Du hättest mir glauben können!
Du hättest mir glauben sollen.
Du hättest mir glauben müssen.

7. Sie saß mir gegenüber.[2]
Er saß ihr gegenüber.
Wer wohnt in dem Haus gegenüber?
Wer steht Ihnen gegenüber?

8. Meiner Meinung [3] nach [4] hätten Sie gestern Ihren Eltern schreiben sollen.
Seiner Meinung nach hätte ich gestern studieren sollen.
Unserer Meinung nach hätten Sie mit uns aufs Land fahren sollen.

9. Einem Gerücht [5] zufolge [6] wird dieser berühmte Filmstar sich bald zum siebenten Mal verheiraten.
Einer verläßlichen Quelle [7] zufolge soll die Konferenz der Westmächte verschoben [8] werden.

English to German

Prepare this exercise in writing.

1) They were able to do it. **vs/vl**
They have not been able to do it. **vs/vl**
They would not have been able to do it. **vs/vl**

2) They have had to do it. **vs/vl**
They would have had to do it. **vs/vl**

3) They should have done it. **vs/vl**
She should not have said that. **vs/vl**

4) What would [9] he do **vs/vl** if he had money? **vl**
What would he have done **vs/vl** if he had had money? **vl**
What could he have done? **vs/vl**

[1] **eben** just, simply (*intensifies a statement*) [2] **gegenüber** opposite, vis-à-vis [3] **die Meinung** opinion [4] **nach** *here:* according to [5] **das Gerücht** rumor [6] **zufolge** according to [7] **die verläßliche Quelle** reliable source [8] **verschieben** postpone [9] *For* "would" *and the infinitive use the conditional.*

Translate the following sentences without the aid of the key:

5) Would you like to go to the movies?
Would she have gone to the movies?
Could she have gone to the movies?

6) It looked as if it would rain.

GRAMMAR

44. Past Imaginative of Modals

In many of the previous illustrations of the imaginative subjunctive, we have seen the important part that an umlaut can play in transforming fact to fancy, the real to the unreal. This is vividly illustrated especially in the past imaginative of the modal auxiliaries. Note, for example, the difference between:

Sie hatten sich retten können.
They had been able to save themselves.

and

Sie hätten sich retten können.
They would have been able to save themselves (or *could have saved themselves*). (*But didn't.*)

Illustrations of other modals in the past imaginative

Ich hätte um halb acht abfahren sollen.	*I should have left at half past seven.*
Er hätte das tun mögen.	*He would have liked to do that.*
Er hätte im Juli in Salzburg bleiben wollen.	*He would have wanted to stay in Salzburg in July.*
Wir hätten umkehren müssen, wenn das Wetter nicht gewechselt hätte.	*We would have had to turn back if the weather had not changed.*
Wenn ihr die Aufgaben fertig gemacht hättet, hättet ihr ins Kino gehen dürfen.	*If you had finished your homework, you would have been permitted to go to the movies.*

45. Postpositive Prepositions

This is a group of prepositions that frequently follow rather than precede the noun or pronoun they govern:

gegenüber opposite, facing (*with preceding dative*)
nach according to, on the authority of (*with preceding dative*)
zufolge according to, by virtue of, owing to (*with preceding dative*)
wegen because of, on behalf of, regarding (*with genitive*)

Illustrations

Ihm gegenüber saß das junge Mädchen, das ihn lächelnd anschaute.	*Opposite him sat the young girl, who looked at him smiling.*

Seinem Aussehen nach mochte er ein reicher Mann gewesen sein.	*According to* (i.e. *to judge by*) *his appearance, he might* (*possibly*) *have been a rich man.*
Die Rechnung ist **meiner Meinung nach** falsch.	*The calculation* (or *bill*) *is, in my opinion, inaccurate.*
Unserem Psychologieprofessor zufolge wird die gesamte Menschheit einst durch Psychiatrie geheilt werden.	*According to our psychology professor, all humanity will some day be healed through psychiatry.*
Der Flug wurde **des schlechten Wetters wegen** abgesagt.	*The flight was cancelled because of bad weather.*

46. Extended Participial Phrases

In German and English a *relative clause* together with the antecedent of the relative pronoun can often be reduced to a single *phrase* containing, for example, definite (or indefinite) article, attributive adjective, and noun:

das Buch, das alt ist — das alte Buch
the book that is old — the old book

eine Methode, die völlig neu ist — eine völlig neue Methode
a method that is entirely new — an entirely new method

The attributive adjective can be, and often is, a participle, present or past:

das Kind, welches ruhig schläft — das ruhig **schlafende** Kind
the child that is peacefully asleep — the peacefully ***sleeping*** *child*

ein Kind, welches höchst aufgeregt ist — ein höchst **aufgeregtes** Kind
a child that is most excited — a most ***excited*** *child*

Up to this point in the above phrases there is no difference in speech pattern between German and English. However, German can stretch phrases, even of the participial type, to points where English cannot venture. The presence, for example, of a *prepositional phrase* can be accommodated within a single, self-contained *participial phrase* in German, but not in English, as indicated here:

RELATIVE CLAUSE	PARTICIPIAL PHRASE
das Kind, welches **im Bett** ruhig schläft —	das **im Bett** ruhig schlafende Kind
the child that is peacefully sleeping ***in the bed***	

It would be a violation of accepted English word order and idiom here to insist on following the German participial phrase pattern, „das im Bett ruhig schlafende Kind"; "the in the bed peacefully sleeping child" is obviously unacceptable English.

German writers often use (notably in expository prose) extended participial phrases of the kind we have been discussing. They are used, as indicated above, to replace relative clauses — for the purpose of linguistic economy.

Illustrations

1. Das Geschichtsbuch, welches Professor Braun schrieb, ist überall bekannt.
   Das **von Professor Braun geschriebene** Geschichtsbuch ist überall bekannt.
2. Sie verglichen die verschiedenen **im Lauf der Jahre aufgetretenen** Titelhelden des „Jedermann."
3. Der **1946 aus der amerikanischen Gefangenschaft entlassene** Ruprecht D. baute sich in Regensburg eine neue Existenz auf.
4. Der **wegen Bigamie angezeigte** Klempner wurde zu sechs Monaten Gefängnis verurteilt.
5. Der **am 3. Mai im Krankenhaus eingelieferte** siebzehnjährige Otto H. erholte sich nach wenigen Wochen.
6. Einer verläßlichen Quelle zufolge soll die **ursprünglich** (*originally*) **im Juni angesetzte** (*scheduled*) Konferenz der Westmächte verschoben werden.

Whereas the above illustrations are taken from or based upon material already dealt with in preceding units, the following examples will be found in the Readings of the next lessons:

7. Ein **im atlantischen Ozean versenkter** Süßwassersee ist eine Anomalie.

   A fresh water lake ***that became submerged in the Atlantic Ocean*** *is an anomaly.*

8. Das **später von anderen berichtigte, modifizierte und weiter ausgearbeitete** Sprachgesetz von Jakob Grimm hat im Grunde zwei Teile.

   The linguistic law (formulated) by Jacob Grimm, (***which was***) ***later corrected, modified, and elaborated by others,*** *has basically two parts.*

9. Als diese **lose zur Einheit gefügte** Ursprache zu zerfallen begann, traten immer schärfer Spaltungen und Unterschiede zu Tage.

   As this ***loosely united*** *primitive language began to break up, divisions and differences became more and more sharply evident.*

10. Englisch und Deutsch sind nur zwei Angehörige einer beträchtlichen Anzahl von **organisch miteinander verbundenen** Sprachen innerhalb einer großen Sprachfamilie, deren weitreichende Wirkung im Laufe der Geschichte kaum zu ermessen ist.

    English and German are only two (members) of a large number of ***organically interrelated*** *languages within a big family of languages, whose far-reaching effect through the course of history can hardly be calculated.*

24. Aufgabe

VOCABULARY BUILDING

The following strong and irregular verbs are from Units VII and VIII, where they appear as new verbs. Frequent reference to their principal parts will help you in the formation of the past tenses.

CLASS 1

ei ie ie

schreien *shriek, scream, shout*
betreiben *engage* or *participate in*
besteigen *climb, scale*

ei i i

begreifen *grasp, comprehend*

CLASS 2

ie o o

verschieben *postpone;* (refl.) *shift*

CLASS 3

i a o

gewinnen *win, gain*

i a u

klingen *sound, ring (clang)*
springen *jump, spring*
verbinden *unite, bind*

CLASS 4

e (i) a e

(sich) ergeben *come to pass (to light), surrender*
ermessen *estimate*

e (i) a o

gelten *be worth;* gelten für *be true of*
entsprechen *correspond*

CLASS 5

a (ä) i a

empfangen *receive*

a (ä) ie a

enthalten *hold, contain*
zerfallen *fall apart, break up*

a (ä) u a

graben *dig*

IRREGULARS

bekommen, bekam, bekommen *get, receive*
bestehen, bestand, bestanden *pass* (a test); bestehen aus *consist of*
vergehen, verging, vergangen *pass* (of time)

The following words are based on strong and irregular verb stems. (Almost all of these are used in the next reading selection.)

der Abkömmling (kommen) *descendant*
ab *from*
kommen *come*
-ling (*masc. dim. suffix*)

die Ansicht (sehen) *view, opinion*
an *at*
sehen *look*

ausgestorben (sterben) *extinct*
aus *out*
gestorben *died*

bekanntlich (kennen) *as is well known*
bekannt *well known*
-lich (*adj.-adv. suffix*)

der Beweis (weisen *show*) *proof, evidence*
beweisen *prove*

entlegen (liegen) *distant, removed, remote*
ent- *away from*
gelegen *lain, situated*

entschieden (entscheiden *decide*) *decided(ly)* (*p.p. used as adj. or adv.*)

entsprechend (entsprechen *correspond*) *corresponding(ly)*
(*pres. p. used as adj. or adv.*)

der Gang (gehen: gegangen) *gait, passage, course*

die Gewißheit (wissen) *certainty*
gewiß *certain*
–heit (*abstract suffix*)

die Herkunft (kommen) *"coming hither," origin, descent*
her *here* (i.e., from there, hence)
–kunft = das Kommen

(*See:* die Ankunft *arrival*
die Wiederkunft *return*
die Zukunft *future*
künftig *future*)

der Leitgedanke (denken) *guiding thought*
leit(en) *lead, guide*
der Gedanke *thought*

schriftlich (schreiben) *in writing, written*
die Schrift *script, writing*
–lich (*adj.-adv. suffix*)

selbstverständlich (verstehen) *self-evident*
selbst *self*
verständlich *understandable, evident*

sogenannt (nennen *call*) *so-called*
genannt *called*

die Sprachkunde (kennen) *science of language, linguistics*
die Sprache *language*
die Kunde *knowledge* (often scientific)

(*See:* die Heilkunde *science of healing, medicine*)

sprachlich (sprechen) *linguistic*
die Sprache *language*

das Überbleibsel (bleiben) *remainder, remnant*
über *over*
bleiben *remain*
–sel (*dim. suffix*)

der Unterschied (scheiden *part, separate*) *difference, distinction*
unterscheiden *distinguish, differentiate*

der Ursprung (springen) *origin*
ur– (*prefix denoting "out of," referring to source* or *origin*)
der Sprung *leap, spring*

(*See:* ursprünglich *original*
die Urform *primitive form*
die Ursprache *primitive language*)

vergleichend (gleichen *liken, resemble*) *comparative*
vergleichen *compare*

vollständig (stehen) *complete*
voll *full*
der Stand *state*
–ig (*adj.-adv. suffix*)

der Vorzug (ziehen: zog) *priority, preference, superiority*
vor *before, in front of, ahead of*
ziehen *move, pull, draw*

(*See:* die Vorzugsstellung *privileged position*)

das Wesentliche (sein: gewesen) *the essential*
das Wesen (*from* "wesen," *archaic inf. now replaced by* sein) *being, existence, nature, essence*

WORD STUDY

WORD LIST (from next reading selection)

bilden form, shape, cultivate (*a person*)
die Ebene the plain (*based on* **eben** even, level)
das Geheim'nis secret, secrecy (*based on* **heim** home; **das Geheimnis:** *that which takes place within one's home*)
irgend any, some (*combines with* **ein, jemand, wo, wer, was, wie, wann,** etc.)
die Mitteilung communication (**mit** with; **teilen** share)
die schriftliche Mitteilung written communication
die mündliche Mitteilung oral communication (**der Mund** mouth)

WORDS BASED ON ein (*a, an, one*)

Many of these words have already been used. Most of them will appear in the reading selection immediately following.

Einander (*one another*) is frequently found in combination with prepositions, for example:

gegeneinander toward (*or* against) each other
miteinander with each other
nebeneinander next to each other
zueinander to each other

ein as verbal prefix = *in, into:*

einbringen bring in
der Einfluß influence
der Eingang entrance

ein (as equivalent to English *uni–*):

die Einheit unit, unity
einheitlich uniform
einig united, at one (*See* **die Vereinigten Staaten**)
einzig only, single; unique
einzigartig unique
die Einzigartigkeit uniqueness

Note also the following:

einerlei (ein + **–erlei** kind of) one and the same
Es ist mir einerlei. It is all the same to me.
einfach (ein + **–fach** department, division) simple
einige some, a few
einsam lonesome, alone (*see* **allein**)
einzeln single, individual (*see* **einzig** *above*)

IDIOMATIC EXPRESSIONS

All but the first in this series occur in the readings immediately following.

als (ob) *as if*
Mir scheint, als **hättest** du das schon oft gesagt.
Mir scheint, als ob du das schon oft gesagt **hättest.**
It seems to me as if you had often said that before.

Note the position of **hättest** in each of the above sentences, depending upon the presence or absence of **ob.**

Sein, when in direct association with a negative (**nicht, nichts, kaum**) and **zu** plus infinitive, frequently assumes the meaning of **können:**

Es ist eine Sprache, deren weitreichende Wirkung im Laufe der Geschichte kaum zu ermessen ist. *It is a language whose far-reaching effect in the course of history* ***can hardly be calculated.***

Note that English requires passive infinitive, whereas German uses **zu** plus active infinitive.

zu Tage treten *become evident*
Solche Unterschiede **traten** immer schärfer **zu Tage.** *Such differences* ***became*** *more and more sharply* ***evident.***

genau genommen *strictly speaking*
Genau genommen steht nur die indoiranische Gruppe außerhalb der Grenzen Europas. *Strictly speaking, only the Indo-Iranian group (of languages) stands outside the boundaries of Europe.*

gelten für *be true of, be said for*
Die Basken gehören wohl zu dem ältesten überlebenden Rassebestand Europas. Dasselbe mag auch für ihre Sprache gelten. *The Basques probably belong to the oldest surviving racial stock of Europe. The same may be true of their language too.*

sich niederlassen *settle (down)*
Die ursprünglichen Indoeuropäer ließen sich längs des Schwarzen Meeres nieder. *The original Indo-Europeans settled along the Black Sea.*

Reading

Aus Goethes *Sprüchen* *

Man könnt' erzogene Kinder gebären,
Wenn die Eltern erzogen wären.

Hätte Gott mich anders gewollt,
So hätt' er mich anders gebaut . . .

5 Es wäre nicht der Mühe wert, siebzig Jahr alt zu werden,
wenn alle Weisheit der Welt Torheit wäre vor Gott.

Was wär' ein Gott, der nur von außen stieße,
Im Kreis das All am Finger laufen ließe!

Wär' nicht das Auge sonnenhaft,
10 Die Sonne könnt' es nie erblicken;
Läg' nicht in uns des Gottes eigne Kraft,
Wie könnt' uns Göttliches entzücken!

Mir gäb' es keine größre Pein,
Wär' ich im Paradies allein.

* der Spruch — *epigram*

LINE
1 erzogen — *well bred*
5 der Mühe wert — *worth the trouble*
6 die Torheit — *folly*
7 stieße — *thrust*
8 der Kreis — *circle*
das All — *the universe*

LINE
9 sonnenhaft — *sun-like, radiant, capable of holding sunlight*
11 die Kraft — *power*
12 Göttliches — *the divine*
entzücken — *delight, enthrall*
13 die Pein — *pain, torture*

Aus Franz Werfels *Sinngedichten* *

Wenn mich der trockne heiße Durst nicht brennte,
So könnte nie ein eisiger Trank mich kühlen.
Wenn ich nicht durch den Wald der Krankheit rennte,
Genesung könnt' ich nie als Durchbruch fühlen.

Volkslied

Wenn ich ein Vöglein wär' 5
Und auch zwei Flüglein hätt',
Flög' ich zu dir;
Weil's aber nicht kann sein,
Bleib ich allhier.

READING DRILL

The purpose of this section is to anticipate the reading. The sentences are given bilingually and may be treated in much the same way as the basic dialogues, except that they are not to be memorized. For the sake of readier comprehension, the complex German sentences need to be divided into convenient units, as indicated below.

1. Als mündliche Mitteilung / reicht die Sprache ohne Zweifel zurück / bis in die tiefste, dunkelste Epoche der menschlichen Geschichte.

   Language as oral communication reaches back no doubt into the deepest, dimmest period of human history.

2. Man nimmt an, / daß die früheste schriftliche Mitteilung / nicht älter sei als siebentausend Jahre. Allerdings könnte wohl niemand genau angeben, / wie weit verbreitet die schriftliche Mitteilung / in dieser entlegenen Epoche war.

   It is estimated that the earliest written communication goes back no more than seven thousand years. It would be impossible, of course, to say exactly how widespread written communication was in that remote period.

3. Diese rätselhafte Einzigartigkeit der baskischen Sprache / bleibt bestehen, / trotz mancher Theorien und Spekulationen, / die eine rassenmäßige oder kulturelle Verwandtschaft / zwischen den Basken und anderen Völkern nahelegen.

   This mysterious uniqueness of the Basque language persists despite a number of theories and speculations suggesting a racial or cultural affinity between the Basques and other peoples.

* das Sinngedicht — *epigram* (*in verse*)

LINE
1 trocken — *dry*
der Durst — *thirst*
2 der Trank — *drink*
3 die Krankheit — *sickness*
4 die Genesung — *recovery, convalescence*

LINE
4 der Durchbruch — *break-through*
5 das Vöglein — *little bird*
6 das Flüglein — *little wing*
9 allhier = hier

4. Nicht weniger interessant, / wenn auch nicht ganz so verwirrend, / ist das Geheimnis, / welches Zeit und Ort des Ursprungs / der indoeuropäischen Sprachen umgibt / und damit die Frage, / welche Sprache dieser Familie die älteste ist / und also der Muttersprache am nächsten steht.

   Not less interesting, even if not quite so baffling, is the mystery surrounding the time and place of origin of the Indo-European languages and with it the question as to which language of this family might be the most ancient and therefore closest to the mother tongue.

SPRACHEN I

Die menschliche Sprache ist den meisten Menschen so selbstverständlich wie die Luft, die sie atmen. Und doch ist die Sprache eines der erstaunlichsten Phänomene, die dem Menschen vom Menschen bekannt sind. Ihr Ursprung ist ein tief verhülltes Geheimnis. Sie offenbart eine wunderbare Ordnung und eigenartige
5 Subtilität. Sie besitzt größte Mannigfaltigkeit, sowohl in den einzelnen Sprachen wie im Verhältnis der Sprachen zueinander.

Als mündliche Mitteilung reicht die Sprache ohne Zweifel zurück bis in die tiefste, dunkelste Epoche der menschlichen Geschichte. Die geschriebene Sprache ist verhältnismäßig jungen Datums. Man nimmt an, daß die früheste schriftliche
10 Mitteilung nicht älter sei als siebentausend Jahre. Allerdings könnte wohl niemand genau angeben, wie weit verbreitet die schriftliche Mitteilung in dieser entlegenen Epoche war. Einer vernünftigen Schätzung zufolge, dürfte ihr Bereich sehr eng begrenzt gewesen sein. Heute umfassen die Grenzen bekanntlich fast die ganze Erde. Einen deutlichen Beweis dafür liefern, zum Beispiel, die zwei Sprachen,
15 mit denen wir es in diesem Kurs zu tun haben. Englisch und Deutsch sind aber nur zwei Angehörige einer beträchtlichen Anzahl von organisch miteinander verbundenen Sprachen innerhalb einer großen Sprachfamilie, deren weitreichende Wirkung im Laufe der Geschichte kaum zu ermessen ist.

Den Sprachforschern zufolge gab es vor ungefähr fünftausend Jahren, etwa im
20 dritten Jahrtausend vor Christi Geburt, also in der jüngeren Steinzeit, eine mehr oder weniger einheitliche Sprache. Heute nimmt man im Allgemeinen an, daß diese Sprache die Urform für die Mehrzahl der Sprachen war, die gegenwärtig von vielen Millionen Menschen gesprochen werden — in Europa, den Amerikas, Asien, Australien, Neuseeland und Südafrika. Als diese lose zur Einheit gefügte
25 Ursprache zu zerfallen begann, traten immer schärfer Spaltungen und Unterschiede zu Tage, bis endlich in dem langen, langsamen Gang der Zeit klar be-

LINE
2 erstaunlich — *astonishing*
3 der Ursprung — *origin*
4 verhüllt — *enshrouded*
offenbaren — *reveal*
eigenartig — *unique*
5 die Mannigfaltigkeit — *variety*
5–6 sowohl . . . wie — *as well as*
6 das Verhältnis — *relation*
9 verhältnismäßig — *relatively*
man nimmt an — *it is assumed* or *estimated*
11 angeben — *state, declare*
entlegen — *remote*

LINE
12 eine vernünftige Schätzung — *a reasonable estimate*
12–13 dürfte . . . gewesen sein — *its range would seem to have been very narrowly limited*
14 der Beweis — *proof*
19 der Sprachforscher — *linguistic scientist* or *scholar*
ungefähr — *about, approximately*
21 einheitlich — *uniform*
im Allgemeinen — *in general, generally*
22 gegenwärtig — *at present*

stimmte, eindeutig unterschiedene Einheiten gebildet wurden. In ihrer Gesamtheit wurden diese Spracheinheiten als die indoeuropäische Sprachfamilie identifiziert, die im Wesentlichen aus acht bis zwölf Hauptgruppen besteht. Von diesen Hauptgruppen sind die meisten in kleinere Gruppen untergeteilt, die ihrerseits in einzelne Spracheinheiten oder bestimmte Sprachen zerfallen. Die folgende Tafel, die 5 keineswegs vollständig ist, gibt Beispiele für die Verbreitung der indoeuropäischen Sprachfamilie.

Die indoeuropäischen Sprachen

UNTERFAMILIE	GRUPPE	SPRACHEN
I. Indoiranisch	Indisch	Vedisch,* Sanskrit,* Indisch
	Iranisch	Persisch
II. Armenisch		
III. Albanisch		
IV. Griechisch		
V. Italisch	Latein	
	Romanische Sprachen	Italienisch, Spanisch, Portugiesisch, Französisch
VI. Keltisch	Bretonisch	Walisisch
	Gälisch	Irisch
VII. Germanisch	Ostgermanisch	Gotisch *
	Nordgermanisch	Schwedisch, Norwegisch, Dänisch, Isländisch, Altnordisch *
	Westgermanisch	
	Hochdeutsch	Alt-,* Mittel-* und Neuhochdeutsch, Jiddisch, Pennsylvania Dutch
	Niederdeutsch	Holländisch, Flemisch, Friesisch, Altsächsisch oder Niederdeutsch, Englisch: Altenglisch,* Mittelenglisch,* (Neu-)Englisch
VIII. Baltisch		Litauisch, Lettisch
IX. Slawisch (Slawonisch)	Südslawisch	Serbokroatisch
	Westslawisch	Polnisch, Tschechisch
	Ostslawisch	Russisch, Ukrainisch
X. Tocharisch *		
XI. Anatolisch *		Hettitisch *

* Bezeichnet eine ausgestorbene Sprache.

LINE
1 eindeutig — *clearly, unequivocally*
in ihrer Gesamtheit — *taken together*
3 im Wesentlichen — *essentially*
bestehen (aus) — *consist (of)*

LINE
4 untergeteilt — *subdivided*
ihrerseits — *for their part, in turn*
6 vollständig — *complete, all-inclusive*
die Verbreitung — *spread, range*

In der historischen Entwicklung des Englischen wie des Hochdeutschen unterscheidet man drei Perioden, die einander chronologisch entsprechen. Die Periode des Altenglischen (Angelsächsischen) und des Althochdeutschen erstreckt sich ungefähr von 800 bis 1100, die Periode von Mittelenglisch und Mittel-
5 hochdeutsch reicht von 1100 bis 1500. Um 1500 beginnt die Entwicklung des modernen Englisch und des Neuhochdeutschen.

Innerhalb der indoeuropäischen Familie steht, genau genommen, nur die indoiranische Gruppe außerhalb der Grenzen Europas. Hingegen gibt es in Europa heute nur wenige Sprachen, die nicht zur indoeuropäischen Familie gehören. Die
10 wichtigsten darunter sind die finnougrische Gruppe, zu der, außer Finnisch, auch Lappländisch, Estnisch und Magyarisch (Ungarisch) gehören, sowie die Gruppe der türkischen Sprachen und Baskisch.

Magyarisch, die offizielle Sprache Ungarns, ist mit dem Türkischen verwandt, besonders durch einzelne Wörter und Formen, die aus dem Bereich des Türkischen
15 entlehnt sind. Baskisch hingegen scheint mit keiner anderen Sprache der Welt organisch verwandt zu sein. Diese rätselhafte Einzigartigkeit bleibt bestehen, trotz mancher Theorien und Spekulationen, die eine rassenmäßige oder kulturelle Verwandtschaft zwischen den Basken und anderen Völkern nahelegen — lebenden oder ausgestorbenen, historischen oder mythischen. Vielleicht ergibt sich eines
20 Tages, daß die Basken Abkömmlinge des Cro-Magnon Menschen sind, oder verschlagene Besucher von der Insel Kreta, oder gar ein Überbleibsel der legendären, verschwundenen Bewohner von Atlantis, aber niemand hat bisher das Rätsel gelöst, das ihre rassische Herkunft und den Ursprung ihrer Sprache umgibt. Jedenfalls dürfte gewiß sein, daß die Basken zu dem ältesten überlebenden Rasse-
25 bestand Europas gehören. Dasselbe mag auch für ihre Sprache gelten. Aber wer könnte das mit Gewißheit behaupten!

Nicht weniger interessant, wenn auch nicht ganz so verwirrend, ist das Geheimnis, welches Zeit und Ort des Ursprungs der indoeuropäischen Sprachen umgibt und damit die Frage, welche Sprache dieser Familie die älteste ist und
30 also der Muttersprache am nächsten steht. In der Nachfolge von Gelehrten wie Jakob Grimm, einem der ersten großen Philologen auf dem Gebiet der vergleichenden Sprachkunde, waren die Sprachwissenschaftler des neunzehnten

LINE

13 Ungarns — *of Hungary*
14 der Bereich — *realm*
15 entlehnt — *borrowed, taken from*
16 diese rätselhafte Einzigartigkeit — *this mysterious uniqueness*
bleibt bestehen — *persists*
17 rassenmäßig — *racial*
18 nahelegen — *suggest*
19 ausgestorben — *extinct*
ergibt sich — *it turns out*
20 die Abkömmlinge — *descendants*
21 verschlagen — *lost, wayward*
das Überbleibsel — *survivors, remnant*
22 der Bewohner — *inhabitant*

LINE

23 die Herkunft — *descent*
umgeben — *surround, include*
24 jedenfalls — *in any case*
24–5 (der) überlebende Rassebestand — *surviving racial stock*
26 behaupten — *maintain*
27 verwirrend — *baffling, bewildering, confusing*
30 in der Nachfolge von Gelehrten — *following the lead of scholars*
31–2 auf dem Gebiet . . . Sprachkunde — *in the field of comparative linguistics*
32 der Sprachwissenschaftler — *linguist, linguistic scientist*

Jahrhunderts davon überzeugt, daß der Ursprung des Indoeuropäischen, ja der Sprache überhaupt, irgendwo im Osten zu suchen sei. Kein Wunder, daß man, diesem Leitgedanken entsprechend, Sanskrit, den ältesten östlichen Zweig des Indoeuropäischen, als ursprüngliche Muttersprache bezeichnete und daß daher Indien als Ursprungsort des Indoeuropäischen galt. 5

Gegen Ende des ersten Viertels des zwanzigsten Jahrhunderts verschob sich aber die Aufmerksamkeit der Sprachforscher entschieden vom Osten nach dem Westen. Dies geschah auf Grund einer genauen Überprüfung von archäologischen, botanischen und anthropologischen Befunden in dem Gebiet von Litauen. Auch hatte sich ergeben, daß Altlitauisch nicht nur dem Sanskrit eng verwandt war, 10 sondern noch archaischere Züge aufwies als dieses. Daher mußte die Theorie über den Ort des indoeuropäischen Ursprungs grundlegend geändert werden. Man gab nun den weiten Ebenen im Nordosten Europas den Vorrang.

In jüngerer Zeit ist aber auch die Vorzugstellung dieses europäischen Gebietes wieder angezweifelt worden. Man neigt nun immer mehr zu der folgenden 15 Ansicht: Die ursprünglichen Indoeuropäer wanderten aus dem Südwesten Asiens aus, kamen über den Kaukasus nach Europa, ließen sich längs des Schwarzen Meers nieder und gewannen erst später sprachlichen Einfluß auf das übrige Europa.

FRAGEN

1. Kennt man den Ursprung der Sprache? 2. Seit wann gibt es eine geschriebene Sprache? 3. Wie alt ist die indoeuropäische Sprachfamilie? 4. Welche Perioden unterscheidet man in der Entwicklung der hochdeutschen und der englischen Sprache? 5. Welche Theorien über den Ursprungsort des Indoeuropäischen sind Ihnen bekannt? 6. Wovon waren die Sprachwissenschaftler des vorigen (*preceding*) Jahrhunderts überzeugt? 7. Warum verschob sich das Interesse der Forscher vom Osten nach dem Westen? Zu welcher Ansicht neigt man heute?

TROSTLIED IM KONJUNKTIV

Wär ich ein Baum, stünd ich droben am Wald.
Trüg Wolke und Stern in den grünen Haaren.
Wäre mit meinen dreihundert Jahren
noch gar nicht sehr alt.

LINE

1 überzeugt — *convinced*
2 irgendwo — *somewhere*
3 diesem Leitgedanken entsprechend — *with this as a guiding principle* or *thought*
der Zweig — *branch*
4 bezeichnen — *designate*
6–7 verschob sich . . . die Aufmerksamkeit — *the attention* or *focus shifted*
7 entschieden — *definitely, radically*
8 auf Grund — *on the basis*
die Überprüfung — *scrutiny*

LINE

9 der Befund — *finding, evidence*
Litauen — *Lithuania*
11 Züge aufwies — *revealed characteristics*
12 grundlegend — *fundamentally*
13 gab . . . Vorrang — *gave preference* (*to*)
14 die Vorzugstellung — *privileged position*
15 angezweifelt — *questioned, doubted*
neigen — *tend to, be inclined*
16 die Ansicht — *view*
17–18 ließen sich nieder — *settled*
18 das übrige — *the rest of*

Wildtauben grüben den Kopf untern Flügel.
Kriege ritten und klirrten im Trab
querfeldein und über die Hügel
ins offene Grab.

Humpelten Hunger vorüber und Seuche.
Kämen und schmölzen wie Ostern und Schnee.
Läg ein Pärchen versteckt im Gesträuche
und tät sich süß weh.

Klängen vom Dorf her die Kirmesgeigen.
Ameisen brächten die Ernte ein.
Hinge ein Toter in meinen Zweigen
Und schwänge das Bein.

Spränge die Flut und ersäufte die Täler.
Wüchse Vergißmeinnicht zärtlich am Bach.
Alles verginge wie Täuschung und Fehler
und Rauch überm Dach.

Wär ich ein Baum, stünd ich droben am Wald.
Trüg Sonne und Mond in den grünen Haaren.
Wäre mit meinen dreihundert Jahren
nicht jung und nicht alt . . .

Erich Kästner

SONG OF SOLACE IN SUBJUNCTIVE

Were I a tree, near the woods I'd stand high,
Wear clouds and stars in my emerald hair.
At three hundred years I'd still be fair —
Not ancient, not I.

Wild doves under wing their heads would hide.
Wars would charge clanking wave after wave
Across the hills and the meadows wide
Into the yawning grave.

Sickness and famine would hobble by,
Would come and would go like Easter and snow.
Hidden in underbrush lovers would lie
Exchanging sweet woe.

Fiddles would shrill from the village fair.
Ants would be hauling their winter's supply.
A dead man would dangle and jerk in midair
From my branches high.

Rivers would leap, drowning lands in confusion,
By the brook grow forget-me-not, tender, sedate.
All things would pass like error, delusion,
Like smoke across slate.

Were I a tree, I'd stand high near the wold,
Wear sun and moon in my emerald hair.
At three hundred years I'd still be fair —
Not young and not old.

NEUNTER TEIL

Berlin: Ernst-Reuter-Platz

Berlin: Kongreßhalle

Berlin: Luftbrückendenkmal. (*Monument to the Airlift of 1948–1949*)

25. Aufgabe

DEUTSCHLANDS POLITISCHE LAGE

Read the following dialogue and memorize the bracketed area only. The rest (see page 215) is to be treated as reading assignment.

OLSON: War jemand von euch bei der Diskussion über Deutschland, die gestern in unserem deutschen Klub abgehalten wurde?

EVANS: Ja, Foster und ich waren anwesend. Zwei deutsche Austauschstudenten, Schulze und Meier, sprachen über Deutschlands politische Lage.

[OLSON: Ich wünschte, Sie könnten mir berichten, was die beiden zu sagen hatten.

EVANS: Der erste Vortragende, Meier, meinte, das nationalsozialistische Deutschland sei an der Katastrophe des zweiten Weltkriegs hauptsächlich schuld gewesen.

OLSON: Nun, das ist nicht gerade neu.

EVANS: Seit dem Krieg habe Deutschland sich aber so schnell erholt, daß es innerhalb Europas bald wieder eine führende Rolle spielte.

OLSON: Auch das ist uns bekannt.

FOSTER: Schulze hingegen betonte die einstige Größe Deutschlands. Im neunzehnten Jahrhundert, wie im Mittelalter, — so sagte er — sei Deutschland die Mitte Europas gewesen.]

GERMANY'S POLITICAL SITUATION

OLSON: Were any of you at the discussion on Germany that was held at our German Club yesterday?

EVANS: Yes, Foster and I were present. Two German exchange students, Schulze and Meier, spoke about Germany's political situation.

OLSON: I wish you could tell me what the two had to say.

EVANS: The first lecturer, Meier, thought that Nazi Germany (National Socialist Germany) was chiefly to blame for the catastrophe of the second World War.

OLSON: Well, that is not exactly new.

EVANS: However, since the war Germany had recovered so quickly, that soon it was playing a leading role in Europe again.

OLSON: We know that too. (That too is known to us.)

FOSTER: Schulze, on the contrary, emphasized Germany's former greatness. In the nineteenth century, as in the Middle Ages — so he said — Germany had been the center of Europe.

OLSON: Mag sein. Jedenfalls entwickelte sich im neunzehnten Jahrhundert das jahrhundertelang zersplitterte Deutschland zu einer Großmacht.

FOSTER: Deutschlands Niedergang, meinte Schulze, begann mit dem ersten Weltkrieg. Heute, sagte er, gebe es Deutschland als eine politische Einheit eigentlich gar nicht. Land und Volk seien in ungleiche Teile gespalten. 5

EVANS: Die westdeutsche Republik, so sagte auch Meier, sei ein Grenzland der westlichen Welt.

OLSON: Und die DDR, die „deutsche demokratische Republik"? 10

FOSTER: Das sei nur ein Deckname für die kommunistische Diktatur, sagte Schulze.

EVANS: Das meinte Meier auch. Dennoch hielt er die Wiedervereinigung der beiden Teile Deutschlands für möglich.

FOSTER: Und beide glaubten an die zukünftige Einheit Europas. 15

OLSON: Schön wäre es ja. Wenn man nur wüßte, was die Zukunft bringt!

DRILL PATTERNS

Repeat the following drills after your instructor or after the speaker on the tape. Imitate the pronunciation very carefully.

1. Sie sagte, das wisse sie schon lange.
Er sagte, das habe sie schon lange gewußt.
Sie sagte, daß er das schon lange wüßte.
Sie sagte, das hätten sie schon lange gewußt.

2. Meint er, das sei neu?
Meint er, das sei etwas Neues?
Meint ihr, das wäre etwas Neues?
Meint ihr, das sei etwas Neues gewesen?
Meinen Sie, daß das etwas Neues gewesen wäre?
Würde das etwas Neues sein?

3. Sie sagte, ich sollte ihr alles genau berichten.
Sie sagte, ich müßte ihr alles genau berichten.
Sie sagte, ich hätte ihr alles erzählen sollen.
Sie sagte, ich hätte ihr alles erzählen müssen.

LINE
3 die Großmacht — *major power*
4 der Niedergang — *downfall*
7 spalten — *split*

LINE
8 das Grenzland — *borderland*
11 der Deckname — *disguise, cloak, decoy*
13 die Wiedervereinigung — *reunification*

4. Meier meinte, Deutschland spiele eine führende Rolle in Europa.
Meinte Meier, Deutschland habe eine führende Rolle in Europa gespielt?
Meier meinte, Deutschland werde eine führende Rolle in Europa spielen.

5. Meier meinte, daß Deutschland eine führende Macht [1] in Europa sei.
Meier meinte, daß Deutschland eine führende Macht in Europa gewesen sei.
Meier meinte, daß Deutschland eine führende Macht in Europa sein werde.

6. Er sagte, die Deutschen seien daran schuld.
Er sagte, daß die Russen daran schuld seien.
Er sagte, die Amerikaner seien daran schuld gewesen.
Er sagte, daß die Franzosen daran schuld gewesen seien.

7. Damals, sagte er, habe es Deutschland als eine politische Einheit noch gar nicht gegeben.
Heute, sagte er, gebe es Deutschland als eine politische Einheit nicht mehr.
In Zukunft, sagte er, werde es Deutschland als eine politische Einheit nicht geben.

8. Er sagte, Deutschland erhole sich schnell.
Er sagte, Deutschland habe sich schnell erholt.
Er sagte, Deutschland werde sich schnell erholen.

9. Er sagte, er sei krank.[2]
Er sagte, daß er krank sei.
Er sagte, er wäre krank.
Er sagte, daß er krank wäre.

10. Er sagte, er sei krank gewesen.
Er sagte, daß er krank gewesen sei.
Er sagte, er wäre krank gewesen.
Er sagte, daß er krank gewesen wäre.

11. Ich fragte, ob es etwas Neues gebe.
Ich fragte, ob es etwas Neues gäbe.
Ich fragte, ob es etwas Neues gegeben habe.
Ich fragte, ob es etwas Neues gegeben hätte.
Ich fragte, ob es etwas Neues geben werde.
Ich fragte, ob es etwas Neues geben würde.

12. Glaubt er, daß die Wiedervereinigung zustandekommen [3] wird?
Er glaubte, daß die Wiedervereinigung zustandekommen werde.
Er glaubte, daß die Wiedervereinigung zustandekommen würde.
Er glaubt, daß die Wiedervereinigung damals beinah [4] zustandegekommen wäre.

13. Er betonte, daß er davon nichts wisse.
Er betonte, daß er davon nichts wüßte.
Er betonte, daß er davon nichts gewußt habe.
Er betonte, daß er davon nichts gewußt hätte.
Er betonte, daß er davon nichts weiß.

14. Das wäre schön.
Schön wäre es ja.
Das wäre schön gewesen.
Schön wäre es ja gewesen.

[1] **die Macht** power [2] **krank** sick [3] **zustandekommen** come about [4] **beinah(e)** almost

15. Herr Doktor, Sie wären beinahe zu spät gekommen.
Der Patient wäre ja beinahe gestorben.
Ich wünschte, Sie wären früher[1] gekommen.
Ich wünschte, Sie kämen das nächste Mal früher.

EXERCISE

Note the following examples:

I. *Direct Discourse:* Er sagte: „Ich bin Student."
Indirect Discourse: Er sagte, er {sei / wäre} Student.

II. *Direct Discourse:* Er sagte: „Ich war krank."
or „Ich bin krank gewesen."
or „Ich war krank gewesen."
Indirect Discourse: Er sagte, er {sei / wäre} krank gewesen.

III. *Direct Discourse:* Er sagte: „Ich werde Meier morgen besuchen."
Indirect Discourse: Er sagte, er {werde / würde} Meier morgen besuchen.

Change to indirect discourse:

1. Müller sagte: „Das weiß ich schon."
Müller sagte: „Das habe ich nicht gewußt."
Müller sagte: „Das werde ich morgen wissen."

2. Schmidt fragte: „Wer war gestern in unserem deutschen Klub?"
Müller antwortete: „Fischer und ich waren anwesend."

Note: In changing the following phrases use **ob (Wir fragten, ob . . .).**

3. Wir fragten: „Ist das ein Vorteil[2] für Europa?"
Wir fragten: „War das ein Vorteil für Europa?"
Wir fragten: „Wird das ein Vorteil für Europa sein?"

English to German

Study the grammar section of this lesson before preparing this exercise in writing.

1) I told him **vs** I knew that. **vl** (*use* **daß**)
I told him **vs** I had known that. **vl** (*use* **daß**)
I told him **vs** I would know that tomorrow. **vl** (*use* **daß**)

Note: *Whenever* **daß** *is expressed in sentences under* **2** *and* **3**, *the word order of the* **daß**-*clause will of course be* **vl.**

2) We told her **vs** we had to know that. **vs / vl**

[1] **früher** earlier [2] **der Vorteil** advantage

She told us **vs** we should know that. **vs/vl**

3) He said **vs** he was sick. **vs**
I said **vs** they had been sick. **vs/vl**
We knew **vs** she would come. **vs/vl**

4) I asked **vs** whether there was something new. **vl**
He asked me **vs** whether they had come. **vl**
We asked her **vs** whether there would be any news tomorrow. **vl**

Translate the following sentences without the help of the key:

5) They said we should report everything to them.
They said we should have reported everything to them.
We said we would report everything to them.

6) He almost died. (*use subjunctive*)
That would have been sad.

GRAMMAR

47. Subjunctive of Indirect Discourse

A thorough review of the subjunctive and imaginative forms is indispensable at this point!

a. In German (unlike modern English) the use of subjunctive forms is required in indirect discourse clauses, *notably when the governing verb expresses past time:*

Werner sagte, er **habe** Karl etwas Wichtiges mitzuteilen.	*Werner said he **had** something important to tell Karl.*
Der Arzt sagte, Otto **sei** erst gestern eingeliefert worden.	*The doctor said Otto **had** been brought in only yesterday.*
Die Grenzwache meinte, der Paß **sei** nicht in Ordnung.	*The border watch said the passport **was** not in order.*

Note within each pair the difference between German and English in the matter of verb tenses.

In German the tense of the governed verb is normally determined by the tense it would assume in the direct discourse statement. Compare the following with the indirect statements above.

Werner sagte: „Ich **habe** dir etwas mitzuteilen, Karl."
Der Arzt sagte: „Otto **ist** erst gestern eingeliefert worden."
Die Grenzwache meinte: „Der Paß **ist** nicht in Ordnung."

Other Illustrations

Der Fremdenführer erklärte: „Diese Wachen **sind** ausgesuchte Soldaten."
Der Fremdenführer erklärte, daß diese Wachen ausgesuchte Soldaten **seien.**

Der Reiter sagte: „Stundenlang **muß** man die verfluchten Stiefel putzen."
Der Reiter sagte, daß man die verfluchten Stiefel stundenlang putzen **müsse.**

Der feine Herr fragte: „Wer von den Herrschaften **vermißt** seinen Fahrtausweis?"
Der feine Herr fragte, wer von den Herrschaften seinen Fahrtausweis **vermisse.**

Adler fragte Berger: „Was **gibt** es Neues?"
Adler fragte Berger, was es Neues **gebe.**

Sokrates erklärte, alles was er wisse, sei, daß er nichts wisse.
Socrates declared that all he knew was that he knew nothing.

Adler sagte zu Berger: „Es **wird** immer Kriege **geben,** weil es immer Kriege **gegeben hat.**"
Adler sagte zu Berger, es **werde** immer Kriege **geben,** weil es immer Kriege **gegeben habe.**

Ruprecht D. heiratete 1952 in der Annahme, daß seine erste Frau tot **sei,** eine Landwirtstochter.
Ruprecht D. married a farmer's daughter in 1952, assuming that his first wife **was** *dead.*

b. It is permissible to substitute the *present imaginative for the present subjunctive:*

Der Fremdenführer erklärte, daß die Wachen ausgesuchte Soldaten **wären (seien).**
Der Reiter sagte, daß man die verfluchten Stiefel stundenlang putzen **müßte (müsse).**
Der feine Herr fragte, wer von den Herrschaften seinen Fahrtausweis **vermißte (vermisse).**
Adler fragte Berger, was es Neues **gäbe (gebe).**

c. It is permissible to substitute the *past imaginative for the present perfect subjunctive;* also the *conditional* forms for the *future subjunctive* forms:

Adler sagte zu Berger, es **würde (werde)** immer Kriege **geben,** weil es immer Kriege **gegeben hätte (habe).**

This shift is required when the subjunctive happens not to be distinguishable from the indicative form:

Der Arzt sagte: „Otto und sein Freund **haben** den Sturm ja nicht kommen sehen."
(Der Arzt sagte, Otto und sein Freund **haben** den Sturm ja nicht kommen sehen.)
Der Arzt sagte, Otto und sein Freund **hätten** den Sturm ja nicht kommen sehen.

d. When the subject of the governing verb is **ich** or **wir,** the subjunctive forms have a tendency to give way to the indicative forms:

Ich sagte, daß ich davon nichts wußte.
Wir meinten, daß alles in Ordnung war.

If the context indicates doubt, uncertainty, surprise, or the like in the mind of the speaker (or speakers), the subjunctive or imaginative forms are likely to be used:

Wir glaubten, daß nun alles mit ihm in Ordnung sei (wäre).
We believed (fancied) that everything was all right with him now.

e. Subjunctive (or imaginative) forms in indirect commands with the auxiliary **sollen:**

Plötzlich befahl ihm der junge Mann: „Rufen Sie auch!"
Plötzlich befahl ihm der junge Mann, daß er auch rufen solle (sollte).

The young man commanded him suddenly: "You shout too!"
The young man suddenly commanded him to shout, too.

„So halten Sie sich doch ruhig!" fuhr ihn der junge Mann an.
Der junge Mann fuhr ihn an, er solle (sollte) sich doch ruhig halten.

"Why don't you keep quiet!" the young man angrily said to him.
The young man angrily told him just to keep quiet.

48. Other Uses of the Subjunctive and Imaginative Forms

a. *Present subjunctive* expressing wish or hope:

Es lebe die Freiheit!	*Long live liberty!*
Hoch lebe der König!	*Long live the king!*

b. *Present subjunctive* expressing exhortation, advice, instruction, command, concession. Some of the following illustrations have an archaic flavor, but they, and others like them, will be encountered, particularly in the written language.

Jedermann folge mir!	*(Let) everyone follow me.*
Der Herr trete ein!	*Come in, Sir!*
Dem sei, wie ihm wolle!	*Be that as it may.*

c. *Past imaginative* (with **beinahe** *almost*) expressing an all but consummated event:

Beinahe hätte ich ihr den Ring gekauft.	*I came near buying her the ring.* (*I almost bought her the ring*).
Ich wäre beinahe abgestürzt.	*I almost plunged down* (*the precipice, the elevator shaft*) or *off* (*the roof, the ladder, etc.*).
Ich wäre beinahe gestorben.	*I came near dying.* (*I could have died.*)

26. Aufgabe

WER BIN ICH?

I.

SAMPLE ANSWERS AND SUGGESTIONS

a. Wie sind Sie angezogen?

Ich bin leicht angezogen. / warm angezogen.

Zieht[1] man sich[1] im Winter bei Ihnen leicht an?[1]

Nein, im Winter zieht man sich . . . an.

Oder sind Sie im Winter warm angezogen?
Trägt[2] man im Sommer einen Pelzmantel?[3]
Oder ist man im Sommer leicht bekleidet?[4]
Geht man in einem Abendkleid[5] in die Berge?
Kommen Sie in einem Frack[6] — in einem Straßenanzug[7] — in Lederhosen[8] — in einem einfachen Kostüm — im Badeanzug[9] — in die Klasse?
Geht man in kurzen Hosen auf einen Ball?
Tragen Sie bei gutem Wetter einen Regenmantel?
Haben Sie einen Hut?[10] — einen Regenschirm?[11] — einen Schlips?[12] — ein Paar Handschuhe?[13] — einen Schlafrock?[14] — ein Paar Socken?[15] — ein Paar Strümpfe?[16]

Ja, ich habe . . .

Tragen Sie heute einen Rock?[17] — ein Paar lange Hosen? — ein Hemd[18] mit kurzen oder langen Ärmeln?[19] — eine Bluse? — eine Jacke?

b. Waschen[20] Sie sich[20] jeden Morgen?

Ich wasche mich . . .

Brausen[21] Sie gerne oder nehmen Sie lieber ein Bad?[22]
Putzen[23] Sie sich morgens und abends die Zähne?[24]

Ich putze mir . . . die Zähne.

Lassen Sie sich die Schuhe putzen oder putzen Sie sich die Schuhe selber?

Ich lasse mir die Schuhe putzen. Ich putze mir die Schuhe selber.

Lassen Sie Ihre Hemden waschen oder waschen Sie Ihre Hemden selber?

Ich lasse meine Hemden waschen. Ich wasche sie selber.

Wie oft lassen Sie sich die Haare schneiden?[25]

Ich lasse mir die Haare alle 14 Tage (zweimal im Monat) schneiden.

Note: With nouns referring to parts of the body, the tendency in German is to use the definite article in place of the possessive adjective, especially when a dative of interest or possession is involved, e.g., **Ich habe mir in den Finger geschnitten.**

[1] **sich anziehen** dress, get dressed [2] **tragen** wear [3] **der Pelz** fur; **der Mantel** coat [4] **bekleidet** dressed [5] **das Abendkleid** evening dress [6] **der Frack** dinner jacket [7] **der Straßenanzug** business *or* everyday suit [8] **das Leder** leather; **die Hose(n)** pants, trousers [9] **der Badeanzug** bathing suit [10] **der Hut** hat [11] **der Regenschirm** umbrella [12] **der Schlips** tie [13] **der Handschuh** glove [14] **der Schlafrock** housecoat, robe [15] **die Socke** sock [16] **der Strumpf** stocking [17] **der Rock** skirt [18] **das Hemd** shirt [19] **der Ärmel** sleeve [20] **sich waschen** wash [21] **brausen** take a shower [22] **das Bad** bath [23] **putzen** clean, brush [24] **der Zahn** tooth [25] **sich die Haare schneiden lassen** get a haircut

Berlin: Kurfürstendamm. Ruine und Neubau der Kaiser-Wilhelm-Gedächtniskirche.

Sind Sie letzte Woche zum Friseur [1] gegangen?	
Lassen Sie sich Dauerwellen [2] legen?	*Ich lasse mir (keine) Dauerwellen legen.*

II.

An den Leser: Sie brauchen die folgenden Fragen nicht wahrheitsgemäß [3] zu beantworten.[4] Antworten Sie, was Ihnen einfällt! [5] Die Hauptsache [6] ist, daß die Antwort sinnvoll [7] und grammatisch richtig ist.

Ein Fragebogen [8]

	SAMPLE ANSWERS AND SUGGESTIONS
Halten Sie sich für glücklich? — erfolgreich? [9] — beliebt? [10]	*Ich halte mich für . . .*
Lädt [11] man Sie oft zu Gesellschaften [12] ein? [11]	*Man lädt mich (nicht) oft . . . ein.*
Haben Sie viele Bekannte?	
Gibt es Menschen, mit denen Sie eng befreundet sind?	*Es gibt viele (wènige, keine) Menschen, mit denen ich . . . bin.*
Sind Sie verliebt? — verlobt? [13] — verheiratet? [14]	
Liegt Ihnen daran,[15] bei Ihren Kollegen — Kolleginnen — Lehrern beliebt zu sein?	*Mir liegt (nicht) daran, . . .*
Gehören [16] Sie einer Studentenorganisation an? [16]	*Ich gehöre . . . an.*
Sind Sie je in einen Klub oder in eine Verbindung [17] aufgenommen [18] worden?	*Ja, ich bin . . . aufgenommen worden. Nein, ich bin nie . . . aufgenommen worden.*
Lassen Sie sich von Ihren Kollegen (Kolleginnen) gerne helfen?	*Ich lasse mir von . . . (nicht) gerne helfen.*
Oder helfen Sie Ihren Kollegen (Kolleginnen) lieber?	
Glauben Sie, daß Sie den meisten Menschen gefallen? (*. . . that most people like you?*)	*Ich glaube, daß ich den meisten Menschen (nicht) gefalle.*
Gefallen Ihnen die meisten Menschen? (*Do you like most people?*)	*Mir gefallen . . . (nicht).*
Wollen Sie gerne überall mit dabei sein? [19]	
Oder fühlen Sie sich wohler, wenn man Sie in Ruhe läßt?	*Ich fühle mich wohler, wenn . . .*
Glauben Sie alles — das Meiste — nichts —, was man Ihnen sagt?	
Folgen Sie gerne dem Rat [20] Ihrer Freunde?	
Oder ziehen [21] Sie es vor,[21] wenn man Ihrem Rat folgt?	

[1] **der Friseur** barber [2] **die Dauerwelle** permanent (wave) [3] **wahrheitsgemäß** truthfully [4] **beantworten** (*with acc.*) answer [5] **einfallen** (*with dat.*) occur [6] **die Hauptsache** the main thing [7] **sinnvoll** meaningful [8] **der Fragebogen** questionnaire [9] **erfolgreich** successful [10] **beliebt** popular, well-liked [11] **einladen** invite [12] **die Gesellschaft** party [13] **verlobt** engaged [14] **verheiratet** married [15] **liegt Ihnen daran** does it matter to you [16] **angehören** belong to [17] **die Verbindung** association [18] **aufnehmen** accept [19] **mit dabei sein** be present [20] **der Rat** advice [21] **vorziehen** prefer

	SAMPLE ANSWERS AND SUGGESTIONS
Sind Sie leicht verletzt? [1]	
Oder macht es Ihnen nicht viel, wenn man Sie kritisiert? (*Or don't you mind if . . .*)	*Es macht mir nicht viel, . . .*
Fällt Ihnen je ein, daß Sie im Unrecht sein könnten?	*Mir fällt nie* (*oft, selten*) *ein, daß ich . . . könnte.*
Oder sind Sie davon überzeugt, [2] daß Sie immer im Recht sind?	
Sind Sie mit dem Eindruck,[3] den Sie auf andere machen, zufrieden? [4]	
Sind Sie mit sich selbst zufrieden?	*Ich bin mit mir selbst* (*nicht*) *zufrieden.*

DRILL PATTERNS

Repeat the following drills after your instructor or after the speaker on the tape. Imitate the pronunciation very carefully.

1. Das sind Fragen, die ich nicht beantworten will.
Das sind Fragen, die man nicht beantworten muß.
Das sind Fragen, die sich nicht beantworten lassen.
Das sind Fragen, die niemand beantworten kann.

2. Wird man diese Frage je beantworten können? [5]
Wird sich diese Frage je beantworten lassen? [5]
Das ist eine Frage, die kein Mensch je beantwortet hat.
Das ist eine Frage, die nie beantwortet werden wird.

3. Wie macht man das?
Wie läßt sich das machen?
Wie wird das gemacht?
Wie wird sich das machen lassen? [6]

4. Sollte man ihm nicht helfen?
Hat man ihm je geholfen?
Wird man ihm helfen?
Könnte ihm nicht geholfen werden?

5. Ihm wird nie geholfen.
Ihm wird nie geholfen werden.
Ihm ist nie geholfen worden.

6. Ich weiß nicht, was ihm eingefallen ist.
Warum ist ihm das nie eingefallen?
Das fiel mir bisher [7] nie ein.

7. Was hat man dazu gesagt?
Was sagen Sie dazu?
Was soll man dazu sagen?
Was ist dazu noch zu sagen?

8. Das Kleid paßt [8] ihr nicht.
Der Anzug gefällt mir nicht.
Der Regenschirm gehört ihm nicht.

9. Es gelingt ihr nicht.
Es gelang ihr nicht.
Es war ihr nicht gelungen.
Es ist ihr nicht gelungen.
Es wird ihr nicht gelingen.

[1] **verletzt** hurt, offended [2] **überzeugt** convinced [3] **der Eindruck** impression [4] **zufrieden** satisfied
[5] **Wird man . . . können? Wird sich . . . lassen?** Will it ever be possible to answer this question?
[6] **Wie wird sich . . . lassen?** How will it be possible to do it? [7] **bisher** up to now [8] **passen** fit

10. Lassen Sie sich die Haare schneiden!
Ich habe mir gestern die Haare schneiden lassen.
Wann wird er sich die Haare schneiden lassen?

11. Er läßt sich hier selten sehen.
Gestern hat man ihn hier gesehen.
Heute ist hier kein Mensch zu sehen.
In diesem Anzug dürfen Sie sich nicht sehen lassen.

12. Ist sein Hemd gewaschen?
Wer hat das Hemd gewaschen?
Ist das Hemd von Ihnen selbst gewaschen worden?

13. Sind seine Schuhe geputzt?
Hat man ihm die Schuhe geputzt?
Von wem sind die Schuhe geputzt worden?

14. Hat er sich die Zähne geputzt?
Hat man dem Kind die Zähne geputzt?
Hat er sich die Hände gewaschen?
Sind dem Kind die Hände gewaschen worden?

15. Um die Jahrhundertwende [1] wurden nur lange Kleider getragen.
In den zwanziger Jahren war es die Mode, kurze Röcke zu tragen.
Was trägt man heute?
Was wird man morgen tragen?

English to German

Study the grammar sections in this lesson before preparing the following exercise in writing.

1) This question cannot be answered. (*use* [1] *the passive*, [2] **man**) (*in either case* **vs/vl**)
This question has never been answered. (*use* [1] *the passive*, [2] **man**) (*in either case* **vs/vl**)

2) What can be said about it? [2] **vs/vl** (*use* **man**)
This has never occurred to me. **vs/vl**

3) We cannot help her. **vs/vl**
She cannot be helped. **vs/vl** (*use* [1] *the passive*, [2] **man**)

4) Why don't you get a haircut? **vs/vl**
Why don't you brush your teeth? **vs**
Why don't you have your shoes polished? **vs/vl**
Why don't you wear a hat? **vs**

5) This book belongs to her. **vs**
Doesn't she like it? **vf**
Why don't you answer me? **vs**

6) She succeeds in everything.[3] **vs**
We lack money. **vs**
This suit does not fit him. **vs**
Their children do not obey [4] them. **vs**

7) Do you belong to a student organization? **vf**

Translate the following sentences without the help of the key:

8) Why didn't they show up? (*Why didn't they let themselves be seen?*) (*use pres. perf.*)
She was seen here last night.[5] (*use* **man**)
No one is to be seen here today.
You shouldn't let yourself be seen in this dress.

[1] **die Jahrhundertwende** turn of the century [2] about it **darüber** [3] in everything *here:* **alles**
[4] obey **folgen** (*with dat. obj.*) [5] last night **gestern abend**

9) The shirts are washed.
The shirts were washed by her last night.

10) Give the glass of beer[1] to your father.
Give him the glass of beer.
Give it to him.

GRAMMAR

49. Actional versus Statal Passive

The difference between the actional passive and the so-called statal passive may be readily seen from the following examples. Note that the statal passive uses as auxiliary not **werden,** but **sein.**

1. Die Ringe werden aus Gold gemacht.	*The rings are* **being** *made of gold.*
2. Die Ringe sind aus Gold gemacht.	*The rings are* **made** *of gold* (i.e., *they are gold rings*).

No. 1 describes a process; No. 2 describes the state of completion of the process.

Der Brief wird geschrieben.	*The letter is* **being** *written.*
Der Brief ist geschrieben.	*The letter is written.*

50. Passive Voice Substitutes

The indefinite pronoun **man** is used very frequently with active voice verbs as a simple replacement for the passive voice:

Man sah ihn in den Aufzug einsteigen.	*He was seen* (*One saw him*) *getting into the elevator.*
Wenn man die Prüfung nur aufschieben könnte!	*If only the examination could be postponed.*
Man sagt, Karl habe es getan.	*It is said* (*reported*) *that Karl did it.*
Man erklärte ihm nie, warum man ihn eingesperrt habe.	*It was never explained to him why he was locked up.*

Reflexive verbs are sometimes used in a passive voice sense:

Die Gardinen zogen sich langsam zu.	*The curtains were slowly pulled shut.*

The reflexive of **lassen** plus infinitive is frequently used with passive meaning:

Er ließ sich nicht sehen.	*He did not let himself be seen.*
Lassen Sie sich nicht stören!	*Do not let yourself be disturbed.*

Sein plus **zu** plus infinitive has a similar effect:

Es war nichts im Keller zu sehen.	*Nothing was to be seen in the cellar.*
Nur ein kleines Pünktchen Licht war noch zu sehen.	*Only a tiny little point of light was still visible* (*to be seen*).

[1] the glass of beer **das Glas Bier**

51. Impersonal Passive

Es wird in dieser Klasse nicht viel gearbeitet. In dieser Klasse wird nicht viel gearbeitet.	*Not much work is being done in this class.*

Note the omission of **es** in the second version of the above sentence.

Es wurde oft von ihm gesprochen.	*He was often talked about.* *(People often talked about him.)*
Es wird heutzutage viel vom Frieden geredet.	*Nowadays there is much talk about peace.*

52. Verbs Taking the Dative

The following sentences illustrate a series of verbs that take the dative.

Sie **antwortet** ihm nicht.
Ich bin ihr auf dieser Straße **begegnet** (*met*).
Ich **danke** Ihnen.
Das Kind **folgt** (*follows* or *obeys*) dem Vater.
Das **gefällt** mir nicht. *I don't like that.*
Er **hilft** ihr mit allem.

Er **gehört** keiner Studentenverbindung **an.**	*He belongs to no student organization.*
Ich weiß nicht, was ihm **eingefallen** (*occurred*) ist.	*I don't know what's come over him.*
Es **fehlt** ihm der Mut dazu.	*He lacks the courage to do it.*
Der Wagen **gehört** (*belongs*) meinem Vater.	
Es ist mir nicht ganz **gelungen.**	*I didn't quite succeed.*
Das schwarze Kleid **paßt** ihr überhaupt nicht.	*The black dress doesn't fit her at all.*

Verbs prefixed by **ent**– frequently take the dative:

Das ist mir leider entgangen.	*Unfortunately that escaped me (my notice).*
Die Antwort entspricht meinen Erwartungen nicht.	*The answer does not correspond to (come up to) my expectations.*

Verbs that take the dative retain the dative form in passive voice.

Sie hilft **ihm** nicht.
Ihm wird von ihr nicht geholfen.

Compare with:

Sie liebt **ihn** nicht.
Er wird von ihr nicht geliebt.

53. Position of Direct and Indirect Objects

Verbs expressing saying, telling, giving, offering, depriving, and the like, can of course take both dative and accusative. Notice the position of the nouns and/or pronouns involved. The dative (indirect object) precedes the accusative unless the accusative (direct object) is a personal pronoun.

Die Mutter erzählt den Kindern ein Märchen.
Die Mutter erzählt ihnen ein Märchen.
Die Mutter erzählt es den Kindern.
Die Mutter erzählt es ihnen.

Der Vater schenkt der Tochter ein neues Kleid zum Geburtstag.
Der Vater schenkt ihr ein neues Kleid zum Geburtstag.
Der Vater schenkt es der Tochter zum Geburtstag.
Der Vater schenkt es ihr zum Geburtstag.

54. Uses of the Present Perfect

The present perfect tense is employed more widely and variously in German than in English. It is frequently used, for example, to refer to isolated situations, actions, or events, completed in past time. (It often appears therefore in conversational German.)

Ich habe das nicht gewußt.	*I did not know that.*
Er hat es vorausgesehen.	*He foresaw it.*

Depending on circumstances, the last two sentences could be rendered more literally: *I have not known that. He has foreseen it.*

In the following examples, however, the time references exclude all possibility of English present perfect:

Gestern hat Professor Braun eine Vorlesung über Goethes *Faust* gehalten.	*Yesterday Professor Braun gave a lecture on Goethe's* Faust.
Goethe ist im Jahre 1832 gestorben.	*Goethe died in* 1832.

Note that the simple past tense is used in narration. This agrees generally with English usage.

27. Aufgabe

VOCABULARY BUILDING I

This is a list of weak verbs from Unit IX based on or related to *nouns* or *adjectives*. Most of them you have encountered at least once before this point. The starred items should be part of your active vocabulary.

abstürzen *plunge down:* der Sturz *plunge, sudden fall*
* antworten *answer:* die Antwort *answer*
atmen *breathe:* der Atem *breath*
* bauen *build:* der Bau *structure;* das Gebäude *building*
bedecken *cover:* die Decke *cover, ceiling*
* berichten *report, inform:* der Bericht *report*
beruhigen *calm, pacify:* die Ruhe *calm, quiet, rest*
beunruhigen *disturb, disquiet:* die Unruhe *unrest*
bilden *form, shape, cultivate:* das Bild *picture;* die Bildung *education, culture*
deuten *point, explain, interpret:* die Bedeutung *meaning, significance*
drücken *press:* der Druck *pressure* (*see:* der Ausdruck *expression;* der Eindruck *impression*)
einbüßen *suffer loss from, pay penalty:* die Buße *penance, fine*
* enden *end:* das Ende *end*
entfernen *take away, withdraw* (*when used with refl.*): die Ferne *distance;* fern *distant*
* erklären *declare, explain:* klar *clear*
ermüden *tire, exhaust:* müde *tired*
* erzählen *tell, relate, recount:* die Zahl *number, figure* (*see:* "*tale*," "*tally*")
* folgen (*with dat.*) *follow, obey:* die Folge *result, consequence*
* fragen *ask:* die Frage *question*
* fürchten (*refl.*) *fear:* die Furcht *fear*
* glauben *believe:* der Glaube *faith, belief*
leuchten *gleam, give light, shine:* das Licht *light* (*see:* die Leuchte *anything that gives light,* e.g., *beacon, lamp, sun, star*)
* öffnen *open:* offen *open;* die Öffnung *opening*
* reden *speak, talk:* die Rede *speech, talk*
schämen (*refl.*) *be ashamed:* die Scham *shame, modesty*
schwindeln *become dizzy, swindle:* der Schwindel *dizziness, fraud*
spüren *feel, sense, track:* die Spur *track, trace*
* stellen *place:* die Stelle *place, position*
überraschen *surprise, startle:* rasch *quick, hasty, impetuous*
verfluchen *curse:* der Fluch *curse*
versichern *assure, insure:* sicher *sure, secure, certain*
verstummen *become silent:* stumm *dumb, mute, silent*
verursachen *cause:* die Ursache *cause*
vorbereiten *prepare:* bereit *ready*

The following *weak verb–noun* pairs comprise a selection from preceding units. Test your memory regarding them.

arbeiten — die Arbeit
begrüßen — der Gruß
bezahlen — die Zahl
blicken — der Blick
danken — der Dank
donnern — der Donner
entschuldigen — die Schuld
freuen — die Freude
frühstücken — das Frühstück
führen — der Führer
leben — das Leben
meinen — die Meinung
reisen — die Reise
ruhen — die Ruhe
spielen — das Spiel
warnen — die Warnung
wohnen — die Wohnung
wünschen — der Wunsch

SYNONYMS AND ANTONYMS

The left-hand column of the following word lists contains vocabulary from **Der Schacht,** the first reading selection in this unit. The middle column contains synonyms and the right-hand column antonyms of these words. Given the meaning of the antonyms, try to derive the meanings of the other words.

Der Schacht

VOCABULARY		SYNONYMS	ANTONYMS
bedecken	________	verhüllen	entdecken *discover*
böse	________	übel	gut *good*
dunkel	________	finster	hell *bright*
eng	________	schmal	breit *broad*
erwidern	________	antworten	fragen *ask*
gefährlich	________	gewagt	sicher *safe*
glauben	________	meinen	zweifeln *doubt*
mitnehmen	________	mitbringen	zurücklassen *leave behind*
nachher	________	später	vorher *beforehand*
plötzlich	________	auf einmal	allmählich *gradually*
riesig	________	gigantisch	winzig *minute; tiny*
ruhig	________	gelassen	rastlos *restless*
streng	________	hart	sanft *gentle*
der Fremde	________	der Unbekannte	der Bekannte *acquaintance*
der Gastgeber	________	der Wirt	der Gast *guest*
die Nässe	________	die Feuchtigkeit	die Trockenheit *aridity*
die Seligkeit	________	die Freude	das Elend *misery*

Each German word in the left-hand column below has a *synonym* somewhere among the German words in the right-hand column (from **Der Schacht**). Match them.

bloß *merely*	allein	________
deshalb *therefore*	kräftig	________
einsam *lonely*	geschlossen	________
hinab *down(ward)*	daher	________
schnell *quickly*	immer	________
stark *strong*	rasch	________
stets *constantly*	abwärts	________
zeitig *early*	nur	________
zu *closed*	früh	________
zumachen *close*	schließen	________

IDIOMATIC EXPRESSIONS

The following idiomatic expressions are from **Der Schacht:**

in die Länge ziehen *draw out (full length), protract*
Es hat sich in die Länge gezogen. *It was long drawn-out.*
Der in die Länge gezogene gastliche Abend hatte ihn ermüdet. *The long-drawn-out convivial evening had tired him. (The convivial evening, which had been long drawn-out, had tired him.)*

schwindeln *cheat, tell a lie; become dizzy*
Er schwindelt. *He is not telling the truth. (He is cheating.)*

But: **Ihm** schwindelt. *He is getting dizzy.*

Note that in this last German example the dative is used and that there is no apparent subject. English speech pattern of course requires one. It is also permissible to say: **Es schwindelt mir.**

See: **beschwindeln** *swindle, defraud*

Es ist nicht immer der Reiche, der die Armen beschwindelt. *It is not always the rich man who cheats the poor.*

lassen *let, allow,* but here "*have*" in the sense of "*cause*"

Der Gast hat sich die Hausschlüssel von seinem Gastgeber geben lassen. *The guest had the house keys given to him by his host.*

reichen *reach, extend,* but also: *suffice, last, hold out*

Die Luft (das Geld, der Wein) wird nicht reichen. *There will not be enough air (money, wine).*

die Meinung *opinion* (Note use of gen. without prep. in German)

Er war der Meinung, das Fahrstuhlgehäuse könne unmöglich von jeder Luftzufuhr abgeschlossen sein. *He was of the opinion that the elevator cage could hardly be sealed tight against every possible source of air.*

bei sich sein, zu sich kommen

Der Patient war noch nicht völlig **bei sich.** Nach einigen Minuten aber war er **zu sich** gekommen. *The patient was not yet fully conscious. After a few minutes, however, he had regained consciousness (had come to).*

Reading I

WERNER BERGENGRUEN

WERNER BERGENGRUEN, born in Riga, Latvia, on September 16, 1892, is a leading German author still actively engaged as a creative artist. He is deeply concerned with religious themes, with historical subjects, and with issues emerging from events enacted on the contemporary scene. Among his best known novels are *Der Großtyrann und das Gericht* and *Am Himmel wie auf Erden.* He has written many short stories of distinction (*Der Tod von Reval*) as well as lyric poetry, notably *Dies Irae. Der Schacht,* the brief psychological story introduced here, typifies the author's manner and skill in handling the short anecdotal medium: The psychological revelation is disclosed not so much through analytical probing as through action, through an event.

DER SCHACHT *

Das riesige Hochhaus, welches den Schauplatz dieser Geschichte bildet, enthält fast nur Büroräume. Daher liegt es schon am frühen Abend totenstill und wird zeitig geschlossen. Nur das Dachgeschoß ist zu Wohnungen ausgebaut.

* der Schacht — *pit, (elevator) shaft, gorge, ravine*

LINE
1 riesig — *gigantic*
der Schauplatz — *setting, scene of action*
enthalten — *contain, house*
2 der Büroraum — *office*

LINE
2 daher — *therefore*
3 zeitig — *early*
das Dachgeschoß — *top floor*
ausgebaut — *designed, made into*

Aus einer dieser Wohnungen trat Kleinsieper, rückwärts gehend und sich noch in der Tür von dem Ehepaar verabschiedend, bei welchem er den Abend verbracht hatte.

Beim Niedersteigen hörte er das näherkommende Summen des aufwärtsgleiten-5 den Fahrstuhls und empfand eine flüchtige Verwunderung darüber, denn es war schon fast Mitternacht.

Das Summen verstummte in demselben Augenblick, in welchem Kleinsieper den Treppenabsatz des zweitobersten Stockwerks erreicht hatte. Vor dem Aufzug stand ein junger Mann, eine Aktenmappe unter dem Arm. Er öffnete gerade die 10 Aufzugstür, um einzusteigen, hielt aber inne, als er Kleinsieper bemerkte.

„Sie wollen abwärts? Bitte."

Kleinsieper hatte eine Abneigung gegen die engen Behältnisse, in denen ihm das Fahren Beängstigung, das Anlangen aber ein widriges Gefühl in der Magengrube verursachte. Allein es wäre schwierig gewesen, die Höflichkeit des Fremden 15 zurückzuweisen und gar diese Zurückweisung zu erklären, auch hatte der in die Länge gezogene gastliche Abend Kleinsieper ermüdet.

Und wer schämt sich nicht, einem kräftigen jungen Mann Beängstigungen einzugestehen? Kleinsieper griff an den Hut, sagte: „Vielen Dank!" und trat ein. Der Fremde folgte ihm.

20 Kleinsieper spürte eine Beklemmung und wider seinen Willen deutete sein Körper fast unmerklich die Bewegung eines Fluchtversuches an.*

Aber da hatte der junge Mann bereits die Tür zugezogen; er drückte auf den Knopf und die Fahrt begann. Kleinsieper schloß die Augen. Ihm schwindelte und er spürte, wie seine Stirn sich mit kleinen eiskalten Tröpfchen bedeckte.

25 Mit einem Ruck brach die Fahrt ab. Kleinsieper öffnete die Augen: alles war dunkel.

„Nanu!" rief der junge Mann zornig. Kleinsieper war erschrocken.

„Was ist denn?" fragte er zaghaft.

* *Kleinsieper felt a tightness inside him, and against his will his body made an almost imperceptible movement as if to try to escape.*

LINE

1–2 sich verabschiedend — *taking leave*
2 das Ehepaar — *married couple*
4 beim Niedersteigen — *as he was going down the stairs*
das Summen — *humming*
aufwärtsgleiten — *glide upward*
5 der Fahrstuhl — *elevator*
empfand eine flüchtige Verwunderung darüber — *experienced a fleeting sense of surprise about this*
7 verstummen — *grow silent, stop*
8 den Treppenabsatz des zweitobersten Stockwerks — *the landing on the second last floor*
der Aufzug — *see* Fahrstuhl
9 die Aktenmappe — *briefcase*
10 innehalten — *stop*
12 die Abneigung — *aversion*

LINE

12 die engen Behältnisse — here: *close-quarter conveyances*
13 die Beängstigung — *anxiety*
das Anlangen — *arrival*
widrig — *unpleasant*
13–14 die Magengrube — *pit of the stomach*
14 die Höflichkeit — *courteous offer*
15 zurückweisen — *refuse*
die Zurückweisung — *refusal*
17–18 eingestehen — *confess*
18 griff an den Hut — *touched (his hand to) his hat*
23 der Knopf — *button*
24 das Tröpfchen — *small drop*
25 der Ruck — *jerk*
27 Nanu! — *Well, now!*
28 zaghaft — *timidly*

„Irgendeine Schweinerei,“ antwortete der andere grob. „Kurzschluß, was weiß ich. Steckengeblieben sind wir. Vielleicht ist eins von den Drahtseilen gerissen.“

„Abstürzen?“ keuchte Kleinsieper. „Abstürzen? Wieso sind wir dann nicht abgestürzt? Wir können doch jeden Augenblick abstürzen!“ 5

„Ach was,“ erwiderte der junge Mann wegwerfend, „was wollen Sie denn immer mit Ihrem Abstürzen? Dafür ist doch die selbsttätige Fangvorrichtung da. Haben Sie Streichhölzer?“

„Nein, nur ein Feuerzeug.“

Es gab ein kratzendes Metallgeräusch, dann glomm die Lunte, die nichts zu 10 erleuchten vermochte als einen handbreiten Umfang.*

„Nützt nichts!“ sagte der junge Mann. „Wir müssen rufen. — Halloh! Hallooh!“

Das langgezogene „o“ prallte von den Wänden zurück und erfüllte den engen Raum mit Schrecken. 15

„Rufen Sie auch!“

Kleinsieper gehorchte. Es wurde ein Angstgebrüll. Die Stimme versagte ihm.

Eine halbe Stunde später erklärte der junge Mann heiser: „Es hat keinen Zweck. Niemand hört uns. Wir werden warten müssen, bis es Morgen wird.“

Sie sprachen nun miteinander über die Gebräuche des Hauses, die es unwahr- 20 scheinlich machten, daß zur Nachtzeit zufällig ein Mensch vorüberkomme, der sie hören könnte. Der junge Mann erzählte, sein Chef habe ihn mitten in der Nacht mit den Schlüsseln hergeschickt, um einige Akten zu holen, die er morgen früh auf einer Geschäftsreise mitnehmen wollte. Kleinsieper aber hatte seinen Gastgebern die Mühe der Begleitung ersparen wollen und sich daher die Haus- 25 schlüssel von ihnen geben lassen.

Der junge Mann sagte: „Ein verfluchtes Pech, hier stundenlang im Schacht hocken zu müssen.“

* *There was a grating metallic sound; then the wick flared up, but was capable of illuminating only a tiny little area.*

LINE

1 irgendeine Schweinerei — *something's fouled up*
der Kurzschluß — *short circuit*
2 steckenbleiben — *get stuck*
das Drahtseil — *cable*
4 abstürzen — *plunge down*
keuchen — *pant, gasp*
6 erwidern — *reply*
wegwerfend — *contemptuously*
7 die selbsttätige Fangvorrichtung — *automatic safety catch*
8 das Streichholz — *match*
9 das Feuerzeug — *lighter*
12 Nützt nichts! — *No use!*
14 langgezogen — *long-drawn-out*
zurückprallen — *re-echo*
15 der Schrecken — *terror*

LINE

17 das Angstgebrüll — *cry of terror*
versagen — *fail*
18 heiser — *hoarse*
19 der Zweck — *purpose*
20 die Gebräuche des Hauses — *the daily routine ("customs") of the building*
21 zufällig — *by chance*
23 der Schlüssel — *key*
herschicken — *send here*
einige Akten — *some papers*
24 die Geschäftsreise — *business trip*
25 der Gastgeber — *host*
die Mühe der Begleitung — *the trouble of accompanying him*
ersparen — *spare*
27 verfluchtes Pech — *rotten luck*
28 hocken — here: *"be cooped up"*

„Im Schacht?" rief Kleinsieper bestürzt, „Im Schacht, wieso im Schacht?"

Der andere konnte sich das Entsetzen nicht erklären, das in Kleinsiepers Stimme lag. „Natürlich, im Fahrschacht, wie nennen Sie es denn?"

„Schacht . . . Schacht . . ." murmelte Kleinsieper. „Also im Schacht. Ich hatte 5 gemeint, ein Schacht wäre in Bergwerken oder . . . oder im Gebirge, so . . . so zwischen Felsen, wissen Sie."

Der junge Mann schwieg.

„Schacht . . . Schacht . . ." wiederholte Kleinsieper nach einer Weile. Plötzlich begann er zu schnaufen. Er sprach in kurzen, gekeuchten Sätzen, zwischen denen 10 Pausen lagen: „Die Luft ist dumpf. Es ist so eng hier. Die Luft wird nicht reichen. Bis morgen warten? Wir werden ersticken. Hier im Schacht."

„So halten Sie sich doch ruhig," fuhr ihn der junge Mann an. „Wissen Sie denn nicht, daß jede Bewegung Sauerstoff kostet? Man muß es machen, wie die Leute in den Unterseebooten, sich nicht unnütz rühren, nicht zu tief atmen, verstanden?"

15 Im Grunde hielt der junge Mann die Lage nicht für sehr gefährlich, da er der Meinung war, das Fahrstuhlgehäuse könne unmöglich von jeder Luftzufuhr abgeschlossen sein.

„Regen Sie sich nicht auf," sagte er streng. „Es ist gar keine Gefahr vorhanden. Halten Sie sich ruhig!"

20 Kleinsieper versuchte zu gehorchen, aber am Geklapper seiner Manschettenknöpfe merkte der junge Mann, daß jener zitterte. Plötzlich begann Kleinsieper zu reden, ohne sich von dem andern unterbrechen zu lassen. Er flüsterte rasch, dringlich, beschwörend, sein wirres Gerede gelegentlich kurz unterbrochen durch sein Keuchen:

25 „Ja, Sie sind noch jung. Sie haben damals noch keine Zeitungen gelesen, und heute redet kein Mensch mehr davon, es war nämlich auch ein Schacht, das heißt, erst hieß es immer nur Spalte oder Kamin, nachher nach dem Lokaltermin kam erst die Bezeichnung Schacht in Gebrauch. Wenn ich doch Luft hätte! — Ersticken muß ich! — Erzählen muß ich, ich ersticke ja nicht nur von außen, darum 30 muß ich es erzählen, keinem Menschen habe ich es erzählt, aber weil ich doch ersticken muß, verstehen Sie, weil ich ersticken muß! Ja, die haben mir freilich

LINE
1 bestürzt — *startled*
2 das Entsetzen — *horror, terror*
9 schnaufen — *breathe heavily*
der Satz — *sentence*
11 reichen — *be sufficient, last*
ersticken — *suffocate*
12 anfahren — *say angrily*
13 die Bewegung — *motion*
der Sauerstoff — *oxygen*
14 das Unterseeboot — *submarine*
sich rühren — *move*
unnütz — *unnecessarily*
15 im Grunde — *actually*
die Lage — *situation*
gefährlich — *dangerous*
16 das Fahrstuhlgehäuse — *elevator cage*
die Luftzufuhr — *supply of air*

LINE
17 abgeschlossen — *sealed off*
18 sich aufregen — *get excited*
vorhanden — *imminent*
20–1 Geklapper seiner Manschettenknöpfe — *clicking of his cuff links*
21 zittern — *tremble*
22 unterbrechen — *interrupt*
23 dringlich — *urgently*
beschwörend — *imploringly*
wirr — *confused*
das Gerede — *talk*
gelegentlich — *occasionally*
27 die Spalte — *crevice, crevasse*
nach dem Lokaltermin — *after the court hearing*
28 die Bezeichnung — *term*

nichts nachweisen können, mußten mich loslassen, halbes Jahr Untersuchung, die Gesellschaft mußte die Versicherung zahlen, ich hatte meine Frau doch ordnungsgemäß versichert, kurz bevor wir in die Alpen fuhren. Ja, da war eine Spalte, meinetwegen ein Schacht, ich hatte mir den Platz vorher ausgesucht, den Schacht! Den Schacht!" Sein Sprechen, das immer hastiger und wilder geworden, ging plötzlich in Gebrüll über. „Freispruch! Versicherungssumme! Aber Luft brauche ich. Luft! Gebt mir doch Luft! Ich ersticke ja! Innen ersticke ich, innen! Luft! Luft!"

Dieses Wort „Luft!" schrie er sieben oder acht Male hintereinander. Dann wurde er plötzlich still.

Kleinsieper spürte einen scharfen Reiz in der Kehle, kalte Nässe auf seiner Stirn und grelles Licht vor seinen Augen. Gleich darauf erkannte er, daß eine Hand ein Schnapsglas von seinen Lippen entfernte.

Er schloß wieder die Augen und genoß die Seligkeit des Atmens. Er hörte Stimmen, unter denen er die seines Gastgebers zu erkennen glaubte. Nach einigen Minuten war er völlig bei sich.

„Gott sei Dank, Herr Kleinsieper! Gott sei Dank!" sagte sein Gastgeber. „Na, das war eine böse Geschichte, Herr Kleinsieper, was?"

Durch die Fenster der Portierswohnung dämmerte der Tag.

Der junge Mann stand neben dem Fenster und durchsuchte seine Taschen, um dem Portier ein Geschenk zu machen. Als er sah, daß Kleinsieper zu sich gekommen war, trat er zu dem Sofa, auf dem Kleinsieper immer noch lag, und sagte: „Sie haben mir da vorhin eine interessante Geschichte erzählt, Herr Kleinsieper. Sie hatten nur vergessen, mir Ihren Namen zu nennen, Herr Kleinsieper. Jetzt habe ich ihn gehört. — Wir sehen uns wieder, Herr Kleinsieper!"

FRAGEN

1. Was wissen Sie über Werner Bergengruen? 2. Beschreiben Sie den Schauplatz seiner Erzählung! 3. Worin bestand (bestehen in *consist of*) „die Höflichkeit des Fremden"? 4. Wie fühlte sich Kleinsieper in dem Aufzug? 5. Wovor fürchtete sich Kleinsieper, nachdem der Aufzug steckengeblieben war? 6. Wie erklären Sie sich, daß Kleinsieper bei dem Wort „Schacht" sogleich an einen Schacht in den Bergen dachte? 7. Was gestand Kleinsieper und warum machte er sein Geständnis (*confession*) gerade in dieser Nacht? 8. Warum lag dem Fremden daran, Kleinsiepers Namen zu kennen?

LINE
1 nachweisen — *prove*
die Untersuchung — *investigation*
2 die Gesellschaft — *company*
die Versicherung — *insurance*
2–3 ordnungsgemäß — *duly*
4 meinetwegen — *if you want to call it that, for all I care*
aussuchen — *select, pick*
6 das Gebrüll — *roaring*
der Freispruch — *acquittal*

LINE
11 der Reiz — *pain, irritation*
die Kehle — *throat*
die Nässe — *moisture*
12 grell — *glaring*
13 das Schnapsglas — *glass of brandy*
entfernen — *remove*
14 genießen — *enjoy*
die Seligkeit — *delight*
19 der Portier — *doorkeeper*
21 das Geschenk — *gift, tip*

VOCABULARY BUILDING II

ANTONYMS

Each German word in the left-hand column has an *antonym* somewhere among the German words in the right-hand column (from **Lutezia,** the next reading selection). Pair them and give the meaning of the antonym in each case.

besänftigen *pacify*	die Zukunft	______
das Elend *misery*	ziehen	______
freudig *joyful*	geheim	______
glücklicherweise *fortunately*	leider	______
hart *hard*	das Glück	______
offenbar *obvious*	die Niederlage	______
selten *seldom*	gewöhnlich	______
stoßen *push*	sanft	______
der Sieg *victory*	elend	______
die Vergangenheit *past*	beunruhigen	______

IDIOMATIC EXPRESSIONS

The following idiomatic expressions are from **Lutezia** *and* **Atlantis,** *in Reading II of this lesson.*

aus den Augen verlieren *lose sight of*
Wir dürfen ihn nie aus den Augen verlieren. *We must never lose sight of him.*

zugrunde richten *destroy*
Diese beiden Völker können in einem gewöhnlichen politischen Kriege nicht ganz zugrunde gerichtet werden. *These two nations cannot be completely destroyed in an ordinary political war.*

Seiner Meinung **nach** brachte eine warme Strömung aus dem Süden Feuchtigkeit nach Nordafrika und Südwesteuropa, solange der Golfstrom **daran** verhindert war, Europa **zu erreichen.** *According to his opinion, a warm current from the South brought moisture to North Africa and Southwest Europe as long as the Gulf Stream was prevented from reaching Europe.*

NOTE: (1) The postpositive preposition **nach** (*according to*);
(2) the prepositional compound **daran**, which serves to anticipate the final phrase;
(3) the difference in speech pattern between German and English in their treatment of the verb in the final phrase: Whereas German uses an infinitive phrase **zu erreichen** (lit. "*to reach*"), English employs a participial phrase *from reaching*. The difference in prepositional usage is striking also: **zu** (lit. "*to*") as against "*from.*"

werden + zu = *become, be changed to, change to, turn to*
Die Erde wurde **zur** Wüste. *The earth became (was changed to)* ***a*** *desert.*
Das Eis wurde zu Wasser. *The ice became (turned to) water.*
Das Holz wurde zu Stein. *The wood became (turned to) stone.*
Die Antwort wurde zur Frage. *The answer became (changed to) a question.*

Note that with a feminine noun **zur** is used, that is, the contraction of **zu** and the definite article.

Reading II

1. Aus Heinrich Heines LUTEZIA (1840/43; 1854)

Kommunismus ist der geheime Name des furchtbaren Antagonisten, der die Proletarierherrschaft in allen ihren Konsequenzen dem heutigen Bourgeoisieregimente entgegensetzt. Es wird ein furchtbarer Zweikampf sein. Wie möchte er enden? Das wissen die Götter und Göttinnen, denen die Zukunft bekannt ist. Nur so viel wissen wir, der Kommunismus, obgleich er jetzt wenig besprochen wird und in verborgenen Dachstuben auf seinem elenden Strohlager hinlungert, so ist er doch der düstere Held, dem eine große, wenn auch vorübergehende Rolle beschieden in der modernen Tragödie und der nur des Stichwortes harrt, um auf die Bühne zu treten. Wir dürfen daher diesen Akteur nie aus den Augen verlieren, und wir wollen zuweilen von den geheimen Proben berichten, worin er sich zu seinem Debüt vorbereitet.

Ich fürchte mich immer im ersten Anfang, wenn ich die Dämonen der Umwälzung entzügelt sehe, späterhin bin ich sehr gefaßt, und die tollsten Erscheinungen können mich weder beunruhigen noch überraschen, eben weil ich sie vorausgesehen. Was wäre das Ende dieser Bewegung, wozu Paris wieder, wie immer, das Signal gegeben? Es wäre der Krieg, der gräßlichste Zerstörungskrieg, der leider die beiden edelsten Völker der Zivilisation in die Arena riefe zu beider Verderben; ich meine Deutschland und Frankreich. England, die große Wasserschlange, die immer in ihr ungeheures Wassernest zurückkriechen kann, und Rußland, das in seinen ungeheuren Föhren, Steppen und Eisgefilden ebenfalls die sichersten Verstecke hat, diese beiden können in einem gewöhnlichen politischen Kriege, selbst durch die entschiedensten Niederlagen, nicht ganz zugrunde gerichtet werden — aber Deutschland ist in solchen Fällen weit schlimmer bedroht, und gar Frank-

LINE
2 die Herrschaft — *rule*
3 entgegensetzen — *oppose*
der Zweikampf — *duel*
möchte — *might, could*
6 in verborgenen Dachstuben — *in hidden garrets*
auf seinem elenden Strohlager — *on a miserable bed of straw*
hinlungern — *lounge*
7 düster — *dark, sombre*
8 beschieden (*read:* beschieden ist) — *is destined*
das Stichwort — *cue*
harren — *await*
9 die Bühne — *stage*
10 zuweilen — *from time to time*
die Probe — *rehearsal*
12 Dämonen der Umwälzung — *demons of revolution*
13 entzügelt — *unchained*
gefaßt — *composed, calm*

LINE
13 die tollsten Erscheinungen — *the maddest apparitions*
14 beunruhigen — *disturb*
voraussehen — *anticipate*
vorausgesehen (*read:* vorausgesehen habe)
15 die Bewegung — *movement*
16 gegeben (*read:* gegeben hat)
der gräßlichste Zerstörungskrieg — *the ghastliest war of destruction*
17 edel — *noble*
zu beider Verderben — *to the detriment or undoing of both*
18 die Wasserschlange — *water snake*
19 ungeheuer — *immense*
20 die Föhren — *firs, forests (of fir trees)*
20–1 das Versteck — *hiding place, retreat*
21 selbst — *even*
22 die entschiedensten Niederlagen — *the most decisive defeats*
23 bedrohen — *threaten*

reich könnte in der kläglichsten Weise seine politische Existenz einbüßen. Doch das wäre nur der erste Akt des großen Spektakelstücks, gleichsam das Vorspiel. Der zweite Akt ist die europäische, die Weltrevolution, der große Zweikampf der Besitzlosen mit der Aristokratie des Besitzes, und da wird weder von Nationalität
5 noch von Religion die Rede sein; nur Ein Vaterland wird es geben, nämlich die Erde, und nur Einen Glauben, nämlich das Glück auf Erden.

Werden die religiösen Doktrinen der Vergangenheit in allen Landen sich zu einem verzweiflungsvollen Widerstand erheben, und wird etwa dieser Versuch den dritten Akt bilden? Wird gar die alte absolute Tradition nochmals auf die Bühne treten,
10 aber in einem neuen Kostüm und mit neuen Stich- und Schlagwörtern? Wie würde dieses Schauspiel schließen? Ich weiß nicht, aber ich denke, daß man der großen Wasserschlange am Ende das Haupt zertreten und dem Bären des Nordens das Fell über die Ohren ziehen wird. Es wird vielleicht alsdann nur Einen Hirten und Eine Herde geben, ein freier Hirt mit einem eisernen Hirtenstabe und eine gleich-
15 geschorene, gleichblökende Menschenherde! Wilde, düstere Zeiten dröhnen heran, und der Prophet, der eine neue Apokalypse schreiben wollte, müßte ganz neue Bestien erfinden, und zwar so erschreckliche, daß die älteren Johanneischen Tiersymbole dagegen nur sanfte Täubchen und Amoretten wären.

2. EINSTELLUNG DER KERNWAFFENVERSUCHE? *

In einem Gespräch mit einer Delegation der Weltföderation der Wissenschaftler
20 in Moskau sagte der russische Ministerpräsident: „Wir wären sehr erfreut, wenn es gelänge, bis Ende dieses Jahres in Genf ein Abkommen über die Einstellung der Kernwaffenversuche zu erzielen.“ Es wird berichtet, daß der russische Ministerpräsident betont habe, er sehe keine Hindernisse, die einen raschen Abschluß eines Abkommens über die Kernwaffenversuche hindern würden. Die Frage der Zahl
25 der Kontrollposten und ihres Personals biete keine großen Schwierigkeiten. Bei einer Kontrolle könne man mit Erfolg „die Methode der Stichproben“ anwenden.

Aus der *Süddeutschen Zeitung*, 24. Mai 1959

* *Cessation of nuclear tests*

LINE

1 kläglich — *pitiful, miserable*
einbüßen — *lose*
2 das Spektakelstück — *spectacular play*
gleichsam — *as it were, so to speak*
4 die Besitzlosen — *the poor, the proletariat*
7–8 sich . . . erheben — *rise up*
8 verzweiflungsvoll — *desperate*
der Widerstand — *resistance*
der Versuch — *attempt*
10 das Schlagwort — *slogan*
13 das Fell — *skin*
der Hirt(e) — *shepherd*
14 der Stab — *staff, rod*
14–15 eine gleichgeschorene . . . Menschenherde — *a human herd, uniformly shorn and bleating in unison*

LINE

15 dröhnen — *roar, thunder*
17–18 die Johanneischen Tiersymbole (*refers to animal symbols in the Revelation of St. John*)
18 dagegen — *by comparison*
das Täubchen — *little dove*
die Amoretten — *little cupids*
20 der Ministerpräsident — *prime minister*
erfreut — *pleased*
21 das Abkommen — *agreement, pact*
22 erzielen — *achieve*
23 betonen — *emphasize*
das Hindernis — *obstacle*
der Abschluß — *conclusion*
24 hindern — *obstruct*
25 bieten — *present*
26 die Stichprobe — *spot check*

3. EINE NEUE THEORIE ÜBER DAS VERLORENE ATLANTIS

Ein im atlantischen Ozean versenkter Süßwassersee ist eine Anomalie. Aber das Phänomen wird erklärlich, wenn sich herausstellt, daß der See sich einst auf dem Festland befand und daß das Land versank und von Seewasser bedeckt wurde. Schwedische und amerikanische Geologen stellten die Tatsache dieses Versinkens vor Jahren fest. Der versunkene Erdteil ist als die mittelatlantische Landbrücke 5 bekannt.

Dr. René Malaise vom Riksmuseum in Stockholm berichtet in dem schwedischen Magazin für Geographie, *Ymer*, daß sein Kollege, Dr. P. W. Kolbe, den definitiven Beweis für dieses Versinken erbracht habe, und zwar durch seine Forschungen über die Diatomeen, mikroskopische Algen, die sowohl in Süßwasser wie in 10 Salzwasser vorkommen. Wenn die Algen sterben, so sinken sie zu Boden und ihre harten toten Schalen sammeln sich im Sediment und Schlick an. Dr. Kolbe prüfte Diatomeen in einem Kerngehäuse, das von schwedischen Wissenschaftlern in einer Tiefe von 12 000 Fuß dem tropischen Bereich des atlantischen Ozeans entnommen worden war. Einige der Diatomeen in diesem Kerngehäuse waren 15 ausschließlich von der Süßwasserart, was beweist, daß das Sediment, aus dem sie stammten, einst ein Teil eines Sees war.

Eine Schranke* für den Golfstrom

Dr. Malaise zufolge können die Süßwasserdiatomeen auf dem Grund des Ozeans nur durch die Annahme erklärt werden, daß es einst eine mittelatlantische Landbrücke gab, die über dem Meeresspiegel quer durch den Ozean verlief. Das 20 Kerngehäuse, welches die schwedische Expedition mitbrachte, befand sich ursprünglich auf dem Grund eines Süßwassersees, der zu der mittelatlantischen Landbrücke gehörte. Diese Brücke bildete eine Schranke für den Golfstrom, sodaß der arktische Ozean von Europa bis Grönland vor nicht mehr als zehn bis zwölftausend Jahren ein Binnenmeer war. Als die Landschranke versank, konnte 25 der Golfstrom den arktischen Ozean erreichen, und so endete die Eiszeit. Diese Folgerung ist von russischen Wissenschaftlern bestätigt worden, die auf dem Eisbrecher Sadko Forschungen auf dem Grund des Ozeans betrieben.

* die Schranke — *barrier*

LINE
- 2 wenn sich herausstellt — *when it turns out*
- 2–3 sich befinden — *be situated*
- 4–5 feststellen — *establish*
- 5 die mittelatlantische Landbrücke — *the Mid-Atlantic Ridge*
- 8–9 den . . . Beweis . . . erbracht habe — *had furnished . . . proof*
- 9–10 die Forschungen — *research*
- 11 vorkommen — *occur*
- 12 die Schale — *shell*
  sich ansammeln — *collect*
  Sediment und Schlick — *sediment and ooze*

LINE
- 13 das Kerngehäuse — *core*
- 15 entnommen worden war — *had been taken from*
- 16 ausschließlich — *exclusively*
  was beweist — *(a fact) which proves*
- 19 die Annahme — *hypothesis, assumption*
- 20 der Meeresspiegel — *surface of the sea*
- 24–5 vor nicht mehr als . . . Jahren — *no more than . . . years ago*
- 25 das Binnenmeer — *land-locked sea*
- 27 die Folgerung — *conclusion*
  ist . . . bestätigt worden — *was confirmed*
- 28 betreiben — *carry out*

Dr. Malaise glaubt, daß die bekannten unterseeischen Schluchten von großen Überschwemmungen gebildet wurden, die von der Meerenge von Dänemark ausgingen. Sie wurden nicht vom Hudson, Niger, Kongo und von anderen Flüssen ausgegraben, sondern von nördlichen Überschwemmungen, die ihren Abfluß fan-
5 den, als die mittelatlantische Landbrücke versank. All das stimmt im Wesentlichen mit Theorien überein, die Professor Nils H. Odhner schon vor langer Zeit entwickelte. Diese Theorien erklären, wieso manche Mollusken des Mittelmeers in Südafrika zu finden sind.

Die Legende von dem verlorenen Atlantis

Dr. Malaise erwägt die möglichen Folgerungen, die man aus seinen Funden
10 ziehen kann. Seiner Meinung nach brachte eine warme Strömung aus dem Süden Feuchtigkeit nach Nordafrika und Südwesteuropa, solange der Golfstrom daran verhindert war, Europa zu erreichen. Als der Golfstrom die Schranke durchbrach und die Arktis erreichte, verdrängte sein kälterer, südlicher Ast, der Kanaristrom, die warme Strömung, und die Sahara wurde zur Wüste. Dr. Malaise glaubt, daß
15 dieser Umstand hungernde Menschen aus Lybien und Nordwestafrika dazu bewegte, langsam gegen Ägypten hin abzuwandern. Die Eindringlinge wurden von Ramses III im Jahre 1195 v. Chr. geschlagen. Die Erzählungen der Gefangenen mögen die Grundlage für Platos Erzählungen von den überlebenden Einwohnern von Atlantis gewesen sein. Ihre Vorfahren, meint Dr. Malaise, mögen wohl
20 tausende Jahre vor der Wanderung auf der mittelatlantischen Landbrücke gelebt haben.

Nach einem Bericht der *New York Times*
vom 23. September 1956

DER LATTENZAUN	THE PICKET FENCE
Es war einmal ein Lattenzaun mit Zwischenraum, hindurchzuschaun.	*There was a fence one time I knew* *With spacebetween for peeking through.*
Ein Architekt, der dieses sah, stand eines Abends plötzlich da —	*An architect who saw this thing* *Stood there one sudden evening* —

LINE
1 die bekannten unterseeischen Schluchten — *the well-known submarine canyons*
2 die Überschwemmung — *inundation*
die Meerenge von Dänemark — *Denmark Strait*
4 ausgraben — *gouge out, dig out*
der Abfluß — *outlet*
5–6 übereinstimmen — *agree*
im Wesentlichen — *essentially*
7 entwickeln — *develop, advance*
wieso — here: "*why*"
8 zu finden sind — *are (to be) found*
9 erwägen — *consider, speculate on*
die Funde — *findings*

LINE
10 die Strömung — *current*
11 die Feuchtigkeit — *moisture*
12 verhindert war — *was prevented*
13 verdrängte sein ... südlicher Ast — *its southern branch displaced*
14 die Wüste — *desert*
15 der Umstand — *circumstance*
16 bewegen — *cause, induce*
abwandern — *migrate*
der Eindringling — *intruder, invader*
17–18 der Gefangene — *captive*
18 die Grundlage — *basis*
überlebend — *surviving*
19 die Vorfahren — *ancestors*

und nahm den Zwischenraum heraus
und baute draus ein großes Haus.

Der Zaun indessen stand ganz dumm,
mit Latten ohne was herum.

Ein Anblick gräßlich und gemein.
Drum zog ihn der Senat auch ein.

Der Architekt jedoch entfloh
nach Afri- od. Ameriko.

Christian Morgenstern

And pulled the spacebetween "heraus"
And built himself a nice big house.

The fence meanwhile stood in disgrace,
Pickets apart but minus space.

A sight quite vulgar, and a sin.
So the police they pulled it in.

The architect he ran off though
To Afri- or Americo.

ZEHNTER TEIL

„Der singende Mann“ (Barlach)

Kunstausstellung in Kassel

„Schachspieler am Zug“ (Baumeister)

Herbert von Karajan (mit erhobenem Zeigefinger) leitet einen Dirigentenkurs in der West-Berliner Hochschule für Musik.

28. Aufgabe

GESPRÄCH ÜBER DIE MUSIK

Of the following dialogue memorize only the section on this page. The rest (see page 247) is to be treated as reading assignment.

HANS: Sag mal, Heinz, wie bist du denn eigentlich darauf gekommen, klassische Musik zu studieren?

HEINZ: Warum sollte ich mich nicht für klassische Musik interessieren!

HANS: Hat denn ein solches Studium einen praktischen Wert? Dafür interessiert sich doch heute kein Mensch.

HEINZ: Anscheinend doch! Oder willst du behaupten, ich sei der einzige Mensch, der Musiker werden will?

HANS: Na schön. Es muß wohl auch unpraktische Menschen geben. Das ist es ja nicht, was ich nicht verstehe.

HEINZ: Was ist es also?

HANS: Ich begreife nicht, wie man sich, zum Beispiel, für die deutsche Musik so begeistern kann wie du. Dieser Bach und dieser Händel, dieser Haydn, dieser Mozart —

HEINZ: Ja, und dieser Beethoven, dieser Schubert, dieser Brahms!

HANS: Und wie sie alle heißen mögen!

CONVERSATION ON MUSIC

HANS: Tell me, Heinz, just how did it occur to you to study classical music?

HEINZ: Why shouldn't I be interested in classical music?

HANS: Is there any practical value to this kind of study? After all, no one is interested in that (sort of thing) nowadays.

HEINZ: Apparently (there are some people who are). Or do you wish to maintain that I am the only person who wants to become a musician?

HANS: All right. I guess there must be unpractical people too. That's really not the thing that puzzles me. (*lit.* "That isn't what I don't understand.")

HEINZ: What is it, then?

HANS: It is beyond me (I do not comprehend) how, for instance, anyone can get as enthusiastic about German music as you (do). This (fellow) Bach, and Handel, (and) Haydn, (and) Mozart —

HEINZ: Yes, and Beethoven, (and) Schubert, (and) Brahms!

HANS: And whatever their names may be!

HEINZ: Wenn du sagen willst, daß ich mich nur für deutsche Musik interessiere, so irrst du dich übrigens. Die deutsche Musik ist ein Teil der abendländischen Tradition.

HANS: Das will ich ja nicht bestreiten.

HEINZ: Und gerade die klassische Musik macht die kulturelle Verbundenheit der westlichen Welt erst recht deutlich. 5

HANS: Aber was kann einem denn diese Musik viel sagen?

HEINZ: Dem, der Ohren hat zu hören, kann sie fast alles sagen. Ist die Musik nicht eine Sprache über allen Sprachen? Erhebt die Musik sich nicht über alle Landesgrenzen? 10

HANS: Soll das deine Antwort sein?

HEINZ: Vielleicht. Jedenfalls liebe ich die Musik, weil sie zu jedermann sprechen will und weil sie ans Herz rührt, kurz: weil sie eine Sprache ist — *ohne* Worte!

DRILL PATTERNS

Repeat the following drills after your instructor or after the speaker on the tape. Imitate the pronunciation very carefully.

1. Ich darf das nicht leugnen.[1]
Ich will das nicht leugnen.
Ich werde das nicht leugnen.
Ich möchte das nicht leugnen.
Ich kann das nicht leugnen.
Ich brauche das nicht zu leugnen.

2. Will er das nicht begreifen?
Wird er das nicht begreifen?
Sollte sie das nicht begreifen?
Muß sie das nicht begreifen?

3. Soll ich das nicht sagen?
Nein, das darfst du nicht sagen.
Muß ich das nicht sagen?
Nein, das kannst du nicht sagen.

4. Will er das? Wollte er das?
Möchte er das? Mag er das?
Darf er das? Dürfte er das?
Muß er das? Müßte er das?
Kann er das? Könnte er das?
Soll er das? Sollte er das?

[1] **leugnen** deny

LINE
2 sich irren — *be wrong*
übrigens — *incidentally*
3 abendländisch — *occidental, Western*
4 bestreiten — *dispute*
5–6 die Verbundenheit — *unity*
6 westlich — *Western*
6 deutlich — *clear*
8 fast — *almost*
9–10 sich erheben (über) — *rise beyond, transcend*
13 rühren (an) — *touch, move*

5. Hat er das gewollt?
Hat er das gedurft?
Hatte sie das gemocht?
Hatte sie das gekonnt?

6. Habt ihr das tun müssen?
Haben wir das tun können?
Hatten sie das tun dürfen?
Hatte sie das tun wollen?

7. Wir hätten das nicht tun können.
Ihr hättet das nicht tun dürfen.
Er hätte das tun sollen.
Sie hätte das tun müssen.

8. Was soll das?
Was soll das bedeuten?
Was mag das heißen?
Was kann das bedeuten?

9. Er soll ihr das nicht sagen.
Er soll ihr das gesagt haben.
Er muß ihr das gesagt haben.
Er hätte ihr das nicht sagen sollen.
Er sagte ihr, sie solle nach Hause gehen.

10. Das mag wohl sein.
Das kann nicht sein.
Sollte das möglich sein?
Das dürfte richtig sein.
Muß das sein?

11. Diese Leute mögen sagen, was sie wollen.
Ich mag diese Leute nicht.
Ich kann [1] diese Leute nicht leiden.[1]
Ich will mit diesen Leuten nichts zu tun haben.

12. Mögen Sie ihn?
Haben Sie ihn gern?
Sind Sie mit ihm befreundet?
Lieben Sie ihn?

13. Kann er Deutsch?
Wissen Sie, ob er Deutschland kennt?
Möchten Sie ihn kennenlernen?
Wissen Sie, was er uns gestern erzählt hat?

14. Die Musik ist eine Sprache ohne Worte. Sie rührt die Herzen aller Menschen.
Ist die Musik auch eine Sprache ohne Worte, so rührt sie doch die Herzen aller Menschen.
Wäre die Musik nicht eine Sprache ohne Worte, wie könnte sie die Herzen aller Menschen rühren!

15. Mag der Hans auch in die Grete verliebt sein, heiraten wird er sie nicht.
Heinz mag sagen, was er will! Hans wird ihn doch nie verstehen.

16. Wenn Sie ihm das versprochen haben, so müssen Sie es auch tun.
Haben Sie ihm das versprochen, so müssen Sie es auch tun.
Wenn Sie gestern in der Klasse gewesen wären, würden Sie diese Frage nicht stellen.[2]
Wären Sie gestern in der Klasse gewesen, so würden Sie diese Frage nicht stellen.

17. Darauf ist niemand gekommen.
Darauf werden gerade Sie nicht kommen!
Wenn sie nur nicht darauf kommt!
Nein, darauf wird auch sie nicht gekommen sein.

18. Er hält nicht viel von uns.
Er hält nicht viel davon.
Er hält nicht viel davon, daß ich Philosophie studieren will.

[1] **kann nicht leiden** cannot stand [2] **eine Frage stellen** pose *or* ask a question

19. Wie kamen Sie darauf, Chemie zu studieren?
Was hielten Sie davon, Physik zu studieren?
Was würden Sie dazu sagen, wenn ich Philosophie studieren wollte?

20. Wäre es praktischer gewesen, etwas anderes zu studieren?
Hätten Sie nicht lieber etwas anderes studieren sollen?
Wollen Sie wirklich behaupten, das wäre besser gewesen?
Sollte das wirklich der Fall [1] sein?
Sollte das wirklich der Fall gewesen sein?

21. Was sagen Sie dazu, daß Heinz Musik studieren will?
Ich wäre nie darauf gekommen, daß er Musik studieren könnte.
Wie ist er darauf gekommen, Musik zu studieren?
Es dürfte ihm nicht leicht fallen,[2] uns darauf eine vernünftige [3] Antwort zu geben.
Es muß wohl auch Menschen geben, die Musik studieren!
Ich weiß nicht, woran es liegt,[4] daß ich Heinz nicht verstehen kann.

22. Er liebt die Musik eben darum,[5] weil sie ihn die Wirklichkeit vergessen läßt.
Er hat seine Arbeit nur darum vernachlässigt,[6] weil er verliebt ist.
Es geht hier nicht darum,[7] ob er recht hat oder nicht.

23. Herr Müller, für diese Stellung [8] sollten Sie sich interessieren!
Bin ich nicht zu alt dazu, um mich dafür noch zu interessieren?
Sollten Sie sich für diese Stellung interessieren, so würde ich Sie gerne empfehlen.[9]

English to German

Study the grammar section of this lesson before you prepare this exercise in writing (without the aid of the key).

1) I can't say it.
I don't want to say it.
He is permitted to say it.
He likes to say it.
He must say it.
He is supposed to say it.

2) I was able to do it.
I didn't want to do it.
He was permitted to do it.
He liked to do it.
He had to do it.
He was supposed to do it.

3) I have not been able to do it.
I have not wanted to do it.
He has been permitted to do it.
He (has) liked to do it.
He has had to do it.
He had been obliged to do it.

4) They had been permitted to do it.
They had had to do it.
They had been obliged to do it.

5) She would have been able to do it.
He could not have done it.
We should have done it.

[1] **der Fall** case [2] **(jemandem) leicht fallen** be an easy matter (for someone) [3] **vernünftig** rational [4] **an (etwas) liegen** be due to (something); **Ich weiß nicht, woran es liegt, daß . . .** I don't know the reason why . . . [5] **eben darum, (weil)** *here:* just because [6] **vernachlässigen** neglect [7] **es geht darum, (ob)** it is a question (whether) [8] **die Stellung** position, job [9] **empfehlen** recommend

6) Would you like to deny that?
You must not deny it.
You need not deny it.

7) That may well be true.
It may rain today.
What is that supposed to mean?
She must have told him that.
She is supposed to have told her that.

8) If you have promised him (that), then you have to do it. (*Write the sentence* [1] *with* **wenn,** [2] *without* **wenn.**)

9) How did he come to the idea of studying music?
She doesn't know why it is that she cannot understand him.

10) What do you think of him?
What do you think of it?
What do you think of the fact that he is studying music?

GRAMMAR

55. Modals

Modals were employed early in this book, in fact in the very first basic dialogue the phrase **„Das möchte ich auch"** is included. Up to now there has been no attempt made in this text to "explain" this form. All that you were required to do at that time was to "absorb" it. You know the English equivalent as a matter of habit by now.

The difference in speech pattern between German and English in this case is admittedly quite radical: **Ich möchte** *I should like to.* The modal auxiliaries present us with striking instances of such differences:

Ich **mußte** es ihm sagen.	*I* ***had to*** *tell it to him.*
Ich habe es ihm sagen **müssen.**	*I have* ***had to*** *tell it to him.*
Ich hatte es tun **können.**	*I had* ***been able to*** *do it.*
Ich **hätte** es tun **können.**	*I* ***would have been able to*** *do it.* or *I* ***could have done*** *it.*

With respect to the modals, not only are there differences in speech pattern and idiom between German and English, but also within each language considered separately. For example: *He may do it.* Taken out of context this can mean either *he has permission to do it* or *it is possible that he'll do it.* — *He must come* indicates compulsion; *he must have come* indicates probability.

The possibilities of multiple meanings of this kind are even more frequent in German than in English. Thus, **sollen,** for example, though the essential idea behind it is one of moral obligation (**Du sollst nicht töten** — *Thou shalt not kill*), may also be used to give expression to rumor or report:

In seiner Jugend soll er sehr arm gewesen sein.	*He is said to have been very poor in his youth.*
Jetzt soll er sehr reich sein.	*Now he is said to be very rich.*

Some other meanings of **sollen:**

"*Is to*"

Dieses alte Gebäude soll morgen abgerissen werden. — *This old building is to be torn down tomorrow.*

"*Is supposed to*"

Was soll das bedeuten? — *What is that supposed to mean?*

Sollen + **nur** expresses a threat or a dare:

Er soll es nur anrühren! — *Let him just touch it (and see what happens).*

Indirect commands:

Der Vater sagte ihr, sie solle sogleich nach Hause gehen. — *Her father told her to go home right away.*

The basic meaning of **dürfen** is *may, be permitted to:* **Er darf es sehen.** *He may see it.* Note the following idiomatic uses:

dürfen + **nicht** = *must not*

Ihm darf man das nicht erzählen. — *We must not tell him that.* (*He must not be told.*)

Present imaginative meaning:

Das dürfte wahr sein. — *That might well be true.*

dürfen + **nur** = *need only to*

Man darf es nur anrühren und es zerfällt. — *You need only touch it and it crumbles.*

The basic meaning of **können** is *can, be able to:* **Er kann kaum noch gehen.** *He can hardly walk any more.* Note the following idiomatic uses:

Possibility, "*may*"

Das kann wahr sein. — *That may be true.*
Er kann es doch gesehen haben. — *It's possible that he really did see it.*
Das könnte mir große Sorge machen. — *It might cause me great concern.*

Capacity, "*to know*" (in the sense of having a well-rounded knowledge of):

Er kann Deutsch (sprechen, lesen, schreiben). — *He knows German* (i.e., *he can speak it, read it, write it*).

Note the distinctions in the following sentences:

Er kann Russisch.
Er kennt Rußland.
Er weiß, daß sie Russisch kann.

The basic meaning of **mögen** is *like, care for, like to:* **Sie mag ihn nicht.** *She does not like (care for) him.* **Er mag es nicht zugeben.** *He does not like to admit it.* **Er möchte (gern) Anthropologie studieren.** *He would like (very much) to study anthropology.* Note the following idiomatic uses:

Likelihood, possibility:

Er mag (kann wohl) recht haben.	*He may well be right.*
Es mochten wohl fünfzig Leute da gewesen sein.	*There were probably fifty people there.*

Present indicative or subjunctive with meaning of "*let,*" "*may*":

Er mag sich in acht nehmen!	*Let him beware.*
Möge es ihm wohl bekommen!	*May it do him some good.*
Möge es die ganze Welt wissen!	*Let the whole world know about it.*

The basic meaning of **müssen** is *must, have to:* **Er muß mitkommen.** *He must come along.* Note the following idiomatic meanings:

Likelihood, probability:

Er muß sie sehr geliebt haben.	*He must have loved her very much.*

müssen (+ **nicht**) = *need* (*not*)

Du mußt das ja nicht tun, du mußt es nur verstehen.	*You do not need to do that, you only need to understand it.*

The basic meaning of **wollen** is *want, want to, intend to, be determined to:* **Er will es nicht.** *He does not want it.* **Er will es nicht tun.** *He does not want to do it.* Note the following idiomatic meanings:

wollen = *claim* or *profess:*

Er will krank gewesen sein.	*He claims to have been sick.*

In present subjunctive, expressing a concession:

Dem sei wie ihm wolle.	*However that may be.*

56. Conditional Inversions

The omission of **wenn** has already been noted. Some of the familiar examples are:

Wär' nicht das Auge sonnenhaft,
Die Sonne könnt' es nie erblicken . . .
Goethe

Hätte sie ihn geliebt, so hätte sie das nicht tun können.
Hätte ich dir nur geglaubt!
Wäre ich reich gewesen, so hätte ich mir ein größeres Haus gekauft.

The practice of omitting **wenn** in contrary-to-fact situations corresponds to the practice of omitting *if* in similar English statements. Whereas English limits this practice to contrary-to-fact clauses, German goes beyond such limits, and very frequently. Almost any conditional clause, indicative or subjunctive, could get along without the subordinating conjunction. However, whenever **wenn** is omitted, the *if*-clause should precede the conclusion.

Note that the usual connecting link between the clauses is **so** or **dann.** It is not always indispensable, but its presence is important for the sake of sentence rhythm or clarification, or both.

Illustrations

Wenn er Geld hat, kauft er sich wohl einen Wagen.
Hat er Geld, so kauft er sich wohl einen Wagen.

Wenn er das gesagt hat, ist er ein Lügner.
Hat er das gesagt, dann ist er ein Lügner.

Kenne ich mein Verhältnis zu mir selbst und zur
Außenwelt, so heiß' ich's Wahrheit . . .
Goethe: *Maximen und Reflexionen*

If I know my relationship to myself and to the external world, I call it truth.

Willst du ins Unendliche schreiten,
Geh nur im Endlichen nach allen Seiten.
Goethe: *Sprüche in Reimen*

If you want to move into the infinite,
Go in all directions within the finite.

Kannst du lesen, so sollst du verstehen; kannst du schreiben, so mußt du etwas wissen; kannst du glauben, so sollst du begreifen; wenn du begehrst, wirst du sollen; wenn du forderst, wirst du nicht erlangen, und wenn du erfahren bist, sollst du nutzen.
Goethe: *Maximen und Reflexionen*

If you can read, you ought to understand; if you can write, you must necessarily know something; if you can believe, then you should comprehend; if you desire, then you will be under obligations; if you demand, you will not attain your purpose, and if you are experienced, then you are obliged to be of use.

Wenn, in past time, meaning "*whenever*":

Wenn ihn Alexander Weill besuchte, langweilte sich Heine immer.
Besuchte ihn Alexander Weill, so langweilte sich Heine immer.

57. Anticipative Pronouns and Compounds

German and English frequently use the pronouns **es** and *it* respectively to prepare the way for an entire clause or infinitive phrase:

Es ist unmöglich, das alles zu verstehen.	*It is impossible to understand all that.*
Es würde mir viel Vergnügen machen, Sie morgen wieder zu sprechen.	*It would be a great pleasure (for me) to speak to you again tomorrow.*

By no means always will German and English agree in specific cases involving this stylistic device:

Es ist Unsinn, was du da sprichst.	*What you are saying is nonsense.*
Er will **es** ihr einfach nicht sagen, daß er gestern bei uns war.	*He simply does not want to tell her that he was at our house yesterday.*

The use of *anticipative compounds with* **da**– *or* **wo**– is a peculiarly German device. Note the following examples:

Er besteht **darauf,** ihn zu sprechen.	*He insists upon speaking to him.*
Er denkt **daran,** diesen kommenden Sommer in Deutschland zu verbringen.	*He is thinking of spending this coming summer in Germany.*
Ich erinnere mich **daran,** daß er ein vorzüglicher Mensch war.	*I remember that he was an excellent person.*
Woran liegt es, daß er immer so ungeduldig ist?	*What is the reason that he is always so impatient?* (*Why is he always so impatient?*)

Illustrations from preceding lessons

Solange der Golfstrom **daran** verhindert war, Europa zu erreichen, brachte eine warme Strömung aus dem Süden Feuchtigkeit nach Nordafrika und Südwesteuropa.

Dr. Malaise glaubt, daß dieser Umstand hungernde Menschen aus Lybien und Nordwestafrika **dazu** bewegte, langsam gegen Ägypten hin abzuwandern.

In der Nachfolge von Gelehrten wie Jakob Grimm waren die Sprachwissenschaftler des neunzehnten Jahrhunderts **davon** überzeugt, daß der Ursprung des Indoeuropäischen, ja der Sprache überhaupt, irgendwo im Osten zu suchen sei.

DIE LORELEI	THE LORELEI
Ich weiß nicht, was soll es bedeuten, Daß ich so traurig bin; Ein Märchen aus alten Zeiten, Das kommt mir nicht aus dem Sinn.	*I know not what it should signify, This mournfulness in me; An ancient tale I can't deny Runs through my memory.*
Die Luft ist kühl, und es dunkelt, Und ruhig fließt der Rhein; Der Gipfel des Berges funkelt Im Abendsonnenschein.	*The air is cool, and it's darkling, And calmly flows the Rhine; The mountain peak is sparkling In sunset's deepening shine.*
Die schönste Jungfrau sitzet Dort oben wunderbar, Ihr goldnes Geschmeide blitzet, Sie kämmt ihr goldenes Haar.	*Up yonder sits a maiden, Miraculously fair; Her jewels splendor-laden, She combs her golden hair.*
Sie kämmt es mit goldenem Kamme Und singt ein Lied dabei; Das hat eine wundersame, Gewaltige Melodei.	*She combs with a comb gold-gleaming And sings a song the while; Its melody wondrous-seeming Has the power to beguile.*

Den Schiffer im kleinen Schiffe
Ergreift es mit wildem Weh;
Er schaut nicht die Felsenriffe,
Er schaut nur hinauf in die Höh'.

Ich glaube, die Wellen verschlingen
Am Ende Schiffer und Kahn;
Und das hat mit ihrem Singen
Die Lorelei getan.

Heinrich Heine

The sailor sailing his skiff
Is gripped with a passion wild;
He sees not the rocky reef,
He looks only upward beguiled.

The waters at last must devour
The ship and the sailor strong —
All deftly done through the power
Of Lorelei's love song.

Die Wiener Staatsoper nach dem Wiederaufbau im Jahre 1955.

29. Aufgabe

WER BIN ICH?

SAMPLE ANSWERS AND SUGGESTIONS

a. Nehmen Sie an, Sie wären in einer großen deutschen Stadt und hätten den Nachmittag und den Abend frei. —

Wohin würden Sie lieber gehen: — *Ich würde lieber in . . . gehen.*
in eine Ausstellung?[1] in ein Museum?
ins Theater? in die Oper?
in ein Konzert? ins Kino?

Könnten Sie nicht sowohl[2] in eine Ausstellung (in ein Museum) als auch[2] ins Theater (in die Oper, in ein Konzert) gehen?

Glauben Sie nicht, daß die Museen am Nachmittag offen sind?

Gibt es in Deutschland viele Museen?

Was für ein Museum würden Sie am liebsten besuchen: — *Ich würde am liebsten ein . . . besuchen.*
ein naturhistorisches Museum?[3]
ein technisches Museum?
ein kunsthistorisches Museum?[4]

b. Nehmen Sie an, Sie wären in einem kunsthistorischen Museum. —

Würden Sie gerne griechische Skulpturen[5] sehen?

Oder ziehen[6] Sie die alten Ägypter vor?[6]

Interessieren Sie sich für die Kunst der Gotik? — *Ja, ich interessiere mich für . . .*
für die Renaissance? für das Barock?
für den französischen Impressionismus?
für die deutschen Expressionisten?

Sehen Sie lieber moderne Malerei,[7] oder ziehen Sie die alten Meister vor?

Kennen Sie den Namen eines deutschen Malers?[8]
eines deutschen Bildhauers?[9]

c. Nehmen Sie an, Sie wollen nun ins Theater gehen. —

Wird in Deutschland viel Theater gespielt?

Hätten Sie etwas dagegen,[10] sich ein Trauerspiel[11] anzusehen? — *Nein, ich hätte nichts dagegen, mir . . .*

[1] **die Ausstellung** exhibition [2] **sowohl . . . als auch** as well as [3] **das naturhistorische Museum** museum of natural history [4] **das kunsthistorische Museum** museum of art (history) [5] **die Skulptur** sculpture [6] **vorziehen** prefer [7] **die Malerei** painting [8] **der Maler** painter [9] **der Bildhauer** sculptor [10] **etwas dagegen haben** object to (something); **Hätten Sie etwas dagegen?** Would you object . . .? [11] **das Trauerspiel** tragedy

Würden Sie eine Komödie vorziehen?
Was wäre Ihnen lieber: ein klassisches Theaterstück [1] oder ein modernes Theaterstück?
Kennen Sie den Namen eines klassischen deutschen Dichters?
Kennen Sie den Namen eines klassischen deutschen Dramatikers?
Kennen Sie den Titel eines klassischen deutschen Stücks?
Kennen Sie den Namen eines modernen Autors (Dramatikers)? den Titel eines modernen deutschen Stücks?
Haben Sie auch nicht vergessen, sich Theaterkarten reservieren zu lassen?

DRILL PATTERNS

Repeat the following drills after your instructor or after the speaker on the tape Imitate the pronunciation very carefully.

1. Er geht nicht gern ins Museum.
   Was sollte er dagegen haben, sich das kunsthistorische Museum anzusehen? [2]
   Warum sollte er etwas dagegen haben, heute nachmittag mit Ihnen in das kunsthistorische Museum zu gehen?
   Ich kann mir nicht vorstellen, was er dagegen haben könnte, sich mit Ihnen heute nachmittag das kunsthistorische Museum anzusehen.
   Hätte er gestern nicht bis fünf Uhr arbeiten müssen, so hätte er, meiner Meinung nach, bestimmt nichts dagegen gehabt, sich mit uns zusammen das kunsthistorische Museum anzusehen.

2. Er will ins Kino.
   Warum will er nicht ins Theater gehen?
   An seiner Stelle ginge ich lieber ins Theater.
   Würden Sie an seiner Stelle heute abend nicht lieber ins Theater gehen?
   Sagten Sie nicht, daß Sie an seiner Stelle heute abend lieber ins Theater gehen würden als ins Kino?

3. Läßt er sich eine Karte (einen Sitz, einen Tisch) reservieren?
   Haben Sie sich Theaterkarten reservieren lassen?
   Warum haben Sie mich das nicht tun lassen?
   Sie hätten mich das tun lassen können.
   Er ließ uns sagen, er hätte Theaterkarten für uns reservieren lassen.

4. Sind noch Karten zu haben?
   Sind noch Karten für die erste Reihe [3] zu haben?
   Vor dem Beginn der Vorstellung [4] sind oft noch einige Karten für die vordersten Reihen [3] zu haben.

[1] **das Theaterstück (das Stück)** play [2] **sich etwas ansehen** look at something [3] **die Reihe** row; **die vorderste Reihe** front row [4] **die Vorstellung** performance

Für die heutige Vorstellung sind glücklicherweise [1] noch einige Karten für die vordersten Reihen zu haben.
Werden Ihnen die Karten für die vordersten Reihen, die für die heutige Abendvorstellung noch zu haben sind, nicht zu teuer sein?

5. Wären sie früher gekommen, hätten sie billigere [2] Karten bekommen.
Wenn sie die Karten rechtzeitig [3] hätten reservieren lassen, hätten sie die Erstaufführung [4] dieses Stücks sehen können.
Um der Première dieses Stücks beizuwohnen, [5] hätten sie sich schon vor zwei Monaten Karten reservieren lassen müssen.

6. Hans interessiert sich weder [6] für Ausstellungen noch [6] für Konzerte.
Heinz interessiert sich sowohl für Ausstellungen als auch für Konzerte.
Hans dürfte sich weder für Theaterstücke noch für Opern interessieren.[7]
Heinz dürfte sich sowohl für das Theater wie für die Oper interessieren.

7. Da Hans sich für Dürer und Grünewald ebenso wenig [8] interessierte wie [8] für Breughel oder für Rembrandt, zog er es vor, statt [9] ins Museum ins Kino zu gehen.
Da Heinz sich für gotische Kathedralen ebenso sehr wie für die Architektur der Renaissance und des Barock interessierte, besichtigte [10] er täglich die Kirchen und Paläste dieser alten Stadt.
Während Heinz sich [11] über klassische deutsche Dichter wie Lessing, Goethe und Schiller unterhielt,[11] zog unser Freund Hans es vor, sich über das deutsche Bier und die deutschen Weine zu unterhalten.
Wenn Heinz über moderne deutsche Dramatiker wie Hauptmann, Hofmannsthal und Brecht, oder über die Romane von Thomas Mann und Kafka sprach, war Hans immer nahe daran, einzuschlafen.

English to German

Prepare this exercise in writing (without the aid of the key).

1) Would she like to go to the opera?
Would you (*3 ways*) like to go to an exhibition?

2) Would she rather go to the theater?
I think he would rather go to the movies.

3) Couldn't we go to a museum?
Shouldn't we go to the museum of natural history?

4) Are you (*3 ways*) interested in Greek sculpture?
If he were interested in Gothic art, he would come with us.

5) She prefers modern painting.
I thought she preferred modern painting.

[1] **glücklicherweise** fortunately [2] **billig** inexpensive, cheap [3] **rechtzeitig** in time [4] **die Erstaufführung** première [5] **beiwohnen** attend [6] **weder . . . noch** neither . . . nor [7] **dürfte sich . . . interessieren** might (well) be interested [8] **ebenso wenig . . . wie** as little as [9] **statt** instead of [10] **besichtigen** visit (inspect) [11] **sich unterhalten (über)** talk about

6) He had some tickets reserved for them.
He could have had some tickets reserved for them.

7) Why didn't they let him do that? (*use pres. perf.*)
They should have let us do that.

8) I am interested in concerts as well as in plays.
He is neither interested in concerts nor in plays.

9) In my opinion the tickets for tonight's performance are too expensive.

10) While Heinz was talking about modern German painting, Hans fell asleep.

GRAMMAR

58. Nouns and Noun Suffixes

CLASS 4 NOUNS

1. The majority of this class (characterized by –**n** or –**en** ending in the plural) are *feminine*.

   Some familiar examples:

die Frau	die Symphonie′	die Erzählung
die Schwester	die Krankheit	die Naturwissenschaft
die Tante	die Streitigkeit	die Freundin

2. There are *some masculines* in this class. One major group of masculines is characterized by –**en** endings in all forms except the nominative singular. (Most of these have accent on the last syllable.)

der Mensch	der Patient′	der Kamerad′
der Student′	der Soldat′	der Philosoph′

Illustration

Das ist der Student, der die besten Noten bekommt.
Ich kenne den Studenten nicht.
Ich sage dem Studenten gar nichts.
Das Buch des Studenten ist verloren.
Das sind die Studenten, die die besten Noten bekommen.
Ich kenne die Studenten nicht.
Ich sage den Studenten gar nichts.
Die Bücher der Studenten sind verloren.

3. Some other masculines of this class show only one change in the singular: an –**s** ending in the genitive. The plural forms conform to the regular pattern typical of this class:

der Profes′sor	der Autor	der Vetter (*cousin*)
der Doktor	der See	

Illustration

Der Professor ist streng.	Die Professoren sind streng.
Den Professor habe ich nicht gern.	Die Professoren habe ich nicht gern.
Dem Professor geht es nie gut.	Den Professoren geht es nie gut.
Des Professors Bücher kosten viel Geld.	Der Professoren Bücher kosten viel Geld.

4. *Four familiar neuter nouns* follow the above pattern, except that the genitive singular ends in –(**e**)**s.**

das Auge, des Auges, die Augen
das Ohr, des Ohres, die Ohren
das Ende, des Endes, die Enden
das Bett, des Bettes, die Betten

5. A few masculines of Class 4 have a genitive singular –**ns.** The remaining forms, except the nominative singular, end in –**en.**

der Name, des Namens, die Namen
der Glaube, des Glaubens, die Glauben

One noun of this class offers a choice in the genitive singular. The other forms, except the nominative, end in –**n.**

der Bauer (*farmer, peasant*), {des Bauers / des Bauern}, die Bauern

One noun of this class deviates from the regular pattern by showing a singular –**n** and a plural –**en.**

Nom.	der Herr	die Herren
Acc.	den Herrn	die Herren
Dat.	dem Herrn	den Herren
Gen.	des Herrn	der Herren

One noun of this class is quite irregular in the singular. The plural forms go according to the normal pattern.

Nom.	das Herz	die Herzen
Acc.	das Herz	die Herzen
Dat.	dem Herzen	den Herzen
Gen.	des Herzens	der Herzen

NOUN SUFFIXES

The following suffixes form in most cases abstract nouns, all of which are *feminine.**

–**schaft** (cf. English *–ship, –hood, –y*)

die Freundschaft	die Nachbarschaft (*neighborhood*)
die Herrschaft (*mastery, authority*)	die Naturwissenschaft
die Mannschaft (*group of men*)	die Reisegesellschaft

* The suffixes –**heit,** –**keit,** and –**ung** are not included here. They have already been discussed. (See 15. Aufgabe, pages 119–120.)

–tät (= *–ty*)

die Universität′
die Majestät′
die Qualität′
die Quantität′

–ion preceded by **t, kt, x, s, ss**

die Nation′
die Zivilisation′
die Reflexion′
die Funktion′

–ie (= *–y*) This suffix forms nouns, many of which pertain to branches of learning technology, business, professions:

die Philosophie′
die Chemie′
die Biologie′
die Theorie′
die Poesie′
die Melodie′

–ik (often *–ics, –icism*)

die Politik′
die Kritik′
die Ästhe′tik
die Gramma′tik

The following endings are found in both concrete and abstract nouns:

–ei, –erei (= *–y*)

die Partei′
die Bäckerei′

–in, often attached to **–er** or **–or**, changes masculine nouns to feminines. The plural is formed by attaching **–nen** to the singular:

die Lehrerin
die Freundin
die Chemikerin
die Dokto′rin
die Engländerin
die Journalis′tin

–e is a frequently occurring feminine ending:

die Erde
die Frage
die Schule
die Sonne
die Geschichte
die Stunde
die Seite
die Dame

There are some commonly used **–e** nouns that are masculine or neuter:

der Junge
der Knabe
der Gedanke (*thought, idea*)
das Ende
das Gebirge
das Auge
das Gebäude (*building*)

Nouns prefixed by **Ge–** and suffixed by **–e** are for the most part neuter. (The **Ge–** prefix is related to English *co–, con–, com–* [Latin: *cum*], meaning "with" in the sense of accompaniment or in the collective sense.

das Gebirge (*mountain chain*)

Nouns formed in this manner, if neuter and capable of plural forms, belong to Class 1: das Gebäude, die Gebäude.

Feminine and masculine nouns of this group belong to Class 4: die Geschichte, die Geschichten; die Gemeinde (*community*), die Gemeinden; der Geselle (*companion*), die Gesellen; der Gedanke (*idea*), die Gedanken.

–**sucht** (from **siech** = *sick;* **die Sucht** = *sickness, mania, passion*)

die Habsucht (*greed*)
die Sehnsucht (*longing, passionate desire, pining* [sehnen *long*])
die Schwindsucht (*consumption*)

Suffixes forming *masculine* nouns:

German and English use a few noun suffixes that are identical in spelling and function. For example:

–**or** or –**er** (to form personal agent nouns):

der Sänger (*singer*)
der Läufer (*runner*)
der Redner (*speaker, orator*)

der Autor (*author*)
der Doktor (*doctor*)
der Profes′sor (*professor*)

The –**er** nouns belong to Class 1: der Sänger, die Sänger; the –**or** nouns belong to Class 4: der Doktor, die Dokto′ren.

–**ist** (usually nouns of foreign origin):

der Journalist′ (*journalist*)
der Optimist′ (*optimist*)

der Pessimist′ (*pessimist*)
der Komponist′ (*composer*)

The –**ist** nouns belong to Class 4: der Journalist, die Journalisten.

NOTE:

–**er,** –**or,** –**ist** nouns can often be changed to feminines by adding –**in.**

–**ling** (often with diminutive force):

der Jüngling (*young man, youth*)
der Frühling (*spring*)

der Lehrling (*apprentice*)
der Feigling (*coward*)

The –**ling** nouns belong to Class 2: der Jüngling, die Jünglinge.

Suffixes forming *neuter* nouns:

–**lein,** –**chen** (umlaut whenever possible). As a rule, these nouns are diminutives (and, frequently, terms of endearment). Note, however, that **das Fräulein** and **das Mädchen** have lost this diminutive quality.

das Äuglein
das Büchlein

das Zimmerchen
das Blümchen

The –**lein** and –**chen** nouns belong to Class 1: das Äuglein, die Äuglein.

–tum (See English *–dom* referring to authority, realm, dominion, e.g., kingdom)

das Eigentum (*property, possession*)
das Altertum (*antiquity*)
das Priestertum (*clergy, priesthood*)

The **–tum** nouns that have plurals conform to Class 3: das Eigentum, die Eigentümer.

–nis forms some feminine as well as neuter nouns:

das Gefängnis (*prison*)
das Geheimnis (*secret, mystery*)
das Hindernis (*hindrance*)
das Mißverständnis (*misunderstanding*)
die Finsternis (*darkness*)
die Erkenntnis (*knowledge, perception, realization*)

The –**nis** nouns that have plurals conform to Class 2: das Gefängnis, die Gefängnisse. (Note the double–s in the plural.)

30. Aufgabe

Reading

BEETHOVEN UND NAPOLEON

Im Jahre 1802 komponierte Beethoven in Heiligenstadt, einem anderthalb Stunden von Wien gelegenen Dorfe, seine dritte Symphonie (jetzt unter dem Titel: *Sinfonia eroica* bekannt). Beethoven dachte sich bei seinen Kompositionen oft einen bestimmten Gegenstand, obschon er über musikalische Malereien häufig lachte und schalt, besonders über kleinliche der Art... Bei seiner dritten Sym- 5
phonie hatte er an Buonaparte gedacht, aber an diesen, als er noch erster Konsul war. Beethoven schätzte ihn damals außerordentlich hoch und verglich ihn den größten römischen Konsuln. Sowohl ich als mehrere seiner näheren Freunde haben diese Symphonie schon in Partitur abgeschrieben auf seinem Tische liegen sehen, wo ganz oben auf dem Titelblatte das Wort „Buonaparte," und ganz 10
unten „Luigi van Beethoven" stand, aber kein Wort mehr. Ob und womit die Lücke hat ausgefüllt werden sollen, weiß ich nicht. Ich war der erste, der ihm die Nachricht brachte, Buonaparte habe sich zum Kaiser erklärt, worauf er in Wut geriet und ausrief: „Ist der auch nichts anders, wie ein gewöhnlicher Mensch! Nun wird er auch alle Menschenrechte mit Füßen treten, nur seinem Ehrgeize 15
frönen; er wird sich nun höher wie alle andern stellen, ein Tyrann werden!" Beethoven ging an den Tisch, faßte das Titelblatt oben an, riß es ganz durch und warf es auf die Erde. Die erste Seite wurde neu geschrieben, und nun erst erhielt die Symphonie den Titel: *Sinfonia eroica.*

Aus: Wegeler und Ries: *Biographische Notizen über Ludwig van Beethoven.* Berlin–Leipzig 1906, Seite 92–94

LINE
3 „eroica" — *heroic*
4 einen bestimmten Gegenstand — *a definite subject*
musikalische Malerei — *"musical painting," program music, illustrative* or *descriptive music*
5 schelten — *scold*
kleinliche der Art — *petty works of this kind*

LINE
6 Napoleon Buonaparte ([1769–1821] *was nominated "first consul" of the French republic before he crowned himself in 1804 and assumed the title "emperor."*)
9 die Partitur — *score*
12 die Lücke — *gap*
13–14 in Wut geraten — *become enraged*
15 der Ehrgeiz — *ambition*
16 frönen — *indulge*

VOM WESEN * DES GENIES

Aus Eckermanns *Gesprächen mit Goethe*

1.

„Merkwürdig ist," sagte ich, „daß sich von allen Talenten das musikalische am frühesten zeigt, so daß Mozart in seinem fünften, Beethoven in seinem achten und Hummel in seinem neunten Jahre schon die nächste Umgebung durch Spiel und Kompositionen in Erstaunen setzten."

5 „Das musikalische Talent," sagte Goethe, „kann sich wohl am frühesten zeigen, indem die Musik ganz etwas Angeborenes, Inneres ist, das von außen keiner großen Nahrung und keiner aus dem Leben gezogenen Erfahrung bedarf. Aber freilich, eine Erscheinung wie Mozart bleibt immer ein Wunder, das nicht weiter zu erklären ist. Doch wie wollte die Gottheit überall Wunder zu tun Gele-
10 genheit finden, wenn sie es nicht zuweilen in außerordentlichen Individuen versuchte, die wir anstaunen und nicht begreifen, woher sie kommen!"

2.

„. . . Was ist Genie anders als jene produktive Kraft, wodurch Taten entstehen, die vor Gott und der Natur sich zeigen können und die eben deswegen Folgen haben und von Dauer sind. Alle Werke Mozarts sind dieser Art; es liegt in ihnen eine
15 zeugende Kraft, die von Geschlecht zu Geschlecht fortwirkt und sobald nicht erschöpft und verzehrt sein dürfte. Von anderen großen Komponisten und Künstlern gilt dasselbe. Wie haben nicht Phidias und Raphael auf nachfolgende Jahrhunderte gewirkt, und wie nicht Dürer und Holbein! — Derjenige, der zuerst die Formen und Verhältnisse der altdeutschen Baukunst erfand, so daß im Laufe
20 der Zeit ein Straßburger Münster und ein Kölner Dom möglich wurde, war auch

* Vom Wesen — *concerning the nature (of)*

LINE
1 merkwürdig — *strange*
1–2 sich . . . zeigt — *shows itself*
3 die nächste Umgebung — *the people in their immediate surroundings*
4 in Erstaunen setzen — *astonish*
6 angeboren — *inborn*
7 die Nahrung — *food, nourishment*
die Erfahrung — *experience*
bedürfen (*with gen.*) — *be in need of*
8 die Erscheinung — *phenomenon*
9 die Gottheit — *deity, divinity*
überall — here: *at all*
9–10 die Gelegenheit — *occasion, opportunity*
10 zuweilen — *at times*
11 anstaunen — *gaze at in admiring astonishment*
begreifen — *grasp, comprehend*

LINE
12 anders als — here: *other than, else but*
13 eben deswegen — *for that very reason*
Folgen haben — *be of consequence*
14 von Dauer sein — *last, have a lasting effect*
15 zeugende Kraft — *creative power*
das Geschlecht — *generation*
fortwirken — *continue to be effectual*
16 erschöpft — *exhausted*
verzehrt — *consumed*
17 gilt dasselbe — *the same holds true*
18 wirken — *have* or *produce an effect, be effective*
derjenige, der — *he who, the man who*
19 die Verhältnisse — *proportions*
die altdeutsche Baukunst — here: *Gothic architecture*

ein Genie, denn seine Gedanken haben fortwährend produktive Kraft behalten und wirken bis auf die heutige Stunde . . ."

3.

„Im Grunde sind wir alle kollektive Wesen, wir mögen uns stellen wie wir wollen. Denn wie weniges haben und sind wir, das wir im reinsten Sinne unser Eigentum nennen! Wir müssen alle empfangen und lernen, sowohl von denen, 5 die vor uns waren, als von denen, die mit uns sind. Selbst das größte Genie würde nicht weit kommen, wenn es alles seinem eigenen Innern verdanken wollte. Das begreifen aber viele sehr gute Menschen nicht und tappen mit ihren Träumen von Originalität ein halbes Leben im Dunkeln. Ich habe Künstler gekannt, die sich rühmten, keinem Meister gefolgt zu sein, vielmehr alles ihrem eigenen Genie zu 10 danken zu haben. Die Narren! Als ob das überall anginge! Und als ob sich die Welt ihnen nicht bei jedem Schritt aufdränge und aus ihnen, trotz ihrer eigenen Dummheit, etwas machte! Ja, ich behaupte, wenn ein solcher Künstler nur an den Wänden dieses Zimmers vorüberginge und auf die Handzeichnungen einiger großer Meister, womit ich sie behängt habe, nur flüchtige Blicke würfe, er müßte, 15 wenn er überall einiges Genie hätte, als ein anderer und Höherer von hier gehen."

„Und was ist denn überhaupt Gutes an uns, wenn es nicht die Kraft und Neigung ist, die Mittel der äußeren Welt an uns heranzuziehen und unseren höheren Zwecken dienstbar zu machen. Ich darf wohl von mir selber reden und bescheiden sagen, wie ich fühle. Es ist wahr, ich habe in meinem langen Leben mancherlei getan und 20 zustande gebracht, dessen ich mich allenfalls rühmen könnte. Was hatte ich aber, wenn wir ehrlich sein wollen, das eigentlich mein war, als die Fähigkeit und Neigung zu sehen und zu hören, zu unterscheiden und zu wählen, und das Gesehene und Gehörte mit einigem Geist zu beleben und mit einiger Geschicklichkeit wieder zu geben. Ich verdanke meine Werke keineswegs meiner eigenen Weisheit allein, 25 sondern tausenden von Dingen und Personen außer mir, die mir dazu das Material

LINE
1 haben fortwährend produktive Kraft behalten — *have preserved throughout the ages their productive force*
3–4 wir mögen uns stellen wie wir wollen — *whatever attitude we may assume*
5 das Eigentum — *property*
empfangen — *receive*
7 seinem eigenen Innern — (*to*) *his innermost being* or *self*
verdanken — *owe, attribute*
8 tappen — *grope*
9–10 sich rühmen — *boast*
11 der Narr — *fool*
Als ob das überall anginge — *as if that were at all possible*
11–12 sich aufdrängen — *intrude upon*
14 die Zeichnung — *drawing*
15 flüchtig — *fleeting, cursory*

LINE
16 wenn er überall einiges Genie hätte — *if he had any genius at all*
17 die Neigung — *inclination*
18 das Mittel — *means*
heranziehen — *draw upon*
19 dienstbar — *serviceable*
bescheiden — *modestly*
20 mancherlei — *some things*
21 zustande bringen — *accomplish*
allenfalls — *perhaps*
22 ehrlich — *honest*
die Fähigkeit — *capacity, ability*
23 unterscheiden — *distinguish*
23–5 das Gesehene und Gehörte mit einigem Geist zu beleben und mit einiger Geschicklichkeit wieder zu geben — *animate what I had seen and heard with some spirit and to reproduce it with some skill*

boten. Es kamen Narren und Weise, helle Köpfe und bornierte, Kindheit und Jugend, wie das reife Alter; alle sagten mir, wie es ihnen zu Sinne sei, was sie dachten, wie sie lebten und wirkten und welche Erfahrungen sie sich gesammelt, und ich hatte weiter nichts zu tun als zuzugreifen und das zu ernten, was andere
5 für mich gesäet hatten."

„Es ist im Grunde auch alles Torheit, ob einer etwas aus sich habe, oder ob er es von anderen habe; ob einer durch sich wirke, oder ob er durch andere wirke; die Hauptsache ist, *daß man ein großes Wollen habe und Geschick und Beharrlichkeit besitze, es auszuführen;* alles übrige ist gleichgültig."

ERNST BARLACH (1870–1938)

Ernst Barlachs schöpferische Begabung zeichnete sich durch Vielseitigkeit aus. Im Ausland vor allem als Bildhauer bekannt, wurde er in Deutschland ebenso als Graphiker geschätzt. Seine Dramen, darunter *Die Sündflut* (1924), erregten durch ungewöhnliche Eindringlichkeit und Kraft das Aufsehen der Kritik.

Der erste der folgenden Auszüge aus den Briefen des Künstlers behandelt Barlachs inniges Verhältnis zu der Kunst der Holzschnitzerei, der er sein Leben lang treu blieb. Der zweite Brief enthält eine ernste, ja leidenschaftliche Auseinandersetzung mit der abstrakten Kunst, zumal mit dem russischen Maler Vassily Kandinsky (1866–1944), einem Zeitgenossen Barlachs, der, zusammen mit Paul Klee (1879–1940), eine führende Rolle in der expressionistischen Bewegung spielte.

Die abstrakte Kunst, wie Kandinsky sie empfahl, sieht von der Darstellung konkreter Gegenstände ab. Sie will allein durch Linie und Farbe wirken. Barlach hingegen * besteht darauf, daß die schöpferische Nachahmung der Gegenstände und Formen der uns bekannten Welt, vor allem der Gestalt und der Form des menschlichen Körpers, die eigentliche Aufgabe der Malerei und der Skulptur sei.

Ernst Barlach's creative talent was distinguished by versatility. Beyond the boundaries of Germany he was noted particularly as a sculptor; within Germany he was equally esteemed as a graphic artist. His dramatic works, among them *The Flood* (1924), impressed the critics with their unusual penetration and power.

The first of the following excerpts from the letters of the artist contains an account of Barlach's deep and lasting attachment to the art of wood sculpturing. In the second letter he takes serious and passionate issue with abstract art, and particularly with the Russian painter Vassily Kandinsky (1866–1944), a contemporary of Barlach who, together with Paul Klee (1879–1940), played a leading part in the expressionist movement.

Abstract art, as recommended by Kandinsky, is nonrepresentational (excludes the representation of concrete objects). It is meant to depend for its effect exclusively on line and color. Barlach, on the contrary, insists that painting and the plastic arts should imitate creatively the objects and forms in the world as we know it, and above all the shape and form of the human body.

* *Ernst Barlach: Leben und Werk in seinen Briefen.* R. Piper, München, 1952, p. 64.

LINE
1 bieten — *offer*
borniert — *narrow-minded*
2 wie es ihnen zu Sinne sei — *how they felt*
3 sammeln — *collect*
sie sich gesammelt = sie sich gesammelt hatten
4 zugreifen — *stretch out one's hand, seize*
ernten — *harvest*

LINE
5 säen — *sow*
6 die Torheit — *foolishness*
8 ein großes Wollen — here: *a strong will directed toward a great* (or *worthy*) *object*
das Geschick — *skill, dexterity*
8–9 die Beharrlichkeit — *tenacity*
9 ausführen — *carry out*
gleichgültig — *irrelevant*

Auch meint er, daß er als Künstler selbst Gefühle wie Mitleid oder Freude empfinden müsse. Diese Gefühle könne er aber durch Abstraktion weder erleben noch vermitteln, sondern allein durch die Darstellung von Menschen in Bewegung und Handlung, mögen sie singen, leiden, tanzen, oder beten.

Moreover, he believes that he himself must experience as an artist emotions like compassion or joy, and these, he claims, he can neither feel nor represent in abstraction, but only by portraying human beings in motion and action, singing, suffering, dancing, or praying.

I. An Dr. Artur Eloesser:

... In Holz habe ich immer nach einem meistens sehr kleinen Modell gearbeitet. Sie müssen wissen, anno 1907 fing ich mit Holz an, ungelernt. Die sogenannten „Holzbildhauer," handwerkliche Ornamentschnitzer an Bauten oder Möbeln, haben noch so etwas wie Berufstradition, ihre Werkzeuge sind aus alten Zeiten überkommen, und sie wissen sie zu handhaben, es geht halt um Stundenlohn bei 5 ihnen und nach Stück und Metern, es sind ungemein routinierte Leute, die sich über meine Art zunächst krank lachten. So einer besorgte mir das Geschirr — ich wußte von nichts und fuhr mir zunächst mit einem flotten Stich tief in die Hand. Ich habe aber doch nicht eine einzige Arbeit als mißlungen liegen lassen müssen, wenn es auch oft auf kuriose Art herging, so fing ich längere Zeit mit Sägen an und 10 darf sagen, daß die frisch angesägten Arbeiten recht sehr nach etwas aussahen, hätte ichs dabei bewenden lassen und die Stücke ausgestellt, wer weiß was für Furor es gegeben hätte. So aber trachtete ich nach dem Vollenden und hatte die Genugtuung, daß manches als besonders angesehen wurde, was zunächst nur ungeschickt war. Alles in allem habe ich mir's sauer genug werden lassen, ca. 70 Holzar- 15 beiten, darunter ziemlich große, ehe ich es mir einmal gönnte, das Grobe nach Modell vorarbeiten zu lassen. Jahrelang war es meine Lust, mit der Axt, sagen

LINE
2 ungelernt — *without training* or *experience*
3 handwerkliche Ornamentschnitzer — *craftsmen who carve out ornaments*
die Möbel — *furniture*
4 die Berufstradition — *professional tradition*
das Werkzeug — *tool*
4–5 sind ... überkommen — *have been handed down*
5 handhaben — *handle*
5–6 es geht halt um ... (nach) — *it is just a matter of*
6 Stück und Metern — *the number of pieces and the area (meters) covered*
ungemein routinierte Leute — *people of extraordinary technical skill and experience*
7 besorgte mir das Geschirr — *got the tools for me*
8 fuhr mir ... in die Hand — *cut my hand*
flott — *quick*
9 als mißlungen liegen lassen — *leave unfinished* or *give up as failure*

LINE
10 wenn es auch auf kuriose Art herging — *even though my work proceeded in an odd manner*
(ich) fing mit Sägen an — *I began by working with the saw*
11 die frisch angesägten Arbeiten — *the pieces (of work) that I had just worked on with the saw*
recht sehr nach etwas aussahen — *weren't bad looking at all*
12 hätte ich's dabei bewenden lassen — *had I left it at that*
13 trachten — *strive for*
das Vollenden — *the final* or *perfect form, perfection*
13–14 die Genugtuung — *satisfaction*
14 manches — *many a piece*
als besonders — *as something special*
ungeschickt — *clumsy*
16 ehe ich es mir ... gönnte — *before I gave myself permission*
16–17 nach Modell — *according to a model*

wir mit dem Beil, vorzuarbeiten, und geschliffen habe ich die sämtlichen Eisen bis 1927 auf einem Küchenschleifstein!

II. An Reinhard Piper:

. . . Wir könnten uns tausend Jahre unterhalten ohne Verständigung . . .

Wir müssen uns doch auf ein Sprechen einigen, um überhaupt etwas zu wissen: 5 einer könnte das Schönste, Herrlichste auf chinesisch sagen, und ich würde nicht die Ohren spitzen. Wenn ich also ein seelisches Erlebnis nachfühlen soll, so muß es eine Sprache sprechen, in der ich das Tiefste und Verborgenste nacherleben kann. Meine Muttersprache ist die geeignetste, und meine künstlerische Muttersprache ist nun mal die menschliche Figur oder das Milieu, der Gegenstand, durch das 10 oder in dem der Mensch lebt, leidet, sich freut, fühlt, denkt. Darüber komme ich nicht hinaus. Auf eine Esperanto-Kunst kann ich mich auch nicht einlassen. Gerade das Vulgäre, das Allgemein-Menschliche, die Urgefühle aus der Rasse, das sind die großen, die ewigen. Was der Mensch gelitten hat und leiden kann, seine Größe, seine Angelegenheiten (inklusive Mythos und Zukunftstraum), dabei 15 bin ich engagiert, aber mein Spezialgefühlchen oder meine mir eigenste Sensation ist ja belanglos, ist bloße Laune, wenn ich dabei aus dem Ring des Menschlichen heraustrete . . . Ich glaube auch nicht, daß man eine neue Kunstweise logisch darstellen kann, so wie der Herr Kandinsky denkt — außer als Literatur, als gedankliche Leistung . . .

DIE ABSCHIEDSSYMPHONIE *

Nach C. F. Pohls *Joseph Haydn*

20 Joseph Haydn (1732–1809), der Schöpfer der Formen der klassischen Instrumentalmusik, lebte zu einer Zeit, in der die Musiker meist noch als Diener und Angestellte dem patriarchalischen Haushalt aristokratischer Familien angehörten. Die folgende Anekdote

* der Abschied — *farewell*

LINE

1 das Beil — *hatchet*
schleifen — *grind*
2 der Küchenschleifstein — *kitchen grindstone*
4 ein Sprechen — *a language, a mode of communication*
6 die Ohren spitzen — *prick up one's ears*
ein seelisches Erlebnis nachfühlen — *enter into a deep inner experience*
7 das Verborgenste (verborgen) — *the most recondite* or *the least accessible things*
8 geeignet — *suitable*
9 ist nun mal — *happens to be*
11 auf . . . kann ich mich nicht einlassen — *I (can) have nothing to do with*

LINE

12 das Allgemein-Menschliche — *the universally human*
14 die Angelegenheit — *concern, affair*
15 das Spezialgefühlchen — *little private sentiment*
16 belanglos — *irrelevant*
die Laune — *mood, whim*
der Ring — *circle*
18 darstellen — *represent*
18–19 die gedankliche Leistung — *intellectual achievement*
20 der Schöpfer — *creator*
21 Diener und Angestellte — *servants and employees*
22 angehören — *belong to*

ist ebenso charakteristisch für die gesellschaftlichen Verhältnisse jener Epoche wie für Haydns heitere Originalität und sein harmonisches Temperament. Der Schauplatz ist Esterház, der Landsitz des ungarischen Fürsten von Esterházy, in dessen reichem und prächtigem Schloß Haydn als Kapellmeister und Komponist dreißig Jahre lang tätig war.

Aus der Beschreibung von Esterház ist zu ersehen, daß das Musikgebäude für alle Mitglieder der Kapelle kaum ausreichte und umso weniger, wenn dieselben auch noch Platz für Frau und Kinder beanspruchten. Der Fürst von Esterházy mochte wohl wünschen, diesem Raummangel sowohl als auch den unausweichlichen Verdrießlichkeiten abzuhelfen, die das nahe Zusammenleben ganzer Familien in ein und demselben Hause erzeugten. Demgemäß machte er im Januar 1772 durch seinen Wirtschaftsrat von Rahier den Musikern schriftlich zu wissen, daß er „künftighin ihre Weiber und Kinder nicht einmal auf vierundzwanzig Stunden in Esterház sehen wolle“ und daß diejenigen, denen diese Verordnung nicht behage, sich melden sollten, um ihre Dimission entgegenzunehmen. Zugleich mußte dem Fürsten eine Liste der Kapelle vorgelegt werden, in der er diejenigen bezeichnete, welche er von dem Verbot ausgeschlossen wissen wollte. Es waren dies Kapellmeister Haydn, die beiden Kammersänger Fribert und Dichtler und der erste Violinist Tommasini. Die nächste Folge der fürstlichen Verordnung war, daß die Musiker, nunmehr gezwungen doppelte Ménage zu führen, um eine Aufbesserung ihres Gehaltes baten, die ihnen auch bewilligt wurde. Sie erhielten ein jeder 50 Gulden jährliche Zulage mit der ausdrücklichen Bemerkung, daß sie sich nicht unterfangen sollten, den Fürsten weiterhin zu belästigen oder ihre Weiber und Kinder etwa in des Fürsten Abwesenheit dennoch nach Esterház kommen zu

LINE

1 die gesellschaftlichen Verhältnisse — *social conditions*
3 der Fürst — *prince*
4 prächtig — *magnificent*
der Kapellmeister — *orchestra leader, conductor*
tätig sein — *be active*
5 aus der Beschreibung — *from the description*
ist zu ersehen — *it is apparent*
6 ausreichen — *be adequate*
umso weniger — *the less so*
dieselben — *the latter*
7 beanspruchen — *demand*
8 der Mangel — *lack*
unausweichlich — *inevitable*
9 die Verdrießlichkeit — *annoyance*
abhelfen — *remedy*
10 erzeugen — *cause, create*
demgemäß — *accordingly*
11 der Wirtschaftsrat — *"economic counselor," manager*
12 künftighin — *in the future*
13 die Verordnung — *ruling, order*
behagen — *please*

LINE

14 sich melden — *report*
entgegennehmen — *receive, accept*
zugleich — *at the same time*
15 vorlegen — *present*
bezeichnen — *designate*
16 das Verbot — *prohibition, restriction*
ausgeschlossen — *exempted*
17 der Kammersänger — *(court) singer*
19 nunmehr = nun
gezwungen — *compelled*
doppelte Ménage zu führen — *to support two households*
19–20 Aufbesserung des Gehaltes — *raise in salary*
20 bewilligen — *grant*
21 die Zulage — *addition, increment*
mit der ausdrücklichen Bemerkung — *with the express statement* or *condition*
21–2 sich unterfangen — *dare, venture, presume*
22 weiterhin — *any more*
belästigen — *molest, pester*
23 etwa — *by any chance*
die Abwesenheit — *absence*

lassen, widrigenfalls diese Wohltat sogleich aufhören würde. Als einzigen Trost stellte es ihnen der Fürst frei, die Zeit seiner Abwesenheit von Esterház nach vorangegangener Bewilligung zur Reise nach Eisenstadt benutzen zu dürfen. Dem Fürsten schien aber gerade damals der Aufenthalt in Esterház so sehr behagt zu
5 haben, daß er nicht ans Fortgehen dachte und überdies denselben weit über den Herbst hinausdehnte.

Der Seufzer und Klagen war nun kein Ende; sie fanden ihren Weg nach Eisenstadt und hallten von dort als getreues Echo in noch trostloserer Weise zurück. Vergebens wandten sich die armen Ehemänner an ihren Papa Haydn, der gegen
10 seine Gewohnheit es diesmal nicht unternahm, der Fürsprecher seiner Kapelle zu sein. Er hatte für die Musiker nichts als etwa ein schalkhaftes Lächeln, aus dem sie nicht klug wurden, bis ihnen bei einer Probe zum nächsten Orchesterkonzert unerwartet ein Hoffnungsstrahl leuchtete. Der Tag der Aufführung kam, und klopfenden Herzens begann die Kapelle als Schlußnummer eine neue Symphonie
15 ihres verehrten Führers, dem dabei selber bange ums Herz war. Schon die Tonart, Fis-Moll, war eine ungewöhnliche. Der erste Satz strebt entschlossene Haltung an; im Adagio herrscht Weichheit und Milde; Menuett und Trio, beide kurz gehalten, suchen wohl den herkömmlichen Charakter beizubehalten, aber die gewohnte freudige Sorglosigkeit kommt nicht recht zum Durchbruch; das Finale
20 (Presto) redet sich gewaltsam in den sonst hier sprudelnden Frohsinn hinein; nach kaum hundert Takten machen alle Instrumente plötzlich Halt, und statt der erwarte-

LINE

1 widrigenfalls — *otherwise*
die Wohltat — *benefit*
sogleich — *immediately*
der Trost — *consolation*
2 jemandem etwas frei stellen — *give someone the choice, allow someone*
2–3 nach vorangegangener Bewilligung — *after having obtained the permission*
3 Eisenstadt (*the capital of the Austro-Hungarian province, where the wives and children of the musicians were living*)
4 der Aufenthalt — *the stay*
behagen (*with dat.*) — *please*
5 überdies — *besides*
6 hinausdehnen — *extend*
7 Seufzer und Klagen — *sighs and complaints*
8 hallten . . . zurück — *resounded, came back*
getreu — *faithful*
in noch trostloserer Weise — *in an even more despondent fashion* or *tune*
9 vergebens — *in vain*
10 die Gewohnheit — *custom, customary manner*
der Fürsprecher — *spokesman*
11 schalkhaft — *sly*
11–12 aus dem sie nicht klug wurden — *which they could not make out, which merely mystified* or *puzzled them*

LINE

12 die Probe — *rehearsal*
13 die Aufführung — *performance*
14 klopfenden Herzens — *with a throbbing heart, anxiously*
15 dem dabei selber bange ums Herz war — *who was himself rather uneasy*
schon die Tonart — *the very key* (*in which the symphony was composed*), *even the key*
16 Fis-Moll — *F sharp minor*
der Satz — *movement*
16–17 strebt entschlossene Haltung an — *attempts to strike a determined attitude*
17–18 beide kurz gehalten — *both kept brief*
18 den herkömmlichen Charakter beizubehalten — *to preserve their traditional character*
19 gewohnt — *accustomed*
kommt nicht . . . zum Durchbruch — *does not come into full display, cannot break through* or *assert itself fully*
19–20 das Finale redet sich gewaltsam in den sonst hier sprudelnden Frohsinn hinein — paraphrase: "*it takes some violent self-persuasion before the finale gets into the spirit of joviality and good cheer that usually bubble over in the concluding movements of Haydn's symphonies*"
21 Halt machen — *stop*

ten Tonart, tritt Takt und Tonart des zweiten Satzes (Adagio) ein. Noch eine kurze Weile und etwas bis dahin Unerhörtes geschieht: der zweite Hornist und erste Oboist, getreu ihrer Vorschrift,* packen ihre Instrumente ein und verlassen das Podium; elf Takte weiter greift der bisher unbeschäftigte Fagottist zu seinem Instrument, aber nur, um im Unisono mit der 2. Violine zweimal die Anfangstakte 5 des ersten Motivs zu blasen, dann löscht er das Licht an seinem Pulte aus und geht gleichfalls ab. Nach sieben Takten folgt ihm der erste Hornist und zweite Oboist. Nun löst sich endlich das Violoncell vom Basse los: beide gehen geraume Zeit jedes seinen eigenen Weg, bis auch der Bass das Weite sucht. In kurzen Zwischenräumen verschwinden nun Cellist, dritter und vierter Violinist und 10 Bratschist.

Es ist fast finster geworden im Orchesterraum; nur an einem Pulte brennen noch zwei Lichter; hier sitzen Tommasini (des Fürsten Liebling) und ein zweiter Violinist, denen das letzte Wort zugefallen ist. Leise und gedämpft erklingt ihr Wechselgesang, zuletzt in Terzen und Sexten sich verschlingend wie im leisesten 15 Hauch ersterbend. — Die letzten Lichter erlöschen, die letzten Geiger gehen, und auch Haydn ist im Begriff, ihnen zu folgen, als der Fürst, der dem Vorgang anfangs befremdet gefolgt war, auf ihn hinzutritt, ihm gerührt die Hand reicht und mit den Worten anredet: „Ich habe Ihre Absicht wohl durchschaut, die Musiker sehnen sich nach Hause — nun gut — morgen packen wir ein.“ 20

Im Vorsaale aber harrte die Kapelle in banger Erwartung ihres Führers und als nun dieser unter sie tritt und sein leuchtender Blick ihnen den glücklichen Ausgang verrät — bedarf es noch der Worte, die nun folgende Scene zu schildern, wie alle, die Junggesellen mit inbegriffen, sich herzu drängen, seine Hände zu drücken und Haydn selbst die Rührung kaum verbergen kann — ein glücklicher Vater unter 25 glücklichen Kindern!

* getreu ihrer Vorschrift — *faithful to their instructions* (In der Partitur: „Nichts mehr,“ in den Auflagestimmen: „Geht ab.“ *In the score it says: “Nothing more,” in the parts for the instruments the instruction reads: “Exit.”*)

LINE

1 tritt Takt und Tonart des zweiten Satzes . . . ein — *the measure and key of the second movement are reintroduced*
2 etwas bis dahin Unerhörtes geschieht — *something happens that had hitherto been unheard of*
4 der bisher unbeschäftigte Fagottist — *the bassoon player, idle until that moment*
6 blasen — *blow*
das Pult — *desk*
7 abgehen — *leave*
gleichfalls — *likewise*
8 sich loslösen — *separate*
8–9 geraume Zeit — *for a good while*
9 das Weite sucht — *“takes off”*
9–10 in kurzen Zwischenräumen — *at short intervals*
11 der Bratschist — *viola player*
13 der Liebling — *favorite*
15 der Wechselgesang — *alternating song*

LINE

15 zuletzt — *finally*
Terzen — *thirds*
sich verschlingend — *interlacing*
15–16 wie im leisesten Hauch ersterbend — *as if they were dying away in the softest breath*
17 ist im Begriff . . . zu folgen — *is about to follow*
der Vorgang — *event, goings on*
18 befremdet — *with surprise*
gerührt — *touched, moved, with emotion*
19–20 sich sehnen — *long*
21 harren — *wait*
22 sein leuchtender Blick — *his beaming eyes*
der Ausgang — *solution, ending*
23 schildern — *describe*
24 der Junggeselle — *bachelor*
mit inbegriffen — *included*
25 verbergen — *conceal*

GEISS UND SCHLEICHE

Die Schleiche singt ihr Nachtgebet,
die Waldgeiß staunend vor ihr steht.

Die Waldgeiß schüttelt ihren Bart
wie ein Magister hochgelahrt.

Sie weiß nicht, was die Schleiche singt,
sie hört nur, daß es lieblich klingt.

Die Schleiche fällt in Schlaf alsbald.
Die Geiß geht sinnend durch den Wald.

Christian Morgenstern

GOAT AND BLINDWORM

The blindworm sings its vesper prayer,
The woodgoat stands astounded there,

Inclines its beard with learned nod
Before the worm intent on God.

It knows not what the words convey,
Hears but sweet sound of roundelay.

The worm soon nods its head for good,
The goat goes pensive through the wood.

APPENDIX I

ADDITIONAL READING

THE GERMAN ALPHABET

German Letters		Roman Letters		German Name	German Letters		Roman Letters		German Name
𝔄	𝔞	A	a	[ah]	𝔑	𝔫	N	n	[en]
𝔅	𝔟	B	b	[bay]	𝔒	𝔬	O	o	[oh]
ℭ	𝔠	C	c	[tsay]	𝔓	𝔭	P	p	[pay]
𝔇	𝔡	D	d	[day]	𝔔	𝔮	Q	q	[koo]
𝔈	𝔢	E	e	[ay]	ℜ	𝔯	R	r	[air]
𝔉	𝔣	F	f	[ef]	𝔖	ſ 𝔰[1]	S	s	[ess]
𝔊	𝔤	G	g	[gay]	𝔗	𝔱	T	t	[tay]
ℌ	𝔥	H	h	[hah]	𝔘	𝔲	U	u	[oo]
ℑ	𝔦	I	i	[ee]	𝔙	𝔳	V	v	[fow]
𝔍	𝔧	J	j	[yot]	𝔚	𝔴	W	w	[vay]
𝔎	𝔨	K	k	[kah]	𝔛	𝔵	X	x	[iks]
𝔏	𝔩	L	l	[el]	𝔜	𝔶	Y	y	[ipsilon]
𝔐	𝔪	M	m	[em]	ℨ	𝔷	Z	z	[tset]

Combined Letters

𝔠𝔥	[tsay-hah]	ß	[ess-tset]
𝔠𝔨	[tsay-kah]	𝔱𝔷	[tay-tset]

Modified Vowels

𝔄̈	ä	[ah-umlaut]	𝔒̈	ö	[oh-umlaut]
𝔄̈𝔲	äu	[ah-umlaut-oo]	𝔘̈	ü	[oo-umlaut]

NOTE 1 Of the two small letters for *s* (ſ and 𝔰), the latter is called "final *s*." It is used at the end of a word or syllable. The other *s* (ſ) is called "long *s*" and is used in all other positions.

GERMAN TYPE

The so-called Gothic type introduced at this point is known in German as **Fraktur** and was until recent years widely used by German printers, and also by American publishers of German textbooks. Since many older German literary works printed in **Fraktur** still exist, it seems only appropriate to introduce it, alphabetically and by way of the following reading selections, so that you may at least become acquainted with it.

READING DRILL

As in Unit VIII, the purpose of this section is to anticipate the reading. For the sake of readier comprehension, the complex German sentences need to be divided into convenient units, as indicated below.

1. Dieſe Entwicklung, / bewirkt von einer Urſache, / die den beſten Kennern unter den Sprachwiſſenſchaftlern / noch heute ein Rätſel iſt, / betraf im beſonderen, / — obſchon nicht ausſchließlich, — / die ſtimmhaften und ſtimmloſen Verſchlußlaute / **b, d, g** und **p, t, k.**

   This development, operating by way of some cause still baffling to the best observers among language scientists, involved particularly, though not exclusively, the voiced and unvoiced stops, b, d, g *and* p, t, k.

2. Der Philologe Jakob Grimm, / der bekannte Sammler der Volksmärchen, / war unter den erſten, / welche die klare Evidenz / einer ſyſtematiſchen Reihe / von Konſonantenveränderungen erkannten, / die einſt innerhalb der indoeuropäiſchen Sprachgemeinſchaft / wirkſam geweſen waren.

   The philologist, Jacob Grimm, the well-known collector of folk tales, was among the first to see unmistakable evidence of a systematic series of consonant changes, once actively operative within the Indo-European language community.

3. Die zweite Lautverſchiebung / (etwa von 350 bis 750 n. Chr.) / fand innerhalb der weſtgermaniſchen Gruppe der germaniſchen Unterfamilie ſtatt / und war weſentlich daran beteiligt, / den Unterſchied zwiſchen dem Niederdeutſchen / (zum Beiſpiel, der engliſchen Sprache) / und dem Hochdeutſchen zu begründen.

   The second sound shift (*ca. 350–750 A.D.*) *occurred within the West-Germanic group of the Germanic subfamily and was instrumental in producing the difference between Low German* (*for example, English*) *and High German.*

4. Gotiſch iſt ein wichtiger Schlüſſel / zur Entdeckung und zum Verſtändnis / jener „unſichtbaren Strömung" / innerhalb der indoeuropäiſchen Familie, / obgleich nur ein Teil der Sprache / uns erhalten geblieben iſt.

   Gothic is an important key to the discovery and understanding of that "invisible drift" within the Indo-European family, although only a part of the language has been preserved for us.

5. Die folgende Tafel / mag in vereinfachter Form andeuten, / wie ſich in den zwei Lautverſchiebungen nacheinander / die Entwicklung vom Indoeuropäiſchen zum Germaniſchen, / vom Germaniſchen zum Hochdeutſchen vollzog.

   The following table may suggest in simplified form how the two sound shifts brought about successively the development from Indo-European to Germanic and from Germanic to High German.

Sprachen II *

Das einzig Konstante an den Sprachen ist ihre Veränderlichkeit. „In der Sprache ist nichts vollkommen statisch. Jedes Wort, jedes grammatische Element, jeder Ausdruck, jeder Laut, jeder Akzent ist eine langsam wechselnde Gestalt, geformt von der unsichtbaren und unpersönlichen Strömung, die das
5 Leben der Sprache ist.“ † Wenn das für die heutigen Sprachen gilt, so galt es in noch weit stärkerem Ausmaß für die Sprachen früherer Zeitalter. Im Falle des Indoeuropäischen begann, zum Beispiel, vor viertausend Jahren eine Reihe von Veränderungen, die so grundlegend waren, daß sie eine scharfe Trennung innerhalb dieser Sprachgemeinschaft bewirkten. Das Ergebnis war,
10 daß sich nach und nach innerhalb der indoeuropäischen Sprachfamilie ein Segment bildete, das sich deutlich von dem Rest der indoeuropäischen Sprachen unterschied. Dieses bedeutende Segment wird heute als die germanische Unterfamilie der indoeuropäischen Sprachen bezeichnet.

Man nimmt an, daß die Entwicklung, welche diese germanische Unter-
15 familie begründete, im zweiten Jahrtausend vor Christi Geburt anfing. Um Fünfhundert war sie im wesentlichen abgeschlossen. Ihr letztes Stadium reichte von etwa 500 v. Chr. bis gegen 250 n. Chr. Diese Entwicklung, bewirkt von einer Ursache, die den besten Kennern unter den Sprachwissenschaftlern noch heute ein Rätsel ist, betraf im besonderen, — obschon nicht ausschließ-
20 lich, — die stimmhaften und stimmlosen Verschlußlaute **b, d, g** und **p, t, k.**

Jakob Grimm, der bekannte Sammler der Volksmärchen, war unter den ersten, welche die klare Evidenz einer systematischen Reihe von Konsonantenveränderungen erkannten, die einst innerhalb der indoeuropäischen Sprachgemeinschaft wirksam gewesen waren. So durchgehend und ausgeprägt inner-
25 halb des Indoeuropäischen waren die Veränderungen, die Grimm beobachtete, und so regelmäßig wiederholten sie sich, daß er (ebenso wie sein dänischer Zeitgenosse Rasmus Rask) zu dem Schluß kam, daß diese Veränderungen

* The first part ("Sprachen I") of this language discussion as well as a condensed version in English of the two parts ("Linguistic Kinship between German and English") may be found on pages 206–209 and pages 17–18 respectively.
† See footnote on page 17.

LINE

1 die Veränderlichkeit — *changeability*
3 der Ausdruck — *expression, locution*
6 das Ausmaß — *measure, extent*
das Zeitalter — *age*
8 die Veränderung — *change*
9 die Trennung — *separation*
die Sprachgemeinschaft — *language community*
bewirken — *effect, bring about*
das Ergebnis — *result*
10 nach und nach — *gradually*
14 die Entwicklung — *development*

LINE

15 begründen — *establish, produce*
16 abgeschlossen — *completed, concluded*
das Stadium — *stage*
19 betreffen — *concern, affect*
19–20 ausschließlich — *exclusively*
20 stimmhaft — *voiced*
der Verschlußlaut — *stop*
24 wirksam — *operative*
durchgehend — *pervasive*
ausgeprägt — *pronounced*
26 regelmäßig — *regularly*
27 der Zeitgenosse — *contemporary*

einem sprachlichen Gesetz folgten. Grimm leistete einen großen Beitrag zur Sprachwissenschaft, indem er ein solches Gesetz formulierte. Er wurde damit zu einem der Begründer der vergleichenden Philologie.

Das später von anderen berichtigte, modifizierte und weiter ausgearbeitete Gesetz von Jakob Grimm hat im Grunde zwei Teile. Beide betreffen die Veränderungen von Konsonanten oder „Lautverschiebungen." Die erste Lautverschiebung war ein wesentlicher Faktor in der Differenzierung des Germanischen vom Indoeuropäischen. Die zweite Lautverschiebung (etwa von 350 bis 750 n. Chr.) fand innerhalb der westgermanischen Gruppe der germanischen Unterfamilie statt und war wesentlich daran beteiligt, den Unterschied zwischen dem Niederdeutschen (zum Beispiel, der englischen Sprache) und dem Hochdeutschen zu begründen.

„Hoch" und „nieder" sind rein geographische Bezeichnungen, die sich auf niedrig gelegene Ebenen und Hochland beziehen. Englisch, zum Beispiel, ist seit den germanischen Invasionen des 5. Jahrhunderts besonders eng mit den Sprachen verwandt, die auf den niedrig gelegenen friesischen Inseln nahe den „Niederlanden" gesprochen werden. Das Englische ist daher im Grunde eine „niederdeutsche" Sprache, allerdings seit dem 12. Jahrhundert, in der Folge der Eroberung durch die Normannen, mit wesentlichen „Entlehnungen" aus lateinischen Wurzeln. Man schätzt, daß Englisch heute etwa 50% lateinische, 30% germanische, 10% griechische und 10% diverse andere Wurzeln enthält.

Unter den germanischen Sprachen bildet Ostgermanisch, nämlich Gotisch, den ältesten erhaltenen Rest. Gotisch ist ein wichtiger Schlüssel zur Entdeckung und zum Verständnis jener „unsichtbaren Strömung" innerhalb der indoeuropäischen Familie, obgleich nur ein Teil der Sprache uns erhalten geblieben ist: — Fragmente einer Bibelübersetzung ins Gotische, die der gotische Bischof Ulfilas nach seiner Bekehrung zum Christentum im vierten Jahrhundert unternahm.

Es würde in dem Rahmen unseres Kurses zu weit führen, wenn wir auf Grimms Gesetz, die zwei Lautverschiebungen und die späteren Modifikationen im einzelnen eingehen wollten. Die folgende Tafel mag aber in vereinfachter Form andeuten, wie sich in den zwei Lautverschiebungen nacheinander die Entwicklung vom Indoeuropäischen zum Germanischen, vom Germanischen zum Hochdeutschen vollzog. Lateinische Beispiele repräsentieren die indo-

LINE

1 leistete . . . Beitrag — *made . . . contribution*
2 indem — *by* (with participial constr.)
6 die Lautverschiebung — *sound shift*
9–10 fand . . . statt — *took place*
10 war . . . beteiligt — *was instrumental*
13–14 sich beziehen (auf) — *refer to*
18–19 in der Folge der Eroberung — *following the conquest*
19 die Entlehnung — *borrowing*
20 die Wurzel — *root*
man schätzt — *it is estimated*
23 der älteste erhaltene Rest — *the oldest preserved remnant*
23–4 die Entdeckung — *discovery*
24 das Verständnis — *understanding*
27 die Bekehrung — *conversion*
29 der Rahmen — *frame(work), limits*
31 eingehen (auf) — *go into*

europäische Sprachfamilie, gotische und englische Beispiele die germanische Gruppe. Dabei ist folgendes zu beachten: (1) Die Entsprechungen zwischen Konsonanten beziehen sich auf phonetische Laute, nicht auf bloße Buchstaben des Alphabets. So kennt, zum Beispiel, die lateinische Orthographie kaum den
5 Buchstaben k, aber der k-Laut erscheint in der Schrift als c oder q. (2) Das Folgende ist nur eine Auswahl der möglichen Entsprechungen zwischen den Konsonanten. (3) Die stammverwandten Wörter müssen nicht die gleiche Bedeutung haben. (4) Die Vokalwerte der stammverwandten Wörter stimmen nicht notwendigerweise überein, denn das System der Vokalveränderungen
10 ist weitgehend unabhängig von der Konsonantenverschiebung.

Indoeuropäisch (Lateinisch)	Germanisch (Gotisch, Englisch)	Hochdeutsch (Neuhochdeutsch)
p	**f**	**f (v)**
ped(is)	fōtus, *foot*	Fuß
pater	fadar, *father*	Vater
pro	faúr, *for*	für
pell(is)	fill, *fell* (= *skin*)	Fell
pecus	faíhu, *fee*	Vieh (*cattle*)
k	**h**	**h**
cornu	haúrn, *horn*	Horn
capere	haban, *have*	haben
cord(is)	haírto, *heart*	Herz
canis	hunds, *hound*	Hund
canare	hana, *hen*	Hahn (Henne)
centum	hund, *hundred*	hundert
pecus	faíhu, *fee*	Vieh (*cattle*)
decem	taíhun, *ten*	zehn
d	**t**	**z, s, ſ, ſſ, ß, tz**
cord(is)	haírtō, *heart*	Herz
sedere	sitan, *sit*	sitzen
duo	twai, *two*	zwei
domare	tamjan, *tame*	zähmen
domus	timrjan, *timber*	Zimmer
ducere	tiuhan, *tug*	Zug
istud	þata, *that*	das
quod	hwaet, *what*	was
edere	itan, *eat*	essen
ped(is)	fōtus, *foot*	Fuß
decem	taíhun, *ten*	zehn

LINE

2 Dabei ist folgendes zu beachten — here: *In examining this table the following must be borne in mind*
die Entsprechung — *correspondency*
6 die Auswahl — *selection, selected list*
8 stammverwandt — *cognate*

LINE

8–9 stimmen nicht notwendigerweise überein — *do not necessarily correspond* (or *coincide*)
10 weitgehend unabhängig von — *largely independent of*

Indoeuropäisch (Lateinisch)	Germanisch (Gotisch, Englisch)	Hochdeutsch (Neuhochdeutsch)
t	**þ, th**	**d**
tu	þu, *thou*	du
tres	þreis, *three*	drei
tonare	þeihvō, *thunder*	donnern
tenuis	þunnus, *thin*	dünn
turba	þaúrp, *thorp*	Dorf
tectum	* þak, *thatch*	Dach
tunc	þan, *then*	dann
g	**k, c**	**k, ck**
ager	akrs, *acre*	Acker
genu	kniu, *knee*	Knie
granum	kaúrn, *corn*	Korn
genus	kuni, *kin(d)*	Kind

* Hypothetische indoeuropäische Form

HEINRICH BÖLL

Heinrich Böll (geb. 1917 in Köln) ist einer der führenden deutschen Autoren der Gegenwart. Seine Romane, Novellen, Kurzgeschichten und Prosasatiren dienen der Auseinandersetzung mit den geistigen, seelischen und materiellen Problemen der jüngsten deutschen Vergangenheit. So behandeln etwa der Roman „Wo warst du, Adam?" (1950) oder die Kurzgeschichten, die unter den Titeln „Wanderer, kommst du nach Spa . . .?" (1950) und „Nicht nur zur Weihnachtszeit" (1952) erschienen, den zweiten Weltkrieg und seine Folgen; die Romane „Und sagte kein einziges Wort" (1953) und „Haus ohne Hüter" (1954) das wirtschaftliche und seelische Elend der ersten Nachkriegszeit; der Roman „Billard um halb zehn" (1959) den Konflikt zwischen christlicher Friedensliebe und totalitärem Machtstreben. Die folgende Satire aus der Sphäre des deutschen „Wirtschaftswunders" gilt dem mechanischen, sinn- und seelenlosen Betrieb der modernen Arbeitswelt überhaupt. Sie ist der Sammlung „Doktor Murkes gesammeltes Schweigen" (1958) entnommen.

HEINRICH BÖLL (born 1917 in Cologne) is one of the leading contemporary German writers. His novels, "Novellen," short stories, and prose satires serve as a means of coming to terms with the intellectual, spiritual, and material problems of Germany's most recent past. Thus, for example, the novel *Wo warst du, Adam?* (1950) or the short stories that appeared under the titles *Wanderer, kommst du nach Spa . . .?* (1950) and *Nicht nur zur Weihnachtszeit* (1952) deal with the Second World War and its consequences. The novels *Und sagte kein einziges Wort* (1953) and *Haus ohne Hüter* (1954) deal with the economic and spiritual misery of the period immediately following the war. The novel *Billard um halb zehn* (1959) deals with the conflict between Christian love of peace and the totalitarian drive for power. The following satire issuing from the realm of the "economic miracle" in Germany is concerned with the mechanical, meaningless, and soulless activity of the modern working world in general. It is taken from a collection entitled *Doktor Murkes gesammeltes Schweigen* (1958).

Es wird etwas geschehen

(Eine handlungsstarke Geschichte) *

Zu den merkwürdigsten Abschnitten meines Lebens gehört wohl der, den ich als Angestellter in Alfred Wunsiedels Fabrik zubrachte. Von Natur bin ich mehr dem Nachdenken und dem Nichstun zugeneigt als der Arbeit, doch hin und wieder zwingen mich anhaltende finanzielle Schwierigkeiten — denn 5 Nachdenken bringt sowenig ein wie Nichtstun —, eine sogenannte Stelle anzunehmen. Wieder einmal auf einem solchen Tiefpunkt angekommen, vertraute ich mich der Arbeitsvermittlung an und wurde mit sieben anderen Leidensgenossen in Wunsiedels Fabrik geschickt, wo wir einer Eignungsprüfung unterzogen werden sollten.

10 Schon der Anblick der Fabrik machte mich mißtrauisch: die Fabrik war ganz aus Glasziegeln gebaut, und meine Abneigung gegen helle Gebäude und helle Räume ist so stark wie meine Abneigung gegen die Arbeit. Noch mißtrauischer wurde ich, als uns in der hellen, fröhlich ausgemalten Kantine gleich ein Frühstück serviert wurde: hübsche Kellnerinnen brachten uns Eier, Kaffee und 15 Toaste, in geschmackvollen Karaffen stand Orangensaft; Goldfische drückten ihre blasierten Gesichter gegen die Wände hellgrüner Aquarien. Die Kellnerinnen waren so fröhlich, daß sie vor Fröhlichkeit fast zu platzen schienen. Nur starke Willensanstrengung — so schien mir — hielt sie davon zurück, dauernd zu trällern. Sie waren mit ungesungenen Liedern so angefüllt wie Hühner 20 mit ungelegten Eiern. Ich ahnte gleich, was meine Leidensgenossen nicht zu ahnen schienen: daß auch dieses Frühstück zur Prüfung gehöre; und so kaute ich hingebungsvoll, mit dem vollen Bewußtsein eines Menschen, der genau weiß, daß er seinem Körper wertvolle Stoffe zuführt. Ich tat etwas, wozu

* eine handlungsstarke Geschichte — *a story full of action*

LINE

1 merkwürdig — *notable*
der Abschnitt — *period, chapter*
2 der Angestellte — *employee*
die Fabrik — *factory*
zubringen — *spend*
3 zugeneigt (*plus dat.*) — *inclined to*
3–4 hin und wieder — *now and then*
4 anhaltend — *persistent*
5 sogenannt — *so-called*
die Stelle — *position*
6 der Tiefpunkt — *low point*
7 vertraute ich mich der Arbeitsvermittlung an — *I confided my troubles to the employment agency*
8 der Leidensgenosse — *fellow-sufferer*
die Eignungsprüfung — *aptitude test*
9 unterzogen werden — *be subjected to*
10 der Anblick — *sight*
mißtrauisch — *suspicious*

LINE

11 der Glasziegel — *glass block* (or *brick*)
12 die Abneigung — *aversion*
13 fröhlich ausgemalt — *painted in cheerful colors*
die Kantine — *cafeteria*
15 die Karaffe — *carafe*
16 blasiert — *blasé*
17 die Fröhlichkeit — *cheerfulness, cheer*
platzen — *burst*
18 die Willensanstrengung — *effort* (*of will*)
19 trällern — *hum*
20 ungelegt — *unlaid*
ahnen — *suspect*
21 kauen — *chew*
22 hingebungsvoll — *with dedication, devotedly*
das Bewußtsein — *consciousness*
23 wertvoll — *valuable*
der Stoff — *substance*

mich normalerweise keine Macht dieser Welt bringen würde: ich trank auf den nüchternen Magen Orangensaft, ließ den Kaffee und ein Ei stehen, den größten Teil des Toasts liegen, stand auf und marschierte handlungsschwanger in der Kantine auf und ab.

So wurde ich als erster in den Prüfungsraum geführt, wo auf reizenden 5 Tischen die Fragebogen bereitlagen. Die Wände waren in einem Grün getönt, das Einrichtungsfanatikern das Wort „entzückend" auf die Lippen gezaubert hätte. Niemand war zu sehen, und doch war ich so sicher, beobachtet zu werden, daß ich mich benahm, wie ein Handlungsschwangerer sich benimmt, wenn er sich unbeobachtet glaubt: ungeduldig riß ich meinen Füllfederhalter aus 10 der Tasche, schraubte ihn auf, setzte mich an den nächstbesten Tisch und zog den Fragebogen an mich heran, wie Choleriker Wirtshausrechnungen zu sich hinziehen.

Erste Frage: Halten Sie es für richtig, daß der Mensch nur zwei Arme, zwei Beine, Augen und Ohren hat? 15

Hier erntete ich zum ersten Male die Früchte meiner Nachdenklichkeit und schrieb ohne Zögern hin: „Selbst vier Arme, Beine, Ohren würden meinem Tatendrang nicht genügen. Die Ausstattung des Menschen ist kümmerlich."

Zweite Frage: Wieviel Telefone können Sie gleichzeitig bedienen?

Auch hier war die Antwort so leicht wie die Lösung einer Gleichung ersten 20 Grades. „Wenn es nur sieben Telefone sind," schrieb ich, „werde ich ungeduldig, erst bei neun fühle ich mich vollkommen ausgelastet."

Dritte Frage: Was machen Sie nach Feierabend?

Meine Antwort: „Ich kenne das Wort Feierabend nicht mehr — an meinem

LINE

1 normalerweise — *normally, ordinarily*
1–2 auf den nüchternen Magen — *on an empty stomach*
3 handlungsschwanger — *filled with the spirit of action*
5 reizend — *charming, attractive*
6 bereitliegen — *lie in readiness*
7 getönt — *shaded, colored*
der Einrichtungsfanatiker — *fanatic about interior decorating*
entzückend — *delightful*
8 zaubern — *impel, summon up* (as if magically)
beobachten — *observe*
9 sich benehmen — *behave*
10 der Füllfederhalter — *fountain pen*
11 die Tasche — *pocket*
12 die Wirtshausrechnung — *bill* (for a meal in a restaurant)

LINE

16 ernten — *reap*
die Nachdenklichkeit — *thoughtfulness*
17 das Zögern — *hesitation*
selbst — here: *even*
18 der Tatendrang — *thirst for action*
die Ausstattung — *equipment*
kümmerlich — *meager*
19 gleichzeitig — *at the same time, simultaneously*
20 die Lösung — *solution*
die Gleichung — *equation*
21 der Grad — *degree, grade, power*
22 vollkommen ausgelastet — *wholly satisfied, working to my full capacity*
23 der Feierabend — *rest period* (following the day's work)
nach Feierabend — *in your free time* (after work)

fünfzehnten Geburtstag strich ich es aus meinem Vokabular, denn am Anfang war die Tat."

Ich bekam die Stelle. Tatsächlich fühlte ich mich sogar mit den neun Telefonen nicht ganz ausgelastet. Ich rief in die Muscheln der Hörer: „Handeln
5 Sie sofort!" oder: „Tun Sie etwas! — Es muß etwas geschehen — Es wird etwas geschehen — Es ist etwas geschehen — Es sollte etwas geschehen." Doch meistens — denn das schien mir der Atmosphäre gemäß — bediente ich mich des Imperativs.

Interessant waren die Mittagspausen, wo wir in der Kantine, von lautloser
10 Fröhlichkeit umgeben, vitaminreiche Speisen aßen. Es wimmelte in Wunsiedels Fabrik von Leuten, die verrückt darauf waren, ihren Lebenslauf zu erzählen, wie eben handlungsstarke Persönlichkeiten es gern tun. Ihr Lebenslauf ist ihnen wichtiger als ihr Leben, man braucht nur auf einen Knopf zu drücken, und schon erbrechen sie ihn in Ehren.

15 Wunsiedels Stellvertreter war ein Mann mit Namen Broschek, der seinerseits einen gewissen Ruhm erworben hatte, weil er als Student sieben Kinder und eine gelähmte Frau durch Nachtarbeit ernährt, zugleich vier Handelsvertretungen erfolgreich ausgeübt und dennoch innerhalb von zwei Jahren zwei Staatsprüfungen mit Auszeichnung bestanden hatte. Als ihn Reporter gefragt
20 hatten: „Wann schlafen Sie denn, Broschek?", hatte er geantwortet: „Schlafen ist Sünde!"

Wunsiedels Sekretärin hatte einen gelähmten Mann und vier Kinder durch Stricken ernährt, hatte gleichzeitig in Psychologie und Heimatkunde promoviert, Schäferhunde gezüchtet und war als Barsängerin unter dem Namen „Vamp 7"
25 berühmt geworden.

Wunsiedel selbst war einer von den Leuten, die morgens, kaum erwacht,

LINE

1–2 „Am Anfang war die Tat" — "*In the beginning was the deed*" (a reference to Faust's significant mistranslation of St. John 1:1)
4 die Muschel — *mouth-piece* (telephone)
der Hörer — *receiver* (telephone)
5 sofort — *immediately*
7 gemäß — *in keeping with*
9 lautlos — *soundless*
11 verrückt darauf — *madly intent upon*
12 handlungsstarke Persönlichkeiten — *persons with a drive for action*
der Lebenslauf — *career*
13 der Knopf — *button*
14 erbrechen — *spill out*
ihn — (refers to Lebenslauf above)
in Ehren — *respectfully, with dignity*
15 der Stellvertreter — *representative, the second in command*
16 der Ruhm — *fame*
erwerben — *acquire*

LINE

17 gelähmt — *lame*
ernähren — *feed, support*
zugleich — *at the same time*
17–18 vier Handelsvertretungen erfolgreich ausgeübt — *had been the successful sales representative for four different firms*
19 die Staatsprüfung — *state* or *civil service examination* (an examination in the sphere of higher education, qualifying for legal practice, teaching positions, etc.)
21 die Sünde — *sin*
23 das Stricken — *knitting*
die Heimatkunde — *study of one's native country* (or *region*)
promovieren — *get a degree*
24 der Schäferhund — *German shepherd dog*
züchten — *raise*

schon entschlossen sind zu handeln. „Ich muß handeln," denken sie, während sie energisch den Gürtel des Bademantels zuschnüren. „Ich muß handeln," denken sie, während sie sich rasieren, und sie blicken triumphierend auf die Barthaare, die sie mit dem Seifenschaum von ihrem Rasierapparat abspülen: Diese Reste der Behaarung sind die ersten Opfer ihres Tatendranges. Auch 5
die intimeren Verrichtungen lösen Befriedigung bei diesen Leuten aus: Wasser rauscht, Papier wird verbraucht. Es ist etwas geschehen. Brot wird gegessen, dem Ei wird der Kopf abgeschlagen.

Die belangloseste Tätigkeit sah bei Wunsiedel wie eine Handlung aus: wie er den Hut aufsetzte, wie er — bebend vor Energie — den Mantel zuknöpfte, 10
der Kuß, den er seiner Frau gab, alles war Tat.

Wenn er sein Büro betrat, rief er seiner Sekretärin als Gruß zu: „Es muß etwas geschehen!" Und diese rief frohen Mutes: „Es wird etwas geschehen!" Wunsiedel ging dann von Abteilung zu Abteilung, rief sein fröhliches: „Es muß etwas geschehen!" Alle antworteten: „Es wird etwas geschehen!" 15
Und auch ich rief ihm, wenn er mein Zimmer betrat, strahlend zu: „Es wird etwas geschehen!"

Innerhalb der ersten Woche steigerte ich die Zahl der bedienten Telefone auf elf, innerhalb der zweiten Woche auf dreizehn, und es machte mir Spaß, morgens in der Straßenbahn neue Imperative zu erfinden oder das Verbum 20
„geschehen" durch die verschiedenen Tempora, durch die verschiedenen Genera, durch Konjunktiv und Indikativ zu hetzen; zwei Tage lang sagte ich nur den einen Satz, weil ich ihn so schön fand: „Es hätte etwas geschehen müssen," zwei weitere Tage lang einen anderen: „Das hätte nicht geschehen dürfen."

So fing ich an, mich tatsächlich ausgelastet zu fühlen, als wirklich etwas 25
geschah. An einem Dienstagmorgen — ich hatte mich noch gar nicht richtig zurechtgesetzt — stürzte Wunsiedel in mein Zimmer und rief sein „Es muß etwas geschehen!" Doch etwas Unerklärliches auf seinem Gesicht ließ mich zögern, fröhlich und munter, wie es vorgeschrieben war, zu antworten: „Es

LINE

2 der Gürtel — *belt*
der Bademantel — *bathrobe*
zuschnüren — *tie*
4 der Bart — *beard*
der Seifenschaum — *soap lather*
der Rasierapparat — *razor*
abspülen — *wash off, rinse off*
5 das Opfer — *victim*
6 die Verrichtung — *activity*
auslösen — *cause, induce*
die Befriedigung — *satisfaction*
7 rauschen — *roar*
verbrauchen — *use (up)*
8 den Kopf abschlagen — *behead*
9 belanglos — *insignificant, trivial*
10 aufsetzen — *put on*

LINE

10 bebend vor — *trembling with*
zuknöpfen — *button*
12 das Büro — *office*
der Gruß — *greeting*
14 die Abteilung — *department*
18 innerhalb — *within*
steigern — *increase*
20 die Straßenbahn — *streetcar*
erfinden — *invent*
21 Tempora — *tenses* (Lat.)
Genera — *genders* (Lat.)
22 hetzen — *chase, pursue*
26–7 sich zurechtsetzen — *settle down*
28 etwas Unerklärliches — *something unexplainable, something mysterious*
29 vorgeschrieben — *prescribed*

wird etwas geschehen!" Ich zögerte wohl zu lange, denn Wunsiedel, der sonst selten schrie, brüllte mich an: „Antworten Sie! Antworten Sie, wie es vorgeschrieben ist!" Und ich antwortete leise und widerstrebend wie ein Kind, das man zu sagen zwingt: ich bin ein böses Kind. Nur mit großer Anstren-
5 gung brachte ich den Satz heraus: „Es wird etwas geschehen," und kaum hatte ich ihn ausgesprochen, da geschah tatsächlich etwas: Wunsiedel stürzte zu Boden, rollte im Stürzen auf die Seite und lag quer vor der offenen Tür. Ich wußte gleich, was sich mir bestätigte, als ich langsam um meinen Tisch herum auf den Liegenden zuging: daß er tot war.

10 Kopfschüttelnd stieg ich über Wunsiedel hinweg, ging langsam durch den Flur zu Broscheks Zimmer und trat dort ohne anzuklopfen ein. Broschek saß an seinem Schreibtisch, hatte in jeder Hand einen Telefonhörer, im Mund einen Kugelschreiber, mit dem er Notizen auf einen Block schrieb, während er mit den bloßen Füßen eine Strickmaschine bediente, die unter dem Schreibtisch
15 stand. Auf diese Weise trägt er dazu bei, die Bekleidung seiner Familie zu vervollständigen. „Es ist etwas geschehen," sagte ich leise. Broschek spuckte den Kugelstift aus, legte die beiden Hörer hin, löste zögernd seine Zehen von der Strickmaschine.

„Was ist denn geschehen?" fragte er.

20 „Herr Wunsiedel ist tot," sagte ich.

„Nein," sagte Broschek.

„Doch," sagte ich, „kommen Sie!"

„Nein," sagte Broschek, „das ist unmöglich," aber er schlüpfte in seine Pantoffeln und folgte mir über den Flur.

25 „Nein," sagte er, als wir an Wunsiedels Leiche standen, „nein, nein!" Ich widersprach ihm nicht. Vorsichtig drehte ich Wunsiedel auf den Rücken, drückte ihm die Augen zu und betrachtete ihn nachdenklich.

Ich empfand fast Zärtlichkeit für ihn, und zum ersten Male wurde mir klar, daß ich ihn nie gehaßt hatte. Auf seinem Gesicht war etwas, wie es auf den
30 Gesichtern der Kinder ist, die sich hartnäckig weigern, ihren Glauben an den

LINE

3 widerstrebend — *resisting*
4 zwingen — *compel, force*
4–5 die Anstrengung — *effort*
5 herausbringen — *utter*
6–7 stürzte zu Boden — *fell to the floor*
8 was sich mir bestätigte — *what I soon found confirmed*
10 kopfschüttelnd — *shaking (my) head*
11 der Flur — *corridor, hallway*
anklopfen — *knock (at a door)*
12 der Schreibtisch — *(writing) desk*
13 der Kugelschreiber — *ball-point pen*
der Block — *pad*
14 bloß — *bare*
die Strickmaschine — *knitting machine*

LINE

15 auf diese Weise — *in this manner*
(zu etwas) beitragen — *add to, help*
die Bekleidung — *apparel, clothing*
16 vervollständigen — *complete*
16–17 ausspucken — *spit out*
22 Doch — *Oh yes, he is*
23 schlüpfen — *slip*
23–4 der Pantoffel — *slipper*
25 die Leiche — *corpse, body*
26 widersprechen — *contradict*
27 zudrücken — *close, press shut*
28 die Zärtlichkeit — *tenderness*
30 hartnäckig — *obstinately*
weigern — *refuse*

Weihnachtsmann aufzugeben, obwohl die Argumente der Spielkameraden so überzeugend klingen.

„Nein," sagte Broschek, „nein."

„Es muß etwas geschehen," sagte ich leise zu Broschek.

„Ja," sagte Broschek, „es muß etwas geschehen."

Es geschah etwas: Wunsiedel wurde beerdigt, und ich wurde ausersehen, einen Kranz künstlicher Rosen hinter seinem Sarg herzutragen, denn ich bin nicht nur mit einem Hang zur Nachdenklichkeit und zum Nichtstun ausgestattet, sondern auch mit einer Gestalt und einem Gesicht, die sich vorzüglich für schwarze Anzüge eignen. Offenbar habe ich — mit dem Kranz künstlicher Rosen in der Hand hinter Wunsiedels Sarg hergehend — großartig ausgesehen. Ich erhielt das Angebot eines eleganten Beerdigungsinstitutes, dort als berufsmäßiger Trauernder einzutreten. „Sie sind der geborene Trauernde," sagte der Leiter des Instituts, „die Garderobe bekommen Sie gestellt. Ihr Gesicht — einfach großartig!"

Ich kündigte Broschek mit der Begründung, daß ich mich dort nicht richtig ausgelastet fühle, daß Teile meiner Fähigkeiten trotz der dreizehn Telefone brachlägen. Gleich nach meinem ersten berufsmäßigen Trauergang wußte ich: Hierhin gehörst du, das ist der Platz, der für dich bestimmt ist.

Nachdenklich stehe ich hinter dem Sarg in der Trauerkapelle, mit einem schlichten Blumenstrauß in der Hand, während Händels „Largo" gespielt wird, ein Musikstück, das viel zu wenig geachtet ist. Das Friedhofscafé ist mein Stammlokal, dort verbringe ich die Zeit zwischen meinen beruflichen Auftritten, doch manchmal gehe ich auch hinter Särgen her, zu denen ich nicht beordert bin, kaufe aus meiner Tasche einen Blumenstrauß und geselle mich zu dem

LINE

1 der Weihnachtsmann — *Santa Claus*
2 überzeugend — *convincing*
6 beerdigen — *bury*
wurde ausersehen — *was selected*
7 der Kranz — *wreath*
künstlich — *artificial*
7–8 ausgestattet sein — *be furnished with*, here: *have by nature*
8 der Hang — *inclination*
9 die Gestalt — *figure*
9–10 sich vorzüglich eignen für — *go* (or *fit*) *well with*
10 offenbar — *evidently*
11 großartig — *magnificent, splendid*
12 das Angebot — *offer*
das Beerdigungsinstitut — *funeral home*
12–13 berufsmäßig — *professional*
13 der Trauernde — *mourner*
14 die Garderobe bekommen Sie gestellt — *clothes will be furnished to you*
16 kündigen — *give notice* (*of resignation*)

LINE

16 die Begründung — *reason, explanation*
16–17 nicht richtig ausgelastet — *not wholly satisfied* (*with my job*)
17 die Fähigkeit — *ability*
18 brachliegen — *lie fallow, be wasted*
der Trauergang — *funeral procession*
19 bestimmt für — *meant for;* here: *intended for*
20 der Sarg — *coffin*
die Trauerkapelle — *funeral chapel*
21 schlicht — *simple*
der Blumenstrauß — *wreath*
22 achten — *respect*
das Friedhofscafé — *coffee shop near the cemetery*
23 das Stammlokal — *favorite café* or *restaurant*
der Auftritt — *appearance*
24 beordert — *assigned*
25 ich geselle mich zu — *I join*

Wohlfahrtsbeamten, der hinter dem Sarg eines Heimatlosen hergeht. Hin und wieder auch besuche ich Wunsiedels Grab, denn schließlich verdanke ich es ihm, daß ich meinen eigentlichen Beruf entdeckte, einen Beruf, bei dem Nachdenklichkeit geradezu erwünscht und Nichtstun meine Pflicht ist.

5 Später erst fiel mir ein, daß ich mich nie für den Artikel interessiert habe, der in Wunsiedels Fabrik hergestellt wurde. Es wird wohl Seife gewesen sein.

LINE

1 der Wohlfahrtsbeamte — *official of a welfare organization*
der Heimatlose — *homeless man, displaced person*
2 schließlich — *after all, in the final analysis*
verdanken — *owe*
3 der Beruf — *profession*

LINE

3–4 die Nachdenklichkeit — *meditativeness*
4 geradezu — *actually*
erwünscht — *welcome, desirable*
die Pflicht — *duty*
5 der Artikel — *product*
6 herstellen — *produce, manufacture*
die Seife — *soap*

APPENDIX II

GRAMMATICAL PATTERNS

VERB PATTERNS

sein, haben, werden

sein (ist), war, ist gewesen *to be*

PRESENT *I am, etc.*

ich bin		wir sind
du bist	Sie sind	ihr seid
sie		sie sind
es } ist		
er		

PAST *I was, etc.*

ich war		wir waren
du warst	Sie waren	ihr wart
sie		sie waren
es } war		
er		

PRESENT PERFECT *I have been, etc.*

ich bin gewesen		wir sind gewesen
du bist gewesen	Sie sind gewesen	ihr seid gewesen
sie		sie sind gewesen
es } ist gewesen		
er		

PAST PERFECT *I had been, etc.*

ich war gewesen		wir waren gewesen
du warst gewesen	Sie waren gewesen	ihr wart gewesen
sie		sie waren gewesen
es } war gewesen		
er		

FUTURE *I shall be, etc.*

ich werde sein		wir werden sein
du wirst sein	Sie werden sein	ihr werdet sein
sie		sie werden sein
es } wird sein		
er		

FUTURE PERFECT *I shall have been, etc.*

ich werde gewesen sein		wir werden gewesen sein
du wirst gewesen sein	Sie werden gewesen sein	ihr werdet gewesen sein
sie		sie werden gewesen sein
es } wird gewesen sein		
er		

IMPERATIVE *be*

sei! seid! seien Sie!

haben (hat), hatte, hat gehabt *to have*

PRESENT *I have, etc.*

ich habe		wir haben
du hast	Sie haben	ihr habt
sie, es, er hat		sie haben

PAST *I had, etc.*

ich hatte		wir hatten
du hattest	Sie hatten	ihr hattet
sie, es, er hatte		sie hatten

PRESENT PERFECT *I have had, etc.*

ich habe gehabt		wir haben gehabt
du hast gehabt	Sie haben gehabt	ihr habt gehabt
sie, es, er hat gehabt		sie haben gehabt

PAST PERFECT *I had had, etc.*

ich hatte gehabt		wir hatten gehabt
du hattest gehabt	Sie hatten gehabt	ihr hattet gehabt
sie, es, er hatte gehabt		sie hatten gehabt

FUTURE *I shall have, etc.*

ich werde haben		wir werden haben
du wirst haben	Sie werden haben	ihr werdet haben
sie, es, er wird haben		sie werden haben

FUTURE PERFECT *I shall have had, etc.*

ich werde gehabt haben		wir werden gehabt haben
du wirst gehabt haben	Sie werden gehabt haben	ihr werdet gehabt haben
sie, es, er wird gehabt haben		sie werden gehabt haben

IMPERATIVE *have*

habe! habt! haben Sie!

werden (wird), wurde, ist geworden *to become*

PRESENT *I become, etc.*

ich werde	Sie werden	wir werden
du wirst		ihr werdet
sie, es, er } wird		sie werden

PAST *I became, etc.*

ich wurde	Sie wurden	wir wurden
du wurdest		ihr wurdet
sie, es, er } wurde		sie wurden

PRESENT PERFECT *I have become, etc.*

ich bin geworden	Sie sind geworden	wir sind geworden
du bist geworden		ihr seid geworden
sie, es, er } ist geworden		sie sind geworden

PAST PERFECT *I had become, etc.*

ich war geworden	Sie waren geworden	wir waren geworden
du warst geworden		ihr wart geworden
sie, es, er } war geworden		sie waren geworden

FUTURE *I shall become, etc.*

ich werde werden	Sie werden werden	wir werden werden
du wirst werden		ihr werdet werden
sie, es, er } wird werden		sie werden werden

FUTURE PERFECT *I shall have become, etc.*

ich werde geworden sein	Sie werden geworden sein	wir werden geworden sein
du wirst geworden sein		ihr werdet geworden sein
sie, es, er } wird geworden sein		sie werden geworden sein

IMPERATIVE *become*

werde! werdet! werden Sie!

Weak Verb Pattern

sagen (sagt), sagte, hat gesagt *to say*

PRESENT *I say, etc.*

ich sage		wir sagen
du sagst	Sie sagen	ihr sagt
sie / es / er } sagt		sie sagen

PAST *I said, etc.*

ich sagte		wir sagten
du sagtest	Sie sagten	ihr sagtet
sie / es / er } sagte		sie sagten

PRESENT PERFECT *I have said, etc.*

ich habe gesagt		wir haben gesagt
du hast gesagt	Sie haben gesagt	ihr habt gesagt
sie / es / er } hat gesagt		sie haben gesagt

PAST PERFECT *I had said, etc.*

ich hatte gesagt		wir hatten gesagt
du hattest gesagt	Sie hatten gesagt	ihr hattet gesagt
sie / es / er } hatte gesagt		sie hatten gesagt

FUTURE *I shall say, etc.*

ich werde sagen		wir werden sagen
du wirst sagen	Sie werden sagen	ihr werdet sagen
sie / es / er } wird sagen		sie werden sagen

FUTURE PERFECT *I shall have said, etc.*

ich werde gesagt haben		wir werden gesagt haben
du wirst gesagt haben	Sie werden gesagt haben	ihr werdet gesagt haben
sie / es / er } wird gesagt haben		sie werden gesagt haben

IMPERATIVE *say*

sage! sagt! sagen Sie!

Strong Verb Pattern

sehen (sieht), sah, hat gesehen *to see*

PRESENT *I see, etc.*

ich sehe		wir sehen
du siehst	Sie sehen	ihr seht
sie / es / er } sieht		sie sehen

PAST *I saw, etc.*

ich sah		wir sahen
du sahst	Sie sahen	ihr saht
sie / es / er } sah		sie sahen

PRESENT PERFECT *I have seen, etc.*

ich habe gesehen		wir haben gesehen
du hast gesehen	Sie haben gesehen	ihr habt gesehen
sie / es / er } hat gesehen		sie haben gesehen

PAST PERFECT *I had seen, etc.*

ich hatte gesehen		wir hatten gesehen
du hattest gesehen	Sie hatten gesehen	ihr hattet gesehen
sie / es / er } hatte gesehen		sie hatten gesehen

FUTURE *I shall see, etc.*

ich werde sehen		wir werden sehen
du wirst sehen	Sie werden sehen	ihr werdet sehen
sie / es / er } wird sehen		sie werden sehen

FUTURE PERFECT *I shall have seen, etc.*

ich werde gesehen haben		wir werden gesehen haben
du wirst gesehen haben	Sie werden gesehen haben	ihr werdet gesehen haben
sie / es / er } wird gesehen haben		sie werden gesehen haben

IMPERATIVE *see*

sieh! seht! sehen Sie!

Weak-Strong Verbs

kennen (kennt), kannte, hat gekannt *to know*

PRESENT *I know, etc.*

ich kenne		wir kennen
du kennst	Sie kennen	ihr kennt
sie, es, er } kennt		sie kennen

PAST *I knew, etc.*

ich kannte		wir kannten
du kanntest	Sie kannten	ihr kanntet
sie, es, er } kannte		sie kannten

PRESENT PERFECT *I have known, etc.*

ich habe gekannt		wir haben gekannt
du hast gekannt	Sie haben gekannt	ihr habt gekannt
sie, es, er } hat gekannt		sie haben gekannt

PAST PERFECT *I had known, etc.*

ich hatte gekannt		wir hatten gekannt
du hattest gekannt	Sie hatten gekannt	ihr hattet gekannt
sie, es, er } hatte gekannt		sie hatten gekannt

FUTURE *I shall know, etc.*

ich werde kennen		wir werden kennen
du wirst kennen	Sie werden kennen	ihr werdet kennen
sie, es, er } wird kennen		sie werden kennen

FUTURE PERFECT *I shall have known, etc.*

ich werde gekannt haben		wir werden gekannt haben
du wirst gekannt haben	Sie werden gekannt haben	ihr werdet gekannt haben
sie, es, er } wird gekannt haben		sie werden gekannt haben

IMPERATIVE *know*

kenne! kennt! kennen Sie!

Modal Auxiliary Pattern

können (kann), konnte, hat gekonnt *to be able to, "can"*

PRESENT *I can, etc.*

ich kann		wir können
du kannst	Sie können	ihr könnt
sie es } kann er		sie können

PAST *I could, etc.*

ich konnte		wir konnten
du konntest	Sie konnten	ihr konntet
sie es } konnte er		sie konnten

PRESENT PERFECT *I have been able to, etc.*

ich habe gekonnt		wir haben gekonnt
du hast gekonnt	Sie haben gekonnt	ihr habt gekonnt
sie es } hat gekonnt er		sie haben gekonnt

PAST PERFECT *I had been able to, etc.*

ich hatte gekonnt		wir hatten gekonnt
du hattest gekonnt	Sie hatten gekonnt	ihr hattet gekonnt
sie es } hatte gekonnt er		sie hatten gekonnt

FUTURE *I shall be able to, etc.*

ich werde können		wir werden können
du wirst können	Sie werden können	ihr werdet können
sie es } wird können er		sie werden können

FUTURE PERFECT *I shall have been able to, etc.*

ich werde gekonnt haben		wir werden gekonnt haben
du wirst gekonnt haben	Sie werden gekonnt haben	ihr werdet gekonnt haben
sie es } wird gekonnt haben er		sie werden gekonnt haben

Subjunctive Pattern of **sein** *to be*

PRESENT *

ich sei		wir seien
du sei(e)st	Sie seien	ihr seiet
sie, es, er } sei		sie seien

PAST

ich wäre		wir wären
du wärest	Sie wären	ihr wäret
sie, es, er } wäre		sie wären

PRESENT PERFECT

ich sei gewesen		wir seien gewesen
du sei(e)st gewesen	Sie seien gewesen	ihr seiet gewesen
sie, es, er } sei gewesen		sie seien gewesen

PAST PERFECT

ich wäre gewesen		wir wären gewesen
du wärest gewesen	Sie wären gewesen	ihr wäret gewesen
sie, es, er } wäre gewesen		sie wären gewesen

FUTURE

ich werde sein		wir werden sein
du werdest sein	Sie werden sein	ihr werdet sein
sie, es, er } werde sein		sie werden sein

FUTURE PERFECT

ich werde gewesen sein		wir werden gewesen sein
du werdest gewesen sein	Sie werden gewesen sein	ihr werdet gewesen sein
sie, es, er } werde gewesen sein		sie werden gewesen sein

***Sein** is the only verb that deviates from the normal subjunctive ending pattern for all verbs (**–e, –est, –e; –en, –et, –en**). The deviation from this pattern, however, occurs only in the present subjunctive of **sein: —, –(e)st, —; –en, –et, –en.**

CONDITIONAL TENSES

PRESENT

ich würde sein	Sie würden sein	wir würden sein
du würdest sein		ihr würdet sein
sie / es / er } würde sein		sie würden sein

PAST

ich würde gewesen sein	Sie würden gewesen sein	wir würden gewesen sein
du würdest gewesen sein		ihr würdet gewesen sein
sie / es / er } würde gewesen sein		sie würden gewesen sein

Illustrations

Ich wäre glücklich, wenn ich so viel hätte. Ich würde glücklich sein, wenn ich so viel hätte.	*I'd be happy if I had that much.*
Ich wäre glücklich gewesen, wenn ich so viel gehabt hätte. Ich würde glücklich gewesen sein, wenn ich so viel gehabt hätte.	*I would have been happy if I had had that much.*

Subjunctive Pattern of **haben** *to have*

PRESENT

ich habe	Sie haben	wir haben
du habest		ihr habet
sie / es / er } habe		sie haben

PAST

ich hätte	Sie hätten	wir hätten
du hättest		ihr hättet
sie / es / er } hätte		sie hätten

PRESENT PERFECT

ich habe gehabt	Sie haben gehabt	wir haben gehabt
du habest gehabt		ihr habet gehabt
sie / es / er } habe gehabt		sie haben gehabt

PAST PERFECT

ich hätte gehabt		wir hätten gehabt
du hättest gehabt	Sie hätten gehabt	ihr hättet gehabt
sie } es } hätte gehabt er }		sie hätten gehabt

FUTURE

ich werde haben		wir werden haben
du werdest haben	Sie werden haben	ihr werdet haben
sie } es } werde haben er }		sie werden haben

FUTURE PERFECT

ich werde gehabt haben		wir werden gehabt haben
du werdest gehabt haben	Sie werden gehabt haben	ihr werdet gehabt haben
sie } es } werde gehabt haben er }		sie werden gehabt haben

CONDITIONAL TENSES

PRESENT

ich würde haben		wir würden haben
du würdest haben	Sie würden haben	ihr würdet haben
sie } es } würde haben er }		sie würden haben

PAST

ich würde gehabt haben		wir würden gehabt haben
du würdest gehabt haben	Sie würden gehabt haben	ihr würdet gehabt haben
sie } es } würde gehabt haben er }		sie würden gehabt haben

Subjunctive Pattern of **werden** *to become*

PRESENT

ich werde		wir werden
du werdest	Sie werden	ihr werdet
sie } es } werde er }		sie werden

PAST

ich würde	Sie würden	wir würden
du würdest		ihr würdet
sie / es / er } würde		sie würden

PRESENT PERFECT

ich sei geworden	Sie seien geworden	wir seien geworden
du sei(e)st geworden		ihr seiet geworden
sie / es / er } sei geworden		sie seien geworden

PAST PERFECT

ich wäre geworden	Sie wären geworden	wir wären geworden
du wärest geworden		ihr wäret geworden
sie / es / er } wäre geworden		sie wären geworden

FUTURE

ich werde werden	Sie werden werden	wir werden werden
du werdest werden		ihr werdet werden
sie / es / er } werde werden		sie werden werden

FUTURE PERFECT

ich werde geworden sein	Sie werden geworden sein	wir werden geworden sein
du werdest geworden sein		ihr werdet geworden sein
sie / es / er } werde geworden sein		sie werden geworden sein

CONDITIONAL TENSES

PRESENT

ich würde werden	Sie würden werden	wir würden werden
du würdest werden		ihr würdet werden
sie / es / er } würde werden		sie würden werden

PAST

ich würde geworden sein	Sie würden geworden sein	wir würden geworden sein
du würdest geworden sein		ihr würdet geworden sein
sie / es / er } würde geworden sein		sie würden geworden sein

Subjunctive Pattern of Weak Verbs

sagen *to say*

PRESENT

ich sage		wir sagen
du sagest	Sie sagen	ihr saget
sie / es / er } sage		sie sagen

PAST *

ich sagte		wir sagten
du sagtest	Sie sagten	ihr sagtet
sie / es / er } sagte		sie sagten

PRESENT PERFECT

ich habe gesagt		wir haben gesagt
du habest gesagt	Sie haben gesagt	ihr habet gesagt
sie / es / er } habe gesagt		sie haben gesagt

PAST PERFECT

ich hätte gesagt		wir hätten gesagt
du hättest gesagt	Sie hätten gesagt	ihr hättet gesagt
sie / es / er } hätte gesagt		sie hätten gesagt

FUTURE

ich werde sagen		wir werden sagen
du werdest sagen	Sie werden sagen	ihr werdet sagen
sie / es / er } werde sagen		sie werden sagen

FUTURE PERFECT

ich werde gesagt haben		wir werden gesagt haben
du werdest gesagt haben	Sie werden gesagt haben	ihr werdet gesagt haben
sie / es / er } werde gesagt haben		sie werden gesagt haben

* In form there is no difference between the past subjunctive and the past indicative of a weak verb.

CONDITIONAL TENSES

PRESENT

ich würde sagen		wir würden sagen
du würdest sagen	Sie würden sagen	ihr würdet sagen
sie, es, er } würde sagen		sie würden sagen

PAST

ich würde gesagt haben		wir würden gesagt haben
du würdest gesagt haben	Sie würden gesagt haben	ihr würdet gesagt haben
sie, es, er } würde gesagt haben		sie würden gesagt haben

Subjunctive Pattern of Strong Verbs

sehen *to see*

PRESENT

ich sehe		wir sehen
du sehest	Sie sehen	ihr sehet
sie, es, er } sehe		sie sehen

PAST *

ich sähe		wir sähen
du sähest	Sie sähen	ihr sähet
sie, es, er } sähe		sie sähen

PRESENT PERFECT

ich habe gesehen		wir haben gesehen
du habest gesehen	Sie haben gesehen	ihr habet gesehen
sie, es, er } habe gesehen		sie haben gesehen

* The past subjunctive of strong verbs has umlaut if the past indicative stem vowel is **a, o,** or **u: sah — sähe, schloß — schlösse, wusch — wüsche.** The past subjunctive pattern, therefore, of a verb like **gehen (geht; ging, ist gegangen)** is of course without umlaut:

ich ginge		wir gingen
du gingest	Sie gingen	ihr ginget
sie, es, er ginge		sie gingen

The following three verbs show a radical vowel change in the past subjunctive: **helfen (hilft; half, hat geholfen); sterben (stirbt; starb, ist gestorben); stehen (steht; stand, hat gestanden).** In each case the past subjunctive shows **ü** instead of the expected **ä: hülfe, stürbe, stünde.** (**Stände** is also acceptable, but *not* **stärbe.**)

PAST PERFECT

ich hätte gesehen		wir hätten gesehen
du hättest gesehen	Sie hätten gesehen	ihr hättet gesehen
sie / es / er hätte gesehen		sie hätten gesehen

FUTURE

ich werde sehen		wir werden sehen
du werdest sehen	Sie werden sehen	ihr werdet sehen
sie / es / er werde sehen		sie werden sehen

FUTURE PERFECT

ich werde gesehen haben		wir werden gesehen haben
du werdest gesehen haben	Sie werden gesehen haben	ihr werdet gesehen haben
sie / es / er werde gesehen haben		sie werden gesehen haben

CONDITIONAL TENSES

PRESENT

ich würde sehen		wir würden sehen
du würdest sehen	Sie würden sehen	ihr würdet sehen
sie / es / er würde sehen		sie würden sehen

PAST

ich würde gesehen haben		wir würden gesehen haben
du würdest gesehen haben	Sie würden gesehen haben	ihr würdet gesehen haben
sie / es / er würde gesehen haben		sie würden gesehen haben

Subjunctive of Weak-Strong Verbs

kennen *to know*

PRESENT

ich kenne		wir kennen
du kennest	Sie kennen	ihr kennet
sie / es / er kenne		sie kennen

PAST *

ich kennte		wir kennten
du kenntest	Sie kennten	ihr kenntet
sie / es / er } kennte		sie kennten

PRESENT PERFECT

ich habe gekannt		wir haben gekannt
du habest gekannt	Sie haben gekannt	ihr habet gekannt
sie / es / er } habe gekannt		sie haben gekannt

PAST PERFECT

ich hätte gekannt		wir hätten gekannt
du hättest gekannt	Sie hätten gekannt	ihr hättet gekannt
sie / es / er } hätte gekannt		sie hätten gekannt

FUTURE

ich werde kennen		wir werden kennen
du werdest kennen	Sie werden kennen	ihr werdet kennen
sie / es / er } werde kennen		sie werden kennen

FUTURE PERFECT

ich werde gekannt haben		wir werden gekannt haben
du werdest gekannt haben	Sie werden gekannt haben	ihr werdet gekannt haben
sie / es / er } werde gekannt haben		sie werden gekannt haben

CONDITIONAL TENSES

PRESENT

ich würde kennen		wir würden kennen
du würdest kennen	Sie würden kennen	ihr würdet kennen
sie / es / er } würde kennen		sie würden kennen

* Of the weak-strong verbs, **brennen, kennen, nennen, rennen, senden, wenden** have an **e**-stem in the past subjunctive; whereas **bringen** and **denken** show **ä: brächte, dächte.** Also, **senden** and **wenden** add **–et** plus the normal endings to form their past subjunctive:

ich sendete		wir sendeten	ich wendete		wir wendeten
du sendetest	Sie sendeten	ihr sendetet	du wendetest	Sie wendeten	ihr wendetet
sie / es / er } sendete		sie sendeten	sie / es / er } wendete		sie wendeten

PAST

ich würde gekannt haben		wir würden gekannt haben
du würdest gekannt haben	Sie würden gekannt haben	ihr würdet gekannt haben
sie, es, er } würde gekannt haben		sie würden gekannt haben

Subjunctive Pattern of Modals

können *to be able to, "can"*

PRESENT

ich könne		wir können
du könnest	Sie können	ihr könnet
sie, es, er } könne		sie können

PAST *

ich könnte		wir könnten
du könntest	Sie könnten	ihr könntet
sie, es, er } könnte		sie könnten

PRESENT PERFECT

ich habe gekonnt		wir haben gekonnt
du habest gekonnt	Sie haben gekonnt	ihr habet gekonnt
sie, es, er } habe gekonnt		sie haben gekonnt

PAST PERFECT

ich hätte gekonnt		wir hätten gekonnt
du hättest gekonnt	Sie hätten gekonnt	ihr hättet gekonnt
sie, es, er } hätte gekonnt		sie hätten gekonnt

FUTURE

ich werde können		wir werden können
du werdest können	Sie werden können	ihr werdet können
sie, es, er } werde können		sie werden können

* **dürfen, können, mögen,** and **müssen** carry their umlaut into the past subjunctive: **dürfte, könnte, möchte, müßte; sollen** and **wollen** do *not* take umlaut: **sollte, wollte. Wissen,** which is of course *not* a modal but similar to a modal in pattern, also shows umlaut in the past subjunctive: **wüßte.**

FUTURE PERFECT

ich werde gekonnt haben		wir werden gekonnt haben
du werdest gekonnt haben	Sie werden gekonnt haben	ihr werdet gekonnt haben
sie / es / er } werde gekonnt haben		sie werden gekonnt haben

CONDITIONAL TENSES

PRESENT

ich würde können		wir würden können
du würdest können	Sie würden können	ihr würdet können
sie / es / er } würde können		sie würden können

PAST

ich würde gekonnt haben		wir würden gekonnt haben
du würdest gekonnt haben	Sie würden gekonnt haben	ihr würdet gekonnt haben
sie / es / er } würde gekonnt haben		sie würden gekonnt haben

Infinitives

Each transitive verb in English and in German has four infinitives,* two active voice infinitives: present and perfect, and two passive voice infinitives: present and perfect; for example:

	PRESENT INFINITIVE	PERFECT INFINITIVE
	(to) sing	(to) have sung
Active Voice:	**singen**	**gesungen haben**
	(to) be sung	(to) have been sung
Passive Voice:	**gesungen werden**	**gesungen worden sein**

Note the difference in auxiliary between English and German in the *passive voice:* English uses the forms *be* and *have been;* German uses **werden** and **worden sein.**

Note also the difference in word order between English and German, as indicated by the arrows in the perfect infinitive, active voice, and the present and perfect infinitives, passive voice.

Illustrations

Ich muß das Lied **singen.**	*I must* ***sing*** *the song.*
Er muß das Lied **gesungen haben.**	*He must* ***have sung*** *the song.*
Das Lied muß **gesungen werden.**	*The song must* ***be sung.***
Das Lied muß **gesungen worden sein.**	*The song must* ***have been sung.***

* Each intransitive verb has only two infinitives: to be (**sein**), to have been (**gewesen sein**).

Passive Indicative Pattern

PRESENT *I am (being) asked, etc.*

ich werde gefragt		wir werden gefragt
du wirst gefragt	Sie werden gefragt	ihr werdet gefragt
sie, es, er wird gefragt		sie werden gefragt

PAST *I was (being) asked, etc.*

ich wurde gefragt		wir wurden gefragt
du wurdest gefragt	Sie wurden gefragt	ihr wurdet gefragt
sie, es, er wurde gefragt		sie wurden gefragt

PRESENT PERFECT *I have been asked, etc.*

ich bin gefragt worden		wir sind gefragt worden
du bist gefragt worden	Sie sind gefragt worden	ihr seid gefragt worden
sie, es, er ist gefragt worden		sie sind gefragt worden

PAST PERFECT *I had been asked, etc.*

ich war gefragt worden		wir waren gefragt worden
du warst gefragt worden	Sie waren gefragt worden	ihr wart gefragt worden
sie, es, er war gefragt worden		sie waren gefragt worden

FUTURE *I shall be asked, etc.*

ich werde gefragt werden		wir werden gefragt werden
du wirst gefragt werden	Sie werden gefragt werden	ihr werdet gefragt werden
sie, es, er wird gefragt werden		sie werden gefragt werden

FUTURE PERFECT *I shall have been asked, etc.*

ich werde gefragt worden sein		wir werden gefragt worden sein
du wirst gefragt worden sein	Sie werden gefragt worden sein	ihr werdet gefragt worden sein
sie, es, er wird gefragt worden sein		sie werden gefragt worden sein

Passive Subjunctive Pattern

PRESENT

ich werde gefragt		wir werden gefragt
du werdest gefragt	Sie werden gefragt	ihr werdet gefragt
sie, es, er werde gefragt		sie werden gefragt

PAST

ich würde gefragt		wir würden gefragt
du würdest gefragt	Sie würden gefragt	ihr würdet gefragt
sie / es / er } würde gefragt		sie würden gefragt

PRESENT PERFECT

ich sei gefragt worden		wir seien gefragt worden
du sei(e)st gefragt worden	Sie seien gefragt worden	ihr seiet gefragt worden
sie / es / er } sei gefragt worden		sie seien gefragt worden

PAST PERFECT

ich wäre gefragt worden		wir wären gefragt worden
du wärest gefragt worden	Sie wären gefragt worden	ihr wäret gefragt worden
sie / es / er } wäre gefragt worden		sie wären gefragt worden

FUTURE

ich werde gefragt werden		wir werden gefragt werden
du werdest gefragt werden	Sie werden gefragt werden	ihr werdet gefragt werden
sie / es / er } werde gefragt werden		sie werden gefragt werden

FUTURE PERFECT

ich werde gefragt worden sein		wir werden gefragt worden sein
du werdest gefragt worden sein	Sie werden gefragt worden sein	ihr werdet gefragt worden sein
sie / es / er } werde gefragt worden sein		sie werden gefragt worden sein

CONDITIONAL TENSES

PRESENT

ich würde gefragt werden		wir würden gefragt werden
du würdest gefragt werden	Sie würden gefragt werden	ihr würdet gefragt werden
sie / es / er } würde gefragt werden		sie würden gefragt werden

PAST

ich würde gefragt worden sein		wir würden gefragt worden sein
du würdest gefragt worden sein	Sie würden gefragt worden sein	ihr würdet gefragt worden sein
sie / es / er } würde gefragt worden sein		sie würden gefragt worden sein

PRINCIPAL PARTS OF VERBS

The following is a classified list of strong verbs, weak-strong verbs, modals, and irregular verbs drawn from the material in this book. (Included are a good number of inseparable compound verbs and a few frequently used separable compound verbs.)

Strong Verbs

CLASS 1

INFINITIVE	3RD SING. PRES.	1ST & 3RD SING. PAST	PAST PART.	
ei		**i**	**i**	
begreifen	begreift	begriff	begriffen	*understand*
beißen	beißt	biß	gebissen	*bite*
ergreifen	ergreift	ergriff	ergriffen	*grasp, grip*
gleichen (*dat.*)	gleicht	glich	geglichen	*equal, resemble*
gleiten	gleitet	glitt	ist geglitten	*glide*
greifen	greift	griff	gegriffen	*seize, grasp*
kneifen	kneift	kniff	gekniffen	*pinch, nip*
leiden	leidet	litt	gelitten	*suffer*
pfeifen	pfeift	pfiff	gepfiffen	*pipe, whistle*
reißen	reißt	riß	gerissen	*tear*
reiten	reitet	ritt	*(ist) geritten	*ride* (horseback)
schleichen	schleicht	schlich	ist geschlichen	*sneak, creep*
schneiden	schneidet	schnitt	geschnitten	*cut*
schreiten	schreitet	schritt	ist geschritten	*walk, stride*
streiten	streitet	stritt	gestritten	*quarrel*
vergleichen	vergleicht	verglich	verglichen	*compare*
zerreißen	zerreißt	zerriß	zerrissen	*tear to pieces, tear apart*
ei		**ie**	**ie**	
besteigen	besteigt	bestieg	bestiegen	*climb*
betreiben	betreibt	betrieb	betrieben	*manage, carry on*
bleiben	bleibt	blieb	ist geblieben	*remain, stay*
entscheiden	entscheidet	entschied	entschieden	*decide*
scheiden	scheidet	schied	ist geschieden	*depart*
scheinen	scheint	schien	geschienen	*shine; appear*
schreiben	schreibt	schrieb	geschrieben	*write*
schweigen	schweigt	schwieg	geschwiegen	*be silent*
steigen	steigt	stieg	ist gestiegen	*climb*
treiben	treibt	trieb	getrieben	*put in motion, drive*
unterscheiden	unterscheidet	unterschied	unterschieden	*distinguish*
verschweigen (*dat. of person*)	verschweigt	verschwieg	verschwiegen	*keep secret*
verzeihen (*dat. of person*)	verzeiht	verzieh	verziehen	*forgive*
weisen	weist	wies	gewiesen	*show, direct*

* **(ist)** = **ist** or **hat**

CLASS 2

INFINITIVE	3RD SING. PRES.	1ST & 3RD SING. PAST	PAST PART.	
ie, e (i, ä, ö, ü)		**o**	**o**	
beschließen	beschließt	beschloß	beschlossen	*decide*
betrügen	betrügt	betrog	betrogen	*deceive, cheat*
beziehen	bezieht	bezog	bezogen	*refer; cover*
biegen	biegt	bog	gebogen	*bend*
bieten	bietet	bot	geboten	*offer*
entfliehen (*dat.*)	entflieht	entfloh	ist entflohen	*escape, flee from*
erheben	erhebt	erhob	erhoben	*raise*
erlöschen	erlischt	erlosch	ist erloschen	*go out, die out*
erwägen	erwägt	erwog	erwogen	*consider*
erziehen	erzieht	erzog	erzogen	*bring up, educate, train*
fliegen	fliegt	flog	ist geflogen	*fly*
fliehen	flieht	floh	ist geflohen	*escape, flee from*
fließen	fließt	floß	ist geflossen	*flow*
frieren	friert	fror	(ist) gefroren	*freeze*
genießen	genießt	genoß	genossen	*enjoy*
gießen	gießt	goß	gegossen	*pour*
glimmen	glimmt	glomm	geglommen	*glimmer, glow*
heben	hebt	hob	gehoben	*lift*
kriechen	kriecht	kroch	ist gekrochen	*creep, crawl*
lügen	lügt	log	gelogen	*lie (= tell a lie)*
riechen	riecht	roch	gerochen	*smell*
schießen	schießt	schoß	geschossen	*shoot*
schließen	schließt	schloß	geschlossen	*shut*
schmelzen	schmilzt	schmolz	(ist) geschmolzen	*melt, dissolve*
verbieten	verbietet	verbot	verboten	*prohibit, forbid*
verlieren	verliert	verlor	verloren	*lose*
vollziehen	vollzieht	vollzog	vollzogen	*execute, carry out*
ziehen	zieht	zog	(ist) gezogen	*draw, pull, go, move*

CLASS 3

i		**a**	**u, o** [1]	
befinden (*refl.*)	befindet	befand	befunden	*be, feel*
beginnen	beginnt	begann	begonnen	*begin*
dringen	dringt	drang	ist gedrungen	*press forward, penetrate*
empfinden	empfindet	empfand	empfunden	*feel, perceive*
entrinnen (*dat.*)	entrinnt	entrann	ist entronnen	*escape*
erfinden	erfindet	erfand	erfunden	*invent*
erklingen	erklingt	erklang	ist erklungen	*ring out*
finden	findet	fand	gefunden	*find*
gelingen (*dat.*)	gelingt	gelang	ist gelungen	*succeed*
gewinnen	gewinnt	gewann	gewonnen	*win*
klingen	klingt	klang	geklungen	*sound*
mißlingen (*dat.*)	mißlingt	mißlang	ist mißlungen	*be unsuccessful, fail*

[1] **mm** and **nn** stems have **o** instead of **u** in the past participle.

INFINITIVE	3RD SING. PRES.	1ST & 3RD SING. PAST		PAST PART.	
schwimmen	schwimmt	schwamm	(ist)	geschwommen	*swim*
schwingen	schwingt	schwang		geschwungen	*swing*
singen	singt	sang		gesungen	*sing*
sinken	sinkt	sank	ist	gesunken	*sink*
sinnen	sinnt	sann		gesonnen	*reflect, ponder*
springen	springt	sprang	ist	gesprungen	*jump*
trinken	trinkt	trank		getrunken	*drink*
verbinden	verbindet	verband		verbunden	*bind (up), unite, connect*
verschlingen	verschlingt	verschlang		verschlungen	*devour, swallow*
verschwinden	verschwindet	verschwand	ist	verschwunden	*disappear*
versinken	versinkt	versank	ist	versunken	*sink*
zwingen	zwingt	zwang		gezwungen	*force*

CLASS 4

e [1]	**(i, ie)**	**a**		**o**	
befehlen	befiehlt	befahl		befohlen	*command*
besprechen	bespricht	besprach		besprochen	*discuss*
betreffen	betrifft	betraf		betroffen	*affect, concern*
brechen	bricht	brach		gebrochen	*break*
empfehlen	empfiehlt	empfahl		empfohlen	*recommend*
entsprechen (*dat.*)	entspricht	entsprach		entsprochen	*correspond*
erschrecken	erschrickt	erschrak	ist	erschrocken	*be frightened*
gebären	gebiert	gebar		geboren	*give birth to*
gelten	gilt	galt		gegolten	*be true of, be valid*
helfen (*dat.*)	hilft	half		geholfen	*help*
nehmen	nimmt	nahm		genommen	*take*
schelten	schilt	schalt		gescholten	*scold, rebuke*
sprechen	spricht	sprach		gesprochen	*speak*
stehlen	stiehlt	stahl		gestohlen	*steal*
sterben	stirbt	starb	ist	gestorben	*die*
treffen	trifft	traf		getroffen	*meet*
unternehmen	unternimmt	unternahm		unternommen	*undertake*
verbergen	verbirgt	verbarg		verborgen	*hide*
verderben	verdirbt	verdarb	(ist)	verdorben	*spoil*
versprechen	verspricht	versprach		versprochen	*promise*
werfen	wirft	warf		geworfen	*throw*

e [2]	**(i, ie)**	**a**		**e**	
begeben (*refl.*)	begibt	begab		begeben	*happen, go*
besitzen	besitzt	besaß		besessen	*own, possess*
betreten	betritt	betrat		betreten	*enter*
bitten	bittet	bat		gebeten	*ask*
ergeben (*refl.*)	ergibt	ergab		ergeben	*submit, surrender*
essen	ißt	aß		gegessen	*eat*

[1] **gebären** is the only **ä**-stem verb in this series.

[2] **bitten, liegen, sitzen,** and their compounds are the only examples with **i** and **ie** stems.

INFINITIVE	3RD SING. PRES.	1ST & 3RD SING. PAST	PAST PART.	
fressen	frißt	fraß	gefressen	*eat* (ref. to animals)
geben	gibt	gab	gegeben	*give*
geschehen	geschieht	geschah	ist geschehen	*happen*
lesen	liest	las	gelesen	*read*
liegen	liegt	lag	gelegen	*lie, recline*
messen	mißt	maß	gemessen	*measure*
sehen	sieht	sah	gesehen	*see*
sitzen	sitzt	saß	gesessen	*sit*
treten	tritt	trat	ist getreten	*step*
vergessen	vergißt	vergaß	vergessen	*forget*
zertreten	zertritt	zertrat	zertreten	*trample*

CLASS 5

a	**(ä)**	**ie**	**a**	
behalten	behält	behielt	behalten	*keep*
braten	brät	briet	gebraten	*fry, roast, broil*
enthalten	enthält	enthielt	enthalten	*contain*
entlassen	entläßt	entließ	entlassen	*dismiss*
erhalten	erhält	erhielt	erhalten	*receive*
fallen	fällt	fiel	ist gefallen	*fall*
gefallen (*dat.*)	gefällt	gefiel	gefallen	*please*
geraten	gerät	geriet	ist geraten	*get into, fall into*
halten	hält	hielt	gehalten	*hold*
lassen	läßt	ließ	gelassen	*let*
raten	rät	riet	geraten	*guess; suggest, advise*
schlafen	schläft	schlief	geschlafen	*sleep*
verlassen	verläßt	verließ	verlassen	*leave, abandon*
verraten	verrät	verriet	verraten	*betray*
zerfallen	zerfällt	zerfiel	ist zerfallen	*be divided, fall to pieces*

a	**(ä)** [1]	**u**	**a**	
backen	bäckt	buk	gebacken	*bake*
einladen	lädt ein	lud ein	eingeladen	*invite*
erfahren	erfährt	erfuhr	erfahren	*experience*
erschaffen	erschafft	erschuf	erschaffen	*create*
fahren	fährt	fuhr	ist gefahren	*ride, travel, go*
graben	gräbt	grub	gegraben	*dig*
schaffen	schafft	schuf	geschaffen	*create*
schlagen	schlägt	schlug	geschlagen	*strike, hit*
tragen	trägt	trug	getragen	*carry, wear*
wachsen	wächst	wuchs	ist gewachsen	*grow*
waschen	wäscht	wusch	gewaschen	*wash*

a [2]	**(ä)**	**i**	**a**	
anfangen	fängt an	fing an	angefangen	*begin*
empfangen	empfängt	empfing	empfangen	*receive*
fangen	fängt	fing	gefangen	*catch*
hängen	hängt	hing	gehangen	*hang*

[1] All but **schaffen** and its compounds take umlaut in the **du, sie, es, er** forms of the present tense.
[2] **hängen** is the only **ä**-stem verb.

The following verbs belong to Class 5 although neither their present stem vowel nor their past participle stem vowel is **a.**

INFINITIVE	3RD SING. PRES.	1ST & 3RD SING. PAST	PAST PART.	
heißen	heißt	hieß	geheißen	*be called*
laufen	läuft	lief	ist gelaufen	*run*
rufen	ruft	rief	gerufen	*call*
stoßen	stößt	stieß	gestoßen	*push, kick*

Weak-Strong Verbs

brennen	brennt	brannte	gebrannt	*burn*
bringen	bringt	brachte	gebracht	*bring*
denken	denkt	dachte	gedacht	*think*
kennen	kennt	kannte	gekannt	*know*
nennen	nennt	nannte	genannt	*call, name*
rennen	rennt	rannte	ist gerannt	*run*
senden	sendet	sandte (*or* sendete)	gesandt (*or* gesendet)	*send*
wenden (*often refl.*)	wendet	wandte (*or* wendete)	gewandt (*or* gewendet)	*turn*

INSEPARABLE COMPOUNDS BASED ON WEAK-STRONG VERB STEMS

bekennen	bekennt	bekannte	bekannt	*admit, confess*
erkennen	erkennt	erkannte	erkannt	*recognize, realize*
verbringen	verbringt	verbrachte	verbracht	*spend (time)*

Modals

dürfen	darf	durfte	gedurft	*may, be permitted to*
können	kann	konnte	gekonnt	*can, be able to*
mögen	mag	mochte	gemocht	*may, like (to)*
müssen	muß	mußte	gemußt	*must, have to*
sollen	soll	sollte	gesollt	*shall, should, be supposed to*
wollen	will	wollte	gewollt	*want (to), will*
wissen [1]	weiß	wußte	gewußt	*know*

INSEPARABLE COMPOUNDS BASED ON MODALS

bedürfen	bedarf	bedurfte	bedurft	*need*
vermögen	vermag	vermochte	vermocht	*be able to*

Irregulars

gehen	geht	ging	ist gegangen	*go, walk*
haben	hat	hatte	gehabt	*have*
kommen	kommt	kam	ist gekommen	*come*
sein	ist	war	ist gewesen	*be*
stehen	steht	stand	gestanden	*stand*
tun	tut	tat	getan	*do*
werden	wird	wurde	ist geworden	*become*

[1] In form **wissen** follows closely the modal auxiliary pattern.

SEPARABLE AND INSEPARABLE COMPOUNDS BASED ON **gehen**

INFINITIVE	3RD SING. PRES.	1ST & 3RD SING. PAST	PAST PART.	
begehen	begeht	beging	begangen	*commit* (a crime)
entgehen (*dat.*)	entgeht	entging	ist entgangen	*escape*
fortgehen	geht fort	ging fort	ist fortgegangen	*go away*
vergehen	vergeht	verging	ist vergangen	*pass* (*e.g.*, of time)

SEPARABLE AND INSEPARABLE COMPOUNDS BASED ON **kommen**

ankommen	kommt an	kam an	ist angekommen	*arrive*
bekommen	bekommt	bekam	bekommen	*get, receive*
entkommen (*dat.*)	entkommt	entkam	ist entkommen	*escape*

SEPARABLE AND INSEPARABLE COMPOUNDS BASED ON **stehen**

aufstehen	steht auf	stand auf	ist aufgestanden	*get up*
bestehen	besteht	bestand	bestanden	*insist, consist, pass* (ref. to test)
entstehen	entsteht	entstand	ist entstanden	*arise*
gestehen	gesteht	gestand	gestanden	*confess*
mißverstehen	mißversteht	mißverstand	mißverstanden	*misunderstand*
verstehen	versteht	verstand	verstanden	*understand*

DECLENSION OF NOUNS

In this book nouns are divided into five classes. Each class can be identified most readily by the ending (or lack of ending) in the nominative plural.

	PLURAL ENDING	SINGULAR	PLURAL	
Class 1	—	der Morgen	die Morgen	*morning*(*s*)
Class 2	–**e**	der Tag	die Tage	*day*(*s*)
Class 3	–**er**	das Feld	die Felder	*field*(*s*)
Class 4	–**n** or –**en**	der Student	die Studenten	*student*(*s*)
Class 5	–**s**	das Auto	die Autos	*car*(*s*)

Practical information (for all classes):

1. Barring the exceptions referred to in Class 4, neuter and masculine nouns take –**s** or –**es** endings in the genitive singular.
2. All nouns except those of Class 5 take –**n** or –**en** endings in the dative plural.
3. No feminine noun of any class will show any endings in the singular.

CLASS 1: Adds no ending to form plurals.

Practical information:

1. Only two feminines belong to this class:
   die Mutter, die Tochter
2. The rest are neuters or masculines.

3. This class adds umlaut in the plural, but unsystematically:

   der Vater, die Väter; der Onkel, die Onkel

4. A great number end in **–el, –en, –er, –chen,** or **–lein:**

   der Apfel (*apple*), das Mädchen (*girl*), der Garten (*garden*), das Fräulein (*miss, young lady*), der Denker (*thinker*), das Kindlein (*little child*)

5. This class has many neuter nouns with prefix **Ge–** and ending **–e:**

   das Gebäude (*building*), das Gebirge (*mountain chain*), das Gemüse (*vegetables*), das Gewerbe (*trade, calling*)

Declensional Patterns:

	SINGULAR			
Nom.	das Fräulein	der Vater	der Onkel	die Tochter
Acc.	das Fräulein	den Vater	den Onkel	die Tochter
Dat.	dem Fräulein	dem Vater	dem Onkel	der Tochter
Gen.	des Fräuleins	des Vaters	des Onkels	der Tochter
	PLURAL			
Nom.	die Fräulein	die Väter	die Onkel	die Töchter
Acc.	die Fräulein	die Väter	die Onkel	die Töchter
Dat.	den Fräulein	den Vätern	den Onkeln	den Töchtern
Gen.	der Fräulein	der Väter	der Onkel	der Töchter

CLASS 2: Adds **–e** to form plurals.

Practical information:

1. All three genders are represented in this class.
2. This class adds umlaut in the plural, but unsystematically.
3. There is an optional **e** in the dative and genitive singular of monosyllabic neuters and masculines.

Declensional Patterns:

	SINGULAR			
Nom.	die Nacht	das Stück	der Tag	der Sohn
Acc.	die Nacht	das Stück	den Tag	den Sohn
Dat.	der Nacht	dem Stück(e)	dem Tag(e)	dem Sohn(e)
Gen.	der Nacht	des Stück(e)s	des Tag(e)s	des Sohn(e)s
	PLURAL			
Nom.	die Nächte	die Stücke	die Tage	die Söhne
Acc.	die Nächte	die Stücke	die Tage	die Söhne
Dat.	den Nächten	den Stücken	den Tagen	den Söhnen
Gen.	der Nächte	der Stücke	der Tage	der Söhne

CLASS 3: Adds **–er** to form plurals.

Practical information:

1. This class has mostly neuters, a few masculines, *no feminines*.

2. In this class, whenever possible, umlaut is added in the plural.
3. There is an optional **–e** in the dative singular of monosyllabics.

Declensional Patterns:

	SINGULAR			
Nom.	das Buch	das Kind	der Reichtum	der Mann
Acc.	das Buch	das Kind	den Reichtum	den Mann
Dat.	dem Buch(e)	dem Kind(e)	dem Reichtum	dem Mann(e)
Gen.	des Buches	des Kindes	des Reichtums	des Mannes
	PLURAL			
Nom.	die Bücher	die Kinder	die Reichtümer	die Männer
Acc.	die Bücher	die Kinder	die Reichtümer	die Männer
Dat.	den Büchern	den Kindern	den Reichtümern	den Männern
Gen.	der Bücher	der Kinder	der Reichtümer	der Männer

CLASS 4: Adds **–n** or **–en** to form plurals.

Practical information:

1. A great number of feminine nouns belong here.
2. A fair number of masculine nouns are included.
3. Very few neuters are in this class.
4. *This class never adds umlaut in forming plurals.*
5. Feminines in **–in** (see **die Freundin** below) add **–nen** to form their plurals.

Declensional Patterns:

Feminines

	SINGULAR			
Nom.	die Freundin	die Frage	die Zeitung	die Illusion
Acc.	die Freundin	die Frage	die Zeitung	die Illusion
Dat.	der Freundin	der Frage	der Zeitung	der Illusion
Gen.	der Freundin	der Frage	der Zeitung	der Illusion
	PLURAL			
Nom.	die Freundinnen	die Fragen	die Zeitungen	die Illusionen
Acc.	die Freundinnen	die Fragen	die Zeitungen	die Illusionen
Dat.	den Freundinnen	den Fragen	den Zeitungen	den Illusionen
Gen.	der Freundinnen	der Fragen	der Zeitungen	der Illusionen

Masculines and Neuters

a) Some masculines in this class show **–en** in all forms except the nominative singular (see **der Student** on page 318).

b) Other masculines and all neuters have **–s** or **–es** in the genitive singular and **–n** or **–en** throughout the plural (see **der Professor, das Auge, das Ohr** on page 318).

	SINGULAR			
Nom.	der Professor	der Student	das Auge	das Ohr
Acc.	den Professor	den Studenten	das Auge	das Ohr
Dat.	dem Professor	dem Studenten	dem Auge	dem Ohr
Gen.	des Professors	des Studenten	des Auges	des Ohres
	PLURAL			
Nom.	die Professoren	die Studenten	die Augen	die Ohren
Acc.	die Professoren	die Studenten	die Augen	die Ohren
Dat.	den Professoren	den Studenten	den Augen	den Ohren
Gen.	der Professoren	der Studenten	der Augen	der Ohren

A few nouns in Class 4 (all masculine) offer an option in the nominative singular, for example:

	SINGULAR	PLURAL
Nom.	der Name(n)	die Namen
Acc.	den Namen	die Namen
Dat.	dem Namen	den Namen
Gen.	des Namens	der Namen

Note: **der Friede(n), der Glaube(n),** and a few others follow the same pattern as **der Name(n).**

The following show varying irregularities in the singular:

	SINGULAR		
Nom.	der Herr	das Herz	der Zyklus
Acc.	den Herrn	das Herz	den Zyklus
Dat.	dem Herrn	dem Herzen	dem Zyklus
Gen.	des Herrn	des Herzens	des Zyklus
	PLURAL		
Nom.	die Herren	die Herzen	die Zyklen
Acc.	die Herren	die Herzen	die Zyklen
Dat.	den Herren	den Herzen	den Zyklen
Gen.	der Herren	der Herzen	der Zyklen

Note: **der Bauer** offers an option in the genitive singular; also in the accusative and dative singular. (**Der Nachbar** [*neighbor*] follows the pattern of **der Bauer**.)

	SINGULAR	PLURAL
Nom.	der Bauer	die Bauern
Acc.	den Bauer(n)	die Bauern
Dat.	dem Bauer(n)	den Bauern
Gen.	des Bauers (*or* –n)	der Bauern

CLASS 5: Adds **–s** to form plurals.

This class comprises borrowings from non-German sources. They all follow the pattern of **das Auto:**

	SINGULAR	PLURAL
Nom.	das Auto	die Autos
Acc.	das Auto	die Autos
Dat.	dem Auto	den Autos
Gen.	des Autos	der Autos

See also:

das Hotel, der Karton, das Kino, das Restaurant, der Perron, der Portier

Note that this is the only class of nouns in which the dative plural does not end in **–n** or **–en.**

DEFINITE ARTICLE, PRONOUNS

Definite Article

	SINGULAR			PLURAL
	FEM.	NEUT.	MASC.	ANY GENDER
Nom.	die	das	der	die
Acc.	die	das	den	die
Dat.	der	dem	dem	**den**
Gen.	**der**	**des**	**des**	**der**

Relative Pronouns and **die, das, der** as Demonstrative Pronouns

	SINGULAR			PLURAL
	FEM.	NEUT.	MASC.	ANY GENDER
Nom.	die; welche	das; welches	der; welcher	die; welche
Acc.	die; welche	das; welches	den; welchen	die; welche
Dat.	der; welcher	dem; welchem	dem; welchem	**denen;** welchen
Gen.	**deren**	**dessen**	**dessen**	**deren**

The boldface forms reveal the only pattern differences between the definite article on the one hand and the relative (and demonstrative) pronoun on the other.

Remember that as relative pronouns, **deren, dessen, dessen, deren** (in the order given above) mean simply *whose*, but as demonstrative pronouns they mean (strongly stressed) *her, its, his, their;* **denen** as a relative pronoun means (*to, for, etc.*) *whom;* as a demonstrative it means (*to, for, etc.*) *them.*

As a demonstrative, the genitive plural **deren** changes its form to **derer** when followed by a relative pronoun:

Die Liebe derer, die uns nahe stehen, ist uns unentbehrlich von Kindheit an.	*The love of those who are close to us is indispensable to us from our very childhood.*

Personal Pronoun

SINGULAR

	1ST PERSON	2ND PERSON		3RD PERSON		
Nom.	ich	du	Sie	sie	es	er
Acc.	mich	dich	Sie	sie	es	ihn
Dat.	mir	dir	Ihnen	ihr	ihm	ihm
Gen.	(meiner)	(deiner)	(Ihrer)	(ihrer)	(seiner)	(seiner)

PLURAL

Nom.	wir	ihr	Sie	sie
Acc.	uns	euch	Sie	sie
Dat.	uns	euch	Ihnen	ihnen
Gen.	(unser)	(euer)	(Ihrer)	(ihrer)

Interrogative Pronoun

Nom.	wer?	was?
Acc.	wen?	was?
Dat.	wem?	
Gen.	wessen?	

DEFINITE ARTICLE, dies-WORDS, mein-WORDS

Definite Article

	SINGULAR			PLURAL
	FEM.	NEUT.	MASC.	ANY GENDER
Nom.	d [ie]	d [as]	d er	d [ie]
Acc.	[ie]	[as]	en	[ie]
Dat.	er	em	em	en
Gen.	er	es	es	er

dies-word

Nom.	dies [e]	dies [es]	dies er	dies [e]
Acc.	[e]	[es]	en	[e]
Dat.	er	em	em	en
Gen.	er	es	es	er

mein-word

Nom.	mein e	mein [—]	mein [—]	mein e
Acc.	e	mein [—]	en	e
Dat.	er	em	em	en
Gen.	er	es	es	er

Note the difference between the **dies**-word and the definite article as indicated in the corresponding boxes. Other words that follow the **dies**-word pattern are:

jed– (*each*), **jen**– (*that*), **manch**– (*many a, some*), **solch**– (*such*), **welch**– (*which*)

The **mein**-words differ in pattern from the **dies**-words in only three instances: he nominative and accusative neuter singular and the nominative masculine singular, where the **mein**-words have no endings. (See boxes in **mein**-word pattern.)

The **dies**-word forms may be used both as adjectives and as pronouns; the **mein**-word pattern also has this dual function, except that the three uninflected forms are *exclusively adjectival.*

To change these forms to pronouns, simply attach the corresponding **dies**-word endings: dies**es** (nom. and acc. neut.), dies**er** (nom. masc.).

Illustrations

Wessen Buch ist das?
Dieses Buch ist meines (*or* meins).

Wer will dieses Buch (mein Buch)?
Wer will dieses (meines *or* meins)?

Wessen Stuhl ist das?
Dieser Stuhl ist meiner.

Other **mein**-words are:

dein (*your*), **Ihr** (*your*), **ihr** (*her, their*), **sein** (*his, its*), **unser** (*our*), **euer** (*your*), **ein** (*a, an*), **kein** (*no, not any*)

CHART OF ADJECTIVE ENDINGS

1. Know whether the noun is singular or plural.
2. Know the gender of the noun *if singular.*
3. Know the case of the noun.

(*See patterns on page 322.*)

	dies-word or mein-word preceding →				attributive adjectives				noun
	1. F.	2. N.	3. M.	4. PL.	1. F.	2. N.	3. M.	4. PL.	
Nom.	**e**	**es** (–) *	**er** (–) *	**e**	**e**	**e** (**es**)	**e** (**er**)	**en**	
Acc.	**e**	**es** (–) *	**en**	**e**	**e**	**e** (**es**)	**en**	**en**	
Dat.	**er**	**em**	**em**	**en**	**en**	**en**	**en**	**en**	
Gen.	**er**	**es**	**es**	**er**	**en**	**en**	**en**	**en**	
	no dies-word or mein-word preceding →								
Nom.					**e**	**es**	**er**	**e**	
Acc.					**e**	**es**	**en**	**e**	
Dat.					**er**	**em**	**em**	**en**	
Gen.					**er**	**en**	**en**	**er**	

* The **dies**-word and the **mein**-word endings are the same except for the starred items, where the **mein**-word shows *no* ending.

ADJECTIVE–NOUN PATTERNS

	SINGULAR			PLURAL
	FEMININE	NEUTER	MASCULINE	ANY GENDER
Nom.	die (diese) schöne Frau	das (dieses) kleine Mädchen	der (dieser) große Mann	die (diese) guten Frauen, Mädchen, Männer
Acc.	die (diese) schöne Frau	das (dieses) kleine Mädchen	den (diesen) großen Mann	die (diese) guten Frauen, Mädchen, Männer
Dat.	der (dieser) schönen Frau	dem (diesem) kleinen Mädchen	dem (diesem) großen Mann	den (diesen) guten Frauen, Mädchen, Männern
Gen.	der (dieser) schönen Frau	des (dieses) kleinen Mädchens	des (dieses) großen Mannes	der (dieser) guten Frauen, Mädchen, Männer
Nom.	meine liebe Mutter	sein armes Kind	dein alter Vater	keine kranken Mütter, Kinder, Väter
Acc.	meine liebe Mutter	sein armes Kind	deinen alten Vater	keine kranken Mütter, Kinder, Väter
Dat.	meiner lieben Mutter	seinem armen Kinde	deinem alten Vater	keinen kranken Müttern, Kindern, Vätern
Gen.	meiner lieben Mutter	seines armen Kindes	deines alten Vaters	keiner kranken Mütter, Kinder, Väter
Nom.	saure Milch	frisches Brot	guter Wein	lange Stunden, Jahre, Tage
Acc.	saure Milch	frisches Brot	guten Wein	lange Stunden, Jahre, Tage
Dat.	saurer Milch	frischem Brot	gutem Wein	langen Stunden, Jahren, Tagen
Gen.	saurer Milch	frischen Brot(e)s	guten Weines	langer Stunden, Jahre, Tage
Nom.	jene warme Nacht	das wärmere Wetter	unser wärmster Sommer	solche warmen Tage
Acc.	jene warme Nacht	das wärmere Wetter	unseren wärmsten Sommer	solche warmen Tage
Dat.	jener warmen Nacht	dem wärmeren Wetter	unserem wärmsten Sommer	solchen warmen Tagen
Gen.	jener warmen Nacht	des wärmeren Wetters	unseres wärmsten Sommers	solcher warmen Tage

VOCABULARY

EXPLANATORY NOTES

Nouns: Except for the genitive singular of **die**-nouns (feminine), the nominative singular genitive singular, and nominative plural of all nouns are given.

Verbs: The principal parts of irregular (strong) verbs are given as follows: Infinitive **sehen;** third person singular, present tense, only listed if irregular: **sieht;** first or third person singular, past tense: **sah;** past participle: **gesehen.** The past participle of verbs that use the auxiliary **sein** instead of **haben** in the perfect tense is given with **ist: ist gegangen.**

Of regular (weak) verbs only the infinitive is given. Verbs that use the auxiliary **sein** instead of **haben** are listed as follows: **stürzen (sein).**

Verbs with a separable prefix are listed with a hyphen: **an-sehen.**

Stress marks: Whenever a word is not stressed on the first syllable, a stress mark appears after the syllable carrying the main stress: **Student′, studie′ren.**

Adjectives: The comparative and superlative forms of adjectives are given only if some stem change or irregularity occurs: **lang, länger, längst–.** A dash at the end of a word indicates that it occurs only with an appropriate ending.

Endings: Note that endings are listed in the following order: feminine, neuter, masculine, e.g., **dies (–e, –es, –er).**

ABBREVIATIONS

acc.	accusative	*inf.*	infinitive
adj.	adjective	*interr.*	interrogative
adv.	adverb	*intrans.*	intransitive
art.	article	*masc.*	masculine
coll.	colloquial	*neut.*	neuter
comp.	comparative	*nom.*	nominative
conj.	conjunction	*pers.*	person
coord.	coordinating	*plur.*	plural
dat.	dative	*poss.*	possessive
def.	definite	*prep.*	preposition
demonst.	demonstrative	*pron.*	pronoun
fam.	familiar	*refl.*	reflexive
fem.	feminine	*rel.*	relative
form.	formal	*sing.*	singular
gen.	genitive	*sub.*	subordinating
ind.	indicative	*subj.*	subjunctive
indef.	indefinite	*temp.*	temporal

GERMAN–ENGLISH VOCABULARY

A

ab away, down, off, from
ab-brechen (bricht ab), brach ab, abgebrochen interrupt, break off
der **Abend, –s, –e** evening; das **Abendessen, –s, —** supper, evening meal; das **Abendkleid, –es, –er** evening dress; der **Abendsonnenschein, –s** evening sunset glow; **abendländisch** Western, occidental; **abends** in the evening; die **Abendvorstellung, –en** evening performance
das **Abenteuer, –s, —** adventure
aber (*coord. conj.*) but, however
ab-fahren (fährt ab), fuhr ab, ist abgefahren depart, leave; die **Abfahrt, –en** departure
ab-fliegen, flog ab, ist abgeflogen fly away, take off
der **Abfluß, –flusses, –flüsse** outlet
ab-geben (gibt ab), gab ab, abgegeben hand in
abgegriffen worn (by handling)
ab-gehen, ging ab, ist abgegangen leave, go away; **Es geht nicht ohne Schwierigkeiten ab.** It is beset with difficulties.
abgeschlossen completed, concluded
ab-halten (hält ab), hielt ab, abgehalten hold, hold off (*or* back); **abgehalten werden** be held, take place (*of events*)
ab-helfen (hilft ab), half ab, abgeholfen remedy
das **Abkommen, –s, —** agreement, pact
der **Abkömmling, –s, –e** descendant
ab-lösen relieve
ab-nehmen (nimmt ab), nahm ab, abgenommen take off
die **Abneigung, –en** aversion
der **Abort′, –(e)s, –e** washroom
ab-reisen (sein) depart, leave; die **Abreise, –n** departure
ab-reißen, riß ab, abgerissen tear down *or* off
ab-sagen refuse, cancel
der **Absatz, –es, ⸚e** paragraph
ab-schätzen estimate, appraise; **nicht abzuschätzen sein** be incalculable
abscheu′lich horrible, disgusting
der **Abschied, –(e)s, –e** departure, farewell; **Abschied nehmen** take leave (of one another); **den Abschied geben** dismiss; die **Ab′schiedssymphonie′** the Farewell Symphony (*by Haydn*)
ab-schließen, schloß ab, abgeschlossen seal off, conclude, finish, fulfil; der **Abschluß, –schlusses, –schlüsse** conclusion
der **Abschnitt, –(e)s, –e** section, selection
ab-schreiben, schrieb ab, abgeschrieben copy
die **Abschußerlaubnis** shooting *or* hunting license
ab-schwören, schwur ab, abgeschworen renounce
ab-sehen (sieht ab), sah ab, abgesehen (von etwas) take no account (of a thing); **abgesehen davon, daß** without mentioning that
(sich) ab-seilen lower (oneself) by ropes
ab-setzen remove, discard
die **Absicht, –en** intention, purpose
absolut′ absolute(ly)
Abstand: mit Abstand by far
ab-steigen, stieg ab, ist abgestiegen descend, put up (*at a hotel, etc.*)
abstrakt′ abstract; die **Abstraktion′, –en** abstraction
ab-stürzen (sein) plunge down
das **Abteil′, –s, –e** compartment; der **Abtei′lungsleiter, –s, —** department manager
ab-wandern (sein) migrate
ab-warten wait and see; **Das muß man abwarten.** One has to wait and see about that.
abwärts down(ward)
(sich) ab-wenden, wandte (*or* **wendete**) **(sich) ab, abgewandt** (*or* **abgewendet**) turn away
die **Abwesenheit** absence
ab-zählen count off
ach oh, ah, alas; **ach so** oh, I see
acht eight
acht: sich in acht nehmen watch out, take care; **achten** pay attention; **acht-geben (gibt acht), gab acht, achtgegeben** pay attention; die **Achtung** attention
achtzehn eighteen
der **Acker, –s, ⸚** acre, field
das **Ada′gio, –s, –s** adagio
der **Advokat′, –en, –en** lawyer
der **Affe, –n, –n** monkey, ape
(das) **Afrika, –s** Africa
(das) **Ägyp′ten, –s** Egypt; der **Ägyp′ter, –s, —** Egyptian
der **Ahn, –(e)s** *or* **–en, –en** ancestor
die **Ahnung, –en** premonition, inkling, suspicion; **ahnungslos** unsuspecting
der **Akt, –(e)s, –e** act (*of a play*)
die **Akten** (*plur.*) papers, documents; die **Aktenmappe, –n** briefcase
der **Akteur′, –s, –e** actor, protagonist
albern silly
die **Alge, –n** algae, seaweed
das **All, –s** universe

alle (*plur. of* **alles**) all, everybody
allein′ alone, only; (*coord. conj.*) but, however
allenfalls′ if need be, at the most, perhaps
allerdings′ to be sure, indeed, certainly
alles everything, all; **alles im Hause** everything included; **alles in allem** all things considered
allgemein′ general; universal; **im allgemei′nen** in general
allhier′ here
allmäh′lich gradually
das **Alltagsleben, –s** everyday routine
die **Alpen** (*plur.*) Alps
als (*sub. conj.*) as,(*temp.*) when; **als** (*conj. in comparisons*) than; **als ob** (*sub. conj.*) as if; **als wenn** (*sub. conj.*) as if
alsbald′ thereupon, presently, soon, at once
alsdann′ then
also thus, hence, therefore, so, well, accordingly; **also gut** very well, all right (then)
alt, älter, ältest- old; der **Alte, –n, –n** old man; die **Alte, –n, –n** old woman; das **Alter, –s, —** age; das **Altertum, –s** antiquity; **altertümlich** old; ancient
altdeutsch Old German
altenglisch Old English
althochdeutsch Old High German
altlitauisch Old Lithuanian
altrosa old rose
am = **an dem**
die **Ameise, –n** ant
(das) **Ame′rika, –s, –s** America; der **Amerika′ner, –s, —** American (*masc.*); die **Amerika′nerin, –nen** American (*fem.*); **amerika′nisch** American (*adj.*)
die **Amme, –n** nurse
die **Amoret′te, –n** little cupid
amtlich official
an (*prep. dat.*) at, by, near, on; (*prep. acc.*) to, in (*e.g.:* **glauben an** believe in); of (*e.g.:* **denken an** think of); **an . . . vorü′ber** (*with dat.*) past
anato′misch anatomical
der **Anbeter, –s, —** admirer
der **Anblick, –(e)s, –e** sight
an-brüllen shout at, yell at
ander (–e, –es, –er) other; **der andere** the other (one); **nichts anderes** nothing else
andererseits (anderseits) on the other hand
ändern change
anders different(ly), otherwise
anderthalb one and a half
an-deuten suggest, intimate
die **Anekdo′te, –n** anecdote
an-fahren (fährt an), fuhr an, angefahren address angrily
der **Anfang, –(e)s, ⸚e** beginning; **Aller Anfang ist schwer.** The first step is the hardest; **anfangs** at first; der **Anfangstakt, –(e)s, –e** opening measure; **an-fangen (fängt an), fing an, angefangen** start, begin
an-fassen, faßte an, angefaßt seize, take hold of
an-gaffen gape at, stare at
an-geben (gibt an), gab an, angegeben state, declare
angeblich alleged(ly)
angeboren inborn
an-gehen, ging an, ist angegangen (*with acc.*) concern, apply, be the case
an-gehören (*dat.*) belong to; der **Angehörige, –n, –n** relative, member
die **Angelegenheit, –en** affair, matter, concern
(das) **Angelsächsisch, –en** Anglo-Saxon (*language*)
angesägt sawed
der **Angestellte, –n, –n** employee
sich an-gewöhnen get accustomed to
an-greifen, griff an, angegriffen attack; der **Angriff, –s, –e** attack
die **Angst, ⸚e** anxiety; das **Angstgebrüll –s** cry of terror; **ängstlich** timid, anxious
an-kommen, kam an, ist angekommen arrive; die **Ankunft, ⸚e** arrival
das **Anlangen, –s** arrival
die **Anmut** charm, gracefulness
die **Annahme, –n** assumption, supposition, hypothesis; **an-nehmen (nimmt an), nahm an, angenommen** assume, accept
die **Anomalie′, –n** anomaly
an-ordnen order
an-reden address, speak to
an-rühren touch
ans = **an das**
sich an-sammeln collect
an-schalten turn on (*a switch, light*)
an-schauen look at
der **Anschein, –(e)s** appearance; **anscheinend** apparently
an-sehen (sieht an), sah an, angesehen look at; look upon; **sich** (*dat.*) **etwas ansehen** look at something
an-setzen schedule
die **Ansicht, –en** view, opinion
die **Ansichtskarte, –n** picture postcard
anstatt′ instead of
an-staunen gaze at in (admiring) astonishment
an-streben attempt, strive for
der **Antagonist′, –en, –en** antagonist
die **Anthologie′, –n** anthology
anthropolo′gisch anthropological
das **Antlitz, –es, –e** face
an-treffen (trifft an), traf an, angetroffen meet
die **Antwort, –en** answer; **antworten** answer; **auf eine Frage** (*acc.*) **antworten** answer a question; **jemandem** (*dat.*) **antworten** answer someone

an-wenden (*see* **wenden**) use, employ
anwesend present
die **Anzahl** number
an-zeigen point out, denounce, report; **jemanden wegen . . .** (*with gen.*) **anzeigen** charge someone with . . .
an-ziehen, zog an, angezogen dress; **sich anziehen** get dressed
der **Anzug, –(e)s, ⸚e** suit
an-zweifeln question, doubt
der **Apfel, –s, ⸚** apple; der **Apfelkuchen, –s, —** apple cake
die **Apokalyp′se** apocalypse
der **April′, –s** April
die **Arbeit, –en** work; **arbeiten** work; das **Arbeitszimmer, –s, —** workroom, study
archa′isch archaic
archäolo′gisch archeological
der **Architekt′, –en, –en** architect; die **Architektur′** architecture
die **Are′na,** (*plur.*) **Are′nen** arena
ärgern annoy; **sich ärgern** get *or* be angry, lose one's temper
das **Ärgste, –n** the worst
die **Aristokratie′, –n** aristocracy; **aristokra′tisch** aristocratic
die **Arithme′tik** arithmetic
die **Arktis** Arctic; **arktisch** arctic
der **Arm, –es, –e** arm
arm, ärmer, ärmst– poor
das **Armband, –(e)s, ⸚er** bracelet; die **Armbanduhr, –en** wrist watch
der **Ärmel, –s, —** sleeve
die **Armut** poverty
die **Art, –en** manner, kind, species
artig well-behaved, nice, good
die **Artillerie′** artillery
der **Arzt, –es, ⸚e** doctor; die **Ärztin, –nen** doctor (*fem.*)
(das) **Asien, –s** Asia
der **Ast, –(e)s, ⸚e** branch
die **Ästhe′tik** aesthetics
der **Atem, –s** breath; **atmen** breathe
(das) **Atlan′tis** Atlantis; **atlan′tisch** Atlantic
der **Atom′krieg, –(e)s, –e** atomic war
auch also, too; **auch wenn** even if, even when; **auch nicht** not . . . either, neither, nor
auf (*prep. dat. or acc.*) on, upon, at, to; **auf einmal** suddenly
die **Aufbesserung, –en** improvement; raise (*salary*)
sich auf-drängen intrude upon
der **Aufenthalt, –es, –e** stay
die **Aufführung, –en** performance
die **Aufgabe, –n** task, lesson, assignment, homework
auf-geben (gibt auf), gab auf, aufgegeben give up; assign
auf-halten (hält auf), hielt auf, aufgehalten keep open; hold up, stop, delay
auf-heben, hob auf, aufgehoben pick up, reserve, keep
auf-hören end, stop
die **Auflage, –n** edition
auf-lauern lie in wait
auf-machen open
die **Aufmerksamkeit, –en** attention
auf-nehmen (nimmt auf), nahm auf, aufgenommen take up, accept
auf-passen, paßte auf, aufgepaßt pay attention
der **Aufputz, –es** finery
auf-regen excite; **sich auf-regen** get excited
auf-reißen, riß auf, aufgerissen tear open, open violently
aufrichtig sincere
auf-rufen, rief auf, aufgerufen call up *or* on; call out
aufs = auf das
auf-schieben, schob auf, aufgeschoben postpone, delay
auf-schlagen (schlägt auf), schlug auf, aufgeschlagen open (*a book, eyes, etc.*); turn to (*a page*)
das **Aufsehen, –s** sensation, attention
auf-stehen, stand auf, ist aufgestanden get up
der **Aufstieg, –(e)s, –e** ascent
auf-treiben, trieb auf, aufgetrieben find, produce
auf-treten (tritt auf), trat auf, ist aufgetreten appear
aufwärts-gleiten, glitt aufwärts, ist aufwärtsgeglitten glide upward
auf-weisen, wies auf, aufgewiesen reveal
der **Aufzug, –(e)s, ⸚e** elevator; die **Aufzugstür, –en** elevator door
das **Auge, –s, –n** eye; **aus den Augen verlieren** lose sight of; der **Augenball, –(e)s, ⸚e** eyeball; der **Augenblick, –s, –e** moment; die **Augenbraue, –n** eyebrow; das **Augenlid, –(e)s, –er** eyelid; das **Äuglein, –s, —** little eye
der **August′, –s** August
aus (*prep. dat.*) out, out of, from, (made) of
aus-arbeiten elaborate
aus-brechen (bricht aus), brach aus, ist ausgebrochen break away, venture out; burst out
aus-breiten spread
der **Ausdruck, –(e)s, ⸚e** expression, locution
ausdrücklich express(ly), especially
auseinan′der-liegen, lag auseinander, auseinandergelegen lie apart
auseinan′der-rücken (sein) move apart; spread out, scatter
die **Auseinan′dersetzung, –en** controversy, discussion, explanation
der **Ausflug, –(e)s, ⸚e** excursion, trip
aus-führen carry out
aus-füllen fill out

der **Ausgang, –(e)s, ¨–e** solution, ending; exit
ausgebaut designed, made into
aus-geben (gibt aus), gab aus, ausgegeben spend (money)
aus-gehen, ging aus, ist ausgegangen go out; be exhausted; start, proceed; end; **gut ausgehen** turn out well
ausgeprägt pronounced, distinct
ausgeschlossen excluded; out of the question
ausgestorben extinct
ausgezeichnet excellent, distinguished, good, fine
aus-graben (gräbt aus), grub aus, ausgegraben dig out, gouge out
aus-halten (hält aus), hielt aus, ausgehalten endure
die **Auskunft, ¨–e** information
das **Ausland, –(e)s** foreign country; **im Ausland** abroad; der **Ausländer, –s, —** foreigner
aus-löschen extinguish, put out
aus-machen arrange; turn off (*light, switch*); **Ich habe es mit ihm ausgemacht.** I arranged it with him.
das **Ausmaß, –es, –e** measure, extent
aus-reichen be sufficient, be adequate
aus-rufen, rief aus, ausgerufen call out, shout, cry
(sich) aus-ruhen relax, rest
aus-schalten turn off (*light, switch*)
aus-schließen, schloß aus, ausgeschlossen lock out; exclude, exempt; **ausschließlich** exclusive(ly)
aus-sehen (sieht aus), sah aus, ausgesehen look like, appear, seem; das **Aussehen, –s** appearance
außen (*adv.*) outside; die **Außenwelt** world outside, external world
außer (*prep. dat.*) outside of, beside, except; besides; **außerdem** besides
außerhalb (*prep. gen.*) outside of
außerordentlich extraordinary
äußerst extremely, very
aus-steigen, stieg aus, ist ausgestiegen get off
aus-stellen exhibit; die **Ausstellung, –en** exhibition
aus-suchen select, pick; **ausgesucht** choice
aus-tauschen exchange; der **Aus′tausch-student′, –en, –en** exchange student
(das) **Austra′lien, –s** Australia
die **Auswahl** selection, selected list
aus-wandern (sein) emigrate, migrate
auswendig by heart; **auswendig lernen** learn by heart
aus-wischen wipe out; **jemandem eins auswischen** strike someone, hit out at a person
sich aus-zeichnen distinguish oneself, be (*or* become) distinguished
der **Auszug, –(e)s, ¨–e** excerpt
das **Auto, –s, –s** car
die **Au′tobiographie′, –n** autobiography
der **Autobus, –busses, –busse** bus
der **Autor, –s,** (*plur.*) **Auto′ren** author
die **Axt, ¨–e** ax

B

der **Bach, –es, ¨–e** brook; die **Bachforelle, –n** brook trout
backen (bäckt), buk, gebacken bake; der **Bäcker, –s, —** baker; die **Bäckerei′, –en** bakery; das **Backhuhn, –s, ¨–er** fried *or* roast chicken
das **Bad, –es, ¨–er** bath; der **Badeanzug, –s, ¨–e** bathing suit; das **Badezimmer, –s, —** bathroom
(das) **Bad Reichenhall′** *resort in Bavaria*
die **Bahn, –en** railroad; road; course; der **Bahndamm, –(e)s, ¨–e** railway embankment; der **Bahnhof, –s, ¨–e** (railroad) station; der **Bahnübergang, –(e)s, ¨–e** railroad crossing
der **Bak′teriolog′(e), –en, –en** bacteriologist
bald soon
der **Ball, –(e)s, ¨–e** ball (*dance*); ball
bang uneasy, anxious
bangen be afraid
die **Bank, ¨–e** bench
der **Bär, –en, –en** bear
barfuß barefoot
(das) **Barock′, –s** Baroque
der **Bart, –(e)s, ¨–e** beard
baskisch Basque
der **Baß, Basses, Bässe** bass, bass viol, double bass
der **Bau, –(e)s,** (*plur.*) **Bauten** building, structure; cultivation; **als seien sie vom Bau** as if they were experts
der **Bauch, –(e)s, ¨–e** belly, stomach
bauen build
der **Bauer, –s** *or* **–n, –n** peasant, farmer
die **Baukunst** architecture
der **Baum, –(e)s, ¨–e** tree
die **Bauten** (*see* **Bau**)
bay(e)risch Bavarian; (das) **Bayern, –s** Bavaria
(das) **Bayreuth′, –s** *city in Northern Bavaria*
beab′sichtigen intend
beach′ten notice, pay attention to
die **Beängs′tigung, –en** anxiety
bean′spruchen demand
beant′worten answer
der **Becher, –s, —** beaker, cup, glass
bedacht′ (*adj.*) thoughtful (of), intent; **auf etwas** (*acc.*) **bedacht′ sein** be intent on something
bedau′ern pity
bede′cken cover; **bedeckt′** covered

bedeu′ten mean, signify; **bedeu′tend** important, significant; die **Bedeu′tung, –en** meaning, significance
bedie′nen serve
bedro′hen threaten
bedür′fen (bedarf), bedurfte, bedurft require, need; **bedür′fen** (*with gen.*) be in need of
befeh′len (befiehlt), befahl, befohlen command; **jemandem etwas befehlen** order someone to do something
befin′den, befand, befunden consider; **sich befinden** be, feel; be situated
befrei′en free, liberate
befrem′det with surprise, surprised
befreun′det sein (mit) be friendly (with)
befrie′digt satisfied
der **Befund′, –(e)s, –e** evidence, finding
die **Bega′bung, –en** talent
sich bege′ben (begibt), begab, begeben go; happen
begeg′nen (sein) (*with dat.*) meet
bege′hen, beging, begangen commit (*an error, crime, etc.*)
begeh′ren desire
begei′stern inspire; **sich begeistern** get excited, get enthusiastic
der **Beginn′, –s** beginning; **begin′nen, begann, begonnen** begin
beglei′ten accompany; die **Beglei′tung** accompaniment
begrei′fen, begriff, begriffen comprehend, understand; der **Begriff′, (–e)s, –e** concept, idea, notion; **im Begriff sein** be about to
begren′zen limit
begrün′den found, establish; give reasons for
begrü′ßen greet
beha′gen (*with dat.*) please
behal′ten (behält), behielt, behalten keep, retain, maintain
das **Behält′nis, –ses, –se** container; conveyance
behan′deln treat
behän′gen, behing, behangen (*or weak*) cover, decorate
die **Beharr′lichkeit** tenacity, perseverance
behaup′ten maintain, assert; die **Behaup′tung, –en** assertion
bei (*prep. dat.*) by, at, near, with, at the home of; **bei sich sein** be conscious; **bei weitem** by far
bei-behalten (behält bei), behielt bei, beibehalten preserve
beide both; die **beiden** the two, both
das **Beil, –(e)s, –e** hatchet, ax
beim = bei dem; beim Vornamen by the first name
das **Bein, –(e)s, –e** leg; **jemandem ein Bein stellen** trip someone up
beinahe almost
beisei′te aside
das **Beispiel, –s, –e** example, instance; **zum Beispiel** (*abbreviation:* **z.B.**) for example, for instance
beißen, biß, gebissen bite
der **Beitrag, –(e)s, ⸚e** contribution
bei-wohnen attend
bekannt′ known, well-known; der **Bekann′te, –n, –n** acquaintance; **bekannt′lich** as is well known
die **Bekeh′rung, –en** conversion
beklei′det dressed
die **Beklem′mung, –en** tightness, anguish, inner pressure
bekom′men, bekam, bekommen get, receive; **Möge es ihm wohl bekommen.** May it do him some good.
belang′los irrelevant, unimportant
beläs′tigen molest, annoy
bele′ben animate
bele′gen reserve; **einen Kurs bele′gen** take a course
beleh′ren instruct, enlighten
das **Belie′ben, –s** wish, pleasure
beliebt′ popular, well-liked
beloh′nen reward
bemer′ken notice, remark; die **Bemer′kung, –en** remark, statement
bemit′telt well-to-do
das **Beneh′men, –s** behavior
benut′zen (*or* **benützen**) use
bepackt′ loaded down
(das) **Berchtesga′den, –s** *town in Bavaria*
das **Bereich′, –(e)s, –e** realm, region, area
bereit′ ready; **bereits′** already; **bereit′willig** ready, willing
der **Berg, –(e)s, –e** mountain; die **Bergschlucht, –en** gorge; der **Bergsteiger, –s, —** mountain climber; die **Bergwacht** mountain watch; das **Bergwerk, –(e)s, –e** mine
der **Bericht′, –(e)s, –e** report; **berich′ten** inform, report
berich′tigen correct
der **Beruf′, –(e)s, –e** profession, calling; die **Berufs′tradition′, –en** professional tradition
beru′higen calm, pacify
berühmt′ famous
besa′gen mean, signify, suggest
besänf′tigen pacify
beschei′den, beschied, beschieden destine, assign; inform
beschei′den (*adj.*) modest
die **Beschlag′nahme** seizure, confiscation
beschlie′ßen, beschloß, beschlossen conclude, decide
beschrei′ben, beschrieb, beschrieben describe; die **Beschrei′bung, –en** description
beschwin′deln defraud
beschwö′ren implore

bese′hen (besieht), besah, besehen look at, examine
beses′sen possessed, mad
besich′tigen visit, examine, inspect
der **Besitz′, –es, –e** possession; **besit′zen, besaß, besessen** own; die **Besitz′losen** (*plur.*) the poor, the proletariat
beson′ders especially; special
besor′gen take care of, do, look after; get
bespre′chen (bespricht), besprach, besprochen discuss
besser (*see* **gut**) better
best– (*see* **gut**) best; **aufs beste** most cordially, in the best possible way
bestä′tigen confirm
beste′hen, bestand, bestanden pass (*a test*); **beste′hen** (*with* **auf**) insist upon; **beste′hen** (*with* **aus**) consist of; **beste′hen bleiben** (**sein**) persist, last
bestei′gen, bestieg, bestiegen climb, scale
bestel′len order
die **Bestie, –n** beast
bestimmt′ definite
bestrei′ten, bestritt, bestritten dispute
bestürzt′ startled
besu′chen visit, attend; der **Besu′cher, –s, —** visitor
betei′ligen give a share to; **betei′ligt sein an** be instrumental in, have a share in
beten pray
beto′nen emphasize
betrach′ten look at, examine
beträcht′lich considerable
betra′gen (beträgt), betrug, betragen amount to
betref′fen (betrifft), betraf, betroffen concern, affect
betrei′ben, betrieb, betrieben pursue, participate in, be engaged in, carry on, do; play; **in Betrieb′ nehmen** *or* **haben** maintain
betre′ten (betritt), betrat, betreten enter
betre′ten (*adj.*) embarrassed
betrü′gen, betrog, betrogen deceive, cheat
das **Bett, –(e)s, –en** bed
beugen decline (*grammatical term*); **(sich) beugen** bend, lean
beun′ruhigen disturb, alarm
bevor′ (*sub. conj.*) before
bewe′gen move; persuade; cause, induce; die **Bewe′gung, –en** movement, motion
der **Beweis′, –es, –e** proof, evidence; **bewei′sen, bewies, bewiesen** prove
bewen′den: dabei bewen′den lassen leave at that, acquiesce in
bewil′ligen grant; die **Bewil′ligung, –en** permission
bewir′ken effect, bring about
der **Bewoh′ner, –s, —** inhabitant
bewun′dernd admiringly
bezah′len pay
bezeich′nen designate; die **Bezeich nung, –en** term, designation
bezie′hen, bezog, bezogen draw *or* receive (*salary, payment*); **sich bezie′hen auf** refer to
der **Bezirk′, –(e)s, –e** district, area, region
die **Bibliothek′, –en** library
das **Bier, –(e)s, –e** beer
bieten, bot, geboten offer, present
die **Bigamie′** bigamy
das **Bild, –es, –er** picture, painting
bilden form, shape, cultivate
der **Bildhauer, –s, —** sculptor
die **Bildung** education; culture
billig cheap, inexpensive
binden, band, gebunden bind, tie
das **Binnenmeer, –(e)s, –e** landlocked sea
biogra′phisch biographical
der **Biolog′(e), –en, –en** biologist; die **Biologie′** biology
bis (*sub. conj., prep.*) until, up to; **bisher′** up to now; **bis auf** up to, excepting
(ein) bißchen a little, a bit
die **Bitte, –n** request; **bitte** please; **Bitte schön!** You're welcome! **bitten, bat, gebeten** ask, request, beg; **bitten um** ask for
blank shiny
blasen (bläst), blies, geblasen blow; play (*a wind instrument*)
das **Blatt, –(e)s, ⸚er** page, leaf
blau blue
das **Blechschild, –(e)s, –er** metal plate
bleiben, blieb, ist geblieben stay, remain
der **Bleistift, –(e)s, –e** pencil
blenden dazzle, blind
der **Blick, –(e)s, –e** glance, view, look; **blicken** look
blind blind
blitzen flash, sparkle
blöken bleat
bloß mere(ly), only; bare
das **Blümchen, –s, —** little flower
die **Blume, –n** flower
die **Bluse, –n** blouse
das **Blut, –(e)s** blood; **bluten** bleed
der **Boden, –s, ⸚** ground, soil, bottom
der **Bodensee, –s** Lake Constance
der **Bogen, –s,** (*plur.*) — *or* ⸚ arc, arch
die **Bombe, –n** bomb
(das) **Bonn, –s** *capital of West Germany*
borniert′ narrow-minded; stupid
böse bad, mean, angry, evil
bota′nisch botanical
das **Bourgeoisie′regiment′, –s** rule of the middle class
der **Braten, –s, —** roast (*meat*); **braten (brät), briet, gebraten** roast, fry
der **Bratschist′, –en, –en** viola player
brauchen need
braun brown

brausen take a shower
brav good, well-behaved
brechen (bricht), brach, gebrochen break
breit broad
bremsen brake, put on the brakes
brennen, brannte, gebrannt burn
die **Brezel, –n** pretzel
(das) **Bridge** (*cards*) bridge
der **Brief, –(e)s, –e** letter
die **Brille, –n** spectacles, pair of glasses
bringen, brachte, gebracht bring
das **Brot, –(e)s, –e** bread
die **Brücke, –n** bridge; die **Mühlenbrücke** mill bridge
der **Bruder, –s, ⸚** brother
brüllen shout, scream
die **Brust, ⸚e** breast, chest
das **Buch, –(e)s, ⸚er** book; der **Bücherschrank, –(e)s, ⸚e** bookcase; das **Büchlein, –s, —** little book, booklet
die **Bühne, –n** stage
bürgen vouch for
die **Bürgerschule, –n** high school
der **Büro′raum, –(e)s, ⸚e** office
der **Bursche, –n, –n** fellow
die **Buße, –n** fine
die **Butter** butter; das **Butterbrot, –(e)s, –e** buttered bread

C

ca. = **cirka** approximately
der **Cellist′, –en, –en** cellist
charakteris′tisch characteristic
der **Chef, –s, –s** boss
die **Chemie′** chemistry; der **Chemiker, –s, —** chemist; die **Chemikerin, –nen** chemist (*fem.*)
chine′sisch Chinese; (das) **Chine′sisch, –en** Chinese (*language*)
chronisch chronic
chronolo′gisch chronological
das **Coupé, –s, –s** compartment (RR)

D

da (*sub. conj.*) when, since (*causal*); as (*temp. or causal*); (*adv.*) here, there; then
dabei′ in this, thereby, in doing that, at this, at the same time; **mit dabei sein** be present
da-bleiben, blieb da, ist dageblieben stay (here, there)
das **Dach, –(e)s, ⸚er** roof; das **Dachgeschoß, –schosses, –schosse** top floor; die **Dachstube, –n** garret, attic
dadurch thereby
dafür for it (that, this, them)
dage′gen on the other hand, by comparison, on the contrary; **etwas dage′gen haben** object to something
daher′ therefore
dahin′ to that place, there (*w. verbs of motion*); **bis dahin** up to this (that) point
dahin′ter behind it (them)
da-lassen (läßt da), ließ da, dagelassen leave (here *or* there)
damals at that time, then
die **Dame, –n** lady
damit′ (*sub. conj. and adv.*) in order that, with it (them)
dämmern grow dark (*or* light)
der **Dämon, –s,** (*plur.*) **Dämo′nen** demon
der **Dampfer, –s, —** steamer
danach′ according to it, after this (that), afterwards
dane′ben-gehen, ging daneben, ist danebengegangen miss (*a target*)
(das) **Dänemark, –s** Denmark
der **Dank, –(e)s** gratitude; **Danke!** *or* **Danke schön!** Thank you; **danken** (*with dat.*) thank
dann then
daran′ in that, on that, near it
darauf′ upon it (that *or* them), afterwards; **daraufhin′** thereupon; **darauf-kommen** hit upon something, come upon an idea, occur
daraus′ out of it (that *or* them)
dar-stellen represent, display; die **Darstellung, –en** representation, performance
darü′ber about it (*or* this), over it (*or* this); **Darüber komme ich nicht hinaus.** Beyond this I cannot go.
darum′ therefore
darun′ter among them
das (*indeclinable demonst. pron.*) that, those
das (die, das, der) (*see* **der**)
daß (*sub. conj.*) that
dassel′be the same
der **Dativ, –s, –e** dative
das **Datum, –s,** (*plur.*) **Daten** date
die **Dauer** duration; **von Dauer sein** be of lasting effect; **dauern** last; **dauernd** lasting; die **Dauerwelle, –n** permanent wave
der **Daumen, –s, —** thumb
davon′ about it (them), from it, of it
davon′-laufen (läuft davon), lief davon, ist davongelaufen run away
dazu′ in addition, besides, for that purpose; to it (that *or* this)
debattie′ren debate
das **Debüt′, –s, –s** debut
die **Decke, –n** ceiling; cover, blanket; **decken** cover; **Der Tisch ist gedeckt.** The table is set; der **Deckname, –ns, –n** disguise, cloak, "blind," decoy
definitiv′ definitive
dein (–e, —, —) your (*fam. sing.*)
die **Delegation′, –en** delegation
dem: dem ist nicht so that's not the case
demgemäß accordingly

demokra'tisch democratic
demzufolge according(ly)
denen (*rel., demonst. pron. dat.*) whom; them
denken, dachte, gedacht think; der **Denker, –s, —** thinker
denn for (= because); *also used to emphasize a question, e.g.:* **Warum arbeitest du denn so viel?** Why in the world are you working so much?
dennoch nevertheless, however
der (die, das, der) (*def. art.; rel. pron.; demonst. pron.*) the; who, which; that, he, she, it, *etc.*
derartig (–e, –es, –er) such
deren (*rel. pron., fem., gen. sing.; also gen. plur. any gender*) whose
derjenige, der he who
dersel'be the same
deshalb therefore, for that reason
dessen (*rel. pron., masc. and neut., gen. sing.*) whose
deswegen therefore, for that reason
der **Detektiv', –s, –e** detective
deuten point (to), explain, interpret
deutlich clear, distinct
deutsch German; (das) **Deutsch, –en** German (*language*); **Er kann Deutsch.** He knows German; **auf deutsch** in German; der **Deutsche, –n, –n** German man; die **Deutsche, –n, –n** German woman; **im Deutschen** in (the) German (language); (das) **Deutschland, –s** Germany
das **Devi'sengesetz, –es, –e** law regulating the exchange of foreign currency
der **Dezem'ber, –s** December
die **Diatomée, –n** diàtom, microscopic algae
dicht dense, thick
der **Dichter, –s, —** poet; die **Dichtung, –en** poetry, fiction
dick thick, fat
die (*see* **der**)
der **Dieb, –es, –e** thief
diejenigen (*plur.*) those
der **Diener, –s, —** servant
der **Dienstag, –s, –e** Tuesday
dienstbar serviceable
dies (*indeclinable demonst.*) this, these
dies (–e, –es, –er) this
diesbezüg'lich in this respect
diesel'be the same
diesmal this time
diesseits (*prep. gen.*) on this side of
die **Diktatur', –en** dictatorship
die **Dimission', –en** dismissal, discharge
das **Ding, –(e)s, –e** thing
der **Diplomat', –en, –en** diplomat
der **Dirigent', –en, –en** conductor
die **Diskussion', –en** discussion
die **Distel, –n** thistle
DM = Deutsche Mark mark (*about 25 cents*)

doch (*coord. conj.; adv.*) but, though, however, nevertheless; after all; **Oh doch!** surely, certainly
der **Doktor, –s,** (*plur.*) **Dokto'ren** doctor; die **Dokto'rin, –nen** doctor (*fem.*)
die **Doktrin', –en** doctrine
das **Dokument', –(e)s, –e** document
der **Dolch, –(e)s, –e** dagger
der **Dom, –(e)s, –e** cathedral; dome
der **Donner, –s** thunder; **donnern** thunder
der **Donnerstag, –s, –e** Thursday
Donnerwetter! (Thunderation!) Hang it all!
das **Dorf, –(e)s, ⸚er** village; der **Dorfplatz, –es, ⸚e** village square; der **Dorfschullehrer, –s, —** village schoolmaster
der **Dorn, –(e)s, –en** thorn
dort there; **dort und dort** over there; **dorthin** to that place, there (*w. verbs of motion*)
das **Drahtseil, –(e)s, –e** cable
das **Drama, –s,** (*plur.*) **Dramen** drama; der **Drama'tiker, –s, —** dramatist
der **Drang, –es** urge, pressure; **drängen** press, crowd
draus = daraus out of it *or* them
draußen outside
drehen turn
drei three
dreizehn thirteen
Dresden, –s *city in Saxony*
dringlich urgent(ly)
dritt (–e, –es, –er) third; das **Drittel, –s, —** the third
droben up there, above
die **Drogerie', –n** pharmacy, drugstore
drohen threaten
dröhnen roar, thunder
drüben yonder, on the other side, over there
der **Druck, –es, –e** pressure, print; **drucken** print
drücken press, squeeze
drum (= darum) therefore
du (*pers. pron.*) (*acc.* **dich,** *dat.* **dir,** *gen.* **deiner**) you (*sing. fam.*)
der **Dudelsack, –s, ⸚e** bagpipe
dulden suffer (patiently), tolerate; der **Duldende, –n, –n** suffering *or* patient person
dumm stupid; die **Dummheit, –en** stupidity; der **Dummkopf, –(e)s, ⸚e** blockhead
dumpf dull, listless, musty, stifling, heavy
dunkel dark; **Es dunkelt.** It is growing dark; **im Dunkeln** in the dark
dunkelgrau dark grey
dünn thin
durch (*prep. with acc.*) through, by, with, by means of
durchbre'chen (durchbricht), durchbrach, durchbrochen (*also separable:* **durchbrechen,** *etc.*) break through; der **Durchbruch, –(e)s, ⸚e** break-through; **zum**

Durchbruch kommen become manifest, appear
durchgehend pervasive
durchgeis'tigt intelligent
durch-hauen give a thrashing
durch-machen undergo
durch-reißen, riß durch, durchgerissen tear up
durchs = **durch das**
durchschau'en penetrate, understand, see through
durchschnittlich on the average
durchsu'chen search thoroughly
der **Durchzug, –(e)s** draft (*of air*)
dürfen (darf), durfte, gedurft be allowed to, be permitted to; **dürfen + nicht** must not
der **Durst, –(e)s** thirst; **dürsten** be thirsty
das **Düsenflugzeug, –(e)s, –e** jet plane
düster dark, mournful
das **Dutzend, –s, –e** dozen
der **D-Zug** (= **Durchgangszug**), **–es, ⁻̈e** through(way) train

E

eben just (*used to intensify a statement*); simply; just now; you see; (*adj.*) level, even; **eben darum** for that reason
die **Ebene, –n** plain
ebenfalls likewise
ebenso likewise; **ebenso . . . wie** just as . . . as
das **Echo, –s, –s** echo
die **Ecke, –n** corner, edge
edel noble; die **Edelfrau, –en** noble lady
ehe (*sub. conj.*) before
der **Ehemann, –(e)s, ⁻̈er** married man, husband; das **Ehepaar, –(e)s, –e** married couple
der **Ehrgeiz, –es** ambition
ehrlich honest
das **Ei, –s, –er** egg; der **Eierkuchen, –s, —** omelet
eifersüchtig jealous
eifrig excited(ly), eager(ly)
eigen own
eigenartig unique, strange, odd
eigensinnig stubborn
eigentlich actually, really
das **Eigentum, –s, ⁻̈er** property
der **Eigenwert, –es, –e** value of its own, intrinsic value
sich eignen (zu) be fit *or* suited (for)
eilen (sein) hurry
das **Eiltempo, –s, –s** great speed
ein (–e, —, —) (*indef. art.*) a, an; one
einan'der one another
ein-bringen, brachte ein, eingebracht bring in
ein-büßen lose, forfeit
eindeutig clear, unequivocal(ly)
die **Eindringlichkeit** insistence, urgency; penetration, impressiveness
der **Eindringling, –s, –e** intruder, invader
der **Eindruck, –s, ⁻̈e** impression
einerlei one and the same, all the same
einfach simple, simply
ein-fallen (fällt ein), fiel ein, ist eingefallen (*dat.*) occur
der **Einfluß, –flusses, –flüsse** influence
der **Eingang, –(e)s, ⁻̈e** entrance; die **Eingangsstelle, –n** take-off point, entrance point; **ein-gehen, ging ein, ist eingegangen (auf)** go into *or* enter into the spirit of
ein-gestehen, gestand ein, eingestanden confess
der **Einheimische, –n, –n** native
die **Einheit, –en** unit, unity; **einheitlich** uniform
ein-holen catch up with
einig united
einige some, few
sich einigen agree
einigermaßen rather, somewhat
ein-laden (lädt ein), lud ein, eingeladen invite
sich ein-lassen auf (läßt ein), ließ ein, eingelassen engage in, enter into
ein-liefern deliver, bring in
einmal (= **ein + Mal**) one time; once; **auf einmal** suddenly; **noch einmal** once more; **Das ist nun einmal so.** It just happens to be that way.
ein-nehmen (nimmt ein), nahm ein, eingenommen occupy
ein-packen pack up
eins one (*cardinal numeral*)
einsam alone, lonely, lonesome
ein-schlafen (schläft ein), schlief ein, ist eingeschlafen fall asleep
ein-sehen (sieht ein), sah ein, eingesehen realize, understand
ein-sperren lock up
einst at one time, some time ago, once (upon a time), some day
ein-steigen, stieg ein, ist eingestiegen enter, board (*a train, bus, etc.*)
die **Einstellung** cessation
die **Einstiegstelle, –n** take-off point
einstig former
ein-treffen (trifft ein), traf ein, ist eingetroffen arrive
ein-treten (tritt ein), trat ein, ist eingetreten enter
einundzwanzig twenty-one
einwandfrei without any doubt; unobjectionable
der **Einwohner, –s, —** inhabitant
die **Einzahl** singular
einzeln single, individual
ein-ziehen, zog ein, eingezogen draft; pull in; arrest

einzig only, single, unique
einzigartig unique (of its kind); die **Einzigartigkeit** uniqueness
das **Eis, –es,** ice; ice cream; der **Eisbrecher, –s, —** icebreaker; das **Eisgefilde, –s, —** ice field; **eisig** icy; **eiskalt** ice-cold; die **Eisnacht, ¨–e** icy cold night; die **Eiszeit, –en** Ice Age
das **Eisen, –s** iron; iron tools
die **Ei′senbahngesell′schaft, –en** railroad company
die **Ei′senbahnverbin′dung, –en** train connection
eisern iron
elas′tisch elastic, agile
der **Elefant′, –en, –en** elephant
elegant′ elegant
elend miserable; das **Elend, –s** misery
elf eleven
der **Ellbogen, –s, —** elbow
die **Eltern** (*plur. noun*) parents
empfan′gen (empfängt), empfing, empfangen receive, welcome
empfeh′len (empfiehlt), empfahl, empfohlen recommend
empfin′den, empfand, empfunden experience; feel; **empfind′lich** sensitive, irritable; sharp
das **Ende, –s, –n** end; **am Ende** finally, in the end; **enden** end; **endlich** finally; das **Endliche, –n** finite
eng narrow, close
engagiert′ engaged, involved
der **Engländer, –s, —** Englishman; die **Engländerin, –nen** English woman; **englisch** English (*adj.*); (das) **Englisch, –en** English (*language*)
entde′cken discover; die **Entde′ckung, –en** discovery
entfer′nen take away, remove; **sich entfernen** withdraw
entflie′hen, entfloh, ist entflohen (*with dat.*) flee, escape
entge′gen-nehmen (nimmt entgegen), nahm entgegen, entgegengenommen receive, accept
entge′gen-setzen oppose
entge′hen, entging, ist entgangen (*with dat.*) escape
enthal′ten (enthält), enthielt, enthalten hold, contain; house; **sich enthalten** (*with gen.*) abstain
entlas′sen (entläßt), entließ, entlassen release, dismiss
entlaust′ deloused
entle′gen distant, removed, remote
entleh′nen (*dat.*) borrow, take from; die **Entleh′nung, –en** borrowing
entneh′men (entnimmt), entnahm, entnommen (*with dat.*) take from *or* away
der **Entomolog′(e), –en, –en** entomologist
entrin′nen, entrann, ist entronnen (*with dat.*) escape
(sich) entschei′den, entschied, entschieden decide; settle; **entschie′den** (*adj.*) definite, radical, decisive
sich entschlie′ßen, entschloß, entschlossen (zu) decide (in favor of *or* upon)
entschlos′sen (*adj.*) resolute
entschul′digen excuse, pardon; die **Entschul′digung, –en** excuse, pardon
das **Entset′zen, –s** terror
entspre′chen (entspricht), entsprach, entsprochen (*with dat.*) correspond; die **Entspre′chung, –en** correspondency
entste′hen, entstand, ist entstanden arise, originate
entwei′chen, entwich, ist entwichen (*with dat.*) escape
entwen′den take away, steal
die **Entwick′lung, –en** development; **entwik′keln** unfold, develop
entzü′cken delight
entzü′geln unchain
die **Epo′che, –n** period
er (*acc.* **ihn,** *dat.* **ihm,** *gen.* **seiner**) he, it
erbeu′ten capture, gain as booty
erbli′cken see, catch sight of
erbrin′gen, erbrachte, erbracht furnish (*proof*)
die **Erbschaft, –en** inheritance, legacy
die **Erbse, –n** pea
die **Erde, –n** earth; ground; der **Erdteil, –(e)s, –e** continent
erden′ken, erdachte, erdacht imagine, invent
das **Ereig′nis, –ses, –se** event
erfah′ren (erfährt), erfuhr, erfahren experience; **erfahren** (*adj.*) experienced; die **Erfah′rung, –en** experience
erfin′den, erfand, erfunden invent, create
der **Erfolg′, –(e)s, –e** success; **erfolg′reich** successful
erfreu′en delight; **erfreut′** pleased
die **Erfrie′rung, –en** frostbite; **leichte Erfrie′rungen** minor frostbites
erfül′len fill up; fulfill, accomplish
(sich) erge′ben (ergibt), ergab, ergeben surrender; result, happen; **erge′ben** (*adj.*) devoted, humble; das **Ergeb′nis, –ses, –se** result
das **Ergöt′zen, –s** delight; **ergöt′zen** delight
ergrei′fen, ergriff, ergriffen seize; comprehend
erhal′ten (erhält), erhielt, erhalten receive, get; preserve; maintain
erhält′lich available
(sich) erhe′ben, erhob, erhoben rise, raise oneself; **erhoben** raised
erhö′hen raise, increase
sich erho′len recover
erin′nern: (jemanden) an (etwas) (*acc.*) **erin-**

nern remind (someone) of (something); **sich erin′nern an (etwas)** (*acc.*) remember (something)
sich erkäl′ten catch a cold
erken′nen, erkannte, erkannt recognize, realize, know; die **Erkennt′nis, –se** knowledge, perception, realization
erklä′ren declare, explain; **für tot erklä′ren lassen** have officially declared dead; die **Erklä′rung, –en** explanation; **erklär′lich** explainable, evident
erklin′gen, erklang, ist erklungen sound, resound
erlan′gen reach, attain
erlau′ben permit, allow
erle′ben experience; das **Erleb′nis, –ses, –se** experience
erle′digen finish, complete, settle
erleuch′ten illuminate
erlö′schen (erlischt), erlosch, ist erloschen be extinguished, die out
ermes′sen (ermißt), ermaß, ermessen estimate, judge, calculate
ermü′den tire, exhaust
erneut′ again
ernst serious; der **Ernst, –es** seriousness
die **Ernte, –n** harvest; **ernten** harvest
ero′bern conquer, win; die **Ero′berung, –en** conquest
erre′gen excite
errei′chen reach, bring about
ersau′fen (ersäuft), ersoff, ist ersoffen drown, be drowned
ersäu′fen (*weak*) submerge, flood, drown
erschaf′fen, erschuf, erschaffen create, produce
erschei′nen, erschien, ist erschienen appear; die **Erschei′nung, –en** phenomenon, apparition
erschöp′fend exhaustive; **erschöpft′** exhausted
erschre′cken (erschrickt), erschrak, ist erschrocken be frightened; **erschreck′lich** terrific, terrible, dreadful
erschüt′tern move deeply
erse′hen (ersieht), ersah, ersehen see, learn
erspa′ren spare, save
erst first, not until, only; **erst recht** all the more, really; der **erste** the first; der **erstere** the former
die **Erstaufführung, –en** première
erstau′nen astonish; **in Erstau′nen setzen** astonish; **erstaun′lich** astonishing
erster′ben (erstirbt), erstarb, ist erstorben die, die away
ersti′cken (sein) suffocate
sich erstre′cken extend, reach
(sich) erträn′ken drown (oneself)
erwa′chen wake up
erwä′gen, erwog, erwogen consider
erwar′ten expect; die **Erwar′tung, –en** expectation
erwer′ben (erwirbt), erwarb, erworben acquire
erwi′dern reply, answer
erwi′schen catch, trap
erzäh′len tell, narrate, ("recount"); der **Erzäh′ler, –s, —** narrator, writer; die **Erzäh′lung, –en** narration
der **Erzbischof, –s, ⸚e** archbishop
erzeu′gen cause, create, beget; produce
erzie′herisch didactic, pedagogical, educational
erzie′len achieve, obtain, arrive at
erzo′gen well-bred
es (*pers. pron.*) (*acc.* **es**, *dat.* **ihm**, *gen.* **seiner**) it
der **Esel, –s, —** donkey, jackass
das **Essen, –s, —** food, meal; **essen (ißt), aß, gegessen** eat; **zu Abend essen** have dinner; **zu Mittag essen** have lunch
estnisch Estonian
etwa maybe, about, approximately; by any chance
etwas something, somewhat, some; **etwas anderes** something else; **so etwas** a thing like this (*or* that)
euer (–e, —, —) your (*plur. fam.*)
(das) **Euro′pa, –s** Europe
ewig eternal; die **Ewigkeit** eternity
die **Existenz′, –en** existence
die **Expedition′, –en** expedition
expressionis′tisch expressionist(ic)

F

die **Fabrik′arbeiterin, –nen** factory worker (*fem.*)
das **Fagott′, –(e)s, –e** bassoon; der **Fagottist′, –en, –en** bassoonist
die **Fähigkeit, –en** ability, capability
fahren (fährt), fuhr, ist gefahren go, travel, ride, drive
die **Fahrkarte, –n** ticket
der **Fahrschacht, –(e)s, ⸚e** elevator shaft; der **Fahrstuhl, –s, ⸚e** elevator; das **Fahrstuhlgehäuse, –s, —** elevator cage
die **Fahrt, –en** trip; der **Fahrtausweis, –es, –e** ticket (*for travel*)
der **Fall, –es, ⸚e** case; fall
die **Falle, –n** trap; **in der Falle sein** be trapped
fallen (fällt), fiel, ist gefallen fall; die
falsch wrong, false
falten fold
die **Fami′lie, –n** family
fangen (fängt), fing, gefangen catch; die **Fangvorrichtung, –en** safety catch
die **Farbe, –n** color; **farblos** colorless; der **Farbton, –(e)s, ⸚e** shade
fassen, faßte, gefaßt grasp, seize, fathom
fast almost

faul lazy
die **Faust, ⸚e** fist
der **Februar,** –s February
die **Feder,** –n pen
fehlen miss, fail, be lacking; **Ihm fehlt nichts.** Nothing is wrong with him.
der **Fehler, –s,** — mistake, error
der **Feierabend,** –s, –e rest period (*after work*)
der **Feigling,** –s, –e coward
fein fine, elegant, fashionable
der **Feind,** –es, –e enemy; die **Feindschaft,** –en hostility
das **Feld,** –es, –er field
die **Feldbahn,** –en military train (R.R.)
das **Fell,** –(e)s, –e skin, fur
der **Fels,** –ens, –en rock; das **Felsenriff,** –(e)s, –e rocky reef
das **Fenster,** –s, — window
die **Ferien** (*plur. only*) vacation
fern distant; die **Ferne,** –n distance
fertig ready
fesseln attract; chain, captivate
fest fixed, firm
(sich) festhalten (hält fest), hielt fest, festgehalten hold firmly to, hold on to
das **Festland,** –es mainland, continent
das **Festpiel,** –(e)s, –e festival (play); die **Festspielzeit,** –en festival (play) season
fest-stellen notice; establish, ascertain; observe; die **Feststellung,** –en observation
das **Fett,** –es, –e fat, grease; der **Fettfleck,** –(e)s, –en grease spot
feucht moist; die **Feuchtigkeit** moisture
das **Feuer,** –s, — fire; das **Feuerzeug,** –(e)s, –e (cigarette) lighter
die **Figur',** –en figure
der **Film,** –(e)s, –e movie, motion picture
das **Fina'le,** –s, –s finale
finden, fand, gefunden find; **Wie finden Sie . . .?** How do you like . . .? **jemanden hübsch finden** think *or* consider someone to be pretty
der **Finger,** –s, — finger; der **Fingernagel,** –s, ⸚ fingernail
finnisch Finnish; **fin'noug'risch** Finno-Ugric; die **finnougrische Gruppe** Finno-Ugric group
finster dark; die **Finsternis,** –se darkness
der **Fisch,** –es, –e fish; **fischen gehen** go fishing; das **Fischen,** –s fishing
(das) **Fis-moll,** –s F sharp minor
flach flat
die **Flasche,** –n bottle
flatterhaft unstable, flirtatious, fickle
flattern flutter; **auf-flattern** flutter up
der **Fleck,** –(e)s, –en spot; der **Fettfleck** grease spot
das **Fleisch,** –es flesh, meat
der **Fleiß,** –es diligence, industry; **fleißig** industrious, diligent, hard-working
fliegen, flog, ist geflogen fly; der **Flieger, –s,** — pilot, flyer, airman
fliehen, floh, ist geflohen flee, escape
fließen, floß, ist geflossen flow
flott quick; gay
der **Fluch,** –(e)s, ⸚e curse
flüchtig fleeting
der **Fluchtversuch,** –(e)s, –e escape attempt
der **Flügel,** –s, — wing; das **Flüglein,** –s, — little wing
der **Flughafen,** –s, ⸚ airport
das **Flugzeug,** –(e)s, –e airplane
die **Flur,** –en meadow
der **Fluß, Flusses, Flüsse** river, stream
flüstern whisper
die **Flut,** –en flood, the waters
die **Fö'deration',** –en federation
die **Föhre,** –n fir (tree)
die **Folge,** –n consequence, result
folgen (*dat.*) obey; **(sein)** follow; **folgend–** following
die **Folgerung,** –en conclusion
folglich consequently
fordern demand
die **Forel'le,** –n trout; der **Forel'lenbach,** –es, ⸚e trout brook
die **Form,** –en form; **formell'** formal; **förmlich** formal, really
der **Forscher,** –s, — researcher, scholar, scientific investigator; die **Forschung,** –en research
fort away, gone
fortan' hereafter, henceforth
fort-gehen, ging fort, ist fortgegangen go away
der **Fortschritt,** –(e)s, –e progress
fortwährend continuously
fortwirken continue to have effect
der **Frack,** –s, ⸚e *or* –s dinner jacket
die **Frage,** –n question; **jemandem eine Frage stellen** ask someone a question; der **Fragebogen,** –s, — *or* ⸚ questionnaire; **fragen** ask (a question)
(das) **Franken,** –s Franconia
(das) **Frankreich,** –s France
die **Franziska'nerkirche** Franciscan Church
der **Franzo'se,** –n, –n Frenchman; (das) **Franzö'sisch,** –en French (*language*); **franzö'sisch** (*adj.*) French
die **Frau,** –en woman, Mrs., wife, lady
das **Fräulein,** –s, — young lady, Miss
frei free; die **Freiheit,** –en liberty, freedom; die **Freistunde,** –n rest period
(das) **Freilas'sing,** –s *town in Bavaria*
freilich to be sure, certainly
der **Freispruch,** –(e)s, ⸚e acquittal
frei-stellen allow
der **Freitag,** –(e)s, –e Friday
die **Freizeit,** –en free time, leisure
fremd strange, alien, alienating, foreign; der

Fremde, –n, –n foreigner, foreign visitor, stranger; der **Fremdenführer, –s, —** guide; die **Fremdsprache, –n** foreign language
fressen (frißt), fraß, gefressen eat (*of animals*), devour
die **Freude, –n** joy, happiness; **freudig** joyful; (**sich**) **freuen** be glad; **sich freuen auf** look forward to
der **Freund, –es, –e** friend; die **Freundin, –nen** friend (*fem.*), girl friend; **freundlich** friendly; die **Freundlichkeit, –en** friendliness; die **Freundschaft, –en** friendship
der **Friede(n), –ns** peace; **jemanden in Frieden lassen** leave someone alone; der **Friedensvertrag, –(e)s, ⸚e** peace treaty
frieren, fror, (ist) gefroren freeze; **Es friert uns.** We are freezing.
der **Friseur′, –(e)s, –e** barber
der **Frohsinn, –(e)s** cheerfulness
frönen indulge
die **Front, –en** front, frontline
die **Frucht, ⸚e** fruit; der **Fruchtsaft, –(e)s, ⸚e** fruit juice
früh early; **früher** earlier, formerly
der **Frühling, –s, –e** spring
das **Frühstück, –s, –e** breakfast; **frühstücken** have breakfast
fügen join
fühlen feel
führen lead, manage, run, support; **ein Tagebuch führen** keep a diary
der **Führer, –s, —** leader; der **Führerschein, –s, –e** driver's license
die **Fülle** fullness, plenty
der **Fund, –es, –e** finding, discovery
fünf five
fünfzehn fifteen
fünfzig fifty
der **Funke, –ns, –n** spark; **funkeln** sparkle
die **Funktion′, –en** function
für (*prep. acc.*) for, on behalf of
die **Furcht** fear; **furchtbar** terrible, terrifying; **fürchten** fear; **sich fürchten** (**vor** *with dat.*) be afraid (of); **fürchterlich** terrible, awful
das **Furo′re, –s** sensation
fürs = für das
der **Fürsprecher, –s, —** spokesman, advocate
der **Fürst, –en, –en** prince; **geistliche Fürsten** church dignitaries
der **Fuß, –es, ⸚e** foot; der **Fußboden, –s, —** *or* ⸚ floor; das **Fußende, –s, –n** foot end, lower end

G

die **Gabe, –n** gift
die **Gabel, –n** fork
die **Galerie′, –n** gallery
der **Gang, –(e)s, ⸚e** corridor, gangway; gait; course; passage
ganz whole, entire, quite, completely; **ganz unten** away at the bottom; das **Ganze, –n, –n** the whole; **gänzlich** completely
gar even, quite, perhaps, at all
die **Gardi′ne, –n** curtain; das **Gardi′nenfeuer, –s** curtain fire
der **Garten, –s, ⸚** garden
die **Gasse, –n** narrow street
der **Gast, –(e)s, ⸚e** guest; der **Gastgeber, –s, —** host; **gastlich** convivial, hospitable
das **Gebäck′, –(e)s** pastry
gebä′ren (gebiert), gebar, geboren give birth to
das **Gebäu′de, –s, —** building
geben (gibt), gab, gegeben give; **es gibt** there is, there are
das **Gebiet′, –(e)s, –e** field, territory, region, district, area
das **Gebir′ge, –s, —** (chain of) mountains
gebo′ren born
der **Gebrauch′, –(e)s, ⸚e** custom, use
das **Gebrüll′, –(e)s** roaring
die **Geburt′, –en** birth; **gebür′tig** born; der **Geburts′ort, –(e)s, –e** birthplace; der **Geburts′tag, –(e)s, –e** birthday
gedämpft′ subdued, muted
der **Gedan′ke, –ns, –n** thought, idea; der **Gedan′kenaustausch, –(e)s** exchange of ideas; **gedank′lich** intellectual
die **Gedenk′tafel, –n** memorial
das **Gedicht′, –(e)s, –e** poem; der **Gedicht′band, –(e)s, ⸚e** volume of poetry
die **Geduld′** patience; **gedul′dig** patient
geeig′net suitable
die **Gefahr′, –en** danger; **gefähr′lich** dangerous
gefal′len (gefällt), gefiel, gefallen (*dat.*) please; **Es gefällt mir.** I like it.
die **Gefal′lenen** (*plur.*) fallen soldiers, the dead
der **Gefan′gene, –n, –n** captive, prisoner; die **Gefan′genschaft** captivity, imprisonment; **in Gefangenschaft geraten (sein)** be captured; das **Gefäng′nis, –ses, –se** prison; die **Gefäng′nisstrafe, –n** penalty of imprisonment
gefaßt′ composed, calm
das **Geflü′gel, –s** fowl, poultry
das **Gefü′ge, –s** structure
das **Gefühl′, –(e)s, –e** feeling
gegen (*prep. acc.*) against, toward; about; **gegen 9 Uhr** about 9 o'clock
die **Gegend, –en** region, district
gegeneinander toward (*or* against) each other
der **Gegenstand, –(e)s, ⸚e** object
gegenü′ber (*postpositive prep. dat.*) opposite, facing
gegenwärtig (at) present
das **Gehalt′, –es, ⸚er** salary
geheim′ secret; das **Geheim′nis, –ses, –se** secret, secrecy
gehen, ging, ist gegangen go; **Wie geht es Ihnen?** How are you? **Es geht mir gut.** I am fine (well); **es geht um** it is a matter

of; **Es geht darum, ob . . .** It is a question whether . . .
das **Gehirn′, –(e)s, –e** brain
das **Gehör′, –(e)s** hearing, ear; attention
gehor′chen (*dat.*) obey
gehö′ren (*dat.*) belong to
das **Gehör′te, –n** that which is heard
der **Geiger, –s, —** violinist, fiddler
die **Geiß, –en** goat
der **Geist, (–e)s, –er** spirit, mind, intellect; **geisteskräftig** with an active mind
geistlich: geistliche Fürsten church dignitaries
das **Geklap′per, –s** clicking, rattling
gelähmt′ paralyzed
das **Gelän′der, –s, —** banister
gelas′sen calm
gelb yellow
das **Geld, –es, –er** money; die **Geldarmut** poverty, indigence; der **Geldmangel, –s, ⸚** lack of money
gele′gen opportune; die **Gele′genheit, –en** opportunity, occasion
gele′gentlich occasionally
der **Gelehr′te, –n, –n** scholar
die **Gelieb′te, –n, –n** beloved
gelin′gen, gelang, ist gelungen (*dat.*) succeed; **Es gelang ihm.** He succeeded in it.
gelten (gilt) galt, gegolten be true of; be worth; concern; **gelten für** apply to
gemein′ common, mean, vulgar
die **Gemein′de, –n** community
gemein′sam in common, together
das **Gemü′se, –s, —** vegetable; die **Gemü′sesuppe, –n** vegetable soup
genau′ precise, exact; **genau genommen** taken precisely, strictly speaking; **genau treffen** guess right
gene′sen, genas, ist genesen recover (*from sickness*); die **Gene′sung** convalescence, recovery
(das) **Genf, –s** Geneva
das **Genie′, –s, –s** genius
genie′ßen, genoß, genossen enjoy
der **Genitiv** (*or* **Genetiv**), **–s, –e** genitive
genug′ enough; die **Genug′tuung** satisfaction
der **Genuß′, –nusses, –nüsse** enjoyment
die **Geographie′** geography
der **Geolog′(e), –en, –en** geologist; die **Geologie′** geology
gera′de straight, even; just
gera′ten (gerät), geriet, ist geraten get into, fall into
geraum′ spacious, ample; **geraume Zeit** for a long time
die **Gerech′tigkeit** justice; das **Gerech′tigkeitsgefühl′, –s** sense of justice
das **Gere′de, –s** talk
das **Gericht′, –(e)s, –e** court, judgment
gern(e), lieber, liebst– gladly; **gern haben** like; **lieber haben** prefer; **am liebsten haben** like best; **gern tun** like to do
das **Gerücht′, –(e)s, –e** rumor
gerührt′ touched, moved
gesamt′ entire; **in ihrer Gesamt′heit** taken together
der **Gesang′, –(e)s, ⸚e** singing, song
das **Geschäft′, –(e)s, –e** shop, business, store; der **Geschäfts′mann, –(e)s,** (*plur.*) **–leute** business man; die **Geschäfts′reise, –n** business trip
gesche′hen (geschieht), geschah, ist geschehen happen
gescheit′ intelligent, clever, bright, sensible
geschei′telt parted (*of hair*)
das **Geschenk′, –(e)s, –e** gift, present
die **Geschich′te, –n** story; history; der **Geschichts′kurs, –es, –e** history course
das **Geschick′, –(e)s, –e** skill, dexterity; fate, destiny
die **Geschick′lichkeit, –en** skill, dexterity
das **Geschirr′, –s, –e** crockery, pots and pans, china, tools
das **Geschlecht′, –(e)s, –er** generation; sex
geschlos′sen closed
das **Geschmei′de, –s, —** jewels
geschützt′ vor (*dat.*) protected from
geschwät′zig garrulous
die **Geschwis′ter** (*plur.*) brother(s) and sister(s)
der **Gesel′le, –n, –n** companion, fellow
die **Gesell′schaft, –en** party, society, company; **gesell′schaftlich** social
das **Gesicht′, –(e)s, –er** face
das **Gespräch′, –s, –e** conversation, talk
gespren′kelt dappled
die **Gestalt′, –en** figure, shape; **gestal′ten** shape, mould
das **Gestampf′, –(e)s** stamping
das **Geständ′nis, –ses, –se** confession
geste′hen, gestand, gestanden confess, admit
gestern yesterday; **gestern abend** last night
das **Gesträuch′, –s** underbrush
gesund′ sound, healthy; die **Gesund′heit** health
getreu′ faithful
gewagt′ risky, dangerous
gewal′tig powerful, huge
gewalt′sam violent, vigorous, vehement
das **Gewehr′, –s, –e** gun, rifle
gewin′nen, gewann, gewonnen win
gewiß′ certain(ly); die **Gewiß′heit** certainty
das **Gewit′ter, –s, —** thunderstorm, storm
die **Gewo′genheit** favorable inclination, favor
die **Gewohn′heit, –en** custom; **gewöhn′lich** common, ordinary, usual; vulgar; **gewohnt′** accustomed
das **Gift, –es, –e** poison

gigan'tisch gigantic
der **Gipfel, –s, —** top, peak
glänzen glisten, shine, sparkle; **glänzend** shiny, brilliant, glistening
das **Glas, –es, ¨–er** glass, spyglass
glatt smooth, sheer
glauben (+ **an** *with acc.*) believe (in); der **Glaube, –ns** belief, faith
gleich immediately; equal to, like; **Das ist mir gleich.** It is all the same to me; **gleichblökend** bleating in unison; **gleichfalls** likewise; **gleichgeschoren** uniformly shorn; **gleichgültig** indifferent, immaterial
gleichen, glich, geglichen liken, resemble
gleichsam as it were, so to speak
gleiten, glitt, ist geglitten glide; **vorü'bergleiten** glide past
das **Glied, –(e)s, –er** limb (*of the body*), member
glimmen, glomm, geglommen glimmer
das **Glockenspiel, –(e)s, –e** chimes, carillon
das **Glück, –es** luck, happiness; **glücklich** happy; **glück'licherwei'se** fortunately
die **Glut, –en** glow
das **Gold, –es** gold; **golden** golden
(das) **Golf, –(e)s** golf; der **Golfplatz, –es, ¨–e** golf course
der **Golfstrom, –(e)s** Gulf Stream
gönnen allow, grant
(die) **Gotik** Gothic; **gotisch** Gothic
der **Gott, –es, ¨–er** god; **Gott sei Dank!** Thank God! die **Gottheit, –en** deity, divinity; die **Göttin, –nen** goddess; **göttlich** divine, godlike
das **Grab, –es, ¨–er** grave
graben (gräbt), grub, gegraben dig
der **Graben, –s, ¨** ditch
der **Grad, –(e)s, –e** degree
grade = gerade
der **Gram, –(e)s** affliction
die **Gramma'tik, –en** grammar; **gramma'tisch** grammatical
der **Grandseigneur', –s, –s** *person of high distinction*
der **Graphiker, –s, —** graphic artist
das **Gras, –es, ¨–er** grass
gräßlich ghastly, horrible, hideous
grau grey
das **Grauen, –s** horror
greifen, griff, gegriffen seize, grasp; **greifen + zu** take (up)
greis old
grell glaring, shrill
die **Grenze, –n** border, boundary; das **Grenzland, –(e)s, ¨–er** borderland; der **Grenzverkehr, –s** border traffic; die **Grenzwache, –n** border guard
der **Grieche, –n, –n** the Greek (*masc.*); (das) **Griechisch, –en** Greek (*language*); **griechisch** (*adj.*) Greek
grob rough, crude, gruff, gross, rude; das **Grobe, –n** the rough (*or* raw) material
(das) **Grönland, –s** Greenland
der **Groschen, –s, —** *small coin*
groß, größer, größt– great, big, large, tall; die **Größe, –n** greatness, size; die **Großmacht, ¨–e** major *or* big power; die **Großmutter, ¨** grandmother; der **Großtyrann, –en, –en** tyrant; der **Großvater, –s, ¨** grandfather
der **Großwildbestand, –(e)s, ¨–e** big-game stock
grün green
der **Grund, –es, ¨–e** reason; ground, bottom; **auf Grund (von)** on the basis (of); **im Grunde** basically, actually
die **Grundlage, –n** basis; **grundlegend** fundamental
der **Grundriß, –risses, –risse** outline, plan, ground plan
die **Gruppe, –n** group
der **Gruß, –es, ¨–e** greeting; **grüßen** greet
der **Gulden, –s, —** guilder, florin
das **Gummibonbon, –s, –s** gum drop
die **Gunst** favor
die **Gurke, –n** cucumber; der **Gurkensalat, –(e)s** cucumber salad
gut, besser, best– good, well; **gut zu (etwas)** good for (something); **zu guter letzt** at long last, finally
das **Gymna'sium, –s, Gymna'sien** secondary school

H

das **Haar, –(e)s, –e** hair
haben (hat), hatte, gehabt have
der **Habenichts, —, –e** penniless man
die **Habsucht** greed
die **Hafenstadt, ¨–e** port (city), harbor
der **Hahn, –(e)s, ¨–e** cock, rooster
halb half; die **Hälfte, –n** half
Hallo! Hello!
der **Hals, –es, ¨–e** neck, throat; die **Halskette, –n** necklace
halt (*adv.*) just, simply
halten (hält), hielt, gehalten hold; stop; **Halt!** "Hold it" (= Stop!); **halten für** consider, take to be; **halten von** think of, think about; have an opinion of (*or* about); **halt-machen** stop; die **Haltung, –en** attitude, posture
(das) **Hamburg, –s** *largest port in Germany*
(das) **Hammerfest, –s** *seaport in Norway*
die **Hand, ¨–e** hand; **handbreit** a few inches, of a hand's breadth
handeln act, deal (with), negotiate, bargain
das **Handgelenk, –s, –e** wrist
die **Handgranate, –n** hand grenade
handhaben, handhabte, gehandhabt handle
die **Handlung, –en** plot, action

der **Handlungsreisende, –n, –n (ein Handlungsreisender)** traveling salesman
der **Handschuh, –s, –e** glove
das **Handwerk, –(e)s, –e** craft, handicraft, trade; **handwerklich** craftsmanlike, professional
die **Handzeichnung, –en** drawing
hängen, hing, gehangen hang
die **Hansestadt, ⸚e** city of the Hansa league
die **Harfe, –n** harp
harmo′nisch harmonious
harren wait, await; (*with gen. or with* **auf** + *acc.*) wait for
hart, härter, härtest– hard
der **Hase, –n, –n** hare
hassen, haßte, gehaßt hate
hasten hasten, be in a hurry; **hastig** hasty
der **Hauch, –(e)s, –e** breath
häufig frequent
das **Haupt, –es, ⸚er** head; **haupt–** main, chief; das **Hauptfach, –(e)s, ⸚er** major subject *or* field; die **Hauptsache, –n** main thing; **hauptsächlich** mainly; die **Hauptspeise, –n** main dish *or* course
das **Haus, –es, ⸚er** house; **Er geht nach Hause.** He goes home. **Er ist zu Hause.** He is at home. **alles im Hause** everything (is) included; **von Hause aus** by nature; die **Hausarbeit, –en** homework; die **Hausfrau, –en** housewife; der **Haushalt, –(e)s, –e** household
hausie′ren go begging, go peddling
der **Hausschlüssel, –s, —** house key; das **Haustor, –s, –e** doorway, gateway; die **Haustür, –en** house door, entrance door
die **Haut, ⸚e** skin
heben, hob, gehoben lift
das **Heft, –(e)s, –e** notebook
die **Heide, –n** heath
heilen cure, save, heal
heilig holy, sainted, sacred; die (der) **Heilige, –n, –n** saint; die **Hei′ligenfigur′, –en** holy image *or* figure
die **Heilkunde** medical science, medicine
heim home; die **Heimat, –en** home land
heim-kommen, kam heim, ist heimgekommen return, come home
die **Heirat, –en** marriage; **heiraten** marry; **heiratslustig** bent on marrying, eager to marry
heiser hoarse
heiß hot
heißen, hieß, geheißen be called; mean; **Wie heißen Sie?** What is your name? **das heißt** (*abbreviation* **d.h.**) that is (to say); **es hieß** it was said; **Wie heißt das auf Deutsch?** What does that mean in German?
heiter cheerful, gay, serene
der **Held, –en, –en** hero
helfen (hilft), half, geholfen (*dat.*) help
hell bright
der **Helm, –(e)s, –e** helmet
das **Hemd, –(e)s, –en** shirt
der **Henker, –s, —** hangman
her here (*direction toward the speaker*); this way; ago; **zehn Jahre her** ten years ago
heran′-ziehen, zog heran, herangezogen (+ an) draw to (*or* upon)
sich heraus′-stellen turn out, prove (to be)
heraus′-treten (tritt heraus), trat heraus, ist herausgetreten step out (*or* outside of)
heraus′-ziehen, zog heraus, herausgezogen draw *or* pull out
der **Herbst, –es, –e** fall, autumn
die **Herde, –n** flock
Herein′! Come in!
herein′-kommen, kam herein, ist hereingekommen come in
her-gehen, ging her, ist hergegangen proceed, happen, go on
her-kommen, kam her, ist hergekommen come here, approach
herkömmlich traditional
die **Herkunft** origin, descent
der **Herr, –n, –en** Mr., sir, master, lord, gentleman; **mein Herr** sir
herrlich magnificent, splendid
die **Herrschaft, –en** mastery, authority, domination, rule; **die Herrschaften** ladies and gentlemen; **herrschen** govern, rule, prevail
her-schicken send here
herum′ around
herum′-liegen, lag herum, herumgelegen lie around
herun′ter down
herun′ter-holen get *or* bring down
das **Herz, –ens, –en** heart; **herzhaft** hearty; **herzig** cute, charming
herzu′ (*separable pref.*) toward (a person *or* place)
das **Heu, –(e)s** hay
heute today; **heutig** of today, today's, modern; **heutzutage** nowadays
hier here
die **Hilfe** help; **um Hilfe rufen** call for help; **hilflos** helpless
der **Himmel, –s, —** heaven, sky
hin (*denoting direction away from speaker*) there, that way; **hin und her** to and fro, back and forth
hinab′ down(ward)
hinab′-schauen look down
hinauf′ up
hinaus′ out
hinaus′-dehnen extend
hinaus′-fliegen, flog hinaus, ist hinausgeflogen fly out *or* away
hinaus′-gehen, ging hinaus, ist hinausgegangen go outside, go out, set out
hinaus′-wehen blow out

hindern hinder, prevent, obstruct; das **Hindernis, –ses, –se** impediment, hindrance, obstacle
hindurch′-schauen look through
hinein′ in, into
(sich) **hinein′-reden** talk one's way into
hin-fallen (fällt hin), fiel hin, ist hingefallen fall down
hinge′gen on the other hand, on the contrary
hin-gehen, ging hin, ist hingegangen go there
hin-kommen, kam hin, ist hingekommen arrive, come, get there
hin-lungern lounge, lie idly
hin-nehmen (nimmt hin), nahm hin, hingenommen accept
hin-sehen (sieht hin), sah hin, hingesehen look to *or* toward (a certain place)
(sich) **hin-setzen** sit down
hinter (*prep. dat. or acc.*) behind, after; **hin′tereinan′der** in (swift) succession
hinterm = **hinter dem**
hinterrücks from the back
hin(zu′)-treten (tritt hin[zu]), trat hin(zu), ist hin(zu)getreten step up to
hinun′ter-spucken spit down
hinwie′derum again, in turn
der **Hirt(e), –en, –en** shepherd; der **Hirtenstab, –(e)s, ⸚e** shepherd's staff
der **Histo′riker, –s, —** historian; **histo′risch** historical
die **Hitze** heat
hoch, höher, höchst– high; **Hoch lebe der König!** Long live the king!
hochdeutsch High German (*correct and modern German*)
hochgelahrt (= **hochgelehrt**) very learned
das **Hochhaus, –es, ⸚er** skyscraper, very tall building
die **Hochschule, –n** institute, academy, etc. (*any institution of higher learning*)
höchst extremely; highest; **höchstens** at most, at best
die **Hochzeitsfeier, –n** marriage celebration
hocken sit hunched, squat
der **Hof, –(e)s, ⸚e** court, yard; farm
das **(Münchner) Hofbräuhaus, –es** *beer garden and restaurant* (*in Munich*)
hoffen hope; **hoffentlich** I hope; die **Hoffnung, –en** hope; der **Hoffnungsstrahl, –(e)s, –en** ray of hope
höflich courteous; die **Höflichkeit, –en** courtesy
die **Höhe, –n** height
die **Hoheit, –en** Highness; aristocratic splendor, majesty, loftiness
hold lovely, gracious
holen go and get, fetch, bring
(das) **Holland, –s** Holland, the Netherlands
das **Holz, –es, ⸚er** wood; die **Holzarbeit, –en** wood carving; der **Holzbildhauer, –s, —** wood carver; die **Holzschnitzerei, –en** wood sculpturing
der **Honig, –s** honey
hören hear
die **Hornbrille, –n** horn-rimmed glasses
der **Hornist′, –en, –en** hornplayer
die **Hose, –n** pair of pants, trousers
hübsch pretty, nice, attractive
die **Hüfte, –n** hip
der **Hügel, –s, —** hill
das **Huhn, –(e)s, ⸚er** hen, chicken; das **Backhuhn, –(e)s, ⸚er** roast (baked *or* fried) chicken
der **Humor′, –s** (sense of) humor
humpeln limp, hobble
der **Hund, –es, –e** dog, hound
hundert hundred
der **Hunger, –s** famine, hunger; **Ich habe Hunger.** I am hungry; **hungern** starve; **hungrig** hungry
der **Hut, –(e)s, ⸚e** hat

I

ich (*acc.* **mich**, *dat.* **mir**, *gen.* **meiner**) I
iden′tifizie′ren identify
ihr (*pers. pron.*) (*acc.* **euch**, *dat.* **euch**, *gen.* **euer**) you (*fam. plur.*)
ihr (*poss. adj.*) her, its, their
Ihr (*poss. adj.*) your (*formal address*)
ihrerseits for their (her, its) part
die **Illusion′, –en** illusion
im = **in dem**
immer always; **immer höher** higher and higher; **immer schöner** more and more beautiful
der **Impressionis′mus, —** impressionism
in (*prep. dat.*) in; (*prep. acc.*) into, to
inbegriffen: mit inbegriffen included, including
indem′ (*sub. conj.*) while, during the time that; since, because
indes′sen meanwhile; however (*coord. conj.*)
(das) **Indien, –s** India
indirekt indirect
das **Indivi′duum, –s,** (*plur.*) **Indivi′duen** individual
der **In′doeuropä′er, –s, —** Indo-European; **in′doeuropä′isch** Indo-European
in′doira′nisch Indo-Iranian
der **Industriel′le, –n, –n (ein Industriel′ler)** industrialist
infol′ge (*prep. gen.*) because of, in consequence of, as a result of
der **Ingenieur′, –s, –e** engineer
inklusiv′ inclusive
inkonsequent′ inconsistent; die **Inkonsequenz′, –en** inconsistency
inne-halten (hält inne), hielt inne, innegehalten stop

innen inside; **inner-** inward, internal; das **Innere, –n** inmost self (*or* being)
innerhalb (*with gen.*) within
innig intimate, sincere
ins = **in das**
die **Insel, –n** island
das **Instrument′, –(e)s, –e** instrument; die **Instrumental′musik′** instrumental music
interessant′ interesting; das **Interes′se, –s, –n** interest; **(sich) interessie′ren für** be interested in
intim′ intimate
inzwi′schen meanwhile
irgend any, some; **irgendein** some kind of; **irgendwo** somewhere, anywhere
iro′nisch ironic
(sich) irren err, be mistaken, be wrong; der **Irrtum, –s, ⁻̈er** error
(das) **Isenbüttel-Gifhorn, –s** *a little town near Braunschweig in Germany*
italie′nisch Italian

J

ja yes; indeed, of course; you see; why! **Ich habe ja ein Buch.** I do have a book.
die **Jacke, –n** coat, jacket
die **Jagdgebühr, –en** hunting fee; der **Jagdschein, –(e)s, –e** hunting license
das **Jagen, –s** hunt(ing)
das **Jahr, –(e)s, –e** year; **jahrelang** for years; **Jahr um Jahr** year after year; **jahraus′, jahrein′** year in, year out
das **Jahrhun′dert, –s, –e** century; **jahrhun′dertelang** for centuries; die **Jahrhun′dertwende, –n** turn of the century
jährlich annual
das **Jahrtau′send, –s, –e** millenium
der **Januar, –s** January
japa′nisch Japanese; (das) **Japa′nisch, –en** Japanese (*language*)
jawohl′ yes indeed
je ever; **je größer desto besser** the bigger the better
jed(–e, –es, –er) every, each
jedenfalls in any case
jedermann everybody
jedoch′ but, though, however
jemals ever
jemand somebody, anybody
jen(–e, –es, –er) that, the former
jenseits (*prep. gen.*) on that side of, on the other side of
jetzt now
Johanne′isch *of or according to St. John*
der **Journalist′, –en, –en** journalist; die **Journalis′tin, –nen** journalist (*fem.*)
die **Jugend** youth
der **Juli, –s** July
jung, jünger, jüngst– young; **in jüngerer Zeit** recently
der **Junge, –n, –n** boy
die **Jungfrau, –en** virgin, maiden
der **Junggeselle, –n, –n** bachelor
der **Jüngling, –s, –e** young man, youth
der **Juni, –s** June
der **Justiz′rat, –(e)s, ⁻̈e** counsellor (*title of an official in the judiciary*)

K

der **Kaffee** (*or* **Kaffee′**), **–s** coffee; der **Kaffeelöffel, –s, —** coffee spoon
der **Kahn, (e)s, ⁻̈e** boat
der **Kaiser, –s, —** emperor, kaiser
das **Kalb, –(e)s, ⁻̈er** calf
(das) **Kalifor′nien, –s** California
kalt, kälter, kältest– cold
der **Kamerad′, –en, –en** companion, comrade
der **Kamin′, –s, –e** chimney
der **Kamm, –(e)s, ⁻̈e** comb, ridge (*of mountains*); **kämmen** comb
die **Kammer, –n** chamber, small room
der **Kammersänger, –s, —** (concert *or* court) singer, private singer to the prince
der **Kampf, –es, ⁻̈e** fight, struggle, battle
der **Kanal′, –(e)s, ⁻̈e** channel, canal
der **Kana′riestrom, –s** Canary Stream
die **Kapel′le, –n** chapel; orchestra; der **Kapell′meister, –s, —** orchestra leader, conductor
der **Kapitalist′, –en, –en** capitalist
die **Karte, –n** ticket; map; card
die **Kartof′fel, –n** potato; der **Kartof′felpuffer, –s, —** potato pancake; der **Kartof′felsalat′, –(e)s** potato salad
der **Käse, –s** cheese; das **Käsebrot, –(e)s, –e** cheese sandwich
der **Kasten, –s, —** box, case
die **Katastro′phe, –n** catastrophe
der **Kater –s, —** tomcat
die **Kathedra′le, –n** cathedral
die **Katze, –n** cat
kauern squat, crouch
kaufen buy
der **Kaukasus, —** Caucasus
kaum hardly
die **Kehle, –n** throat
kein (–e, —, —) no, not any, not a; **Er hat kein Buch.** He has no book. **keiner** nobody; **keineswegs** by no means
der **Keller –s, —** cellar
der **Kellner, –s, —** waiter; die **Kellnerin, –nen** waitress
kennen, kannte, gekannt know (*in the sense of* "be acquainted with," *as distinguished from* "**wissen**" *which refers to factual knowledge*); **Sie kennen sich seit einer Woche.**

They have known each other for a week. **Ich kenne das Buch nicht.** I don't know the book; **kennen-lernen** come to know
der **Kerl, –(e)s, –e** fellow
das **Kerngehäuse, –s, —** core
die **Kernwaffe, –n** nuclear weapon; der **Kernwaffenversuch, –(e)s, –e** nuclear test
die **Kette, –n** chain
keuchen pant, gasp
das **Kind, –es, –er** child; das **Kinderbuch, –(e)s, ¨–er** children's book; das **Kinderfräulein, –s, —** governess; die **Kindergärtnerin, –nen** nursery-school teacher, kindergarten teacher; der **Kinderwagen, –s, —** baby carriage; das **Kinderspielzimmer, –s, —** children's playroom; die **Kindheit** childhood
das **Kinn, –(e)s, –e** chin
das **Kino, –s, –s** movie theater
die **Kirche, –n** church
die **Kirmesgeige, –n** fiddle (*played at village fair*)
die **Klage, –n** complaint
kläglich pitiful, miserable
klappen click, slam
klar clear
die **Klasse, –n** class; das **Klassenzimmer, –s, —** classroom
klassisch classical
klatschen clap, applaud; land with a slap
der **Klee, –s** clover; **jemanden über den Klee loben** praise someone to the skies
das **Kleid, –(e)s, –er** dress; die **Kleidung, –en** dress, clothes
klein small, little; **der kleine Mann** the common man; **kleinlich** petty
der **Klempner, –s, —** plumber
klettern climb; die **Klet′terpartie′, –n** (mountain) climbing excursion
klingen, klang, geklungen sound, ring
die **Klinke, –n** door knob *or* handle
klirren clink, clank, clatter
klopfen beat, pound, throb, knock; **klopfenden Herzens** with pounding heart
der **Klub, –s, –s** club
klug smart, clever, bright; **Sie wurden aus seinen Worten nicht klug.** They didn't make any sense of his words.
der **Knabe, –n, –n** youth, boy
knarren creak
der **Knecht, –(e)s, –e** servant
das **Knie, –s, —** knee
der **Knochen, –s, —** bone
der **Knopf, –es, ¨–e** button
knüpfen tie, unite
knurren growl
der **Koch, –(e)s, ¨–e** cook; **kochen** cook
der **Kolle′ge, –n, –n** colleague; die **Kolle′gin, –nen** colleague (*fem.*)
kollektiv′ collective
(das) **Köln, –s** Cologne; **Kölner** (of) Cologne
das **Kolonial′warengeschäft′, –s, –e** grocery store
die **Kolonna′de, –n** colonnade
komforta′bel comfortable
komisch funny, odd
kommen, kam, ist gekommen come; **auf etwas kommen** get an idea; **in Verle′genheit kommen** get into trouble *or* embarrassment; **zu sich kommen** regain consciousness; **Wie kommt es?** How come?
der **Kommunist′, –en, –en** communist; **kommunis′tisch** communistic
die **Komö′die, –n** comedy; **komö′dienhaft** comic, as in a comedy
die **Kompanie′, –n** company; der **Kompanie′führer, –s, —** commander of a company
komponie′ren compose; der **Komponist′, –en, –en** composer; die **Komposition′, –en** composition
die **Konditorei′, –en** pastry shop, bakery
die **Konferenz′, –en** conference
der **Konflikt′, –(e)s, –e** conflict
(der) **Kongo, –s** Congo
der **König, –s, –e** king
der **Konjunktiv, –s, –e** subjunctive
konkret′ concrete
können (kann), konnte, gekonnt can, be able to, may; know; **Können Sie Deutsch?** Do you know German?
die **Konsequenz′, –en** consequence
der **Konsul, –s, –n** consul
die **Kontrol′le, –n** control; der **Kontroll′posten, –s, —** control station
das **Konzentrations′lager, –s, —** concentration camp
das **Konzert′, –(e)s, –e** concert
der **Kopf, –(e)s, ¨–e** head
das **Korn, –(e)s** grain; das **Kornfeld, –(e)s, –er** wheat field
der **Körper, –s, —** body; **körperlich** physical
die **Kostbarkeit, –en** precious thing
kosten cost
die **Kosten** (*plur.*) expenses
das **Kostüm′, –s, –e** costume, trappings; woman's suit
die **Kraft, ¨–e** power, strength; **kräftig** strong, active
der **Kragen, –s, —** collar; **Kragen und Schlips** starched collar and tie
die **Kralle, –n** claw
der **Krampf, –(e)s, ¨–e** cramp; tension
krank sick; **schwer krank** seriously ill; die **Krankenpflegerin, –nen** nurse; das **Krankenzimmer, –s, —** sickroom; die **Krankheit, –en** sickness, disease
kratzen scratch
die **Kreide, –n** chalk
der **Kreis, –es, –e** circle
kreischend screaming

das **Kreiskrankenhaus, –es, ⸚er** district (county) hospital
(das) **Kreta, –s** Crete
kreuz und quer zigzag, this way and that, crisscross
kreuzen cross
der **Krieg, –(e)s, –e** war
kriegen (*coll.*) get, obtain
der **Krieger, –s, —** warrior; die **Kriegsgefahr, –en** danger of war
die **Kritik′, –en** criticism, critique; der **Kritiker vom Fach** professional critic; **kritisie′ren** criticize
die **Küche, –n** kitchen
der **Kuchen, –s, —** cake
der **Küchenschleifstein, –(e)s, –e** kitchen grindstone, whetstone
die **Küchenuhr, –en** kitchen clock
kühl cool; **kühlen** cool
kulturell′ cultural
der **Kummer, –s** sorrow
die **Kunde** knowledge, information, news
künftig future; **künftighin** henceforth, from now on
die **Kunst, ⸚e** art
kunst′histo′risch pertaining to the history of art
der **Künstler, –s, —** artist; **künstlerisch** artistic; **kunstsinnig** artistic, having appreciation of art; die **Kunstweise, –n** kind *or* style of art
die **Kuppel, –n** dome, cupola
kurios′ curious, odd
der **Kurort, –(e)s, –e** health resort, spa
der **Kurs, –es, –e** course; exchange rate; **einen Kurs bele′gen** take a (university) course
kurz, kürzer, kürzest– short
der **Kurzschluß, –schlusses, –schlüsse** short circuit
die **Kusi′ne, –n** cousin (*fem.*)

L

(**sich**) **laben** refresh (oneself)
lächeln smile; das **Lächeln, –s** smile
lachen laugh; **nichts zu lachen haben** have nothing to laugh about
der **Lackstiefel, –s, —** patent-leather boots
die **Lage, –n** situation
das **Lager, –s, —** camp; bed, couch
das **Lamm, –(e)s, ⸚er** lamb; das **Lämmerheer, –es, –e** flock of lambs
die **Lampe, –n** lamp
das **Land, –es, ⸚er** country; land; region; **auf dem Land** in the country; **aufs Land** to the country; die **Landbrücke, –n** ridge, land bridge
landen land
die **Landesgrenze, –n** national boundary
die **Landschaft, –en** landscape
die **Landschranke, –n** land barrier
der **Landsitz, –es, –e** country seat *or* residence
die **Landwirtstochter, ⸚** farmer's daughter
lang(e), länger, längst– long, for a long time; **lange her** long ago; **noch lange nicht** not by a long shot; **in die Länge ziehen** draw out, protract; **langgezogen** long-drawn-out
lang (*adv.*) for, *e.g.:* **stundenlang** for hours; **jahrelang** for years
längs (*prep. gen. or dat.*) along
langsam slow
die **Langspielplatte, –n** long-playing record
längst long ago, long since
langweilen bore; **sich langweilen** get bored; **langweilig** boring
lappländisch (*adj.*) Lappish, Laplandic
der **Lärm, –(e)s** noise
lassen (läßt), ließ, gelassen let, allow; leave; have (= cause); **Ich lasse mir die Haare schneiden.** I shall have my hair cut. **Es läßt sich machen.** It can be done; **sein Leben lassen** die, lay down one's life
(das) **Latein′, –s** Latin (*the language*); **latei′nisch** Latin
die **Latte, –n** lath; picket; der **Lattenzaun, –es, ⸚e** picket fence
der **Lauf, –(e)s, ⸚e** course; career; run; **laufen (läuft), lief, ist gelaufen** run; der **Läufer, –s, —** runner
die **Laune, –n** mood, whim
der **Lausbub, –en, –en** rascal, rogue
der **Laut, –es, –e** sound
laut loud
lauten sound, read, run; **Die Worte lauten ungefähr so . . .** The words read (run) somewhat like this . . .
lauter pure; nothing but; sheer
die **Lautverschiebung, –en** sound shift
das **Lazarett′, –s, –e** field hospital
das **Leben, –s, —** life; **am Leben sein** be alive; **sein Leben lassen** lay down one's life, die; **leben** live; **leben′dig** alive, lively
die **Leber, –n** liver
das **Leder, –s, —** leather; die **Lederhose(n), –n** leather breeches
leer empty
legen put, place, lay
legendär′ legendary; die **Legen′de, –n** legend
lehnen lean
der **Lehrer, –s, —** teacher (*masc.*); die **Lehrerin, –nen** teacher (*fem.*)
der **Lehrling, –s, –e** apprentice
leicht easy, easily; light (*in weight*); slightly; **leicht fallen** (*w. dat.*) be an easy matter: **Es fällt mir leicht.** It is an easy matter for me.
der **Leichtsinn, –s** thoughtlessness, rashness, levity, frivolity; **leichtsinnig** frivolous

das **Leid, –(e)s, –en** injury, sorrow; **Es tut mir leid.** I am sorry.
leiden, litt, gelitten suffer, tolerate; **an etwas leiden** (*dat.*) suffer from something; der **Leidende, –n, –n** suffering person
leiden können like; **Sie kann ihn nicht leiden.** She doesn't like him (*or* can't stand him).
leidenschaftlich passionate
leider unfortunately
die **Leier, –n** lyre; barrel organ, hurdy-gurdy; der **Leierkasten, –s, ⸚** hand organ, hurdy-gurdy; der **Leiermann, –(e)s, ⸚er** organ grinder, hurdy-gurdy man
der **Leim –(e)s, –e** glue, (bird)lime
leise soft
die **Leistung, –en** achievement, performance
leiten guide, lead; der **Leitgedanke, –ns, –n** main thought, guiding principle
der **Leopard′, –en, –en** leopard
lesen (liest), las, gelesen read; der **Leser, –s,** — reader
letzt: zu guter letzt last, at long last, finally
die **Leuchte, –n** shine, light; **leuchten** gleam, give light, shine
leugnen deny
die **Leute** (*plur.*) people
das **Licht, –(e)s, –er** light; **licht** (*adj.*) bright
lieb dear; **lieb haben** love, hold dear; die **Liebe** love; **lieben** love; **mein Lieber** my dear (fellow)
lieber (*see* **gern**[e]) rather; **Wo studieren Sie lieber?** Where do you prefer to study? **am liebsten** (*see* **gern**[e]) most, (best) of all
die **Liebeserklärung, –en** declaration of love
der **Liebhaber, –s,** — lover, suitor
lieblich lovely; die **Lieblichkeit** loveliness
der **Liebling, –s, –e** favorite, darling
(die) **Liebste, –n** beloved
das **Lied, –es, –er** song; der **Liederzyklus,** —, (*plur.*) **Liederzyklen** song cycle
liefern supply; afford; deliver
liegen, lag, gelegen lie (= be situated); **an (etwas) liegen** be due to (something); **Es liegt an mir.** It depends on me; **Mir liegt daran . . .** It matters to me . . .
die **Linde, –n** linden tree
die **Linie, –n** line, contour
links left, to the left; **von links** from the left
die **Lippe, –n** lip
die **Liste, –n** list
(das) **Litauen, –s** Lithuania
litera′risch literary; die **Literatur′** literature; das **Literatur′geschichts′buch, –(e)s, ⸚er** (book on) literary history
das **Lob, –(e)s** praise; **loben** praise
der **Löffel, –s,** — spoon; **löffeln** ladle out, spoon; **hinein′-löffeln** pour *or* stuff into; der **Löffelzwerg, –(e)s, –e** spoon-eared dwarf
logisch logical
der **Lokal′termin,′ –s, –e** court hearing
der **Lokal′wind, –(e)s, –e** local wind
los free, disengaged, loose; **Es geht los.** It is starting. **Also los!** Go ahead! Get going! **Was ist los?** What is the matter? What is going on?
lose loose; **lösen** solve; **(sich) los-lösen** separate
los-lassen (läßt los), ließ los, losgelassen release
los-ziehen, zog los, ist losgezogen start out, set out (*on an excursion*)
der **Löwe, –n, –n** lion
die **Lücke, –n** gap, blank space
die **Luft, ⸚e** air; die **Luftzufuhr** supply of air
die **Lüftung** ventilation
die **Lüge, –n** lie; **lügen, log, gelogen** lie; der **Lügner, –s,** — liar
die **Lunge, –n** lung
die **Lunte, –n** wick
die **Lust** delight, desire, pleasure, joy; **lustig** jolly, merry, gay, funny
(das) **Lybien, –s** Libya

M

machen make, do; **Das macht mir Mühe.** That gives me trouble.
die **Macht, ⸚e** power
das **Mädchen, –s,** — girl; der **Mädchenname, –ns, –n** maiden name
das **Mädel, –s,** — (*plur. also* –s) girl
das **Magazin′, –s, –e** magazine
die **Magd, ⸚e** maid (*servant*)
der **Magen, –s, ⸚** *or* — stomach; die **Magengrube, –n** pit of the stomach
der **Magis′ter, –s,** — scholar; schoolmaster
magya′risch Magyar
der **Maharad′scha, –s, –s** Maharajah
die **Mahlzeit, –en** meal
der **Mai, –s** May
die **Majestät′, –en** majesty
das **Mal** (point in) time; mark; **zum ersten Mal** for the first time; **einmal** once; **zwanzigmal** twenty times; **zehnmal zehn** ten times ten; **Sagen Sie mal!** Just tell me!
der **Maler, –s,** — painter; die **Malerei′, –en** painting; **malerisch** picturesque
man (*indef. pron.*) one, you, we, they, people
manch (–e, –es, –er) many a; **manche** (*plur.*) some, a number of
mancherlei some things, a number of things
manchmal sometimes
der **Mangel, –s, ⸚** lack
der **Mann, –es, ⸚er** man; **zweitausend Mann** two thousand men (*soldiers*)
die **Mannigfaltigkeit** variety, multiplicity
die **Mannschaft, –en** team, troop, group of men (*soldiers*)

der **Manschet'tenknopf, –(e)s, ⸚e** cuff link
der **Mantel, –s, ⸚** (over)coat
(das) **Marburg, –s** *University town in Germany*
das **Märchen, –s, —** fairy tale; **märchenhaft** enchanting, fabulous
der **Marsch, –(e)s, ⸚e** march; **marschie'ren** march
der **März, –es** March
das **Maschi'nengewehr, –s, –e** machine gun
das **Material', –s, –ien** material, matter; **materiell'** material
die **Mathematik'** mathematics; der **Mathema'tiker, –s, —** mathematician
die **Matrat'zengruft** mattress grave, sick bed
der **Matro'se, –n, –n** sailor
die **Maus, ⸚e** mouse
die **Maxi'me, –n** maxim
das **Meer, –es, –e** ocean, sea; die **Meeresenge, –n** strait; der **Meeresspiegel, –s** surface of the sea
mehr more
mehrere several
die **Mehrzahl** majority, plural
die **Meierei', –en** (dairy) farm
mein (**–e, —, —**) my
meinen think, say, have an opinion, mean
meinetwegen for all I care; for my sake
die **Meinung, –en** opinion
meist most; **meistens** mostly, usually, for the most part
der **Meister, –s, —** master
melancho'lisch melancholy
melden announce; **sich melden** report (oneself present)
die **Melodie', –n** melody
die **Mena'ge, –n** menage, household
mennigrot minium red
die **Mensa** students' dining hall *or* cafeteria
der **Mensch, –en, –en** human being, man, person; die **Menschenherde, –n** human herd; das **Menschenrecht, –(e)s, –e** human right(s); die **Menschheit** mankind; **menschlich** human
das **Menu', –s, –s** menu
das **Menuett', –s, –s** *or* **–e** minuet
merken notice; **sich** (*dat.*) **etwas merken** remember something, take note of
merkwürdig strange, remarkable; **merk'würdigerwei'se** strange to say
das **Messer, –s, —** knife
der **Messingknauf, –s, ⸚e** brass knob
das **Metall', –s, –e** metal; das **Metall'geräusch, –es, –e** metallic sound, grating noise
die **Metamorpho'se, –n** metamorphosis, transformation
das (*or* der) **Meter, –s, —** meter (*measure*)
die **Metho'de, –n** method
die **Miene, –n** expression, look, countenance; **der keine Miene verzog** who did not move a muscle
mikrosko'pisch microscopic
die **Milch** milk; der **Milchkaffee, –s** coffee with milk
die **Milde** mildness, gentleness; **mildern** mitigate, qualify; **mildernde Umstände** extenuating circumstances
das **Milieu', –s** milieu
die **Million', –en** million; der **Millionär', –s, –e** millionaire
der **Min'derwertigkeitskomplex', –es, –e** inferiority complex
die **Mine, –n** mine
der **Minis'terpräsident', –en, –en** prime minister
die **Minu'te, –n** minute
mir: mir ist, als ob . . . I feel as if . . .
die **Mischung, –en** mixture
mißbräuchlich improper, illegal
mißlin'gen, mißlang, ist mißlungen fail
das **Mißverständnis, –ses, –se** misunderstanding
mit (*prep. dat.*) with (*means or accompaniment*); by; at
mit (*adv. or prefix*) along (with); **mit dabei' sein** be one of (member of) a party, be with a group, be included
mit-bringen, brachte mit, mitgebracht bring *or* take along
miteinan'der with one another; **miteinan'der verbun'den** interrelated
mit-gehen, ging mit, ist mitgegangen go along, accompany
das **Mitglied, –(e)s, –er** member (of a group)
mit inbegriffen included, including
mit-kommen, kam mit, ist mitgekommen come along
das **Mitleid, –(e)s** compassion
mit-machen participate, go along
mit-nehmen (nimmt mit), nahm mit, mitgenommen take along
der **Mittag, –s, –e** noon; das **Mittagessen, –s, —** noon meal, dinner
die **Mitte, –n** center, middle
mit-teilen inform, tell, communicate, notify; die **Mitteilung, –en** communication, notice
das **Mittel, –s, —** cure, remedy; means, wealth
das **Mittelalter, –s** Middle Ages
mit'telatlan'tisch Mid-Atlantic
(das) **Mit'teleng'lisch, –en** Middle English (*language*)
(das) **Mit'teleuro'pa, –s** Central Europe
der **Mittelfinger, –s, —** middle finger
mittelhochdeutsch Middle High German
das **Mittelmeer, –s** Mediterranean
mitten (in der Nacht) in the middle (of the night)

die **Mitternacht, ⸚e** midnight; **um Mitternacht** at midnight
der **Mittwoch, –s, –e** Wednesday
die **Möbel** (*plur.*) furniture
möchte (*see* **mögen**) should like to
die **Mode, –n** fashion
das **Modell′, –s, –e** model
modern′ modern
modifizie′ren modify
mögen (mag), mochte, gemocht may (*probability*); like (to), want (to); **Das möchte ich auch.** I should like (to do, to take) that too. **Das mag sein.** That may be. **Ich mag nicht mitgehen.** I don't care (want) to go along.
möglich possible
(das) **Moll, –s** minor (*key*)
die **Mollus′ke, –n** mollusk
der **Monat, –s, –e** month; **monatlich** monthly
der **Mond, –(e)s, –e** moon
der **Montag, –s, –e** Monday
morden murder
der **Morgen, –s, —** morning; **am Morgen** in the morning; **morgen** tomorrow; **morgen früh** tomorrow morning; **heute morgen** this morning; **eines Morgens** one morning; **morgens** mornings
die **Mosel** Moselle (*river in Germany*)
(das) **Moskau, –s** Moscow
das **Motiv′, –s, –e** motif (*music*); motive; subject
die **Mozartkugel, –n** marzipan ball (*candy*)
müde tired
die **Mühe, –n** trouble, effort; **der Mühe wert** worth the trouble
die **Mühle, –n** mill; die **Mühlenbrücke** mill bridge
das **Mühlsturzhorn, –s** *mountain in the Bavarian Alps*
mühselig laboriously, with an effort
(das) **München, –s** Munich; **Münchner** of Munich
der **Mund, –es, ⸚er** mouth; die **Mundharmonika, –s** harmonica, mouth organ; **mündlich** oral
das **Münster, –s, —** cathedral, minster
munter alert, gay
das **Muse′um, –s,** (*plur.*) **Muse′en** museum
die **Musik′** music; **musika′lisch** musical, melodious; der **Musikant′, –en, –en** musician; der **Musiker, –s, —** musician; das **Musik′gebäude, –s, —** music hall
der **Muskel, –s, –n** muscle
müssen (muß), mußte, gemußt must, have to, need to, be compelled to
der **Mut, –(e)s** courage
die **Mutter, ⸚** mother; die **Muttersprache, –n** mother tongue
mythisch mythical; der **Mythos** (*or* **Mythus**), **—,** (*plur.*) **Mythen** myth

N

na (= **nun**) well; **Na schön!** Fine! Well, all right!
nach (*prep. dat.*) after; according to, on the authority of; to, toward
die **Nachahmung, –en** imitation
die **Nachbarschaft, –en** neighborhood
nachdem′ (*sub. conj.*) after
nach-denken, dachte nach, nachgedacht think, ponder
nacheinander one after the other
nacherleben re-experience
die **Nachfolge, –n** succession; **nachfolgend** following
nach-fühlen feel with a person; understand; enter into by way of feeling
nach-gehen, ging nach, ist nachgegangen (*dat.*) follow, go after; be slow; **Er ging ihr nach.** He followed her; **Die Uhr ging nach.** The watch was slow.
nach-helfen (hilft nach), half nach, nachgeholfen (*dat.*) help along, tutor
nachher′ afterwards
nach-kommen, kam nach, ist nachgekommen (*dat.*) follow
der **Nachmittag, –s, –e** afternoon; **am Nachmittag** in the afternoon; **nachmittags** in the afternoon, afternoons
nach-rennen, rannte nach, ist nachgerannt (*dat.*) run after
die **Nachricht, –en** report, news
nach-sehen (sieht nach), sah nach, nachgesehen examine, verify, check
die **Nachspeise, –n** dessert
nach-sprechen (spricht nach), sprach nach, nachgesprochen (*dat.*) repeat (*words*)
nächst– next
die **Nacht, ⸚e** night; das **Nacht′gebet′, –(e)s, –e** evening prayer; das **Nachthemd, –(e)s, –en** nightgown; **nachts** at night, nights; die **Nachtzeit, –en** nighttime; der **Nachtzug, –(e)s, ⸚e** night train
nach-weisen, wies nach, nachgewiesen prove (against)
der **Nagel, -s, ⸚** nail
nah(e), näher, nächst– near; **nahe daran′ sein** be on the point of
nahe-legen suggest, urge upon; make plain
nahe-liegen, lag nahe, nahegelegen suggest itself, be obvious
näherkommend coming nearer, approaching
die **Nahrung** food, nourishment
der **Name, –ns, –n** name; **nämlich** namely, you see, of course
Nanu′! Well now!
der **Narr, –en, –en** fool
die **Nase, –n** nose
die **Nässe** moisture, humidity, wetness
die **Nation′, –en** nation; die **Nationalität′,**

–en nationality; der **National′ökonom′, –en, –en** economist
national′sozialis′tisch National Socialist, Nazi
die **Natur′, –en** nature
natur′historisch pertaining to natural history
natür′lich natural(ly), of course
die **Natur′wissenschaft, –en** natural science
die **Nazizeit** Nazi period
n. Chr. (nach Christi Geburt) A.D.
neben (*prep. dat. or acc.*) near, beside, next to
ne′beneinan′der side by side
der **Neffe, –n, –n** nephew
nehmen (nimmt), nahm, genommen take; **sich in acht nehmen** take care, be cautious; **in Strafe nehmen** penalize
neigen tend to, be inclined; die **Neigung, –en** affection, inclination, love
nein no
nennen, nannte, genannt name, call; **beim Vornamen nennen** call by one's first name
nett nice, pleasant
das **Netz, –es, –e** net
neu new; **von neuem** anew, again; **etwas Neues** something new; das **Neue, –n** that which is new; **Was gibt es Neues?** What is new? **nichts Neues** nothing new; der **Neubau, –s,** (*plur.*) **Neubauten** new building
die **Neugier** curiosity; **neugierig** curious
neuhochdeutsch New High German
neun nine
neunzehn nineteen
(das) **Neusee′land, –s** New Zealand
nicht not; **Nicht wahr?** Isn't it (so)? **nicht einmal** not even
die **Nichte, –n** niece
das **Nicht′raucherabteil, –s, –e** non-smoking compartment; das **Nicht′rauchercoupé, –s, –s** non-smoking compartment
nichts nothing; **nichts anderes** nothing else
nichtsnutzig good-for-nothing
nicken nod
nie never
der **Niedergang, –s** downfall
niedergeschlagen downcast
die **Niederlage, –n** defeat
sich nieder-lassen (läßt nieder), ließ nieder, niedergelassen settle (down)
sich nieder-legen lie down
sich nieder-setzen sit down
das **Niedersteigen: beim Niedersteigen** while climbing down
nieder-treten (tritt nieder), trat nieder, niedergetreten trample underfoot
niedrig low
niemals never
niemand nobody, no one
die **Niere, –n** kidney
nimmer nevermore, never
(das) **Nizza, –s** Nice
noch still (*temp.*); yet, besides; nor; more; **noch einmal** once more; **noch eins** one more thing; **noch immer** = **immer noch** still; **noch jemand** anybody *or* somebody else; **noch nicht** not yet; **weder . . . noch** neither . . . nor
nochmals once again
(das) **Norda′frika, –s** North Africa
norddeutsch North German
der **Norden, –s** north; **nördlich** northern, der **Nordos′ten, –s** northeast; die **Nordsee** North Sea
(das) **Nordwest′afrika, –s** Northwest Africa
(das) **Norwegen, –s** Norway
die **Not, ⁻̈e** need, distress, misery; **zur Not** if necessary
die **Note, –n** grade, mark; note
nötig necessary; **nötig haben** need
die **Notiz′, –en** note; der **Notiz′block, –(e)s, ⁻̈e** note pad
notwendig necessary; **notwendigerweise** necessarily
der **Novem′ber, –s** November
(der *or* das) **Nu** moment; **im Nu** instantly, in a twinkling
die **Nudel, –n** noodle; die **Nudelsuppe, –n** noodle soup
die **Null, –en** zero; **null** zero
die **Nummer, –n** number
nun now, well
nunmehr now, by this time, henceforth
nur only; **immer nur so** rapidly
die **Nuß,** (*plur.*) **Nüsse** nut
nützen be of use; **nützt nichts!** no use!

O

ob (*sub. conj.*) whether, if
oben above, upstairs, at the top
der **Ober, –s, —** headwaiter
(das) **Oberam′mergau, –s** *town in Bavaria*
oberhalb (*prep. gen.*) above
die **Oberschule, –n** secondary (*or* high) school
obgleich′ (*sub. conj.*) although
der **Oboist′, –en, –en** oboist
obschon′ (*sub. conj.*) although
das **Obst, –es** fruit
obwohl′ (*sub. conj.*) although
oder (*coord. conj.*) or
offen open
offenbar obvious
offenba′ren reveal
offiziell′ official
der **Offizier′, –s, –e** officer
öffnen open; die **Öffnung, –en** opening
oft often
ohne (*prep. acc.*) without; **ohne . . . zu** (*with inf.*) without; **ohne das Buch zu öffnen** without opening the book
das **Ohr, –(e)s, –en** ear; **Ich gab ihm eins hinter**

die Ohren. I boxed his ears; **die Ohren spitzen** prick up one's ears
der **Okto'ber, -s** October
der **Onkel, -s** — uncle
die **Oper, -n** opera
der **Optimist', -en, -en** optimist
das **Orches'terkonzert', -(e)s, -e** orchestral *or* symphonic concert; der **Orches'terraum, -s, ¨-e** orchestra pit
ordentlich neat, proper, respectable; thoroughly; die **Ordnung, -en** order; **ordnungsgemäß** orderly, regular
das **Organ', -s, -e** organ (*anatomy*); **orga'nisch** organically
die **Originalität'** originality; **originell'** original
der **Ornament'schnitzer, -s,** — carver of ornaments
der **Ort, -(e)s, -e** (*or* ¨-**er**) place, town; locality; region
(das) **Ostaf'rika, -s** East Africa
ostdeutsch East German
der **Osten, -s** east; **östlich** eastern
(die) **Ostern** Easter; die **Osterferien** (*plur. only*) Easter vacation
(das) **Österreich, -s** Austria; **österreichisch** Austrian
oxyd'grün verdigris
der **Ozean, -s, -e** ocean

P

paar: ein paar a few, a couple, a pair
der **Pädagog'(e), -en, -en** pedagogue, educator
der **Palast', -(e)s, ¨-e** palace
das **Papier', -s, -e** paper
die **Pappe, -n** pasteboard (*ticket*)
das **Paradies', -es** paradise
der **Paragraph', -en, -en** paragraph
das **Pärchen, -s,** — couple
die **Partei', -(e)n** party, faction
die **Partie', -n** game, excursion
die **Partitur', -en** score (*music*)
der **Paß, Passes, Pässe** passport; der **Paßbeamte, -n, -n** passport officer; die **Paßkontrolle, -n** examination of passports
passen, paßte, gepaßt (*dat.*) fit
passie'ren (sein) pass, happen
das **Passions'spiel, -(e)s, -e** passion play
der **Pastor, -s,** (*plur.*) **Pasto'ren** minister, clergyman
der **Patient', -en, -en** patient
patriarcha'lisch patriarchal
die **Pause, -n** pause
das **Pech** pitch; bad luck; **Verfluch'tes Pech!** Rotten luck!
die **Pein** pain, torture
der **Pelz, -es, -e** fur, pelt; der **Pelzmantel, -s, ¨** fur coat
pensioniert' retired
die **Perio'de, -n** period
der **Perron', -s, -s** platform
die **Person', -en** person; das **Personal', -s** personnel; **persön'lich** personal(ly); die **Persön'lichkeit, -en** personality
der **Pessimist', -en, -en** pessimist
die **Pfanne, -n** pan
der **Pfarrer, -s,** — clergyman
der **Pfeffer, -s** pepper
pfeifen, pfiff, gepfiffen whistle, pipe
der **Pfennig, -s, -e** penny (*one-hundredth of a Mark*)
das **Pferd, -es, -e** horse; **zu Pferde** on horseback; das **Pferdegestampf, -(e)s** stamping of horses
(die) **Pfingsten** Pentecost, Whitsuntide
pflegen cultivate, take care of, nurse; be accustomed to
der **Pflock, -(e)s, ¨-e** peg, stake
die **Pfote, -n** paw
das **Pfund, -(e)s, -e** pound
das **Phänomen', -s, -e** phenomenon
der **Philolog'(e), -en, -en** philologist
der **Philosoph', -en, -en** philosopher; die **Philosophie', -n** philosophy
die **Physik'** physics; der **Physiker, -s,** — physicist
der **Physiolog'(e), -en, -en** physiologist
das **Pilsner, -s,** — *famous beer brewed in Pilsen* (*Czechoslovakia*)
die **Platte, -n** record (*phonograph*)
der **Platz, -es, ¨-e** seat, place; space; square, court
plötzlich suddenly
das **Podium, -s,** (*plur.*) **Podien** podium
die **Poesie'** poetry
(das) **Polen, -s** Poland
polie'ren polish
die **Politik'** politics; der **Poli'tiker, -s,** — politician; **poli'tisch** political
die **Polizei'einheit, -en** police unit
der **Polizist', -en, -en** policeman
polnisch Polish; (das) **Polnisch, -en** Polish (*language*)
das **Portal', -s, -e** portal
das **Portemonnaie', -s, -s** purse
der **Portier', -s, -s** doorkeeper; doorman; die **Portiers'wohnung, -en** doorman's quarters (*or* apartment)
der **Portikus, —, -se** portico
die **Pracht** splendor; **prächtig** magnificent, splendid
prahlen brag, boast
praktisch practical
preiswert worth the money, cheap
das **Presto, -s, -s** presto (*music*)
der **Priester, -s,** — priest; das **Priestertum, -s** priesthood; clergy
primitiv' primitive

der **Prinz, –en, –en** prince
das **Privat′flugzeug, –(e)s, –e** private plane
die **Probe, –n** rehearsal; test; trial; **probie′ren** try
produktiv′ productive
der **Profes′sor, –s,** (*plur.*) **Professo′ren** professor (*male*); die **Professo′rin, –nen** professor (*fem.*)
das **Programm′, –s, –e** program; **programm′gemäß** according to plan
die **Proleta′rierherr′schaft** rule of the proletariat
der **Prophet′, –en, –en** prophet
prüfen examine, test; die **Prüfung, –en** examination, test, quiz
der **Psychia′ter, –s, —** psychiatrist
die **Psychiatrie′** psychiatry
der **Psy′choanaly′tiker, –s, —** psychoanalyst
der **Psycholog′(e), –en, –en** psychologist; die **Psychologie′, –n** psychology
das **Publikum, –s** public, audience
der **Puls, –es, –e** pulse
das **Pult, –(e)s, –e** desk
der **Punkt, –(e)s, –e** point; das **Pünktchen, –s, —** small point
putzen clean, shine, polish, brush

Q

quaken croak, quack
quäken squeal, squeak
die **Qual, –en** pain, torture; **quälen** torture
die **Qualität′, –en** quality
die **Quantität′, –en** quantity
das **Quantum, –s,** (*plur.*) **Quanten** quantity; share
der **Quark, –s** whey; trash, rubbish
die **Quart, –en** fourth (*music*)
das **Quartett′, –(e)s, –e** quartet
quatschen chatter, gab, talk nonsense
das **Quecksilber, –s** quicksilver
die **Quelle, –n** well, source, spring; **quellen (quillt), quoll, ist gequollen** well up, spring (from), swell
quer durch (right) through, (diagonally) across
queren cross
querfeldein′ cross-country, across the fields
quieken squeak
quinquillie′ren sing, warble

R

der **Rabe, –n, –n** raven
die **Rache** vengeance
das **Rad, –es, ⸚er** wheel; der **Radfahrer, –s, —** cyclist
ragen rise up
der **Rahmen, –s, —** frame, framework; limit(s); das **Rahmenholz, –es, ⸚er** wooden frame (*e.g., of a window*)
rammen ram
Ramses III. Ram(e)ses III (*Egyptian king*)
rasch quick, hasty, impetuous
rascheln rustle
rasen rage
rasie′ren shave; **sich rasie′ren** shave oneself; **sich rasie′ren lassen** get a shave
die **Rasse, –n** race, breed; der **Rassebestand, –(e)s,** (*plur.*) **Rassenbestände** racial stock; **rassenmäßig** racial; **rassisch** racial
rastlos restless
der **Rat, –es** advice
ratlos perplexed
das **Rätsel, –s, —** riddle, mystery; **rätselhaft** mysterious
der **Raub, –es** theft
der **Rauch, –(e)s** smoke; **rauchen** smoke; das **Rau′cherabteil′, –s, –e** smoking compartment; das **Rauchercoupé, –s, –s** smoking compartment
der **Raum, –(e)s, ⸚e** space; room; der **Raummangel, –s** lack of space
rauschen roar, rush (by), rustle, murmur
rechnen work on a mathematical problem, calculate, compute; die **Rechnung, –en** problem; calculation; bill
das **Recht, –(e)s, –e** right, law, justice
recht right, correct; **recht haben** be right; **Das ist mir recht.** That is all right with me; **Verste′hen Sie mich recht!** Understand me correctly! **recht** (= **sehr**) very; **erst recht** all the more
rechts to the right
rechtzeitig in time
die **Redaktion′, –en** office of the editor
die **Rede, –n** speech, talk; **es ist von . . . die Rede** there is talk of; **reden** talk, speak; der **Redner, –s, —** speaker, orator
die **Reflexion′, –en** reflection
regelmäßig regular(ly)
der **Regen, –s** rain; der **Regenguß, –gusses, –güsse** heavy rainstorm, downpour; der **Regenmantel, –s, ⸚** raincoat; der **Regenschirm, –(e)s, –e** umbrella
regie′ren rule, govern; die **Regie′rung, –en** government
das **Regiment′, –s, –er** regiment; government
reglos motionless
regnen rain
reich rich, wealthy
reichen reach, extend; suffice, last
der **Reichtum, –(e)s, ⸚er** wealth
reif ripe; mature
die **Reihe, –n** series, file, column, row, quite a number of
der **Reim, –(e)s, –e** rhyme
rein pure, clean
der **Reis, –es** rice
die **Reise, –n** trip, journey; die **Rei′sebeschrei′bung, –en** book of travel, trave-

logue; die **Rei′segesell′schaft, –en** travel group; **reisen (sein)** travel
reißen, riß, gerissen tear
reiten, ritt, ist geritten ride (*on horseback*); der **Reiter, –s, —** rider, horseman; die **Reithose(n), –n** riding breeches
der **Reiz, –es, –e** pain, irritation; charm, attraction; **reizend** charming; irritating
die **Religion′, –en** religion; **religiös′** religious
die **Renaissan′ce** the Renaissance
rennen, rannte, ist gerannt run
die **Rente, –n** pension, rent; income
der **Repor′ter, –s, —** reporter
die **Republik′, –en** republic
reservie′ren reserve
der **Rest, –(e)s, –e** rest, remnant
das **Restaurant′, –s, –s** restaurant
retten save; **sich retten vor** escape from, seek shelter from; der **Ret′tungsversuch′, –(e)s, –e** attempt at rescue
der **Rhein, –(e)s** Rhine; der **Rheinwein, –s, –e** Rhine wine
das **Rhino (Rhino′zeros), –s, –s** rhinoceros
richten point, direct; judge; set right; **richten nach** go by, adjust to; **sich nach etwas** (*dat.*) **richten** act according to something
richtig right, correct
riechen, roch, gerochen smell
riesig huge, gigantic
der **Ring, –(e)s, –e** ring, circle
die **Rippe, –n** rib
der **Rock, –(e)s, ¨–e** skirt; coat; jacket
roh coarse, rough, brutal; raw
die **Rolle, –n** part, role; pack
rollen roll
der **Roman′, –s, –e** novel
roman′tisch romantic
römisch Roman
rosig rosy
rostrot rust red
rot red
der **Rote, –n, –n** red wine
das **Rote Kreuz** Red Cross
die **Rotte, –n** gang
der **Rotwein, –(e)s, –e** red wine
routiniert′ experienced, skilful, smart
der **Ruck, –(e)s, –e** jerk
der **Rücken, –s, —** back
die **Rückführung, –en** return; derivation
das **Rückgrat, –(e)s, –e** backbone
rückwärts backwards
der **Ruf, –(e)s, –e** call; reputation; **rufen, rief, gerufen** call, shout, cry
die **Rufverbindung, –en** communication (*established through calling out*)
die **Ruhe** peace, quiet; **in Ruhe lassen** let alone; **ruhen** rest; **ruhig** peaceful, quiet, calm
der **Ruhm, –(e)s** fame; **rühmen** praise; **sich rühmen** boast
rühren (an) (*acc.*) touch, move, stir; die **Rührung** feeling, emotion
die **Rui′ne, –n** ruin(s)
der **Russe, –n, –n** Russian (*man*); die **Russin, –nen** Russian (*woman*); **russisch** Russian; (das) **Russisch, –en** Russian (*language*); (das) **Rußland, –s** Russia; die **Rußland-deutschen** (*plur.*) Russo-Germans

S

der **Saal, –(e)s,** (*plur.*) **Säle** hall
die **Sache, –n** thing; matter, affair; cause
säen sow
der **Saft, –(e)s, ¨–e** juice; der **Fruchtsaft, –(e)s, ¨–e** fruit juice
sagen say
sägen saw
die **Saha′ra** Sahara Desert
der **Salat′, –(e)s, –e** salad
die **Salbe, –n** salve, cream
das **Salz, –es, –e** salt; das **Salzwasser, –s, —** sea (*or* salt) water
(das) **Salzburg, –s** *city in Austria*
sammeln collect; der **Sammler, –s, —** collector
der **Samstag, –s, –e** Saturday
sämtlich all
der **Sandkasten, –s, ¨–** sand box; der **Sandkuchen, –s, —** mud pie
sanft gentle, soft
der **Sänger, –s, —** singer
das **Sanskrit′, –s** Sanskrit
satt satiated, satisfied (with food); **satt werden** (*gen.*) get tired of
der **Satz, –es, ¨–e** sentence; movement (*music*)
die **Sauberkeit** cleanliness
sauer sour; **Ich habe es mir sauer werden lassen.** I took great pains.
der **Sauerstoff, –es** oxygen
sausen rush, race
die **Scene** (*modern spelling:* **Szene), –n** scene
das **Schach, –s** chess; der **Schachspieler, –s, —** chess player
der **Schacht, –(e)s, ¨–e** pit, elevator shaft; ravine, gorge
schade a pity; **Es ist schade, daß . . .** What a pity that . . .; **Es ist schade um dich.** I feel sorry for you.
schaden harm
das **Schaf, –(e)s, –e** sheep
schaffen, schuf, geschaffen create, do
der **Schaffner, –s, —** conductor (R.R.)
die **Schale, –n** shell; cup
schalkhaft sly, roguish, waggish
die **Scham** shame; modesty; **sich schämen** be ashamed
scharf, schärfer, schärfst– sharp
scharlachrot scarlet

der **Schatz, –es, ⸚e** treasure; darling
schätzen esteem, estimate; die **Schätzung, –en** estimate, appraisal
der **Schauder, –s, —** shudder, awe
schauen look, see
der **Schaum, –(e)s, ⸚e** foam
der **Schauplatz, –es, ⸚e** setting
scheiden, schied, ist geschieden depart
der **Schein, –(e)s** appearance; **scheinen, schien, geschienen** shine; seem, appear; **es scheint mir** it seems to me
schelten (schilt), schalt, gescholten scold
der **Schenkel, –s, —** thigh, leg, shank
schenken give
die **Schere, –n** shears, scissors
die **Scheune, –n** barn
das **Schicksal, –s, –e** fate
schiefergrau slate grey
schießen, schoß, geschossen shoot
das **Schiff, –(e)s, –e** boat, ship; der **Schiffer, –s, —** sailor, skipper; der **Schiffs'kapitän', –s, –e** captain of a ship
das **Schild, –(e)s, –er** sign
schildern describe
schimmern shine, shimmer
schimpfen scold, curse
der **Schinken, –s, —** ham; das **Schinkenbrot, –(e)s, –e** ham sandwich
der **Schlafanzug, –(e)s, ⸚e** pajamas
schlafen (schläft), schlief, geschlafen sleep; **schlaflos** sleepless; **schläfrig** sleepy; der **Schlafrock, –(e)s, ⸚e** housecoat, bathrobe; der **Schlafsack, –(e)s, ⸚e** sleeping bag; der **Schlafwagen, –s, —** sleeping car; das **Schlafzimmer, –s, —** bedroom
schlagen (schlägt), schlug, geschlagen strike, hit, beat; defeat
das **Schlagwort, –(e)s, –e** slogan
schlecht bad, poor, low; **schlechte Noten** low (*or* poor) marks
die **Schleiche, –n** blindworm
schleichen, schlich, ist geschlichen creep, sneak
schleifen, schliff, geschliffen grind, sharpen
die **Schleuse, –n** sluice
der **Schlick, –(e)s** ooze, mud
schließen, schloß, geschlossen close
schließlich finally
schlimm bad; das **Schlimmste, –n** the worst
der **Schlips, –es, –e** tie
das **Schlittschuhlaufen, –s** skating
das **Schloß, Schlosses,** (*plur.*) **Schlösser** castle; lock
die **Schlucht, –en** canyon, ravine
der **Schlüssel, –s, —** key
der **Schluß, Schlusses, Schlüsse** conclusion; die **Schlußnummer, –n** concluding number *or* piece
schmal, schmäler, schmälst– (*or without umlaut*) narrow
die **Schmeichelei', –en** flattery; **schmeicheln** flatter
schmelzen (schmilzt), schmolz, ist geschmolzen melt
(sich) schminken put on make-up
(sich) schmücken dress up, put on finery
der **Schmutz, –es** dirt; **schmutzig** dirty
der **Schnabel, –s, ⸚** beak, mouth
das **Schnapsglas, –es, ⸚er** brandy glass
schnaufen breathe heavily, snort
der **Schnee, –s** snow; der **Schnee'orkan', –(e)s, –e** severe blizzard; das **Schneetreiben, –s** blizzard, snowfall
schneiden, schnitt, geschnitten cut, carve
der **Schneider, –s, —** tailor
schneien snow
schnell quick
der **Schnellzug, –(e)s, ⸚e** express train
das **Schnitzel, –s, —** cutlet
schnitzen carve
das **Schöffengericht, –(e)s, –e** jury court
schon already; all right, after all, no doubt
schön beautiful, pretty, nice; das **Schöne, –n** the (that which is) beautiful
schonen spare; treat with caution *or* care
der **Schöpfer, –s, —** creator; **schöpferisch** creative
der **Schrank, –(e)s, ⸚e** closet, cupboard
die **Schranke, –n** barrier
schrecken frighten; der **Schrecken, –s, —** terror; **schrecklich** frightful, terrible, awful; **schrecklich viel** an "awful lot"
schreiben, schrieb, geschrieben write; der **Schreibtisch, –(e)s, –e** desk
schreien, schrie, geschrie(e)n scream, shout
schreiten, schritt, ist geschritten stride, step
die **Schrift, –en** writing, script; **schriftlich** in writing, written; der **Schriftsteller, –s, —** writer, author
der **Schritt, –(e)s, –e** step
der **Schuh, –s, –e** shoe
die **Schularbeit, –en** homework; der **Schulatlas, —** *or* **–ses,** (*plur.*) **–atlasse** *or* **–atlan'ten** school atlas
die **Schuld, –en** guilt, blame; debt; **schuld sein an** (*dat.*) be guilty of
schuldig guilty, due, owing; **Ich bin ihm Geld schuldig.** I owe him money.
die **Schule, –n** school; die **Oberschule, –n** secondary school; die **Volksschule, –n** grammar school
die **Schulter, –n** shoulder
der **Schuster, –s, —** shoemaker, cobbler
schütteln shake
der **Schutz, –es** protection; **schützen** protect
schwach weak
der **Schwamm, –(e)s, ⸚e** sponge, (blackboard) eraser; **Schwamm drüber!** Forget it! Don't worry about it!
schwanken waver, falter

chwarz black
chwätzen gossip
das) **Schweden, –s** Sweden; **schwedisch** Swedish
chweigen, schwieg, geschwiegen be silent
ie **Schweinerei′, –en** mess
ie **Schweiz** Switzerland; **schweizerisch** Swiss
chwer heavy; difficult; severe, serious
ie **Schwester, –n** sister
chwierig difficult, hard; **die Schwierigkeit, –en** difficulty
chwimmen, schwamm, ist geschwommen swim; das **Schwimmbad, –(e)s, ⸗er** swimming pool
er **Schwindel, –s, —** dizziness; swindle, humbug; **schwindeln** swindle; **Er schwindelt.** He is not telling the truth. **Ihm schwindelt.** He is getting dizzy.
chwinden, schwand, ist geschwunden dwindle, disappear, fade away
ie **Schwindsucht** consumption
chwingen, schwang, geschwungen swing, sway, oscillate; **sich schwingen (auf** *or* **in** + *acc.*) jump, vault, leap (onto *or* into)
echs six
echzehn sixteen
echzig sixty
as **Sediment′, –s, –e** sediment
er **See, –s, –n** lake; die **See, –n** ocean, sea; das **Seewasser, –s, —** sea water, salt water
eelisch of the soul; psychological; psychic(al); **seelische Armut** poverty of the soul
ie **Segelregatta, –regatten** race of sailboats
ehen (sieht), sah, gesehen see; **Wir haben uns lange nicht gesehen.** We haven't seen each other for a long time; **sehen auf** look (down) upon; **Er läßt sich sehen.** He lets himself be seen. **Sieh da!** Well, well!
er **Sehende, –n, –n** the seeing person
er **Seher, –s, —** seer
ich sehnen (nach) long (for); die **Sehnsucht** longing, passionate desire
ehr very, very much
ihr) seid (you) are
las **Seil, –(e)s, –e** rope
ein (–e, —, —) his, its, one's
ein (ist), war, ist gewesen be; **aus-sein** be over, be finished; **Dem ist nicht so.** That is not the case.
lie **Seinen** (*plur.*) his (one's) family (people)
eit (*sub. conj.*) since
eit (*prep. dat.*) since, for; **seit acht Tagen** for a week
eitdem′ (*adv. and sub. conj.*) since then; since
lie **Seite, –n** side, page
ler **Sekt, –s** champagne
elber self
elbst itself (herself, himself, *etc.*); even

selbständig independent
selbsttätig automatic
selbstverständ′lich self-evident
die **Seligkeit, –en** bliss, happiness
selten seldom, rare(ly)
das **Semes′ter, –s, —** semester
der **Senat′, –(e)s** senate, civic authorities
senden, sandte (*or* **sendete), gesandt** (*or* **gesendet)** send
senken lower, let down; **sich senken** sink, go down
die **Sensation′, –en** sensation
sentimental′ sentimental
der **Septem′ber, –s** September
servie′ren serve (food)
Servus! (*South German greeting*) Good bye! So long! Hello!
der **Sessel, –s, —** armchair, easy chair, stool
setzen place, set, put; **sich setzen** sit down
die **Seuche, –n** epidemic, contagious disease
der **Seufzer, –s, —** sigh, groan
die **Sexte, –n** sixth (*musical interval*)
sich (*refl. and reciprocal pron.*) himself, herself, itself, oneself, one another, themselves, yourself, yourselves
sicher sure, secure, certain, safe
Sie (*acc.* **Sie,** *dat.* **Ihnen,** *gen.* **Ihrer**) you (*sing. and plur., formal address*)
sie (*acc.* **sie,** *dat.* **ihr,** *gen.* **ihrer**) she; **sie** (*acc.* **sie,** *dat.* **ihnen,** *gen.* **ihrer**) they
das **Sieb, –(e)s, –e** sieve
sieben seven
siebzehn seventeen; **siebzehnjährig** seventeen-year-old
der **Sieg, –(e)s, –e** victory
das **Signal′, –s, –e** signal
das **Silber, –s** silver; der **Silberschmied, –(e)s, –e** silversmith
singen, sang, gesungen sing; der **Singende, –n, –n** one who sings, singer
sinken, sank, ist gesunken sink
der **Sinn, –(e)s, –e** sense, meaning; mind; **Sie sagten mir, wie es ihnen zu Sinne sei.** They told me what they thought (how they felt); das **Sinn′gedicht′, –(e)s, –e** epigram (*in verse*)
sinnen, sann, gesonnen ponder, meditate
sinnvoll meaningful
die **Situation′, –en** situation
der **Sitz, –es, –e** seat; **sitzen, saß, gesessen** sit; der **Sitzplatz, –es, ⸗e** seat
das **Skelett′, –(e)s, –e** skeleton
das **Skilaufen** (*also* **Schilaufen**), **–s** skiing
die **Skulptur′, –en** sculpture
so so, that way, in this manner; **So?** Is that so? **so ein** such, such a; **so bald** (*adv.*) so soon; **so daß** so that
sobald′ (*sub. conj.*) as soon as
die **Socke, –n** sock
sodann′ next, then; in that case

soe′ben just (now)
das **Sofa, –s, –s** couch
sogar′ even, as a matter of fact
sogenannt so-called
sogleich′ immediately, at once
die **Sohle, –n** sole
der **Sohn, –(e)s, ⸚e** son
solan′ge so (*or* as) long as
solch (–e, –es, –er) such, such a
der **Soldat′, –en, –en** soldier
sollen be supposed to; should, shall; be said to; **Er soll gleich kommen.** He is to (should) come right away.
der **Sommer, –s, —** summer; die **Sommerferien** (*plur. only*) summer vacation
sondern (*coord. conj.*) but, on the contrary
der **Sonnabend, –s, –e** Saturday
die **Sonne, –n** sun; **sonnenhaft** sun-like, radiant; capable of holding sunlight; der **Sonnenaufgang, –(e)s, ⸚e** sunrise
der **Sonntag, –(e)s, –e** Sunday; **sonntags** on Sunday, Sundays
sonst otherwise, or else; formerly; usually
die **Sorge, –n** worry, care, sorrow, concern; **(sich)** (*dat.*) **Sorgen machen** worry; **sich sorgen um** be concerned about; die **Sorglosigkeit** unconcern, carefree mood
die **Sorte, –n** sort, kind
soviel as much, so much
so . . . wie as . . . as
sowie′ as well as
sowohl′ . . . wie as well as; **sowohl′ . . . als auch** as well as
der **Soziolog′(e), –en, –en** sociologist
die **Spalte, –n** *also* der **Spalt, –es, –e** crack, crevice, crevasse; **spalten** split; die **Spaltung, –en** split, fissure; division, dissension
spanisch Spanish
spaßhaft teasing, jokingly
spät late; **zu spät kommen** be late; **später** later; afterwards; **späterhin** later on
spedie′ren send on, dispatch
die **Speise, –n** dish, meal, food; der **Speisesaal, –s,** (*plur.*) **–säle** dining hall; der **Speisewagen, –s, —** dining car; das **Speisezimmer, –s, —** dining room
das **Spekta′kelstück, –(e)s, –e** spectacular play
die **Spekulation′, –en** speculation
das **Sperrfeuer, –s, —** barrage
das **Spezial′gefühlchen, –s, —** little private sentiment
der **Spiegel, –s, —** mirror
das **Spiegelei, –s, –er** fried egg
das **Spiel, –(e)s, –e** game, play; **spielen** play; der **Spielplatz, –es, ⸚e** play yard; das **Spielzimmer, –s, —** playroom, toy room; der **Spiel′zeugsoldat′, –en, –en** toy soldier
spießen pierce, stick on a fork
spitz pointed; die **Spitze, –n** point, peak; **spitzen** sharpen; **die Ohren spitzen** prick up (one's) ears
der **Sport, –(e)s** sport
die **Sprache, –n** language; die **Spracheinheit** language unit; die **Sprachfami′lie, –n** family of languages; der **Sprachforscher, –s, —** linguistic scholar, philologist; die **Sprachforschung, –en** linguistic research; die **Sprachgemein′schaft, –en** language community; das **Sprachgesetz, –(e)s, –e** linguistic law; die **Sprachkunde** science of languages, linguistics; **sprachlich** linguistic; das **Sprachrohr, –(e)s, –e** megaphone; der **Sprachwissenschaftler, –s, —** linguist
das **Sprechen, –s** a mode of communication (*see p. 270, l. 4*)
sprechen (spricht), sprach, gesprochen speak; **sprechen über** (*w. acc.*) speak about, discuss
springen, sprang, ist gesprungen jump
spritzen spray, squirt
der **Spruch, –(e)s, ⸚e** epigram
sprudeln bubble
der **Sprung, –es, ⸚e** leap
spucken spit
die **Spur, –en** trace, track, footprint
spüren feel, sense
der **Staat, –(e)s, –en** state; der **Staatsbeamte, –n, –n** state *or* civil official; der **Staatsbürger, –s, —** citizen
der **Stab, –(e)s, ⸚e** staff, rod
das **Stadium, –s,** (*plur.*) **Stadien** stage; stadium
die **Stadt, ⸚e** city, town; das **Städtchen, –s, —** small town
stammen (aus *or* **von** *with dat.*) stem *or* originate from; come from; be born in; **stammverwandt** cognate, kindred
stampfen stamp, pound
der **Stand, –(e)s, ⸚e** state; condition; class
ständig steadily
stark strong
starr stiff, rigid; **mit starren Fingern** with stiff (frozen) fingers
starren stare
die **Station′, –en** station
statt (*prep. gen., sub. conj.*) instead of
stattdes′sen instead of that
statt-finden, fand statt, stattgefunden take place
die **Statue, –n** statue
staunen marvel, be astonished
stecken-bleiben, blieb stecken, ist steckengeblieben get stuck, break down
stehen, stand, gestanden stand; **Es steht in dem Buch.** It says so in the book. **So steht es.** That's the way it is.
stehen-bleiben, blieb stehen, ist stehengeblieben stop
steif stiff
steigen, stieg, ist gestiegen climb, mount

er **Stein** –(e)s, –e stone
ie **Steinzeit, –en** Stone Age
ie **Stelle, –n** place, position; **an ihrer Stelle** in her place
tellen put, place, set; **jemandem ein Bein stellen** trip someone up; **jemandem eine Frage stellen** ask someone a question; **sich stellen** pretend
ie **Stellung, –en** position
ie **Steppe, –n** steppe
terben (stirbt), starb, ist gestorben die
er **Stern, –(e)s, –e** star
tets constantly
er **Stich, –(e)s, –e** stab, thrust, cut
ie **Stichprobe, –n** spot check
as **Stichwort, –(e)s, –e** cue
er **Stiefel, –s, —** boot
ie **Stiege, –n** step, staircase; **über vier Stiegen** four flights up
das) **Stieglbräu, –s** *a restaurant in Salzburg*
tiften establish; initiate; bequeath; make a present of, give (*coll.*)
till quiet, still; **still-stehen** (*see* **stehen**) stand still, stop
ie **Stimme, –n** voice
timmen tune; vote; accord, agree; be correct; **Das stimmt.** That's right; **stimmhaft** voiced (*phonetics*); **stimmlos** voiceless (*phonetics*)
ie **Stimmung, –en** mood
ie **Stirn(e), –en** forehead
as **Stockwerk, –(e)s, –e** floor, story
tolpern (sein) stumble
tören disturb
toßen (stößt), stieß, gestoßen push
ie **Strafe, –n** fine, punishment; **in Strafe nehmen** penalize
trahlen beam, radiate, smile; **strahlend** radiant
traßburger of Strassburg
ie **Straße, –n** street, highway; der **Straßenanzug, –(e)s, ¨–e** everyday suit, business suit
treben (nach) strive *or* aspire (toward)
ie **Strecke, –n** distance; length *or* tract (of land)
as **Streichholz, –es, ¨–er** match
er **Streit, –(e)s** strife, conflict, quarrel; **streitbar** aggressive, valiant; die **Streitigkeit, –en** quarrel, struggle
treng stern, strict, severe
treuen scatter
er **Strick, –(e)s, –e** rope
as **Strohlager, –s, —** bed of straw
er **Strom –(e)s, ¨–e** stream, river; die **Strömung, –en** current
er **Strumpf, –es, ¨–e** stocking
as **Stück, –es, –e** piece; play (*drama*)
er **Student', –en, –en** student (*masc.*); die **Studen'tin, –nen** (*fem.*); das **Studen'tenheim, –(e)s, –e** student dormitory; die **Studen'tenorganisation', –en** student organization
studie'ren study
die **Stufe, –n** step
der **Stuhl, –(e)s, ¨–e** chair
stumm dumb; silent, mute
stumpf dull, apathetic
die **Stunde, –n** hour; class; **von dieser Stunde an** from this hour on, from now on; **stundenlang** for hours; der **Stundenlohn, –(e)s, ¨–e** wage per hour
der **Sturm, –(e)s, ¨–e** storm; **stürmisch** stormy
der **Sturz, –es, ¨–e** plunge, sudden fall; **stürzen (sein)** fall, plunge
die **Subtilität', –en** subtlety
suchen look for, seek; search; try
(das) **Süda'frika, –s** South Africa
(das) **Südame'rika, –s** South America
süddeutsch Southern German
der **Süden, –s** south; der **Süd'kamin', –(e)s, –e** southern chimney *or* fissure; die **Südkante, –n** southern edge; **südlich** southern
(das) **Südeuro'pa, –s** Southern Europe; (das) **Südwest'euro'pa, –s** Southwestern Europe
summen hum; das **Summen, –s** humming
die **Suppe, –n** soup; der **Suppenlöffel, –s, —** soup spoon; der **Suppenteller, –s, —** soup plate
süß sweet; die **Süßspeise, –n** sweets, dessert; das **Süßwasser, –s, —** fresh water; die **Süßwasserart, –en** fresh-water species; der **Süßwassersee, –s, –n** fresh-water lake
symbo'lisch symbolic
die **Symphonie', –n** symphony

T

tadeln rebuke, criticize, censure
die **Tafel, –n** blackboard; table
der **Tag, –(e)s, –e** day; **tagaus', tagein'** day in, day out; das **Tagebuch, –(e)s, ¨–er** diary; die **Tageszeit, –en** time of day; **zu Tage treten** become evident, come to light; **täglich** daily; **tags** in the daytime; **den Tag über** the whole day long; **Guten Tag!** How do you do? Hello!
die **Taille, –n** waistline
der **Takt, –(e)s, –e** measure, beat; tact
das **Tal, –(e)s, ¨–er** valley, dale, glen; **talaus' talein'** in and out of the valley(s)
das **Talent', –(e)s, –e** talent
der **Tank, –(e)s, –s** tank
die **Tante, –n** aunt
der **Tanz, –es, ¨–e** dance; **tanzen** dance; der **Tanzsaal, –(e)s, –säle** dance hall
die **Tape'te, –n** wallpaper
tappen grope
die **Tasche, –n** handbag, pocket; das **Taschentuch, –(e)s, ¨–er** handkerchief; die **Tashenuhr, –en** pocket watch

die **Tasse, –n** cup; **eine Tasse Kaffee** a cup of coffee
die **Tat, –en** act, deed; **tätig** active
die **Tatsache, –n** fact; **tatsächlich** actually, indeed
das **Täubchen, –s, —** little dove; darling; die **Taube, –n** dove
taufen baptize, name
die **Täuschung, –en** deception
tausend thousand
technisch technical, technological
der **Tee, –s** tea; der **Teelöffel, –s, —** teaspoon
der **Teil, –(e)s, –e** part, unit; **teils** partly
telephonie'ren (tele)phone
der **Teller, –s, —** plate, platter
das **Temperament', –s, –e** temperament, temper; spirits
die **Tendenz', –en** tendency, message (*of a play, novel, etc.*)
der **Tennisplatz, –es, ⸚e** tennis court
der **Teppich, –s, –e** carpet, rug
die **Terz, –en** third (*musical interval*)
teuer dear; expensive; beloved, precious
das **Textbuch, –(e)s, ⸚er** textbook
das **Thea'ter, –s, —** theater; die **Thea'terkarte, –n** theater ticket; das **Thea'terstück, –(e)s, –e** play
die **Theorie', –n** theory
tief deep; die **Tiefe, –n** depth
das **Tier, –(e)s, –e** animal; der **Tierarzt, –(e)s, ⸚e** veterinarian; das **Tier'symbol', –(e)s, –e** animal symbol
die **Tinte, –n** ink
der **Tisch, –(e)s, –e** table; das **Tischtuch, –(e)s, ⸚er** tablecloth
der **Titel, –s, —** title; das **Titelblatt, –(e)s, ⸚er** title page; der **Titelheld, –en, –en** actor playing the title *or* leading role
die **Tochter, ⸚** daughter
der **Tod, –es, –e** death; **todmüde** dead tired
toll mad
der **Ton, –(e)s, ⸚e** sound, tone; die **Tonart, –en** key; der **Tondichter, –s, —** composer
das **Tor, –(e)s, –e** gate
der **Tor, –en, –en** fool; die **Torheit, –en** folly; **töricht** foolish
der **Tornis'ter, –s, —** knapsack, pack
die **Torte, –n** cake, tart
tot dead; der **Tote, –n, –n** dead man; **totgesagt** declared dead; **totenstill** deathly still, quiet as death
töten kill
der **Trab, –(e)s** trott
trachten (nach) strive (for *or* toward)
die **Tradition', –en** tradition
tragen (trägt), trug, getragen wear, carry
tragisch tragic
die **Tragö'die, –n** tragedy

die **Träne, –n** tear; **tränenblind** blinded with tears
der **Trank, –(e)s** drink
der **Traubenzucker, –s** grape sugar (tablets)
das **Trauerspiel, –(e)s, –e** tragedy
der **Traum, –(e)s, ⸚e** dream
traurig sad, dreary
treffen (trifft), traf, getroffen meet; hit
trefflich splendid, excellent
treiben, trieb, getrieben drive, push
trennen separate; **Ich kann mich nicht trennen** I cannot tear myself away; die **Trennung, –en** separation
die **Treppe, –n** stairs, stairway; der **Treppenabsatz, –es, ⸚e** landing (of a staircase); **treppauf', treppab'** up and down the stair
treten (tritt), trat, ist getreten step
treu faithful, good; die **Treue** faithfulness, loyalty
der **Trichter, –s, —** shell hole; funnel
der **Trieb, –(e)s, –e** affection, impulse, drive
trinken, trank, getrunken drink
das **Trio, –s, –s** trio (*music*)
der **Tritt, –(e)s, –e** step; **Ohne Tritt!** Break step! (*military*)
trocken dry; die **Trockenheit** aridity; **trocknen** dry
das **Trommelfeuer, –s, —** drumfire
das **Tröpfchen, –s, —** small drop; der **Tropfen, –s, —** drop
tropisch tropical
der **Trost, –(e)s** consolation, comfort; das **Trostlied, –(e)s, –er** song of solace; **trostlos** desolate, desperate, disconsolate
trotten (sein) trot
der **Trotz, –es** defiance
trotz (*prep. dat. or gen.*) despite, in spite of; **trotzdem** (*adv. or sub. conj.*) in spite of the fact that, although; nevertheless
trügen, trog, getrogen deceive
der **Trunkene, –n, –n** drunkard
die **Truppe, –n** troup
das **Tuch, –(e)s, ⸚er** cloth, scarf
die **Tugend, –en** virtue
tun, tat, getan do; **weh-tun, tat weh, wehgetan** (*dat.*) hurt; **so tun, als ob** act as if
die **Tür, –en** door
türkisch Turkish
der **Turm, –(e)s, ⸚e** tower; der **Turmhelm, –(e)s, –e** dome
der **Turnverein, –s, –e** athletic club
der **Tyrann', –en, –en** tyrant

U

übel bad, evil
üben practice
über (*prep. dat. or acc.*) over, above; about; **überall** everywhere
das **Überbleibsel, –s, —** remainder, remnant

überdies′ besides
überein′stimmen agree, correspond
überfal′len (überfällt), überfiel, überfallen pounce upon, attack suddenly
überflüssig superfluous
über-gehen, ging über, ist übergegangen cross, go over, join the other side, flow over
überhaupt′ in general, on the whole; anyway; at all; **überhaupt′ niemand** no one at all
überkom′men, überkam, überkommen be handed down, receive
überle′ben survive
überle′gen consider; (*usually*) **sich** (*dat.*) **(etwas) überle′gen** reflect *or* think about (something)
übermorgen day after tomorrow
die **Überprü′fung, -en** scrutiny
überque′ren cross over
überra′schen surprise, startle
die **Überschwem′mung, -en** inundation, flood
über-setzen ferry across
überset′zen translate
überwäl′tigen overwhelm
überzeu′gen convince
üblich customary, usual
übrig remaining, left; das **Übrige, -n** the rest
übrigens incidentally, besides
die **Uhr, -en** clock, watch; **um zehn Uhr** at ten o'clock; **Um wieviel Uhr?** At what time? **null Uhr** midnight; der **Uhrenschmuggel, -s** watch smuggling
um (*prep. acc.*) around; at; about; for; over; up
um . . . zu (*with inf.*) in order to; **um dich zu besu′chen** in order to visit you
umar′men embrace
der **Umfang, -(e)s, ¨-e** radius, extent
umfas′sen, umfaßte, umfaßt encompass; contain
umge′ben (umgibt), umgab, umgeben surround; include; die **Umge′bung** surroundings, neighborhood
umgekehrt the other way around, vice versa
um-kehren (sein) turn back, turn around
um-kommen, kam um, ist umgekommen perish
ums = **um das**
(**sich**) **um-sehen (sieht um), sah um, umgesehen** look around *or* back
der **Umstand, -(e)s, ¨-e** circumstance; **mildernde Umstände** extenuating circumstances
die **Umwälzung, -en** revolution, upheaval
unausweich′lich inevitable, unavoidable
unbedingt absolute(ly)
unbefleck′bar untarnishable
unbekannt unknown; der **Unbekannte, -n, -n** stranger, unknown person
unbeschäftigt idle
unbeständig inconstant
unbeweglich fixed, motionless
und (*coord. conj.*) and
das **Unend′liche, -n** infinite
unerhört′ unheard of; das **Unerhör′te, -n** the unheard of
unerwartet unexpected
(das) **Ungarn, -s** Hungary; **ungarisch** Hungarian
die **Ungeduld** impatience; **ungeduldig** impatient
ungefähr about, approximately
ungeheuer immense
ungelernt untrained, unskilled
ungemein extraordinary
ungeschickt clumsy
ungewöhnlich unusual
ungezogen ill-mannered
ungleich uneven, unequal
unglücklich unhappy
Uniso′no: im Uniso′no in unison
die **Universität′, -en** university
unmerklich imperceptible
unmittelbar immediate, direct
unmöglich impossible
unnütz unnecessary; useless
unpraktisch impractical
das **Unrecht, -s** wrong, injustice; **im Unrecht sein** be wrong
unromantisch unromantic
die **Unruhe, -n** unrest
die **Unschuld** innocence
unser (-e, —, —) our
der **Unsinn, -s** nonsense
unten below, downstairs, at the bottom
unter (*prep. dat. or acc.*) under, below; among, amid, between; **unter Freunden** among friends; **unter uns (gesagt)** between you and me
unterbre′chen (unterbricht), unterbrach, unterbrochen interrupt
die **Unterfamilie, -n** subfamily (*language*)
sich unterfan′gen (*gen.*) **(unterfängt), unterfing, unterfangen** venture, dare; presume
untergeteilt subdivided
unterhalb (*prep. gen.*) below
unterhal′ten (unterhält), unterhielt, unterhalten entertain; **sich unterhal′ten** converse, talk; **unterhal′tend** entertaining
unterneh′men (unternimmt), unternahm, unternommen undertake, do
unterschei′den, unterschied, unterschieden distinguish, differentiate; der **Unterschied, -(e)s, -e** difference
das **Unterseeboot, -(e)s, -e** submarine; **unterseeisch** (*adj.*) submarine
unterstel′len assume, suppose
die **Untersu′chung, -en** investigation
unter-tauchen (sein) submerge; das **Untertauchen, -s** going underground
ununterbro′chen continual, uninterrupted

unverse′hens inadvertently, suddenly
unwahrscheinlich improbable
die **Urform, –en** primitive form
das **Urgefühl, –(e)s, –e** basic emotion, primordial feeling
die **Ursache, –n** cause
die **Ursprache, –n** primitive language
der **Ursprung, –(e)s, ⸚e** origin; **ursprünglich** original; der **Ursprungsort, –(e)s, –e** place of origin

V

der **Vater, –s, ⸚** father; das **Vaterland, –es, ⸚er** fatherland
(das) **Vene′dig, –s** Venice
sich verab′schieden take leave
die **Verän′derlichkeit** changeability; **(sich) verän′dern** change; die **Verän′derung, –en** change
(sich) verant′worten für (*with acc.*) be responsible for, answer for
verber′gen (verbirgt), verbarg, verborgen hide, conceal
verbie′ten, verbot, verboten forbid; das **Verbot′, –(e)s, –e** prohibition, restriction
verbin′den, verband, verbunden unite, bind; connect; die **Verbin′dung, –en** association, connection
das **Verbor′genste, –n** the most secret thing(s)
verbrei′ten spread; die **Verbrei′tung** spread, dissemination; range
verbrin′gen, verbrachte, verbracht spend (*time*)
die **Verbun′denheit** unity
verdan′ken owe; attribute
das **Verder′ben, –s** detriment, ruin; corruption
verdie′nen deserve, merit; earn
verdrän′gen displace
verdrie′ßen, verdroß, verdrossen sadden; annoy; die **Verdrieß′lichkeit, –en** annoyance
vereh′ren venerate, worship
verein′fachen simplify
die **Verei′nigten Staaten** the United States
vereist′ icy, ice-covered
verfal′len (verfällt), verfiel, ist verfallen decay
verfil′men make into a movie
verflu′chen curse; **verflucht′** blasted, accursed
verfüg′bar available
verfüh′ren entice, seduce
die **Vergan′genheit** past
verge′ben (vergibt), vergab, vergeben forgive; **verge′bens** in vain; die **Verge′bung** forgiveness
verge′hen, verging, ist vergangen go by, pass (*of time*); **vergan′gen** (*adj.*) past, last; die **Vergan′genheit** past
verges′sen (vergißt), vergaß, vergessen forget; das **Vergiß′meinnicht, –(e)s, –e** forget-me-not
verglei′chen, verglich, verglichen compare; **verglei′chend** comparative
das **Vergnü′gen, –s, —** pleasure
verhaf′ten arrest
verha′ken catch, entangle
das **Verhält′nis, –ses, –se** proportion, relation; (*plur. often*) circumstances; **verhält′nismäßig** relatively
sich verhei′raten get married; **verhei′ratet** married
verhe′xen bewitch, enchant
verhin′dern prevent
verhül′len veil, enshroud
der **Verkehr′, –s** traffic; trade, communication
verkrus′tet crusted over
das **Verlan′gen, –s (nach)** desire (for); **verlan′gen** demand
verlas′sen (verläßt), verließ, verlassen leave, abandon; **sich verlas′sen auf** (*w. acc.*) depend upon
verläß′lich reliable
verlau′fen (verläuft), verlief, ist verlaufen run; **sich verlau′fen** lose one's way
verle′ben spend, use up; waste (*time*)
verle′gen (*verb*) misplace
verle′gen (*adj., adv.*) embarrassed; die **Verle′genheit, –en** embarrassment, difficulty; **in Verle′genheit kommen** get into an embarrassing situation
verlet′zen hurt, offend
sich verlie′ben in (*acc.*) fall in love with; **verliebt′** in love
verlie′ren, verlor, verloren lose
verlobt′ engaged
vermis′sen miss
vermit′teln represent; mediate, negotiate
vermö′gen (vermag), vermochte, vermocht can
vernach′lässigen neglect
vernich′ten destroy; die **Vernich′tung, –en** destruction
vernünf′tig reasonable, rational, sensible
die **Verord′nung, –en** ruling, order, mandate
die **Verpfle′gung** food supply
verra′ten (verrät), verriet, verraten betray; tell, show, reveal
verrückt′ crazy
der **Vers, –es, –e** verse
versa′gen fail
verschie′ben, verschob, verschoben delay, postpone; (*refl.*) shift
verschie′den various, different
verschla′gen (*adj.*) lost, wayward
verschlep′pen drag away, transport forcibly, deport
verschlin′gen, verschlang, verschlungen devour; **sich verschlin′gen** interlace
der **Verschluß′laut, –es, –e** stop (*phonetics*);

die stimmhaften und stimmlosen Verschlußlaute the voiced and voiceless stops
verschmä′hen despise, reject
verschmitzt′ clever, cunning
verschwei′gen, verschwieg, verschwiegen keep secret
verschwin′den, verschwand, ist verschwunden disappear
versen′ken (cause to) sink, submerge
versi′chern assure; insure; die **Versi′cherung, –en** insurance; die **Versi′cherungssumme, –n** insurance (sum *or* payment)
versöh′nen reconcile
verspre′chen (verspricht), versprach, versprochen promise
der **Verstand′, –(e)s** understanding, intellect; **Verstan′den?** Understand? **verstän′dig** reasonable; die **Verstän′digung, –en** agreement; **verständ′lich** understandable; das **Verständ′nis, –ses** understanding
das **Versteck′, –(e)s, –e** hiding place, retreat; **verste′cken** hide; **sich verste′cken vor** (*with dat.*) hide from
verste′hen, verstand, verstanden understand
verstum′men become silent, stop, subside
der **Versuch′, –(e)s, –e** attempt, test; **versu′chen** try, attempt; tempt; die **Versu′chung, –en** temptation
vertei′digen defend
sich vertie′fen in (*with acc.*) become engrossed in
sich vertra′gen (verträgt), vertrug, vertra′gen (mit) get along *or* be in agreement (with)
vertun′, vertat, vertan waste
verur′sachen cause
verur′teilen condemn, sentence, fine
verwandt′ related
der **Verwan′dte,** die **Verwan′dte** relative (*masc. and fem.*); **die Verwan′dten** relatives; die **Verwandt′schaft, –en** affinity, relationship
verwen′den, verwandte (*or* **verwendete**), **verwandt** (*or* **verwendet**) use
verwer′fen (verwirft), verwarf, verworfen reject, condemn
verwir′ren confuse; **verwir′rend** confusing, baffling
die **Verwun′derung** surprise
verwüs′tet devastated, desolate; die **Verwü′stung, –en** devastation
verzeh′ren consume
verzei′hen, verzieh, verziehen (*with dat.*) excuse, pardon
(sich) verzie′hen, verzog, verzogen move away, shift; **keine Miene verzie′hen** not move a muscle
verzwei′felt in despair, desperate; **verzweif′lungsvoll** desperate
der **Vetter, –s, –n** cousin (*male*)
das **Vieh, –s** cattle
viel much; **viele** many; **vielgeliebt′** much beloved; **viel′gestal′tig** variously shaped, multiform
vielleicht′ perhaps
vielmehr on the contrary, rather, on the other hand
die **Vielseitigkeit** versatility
vier four
das **Viertel, –s, —** quarter
vierzehn fourteen
die **Violi′ne, –n** violin; der **Violinist′, –en, –en** violinist; das **Violoncel′l(o), –(o)s,** (*plur.*) **–cellos** violoncello
der **Vogel, –s, ¨–** bird; das **Vöglein, –s, —** little bird
das **Volk, –(e)s, ¨–er** people; **volksdeutsch** of German origin (*not citizenship*); der **Volkstanz, –es, ¨–e** folk dance; die **Volkstracht, –en** national costume
die **Volksschule, –n** grammar school
voll (von) full (of)
vollen′den complete; say finally; perfect, finish
völlig complete(ly)
vollkommen complete, perfect
vollständig complete, all-inclusive
(sich) vollzie′hen, vollzog, vollzogen be accomplished; take place
vom = **von dem**
von from, by (*agency*), of; about; **ein Freund von mir** a friend of mine; **von neuem** anew
vor (*prep. dat. or acc.*) in front of (*location*); before (*time*); ago, of, to; **zehn Minu′ten vor neun** ten minutes of (*or* to) nine
vor allem above all
voran′-gehen, ging voran, ist vorangegangen precede
vor-arbeiten prepare
voraus′-sehen (sieht voraus), sah voraus, vorausgesehen anticipate, foresee
vorbei′ over, gone, past; **an dem Hause vorbei′** past the house
vor-bereiten prepare
v. Chr. Geb. (vor Christi Geburt) B.C.
vorderst first
der **Vorfahr(e), –en, –en** ancestor
der **Vorgang, –(e)s, ¨–e** event, proceeding
vor-gehen, ging vor, ist vorgegangen go ahead; **Die Uhr geht vor.** The watch is fast.
vorgestern day before yesterday
vorhan′den available; imminent, present; at hand
der **Vorhang, –(e)s, ¨–e** curtain
vorher before, beforehand
vorhin previously
vorig preceding, previous; last
vor-kommen, kam vor, ist vorgekommen occur; **Das ist mir nie vorgekommen.** That never occurred (happened) to me.
vor-legen present

die **Vorlesung, –en** lecture
vorlieb′-nehmen (nimmt vorlieb), nahm vorlieb, vorliebgenommen mit be content with; put up with
vorm = **vor dem**
vorn(e): nach vorn(e) to the front (of the room, hall)
der **Vorname, –ns, –n** first name
vor-nehmen: sich (*dat.*) **etwas** (*acc.*) **vornehmen (nimmt vor), nahm vor, vorgenommen** resolve on (doing) something; decide (*or* intend) to do (*or* be) something
der **Vorrang, –(e)s** preference; priority
vors = **vor das**
der **Vorsaal, –(e)s,** (*plur.*) **–säle** lobby, antechamber
der **Vorschlag, –(e)s, ⸚e** suggestion, proposal
die **Vorschrift, –en** instruction(s), prescription
vor-singen, sang vor, vorgesungen sing to
die **Vorspeise, –n** appetizer, hors d'œuvre
das **Vorspiel, –(e)s, –e** prelude, overture, prologue
vor-stellen introduce (a person); **sich** (*dat.*) **etwas** (*acc.*) **vor-stellen** imagine something; **Ich kann mir das nicht vorstellen.** I cannot imagine that.
die **Vorstellung, –en** performance
der **Vorteil, –(e)s, –e** advantage
der **Vortragende, –n, –n** lecturer
vorü′ber past
vorü′ber-gehen, ging vorüber, ist vorübergegangen pass by; **vorü′bergehend** passing, temporary
vorü′ber-kommen, kam vorüber, ist vorübergekommen an (*with dat.*) come (go) past
vor-ziehen, zog vor, vorgezogen prefer
der **Vorzug, –(e)s, ⸚e** preference; priority; superiority
vorzüg′lich excellent
die **Vorzugsstellung, –en** privileged position
vulgär′ vulgar, common

W

die **Wache, –n** guard; **wachen** be awake, keep watch; **Wache halten** stand guard
wachsen (wächst), wuchs, ist gewachsen grow
die **Waffe, –n** weapon
der **Waffenrock, –(e)s, ⸚e** tunic
der **Wagen, –s, —** car, automobile, wagon
wagen dare
wählen choose
wahr true; **Nicht wahr?** Isn't it? Hasn't it? Doesn't it? Don't you? Won't he? Can't she? *etc.*
während (*prep. gen.*) during; (*sub. conj.*) while, whereas
die **Wahrheit, –en** truth; **wahr′heitsgetreu′** truthfully; **wahr′heitsgemäß′** truthfully
der **Wahrsager, –s, —** fortuneteller
der **Wald, –(e)s, ⸚er** wood, forest
die **Waldgeiß, –en** woodgoat
die **Wand, ⸚e** wall
wandern (sein) travel, wander, go; die **Wanderung, –en** migration
die **Wanduhr, –en** clock
die **Wange, –n** cheek
wanken reel, sway, waver
wann when
warm, wärmer, wärmst– warm
warnen vor (*dat.*) warn about *or* against; die **Warnung, –en** warning
(das) **Warschau, –s** Warsaw
warten wait; **warten auf** (*acc.*) wait for
der **Wartturm, –(e)s, ⸚e** watchtower
warum′ why
was what; **was für ein** what sort of, what kind of
(sich) waschen (wäscht), wusch, gewaschen wash (oneself)
das **Wasser, –s, —** water; der **Wasserkessel, –s, —** water kettle; das **Wassernest, –(e)s, –er** watery nest; die **Wasserschlange, –n** water snake
der **Weber, –s, —** weaver
der **Wechsel, –s, —** change; der **Wechselgesang, –(e)s, ⸚e** alternating song; **wechseln** change
der **Wecker, –s, —** alarm clock
die **Weckuhr, –en** alarm clock
weder . . . noch neither . . . nor
weg away, gone
der **Weg, –(e)s, –e** way, road; **des Weg(e)s kommen** come along the way
wegen (*prep. gen.*) because of, on behalf of; regarding; on account of
weg-gehen, ging weg, ist weggegangen go away
wegwerfend contemptuously
das **Weh, –s** woe
die **Wehmut** sadness
weh-tun, tat weh, wehgetan (*dat.*) hurt; **Es tut ihr weh.** It hurts her.
das **Weib, –(e)s, –er** woman, wife
weich soft; die **Weichheit** softness; tenderness
die **Weide, –n** pasture
(sich) weihen (*dat.*) dedicate (oneself) to
(die) **Weihnacht** *or plur.* die **Weihnachten** Christmas
weil because
die **Weile** while
weilen linger
der **Wein, –(e)s, –e** wine
weise wise; der **Weise, –n, –n** wise man, seer
die **Weise, –n** manner, way; **auf diese Weise** in this manner
weisen show
die **Weisheit** wisdom
weiß white; der **Weißwein, –s, –e** white wine

weit far, wide
Weite: das Weite suchen take off, run away
weiter further, on; additional
weiter-bestehen, bestand weiter, weiterbestanden continue to exist
das **Weitere, –n** what follows, the following
weiterhin further(more), further on *or* ahead
weithin widely
weitreichend far-reaching
welch (–e, –es, –er) which, what, who
die **Welle, –n** wave
die **Welt, –en** world; die **Welt′föderation′, –en** world federation; der **Weltkrieg, –(e)s, –e** World War; die **Weltreise, –n** trip around the world; die **Welt′revolution′, –en** world revolution; der **Weltteil, –s, –e** continent
wenden, wandte (*or* **wendete**), **gewandt** (*or* **gewendet)** turn; **sich wenden an** (*with acc.*) turn to
wenig little, (*plur.*) few; **weniger** less; minus; **umso weniger** all the less; **wenigst–** least; **wenigstens** at least; **am wenigsten** least of all
wenn (*sub. conj.*) if, when, whenever; **wenn . . . auch** (*or* **auch wenn**) even if
wer (*interr. and rel. pron.*) who, he who, whoever
werden (wird), wurde, ist geworden become, grow, get; shall, will; be; **Er wird alt.** He is growing old. **Es wird spät.** It is getting late. **Es wird Nacht.** Night is setting in; **werden zu** become; be changed to, change, turn to; **Er wird kommen.** He will come. **Das wird so gemacht.** That is done this way.
werfen (wirft), warf, geworfen throw
das **Werk, –(e)s, –e** work
das **Werkzeug, –(e)s, –e** tool
der **Wert, –(e)s, –e** value, worth
der **Werwolf, –(e)s, ⸚e** the wer(e)wolf
das **Wesen, –s, —** being, essence; creature; existence, nature; **wesentlich** essential; considerable; das **Wesentliche, –n** the essential, the point; **im wesentlichen** essentially
westdeutsch West German
der **Westen, –s** west; die **Westküste, –n** West Coast; **westlich** western
die **Westmäche** Western Powers
weswegen why
das **Wetter, –s, —** weather; der **Wettersturz, –es, ⸚e** abrupt change in weather
wichtig important
wider (*prep. acc.*) against, contrary to
der **Widerstand, –(e)s, ⸚e** resistance
widrig unpleasant
widrigenfalls otherwise, failing which (this)
wie (*conj. and adv.*) how, as, like, such as; when (*see* **als**)
wieder again; **schon wieder** once again
wieder-auf′bauen rebuild
wiederho′len repeat
die **Wiederkunft** return
wieder-sehen (sieht wieder), sah wieder, wiedergesehen see again; **Auf Wiedersehen!** Goodbye! So long! See you again (*or* later)!
wiederum again
die **Wie′derverei′nigung, –en** reunification
(das) **Wien, –s** Vienna; der **Wiener, –s, —** Viennese
die **Wiese, –n** meadow, pasture; der **Wiesengrund, –(e)s, ⸚e** meadowland
Wieso′? How come?
wieviel′ how much; **wie viele** how many
wild wild
die **Wildtaube, –n** wild dove
der **Wille, –ns** will
um . . . willen (*gen.*) for the sake of . . .
der **Wind, –(e)s, –e** wind; das **Windgespräch, –(e)s, –e** wind talk
winken wave, signal, beckon
der **Winter, –s, —** winter; die **Winterreise, –n** winter journey
winzig tiny, minute
wir (*acc.* **uns**, *dat.* **uns**, *gen.* **unser**) we
wirken have *or* produce an effect; do work; operate
wirklich really; die **Wirklichkeit, –en** reality
die **Wirkung, –en** effect, impact
wirr confused
der **Wirt, –(e)s, –e** host, innkeeper
der **Wirtschaftsrat, –(e)s, ⸚e** economic and social council
wissen (weiß), wußte, gewußt know (*referring to factual knowledge as distinct from* **kennen**); **Er machte ihnen zu wissen, daß . . .** He informed them that . . .
die **Wissenschaft, –en** science; der **Wissenschaftler, –s, —** scientist
die **Witterung** weather (conditions)
der **Witz, –es, –e** joke, wit; **witzig** witty
wo where, in which; **wodurch′** whereby; **womit′** with what (wherewith); **wofür′** for what (wherefore); **worauf′** on which *or* what (whereupon); **worin′** in which *or* what (wherein)
die **Woche, –n** week; das **Wochenende, –s, –n** weekend; **wöchentlich** weekly
woher′ from where
wohin′ whereto, to what place, where
wohl probably, well, indeed
die **Wohltat, –en** benefit, kindness, blessing
wohnen live (dwell); die **Wohnung, –en** apartment; das **Wohnzimmer, –s, —** living room
der **Wolf, –(e)s, ⸚e** wolf
die **Wolke, –n** cloud
wollen (will), wollte, gewollt want to, intend to, be determined to; claim, profess;

be about to; **ein großes Wollen** a strong will *or* desire
womit′ with what, with which
womög′lich possibly, if possible, perhaps
die **Wonne, –n** bliss
woran′ on (at) it *or* that; **Woran liegt es, daß . . .?** What is the reason that . . .?
worauf′ whereupon, on which *or* what
worin′ in which *or* what, wherein, of what
das **Wort, –es** word, phrase; (*plur.*) **Worte** words (*in context*), phrase(s); **Wörter** (*isolated*) words
wozu′ which, for which; for what purpose
das **Wunder, –s** — wonder, miracle; **Kein Wunder!** Small wonder! This is not surprising! **wunderbar** wonderful, wondrous; **wunderlich** strange; odd; **sich wundern über** (*with acc.*) be surprised at; **wundersam** wondrous, strange
der **Wunsch, –es, ⸚e** wish; **wünschen** wish
würde (*present imaginative of* **werden**) would, should
die **Wurzel, –n** root
die **Wüste, –n** desert
die **Wut** rage, fury; **in Wut gera′ten** become enraged; **wüten** rage

Z

zaghaft timid, scared
die **Zahl, –en** number, figure; **zählen** count
zahlen pay
zahm tame; **zähmen** tame
der **Zahn, –(e)s, ⸚e** tooth; der **Zahnarzt, –es, ⸚e** dentist
zart tender, delicate, soft
zärtlich tender, gentle; affectionate
der **Zaun, –(e)s, ⸚e** fence
die **Zehe, –n** (*or* der **Zeh, –s, –en**) toe
zehn ten; der **Zehnte** the tenth
das **Zeichen, –s,** — sign, token
die **Zeichnung, –en** drawing
der **Zeigefinger, –s,** — index finger
zeigen show
die **Zeile, –n** line (*of print, writing*)
die **Zeit, –en** time; das **Zeitalter, –s,** — age; der **Zeitgenosse, –n, –n** contemporary; **zeitgenössisch** contemporary; **zeitig** early; **im Lauf der Zeit** in the course of time
die **Zeitung, –en** newspaper
zerbre′chen (zerbricht), zerbrach, zerbrochen break to pieces
zerfal′len (zerfällt), zerfiel, ist zerfallen be divided, fall to pieces, break up
zerklüf′tet jagged
zerlumpt′ ragged, shabby
zerrei′ßen, zerriß, zerrissen tear to pieces; **zerris′sen** (*adj.*) torn, ripped
zerschla′gen bruised
zersplit′tern split up
zerstö′ren destroy; der **Zerstö′rungskrieg, –(e)s, –e** war of destruction
zertei′len dispel, split; separate, dissolve
zertre′ten (zertritt), zertrat, zertreten crush, trample underfoot
zeugen beget, produce; testify, witness
zeugend productive
ziehen, zog, gezogen move (*an object*), draw, pull; (*intrans.*) **ziehen, zog, ist gezogen** go, move
zielen aim
ziemlich rather, somewhat
die **Zigaret′te, –n** cigarette
das **Zimmer, –s,** — room; das **Zimmerchen, –s,** — little room, chamber, closet
das **Zinn, –(e)s** tin; pewter
zischen hiss; **zischt hervor** gushes forth
zitie′ren quote
zittern tremble
die **Zivilisation′, –en** civilization
der **Zloty, –s** *Polish monetary unit* (*one dollar = about 25 zlotys*)
zögern hesitate
der **Zoll, –(e)s, ⸚e** toll, duty; customs
die **Zone, –n** zone
die **Zoologie′** zoology
zornig angry
zu (*prefix, conj., prep., adv.*) closed; to, in order to; at, for; too; **Die Tür ist zu.** The door is closed. **Kommen Sie zu uns.** Come to us (to visit us); **zu sich kommen** regain consciousness; **zu Hause** at home; **zu schwierig** too difficult
der **Zubehör, –s, –e** belongings, accessories, incidentals
die **Zubilligung** allowance, compliance, acknowledgment; **unter Zubilligung** (*with gen.*) allowing for
der **Zucker, –s** sugar
zueinan′der to one another, to each other
zuerst′ at first
zu-fallen (fällt zu), fiel zu, ist zugefallen (*with dat.*) fall to one's lot, allot, assign
zufällig by chance, accidentally
zufol′ge (*postpositive prep. dat.*) according to
zufrie′den content, satisfied
zu-fügen (*or, usually,* **hinzu′-fügen**) add, join
der **Zug, –(e)s, ⸚e** feature, trait, characteristic; train; troop; procession; move
der **Zugereiste, –n, –n** stranger, visitor
zugleich′ at the same time
zu-greifen, griff zu, zugegriffen seize, help oneself (*at table*)
zugrun′de-richten destroy
die **Zukunft** future; **zukünftig** future, of the future; der **Zukunftstraum, –(e)s, ⸚e** dream of the future; utopia
die **Zulage, –n** addition, increase
zuletzt′ finally
zum = zu dem

zu-machen shut, close
zumal′ especially
zumu′te: Mir ist schlecht zumu′te. I feel badly (in low spirits).
zunächst′ first of all
die **Zunge, -n** tongue
zur = zu der
(das) **Zürich, -s** *city in Switzerland*
zurück′ back
zurück′-fliegen, flog zurück, ist zurückgeflogen fly back, return (by air)
zurück′-gehen, ging zurück, ist zurückgegangen go back, return
zurück′-hallen resound, echo
zurück′-kehren (sein) return
zurück′-kriechen, kroch zurück, ist zurückgekrochen crawl back
zurück′-lassen (läßt zurück), ließ zurück, zurückgelassen leave behind
zurück′-prallen (von) (sein) re-echo, rebound, reverberate
zurück′-reichen reach back
zurück′-weisen, wies zurück, zurückgewiesen refuse, reject; die **Zurück′weisung, -en** refusal
(sich) **zurück′-ziehen, zog zurück, zurückgezogen** withdraw
zusam′men together
zusam′men-bringen, brachte zusammen, zusammengebracht bring together; achieve
der **Zusam′menklang, -(e)s, ⸚e** harmony
zusam′men-kommen, kam zusammen, ist zusammengekommen come together, gather
zusam′men-leben live together
zu-schauen watch
der **Zuschlag, -(e)s, ⸚e** additional charge
zustan′de-bringen, brachte zustande, zustandegebracht accomplish
zustan′de-kommen, kam zustande, ist zustandegekommen come about, come to pass
zuständig authorized, responsible; **zuständige Stelle** (proper) authorities
zuviel′ too much
zuwei′len from time to time, at times
zu-wenden, wandte zu (*or* **wendete zu**), **zugewandt** (*or* **zugewendet**) turn toward
zu-ziehen, zog zu, zugezogen close, pull shut
zwanzig twenty; der **Zwanzigste** the twentieth; **die zwanziger Jahre** the Twenties
zwar to be sure, indeed, it is true
der **Zweck, -(e)s, -e** purpose
zwei two; **zweierlei** two kinds of; twofold
der **Zweifel, -s, —** doubt; **ohne Zweifel** without a doubt; **zweifeln** doubt; **zweifelsfrei** without doubt
der **Zweig, -(e)s, -e** branch
der **Zweikampf, -(e)s, ⸚e** duel
zweit- second; **zweitens** in the second place, secondly; **zweitoberst** second from the top
zwicken pinch, prick, spur on
zwingen, zwang, gezwungen compel, force
zwischen (*prep. dat. or acc.*) between, among, amid
der **Zwischenraum, -(e)s, ⸚e** space, interval, space-between
zwölf twelve
der **Zyklus, —,** (*plur.*) **Zyklen** cycle

ENGLISH–GERMAN

The English-German vocabulary, more extensive, perhaps, than is customary in basic texts, covers the areas of active command (Basic Dialogues, English-to-German sentences, Questionnaires [*Wer bin ich?*], Drill Patterns, and the pertinent exercises in the Vocabulary Building sections) as well as some additional material designed to promote elementary composition and conversation practice.

A

a, an ein (–e, —, —)
able: be able to können (kann), konnte, gekonnt
about (= concerning, of) über (*prep. acc.*); von (*prep. dat.*); **talk about something** über etwas (*acc.*) *or* von etwas (*dat.*) sprechen; **I heard about it.** Ich habe davon gehört. (= approximately) *adv.* etwa, ungefähr; **about ten years old** etwa (ungefähr) zehn Jahre alt; (= approximately) *prep.* gegen; **about nine o'clock** gegen neun Uhr
above über (*prep. dat. or acc.*); oben (*adv.*); oberhalb (*prep. gen.*)
abrupt plötzlich; **abrupt change in weather** der Wetterumsturz, –(e)s, ⸚e
accept auf-nehmen (nimmt auf), nahm auf, aufgenommen; an-nehmen (nimmt an), nahm an, angenommen
accomplish erle′digen
according to nach (*prep. dat.*), zufol′ge (*with preceding dat.*); **according to plan** programm′gemäß; **accordingly** also
account: on account of wegen (*prep. gen.*)
acquaintance der Bekann′te, –n, –n (ein Bekannter); die Bekann′te, –n, –n
across über (*acc.*); **go across the street** über die Straße gehen; **straight across** quer durch
act tun, tat, getan; **act as if** (so) tun, als ob
actually eigentlich, wirklich
A.D. nach Christi Geburt′ (n. Chr.)
addition: in addition dazu′
admit geste′hen, gestand, gestanden; **admit something to someone** jemandem (*dat.*) etwas (*acc.*) geste′hen
advice der Rat, –(e)s
afraid: be afraid of sich fürchten vor (*dat.*)
after nach (*dat.*); **after school** nach der Schule; **one after another** nacheinan′der; **after a week** nach einer Woche; **after that** danach; **after all** doch; **day after day** Tag für Tag; (*subord. conj.*) nachdem′
afternoon der Nachmittag, –s, –e; **in the afternoon, afternoons** am Nachmittag, nachmittags
again wieder; **once again** noch einmal, schon wieder
against gegen (*acc.*); dage′gen (*prefix; adv.*); **Have you anything against it?** Haben Sie etwas dage′gen?
ago vor (*prep. dat.*); **a year ago** vor einem Jahr
alert munter
all alles, alle; ganz; **all of Europe** ganz Euro′pa
all right gut; **all right, then** also gut; **All right!** Na schön! **It is all right with me.** Es ist mir recht.
allegedly angeblich
almost beinah(e), fast
alone allein′, einsam; **Leave me alone!** Laß mich in Ruh(e)!
along längs (*prep. gen. or dat.*); **go along with** mit-gehen (mit *with dat.*), ging mit, ist mitgegangen; **He went along with us.** Er ging mit uns mit.
Alps die Alpen
already schon, bereits′
also auch
although obgleich′ (*subord. conj.*), obwohl′ (*subord. conj.*)
always immer
a.m. morgens, vormittags
America (das) Ame′rika, –s, –s; **American** (*adj.*) amerika′nisch; **American** (*noun*) der Amerika′ner, –s, —; die Amerika′nerin, –nen
among zwischen, unter (*prep. dat. or acc.*)
amount to betra′gen (beträgt), betrug, betragen
and und
angry zornig, böse
answer (*noun*) die Antwort, –en
answer antworten, beant′worten; **Answer me!** Antworten Sie mir! **answer a question** auf eine Frage antworten *or* eine Frage beant′worten
any irgend (eine, ein, ein); **any** (= every) jed– (–e, –es, –er); **any** (= some) etwas; **Do you have any money?** Haben Sie etwas Geld? **any(one) of you** jemand von euch; **Does anyone of you have money?** Hat jemand von euch Geld?

anyway überhaupt′
apparently anscheinend
appearance das Aussehen, –s
appetizer die Vorspeise, –n
approach sich nähern; her-kommen, kam her, ist hergekommen
approximately etwa, ungefähr
April (der) April′, –s
architecture die Architektur′
arm der Arm, –(e)s, –e
around um (*prep. acc.*)
arrive an-kommen, kam an, ist angekommen
art die Kunst, ⸚e; **museum of art** das kunsthistorische Muse′um
artist der Künstler, –s, —
as wie, als; **as a child (student)** als Kind (Student′); **as in the Middle Ages** wie im Mittelalter; (*subord. conj., temp.*) als; (*subord. conj., causal*) da; **as if** (*subord. conj.*) als ob, als wenn; **as much as** soviel′ wie; **as well as** sowohl′ . . . als auch
aside beisei′te
ask fragen; **ask (for)** bitten (um *with acc.*), bat, gebeten; **ask someone for something** jemanden (*acc.*) um etwas (*acc.*) bitten; **ask of** (= demand) verlan′gen von (*dat.*)
asleep: fall asleep ein-schlafen (schläft ein), schlief ein, ist eingeschlafen
association die Verbin′dung, –en
assume an-nehmen (nimmt an), nahm an, angenommen
at an (*prep. dat.*); **at the door (blackboard)** an der Tür (Tafel); **at work** an der Arbeit; **at the window** am Fenster; **at the University** (*faculty*) an der Universität′; an (*prep. acc.*): **He knocks at the door.** Er klopft an die Tür. auf (*prep. dat.*): **at the University** (*students*) auf der Universität′; **at the Post Office** auf der Post; auf (*prep. acc.*): **at first glance** auf den ersten Blick; bei (*prep. dat.*): **at the baker's** beim Bäcker; **at night** bei Nacht; **at dinner** beim Essen; **at the table** bei Tisch; **at our house (place)** bei uns; um (*prep. acc.*): **at half past seven** um halb acht; zu (*prep. dat.*): **at home** zu Hause; **at the right time** zur rechten Zeit
at all überhaupt′, gar
attend bei-wohnen (*dat.*), besu′chen (*acc.*); **attend a (theatrical) performance** einer Aufführung beiwohnen; **Which classes did you attend?** Welche Klassen besuch′ten Sie?
attention: pay attention to auf-passen auf (*acc.*)
August der August′, –s
aunt die Tante, –n
Austria (das) Österreich, –s
autumn der Herbst, –es, –e
available erhält′lich, erreich′bar
away weg, fort
awful schrecklich; **an 'awful lot'** schrecklich viel

B

back (*noun*) der Rücken, –s, —
back (*prefix; adv.*) zurück′
backbone das Rückgrat, –s
bacteriologist der Bakteriolog′(e), –en, –en
bad schlecht, böse, schlimm
bag (= handbag) die Tasche, –n
bake backen (bäckt), buk *or* backte, gebacken
ball der Ball, –s, ⸚e
barber der Friseur′, –s, –e
bare bloß
Baroque das Barock′, –s
bath das Bad, –(e)s, ⸚er
bathe baden; **bathing suit** der Badeanzug, –s, ⸚e; **bathrobe** der Schlafrock, –s, ⸚e
battle der Kampf, –(e)s, ⸚e
Bavaria (das) Bayern, –s; **Bavarian** bay(e)risch
be sein (ist), war, ist gewesen; sich befin′den, befand, befunden; **there is, there are** es gibt; **There is always something new.** Es gibt immer etwas Neues. **There are people, who . . .** Es gibt Menschen, die . . .; **How are you? — I am fine.** Wie geht es dir? — Es geht mir gut. **Where is Anna?** Wo ist (*or* befin′det sich) Anna? **Where, in the world, is the waiter?** Wo bleibt der Kellner denn? **that is (to say)** das heißt; **be to** *see* (be) supposed (to); **be able to** *see* can; **be up** (= over) um-sein (ist um), war um, ist umgewesen; **The hour (time) is up.** Die Stunde (Zeit) ist um.
beam strahlen
beautiful schön
because (*subord. conj.*) weil; (*coord. conj.*) denn; **because of** wegen (*prep. gen.*); **just because it is wrong** eben darum, weil es falsch ist
become werden (wird), wurde, ist geworden
bed das Bett, –(e)s, –en; **go to bed** zu Bett gehen
beer das Bier, –s
before vor (*prep. dat. or acc.*); (*subord. conj.*) ehe, bevor′
begin an-fangen (fängt an), fing an, angefangen; begin′nen, begann, begonnen
beginning der Anfang, –s, ⸚e; **in the beginning** am Anfang
behind hinter (*prep. dat. or acc.*); **behind it** dahin′ter
believe glauben; **believe someone** jemandem (*dat.*) glauben; **believe something** etwas (*acc.*) glauben; **I don't believe what you are saying.** Ich glaube dir das nicht.

believe in an etwas (*acc.*) glauben; **He believes in God.** Er glaubt an Gott. **He believes in it.** Er glaubt daran′.
belly der Bauch, –(e)s, ⸚e
belong gehö′ren (*dat.*); **It belongs to me.** Es gehört′ mir; **belong to** (= pertain) gehö′ren zu (*dat.*); **This does not belong to the subject.** Das gehört′ nicht zur Sache; **belong to** (*fraternity, club*) an-gehören (*dat.*)
beloved (*noun*) der Gelieb′te, –n, –n; die Gelieb′te, –n, –n
below unter (*prep. dat. or acc.*); unterhalb (*prep. gen.*); unten (*adv.*)
beside neben (*prep. dat. or acc.*); außer (*prep. dat.*); bei (*prep. dat.*)
besides außerdem, (noch) dazu′
best best–
better besser
between zwischen, unter (*prep. dat. or acc.*)
big groß, größer, größt–
bind binden, band, gebunden; verbin′den, verband, verbunden
biologist der Biolog′(e), –en, –en
bit: a bit ein bißchen
bite beißen, biß, gebissen
blackboard die Tafel, –n
blame (*noun*) die Schuld; **be to blame for something** an etwas (*dat.*) schuld sein; **He is to blame for it.** Er ist daran schuld.
blizzard der Schnee′orkan′, –s, –e
blood das Blut, –(e)s
blouse die Bluse, –n
blue blau
boat das Boot, –(e)s, –e; der Dampfer, –s, —; das Schiff, –(e)s, –e
body der Körper, –s, —; der Leib, –es, –er
bomb die Bombe, –n
bone der Knochen, –s, —
book das Buch, –(e)s, ⸚er; **bookcase** der Bücherschrank, –s, ⸚e
born gebo′ren; **He was born in Germany.** Er ist in Deutschland gebo′ren.
both beide; die beiden
bottle die Flasche, –n
bottom der Grund, –es, ⸚e; **at the bottom** unten
boy der Junge, –n, –n
bracelet das Armband, –s, ⸚er
brain das Gehirn′, –s, –e
bread das Brot, –(e)s, –e
break brechen (bricht), brach, gebrochen; **break off** ab-brechen (bricht ab), brach ab, abgebrochen
breakfast das Frühstück, –s, –e
breast die Brust, ⸚e
bridge die Brücke, –n; (*card game*) (das) Bridge, —
bring bringen, brachte, gebracht; **bring in** ein-liefern
brother der Bruder, –s, ⸚; **brother(s) and sister(s)** die Geschwis′ter (*plur. noun*)
brush (one's teeth) (sich die Zähne) putzen
brutal roh
build bauen
burn brennen, brannte, gebrannt
businessman der Geschäfts′mann, –(e)s, (*plur.*) –leute; **business woman** die Geschäfts′frau, –en
busy beschäf′tigt; **I am always busy.** Ich habe immer viel zu tun.
but (= however) aber, doch; (= on the contrary) sondern; (= except) außer (*prep. dat.*)
butter die Butter
button der Knopf, –(e)s, ⸚e
buy kaufen; **He is buying a car** (for himself). Er kauft sich (*dat.*) ein Auto (*acc.*).
by bei; neben; für; mit; nach; von; **He calls her by her first name.** Er nennt sie beim (*dat.*) Vornamen. **She is standing by** (= next to) **him.** Sie steht neben ihm (*dat.*); **step by step** Schritt für Schritt; **He traveled (flew) by plane.** Er flog mit dem (*dat.*) Flugzeug. **I was overtaken by the storm.** Ich wurde von dem Sturm überrascht′; **a book by X** ein Buch von X
by heart auswendig

C

cafeteria (for students) (*student dining hall*) die Mensa
cake die Torte, –n
California (das) Kalifor′nien, –s
call (= name) nennen, nannte, genannt; (= shout) rufen, rief, gerufen; **be called** (= be named) heißen, hieß, geheißen
can können (kann), konnte, gekonnt; **Can it be done?** Kann man das (es) machen? *or* Läßt es sich machen?
captain (*of a ship*) der Schiffs′kapitän′, –s, –e
car der Wagen, –s, —; das Auto, –s, –s
careful vorsichtig; **be careful** auf-passen, paßte auf, aufgepaßt; **Be careful!** Vorsichtig! *or* Paß auf!
carry tragen (trägt), trug, getragen
case der Fall, –es, ⸚e
catastrophe die Katastro′phe, –n
catch fangen (fängt), fing, gefangen; **catch a cold** sich erkäl′ten
cathedral die Kathedra′le, –n
ceiling die Decke, –n
center die Mitte, –n
century das Jahrhun′dert, –s, –e
certain gewiß′, sicher; **certainly** gewiß′, allerdings′, bestimmt′
chair der Stuhl, –(e)s, ⸚e
change ändern, sich ändern; sich verän′dern; wechseln; **This must change.** Das muß sich ändern. **He has changed.** Er hat sich verän′dert; **change money** Geld wechseln

change (*noun*) der Wechsel, –s; **abrupt change in weather** der Wetterumsturz, –(e)s, ⸚e
cheap billig
cheek die Wange, –n
chemist der Chemiker, –s, —
chess (das) Schach, –s
chicken das Huhn, –(e)s, ⸚er; **fried chicken** das Backhuhn
chiefly hauptsächlich
chin das Kinn, –(e)s, –e
church die Kirche, –n
city die Stadt, ⸚e
civil servant der Staatsbeamte, –n, –n (ein Staatsbeamter)
class die Klasse, –n; **classroom** das Klassenzimmer, –s, —
classical klassisch
clean (*verb*) reinigen, putzen
clean (*adj.*) sauber, rein
clear klar
clergyman der Pastor, –s, (*plur.*) Pasto′ren; der Pfarrer, –s, —; der Priester, –s, —
climb steigen, stieg, ist gestiegen; bestei′gen, bestieg, bestiegen; klettern
climb (*climbing expedition*) die Klet′terpartie′, –n
clock die Uhr, –en; **at eleven o'clock** um elf Uhr
close (= shut) schließen, schloß, geschlossen
close (*adj.*) (= near) nah, näher, nächst–; (= intimate) eng; **be close friends** eng befreun′det sein
closet der Schrank, –(e)s, ⸚e
club der Klub, –s, –s
coat (= jacket) die Jacke, –n; der Rock, –(e)s, ⸚e; (= overcoat) der Mantel, –s, ⸚
cold kalt, kälter, kältest–
collar der Kragen, –s, —; (*for dog*) das Halsband, –s, ⸚er
colleague der Kolle′ge, –n, –n; die Kolle′gin, –nen
come kommen, kam, ist gekommen; **come about** *or* **come to pass** zustan′de-kommen, kam zustande, ist zustandegekommen; **Come here!** Komm her! **Come in!** Komm herein′! *or* Herein′! **Come closer** *or* **in!** Treten Sie näher!
comedy die Komö′die, –n
command befeh′len (befiehlt), befahl, befohlen (*dat.*)
compare verglei′chen, verglich, verglichen
complete (*adj.*) ganz
complete (*verb*) erle′digen, vollen′den
comprehend begrei′fen, begriff, begriffen
concern an-gehen (*acc.*), ging an, ist *or* hat angegangen; **That does not concern him.** Das geht ihn nichts an.
concert das Konzert′, –s, –e
conclusion der Schluß, Schlusses, Schlüsse
condemn verur′teilen
conference die Konferenz′, –en
confess geste′hen, gestand, gestanden
conflict der Streit, –(e)s, –e; der Konflikt′, –s, –e
conquer ero′bern
consider halten (für, *acc.*) hielt, gehalten; sich (*dat.*) (etwas [*acc.*]) überle′gen; **I am considering it.** Ich überlege es mir. **Just consider for a moment!** Überle′gen Sie mal!
contain enthal′ten (enthält), enthielt, enthalten
continue (to do something) weiter (+ *verb*); **continue to read** weiter-lesen (liest weiter), las weiter, weitergelesen; **continue to speak** weiter-sprechen (spricht weiter), sprach weiter, weitergesprochen
contrary: on the contrary hinge′gen, im Gegenteil
conversation das Gespräch′, –s, –e
convince überzeu′gen
cook kochen
cordially herzlich; **most cordially** aufs beste
correct richtig
cost kosten
costume das Kostüm′, –s, –e
couch das Sofa, –s, –s
country das Land, –(e)s, ⸚er; **in the country(side)** auf dem Land; **to the country(side)** aufs Land
couple das Paar, –(e)s, –e; **a couple of times** ein paarmal
course der Kurs, –es, –e; **take a course** einen Kurs bele′gen; **of course** natür′lich, ja, doch; allerdings′
court das Gericht′, –(e)s, –e
create schaffen, schuf, geschaffen; erschaf′fen, erschuf, erschaffen
creep schleichen, schlich, ist geschlichen; kriechen, kroch, ist gekrochen
criticize tadeln, kritisie′ren
cry (= weep) weinen; (= call) rufen, rief, gerufen; (= scream) schreien, schrie, geschrien
cucumber die Gurke, –n; **cucumber salad** der Gurkensalat, –s
cup die Tasse, –n; **a cup of coffee** eine Tasse Kaffee (*or* Kaffee′)
cupboard der Schrank, –(e)s, ⸚e
curious neugierig
curtain der Vorhang, –s, ⸚e
cut schneiden, schnitt, geschnitten; **I cut my finger.** Ich habe mir in den Finger geschnit′ten.

D

daily täglich
dark dunkel; **grow dark** dämmern, dunkel werden

day der Tag, –(e)s, –e; **four hours a day** vier Stunden am Tag; **What day in June?** Am wievielten Juni? **Day is breaking.** Es wird Tag.
dead tot; **dead tired** todmüde
dear lieb
deceive betrü′gen, betrog, betrogen
December der Dezem′ber, –s
decide entschei′den, entschied, entschieden; sich entschlie′ßen, entschloß, entschlossen; **I don't know what to decide.** Ich weiß nicht, wozu ich mich entschließen soll.
declaration die Erklä′rung, –en; **declaration of love** die Liebeserklärung
declare erklä′ren
definite bestimmt′
delay verschie′ben, verschob, verschoben
deliver ein-liefern
demand verlan′gen
dentist der Zahnarzt, –(e)s, ⁻̈e
deny leugnen
depart ab-fahren (fährt ab), fuhr ab, ist abgefahren; scheiden, schied, ist geschieden
department manager der Abtei′lungsleiter, –s, —
departure die Abreise, –n
desperate verzwei′felt
dessert die Nachspeise, –n
detective der Detektiv′, –s, –e
devour verschlin′gen, verschlang, verschlungen; fressen (frißt), fraß, gefressen
die sterben (stirbt), starb, ist gestorben
different ander– (–e, –es, –er); anders
difficult schwer, schwierig
dig graben (gräbt), grub, gegraben
diligent fleißig
dine essen (ißt), aß, gegessen
dinner das Abendessen, –s, —; **When do you have dinner?** Um wieviel Uhr essen Sie zu Abend? **dinner jacket** der Frack, –(e)s, –s *or* ⁻̈e
disappear verschwin′den, verschwand, ist verschwunden; schwinden, schwand, ist geschwunden
disclose enthül′len
discussion die Diskussion′, –en
dish die Schüssel, –n; **dish of food** die Speise, –n
distinct(ly) deutlich
district hospital das Kreiskrankenhaus, –es, ⁻̈er
do tun, tat, getan; machen; **How do you do?** Wie geht es Ihnen?
doctor der Arzt, –(e)s, ⁻̈e; der Doktor, –s, (*plur.*) Dokto′ren
door die Tür, –en
dormitory das Studen′tenheim, –s, –e
dramatist der Drama′tiker, –s, —
dress (*noun*) das Kleid, –(e)s, –er
dress (*verb*) (sich) an-ziehen, zog an, angezogen; **The mother dresses the child.** Die Mutter zieht das Kind an. **I get dressed.** Ich ziehe mich an; **dressed** beklei′det, angezogen
drink trinken, trank, getrunken
drive (= travel, go) fahren (fährt), fuhr, ist gefahren; (= push, propel) treiben, trieb, getrieben
due: be due to something an etwas (*dat.*) liegen (liegen, lag, gelegen)
during während (*prep. gen.*)
dwindle schwinden, schwand, ist geschwunden

E

each jed– (–e, –es, –er); **each other** einan′der; **to each other** zueinander
ear das Ohr, –(e)s, –en
early früh, früher, früh(e)st–
(the) **East** der Osten, –s; **Eastern Germany** (das) Ostdeutschland, –s
Easter (die) Ostern (*plur.*); **Easter vacation** die Osterferien (*plur.*)
easy leicht; **It is an easy matter for me.** Es fällt mir leicht.
eat essen (ißt), aß, gegessen; (of animals) fressen (frißt), fraß, gefressen
economist der Ökonom′, –en, –en (*or* National′ökonom)
educator der Erzie′her, –s, —; der Pädagog′(e), –en, –en
egg das Ei, –s, –er
eight acht
eighteen achtzehn
eighty achtzig
eleven elf
else sonst; **or else** sonst; **something else** etwas anderes; **what else?** was noch?
emphasize beto′nen
end (*noun*) das Ende, –s, –n
end (*verb*) auf-hören, enden
engaged verlobt′
engineer der Ingenieur′, –s, –e
English (*adj.*) englisch
English (*language*) (das) Englisch, –en
engrossed: become engrossed in sich vertie′fen in (*acc.*)
enough genug′, genü′gend
entertain unterhal′ten (unterhält), unterhielt, unterhalten
enthusiastic: be *or* **get enthusiastic about** sich begeis′tern für (*acc.*)
entice an-ziehen, zog an, angezogen; reizen, verfüh′ren
entire ganz
entomologist der Entomolog′(e), –en, –en
escape (from) fliehen (vor, *dat.*), floh, ist geflohen; entwei′chen, entwich, ist entwichen; entrin′nen (*dat.*), entrann, ist entronnen

especially beson′ders
essence (= essential character) das Wesen, –s
eternal ewig
Europe (das) Euro′pa, –s; **European** europä′isch
even sogar′, selbst; eben; **even if (when)** wenn . . . auch *or* auch wenn (*sub. conj.*); **not even** nicht einmal′
evening der Abend, –s, –e; **in the evening** am Abend; **Evening is coming** (= dusk is falling). Es wird Abend. **Good evening!** Guten Abend! **evening dress** das Abendkleid, –(e)s, –er; **evenings** abends
ever je
every jed– (–e, –es, –er); **He works every day (every week).** Er arbeitet jeden Tag (jede Woche); **every two weeks** alle vierzehn Tage
everything alles
everywhere überall
exact genau′; **exactly** genau′, gera′de; **That is not exactly new.** Das ist nicht gera′de neu.
examination die Prüfung, –en; das Exa′men, –s, (*plur.*) — *or* Exa′mina; **give an examination** prüfen; **take an examination** geprüft′ werden
example das Beispiel, –s, –e; **for example** zum Beispiel (*abbreviation:* z.B.)
except außer (*prep. dat.*)
exchange student der Aus′tauschstudent′, –en, –en
excite auf-regen; **become excited (about)** sich auf-regen (über, *acc.*)
excuse verzei′hen, verzieh, verziehen; entschul′digen
exhibition die Ausstellung, –en
expensive teuer
explain erklä′ren
explosive explosiv′
exposition die Ausstellung, –en
expressionist der Expressionist′, –en, –en
extremely äußerst
eye das Auge, –s, –n; **eyebrow** die Augenbraue, –n; **eyelid** das Augenlid, –(e)s, –er

F

face das Gesicht′, –s, –er
fall (= season) der Herbst, –es, –e
fall (*verb*) fallen (fällt), fiel, ist gefallen; **fall asleep** ein-schlafen (schläft ein), schlief ein, ist eingeschlafen
famous berühmt′; **famous men** berühm′te (*or* große) Männer
far weit, fern; **by far** bei weitem
fashion die Mode, –n
father der Vater, –s, ¨
fear sich fürchten (vor, *dat.*)
February der Februar, –s
feel fühlen
fellow student der Kolle′ge, –n, –n
festival das Fest, –(e)s, –e; das Festspiel, –s, –e
few wenige; **a few** ein paar, einige
field das Fach, –(e)s, ¨er; **major field** das Hauptfach, –(e)s, ¨er
fifteen fünfzehn
fifty fünfzig
figure die Figur′, –en
film der Film, –(e)s, –e
find finden, fand, gefunden
fine fein, ausgezeichnet, gut; **I feel fine.** Es geht mir gut (ausgezeichnet).
finger der Finger, –s, —; **fingernail** der Fingernagel, –s, ¨
finish erle′digen, vollen′den; **finished** fertig
firm fest
first erst; **at first** zuerst′
fish der Fisch, –(e)s, –e; **fishing** das Fischen, –s
fist die Faust, ¨e
fit passen (*dat.*); **The dress does not fit her.** Das Kleid paßt ihr nicht.
five fünf
fixed fest
flesh das Fleisch, –(e)s
flight der Flug, –(e)s, ¨e
floor der Fußboden, –s, ¨
flow fließen, floß, ist geflossen
fly fliegen, flog, ist geflogen; **fly away** abfliegen, flog ab, ist abgeflogen; **fly back** zurück′-fliegen, flog zurück, ist zurückgeflogen
flyer der Flieger, –s, —
follow folgen (sein) (*dat.*); nach-kommen, kam nach, ist nachgekommen; **the following** das Folgende, folgendes; **Read the following!** Lesen Sie das Folgende!
food das Essen, –s; die Speise, –n
foot der Fuß, –es, ¨e; **foot end** das Fußende, –s, –n
for für (*prep. acc.*): **a present for him** ein Geschenk′ für ihn; seit (*prep. dat.*): **for a week** seit einer Woche, seit acht Tagen; an (*prep. dat.*): **He is to blame for it.** Er ist daran (an dieser Sache) schuld. auf (*prep. acc.*): **We are waiting for our friends.** Wir warten auf unsere Freunde; **(the) hope for something better** die Hoffnung auf etwas Besseres; **for ever, for good** auf immer; aus (*prep. dat.*): **For what reason?** Aus welchem Grund? um (*prep. acc.*): **The conductor is asking for the tickets.** Der Schaffner bittet um die Fahrkarten. **They called for help.** Sie riefen um Hilfe; um . . . willen (*prep. gen.*): **for God's sake** um Gottes willen; **for his sake** um seinetwillen; zu (*prep. dat.*): **for**

the first time zum ersten Mal; **for example** zum Beispiel; **good for something** zu etwas gut
for (*coord. conj.*) denn
forbid verbie′ten, verbot, verboten; **I forbid you to do that.** Ich verbie′te dir das.
forehead die Stirn(e), -en
forget verges′sen (vergißt), vergaß, vergessen
forgive verzei′hen, verzieh, verziehen; **forgive someone for something** jemandem (*dat.*) etwas (*acc.*) verzeihen
formal formell′
former einstig, vorig, früher; **formerly** sonst; früher
fortunately glück′licherwei′se
forty vierzig
four vier
fourteen vierzehn
fowl das Geflü′gel, -s
fraternity die Studen′tenverbin′dung, -en; die Verbin′dung, -en
freeze frieren, fror, gefroren
French (*adj.*) franzö′sisch; **French** (*language*) (das) Franzö′sisch, -en
fresh frisch
Friday der Freitag, -s, -e
friend der Freund, -es, -e; die Freundin, -nen
friendly freundlich; **be on friendly terms with** befreun′det sein mit (*dat.*)
from von (*prep. dat.*): **from now on** von dieser Stunde an; **from Munich to Berlin** von München bis nach Berlin′; vor (*prep. dat.*): **They were protected from** (against) **the storm.** Sie waren vor dem Sturm geschützt′. aus (*prep. dat.*): **from my own experience** aus eigener Erfah′rung; **My mother comes from Bavaria.** Meine Mutter stammt aus Bayern; nach (*prep. dat.*): **from** (judging from) **what I was told** nach dem, was mir gesagt′ worden ist
front: in front of vor (*prep., dat. or acc.*)
fruit das Obst, -(e)s; die Frucht, ⸚e
fur der Pelz, -es, -e
future (*noun*) die Zukunft
future (*adj.*) zukünf′tig

G

gentleman der Herr, -n, -en; **Ladies and gentlemen!** Meine Damen und Herren!
geologist der Geolog′(e), -en, -en
German (*adj.*) deutsch
German (*language*) (das) Deutsch, -en; **in German** auf deutsch; **Translate that into German!** Überset′zen Sie das ins Deutsche!
(the) **German** der Deutsche, -n, -n (ein Deutscher); die Deutsche, -n, -n (eine Deutsche)
Germany (das) Deutschland, -s
get (= receive) bekom′men, bekam, bekommen; erhal′ten (erhält), erhielt, erhalten; (= become, get to be) werden (wird), wurde, ist geworden; **get acquainted with** kennen-lernen; **get dark** dämmern, dunkel werden; **get up** auf-stehen, stand auf, ist aufgestanden; **Get going!** Los!
girl das Mädchen, -s, —; **girl friend** die Freundin, -nen
give geben (gibt), gab, gegeben; schenken; **give birth to** gebä′ren (gebiert), gebar, geboren
glad froh, glücklich; **gladly** gern(e), lieber, liebst-
glass das Glas, -es, ⸚er; **a glass of beer** ein Glas Bier; **a pair of glasses** die Brille, -n
glide gleiten, glitt, ist geglitten
glove der Handschuh, -s, -e
go gehen, ging, ist gegangen; ziehen, zog, ist gezogen; fahren (fährt), fuhr, ist gefahren; sich bege′ben (begibt), begab, begeben; **go along** mit-gehen, ging mit, ist mitgegangen; **go ahead** los-gehen, ging los, ist losgegangen; **go away** fort-gehen, ging fort, ist fortgegangen; **go by car** (*or other vehicle*) fahren (fährt), fuhr, ist gefahren; **He is gone.** Er ist weg (fort).
golf das Golf, -s
good gut, besser, best-; **Good bye!** Auf Wiedersehen!
grade die Note, -n
grandfather der Großvater, -s, ⸚
grape: package of grape sugar tablets die Rolle Traubenzucker
grasp greifen, griff, gegriffen
gray grau
great groß, größer, größt-; **a great deal** viel
greatness die Größe
(the) **Greek** der Grieche, -n, -n
grow wachsen (wächst), wuchs, ist gewachsen; (= become) werden (wird), wurde, ist geworden
guess raten (rät), riet, geraten; **I guess you are right.** Ich glaube, du hast recht.
guilty schuldig, schuld
gun das Gewehr′, -s, -e

H

hair das Haar, -(e)s, -e; **get a haircut** sich (*dat.*) die Haare schneiden lassen
half (*noun*) die Hälfte, -n
half (*adj.*) halb; **in half an hour** in einer halben Stunde
hand die Hand, ⸚e
hand in ab-geben (gibt ab), gab ab, abgegeben
handkerchief das Taschentuch, -(e)s, ⸚er

hang hängen, hing, gehangen
happen gesche'hen (geschieht), geschah, ist geschehen; passie'ren (sein)
happy glücklich, froh
hard schwierig
hat der Hut, –(e)s, ⁻̈e
have haben (hat), hatte, gehabt; **have to** müssen (muß), mußte, gemußt; (= cause) lassen (läßt), ließ, gelassen; **Have your shoes polished!** Laß dir die Schuhe putzen!
he er (*acc.* ihn; *dat.* ihm; *gen.* seiner)
head der Kopf, –es, ⁻̈e; das Haupt, –(e)s, ⁻̈er
headwaiter der Ober, –s, —
hear hören
heart das Herz, –ens, –en
heavy schwer
help helfen (hilft), half, geholfen (*dat.*); **He is helping him.** Er hilft ihm.
helpless hilflos
her ihr (–e, —, —) (*poss. adj.*); **(to) her** ihr (*dat., pers. pron.*)
here hier, da
hesitant zögernd
hesitate zögern
high hoch, höher, höchst–
hip die Hüfte, –n
his sein (–e, —, —) (*poss. adj.*)
historian der Histo'riker, –s, —
history die Geschich'te, –n; **history course** der Geschichts'kurs, –es, –e; **museum of natural history** das natur'historische Muse'um, (*plur.*) Muse'en
hold halten (hält), hielt, gehalten; (*a meeting, exam*) ab-halten (hält ab), hielt ab, abgehalten
home das Heim, –s; **at home** zu Hause, daheim'; **He goes home.** Er geht nach Hause *or* heim.
homework die Hausarbeit, –en; die Schularbeit, –en
hot heiß
hour die Stunde, –n
house das Haus, –es, ⁻̈er; **housecoat** der Schlafrock, –s, ⁻̈e; **housewife** die Hausfrau, –en
how wie; **how much** wieviel'; **how many** wie viele
however aber, doch
human menschlich; **human being** der Mensch, –en, –en
hundred hundert
hungry hungrig; **be hungry** hungrig sein, Hunger haben
hurt verlet'zen

I

I ich (*acc.* mich; *dat.* mir; *gen.* meiner)
if wenn (*sub. conj.*); **as if** als ob, als wenn (*sub. conj.*)
ill-mannered ungezogen
illusion die Illusion', –en
imagine (something) sich (*dat.*) (etwas [*acc.*]) vor-stellen; **I cannot imagine that.** Ich kann mir das nicht vorstellen.
immediately gleich, sogleich', sofort'
impatient ungeduldig
important wichtig
impression der Eindruck, –s, ⁻̈e; **impressionism** der Impressionis'mus, —
in (into) in (*prep. dat.*): **in the room** in dem *or* im Zimmer; **in the German language** in der deutschen Sprache; in (*prep. acc.*): **go into the room** in das *or* ins Zimmer gehen; **out into the wide world** in die weite Welt hinaus'; an (*prep. dat.*): **in the evening** am Abend; **in the beginning** am Anfang; **in the sky** am Himmel; **in the end** am Ende; an (*prep. acc.*): **He believes in a lasting peace.** Er glaubt an einen dauernden Frieden. auf (*prep. dat.*): **in the country** auf dem Lande; **in the street** auf der Straße; **in German** auf deutsch; **Nothing in the world is perfect.** Nichts auf der Welt ist vollkommen; **in the washroom** auf dem Abort'; auf (*prep. acc.*): **in this way** auf diese Weise; nach (*prep. dat.*): **in my opinion** meiner Meinung nach; innerhalb (*prep. gen.*): **in** (within) **Europe** innerhalb Euro'pas
industrialist der Industriel'le, –n, –n
inexpensive billig, preiswert
inform mit-teilen, berich'ten
ink die Tinte, –n
instance: for instance zum Beispiel
instead of anstatt', statt (*prep. gen.*)
intend wollen
interested: be interested in sich interessie'ren für (*acc.*)
interesting interessant'
invite ein-laden (lädt ein), lud ein, eingeladen
irony die Ironie'; **ironic** iro'nisch
it es (*acc.* es; *dat.* ihm; *gen.* seiner); *also* sie (die Tür) *and* er (der Stuhl)

J

jacket die Jacke, –n; der Rock, –(e)s, ⁻̈e; **dinner jacket** der Frack, –(e)s, –s *or* ⁻̈e
January der Januar, –s
jet plane das Düsenflugzeug, –s, –e
job die Stellung, –en
journalist der Journalist', –en, –en
journey die Reise, –n
July der Juli, –s
June der Juni, –s
just gera'de; nur; eben; **He just came.** Er kam gera'de. **If I could just (only) tell you, . . .** Könnte ich dir nur sagen, . . .

K

kidney die Niere, –n
kindergarten teacher die Kindergärtnerin, –nen
kitchen die Küche, –n
knee das Knie, –s, —
knife das Messer, –s, —
know (= be acquainted with a person or fact) kennen, kannte, gekannt; **We know each other.** Wir kennen uns; **get to know** kennen-lernen; (a fact) wissen (weiß), wußte, gewußt; **Do you know German?** Können Sie Deutsch?
known bekannt′

L

lack fehlen (*dat.*); **He lacks experience.** Ihm (*dat.*) fehlt die Erfah′rung (*nom.*).
lady die Dame, –n; **Ladies and gentlemen!** Meine Damen und Herren!
lake der See, –s, –n
lamp die Lampe, –n
land (*noun*) das Land, –(e)s, ¨er
land (*verb*) landen (sein)
language die Sprache, –n
large groß, größer, größt–
last (*adj.*) letzt–; **last winter** im vergan′genen (vorigen) Winter
last (*verb*) dauern
lasting dauernd
late spät, später, spätest–; **He is late.** Er kommt zu spät; **at the latest** spätestens
lawyer der Advokat′, –en, –en
lazy faul
lead führen
learn lernen; **learn by heart** auswendig lernen
least wenigst–, am wenigsten; **at least** wenigstens
leather das Leder, –s, —
leave (= travel, go away) ab-reisen (sein); ab-fahren (fährt ab), fuhr ab, ist abgefahren; hinaus′-gehen, ging hinaus, ist hinausgegangen; ab-fliegen, flog ab, ist abgeflogen; (= let, remain, abandon) lassen (läßt), ließ, gelassen; verlas′sen (verläßt), verließ, verlassen
lecturer der Vortragende, –n, –n
left link–; **to the left** links
leg das Bein, –(e)s, –e
leisure die Freizeit
less weniger
lesson die Aufgabe, –n
let lassen (läßt), ließ, gelassen
library die Bibliothek′, –en
license (driver's) der Führerschein, –s, –e
lie (= recline) liegen, lag, gelegen; **lie down** sich nieder-legen
lie (= tell a lie) lügen, log, gelogen
life das Leben, –s, —
lift heben, hob, gehoben
light (*noun*) das Licht, –(e)s, –er; (= brightness) die Helligkeit
light (*adj.*) leicht; (= bright) hell
like (*adj., adv.*) wie; **like you** wie Sie (du)
like (*verb*) mögen (mag), mochte, gemocht; **should like to** möchte (gerne); **I like him.** Ich habe ihn gern; **like to** (+ *verb*) gern(e) + *verb;* **I like to do it.** Ich tue es gern. **I like to play.** Ich spiele gern. **Who likes to be examined?** Wer läßt sich gern prüfen? (= please) gefal′len (*dat.*) (gefällt), gefiel, gefallen; **I like it** (*lit.* It pleases me). Es gefällt′ mir. **I like them** (*lit.* They please me). Sie gefal′len mir.
likewise ebenfalls, gleichfalls
limb das Glied, –(e)s, –er
line die Zeile, –n
lip die Lippe, –n
list die Liste, –n
listen hören; **listen to** zu-hören; **Listen!** Hören Sie!
literature die Literatur′, –en
little wenig; **little money** wenig Geld; **as little as** so wenig wie; **a little** ein wenig; **a little too expensive** ein wenig zu teuer; (= small) klein
live leben; (= dwell) wohnen
liver die Leber, –n
long lang, länger, längst–; **for a long time** lange; **long ago** (= formerly) einst; **He lived in this city long ago.** Er lebte einst in dieser Stadt; **a long time ago** längst; **He should have done it long ago.** Er hätte das längst tun sollen. **It was a long time ago.** Es ist lange her.
look sehen (sieht), sah, gesehen; **look around** sich (*acc.*) um-sehen (sieht um), sah um, umgesehen; **look at** an-sehen (sieht an), sah an, angesehen; sich (*dat.*) etwas (*acc.*) an-sehen; **He looked at the exhibition.** Er sah sich die Ausstellung an; **look for** (= search) suchen; **look like** aus-sehen (sieht aus), sah aus, ausgesehen
lose verlie′ren, verlor, verloren
loud laut
love (*noun*) die Liebe; **my love** (= dearest) meine Liebste; **be in love** verliebt′ sein; **declaration of love** die Liebeserklärung, –en
love (*verb*) lieben
low niedrig; **low grades** schlechte Noten
lunch das Mittagessen, –s; **When do you have lunch?** Wann essen Sie zu Mittag?
lung die Lunge, –n

M

maiden name der Mädchenname, –ns, –n; **My mother's maiden name is Braun.** Meine Mutter ist eine gebo′rene Braun.

mainly hauptsächlich
maintain behaup'ten
make machen; **make up one's mind** sich (*acc.*) entschlie'ßen, entschloß, entschlossen
man der Mann, –es, ¨er; (= human being) der Mensch, –en, –en
many viele; **many a** manch– (–e, –es, –er)
March der März, –es
mark die Mark, — (*German monetary unit, worth about 25 cents*); (= grade) die Note, –n
married verhei'ratet
master der Meister, –s, —
mathematician der Mathema'tiker, –s, —
mathematics die Mathematik'
matter (*noun*) die Sache, –n
matter (*verb*) darauf an-kommen, kam an, ist angekommen; daran' liegen, lag, gelegen; **It matters to me.** Mir liegt daran'.
may (= possibility) mögen (mag), mochte, gemocht; (= permission) dürfen (darf), durfte, gedurft; **He may** (= is permitted to) **go along.** Er darf mitgehen. **That may be.** Das mag sein.
May der Mai, –s
maybe vielleicht'
meal die Mahlzeit, –en
mean meinen, bedeu'ten
meanwhile inzwi'schen
meat das Fleisch, –es
meet treffen (trifft), traf, getroffen
menu das Menu', –s, –s; die Speisekarte, –n
merchant der Kaufmann, –s, (*plur.*) Kaufleute
merit verdie'nen
middle die Mitte, –n
Middle Ages das Mittelalter, –s
midnight die Mitternacht, ¨e; **at midnight** um Mitternacht, um null Uhr
milk die Milch
million die Million', –en
mind: I don't mind. Es macht mir nichts. **Don't you mind?** Macht es Ihnen nichts?
minister der Pastor', –s, –en
minute die Minu'te, –n
mirror der Spiegel, –s, —
Miss (das) Fräulein, –s
modern modern'
moment der Augenblick, –s, –e
Monday der Montag, –s, –e
money das Geld, –es
month der Monat, –s, –e
mood die Stimmung, –en; die Laune, –n; **He is in a good mood.** Er ist guter Laune.
more mehr; **more and more beautiful** immer schöner
morning der Morgen, –s, —; **Good morning!** Guten Morgen! **in the morning, mornings** am Morgen, morgens; **Sunday morning** Sonntag früh
most meist–; **at most** höchstens; **mostly** meistens
mother die Mutter, ¨
mountain der Berg, –(e)s, –e
move rücken; **move apart** auseinan'derrücken; **Move to the front!** Rücken Sie nach vorn! schieben, schob, geschoben; **Move** (put) **it aside!** Schieben Sie das beisei'te! ziehen, zog, ist gezogen; **He moved to West Berlin.** Er ist nach West-Berlin' gezogen. (= affect) rühren; **That moved me deeply.** Das hat mich sehr gerührt'.
movie der Film, –(e)s, –e; **movie theater** das Kino, –s, –s; **He is going to the movies.** Er geht ins Kino.
Mr. (der) Herr, –n
Mrs. (die) Frau
much viel, mehr, meist–; **as much** (**as**) soviel' (. . . wie)
muscle der Muskel, –s, –n
museum das Muse'um, –s, (*plur.*) Muse'en
music die Musik'
musician der Musiker, –s, —
must müssen (muß), mußte, gemußt; **must not** nicht dürfen (darf), durfte, gedurft; **You must not do that.** Sie dürfen das nicht tun.
my mein (–e, —, —) (*poss. adj.*)

N

name (*noun*) der Name, –ns, –n; **first name** der Vorname, –ns, –n; **What is your name?** Wie heißen Sie?
name (*verb*) nennen, nannte, genannt; **be named** heißen, hieß, geheißen
National Socialist (**Nazi**) der National'sozialist', –en, –en; (*adj.*) national'sozialis'tisch
near an (*prep. dat.*): **near the bridge** an der Brücke; bei (*prep. dat.*): **near the window** beim (*or* bei dem) Fenster; neben (*prep. dat. or acc.*): **He sits near** (next to) **her.** Er sitzt neben ihr.
neck der Hals, –es, ¨e
necklace die Halskette, –n
need brauchen; bedür'fen (*gen.*), (bedarf), bedurfte, bedurft; **Don't you need that?** Brauchst du das nicht? *or* Hast du das nicht nötig? **need to** müssen (muß), mußte, gemußt; **He needs to be treated with care.** Er muß geschont' werden.
neither . . . nor weder . . . noch
nerve der Nerv, –s, –en
never nie, niemals
nevertheless trotzdem, dennoch, doch
new neu; **something new** etwas Neues
news das Neue; die Nachricht, –en; **What's the news?** Was gibt es Neues?
newspaper die Zeitung, –en

next nächst–; **the next time** das nächste Mal; **And what next?** Und was weiter? **He sits (down) next to her.** Er setzt sich zu ihr *or* neben sie.
nice hübsch, schön, nett
night die Nacht, ⸚e; **Night is falling.** Es wird Nacht; **at night** nachts, in der Nacht; **last night** gestern abend
nightgown das Nachthemd, –(e)s, –en
nine neun
nineteen neunzehn
nineteenth neunzehnt–
ninety neunzig
no (= answer to question) nein; (= not a; *adj.*) kein (–e, —, —)
nobody niemand, keiner
nonsense der Unsinn, –s
(the) **North** der Norden, –s
northern nördlich
nose die Nase, –n
not nicht
notebook das Heft, –(e)s, –e; der Notiz′-block, –s, ⸚e
nothing nichts
notice beach′ten, bemer′ken
novel der Roman′, –s, –e
November der Novem′ber, –s
now jetzt, nun
number die Nummer, –n; die Zahl, –en
nurse die Krankenpflegerin, –nen
nursery-school teacher die Kindergärtnerin, –nen

O

obey folgen (*dat.*), gehor′chen (*dat.*); **He does not obey me.** Er folgt *or* gehorcht mir nicht.
object (to something) (etwas) dage′gen haben
obliged: be obliged to sollen (soll), sollte, gesollt
occur (= happen) gesche′hen (geschieht), geschah, ist geschehen; (= get an idea) ein-fallen (*dat.*), (fällt ein), fiel ein, ist eingefallen; **This never occurred to me.** Das ist mir nie eingefallen. **How did it occur to you?** Wie bist du darauf′ ge-kom′men?
ocean das Meer, –es, –e; der Ozean, –s, –e
o'clock: at eleven o'clock um elf Uhr
October der Okto′ber, –s
of von (*prep. dat.*): **a friend of mine** ein Freund von mir; **What do you think of my friend?** Was halten Sie von meinem Freund? **Heidelberg is south of Frankfurt.** Heidelberg liegt südlich von Frankfurt. **There is talk of war.** Es ist von Krieg die Rede. an (*prep. acc.*): **I often think of you.** Ich denke oft an dich; auf (*prep. acc.*): **I'll never give up my hope of** (for) **a better world.** Die Hoffnung auf eine bessere Welt gebe ich nie auf. aus (*prep. dat.*): **made of wood** aus Holz; bei (*prep. dat.*): **the battle of Stalingrad** die Schlacht bei Stalingrad; vor (*prep. dat.*): **He has a great fear of death.** Er hat große Furcht vor dem Tode. "*Of*" *expressed by the genitive only:* **the house of my friend** das Haus meines Freundes
officer der Offizier′, –s, –e
official der Beam′te, –n, –n (ein Beam′ter); die Beam′tin, –nen
often oft
old alt, älter, ältest–
on an (*prep. dat.*): **on the morning of his departure** am Morgen seiner Abreise; **on the shore of the lake** am Ufer des Sees; **the picture on the wall** das Bild an der Wand; **on the streetcorner** an der Straßenecke; **On what day in June?** Am wievielten Juni? **on the tenth of June** am zehnten Juni; an (*prep. acc.*): **write on the blackboard** an die Tafel schreiben; auf (*prep. dat.*): **the windows on the right side of the car** die Fenster auf der rechten Seite des Wagens; **He is on a trip.** Er ist auf einer Reise; **sit on a chair** auf einem Stuhl sitzen; auf (*prep. acc.*): **put something on the table** etwas auf den Tisch legen; bei (*prep.* (*dat.*): **on this occasion** bei dieser Gele′genheit; **Do you have any money on** (with) **you?** Hast du Geld bei dir? in (*prep. dat.*): **on the whole** im Ganzen; zu (*prep. dat.*): **on foot** zu Fuß
once einmal; **once more, once again** noch einmal; **once upon a time** einst
one ein (–e, —, —); (*cardinal number*) eins; (*indef. pron.*) man
only (*adv.*) erst, nur, bloß; **We have known each other only a week.** Wir kennen uns erst seit einer Woche; **only yesterday** erst gestern
only (*adj.*) einzig
open (*verb*) öffnen; **Open your book!** Schlagen Sie Ihr Buch auf! Öffnen Sie Ihr Buch!
open (*adj.*) offen
opera die Oper, –n
opinion die Meinung, –en
opposite gegenü′ber (*with preceding dat.*); **opposite him** ihm gegenü′ber
or oder (*coord. conj.*); **either . . . or** entweder . . . oder
order: give an order to someone jemandem etwas befeh′len; **order something** (*as in a restaurant*) sich (*dat.*) etwas (*acc.*) bestel′len; **in order to** um zu (+ *inf.*); **in order that** damit′ (*sub. conj.*)
organ das Organ′, –s, –e
organization die Organisation′, –en
originate entste′hen, entstand, ist entstanden

other ander–
otherwise sonst; anders
out (*prefix*) hinaus′–, heraus′–
out of aus (*prep. dat.*): **Out of the way!** Aus dem Weg! **run out of the house** aus dem Haus laufen; außer (*prep. dat.*): **be out of breath** außer Atem sein; **He is out of his mind.** Er ist außer sich.
outside draußen (*adv.*); **outside the door** draußen vor der Tür
over über (*prep. dat.*): **The moon is over the mountain.** Der Mond steht über dem Berg; über (*prep. acc.*): **go over the bridge** über die Brücke gehen
over there drüben
overcoat der Mantel, –s, ¨
overtake ein-holen, überra′schen; **I was overtaken by the storm.** Ich wurde vom Sturm überrascht′.
own (*verb*) besit′zen, besaß, besessen
own (*adj.*) eigen

P

page die Seite, –n
painter der Maler, –s, —
painting die Malerei′, –en
palace der Palast′, –es, ¨e
pair das Paar, –(e)s, –e; **a pair of shoes** ein Paar Schuhe; **pair of pants** die Hose, –n
pajamas der Schlafanzug, –(e)s, ¨e
paragraph der Paragraph′, –en, –en; der Absatz, –es, ¨e
pardon verzei′hen, verzieh, verziehen; **pardon someone** jemandem (*dat.*) verzeihen; **pardon something** etwas (*acc.*) verzeihen; **Pardon me, please!** Verzei′hen Sie mir, bitte! *or* Verzeih′ung!
parents die Eltern
part der Teil, –(e)s, –e; (= role) die Rolle, –n
participate: participate in everything überall mit dabei′ sein
partly teils
party (= social gathering) die Gesell′schaft, –en; (= political party) die Partei′, –en
pass (away) verge′hen, verging, ist vergangen; **Time passes.** Die Zeit vergeht′. **pass (a test)** (eine Prüfung) beste′hen, bestand, bestanden
passion play das Passions′spiel, –s, –e
past (*prep.*) an (*dat.*) . . . vorü′ber
patient der Patient′, –en, –en
pause die Pause, –n
pea die Erbse, –n
peace der Friede(n), –ns; die Ruhe
pen die Feder, –n
pencil der Bleistift, –s, –e
penny der Pfennig, –s, –e
people die Menschen, die Leute
performance die Vorstellung, –en
perhaps vielleicht′, etwa, wohl
permanent (wave) die Dauerwelle, –n
permitted: be permitted to dürfen (darf), durfte, gedurft
philosophy die Philosophie′, –n
physicist der Physiker, –s, —
physics die Physik′
physiologist der Physiolog′(e), –en, –en
picture das Bild, –es, –er
piece das Stück, –(e)s, –e; **a piece (sheet) of paper** ein Stück (Blatt) Papier′
pilot (plane) der Flieger, –s, —
place (*noun*) die Stelle, –n; **in her place** an ihrer Stelle
place (*verb*) stellen
plane das Flugzeug, –s, –e
please gefal′len (*dat.*), (gefällt), gefiel, gefallen; **Please!** Bitte! **I'll be pleased to say "du" to you.** Ich sage gerne „du" zu dir.
play (*noun*) das Thea′terstück, –(e)s, –e; das Stück, –(e)s, –e
play (*verb*) spielen
p.m. nachmittags, abends, nachts
pocket die Tasche, –n
poem das Gedicht′, –(e)s, –e
poet der Dichter, –s, —
point die Spitze, –n; **be on the point of** nahe daran′ sein
policeman der Polizist′, –en, –en
polish (shoes) putzen
political poli′tisch
politician der Poli′tiker, –s, —
politics die Politik′
poor arm
popular beliebt′
position die Stellung, –en
possess besit′zen, besaß, besessen
possible möglich
postpone verschie′ben, verschob, verschoben
potato die Kartof′fel, –n
poultry das Geflü′gel, –s
power die Macht, ¨e
practical praktisch
praise loben
prefer lieber haben; vor-ziehen (zieht vor), zog vor, vorgezogen; **prefer to** (+ *verb*) lieber (+ *verb*); **I prefer to study.** Ich studiere lieber.
première die Erstaufführung, –en
prepare vor-bereiten
present (*noun*) das Geschenk′, –(e)s, –e
present (*verb*) schenken
present (*adj.*) anwesend
pretty hübsch
prevent hindern
previous vorig–
priest der Priester, –s, —
primitive primitiv′
private plane das Privat′flugzeug, –s, –e

probably wohl, vielleicht′, wahrschein′lich
professor der Profes′sor, –s, (*plur.*) Professo′ren; die Professo′rin, –nen
promise verspre′chen (verspricht), versprach, versprochen
psychiatrist der Psychia′ter, –s, —
psychologist der Psycholog′(e), –en, –en; **psychoanalyst** der Psy′choanaly′tiker, –s, —
pull ziehen, zog, gezogen
pulse der Puls, –es, –e
pursue betrei′ben, betrieb, betrieben
push stoßen (stößt), stieß, gestoßen
put on (dress) (sich) an-ziehen (zieht an), zog an, angezogen; (make-up) (sich) schminken

Q

quarrel der Streit, –(e)s, –e; die Streitigkeit, –en
quarter das Viertel, –s, —
question die Frage, –n; **pose (ask) a question** eine Frage stellen; **it is a question whether** es geht darum′, ob
questionnaire der Fragebogen, –s, — *or* ¨
quick schnell
quiet still; **Be quiet!** Sei ruhig (still)!
quite ganz
quiz die Prüfung, –en

R

radiate strahlen
radio das Radio, –s, –s
rain (*noun*) der Regen, –s
rain (*verb*) regnen
raincoat der Regenmantel, –s, ¨
raise erhe′ben, erhob, erhoben
rare selten
rather lieber; **I'd rather be young.** Ich wäre lieber jung.
rational vernünf′tig
read lesen (liest), las, gelesen
ready fertig, bereit′
reality die Wirklichkeit, –en
realize ein-sehen (sieht ein), sah ein, eingesehen
really eigentlich, wirklich, denn; **Is that really true?** Ist das denn wahr? **Really?** So?
rebuke tadeln
receive bekom′men, bekam, bekommen; erhal′ten (erhält), erhielt, erhalten; empfan′gen (empfängt), empfing, empfangen; (salary, payment) bezie′hen, bezog, bezogen
recommend empfeh′len (empfiehlt), empfahl, empfohlen
recover sich erho′len
red rot
region die Gegend, –en
reject verwer′fen (verwirft), verwarf, verworfen
reliable verläß′lich
relieve ab-lösen
reluctant zögernd
remain bleiben, blieb, ist geblieben
report (*noun*) der Bericht′, –(e)s, –e
report (*verb*) berich′ten
reporter der Repor′ter, –s, —
reserve reservie′ren; **reserve a table (have a table reserved)** sich (*dat.*) einen Tisch reservie′ren (lassen)
restaurant das Restaurant′, –s, –s
result das Resultat′, –s, –e; die Folge, –n
return zurück′-kehren (sein), um-kehren (sein); **return by air** zurück′-fliegen, flog zurück, ist zurückgeflogen
reunification die Wie′derverei′nigung
Rhine der Rhein, –s; **Rhine wine** der Rheinwein, –s, –e
rib die Rippe, –n
rice der Reis, –es
rich reich
ride (by car, train, *etc.*) fahren (fährt), fuhr, ist gefahren; (on horseback) reiten, ritt, ist geritten
rifle das Gewehr′, –s, –e
right recht, richtig; **That's right.** Das stimmt. Das ist richtig. **He is right.** Er hat recht. **He is** (morally, legally) **right.** Er ist im Recht; **to the right** rechts
ring der Ring, –(e)s, –e
river der Fluß, Flusses, Flüsse
roast der Braten, –s, —
robe der Schlafrock, –s, ¨e
role die Rolle, –n
room das Zimmer, –s, —; der Raum, –(e)s, ¨e
row die Reihe, –n; **front row** die vorderste Reihe
rug der Teppich, –s, –e
rumor das Gerücht′, –(e)s, –e
run laufen (läuft), lief, ist gelaufen; rennen, rannte, ist gerannt
Russia (das) Rußland, –s
Russian (*adj.*) russisch; (*language*) (das) Russisch, –en

S

sad traurig
sailor der Matro′se, –n, –n
salad der Salat′, –s, –e
salesman: traveling salesman der Handlungsreisende, –n, –n (ein Handlungsreisender)
salt das Salz, –es, –e
same: the same dieselbe, dasselbe, derselbe

satisfied zufrie′den
Saturday der Sonnabend, –s, –e; der Samstag, –s, –e
save (someone) retten; (money) sparen
say sagen, meinen; **How do you say that in German?** Wie sagt man das (wie heißt das) auf deutsch?
school die Schule, –n; **grammar school** die Volksschule, –n; **secondary school** die Oberschule, –n; das Gymna′sium, –s, (*plur.*) Gymna′sien
science die Natur′wissenschaft, –en
scientist der Wissenschaftler, –s, —
sculptor der Bildhauer, –s, —
sculpture die Skulptur′, –en
sea die See; der Ozean, –s, –e; das Meer, –es, –e
search (for) suchen (nach)
seat der Platz, –es, ⁻̈e; der Sitz, –es, –e; **Take a seat!** Nehmen Sie Platz!
second zweit–
section der Abschnitt, –(e)s, –e
see sehen (sieht), sah, gesehen; **see again** wieder-sehen (sieht wieder), sah wieder, wiedergesehen; **See you again** (= Goodbye)! Auf Wiedersehen! (= realize, understand) ein-sehen (sieht ein), sah ein, eingesehen
seem scheinen, schien, geschienen; **It seems to me.** Es scheint mir. *or* Mir scheint.
seize greifen, griff, gegriffen
self selbst, selber
semester das Semes′ter, –s, —
send senden, sandte (*or* sendete), gesandt (*or* gesendet)
sentence der Satz, –es, ⁻̈e
separate scheiden, schied, geschieden
September der Septem′ber, –s
serve (a person) (jemanden) bedie′nen; (food) servie′ren
service die Bedie′nung; **Are we going to get service here?** Wird man uns hier bedie′nen?
set out (on an excursion) los-ziehen, zog los, ist losgezogen
seven sieben
seventeen siebzehn; **seventeen-year-old** (*adj.*) siebzehnjährig
seventy siebzig
shall (*auxiliary, future*) werden (wird), wurde, ist geworden; (*modal*) sollen (soll), sollte, gesollt
shave (sich) rasie′ren
she sie (*acc.* sie, *dat.* ihr, *gen.* ihrer)
shine scheinen, schien, geschienen; **shine shoes** die Schuhe putzen
ship das Schiff, –(e)s, –e
shirt das Hemd, –(e)s, –en
shoe der Schuh, –s, –e
shoot schießen, schoß, geschossen
short kurz, kürzer, kürzest– (am kürzesten)
should (= ought to) sollen (soll), sollte, gesollt; **I should like to** ich möchte
shoulder die Schulter, –n
show zeigen; **show up** (of persons) sich sehen lassen
shower: take a shower brausen
sick krank; **sickroom** das Krankenzimmer, –s, —
side die Seite, –n; **on that side of** jenseits (*prep. gen.*); **on this side of** diesseits (*prep. gen.*)
silent: be silent schweigen, schwieg, geschwiegen
simple einfach
since (*sub. conj., temp.*) seit, seitdem′; (*sub. conj., causal*) da; (*prep. dat.*) seit
sincere aufrichtig
sing singen, sang, gesungen
sister die Schwester, –n
sit sitzen, saß, gesessen; **sit down** sich (hin-)setzen; **Sit down!** Setzen Sie sich!
situation die Lage, –n
six sechs
sixteen sechzehn
sixty sechzig
skating das Schlittschuhlaufen, –s
skeleton das Skelett′, –(e)s, –e
skiing das Skilaufen (*or* Schilaufen), –s
skin die Haut, ⁻̈e
skirt der Rock, –(e)s, ⁻̈e
sleep schlafen (schläft), schlief, geschlafen; **fall asleep** ein-schlafen (schläft ein), schlief ein, ist eingeschlafen; **sleeping bag** der Schlafsack, –s, ⁻̈e
sleeve der Ärmel, –s, —
slow langsam
small klein
smell riechen, roch, gerochen
smoke rauchen
snow schneien
so so; **Is that so?** So? **So long!** (Auf) Wiedersehen!
sociologist der Soziolog′(e), –en, –en
sock die Socke, –n
soft (sound) leise; (touch) sanft, weich
soldier der Soldat′, –en, –en
sole die Sohle, –n
some manche (*adj. plur.*); etwas (*pron.*); **some money** etwas Geld
somebody (someone) jemand; **Does somebody else have a question?** Hat noch jemand eine Frage?
something etwas; **something like that** so etwas; **something else** etwas anderes
sometimes manchmal, zuwei′len
somewhat etwas
son der Sohn, –(e)s, ⁻̈e
song das Lied, –(e)s, –er
soon bald; **as soon as** sobald′ (als)
sound klingen, klang, geklungen

soup die Suppe, –n
source die Quelle, –n
(the) **South** der Süden, –s
space der Raum, –(e)s, ⸚e
spare schonen
speak sprechen (spricht), sprach, gesprochen; reden; **speak about (on)** sprechen über (*acc.*); **Speak (Repeat) after me!** Sprechen Sie mir nach!
speech die Rede, –n
spend (time) verbrin′gen, verbrachte, verbracht
spite: in spite of trotz (*prep. dat. or gen.*); **in spite of it (this, that)** trotzdem
sport der Sport, –(e)s
spread out auseinan′der-rücken (sein)
spring (= water) die Quelle, –n; (= season) der Frühling, –s; **in the spring** im Frühling
stand stehen, stand, gestanden; (= tolerate) leiden, litt, gelitten
start an-fangen (fängt an), fing an, angefangen; begin′nen, begann, begonnen; los-gehen, ging los, ist losgegangen
state (*noun*) der Staat, –(e)s, –en
state (*verb*) behaup′ten
stay bleiben, blieb, ist geblieben
steamer der Dampfer, –s, —
step (= staircase) die Treppe, –n; **The first step is the hardest.** Aller Anfang ist schwer.
step (*verb*) treten (tritt), trat, ist getreten
still (*adj.*) still, ruhig; (*adv.*) noch, immer noch, noch immer
stocking der Strumpf, –(e)s, ⸚e
stomach der Magen, –s, ⸚ *or* —
stop stehen-bleiben, blieb stehen, ist stehengeblieben; auf-hören; halten (hält), hielt, gehalten; **Stop!** Halt!
storm der Sturm, –(e)s, ⸚e
stormy stürmisch
story die Geschich′te, –n
straight gera′de
street die Straße, –n
strife der Streit, –(e)s, –e
strike schlagen (schlägt), schlug, geschlagen
struggle der Kampf, –(e)s, ⸚e
student der Student′, –en, –en; die Studen′tin, –nen; **student organization** die Studen′tenorganisation′, –en
study (*noun*) das Studium, –s, (*plur.*) Studien
study (*verb*) studie′ren
subject (= field of study) das Fach, –(e)s, ⸚er; **major subject** das Hauptfach, –s, ⸚er
succeed gelin′gen, gelang, ist gelungen (*impersonal verb with dat.*); **He does not succeed.** Es gelingt′ ihm nicht. **He does not succeed in doing this.** Es gelingt′ ihm nicht, das zu tun.
successful erfolg′reich
such (a) solch (–e, –es, –er); **such a book** ein solches Buch, solch ein Buch, so ein Buch
suddenly plötzlich, auf einmal
suffer leiden, litt, gelitten
sugar der Zucker, –s
suggestion der Vorschlag, –s, ⸚e
suit der Anzug, –s, ⸚e; **everyday suit** der Straßenanzug, –s, ⸚e
summer der Sommer, –s, —; **summer vacation** die Sommerferien (*plur. only*)
sun die Sonne, –n
Sunday der Sonntag, –s, –e
sunrise der Sonnenaufgang, –s, ⸚e
superfluous überflüssig
supposed: be supposed to sollen (soll), sollte, gesollt
sure gewiß′, bestimmt′; **to be sure** zwar
surprise überra′schen
surrender sich erge′ben (ergibt sich), ergab sich, sich ergeben
swim schwimmen, schwamm, ist geschwommen
Switzerland (die) Schweiz

T

table der Tisch, –es, –e
take nehmen (nimmt), nahm, genommen; (a course) studie′ren; **He is taking history.** Er studiert′ Geschich′te; **take along** mitnehmen (nimmt mit), nahm mit, mitgenommen; **take off** (= start) ab-fliegen, flog ab, ist abgeflogen
talk (*noun*) die Rede, –n; das Gespräch′, –(e)s, –e; **There is talk of war again.** Es ist wieder von Krieg die Rede.
talk (*verb*) sprechen (spricht), sprach, gesprochen; reden; **They always talk about literature.** Sie unterhal′ten sich immer über Literatur′.
tall groß, größer, größt–
tea der Tee, –s
teacher der Lehrer, –s, —; die Lehrerin, –nen
tear reißen, riß, gerissen; **tear to pieces** zerrei′ßen, zerriß, zerrissen
technical, technological technisch
tell mit-teilen, erzäh′len, sagen
ten zehn
tennis court der Tennisplatz, –es, ⸚e
terrible schrecklich
test die Prüfung, –en
textbook das Textbuch, –(e)s, ⸚er
than (*in comparisons*) als
thank danken (*dat.*); **Thank you! Thanks!** Danke (schön)!
that (those) das; jen– (–e, –es, –er); **that is (to say)** das heißt; **Those are my parents.** Das sind meine Eltern. (*sub. conj.*) daß; **for that (purpose)** dazu′

the die, das, der
theater das Thea′ter, –s, —
then dann; also, so, da
there dort, da; **there is, there are** es gibt
thereby dadurch
therefore deswegen, darum′, daher′; also
they sie (*acc.* sie, *dat.* ihnen, *gen.* ihrer)
thigh der Schenkel, –s, —
thing das Ding, –(e)s, –e; die Sache, –n; **a thing like this (that)** so etwas
think denken, dachte, gedacht; meinen; **think about** (sich) überle′gen; **think about something** sich (*dat.*) etwas (*acc.*) überle′gen; **think of** denken an (*acc.*); **I often think of it.** Ich denke oft daran! **What do you think of that?** Was halten Sie davon′?
third dritt–
thirteen dreizehn
thirty dreißig
this dies– (–e, –es, –er); **This is my mother.** Das (dies) ist meine Mutter. **These are my parents.** Das (dies) sind meine Eltern.
thoroughly ordentlich
thousand tausend
three drei
throat die Kehle, –n
through durch (*prep. acc.*): **through the door** durch die Tür; **through my fault** durch meine Schuld; (*prep. dat.*) aus: **through fear** aus Furcht
thumb der Daumen, –s, —
Thursday der Donnerstag, –(e)s, –e
ticket die Karte, –n; **theater ticket** die Thea′terkarte, –n
tie der Schlips, –es, –e; die Krawat′te, –n
till bis
time die Zeit, –en; **What time is it?** Wieviel Uhr ist es? *or* Wie spät ist es? **The time is up (over).** Die Zeit ist um; **free time** (= leisure) die Freizeit; **once upon a time (at one time)** einst; **on (in) time** rechtzeitig; **at that time** damals; **point of time** das Mal, –(e)s, –e; **for the first time** zum ersten Mal; **another (some other) time** ein ander Mal; **next time** das nächste Mal; **the assignment for the next time** die Aufgabe für das nächste Mal; **two times two** zweimal zwei; **for a long time** lange, schon lange; **a long time ago** längst
tired müde
title der Titel, –s, —
to zu (*prep. dat.*): **He comes to me.** Er kommt zu mir. **He is going to the city to (visit) his aunt.** Er geht zu seiner Tante in die Stadt; an (*prep. acc.*): **drive to the lake** an den See fahren; **go to the blackboard** an die Tafel gehen; auf (*prep. acc.*): **go to the country** aufs Land gehen; **go to the post office** auf die Post gehen; **(I drink) to your health.** Auf dein Wohl! in (*prep. acc.*): **He is going to school (to church).** Er geht in die Schule (in die Kirche); gegen (*prep. acc.*): **to** (towards) **the west** gegen Westen; mit (*prep. dat.*): **speak to** (with) **a person** mit jemandem sprechen; nach (*prep. dat.*): **He is going to Europe.** Er geht nach Euro′pa; vor (*prep. acc.*): **I say the name to myself.** Ich spreche den Namen vor mich hin; **at a quarter to** (of) **four** um Viertel vor vier
today heute; **of today, today's** heutig
toe die Zehe, –n
together zusam′men, miteinan′der; **All together!** Alle zusam′men!
tomorrow morgen; **day after tomorrow** übermorgen
tongue die Zunge, –n
too (*adv. of degree*) zu; **too difficult** zu schwer; (= also) auch
tooth der Zahn, –(e)s, ⸗e
top: at the top oben
touch berüh′ren; (*in an emotional sense*) rühren
toward gegen (*prep. acc.*): **toward nine o'clock** gegen neun Uhr; nach (*prep. dat.*): **toward the south** nach Süden
town die Stadt, ⸗e
tragedy das Trauerspiel, –s, –e
train der Zug, –(e)s, ⸗e
translate überset′zen
travel fahren (fährt), fuhr, ist gefahren; **traveling salesman** der Handlungsreisende, –n, –n (ein Handlungsreisender)
treat behan′deln; **treat with care** schonen
trip die Reise, –n; **trip around the world** die Weltreise, –n; **take a trip** eine Reise machen
trouble die Mühe, –n; **That gives me trouble.** Das macht mir Mühe.
trousers die Hose, –n
trout die Forel′le, –n
true wahr; **Isn't it true?** Nicht wahr? **It's true, we don't know each other.** Wir kennen uns zwar nicht.
truth die Wahrheit, –en
try versu′chen
Tuesday der Dienstag, –s, –e
turn (*noun*) die Wendung, –en; **turn of the century** die Jahrhun′dertwende, –n
turn (*verb*) wenden, wandte (*or* wendete), gewandt (*or* gewendet); **turn away** (sich) abwenden, wandte ab (*or* wendete ab), abgewandt (*or* abgewendet); **turn to** (*the pages in a book*) auf-schlagen (schlägt auf), schlug auf, aufgeschlagen; **Now turn to page 16!** Schlagen Sie nun Seite 16 auf! **turn back** um-kehren (sein); **turn on** (light) an-schalten, an-machen

twelve zwölf
(the) **twenties** die zwanziger Jahre
twenty zwanzig
twenty-one einundzwanzig
twice (a month) zweimal (im Monat)
two zwei; **the two of them** die zwei, die beiden; **two kinds of** zweierlei

U

umbrella der Regenschirm, –(e)s, –e
uncle der Onkel, –s, —
under unter (*prep. dat.*): **lie under the chair (earth, cover)** unter dem Stuhl (der Erde, der Decke) liegen; unter (*prep. acc.*): **He puts it under the table.** Er stellt es unter den Tisch; bei (*prep. dat.*): **under penalty of death** bei Todesstrafe
understand verste′hen, verstand, verstanden; begrei′fen, begriff, begriffen
unfortunately leider, un′glücklicherwei′se
unit die Einheit, –en
unite verbin′den, verband, verbunden; verei′nigen
United States die Verei′nigten Staaten
university die Universität′, –en; **at the university** (*students*) auf der Universität′; **at the university** (*faculty*) an der Universität′
unpractical unpraktisch
until (*prep. and subord. conj.*) bis
up auf, hinauf′, herauf′; **up to now** bisher′; **up above, upstairs** oben
upon (*see* **on**) auf (*prep. dat. or acc.*)
usually gewöhn′lich, meistens

V

vacation die Ferien (*plur. only*)
value der Wert, –(e)s, –e
veal cutlet (Viennese style) das Wiener Schnitzel, –s, —
vegetable das Gemü′se, –s, —; **vegetable soup** die Gemü′sesuppe, –n
very sehr, recht, äußerst; **very much** sehr, sehr viel; **very well** sehr gut, ausgezeich′net, recht wohl
veterinarian der Tierarzt, –es, ⸚e
Vienna (das) Wien, –s
visit besu′chen, besich′tigen

W

wait (for) warten (auf; *acc.*); **Wait and see!** Warte nur! *or* Paß auf!
waiter der Kellner, –s, —; **headwaiter** der Ober, –s, —
waitress die Kellnerin, –nen
wall die Wand, ⸚e; **wall clock** die Wanduhr, –en; **wallpaper** die Tape′te, –n
want (to) wollen (will), wollte, gewollt
war der Krieg, –(e)s, –e
warm warm, wärmer, wärmst–
warn (against) warnen (vor; *dat.*)
wash waschen (wäscht), wusch, gewaschen
watch die Uhr, –en
way der Weg, –(e)s, –e
we wir (*acc.* uns; *dat.* uns; *gen.* unser)
weak schwach
wear tragen (trägt), trug, getragen
weather das Wetter, –s, —; **abrupt change in weather** der Wetterumsturz, –es, ⸚e
Wednesday der Mittwoch, –s, –e
week die Woche, –n
weekend das Wochenende, –s, –n
welcome: You are welcome! Bitte schön!
well gut, wohl, also; **Well, what else?** Nun, was noch? **Well then** *or* **well now** also
(the) **West** der Westen, –s
western westlich; **Western Powers** die Westmächte
what was, welch– (–e, –es, –er); **what a, what kind of** was für ein; **with what** womit′
when (*sub. conj.*) als, wenn, wie; (*interrog.*) wann
where (*interrog.*) wo; **where . . . to** wohin′
whether (*sub. conj.*) ob
which (*interrog. or rel. pron.*) welch– (–e, –es, –er); (*rel. pron.*) die, das, der
while (*sub. conj.*) während
whistle pfeifen, pfiff, gepfiffen
who (*interrog. pron.*) wer; (*rel. pron.*) die, das, der; welch– (–e, –es, –er)
whole (*noun*) das Ganze, –n
whole (*adj.*) ganz
why (*interrog. pron.*) warum′; **why in the world?** warum′ denn?
wide weit
wife die Frau, –en
will (*aux., fut.*) werden (wird), wurde, ist geworden; (= want to) wollen (will), wollte, gewollt; wünschen
win gewin′nen, gewann, gewonnen
window das Fenster, –s, —
wine der Wein, –(e)s, –e
winter der Winter, –s, —
wise weise
wish wünschen
with mit (*prep. dat.*): **I'm satisfied with him.** Ich bin mit ihm zufrie′den; **cut with a knife** mit einem Messer schneiden; **She came with him.** Sie ist mit ihm gekommen; **with pleasure** mit Vergnü′gen; auf (*prep. acc.*): **He is angry with** (at) **me.** Er ist böse auf mich; bei (*prep. dat.*): **They are living with us** (at our house). Sie wohnen bei uns. **You don't have it with** (on) **you?** Du hast es nicht bei dir?
without ohne (*prep. acc.*); ohne . . . zu (+ *inf.*)

woman die Frau, –en
word das Wort, –es, –e *or* ¨er; *the words of a phrase, sentence:* die Worte; *unrelated words:* die Wörter (*as in* Wörterbuch)
work (*noun*) die Arbeit, –en
work (*verb*) arbeiten
world die Welt, –en; **World War** der Weltkrieg, –(e)s, –e
worry (*noun*) die Sorge, –n
worry about (*verb*) sich (*dat.*) Sorgen machen über (*acc.*)
would würde (*subj. of* werden); **would like to** möchte
wrist das Handgelenk, –s, –e
write schreiben, schrieb, geschrieben
wrong (*noun*) das Unrecht, –s
wrong (*adj.*) falsch, unrichtig
be wrong (*verb*) im Unrecht sein, unrecht haben

Y

year das Jahr, –(e)s, –e
yes ja, jawohl′; **Oh yes!** Oh doch!
yesterday gestern; **day before yesterday** vorgestern
you (*formal sing. and plur.*) Sie (*acc.* Sie; *dat.* Ihnen; *gen.* Ihrer); (*familiar sing.*) du (*acc.* dich; *dat.* dir; *gen.* deiner); (*familiar plur.*) ihr (*acc.* euch; *dat.* euch; *gen.* euer); (*indef. pron.*) man
young jung, jünger, jüngst–
your (*poss. pron.*) Ihr (–e, —, —) (*formal sing. and plur.*); dein (–e, —, —) (*familiar sing.*); euer (–e, —, —) (*familiar plur.*)

Z

zero die Null, –en
zone die Zone, –n
zoology die Zoologie′

INDEX

LIST OF PHOTOGRAPHS

DÄNEMA
Flensburg
SCHLESWIG-
Kiel
NORDSEE
HOLSTEIN
Lübeck
Hamburg
MEC
Bremerhaven
Elbe
Oldenburg
Bremen
NIEDERSACHSEN
Amsterdam
Aller
Ems
Osnabrück
Hannover
Den Haag
NIEDERLANDE
Braunschweig
Münster
Magdebu
NORDRHEIN-
Essen
Dortmund
Weser
Harz
Saale
Duisburg
Ruhr
BELGIEN
Kassel
Wuppertal
Düsseldorf
Brüssel
Köln
Erfurt
Weim
Aachen
WESTFALEN
Jena
Bonn
Rhein
Fulda
Thüringerwald
THÜRINGEN
WESTDEUTSCHLAND
Koblenz
Taunus
HESSEN
Wiesbaden
RHEINLAND-
Frankfurt
Main
Mosel
Bingen
Mainz
LUXEM-
BURG
Trier
PFALZ
Würzburg
Worms
SAARLAND
Mannheim
Nürnberg
Saarbrücken
Heidelberg
Rothenburg
Karlsruhe
BAYER
Baden-Baden
Stuttgart
Regensbur
BADEN-
Donau
Neckar
Ulm
Rhein
Augsburg
Schwarzwald
Lech
Freiburg
WÜRTTEMBERG
Münc
FRANKREICH
Bodensee
Oberammergau
Bayrische
Basel
Zürich
Zugspitze
Innsbr
Luzern
LIECHTEN-
STEIN
Tirol
Ö
Bern
SCHWEIZ
Genfer
See
Rhône
Genf
Matterhorn